Motorcycles
Fundamentals, Service, Repair

by

BRUCE A. JOHNS

and

DAVID D. EDMUNDSON

Publisher
The Goodheart-Willcox Company, Inc.
Tinley Park, Illinois

Library of Congress Catalog Card Number 87-21231
International Standard Book Number 0-87006-654-4

6 7 8 9 10   87   00 99 98 97

Library of Congress Cataloging in Publication Data

Johns, Bruce A.
  Motorcycles: fundamentals, service, repair.

  Includes index.
  1. Motorcycles—Maintenance and repair.
  I. Edmundson, David D.   II. Title.
TL444.J63   1987   629.28'775   87-21231
ISBN 0—87006-654-4

INTRODUCTION

MOTORCYCLES - FUNDAMENTALS, SERVICE, REPAIR is designed to help prepare you to work on motorcycles. It is written in general terms that apply to all motorcycle makes and models. The text and illustrations summarize the most important aspects relating to the operation, construction, design, testing, maintenance, and repair of motorcycle systems and components.

Motorcycles have changed more in recent years than in the previous 50 years. Today's motorcycles use electronic ignition systems, fuel injection, shaft drive, turbochargers, and many other innovations. MOTORCYCLES covers both conventional design features and the latest engineering advances.

All technical terms are defined as soon as they are mentioned. A glossary is also provided in the book. This assures that you can easily understand the many terms essential to motorcycle mechanics.

Each chapter opens with several objectives that tell you what will be learned. Each chapter also prepares you for the chapters that follow. Knowledge builds systematically as you progress through the text.

MOTORCYCLES' easy to understand language and large number of illustrations make the content easy to comprehend and remember. Pictures are generously used to supplement the text.

Many service and repair operations can be dangerous. To stress important safety precautions, all safety rules are printed in color and are located where they apply.

MOTORCYCLES can be used by the novice mechanic to learn "the basics" or by the experienced mechanic as a "refresher course" or reference.

Bruce A. Johns
David D. Edmundson

CONTENTS

IMPORTANT SAFETY NOTICE

Proper service and repair methods are critical to the safe, reliable operation of motorcycles. The procedures described in this textbook are designed to help you use a manufacturer's service manual. A service manual will give the how-to details and specifications needed to do competent work.

This book contains safety precautions which must be followed. Personal injury or part damage can result when basic safety rules are not followed. Also, remember that these cautions are general and do not cover some specialized hazards. Refer to a service manual when in doubt about any service operation!

Today's motorcycles use very precise and complex components to provide a dependable means of transportation. It is important for you to understand all systems of a motorcycle. (Yamaha Motor Corp., U.S.A.)

6

Chapter 1

INTRODUCTION TO MOTORCYCLE SYSTEMS

After studying this chapter, you will be able to:
□ Describe the seven major systems of a motorcycle.
□ Explain the basic parts of each motorcycle system.
□ Identify the most important parts of a motorcycle.
□ List common motorcycle design differences.

Today's motorcycles consist of a number of systems (related group of parts) that work together to provide a safe and dependable means of transportation. Each of these systems performs a particular function. For example, the brake system must stop the motorcycle quickly, yet safely. The fuel system supplies the correct ratio of air and fuel for efficient engine operation. The ignition system must ignite the fuel mixture in the engine to start combustion (burning) and provide a source of energy for the motorcycle.

This chapter will introduce, illustrate, and explain the basic parts of each motorcycle system. As a result, you will be more prepared to comprehend the other specialized chapters of this textbook.

The motorcycle may be divided into seven major systems:
1. Engine.
2. Power transmission.
3. Chassis.
4. Wheels, tires, and brakes.
5. Electrical.
6. Suspension.
7. Fuel.

BASIC ENGINE

Fundamentally, a MOTORCYCLE ENGINE is a group of assembled parts designed to change heat energy (burning fuel) into useful mechanical or rotating energy. The engine provides the power that turns the rear drive wheel. It also generates the electricity needed for the lights, horn, and other electrical devices.

To make an engine operate, we need air, fuel, vacuum (suction), compression (pressure inside engine), and combustion (burning of fuel mixture). When these requirements are provided in proper proportions and sequence, our engine can be made to "run."

BASIC ENGINE PARTS

A SIMPLE ENGINE is made up of a cylinder, piston, connecting rod, crankshaft, and crankcase. Fig. 1-1 illustrates these basic engine components. The piston reciprocates (slides up and down) in the cylinder. The connecting rod and crankshaft change this reciprocating movement into more useful rotating movement. See Fig. 1-2.

Basically, an engine must:
1. Produce a VACUUM which draws air and fuel into the cylinders.
2. COMPRESS the air-fuel mixture to produce a more violent and efficient combustion of the fuel mixture.
3. IGNITE the fuel mixture while under pressure.
4. Use COMBUSTION pressure to do work.
5. EXHAUST (remove) combustion waste products.

For our basic engine to form a vacuum and compress the mixture, a means of sealing the cylinder must be provided. This is accomplished by the cylinder head, piston, and piston rings, Fig. 1-3. They produce a relatively leakproof enclosure and form the combustion chamber (area in engine where fuel mixture is burned). Then, when the piston moves down, a vacuum or low pressure area is developed in the cylinder. When the piston moves up, the mixture is squeezed under pressure.

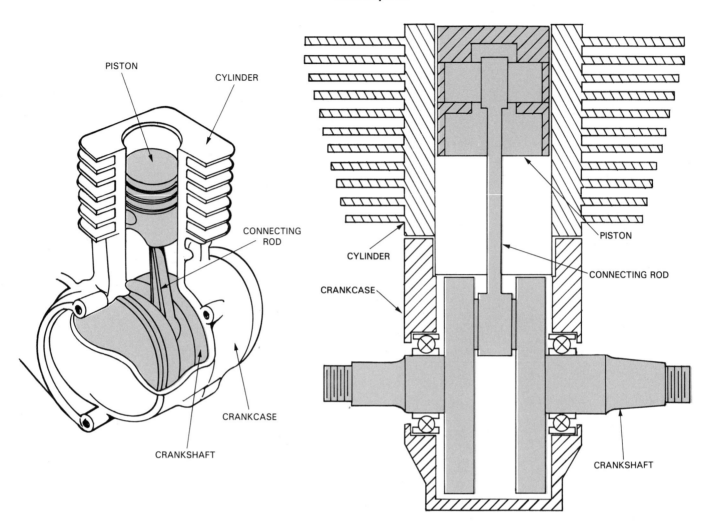

Fig. 1-1. A piston, connecting rod, crankshaft, cylinder, and crankcase are some of the major components of a simple engine.

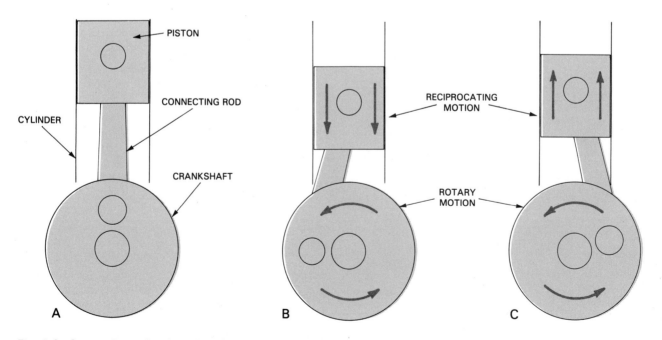

Fig. 1-2. Connecting rod and crankshaft change reciprocating movement of piston into rotating movement. A—Piston is ready to move down in cylinder. B—As piston moves down, connecting rod causes crankshaft to rotate. C—Piston moves back up in cylinder as crankshaft continues to rotate.

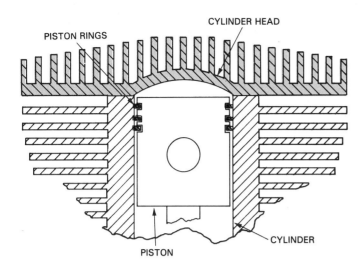

Fig. 1-3. Cylinder is sealed by the piston, piston rings, and cylinder head.

Also, to let the air-fuel mixture into the cylinders, an intake valve and port (passage) are required. A smaller exhaust valve and port allow the burned gases to exit the engine cylinder. Fundamental valve and port action is illustrated in Fig. 1-4. This type of

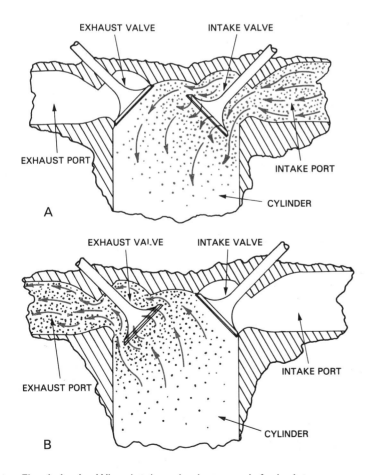

Fig. 1-4. A—When intake valve is open, air-fuel mixture can flow through intake port into cylinder. B—Burned gases leave cylinder by flowing past open exhaust valve into exhaust port.

engine is termed a four-stroke cycle engine.

A two-stroke cycle engine will be discussed later.

FOUR-STROKE CYCLE ENGINE

A FOUR-STROKE CYCLE ENGINE requires four strokes (up or down piston movements) to complete one full cycle. Look at Fig. 1-5. The sequence of events in a four-stroke cycle engine are as follows:

1. INTAKE STROKE is first downward movement of piston while intake valve is open. Fuel mixture is pulled into cylinder.
2. COMPRESSION STROKE is first upward movement of piston which pressurizes fuel mixture.
3. POWER STROKE is second downward movement of piston, caused by combustion heat, expansion, and pressure.
4. EXHAUST STROKE is second upward movement of piston while exhaust valve is open. Burned gases are pushed from engine.

Each STROKE will rotate the crankshaft one-half

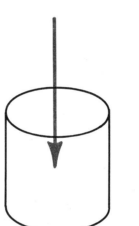
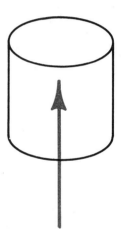

INTAKE STROKE
PISTON MOVES DOWN

COMPRESSION STROKE
PISTON MOVES UP

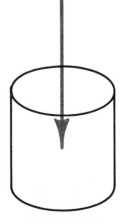
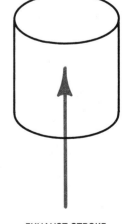

POWER STROKE
PISTON MOVES DOWN

EXHAUST STROKE
PISTON MOVES UP

Fig. 1-5. Four-stroke sequence is intake, compression, power, and exhaust.

revolution (180 deg.). This is shown in Fig. 1-6. To complete one full CYCLE, the crankshaft must make two complete revolutions (720 deg.).

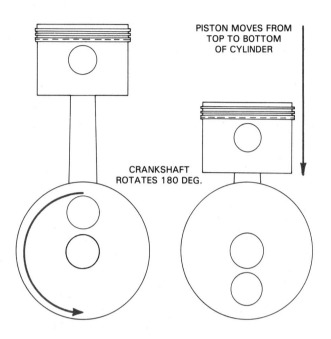

Fig. 1-6. Each stroke moves crankshaft one-half revolution.

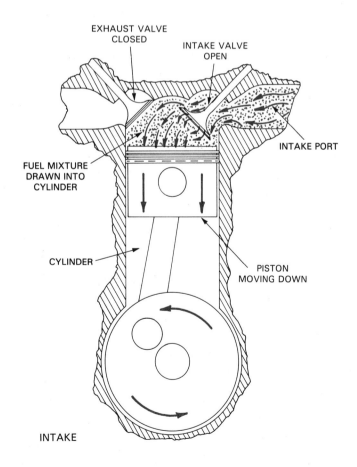

Fig. 1-7. During intake stroke, air and fuel are drawn into cylinder through intake port. Piston is moving down in cylinder.

FOUR-STROKE CYCLE ENGINE OPERATION

To fully comprehend a four-stroke cycle engine, you must be able to visualize valve operation in relation to piston movement. Study what each engine part is doing during the following discussion of the four engine strokes.

Intake stroke

During the INTAKE STROKE, Fig. 1-7, the piston slides down in the cylinder while the intake valve is open and the exhaust valve is closed. Basically, the piston moves from top dead center (TDC or highest piston position) to bottom dead center (BDC or lowest piston position). This creates a vacuum (suction) in the cylinder which draws air and fuel past the open intake valve.

Compression stroke

The next upward movement of the piston (BDC to TDC) is called the COMPRESSION STROKE, Fig. 1-8. During this stroke, both the intake and exhaust valves are closed. This allows the upward movement of the piston to compress the trapped air-fuel mixture. Compression of the air-fuel mixture is needed to cause a more violent combustion of the fuel mixture.

Power stroke

As the piston nears TDC, a spark plug mounted in the cylinder head "fires" and ignites the compressed

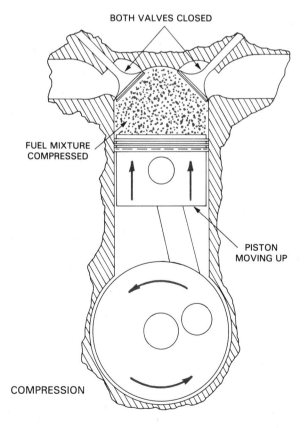

Fig. 1-8. During compression stroke, air-fuel mixture is compressed as piston moves up in cylinder.

air-fuel mixture, Fig. 1-9. This begins the POWER STROKE. As the air-fuel mixture burns, it expands rapidly, causing tremendous pressure and heat. The pressure forces the piston down in the cylinder, transmitting power to the crankshaft.

Exhaust stroke

The last stroke in the four-stroke cycle is the EXHAUST STROKE, Fig. 1-10. As the piston moves up in the cylinder it pushes the burned gases past the open exhaust valve. This leaves the cylinder empty and prepares it for the start of another four-stroke cycle.

VALVE OVERLAP

We have already explained that the intake valve is open while the piston moves down on the intake stroke. To more completely fill the cylinder with fuel mixture, the intake valve actually opens before the piston begins its downward movement (intake valve opens at end of exhaust stroke). Also, the engine exhaust valve remains partially open during the start of the intake stroke.

This period of time, while both valves are open, is called VALVE OVERLAP. Valve overlap helps draw the fresh charge (fuel mixture) into the cylinder, and aids in expelling the spent charge (burned gases). See Fig. 1-11.

Intake valve closing

Once the intake charge is moving into the cylinder, it will continue to move because of INERTIA (tendency to keep moving once in motion).

The fresh charge will flow into the cylinder until pressure in the cylinder overcomes the inertia of the incoming charge. This point in the cycle usually occurs after the piston has started to move up the cylinder on the compression stroke. For this reason, the intake valve remains open during the beginning of the compression stroke to allow for more complete filling of the cylinder.

Exhaust valve opening

At the end of the power stroke, cylinder pressure has decreased to the point that it is no longer useful for making power. By opening the exhaust valve at the end of the power stroke, we can use the tiny remaining pressure to help start the movement of the exhaust gases out the exhaust port. This aids in thoroughly clearing the cylinder. As the piston nears the end of the exhaust stroke, we reach the point of valve overlap again, Fig. 1-12.

FLYWHEEL EFFECT

A FLYWHEEL is a large, round, disc or doughnut shaped weight attached to the crankshaft, Fig. 1-13. It is intended to help keep the engine spinning during

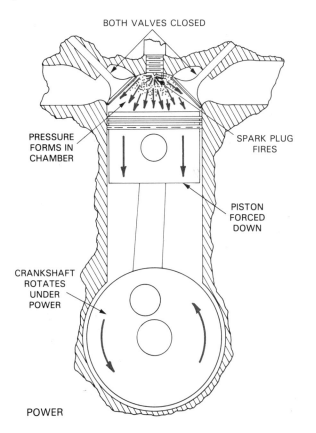

Fig. 1-9. During power stroke, spark plug ignites compressed air-fuel mixture. Combustion pressure and heat drives piston down in cylinder.

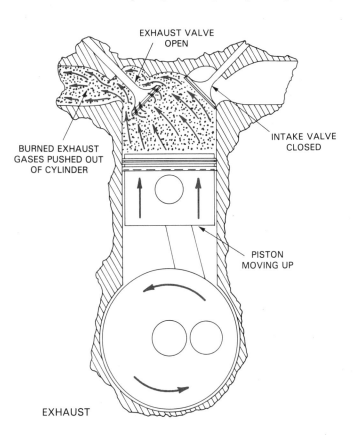

Fig. 1-10. As piston moves up during exhaust stroke, it forces burned gases past open exhaust valve and through exhaust port.

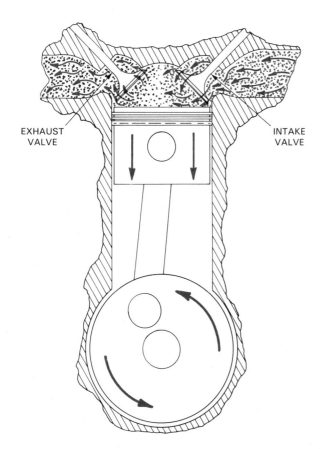

EXHAUST VALVE

INTAKE VALVE

Fig. 1-11. Exhaust valve closes after intake stroke begins. As air-fuel mixture enters cylinder, it helps push last of the burned gases out exhaust port. Valve overlap is the time when intake and exhaust valves are both open.

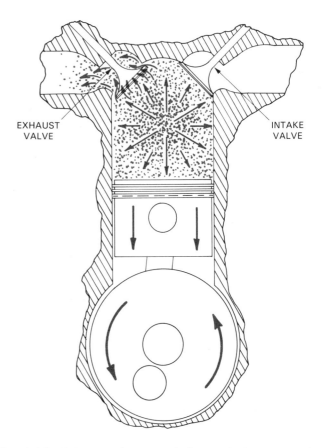

EXHAUST VALVE

INTAKE VALVE

Fig. 1-12. Exhaust valve opens before end of power stroke. This allows combustion pressure to start movement of gases into exhaust port before exhaust stroke begins.

the three non-power producing strokes. Since there is only one power stroke for every two crankshaft revolutions, the flywheel inertia will also aid in smoothing abrupt crankshaft movement during the power stroke.

Some engines may also use a chain or gear-driven counterbalancer. It is designed to add a flywheel effect and to also reduce vibration. See Fig. 1-14.

TWO-STROKE CYCLE ENGINE

A TWO-STROKE CYCLE ENGINE produces power once during each revolution of the crankshaft. It has a power stroke twice as often as a four-stroke cycle engine. Most of the fundamental parts are the same (crankcase, crankshaft, connecting rod, piston, rings, cylinder, and cylinder head). See Fig. 1-15. The primary difference is in the method of controlling fuel mixture flow into and out of the engine.

In a two-stroke cycle engine, the same events take place as in a four-stroke cycle engine. However, the two-stroke cycle events are controlled and overlap differently.

In basic terms, the differences between two-stroke and four-stroke cycle engines are:
1. Two-stroke cycle engines "fire" every crankshaft

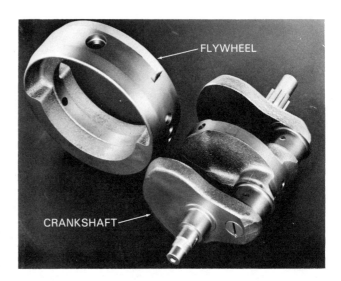

FLYWHEEL

CRANKSHAFT

Fig. 1-13. This flywheel bolts to center of crankshaft. It reduces power pulsations at crankshaft to smooth engine operation.

revolution.
2. Two-stroke cycle engines do NOT use poppet valves.
3. Two-stroke cycle engines pass their air-fuel mixture into the crankcase before reaching the com-

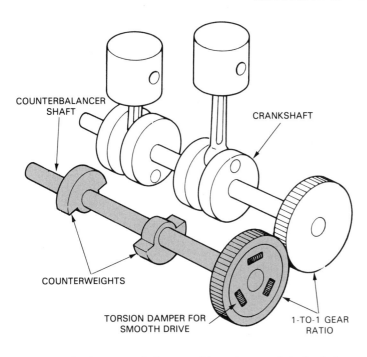

Fig. 1-14. A counterbalancer, driven by crankshaft, helps reduce engine vibration. A chain type drive may also be used. (U.S. Suzuki Motor Corporation)

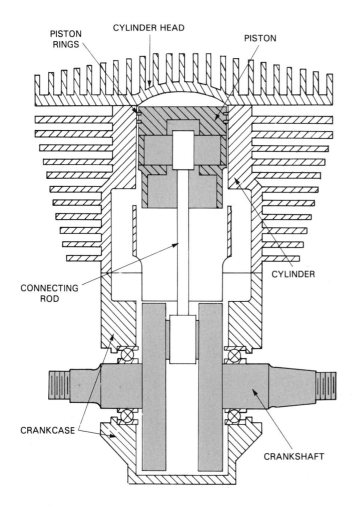

Fig. 1-15. Simple two-stroke cycle engine has many of the same components used in a four-stroke cycle engine.

bustion chamber.

4. Intake and exhaust timing is controlled by the piston, not by the valve mechanism.

TWO-STROKE CYCLE ENGINE OPERATION

Since a two-stroke cycle engine produces power once every revolution, several events must happen at the same time. See Fig. 1-16.

A few two-stroke characteristics should be explained before two-stroke cycle operation can be fully understood:

1. Air-fuel mixture must enter the crankcase below the piston.
2. Air-fuel mixture transfers from the crankcase to the upper cylinder above the piston.
3. Burned air-fuel mixture must exhaust during the power stroke.
4. Flow through the engine is controlled by the piston covering and uncovering ports (openings) in the cylinder wall.

Cylinder ports

Three openings, Fig. 1-17, are used in a two-stroke cycle engine cylinder:

1. Intake port (lets fuel mixture from carburetor flow into crankcase).
2. Transfer port (connects crankcase to upper cylinder).

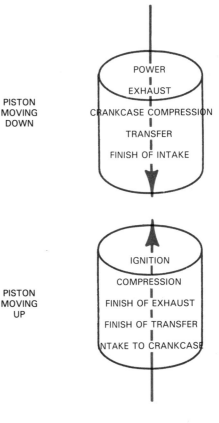

Fig. 1-16. Note series of events during each up and down piston movement in a two-stroke cycle engine.

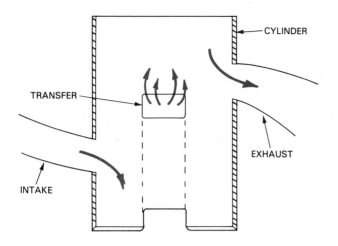

Fig. 1-17. Intake port and transfer port direct air-fuel mixture through two-stroke cycle engine. Exhaust port directs burned gases out of engine.

3. Exhaust port (allows burned gases to leave engine cylinder).

Starting with the piston at TDC, air-fuel mixture is compressed in the combustion chamber and is ready for ignition. At the same time, the crankcase is filled with uncompressed air and fuel. Ignition occurs, driving the piston downward to produce power. See Fig. 1-18.

Moving the fuel charge

As the piston moves down, it uncovers the EXHAUST PORT, allowing burned air-fuel mixture to leave the cylinder. At the same time, downward movement of the piston is causing compression in the crankcase, Fig. 1-19.

As the piston continues downward, the TRANSFER PORT is uncovered. This allows air-fuel mixture from the crankcase to pass upward into the cylinder. The incoming air-fuel charge helps push remaining burned gases out the exhaust port, Fig. 1-20. We have now completed the power, exhaust, and transfer events.

When the piston begins to move up, its bottom edge uncovers the INTAKE PORT. Fresh air-fuel mixture is drawn into the crankcase because vacuum is produced in the crankcase. See Fig. 1-21. As the piston continues upward, the transfer port and exhaust port are closed off. Compression begins as soon as the exhaust port is blocked. When the piston nears

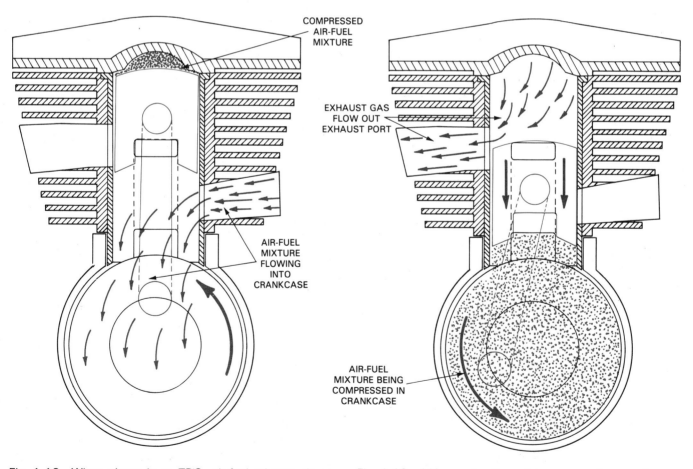

Fig. 1-18. When piston is at TDC, air-fuel mixture above piston is compressed. Compression prepares mixture for ignition. A new charge of air-fuel mixture is also entering crankcase through intake port.

Fig. 1-19. After combustion, piston moves down and opens exhaust port, allowing exhaust gases to flow out of cylinder. Downward movement of piston closes intake port. Fresh air-fuel mixture charge is being compressed in crankcase.

TDC, the spark plug "fires" and the cycle of events begins again.

ENGINE POWER CHARACTERISTICS

Crankshaft rotation produces torque (twisting force) and useful power. Most motorcycle engines produce a great deal of torque and power for their size. In order to do this, the crankshaft must turn at a very high speed.

Work and energy

WORK is performed when an object is moved. Work is measured in foot-pounds (ft-lb) or joules (J).

Work is done when weights are lifted, springs compressed, or shafts are rotated.

ENERGY is the ability to perform work. A gallon of gasoline, for example, has a specific amount of heat energy stored in it. When the gasoline is burned to release energy, work can be done.

Torque

TORQUE is a turning or twisting motion, as when you pull on a wrench handle. Torque is measured in pound-feet (lb-ft) or newton-metres (N·m). See Fig. 1-22. Torque is different from work. Motion is NOT needed to produce torque, while work requires motion.

Power

POWER is a measurement of the amount of work being completed. It is stated in horsepower (hp) or kilowatts (kW). The term power refers to a rate instead of a force.

Horsepower

One HORSEPOWER is the rating for the amount of work needed to lift 33,000 pounds (14 850 kg) a

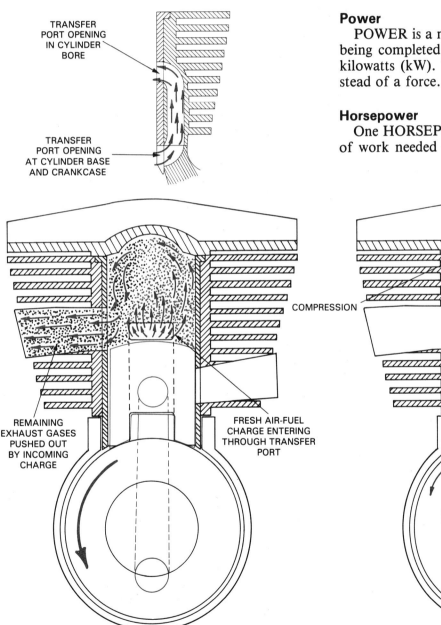

Fig. 1-20. Transfer port is opened as piston continues down. This allows air-fuel mixture to flow from crankcase into cylinder area above piston. Since exhaust port is also open, new charge helps clean last part of exhaust gases out of cylinder.

Fig. 1-21. As piston moves back up, air-fuel charge that was just transferred is compressed. At same time, piston skirt has opened intake port, allowing a new charge of air-fuel mixture to enter crankcase.

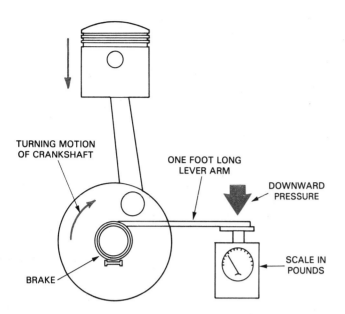

TURNING MOTION
OF CRANKSHAFT

ONE FOOT LONG
LEVER ARM

DOWNWARD
PRESSURE

BRAKE

SCALE IN
POUNDS

Fig. 1-22. Torque can be measured by attaching a brake and a one foot long lever arm to crankshaft. As brake is tightened, lever pushes down on scale. If scale reads 50 pounds, 50 lb-ft of torque is being produced.

distance of one foot (0.30 m) in one minute. This is illustrated in Fig. 1-23. Horsepower equals work divided by time.

BASIC POWER TRANSMISSION

POWER TRANSMISSION, in a motorcycle, sends power from the engine crankshaft to the rear wheel. A series of gears, chains, and/or shafts are used. In order to propel motorcycle, we must be able to make the best use of available power and torque.

To do this, a GEARBOX or transmission is provided to allow the engine to operate in its most efficient power range at all times. A series of gears in the gearbox provides a wide variance in rear wheel speed while the engine operates within a relatively narrow speed range.

Gear action

A combination of gears will accomplish a reduction in speed and a multiplication of torque. Consider, for example, the effect of a ten-tooth gear driving a thirty-tooth gear, Fig. 1-24. The ten-tooth gear will make three revolutions for each revolution of the thirty-tooth gear. With this setup, the large gear will turn at one-third the speed of the small gear.

If the ten-tooth gear is driving the thirty-tooth gear with one foot pound of torque, Fig. 1-25, the thirty-tooth gear will deliver three foot pounds of torque or three times as much torque as the ten-tooth gear. This setup is called a three-to-one gear reduction.

PRIMARY DRIVE

A typical motorcycle power transmission uses a PRIMARY DRIVE to deliver engine power from the crankshaft to the gearbox. To engage and disengage this power to and from the gearbox, a clutch is provided in the primary drive. See Fig. 1-26.

A primary drive serves two main functions:

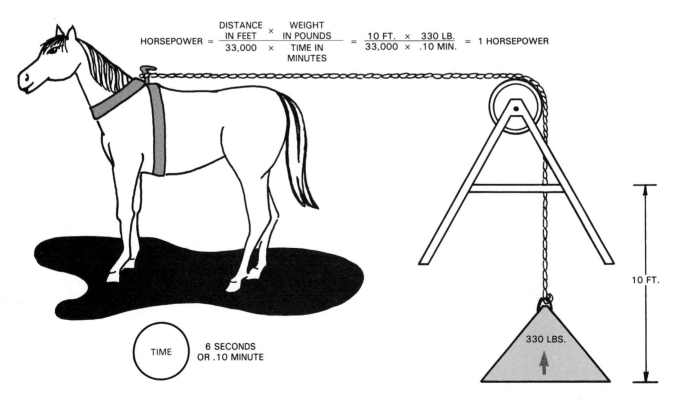

$$\text{HORSEPOWER} = \frac{\text{DISTANCE} \times \text{WEIGHT}}{\text{IN FEET} \quad \text{IN POUNDS}}{33,000 \times \text{TIME IN}} = \frac{10 \text{ FT.} \times 330 \text{ LB.}}{33,000 \times .10 \text{ MIN.}} = 1 \text{ HORSEPOWER}$$

TIME

6 SECONDS
OR .10 MINUTE

330 LBS.

10 FT.

Fig. 1-23. This drawing represents the production of one horsepower.

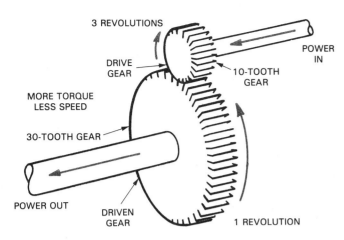

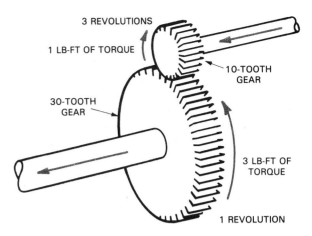

Fig. 1-24. When small gear drives large gear, speed is reduced (large gear rotates slower) and torque is multiplied (large gear has more turning power).

Fig. 1-25. If 10-tooth gear applies 1 lb-ft of torque to a 30-tooth gear, 30-tooth gear will apply 3 lb-ft of torque to its shaft. The small gear will turn three times to make the large gear turn once. This is a 3:1 gear ratio or reduction.

1. It provides a convenient mounting place for the clutch.
2. It provides initial gear reduction, allowing the gearbox to be more compact.

Primary drive reduction

Generally, a primary drive will have a reduction ratio of approximately three to one (3:1).

The need for a primary drive is easily understood if we use an example. Assume that a typical engine is driving a gearbox with a one to one (1:1) ratio. If the engine is turning (crankshaft rotating) at 3000 revolutions per minute (rpm), the gearbox shaft will also turn at 3000 rpm.

In order to reduce this rpm for use at the rear wheel, very large gears would be required in the gear-

box. However, this same engine using a 3:1 primary reduction would now have the gearbox shaft turning at 1000 rpm. This primary reduction allows the use of smaller gears in the gearbox.

CLUTCH

A motorcycle CLUTCH provides a means of connecting and disconnecting the primary drive and the gearbox. As shown in Fig. 1-26, the clutch is located between the primary drive chain or gears and the gearbox.

Anytime the engine is running, the primary drive spins. However, with the clutch disengaged, power does not flow into the gearbox and to the rear wheel. This allows the motorcycle to stand still while in gear

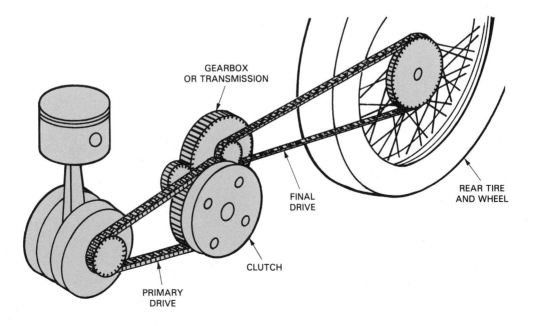

Fig. 1-26. Primary drive transfers power from engine to clutch. Clutch can couple or uncouple engine from gearbox. Gearbox provides various gear ratios. Final drive transfers power from gearbox to rear wheel of motorcycle.

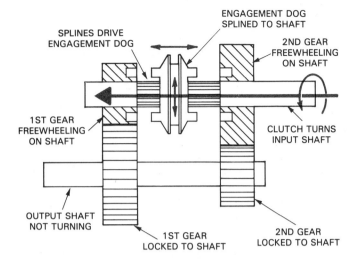

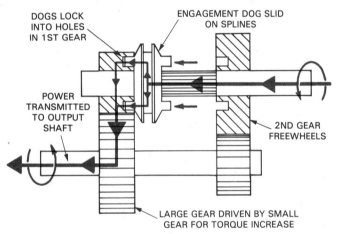

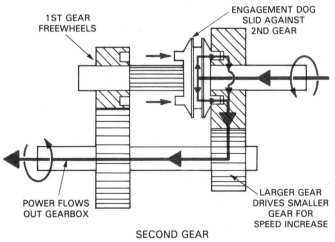

NEUTRAL

A—WHEN GEARBOX IS IN NEUTRAL, INPUT SHAFT AND ENGAGEMENT DOG TURN. SINCE 1ST AND 2ND GEARS ON INPUT SHAFT ARE NOT LOCKED TO SHAFT, THEY DO NOT TURN OR DRIVE OUTPUT SHAFT.

FIRST GEAR

B—FIRST GEAR IS ENGAGED BY SLIDING ENGAGEMENT DOG TO LEFT. PROJECTIONS (DOGS) INDEX OR FIT INTO HOLES IN SIDE OF 1ST GEAR. SINCE ENGAGEMENT DOG IS SPLINED TO INPUT SHAFT, 1ST GEAR NOW TURNS WITH SHAFT AND DRIVES OUTPUT SHAFT.

SECOND GEAR

C—SECOND GEAR IS ENGAGED BY SLIDING ENGAGEMENT DOG TO RIGHT. WHEN DOGS ARE INDEXED INTO HOLES IN SIDE OF 2ND GEAR, 2ND GEAR TURNS WITH INPUT SHAFT AND DRIVES OUTPUT SHAFT.

Fig. 1-27. Note gear position and power flow in each gear: neutral, first, and second.

with the engine running. When the clutch is engaged, the motorcycle is propelled forward.

Basically, the clutch uses spring-loaded plates (round discs) inside a clutch basket (housing). If the springs are pressing the clutch plates together, friction causes power to be transferred through the clutch. If the clutch lever on the handle bar is pulled, a cable operated lever acts against spring pressure to release friction inside the clutch. This uncouples the engine and gearbox.

GEARBOX

A GEARBOX is a set of shafts and gears which connect the primary drive to the final drive (drive mechanism to rear wheel). Motorcycle gearboxes commonly have four to six different speeds or ratios. This is accomplished by engaging and disengaging gears of different sizes (varied number of teeth), as shown in Fig. 1-27.

One recent power transmission design uses a semiautomatic primary and clutch (torque converter) with a two-speed gearbox. This unit is referred to as an AUTOMATIC TRANSMISSION even though it is not fully automatic. See Fig. 1-28.

FINAL DRIVE

The FINAL DRIVE connects the gearbox to the rear wheel. It is the last element in the motorcycle's power transmission system. The three designs commonly used are shaft drive, chain drive, and belt drive. These are pictured in Fig. 1-29.

Generally, the final drive will also have a reduction ratio of approximately 3:1. With chain drive, quick and relatively inexpensive changes in overall ratio can be made by changing sprocket sizes.

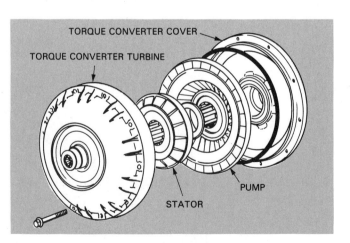

Fig. 1-28. A torque converter (fluid coupling) replaces manual clutch to produce semiautomatic transmission. Engine drives pump. Pump throws oil into turbine. Stator improves oil circulation and torque increases. When engine and pump speed is high enough, turbine is rotated by oil striking blades. Turbine then turns gearbox input shaft.

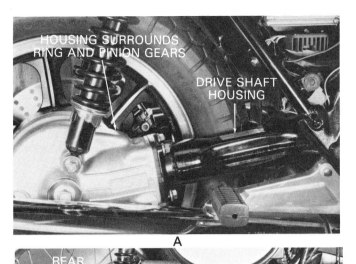

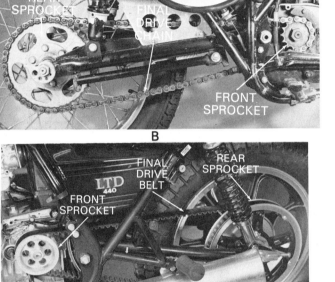

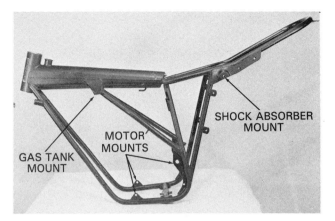

Fig. 1-30. Cradle frame uses tubing surrounding engine to provide rigid mounting and alignment.

Fig. 1-29. The three basic final drive designs are: A—Shaft drive. B—Chain drive. C—Belt drive.

Fig. 1-31. Backbone frame design. Engine hangs from backbone tube and acts as a rigid frame member.

CHASSIS

The CHASSIS of a motorcycle includes everything but the engine, fuel system, and electrical systems. Basically, the frame and suspension form the chassis.

FRAME

The motorcycle FRAME provides a means of rigidly mounting the engine, suspension, and accessories.

Many different frame designs are used. In modern practice, the most common frame is the CRADLE type, Fig. 1-30. Another frame design, called the BACKBONE type, uses the engine as a supporting member. See Fig. 1-31. A STAMPED frame, Fig. 1-32, does not resemble any of the others. This frame is used on many inexpensive, small displacement motorcycles.

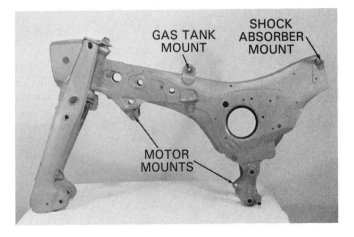

Fig. 1-32. Stamped sheet metal pieces are welded together to fabricate a stamped frame. Notice that this frame uses backbone design as well.

19

Regardless of why a certain frame design is used (low manufacturing cost, lightweight, strength), it must be understood that the frame's job is not easy. The frame must:

1. Provide support for the rider, passenger, and all components.
2. Be rigid enough to assure accurate alignment of the wheels during acceleration, deceleration, and cornering.
3. Be strong enough to resist flexing under adverse conditions (rough surfaces, hard cornering).
4. Provide rigidity between front and rear suspension mounting points.
5. Provide rigid mounting of the engine for accurate alignment of drive train components.
6. Be light enough to provide good performance.

SUSPENSION

The SUSPENSION SYSTEM uses springs and hydraulic dampers to smooth the ride of a motorcycle. Modern motorcycle suspension systems can be classified into two general categories:

1. Suspensions designed for HIGHWAY or ROAD USE.
2. Suspensions designed for OFF-ROAD USE.

In both designs, it is the suspension's job to keep the wheels on the ground over bumps. At the same time, the suspension must absorb the jolts of rough roads before they are transmitted to the frame and rider.

Suspension operation

Suspension operation involves compression and extension. As the wheels roll over a bump, the suspension must compress against a spring, Fig. 1-33. After the spring has absorbed the suspension movement, it tends to rapidly extend the suspension. Unchecked, this will render a bouncing "pogo stick" effect.

To avoid this condition, SUSPENSION DAMPERS are provided inside the suspension components. These dampers are designed to help control the up and down movement of the suspension. Look at Fig. 1-34. Study it closely.

The most common types of motorcycle suspension are composed of TELESCOPING FORKS (tubes) on the front and a SWING ARM with shock absorbers on the rear. This suspension setup is illustrated in Fig. 1-35.

WHEELS, TIRES, BRAKES

WHEELS provide a mounting place for inflatable rubber tires. The WHEEL/TIRE ASSEMBLIES support the motorcycle and provide traction for cornering, braking, and delivery of engine power to the ground.

During the last few years, new wheel designs have emerged. In the past, the traditional spoked wheel offered the most practical service. As modern motorcycles became heavier and more powerful, the need for a stronger wheel arose. To fill this need, manufacturers designed a one-piece cast alloy wheel. This design offers a very rigid, maintenance-free, good-

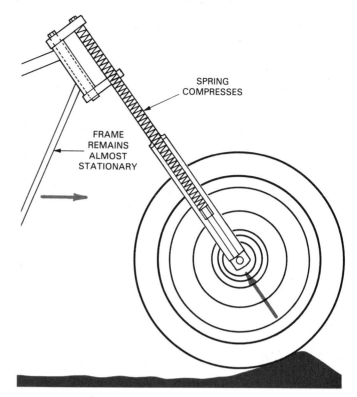

Fig. 1-33. Force applied to front suspension by bump is absorbed by fork springs.

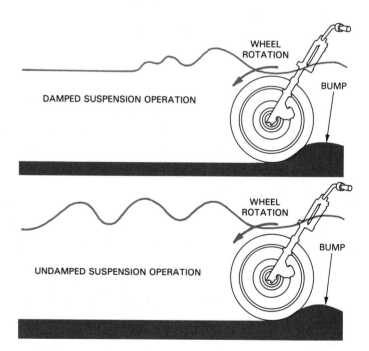

Fig. 1-34. Without suspension damping, motorcycle would be very uncomfortable to ride and hard to control over bumps. Suspension dampers are designed to eliminate uncontrolled bouncing.

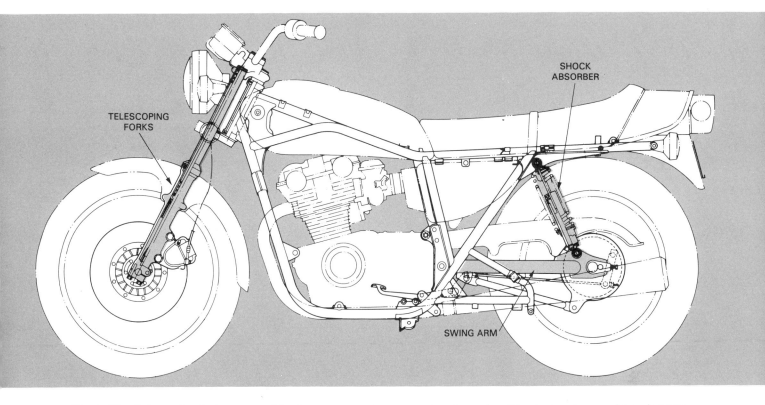

Fig. 1-35. Telescoping forks are used for front suspension on most motorcycles. Shock absorbers and a swing arm are commonly used for rear suspension. (U.S. Suzuki Motor Corporation)

looking wheel, Fig. 1-36.

The spoked wheel still has its place. It is less expensive to manufacture and, in some applications (off-road, for example), its ability to flex is needed. The spoked wheel consists of a hub, spokes, and rim. See Fig. 1-37. This type assembly provides a place to mount the tire, tube, and brake.

TIRES provide traction for moving the motorcycle and to assist the brakes in stopping. Today's tires are made of many different rubber compounds and tread designs. Each tire is designed for a certain use, as shown in Fig. 1-38.

BRAKES provide a controllable means of stopping the motorcycle. Common brake designs are DRUM and DISC types. A in Fig. 1-39 shows a drum brake

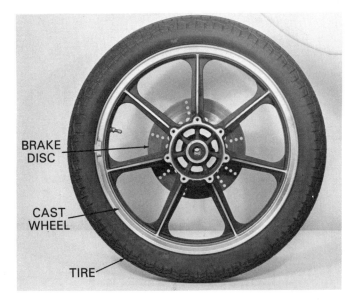

Fig. 1-36. Cast alloy wheel requires very little maintenance, is very strong, and good looking.

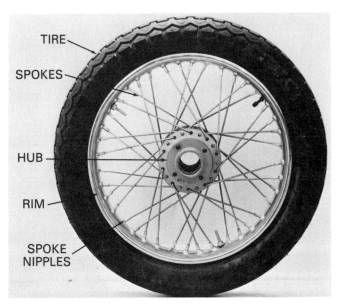

Fig. 1-37. A spoked wheel uses spokes with nipples to attach hub to rim.

Motorcycles

Fig. 1-38. Motorcycle tires vary in rubber compounds, profile, and tread pattern. A—High performance road tire suitable for "sport riding." B—Three universal designs are intended for use on road or in dirt. C—Trials universal design is also dual purpose but not as suitable for road use. D—Knobby design is strictly for off-road, dirt riding.

assembly. B in Fig. 1-39 illustrates disc brakes. Proper wheel, tire, and brake design is necessary for a safe, good-handling motorcycle.

ELECTRICAL SYSTEM

The ELECTRICAL SYSTEM supplies electrical power to various components on the motorcycle. Electrical power is used to "fire" the spark plugs, spin the starting motor and illuminate the lights.

The electrical system is composed of four subsystems:
1. Starting system.
2. Charging system.
3. Ignition system.
4. Accessory system.

Many motorcycles use a BATTERY to store and supply electricity for initial starting, ignition, and lighting. Fig. 1-40 shows the layout of a typical battery powered electrical system.

STARTING SYSTEM

The STARTING SYSTEM is used on many motorcycles to provide engine cranking and initial starting,

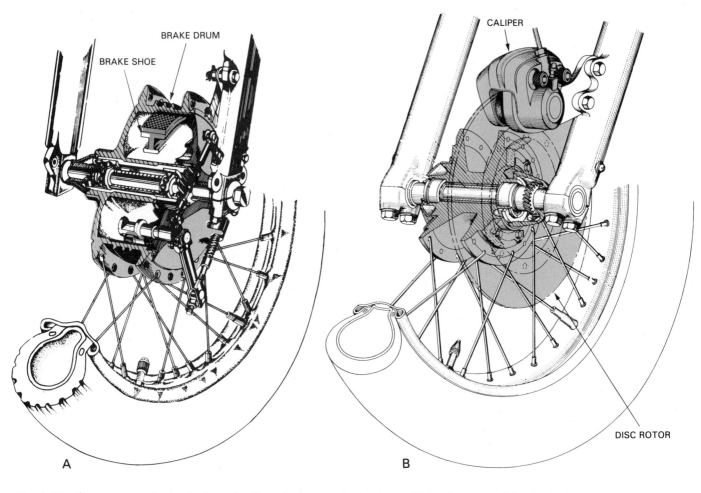

Fig. 1-39. Two common brake designs: A—Drum brakes use brake shoe which rubs on revolving brake drum. B—Disc brakes use brake pads that contact spinning disc. Study their construction.   (Kawasaki Motors Corp., U.S.A.)

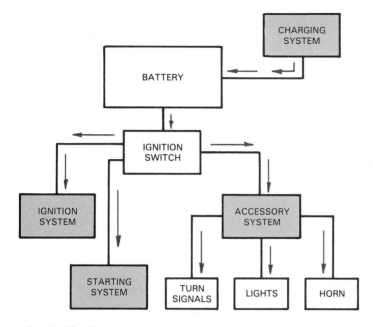

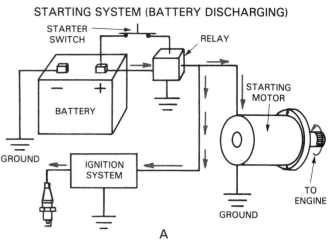

STARTING SYSTEM (BATTERY DISCHARGING)

A

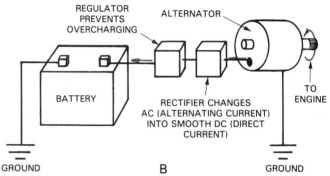

CHARGING SYSTEM (RECHARGING BATTERY)

REGULATOR PREVENTS OVERCHARGING

ALTERNATOR

RECTIFIER CHANGES AC (ALTERNATING CURRENT) INTO SMOOTH DC (DIRECT CURRENT)

B

Fig. 1-40. These are the basic components of a battery-powered electrical system. Battery supplies electrical power to ignition, starting, and accessory systems during engine starting. The charging system recharges the battery and supplies electricity when engine is running.

Fig. 1-41. It eliminates the need to kick the engine over with a foot pedal. The starting system consists of the battery, start switch, solenoid (relay), and starting motor. This is illustrated in Fig. 1-42.

When you push the start switch, a small amount of current flows to the relay. The current activates the relay and contact points in the relay close. The

Fig. 1-42. A—Current flows out of battery and into starting motor and ignition system. Motor spins engine for starting. B—Engine has started. Charging system supplies current to battery for recharging.

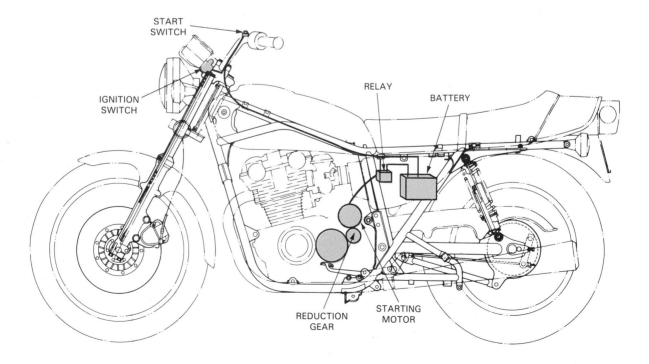

Fig. 1-41. Note the general location and parts of a basic starting system. Electric motor spins engine when activated by start switch, relay, and battery.   (U.S. Suzuki Motor Corp.)

battery-to-starter circuit is completed and a large amount of current flows to the starting motor. The motor spins the engine for starting. As soon as the engine is running, the start switch is released to de-energize the starter.

CHARGING SYSTEM

Since the battery supplies the initial electricity to power the ignition, accessory, and starting systems, it must be recharged. See Fig. 1-43. The charging system uses mechanical energy (engine rotation) to produce electrical energy for battery charging.

An ALTERNATOR, Fig. 1-42, is used on most motorcycles to generate electrical CURRENT (flow) and VOLTAGE (electrical pressure).

A rectifier and voltage regulator are also used in the charging system, Fig. 1-43. The RECTIFIER is needed to change alternating current (AC, flow constantly reverses) produced by the alternator to direct current (DC, flow in only one direction), which is required for the battery.

Since alternator output is directly related to engine speed, a VOLTAGE REGULATOR is used to prevent overcharging of the battery. The regulator matches the charge rate to the needs of the battery and other electrical components.

IGNITION SYSTEM

The IGNITION SYSTEM ignites the air-fuel mixture in the combustion chamber by means of an electrical arc at the spark plug.

Most motorcycle ignition systems are powered by the battery. The ignition system must step up (increase) battery voltage (about 12 volts) to over 20,000 volts. High voltage is needed to "fire" the spark plug. An IGNITION COIL is actually a step-up transformer which provides this high voltage. An ignition coil is shown in Fig. 1-44.

The ignition system must also provide a spark at the proper time during compression of the air-fuel mixture. A switching device driven by the crankshaft or camshaft is used to trigger the coil at the proper time, Fig. 1-45. Contact points or a magnetic triggering device are used. Provisions are made for adjustment of ignition timing to compensate for part wear.

Many dual purpose and off-road "bikes" use the MAGNETO or energy transfer type ignition system. In this system, the ignition is powered directly by the alternator. Fig. 1-46 illustrates a typical magneto ignition system.

ACCESSORY SYSTEM

The ACCESSORY SYSTEM includes all electrical components and wiring other than charging, starting, and ignition systems. Lights, horn, turn signals, and warning lights are some of the components in the accessory system. Fig. 1-47 shows the layout of a typical accessory system. These systems are all powered by the battery or alternator. A FUSE is provided to prevent damage in case of component or wiring failure.

FUEL SYSTEM

The FUEL SYSTEM must store fuel, mix air and fuel together in the proper proportions and, supply

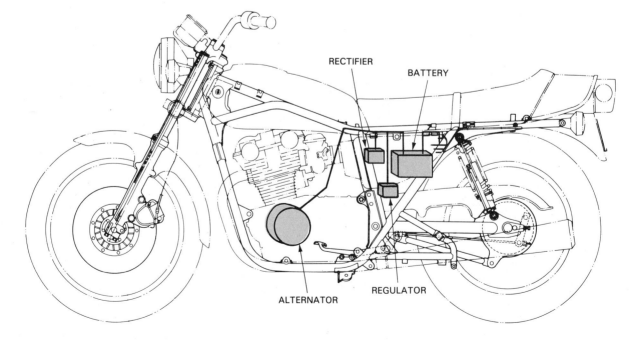

Fig. 1-43. Alternator is spun by engine. Alternator then produces current output that flows back into battery and to electrical system. Note general location of other charging system components.   (U.S. Suzuki Motor Corp.)

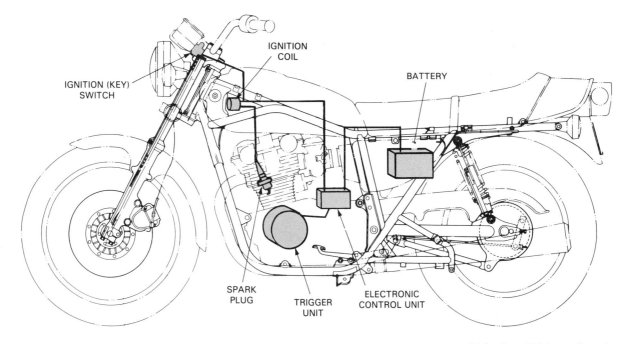

Fig. 1-44. Note general location and fundamental parts of an ignition system.   (U.S. Suzuki Motor Corp.)

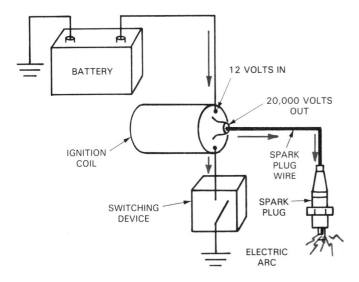

Fig. 1-45. Crankshaft driven switching device (magnetic trigger wheel and electronic control unit or breaker points) operates ignition coil. Coil increases battery voltage (12 volts) to over 20,000 volts. High voltage is needed to make spark jump gap at spark plug.

this mixture to the engine. The fuel system on a motorcycle consists of the fuel tank, fuel shutoff valve, fuel filter, fuel lines, carburetor, and air cleaner. A typical fuel system is shown in Fig. 1-48.

CARBURETOR

The CARBURETOR, Fig. 1-49, is the most complex part of the fuel system. It must supply the engine with an air-fuel mixture of about 15:1 (15 parts air to 1 part fuel by weight).

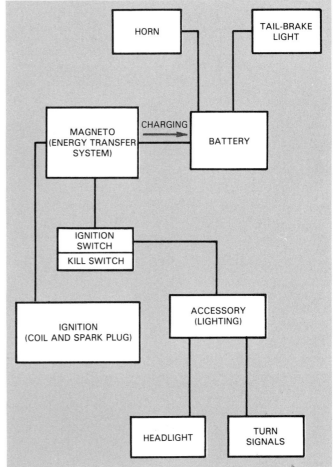

Fig. 1-46. Magneto ignition system is used on many small, dual-purpose motorcycles. If accessories are required, a battery is used along with magneto. A lighting circuit in magneto provides battery recharging.

However, at certain throttle settings, the carburetor is required to vary this ratio. See Fig. 1-50. Under starting conditions, for example, a RICH (high fuel content) air-fuel mixture of 3:1 (3 parts air, 1 part fuel) is needed. While cruising, this ratio can be LEANER (more air, less fuel) or around 16:1 (16 parts air per part fuel).

Carburetor operation

A carburetor relies on pressure differences for operation. It uses a venturi principle to draw fuel into the airstream. Look at Fig. 1-51.

A VENTURI is a restriction formed in the carburetor throat. As air passes through the venturi, it causes an increase in air velocity (speed) and a decrease in pressure (increased vacuum or suction).

Fig. 1-52 shows a simple carburetor using the venturi principle. Notice that outside atmospheric pressure is greater than venturi pressure, causing fuel to be drawn from the carburetor fuel reservoir into the airstream. The fuel is atomized (broken into small droplets) as it enters the airstream.

The THROTTLE TWIST GRIP, connected to the carburetor butterfly or throttle slide, controls airflow through the throat of the carburetor. See Fig. 1-53. As the throttle is opened, more air passes through the carburetor throat, causing more fuel to be drawn into the airstream. This results in increased engine speed and power.

An AIR CLEANER is provided in the fuel system to keep airborne dirt from being carried into the carburetor and engine. The basic action of an air cleaner is shown in Fig. 1-54.

KNOW THESE TERMS

Engine, Four-stroke cycle, Valve overlap, Flywheel, Two-stroke cycle, Work, Energy, Torque,

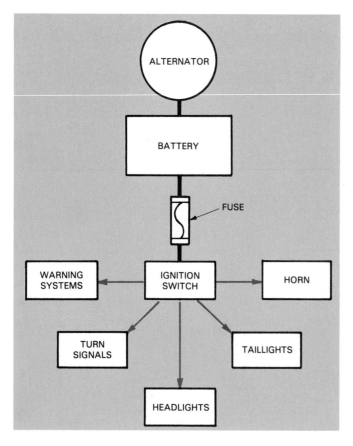

Fig. 1-47. Study this typical accessory system breakdown.

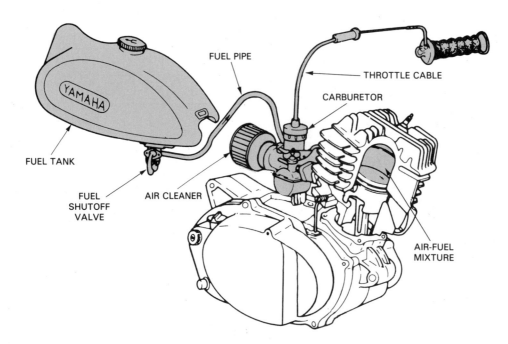

Fig. 1-48. Study basic parts of motorcycle fuel system. These parts regulate and direct air-fuel mixture flow into engine cylinder. (Yamaha Motor Corporation, U.S.A.)

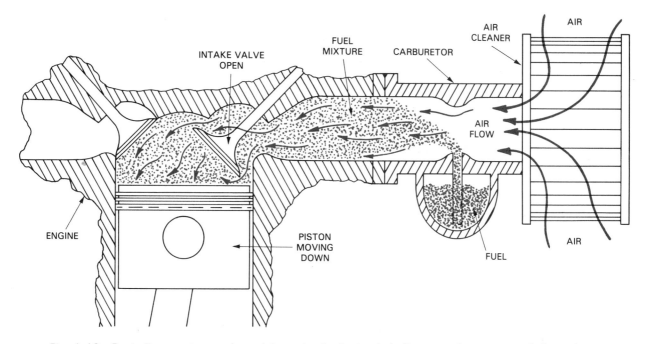

Fig. 1-49. Basically, a carburetor is a mixing valve for fuel and air. Downward movement of piston draws mixture into cylinder.

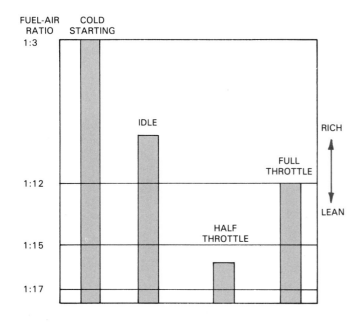

Fig. 1-50. Carburetor must provide different air-fuel ratios, depending upon throttle opening and engine demands.

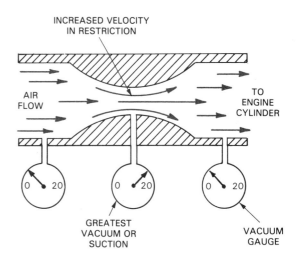

Fig. 1-51. As air passes through venturi, it speeds up, causing a vacuum (suction) in venturi.

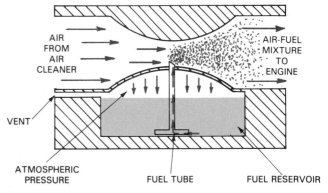

Fig. 1-52. Atmospheric pressure pushes down on fuel in fuel reservoir. When vacuum is produced by venturi airflow, fuel is pushed through fuel tube into airstream.

Power, Horsepower, Primary drive, Clutch, Gearbox, Final drive, Chassis, Frame, Suspension, Wheel, Tire, Brakes, Charging system, Starting system, Ignition system, Accessory system, Fuel system, Carburetor.

REVIEW QUESTIONS—CHAPTER 1

1. List the seven basic motorcycle systems.
2. Name the basic parts of an engine.
3. What is the correct sequence of events for a four-

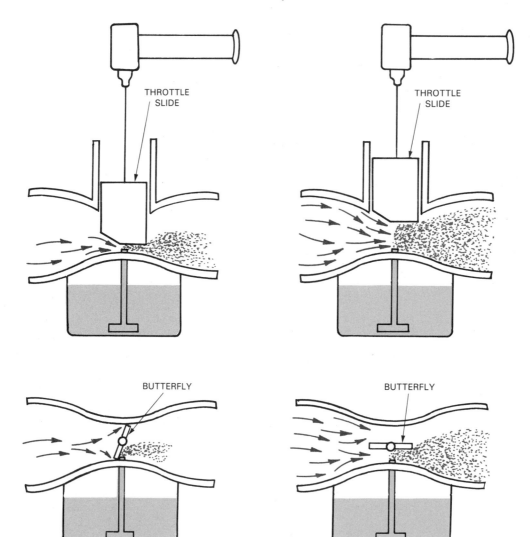

Fig. 1-53. Twist grip controls air and fuel flow through carburetor by changing slide or butterfly position.

stroke cycle engine?
   a. Intake, compression, exhaust, power.
   b. Exhaust, power, compression, intake.
   c. Intake, compression, power, exhaust.
   d. Compression, intake, power, exhaust.
4. When will both valves be closed during four-stroke cycle engine operation?
5. Valve overlap is when both valves are open. True or False?
6. Compression of the intake charge (compression stroke) has no effect on combustion. True or False?
7. How many revolutions of the crankshaft are made during one four-stroke cycle?
8. A flywheel _____ (increases, decreases) inertia of the crankshaft.
9. List two major differences between two-stroke and four-stroke cycle engines.
10. Name three ports in a two-stroke cycle engine.

11. The _____ opens and closes the transfer port in a two-stroke cycle engine.
12. Torque is a _____ force.
13. A _____ allows a motorcycle engine to operate in its most efficient power range at all times.
14. A primary drive connects the _____ to the _____.
15. A _____ engages and disengages power to the gearbox.
16. What are the three common types of final drives?
17. A _____ type frame uses the engine as a primary supporting member.
18. The most common types of suspension systems use _____ on the front and _____ _____ on the rear.
19. A damper is most likely found in a _____ system.
20. List the two types of motorcycle brakes.

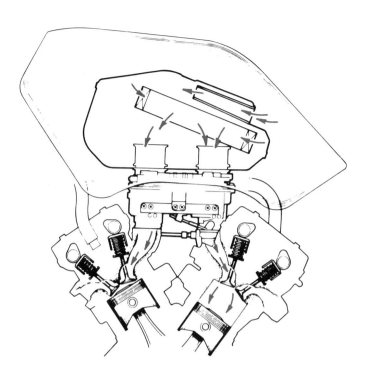

Fig. 1-54. Outside air enters air cleaner, passes through air filter, and flows into carburetors and engine. Filter removes airborne dirt from air, protecting engine from abrasive wear and damage. (Yamaha Motors Corp., U.S.A.)

21. Name the four electrical subsystems.
22. A magneto (energy transfer) is used on _____ type motorcycles.
23. A _____ mixes air and fuel to a ratio of about ____:____ under normal riding conditions.
24. The purpose of the battery in a motorcycle electrical system is to supply initial power for electrical components. True or False?
25. In a charging system, the _____ matches the rate of battery charging to battery needs.
26. The purpose of a carburetor venturi is:
    a. To increase air velocity in the carburetor throat.
    b. To decrease air pressure in the carburetor throat.
    c. To allow atmospheric pressure to push fuel into the carburetor throat.
    d. All of the above.
    e. None of the above.
27. An air cleaner protects both the carburetor and the engine from airborne dirt. True or False?

SUGGESTED ACTIVITIES

1. Make a chart comparing the differences between two-stroke and four-stroke cycle engines.
2. Select three two-stroke and three four-stroke motorcycle engines of the same displacement. Make a chart comparing the following features of the six engines. Use magazine articles, advertising brochures, owner and shop manuals to find the information.
    a. Exact displacement.
    b. Number of cylinders.
    c. Bore size.
    d. Stroke.
    e. Maximum horsepower at rpm.
    f. Maximum torque at rpm.
3. Research and find the most common direction of rotation for vertical, twin four-stroke engines. Then, identify an engine which rotates in the opposite direction and determine why.
4. Inspect any type of motorcycle and list the following information on a sheet of paper.
    a. Number of carburetors used.
    b. Type of air filter.
    c. Location of electrical system fuses.
    d. Type of ignition system.
    e. Type of wheels.
    f. Type of front and rear brakes.
    g. Type of tires.
    h. Frame type.
    i. Type of final drive.
    j. Type of gearbox.

A professional motorcycle mechanic will make a large investment in a full set of tools. This investment will pay off by speeding and simplifying repair work.   (Snap-On Tools)

Chapter 2

TOOLS

After studying this chapter, you will be able to:
☐ Identify the most common hand tools and equipment used by a motorcycle mechanic.
☐ List the safety rules for hand tools and equipment.
☐ Select the correct tool for the job.
☐ Describe the advantages and disadvantages of various tools.

To properly maintain and repair motorcycles, a substantial investment must be made in reliable hand tools. There are many different brands of tools available of varying quality and cost. It is not economical for a serious mechanic to invest in inferior tools. However, it is not always wise to buy the most expensive tools either.

In most cases, a mechanic should invest in good quality tools that are backed by a warranty. Then, if a tool is broken or damaged, the manufacturer's warranty will replace the tool at no cost to the mechanic.

This chapter will help you become familiar with the proper use and selection of motorcycle hand tools and equipment. It will prepare you for the more specialized chapters covering the repair of specific motorcycle systems and components.

The tools and equipment needed for the maintenance, service, and repair of motorcycles can be divided into several categories:
1. Common hand tools.
2. Electrical testing and service tools.
3. Measuring tools.
4. Engine service and repair tools.
5. Special service tools.
6. Fuel system service tools.
7. Wheel, suspension, and frame service tools.
8. Cleaning tools.
9. Power hand tools.
10. General shop equipment.
11. Machining equipment.
12. Miscellaneous tools.

HAND TOOLS

Common hand tools are the tools normally found in a mechanic's tool box. Major tool manufacturers offer tool sets ranging from basic starter sets to master mechanics sets. See Fig. 2-1. Some of the tools normally found in these sets are wrenches, ratchets, sockets, pliers, screwdrivers, and hammers.

Many times, different tools can be used to accomplish the same task. It is important for you to know when to select one type tool over another. As each tool type is discussed, pay close attention to the advantages and disadvantages of each tool.

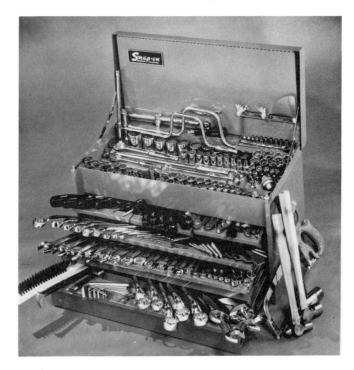

Fig. 2-1. A mechanic's starter set contains a variety of wrenches, sockets, screwdrivers, and miscellaneous hand tools. (Snap-On Tools)

WRENCHES

Various types of wrenches are utilized by the motorcycle mechanic. Wrenches may be broken down into five categories: box end wrenches, open end wrenches, combination wrenches, flare nut wrenches, and adjustable end wrenches. Fig. 2-2

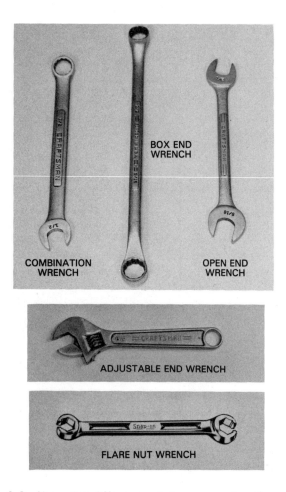

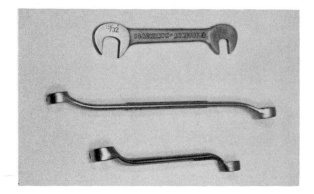

Fig. 2-2. Note the differences between combination, box end, and open end wrenches. An adjustable wrench is good for emergencies, when conventional wrench size is not available. Tubing wrench is used on brake lines and other tube fittings.

Fig. 2-3. Different wrench head angles, offsets, and lengths are available to meet space limitations and unusual applications.

shows each type of wrench. BOX END WRENCHES are closed on both ends. OPEN END WRENCHES have a full opening at both ends. COMBINATION WRENCHES are open on one end and box end on the other.

Box end, open end, and combination wrenches are usually available with various offsets and head angles, Fig. 2-3. Metric and English (American or conventional) sizes are necessary.

On standard fasteners, use a box type wrench whenever possible. It gives better support and reduces the possibility of fastener damage.

Flared tubing nuts (nuts on fuel lines and brake lines) require the use of a FLARE NUT WRENCH, Fig. 2-2. This type of wrench is similar to a box end wrench, but has a slot in the end. The slot allows it to be slipped over tubing and onto the flare nut, Fig. 2-4.

An ADJUSTABLE END WRENCH is an open end wrench which has one movable jaw to accommodate a range of sizes, Fig. 2-2. This type wrench is useful in applications where the proper wrench is NOT available. In motorcycle repair, an adjustable wrench is a "fill in" tool and is the least desirable type of wrench. Its movable jaw provides the least amount of fastener support and can round off the head of a fastener.

Proper use of wrenches

To work safely and prolong wrench and fastener life, you should:
1. Always use the proper size wrench.
2. When loosening or tightening fasteners, always

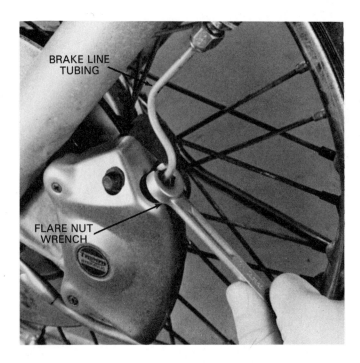

Fig. 2-4. A flare nut wrench gives support needed to tighten or loosen flared nuts. Using an open end wrench on flare nuts can collapse nut head.

pull rather than push the wrench.

3. Whenever possible, use a box end rather than an open end wrench. A box end grips the fastener head better.

4. Never hammer on wrenches to increase loosening or tightening torque.

5. Always replace a cracked or damaged wrench immediately. Never use it.

6. Do not use a pipe as an extension to increase leverage on a wrench. Damage to the tool and fastener may result.

SCREWDRIVERS

Two basic categories of screwdrivers are commonly used for motorcycle repair: STRAIGHT TIP and PHILLIPS TIP (cross point). See Fig. 2-5.

Many different sizes are available for both straight and Phillips screwdrivers. To prevent damage to the head of the fastener, the correct screwdriver TIP

SIZE must be used. Proper and improper examples are given in Fig. 2-6.

Phillips head screws can sometimes be very tight and troublesome to loosen. An IMPACT DRIVER (hammer driver), Fig. 2-7, provides the high torque and inward bit pressure to loosen the screw without damage. The most common Phillips bit sizes used on

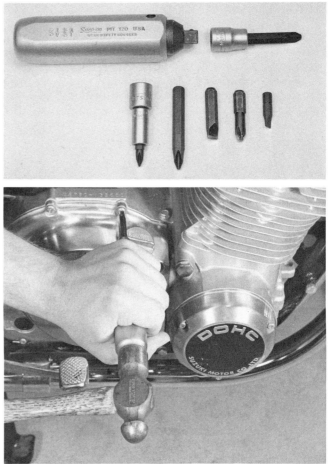

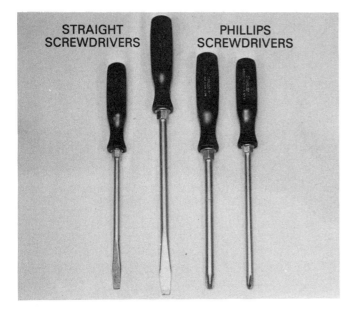

Fig. 2-5. Two general types of screwdrivers are straight tip and Phillips tip.

Fig. 2-7. An impact driver provides necessary inward pressure and torque to loosen stubborn fasteners without damaging them. When driver is hit with a hammer, driver rotates with tremendous force.

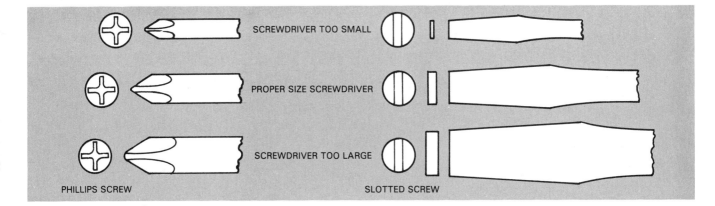

Fig. 2-6. Use correct size screwdriver to avoid damage to fastener or screwdriver.

motorcycles are number 2 and number 3.

WARNING! Always wear eye protection when using an impact driver. Bits of fastener can fly into your face.

Proper use of screwdrivers

To prevent injury and screwhead or screwdriver damage, you should:

1. Always use the proper size screwdriver for the application.
2. Avoid using screwdrivers as pry bars or chisels.
3. Never use a screwdriver so that the screwdriver tip could stab you if it slipped.
4. Do not hammer on screwdrivers.
5. Never use screwdrivers with worn tips. Damage to the fastener or injury may result.

SOCKET DRIVERS AND SOCKETS

SOCKET DRIVERS (ratchets, breaker bars, speed handles) and SOCKETS provide fast means of loosening and tightening fasteners.

A SOCKET is basically a box end wrench designed to be used on a socket handle. See Fig. 2-8. The box end part of the socket fits over the fastener head. The other end of the socket has a square opening that fits onto the driver handle.

A RATCHET is the most commonly used type of socket driver. As shown in Fig. 2-9, a ratchet allows quick selection of turning direction for either loosening or tightening.

Drive size

DRIVE SIZE refers to the dimensions of the square driving head on a ratchet, breaker bar, or speed handle, Fig. 2-10. Different drive sizes are needed because of space limitations and varying torque requirements. There are three drive sizes common to motorcycle mechanics: 1/4 in. drive, 3/8 in. drive, and 1/2 in. drive.

A 3/8 INCH DRIVE is the most frequently used drive size. It is strong, yet not too big and clumsy. A 1/4 INCH DRIVE is needed for very small fasteners. A 1/2 INCH DRIVE is strong enough to handle the larger jobs, requiring a high turning force.

Other drive handles

A breaker bar resembles a ratchet, except that it does not use a ratchet mechanism. See Fig. 2-11. BREAKER BARS are designed to break loose extremely tight fasteners which may overload and damage a ratchet.

A SPEED HANDLE is used for rapid turning of loose fasteners. Look at Fig. 2-12. It is NOT designed to apply final tightening or initial loosening torque.

Fig. 2-10. This is a 3/8 inch drive ratchet with two sockets. Spring-loaded ball prevents socket from falling off driving head.

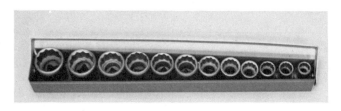

Fig. 2-8. This is a typical socket set and holder.

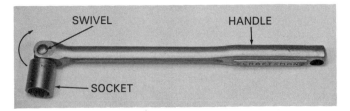

Fig. 2-11. Driving head on a breaker bar swivels but does not ratchet. High twisting force can be applied without breaking handle or swivel.

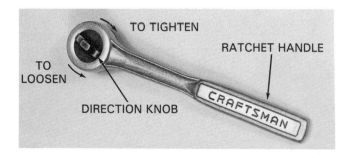

Fig. 2-9. Direction knob selects which way ratchet will rotate socket as handle is swung back and forth.

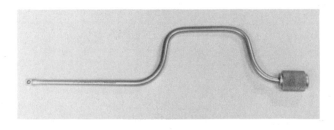

Fig. 2-12. Speed handle can be spun rapidly to run fasteners in or out quickly.

Sockets

There are four common variations of sockets: standard sockets, deep well sockets, 6-point sockets, and 12-point sockets. Sockets are available in metric and conventional sizes.

A STANDARD SOCKET is a short socket. It is the most frequently used type of socket. Figs. 2-10 and 2-11 give examples of standard sockets.

A DEEP WELL SOCKET is longer than a standard socket. It is needed to reach over a long stud bolt, for example. Fig. 2-13 illustrates one utilization of a deep well socket.

The terms 6-POINT and 12-POINT refer to the number of fastener driving edges or corners in the socket. See Fig. 2-14. A 6-point socket is preferable to a 12-point socket since there is less chance of rounding off the fastener head.

Universals and extensions

UNIVERSALS and EXTENSIONS increase the driving capabilities of sockets and driving handles. A UNIVERSAL, also called a swivel joint, allows the ratchet to drive the socket at an angle. An EXTENSION increases the distance between the ratchet and the socket, Figs. 2-15 and 2-16. Both are needed to drive fasteners in hard to reach locations. Universals and extensions are available in several drive sizes and designs to meet varying demands.

Proper use of sockets and socket drivers

There are several rules to remember when working with sockets and socket drivers. These include:
1. Always use the proper size socket and ratchet or breaker bar for the application.
2. When loosening or tightening fasteners with a ratchet or breaker bar, always pull rather than push on the tool.
3. When space permits, use a socket rather than an

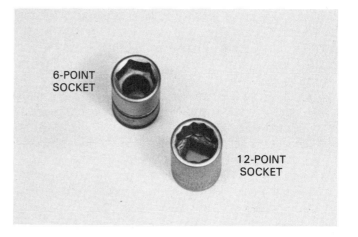

Fig. 2-14. You are less likely to damage a fastener head when using a 6-point socket because it contacts more area on flats of fastener.

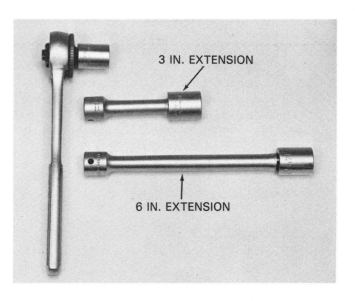

Fig. 2-15. Extensions are available in lengths from one inch to over one foot.

Fig. 2-13. A deep well socket is used to reach over studs or protruding threads to a nut.

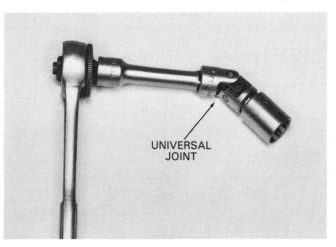

Fig. 2-16. A universal joint is helpful when trying to reach partially hidden fasteners.

open end wrench since it is faster and grips the fastener better.

4. Keep the ratchet as close as possible to the socket. Use extensions and deep well sockets only when necessary.

5. When using extensions, support the ratchet or breaker bar head to prevent applying side load on the socket and fastener.

6. Never hammer on ratchets or breaker bars to increase loosening or tightening torque.

7. Never use a pipe as an extension to improve leverage on a ratchet or breaker bar. Damage to the tool and fastener may result.

8. Always replace damaged sockets, ratchets, and breaker bars.

PLIERS

Pliers fall into an often misused tool category. Pliers should NEVER be used as a substitute for the proper wrench, socket, or screwdriver. PLIERS should only be used for gripping or holding. If pliers are used to grasp the head of a bolt, for example, the bolt head can be rounded off or damaged.

Common types of pliers for motorcycle repair are:

1. Standard or slip joint pliers, Fig. 2-17.
2. Adjustable channel pliers or channel locks, as shown in Fig. 2-18.
3. Locking pliers or vise grips, Fig. 2-19.
4. Side cutters or diagonals, Fig. 2-20.
5. Needle nose pliers, Fig. 2-21.
6. Circlip or snap ring pliers, Fig. 2-22.

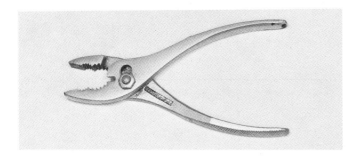

Fig. 2-17. Standard pliers are used to grip, hold, or pull on non-threaded components, such as: removing cotter pins, pulling out chain master-link clips, or when pulling wire.

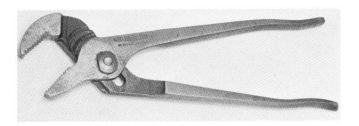

Fig. 2-18. Adjustable channel pliers provide good gripping leverage over a wide range of sizes. They can be opened wide for grasping very large objects.

As you can see, pliers come in various sizes and shapes to accommodate different jobs. Always select the appropriate kind.

Fig. 2-19. Locking pliers provide good gripping leverage and they lock on the workpiece. This will free your hands for other tasks.

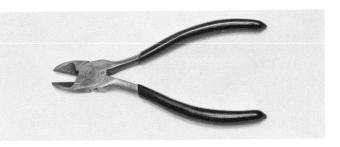

Fig. 2-20. Side cutters are used for cutting wire, pulling cotter pins, cutting small diameter hose, and other similar operations.

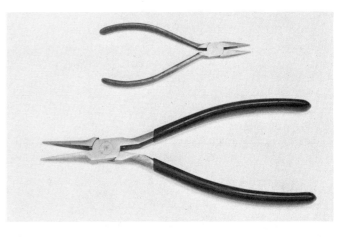

Fig. 2-21. Needle nose pliers are excellent for handling small parts in hard to reach areas.

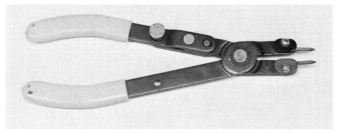

Fig. 2-22. Circlip or snap ring pliers are used to remove and install circlips. These particular circlip pliers have replaceable tips and a hinged handle for inside or outside snap rings.

ALLEN WRENCHES

ALLEN WRENCHES are used to loosen and tighten socket head cap screws. This is illustrated in Fig. 2-23. Allen wrenches come in metric and conventional sizes. They are also available as Allen sockets. ALLEN SOCKETS fit on a ratchet or breaker bar for high torque applications. See Fig. 2-24.

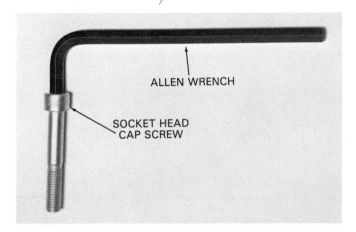

Fig. 2-23. A hexagon shaped Allen wrench is used to drive socket head fasteners. Allen wrench fits into hex cavity in cap screw.

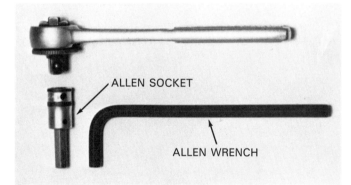

Fig. 2-24. Allen sockets and Allen keys (wrenches) are available.

Proper Allen wrench use

Remember to follow these rules when using Allen wrenches:
1. Always select the correct size Allen wrench for the job. Allen cap screws are easily damaged.
2. Always replace worn Allen wrenches.
3. Never use an air impact wrench on Allen sockets.

HAMMERS

Several different types of hammers are used by the motorcycle mechanic. The major difference in hammers is the material used to make the head and the size of the hammerhead. HAMMER TYPES commonly found in a motorcycle shop are: the ball peen,

brass, plastic, dead blow, rawhide, and rubber hammer. These types of hammers are shown in Figs. 2-25 through 2-30.

Hammerheads are made of soft and hard materials. The heads are available in different weights for specific applications. Generally, a hammerhead should be SOFTER than the material (part) being

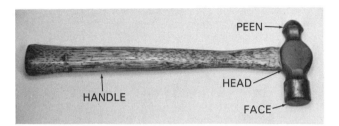

Fig. 2-25. A ball peen hammer is for general striking.

Fig. 2-26. Brass hammer is used for crankshaft trueing, hammering on punches and chisels, and other driving operations. It will provide a powerful striking force, but will not dent thick steel.

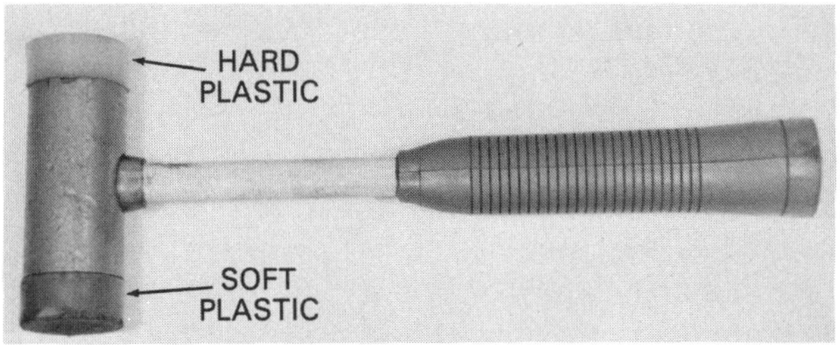

Fig. 2-27. Plastic hammer is good for loosening aluminum covers and other easily marred parts.

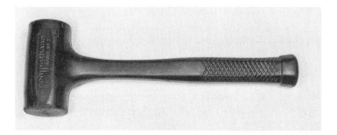

Fig. 2-28. A dead blow hammer's outer surfce is made of plastic, hard rubber or brass. Head of hammer is hollow and contains lead shot (round lead pellets). This prevents hammer from bouncing when object is hit.

Fig. 2-29. A rawhide hammer is handy when removing and installing some types of gearbox shafts.

Fig. 2-30. Rubber hammer can be used on tight fitting exhaust system components. It will not mark or dent thin chrome surface.

hammered on. For instance, a plastic hammer should be used to strike soft aluminum.

Some common examples for utilizing each type of hammer are:
1. Ball peen hammer—striking center punches and chisels.
2. Brass hammer—light blows for making assembled crankshaft alignment.
3. Plastic, dead blow, and rawhide hammers—tapping an axle into place or breaking loose stuck case covers.
4. Rubber hammer—assistance in assembling or disassembling easily dented exhaust systems.

Proper hammer use

To hammer safely, without part or tool damage, you should:
1. Never use a hammer handle as a pry bar.
2. Never use a hammer with a damaged handle (cracked handle, loose head, etc.).
3. Never use a hammer with an oily handle or when oil or grease is on your hands.
4. Use the proper type and size hammer for the job.
5. Always wear safety glasses when hammering.

FILES

FILES are designed to remove small amounts of metal, for smoothing, or shaping parts. Note file use in Fig. 2-31. Files are classified as single cut, double cut, fine, and coarse. These are easily identified by the file tooth pattern. Files come in a variety of shapes and sizes. Fig. 2-32 shows various file cuts and shapes.

File teeth cut in only one direction—on the forward stroke. Generally, large file teeth are for soft materials. Small file teeth are for hard materials. A FILE CARD is used to clean the clogged teeth of a file, Fig. 2-33.

Proper file use

When filing, you should follow these rules to increase file life and working efficiency:
1. Never use a file without a securely attached handle.
2. Always cut away from yourself.
3. Apply light pressure on the cutting stroke (for-

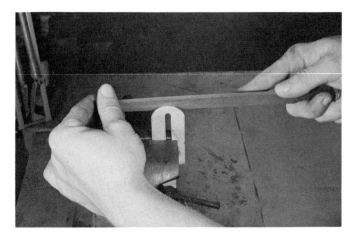

Fig. 2-31. Grasp the file as shown. By pushing it across workpiece, metal can be removed for smoothing or shaping. Files are designed to cut on the forward stroke only. Filing on the backstroke will dull file quickly.

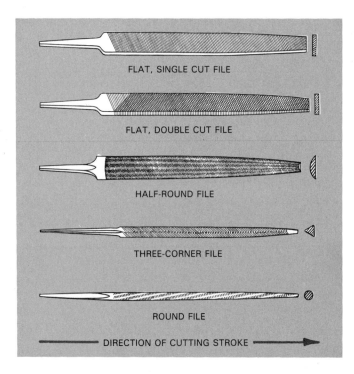

Fig. 2-32. Study various file shapes and cuts. Also note cutting direction.   (Starrett)

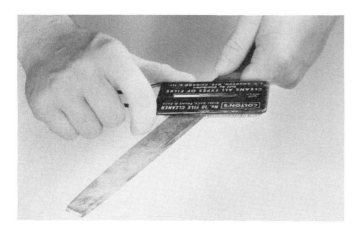

Fig. 2-33. Rub a file card across file to remove metal from clogged teeth.

ward stroke) and do NOT drag the file over the work on the noncutting stroke (backstroke).
4. Always wear safety glasses when filing.
5. Do not use worn (dull) files; replace them.

PUNCHES, CHISELS, AND PRY BARS

Some common types of punches and chisels are shown in Fig. 2-34. A CENTER PUNCH is frequently used to mark parts for reassembly or for indenting parts before drilling. A DRIFT PUNCH is used to drive shafts and bolts out of parts. A CHISEL is sometimes used to cut off damaged fasteners. ALIGNMENT PUNCHES can be inserted in holes in mating parts to shift the parts before starting bolts.

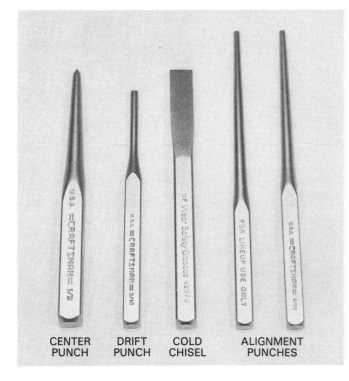

CENTER PUNCH   DRIFT PUNCH   COLD CHISEL   ALIGNMENT PUNCHES

Fig. 2-34. Always wear safety glasses and use a ball peen or brass hammer when striking punches and chisels.

PRY BARS will exert high leverage for lifting or moving heavy or large parts.

Proper use of punches, chisels, and pry bars

Punches, chisels, and pry bars can be very dangerous if misused. To utilize these tools safely, you should:
1. Never use punches or chisels with mushroomed (smashed) ends. Repair the tool by grinding or filing a chamfer on the end.
2. Always wear safety glasses when using punches, chisels, and pry bars.
3. Hold punches, chisels, and pry bars in such a way that you will not injure yourself if the tool slips.
4. Never use punches or chisels to loosen undamaged fasteners.

HACKSAW

A hacksaw is used for cutting metal parts, Fig. 2-35. Hacksaw blades are available in various pitches (number of teeth per inch). COARSE BLADES are for cutting soft metals like aluminum. FINE BLADES are for cutting thin tubing or hard materials. Hacksaw teeth only cut in one direction. The teeth cut on the push stroke. Install the hacksaw blade in the frame with the teeth pointing AWAY from the handle.

Proper hacksaw use

To prolong hacksaw blade life and to avoid injury, you should:
1. Always cut away from yourself and only apply light pressure on the cutting stroke.
2. Be sure the blade is tight.
3. Never use a damaged blade (cracked, kinked, missing teeth).
4. Always wear safety glasses when using a hacksaw.
5. Do not use your thumb to aid in starting a hacksaw. If starting is a problem, use a file to make a starting notch in the work.
6. Use full strokes to get maximum life from the blade.
7. Release downward pressure on the backstroke.

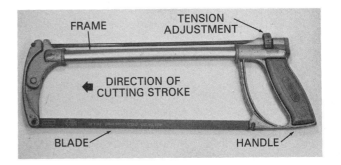

FRAME   TENSION ADJUSTMENT   DIRECTION OF CUTTING STROKE   BLADE   HANDLE

Fig. 2-35. Hacksaws, like files, are designed to cut only on forward stroke. Replacement blades are available with 12, 16, 18, 20, 24, and 32 teeth per inch.

MEASURING TOOLS

Measuring tools are used for a variety of tasks on almost every part of a motorcycle. Some measurements must be extremely precise, crankshaft journal measurement with a micrometer for example. Others require much less precision, like measuring drive chain free play with a six inch scale. Fig. 2-36 shows some of the more common measurement tools.

ENGINE SERVICE AND REPAIR TOOLS

Engine service and repair tools include a variety of tools often used on several engine models. They are needed for motorcycle engine testing, tear down, and assembly. Some of these tools may be provided in factory service tool sets. See Fig. 2-37.

SPECIAL SERVICE TOOLS

Special service tools are also provided in factory service tool sets, Fig. 2-38. Some of these tools are designed to do one specific job on one specific type motorcycle. In some cases, there is no other tool that will work. Other special service tools may be more universal in their use and application.

Factory service manuals often refer to factory service tools by PART NUMBER in their directions for disassembly, assembly, or service procedures.

FUEL SYSTEM SERVICE TOOLS

Fig. 2-39 shows some of the common tools needed to service and repair motorcycle fuel systems. Learn the name of each tool.

WHEEL, SUSPENSION, AND FRAME SERVICE TOOLS

Wheel, suspension, and frame tools are specialized tools frequently used by the motorcycle mechanic. See Fig. 2-40. They are usually not brand oriented but are useful in servicing all motorcycles.

CLEANING TOOLS

Cleaning tools are needed for proper removal of old gaskets, baked on oil or grease, and carbon. Several general types of cleaning tools are pictured in Fig. 2-41.

POWER HAND TOOLS

Power hand tools can be driven by either air pressure or electricity. A few power hand tools are shown in Fig. 2-42. AIR WRENCHES increase work speed or are helpful during removal of stubborn fasteners, Fig. 2-43.

Great care must be exercised in the use of air tools. They can easily overtorque and break fasteners, warp cases, strip threads, and permanently damage com-

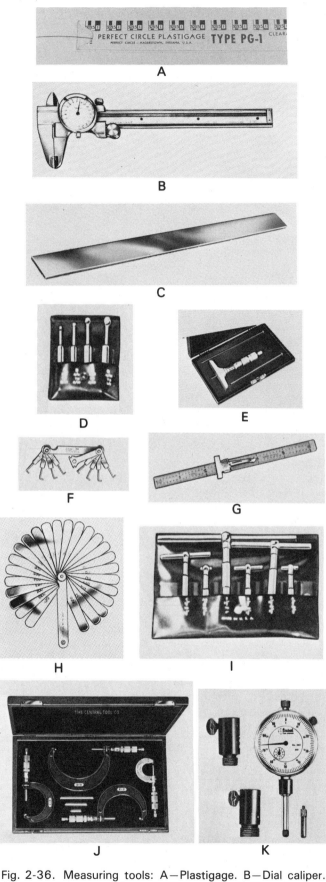

Fig. 2-36. Measuring tools: A—Plastigage. B—Dial caliper. C—Straight edge. D—Small hole gauges. E—Depth micrometer. F—Wire gauge. G—Six inch pocket scale. H—Flat feeler gauge. I—Telescoping gauges. J—Micrometer set. K—Dial indicator.

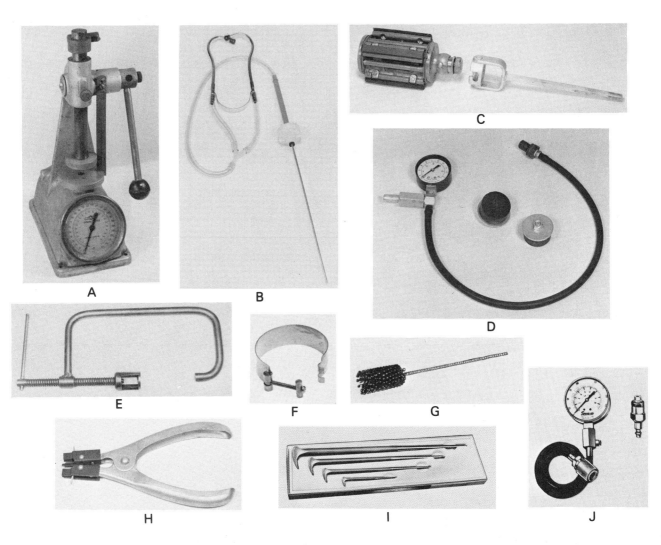

Fig. 2-37. Engine service and repair tools: A—Valve spring tester. B—Stethoscope. C—Cylinder hone. D—Crankcase leak tester. E—Valve spring compressor. F—Ring compressor. G—Cylinder deglazer. H—Ring expander. I—Pry bars. J—Compression tester.

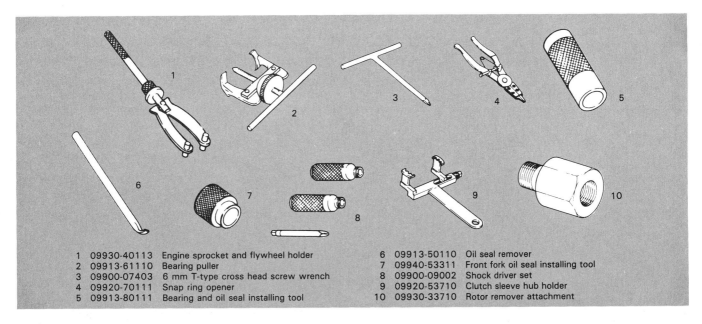

1	09930-40113	Engine sprocket and flywheel holder
2	09913-61110	Bearing puller
3	09900-07403	6 mm T-type cross head screw wrench
4	09920-70111	Snap ring opener
5	09913-80111	Bearing and oil seal installing tool
6	09913-50110	Oil seal remover
7	09940-53311	Front fork oil seal installing tool
8	09900-09002	Shock driver set
9	09920-53710	Clutch sleeve hub holder
10	09930-33710	Rotor remover attachment

Fig. 2-38. Manufacturer's special service tools (factory shop tools) are necessary for some motorcycle repairs. Tools are usually assigned a part number.   (U.S. Suzuki Motor Corp.)

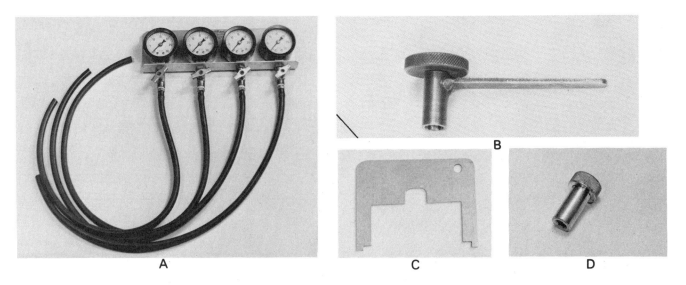

Fig. 2-39. Fuel system service tools: A—Vacuum gauges. B—Synchronization adjustment wrench. C—Float level gage. D—Jet wrench.

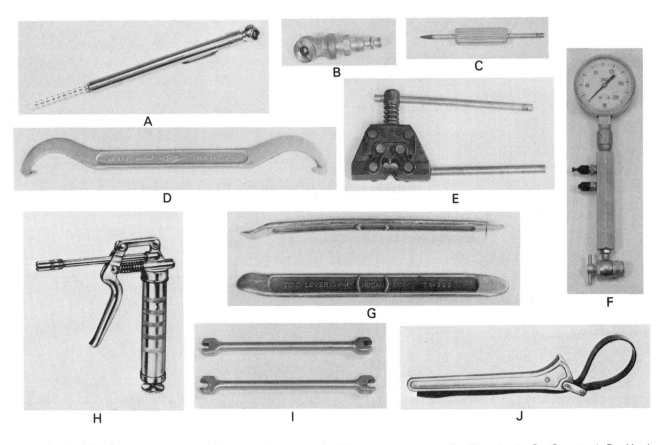

Fig. 2-40. Wheel, suspension, and frame service tools: A—Tire pressure gauge. B—Tire chuck. C—Core tool. D—Hook spanner wrench. E—Chain breaker. F—Fork/shock pressure gauge. G—Tire irons. H—Grease gun. I—Spoke wrenches. J—Strap wrench.

ponents. Special heavy duty impact sockets are designed for use with air impacts.

Note! Never start a bolt or nut with an impact. The fastener could cross thread, causing fastener or part damage. Impact sockets are usually flat black in color.

MISCELLANEOUS TOOLS

Miscellaneous tools are needed for specific types of jobs. Fig. 2-44 shows a variety of miscellaneous tools. Notice that most of these tools can be used on virtually any motorcycle. Directions for use are given in the service manual.

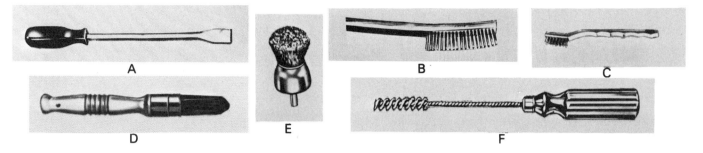

Fig. 2-41. Cleaning tools: A—Gasket scraper. B—Wire brush. C—Wire brush (small). D—Solvent brush. E—Rotary wire brush. F—Valve guide cleaning brush. (Snap-On Tools)

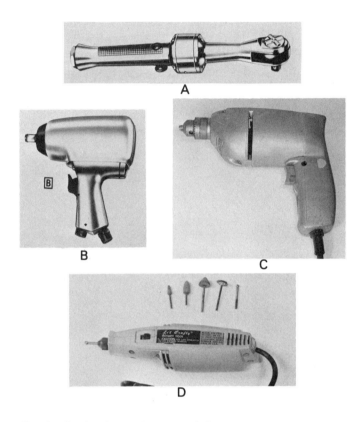

Fig. 2-42. A—Air ratchet with 3/8 in. drive. B—Air impact with 1/2 in. drive. Both can be used to speed up disassembly, but they should not be used for assembly. C—Electric drill. D—Rotary grinder. All are handy power hand tools. (Snap-On Tools)

PROPER CARE AND USE OF TOOLS

Hand tools are only as good as the mechanic using them! It is important to keep your tools well organized, lubricated if necessary, and clean.

The organization of a mechanic's toolbox tells a lot about a mechanic's attitude toward work. A sloppy mechanic usually does sloppy work!

Any motorcycle repair job can be broken down into separate operations—one of them being tool care. A professional mechanic will wipe tools clean and put them away at the completion of each operation. Proper care and organization of tools saves time, extends tool life, and reduces the possibility of tool loss.

GENERAL SHOP EQUIPMENT

GENERAL SHOP EQUIPMENT is normally provided by the motorcycle repair facility. However, some mechanics purchase some of the less expensive equipment. Fig. 2-45 pictures several pieces of shop equipment. Learn their names.

MACHINING EQUIPMENT

Fig. 2-46 shows typical motorcycle machine shop equipment. Most of this equipment is not found in a motorcycle shop because it is very expensive. However, a specialty or high performance shop may have all of this equipment and more.

ELECTRICAL TEST EQUIPMENT

Electrical test equipment is used to diagnose and test the electrical systems of a motorcycle. Fig. 2-47 shows a variety of electrical testing and service tools. Learn to identify each type.

Fig. 2-43. Large, stubborn fasteners, like countershaft sprocket nuts, can be easily loosened with a 1/2 in. drive air impact wrench.

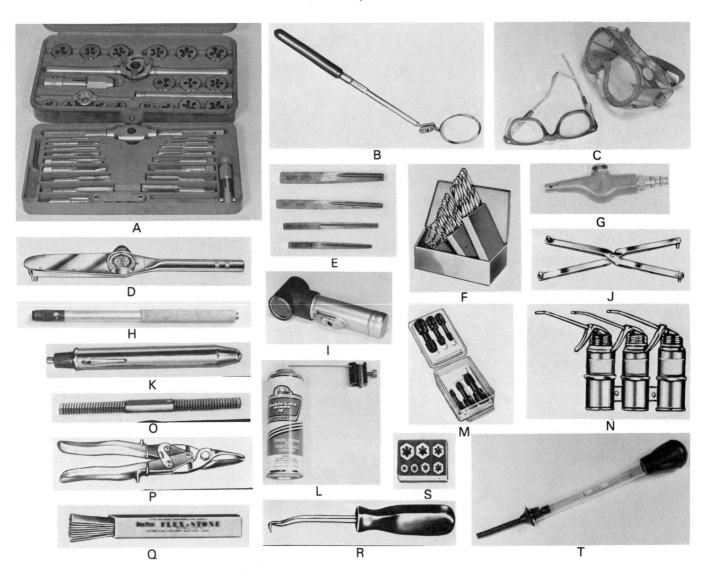

Fig. 2-44. Miscellaneous tools: A—Taps and dies. B—Mirror probe. C—Safety glasses and goggles. D—Torque wrench. E—Screw extractors. F—Drill index. G—Air blow gun. H—Screw starter—magnetic probe. I—Spark plug viewer. J—Pin spanner. K—Pen light. L—Cable lubricator. M—Internal thread chasers. N—Oil squirt cans. O—Thread file. P—Tin snips. Q—Flexstone. R—Cotter pin puller. S—External thread chasers. T—Antifreeze tester.

SHOP SAFETY

To produce a safe working environment and safe working habits, a safety conscious attitude must be developed. Safety in the shop is usually a matter of simple common sense. Taking safety for granted can result in a serious accident or injury.

Remember! You must know what to do in the event of an accident. Knowing the location of fire extinguishers, first aid kits, and emergency telephone numbers can be a "lifesaver."

The following list will help you develop a safety conscious attitude in the motorcycle shop:

1. Store gasoline in properly sealed containers.
2. Do NOT use gasoline as a parts washing solvent.
3. Clean up oil or gasoline spills immediately.
4. Always keep dirty shop towels in an approved container.
5. Never leave parts or tools laying on the floor.
6. Never smoke in the shop area.
7. Do NOT wear jewelry or loose clothing when working in the shop.
8. Always wear safety glasses or goggles when eye protection is required.
9. When mounting an engine or motorcycle on a stand or lift, get help if necessary and be certain the assembly is secure.
10. Use welding equipment only in designated areas and follow safety procedures.
11. Wear insulated gloves when working with heated parts.
12. Discard and replace broken tools.
13. Never run an engine in the shop until provisions are made for exhaust gas removal.
14. Always follow manufacturer operating instructions for special tools and equipment.

Fig. 2-45. General shop equipment: A—Wheel trueing stand. B—Pressure washer. C—Air compressor. D—Shop vacuum. E—Propane torch. F—Wheel dresser. G—Oxyacetylene torch. H—Solvent tank. I—Motorcycle lift. J—vise. K—Bench grinder. L—Scissors jack. M—Oven. (Snap-On Tools)

Note! This list is only a guideline. You must constantly think about safety to maintain a good safety record in your shop.

KNOW THESE TERMS

Tool warranty, Box end wrench, Open end wrench, Combination wrench, Impact driver, Socket driver, Ratchet, Drive size, Breaker bar, Speed handle, Standard socket, Deep well socket, 6-point, 12-point, Universal, Extension, Allen wrench, Philips, File, Center punch, Hacksaw, Air wrench, Safety conscious attitude.

REVIEW QUESTIONS—CHAPTER 2

1. List the three categories of wrenches used by the motorcycle mechanic.

2. Which of the following wrenches provides the best support and is least likely to damage the head of a fastener?
   a. Open end wrench.
   b. Spanner wrench.
   c. Box end wrench.
   d. Adjustable end wrench.

3. Straight tip and _____ tip are the two most common types of screwdrivers used by the motorcycle mechanic.

4. Sockets and wrenches come in conventional and _____ sizes.

5. What are the three common ratchet drive sizes used for motorcycle repair?

6. A tool that resembles a ratchet but does not use a ratchet mechanism is called a _____.

7. Which of the following is NOT one of the

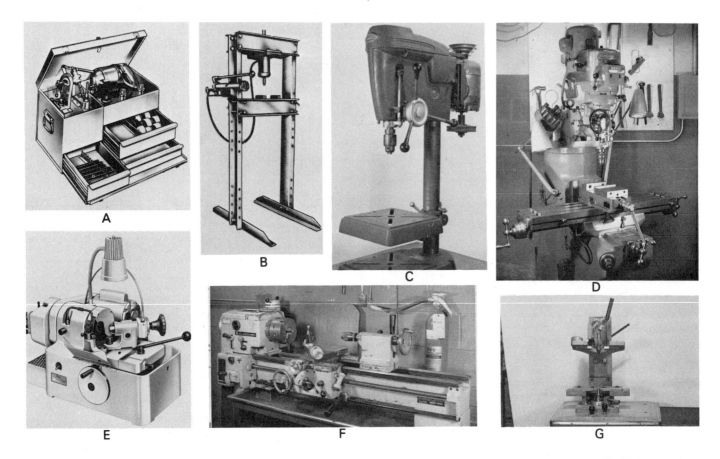

Fig. 2-46. Machining equipment: A—Valve seat grinder. B—Hydraulic press. C—Drill press. D—Vertical mill. E—Valve grinder. F—Lathe. G—Boring bar.

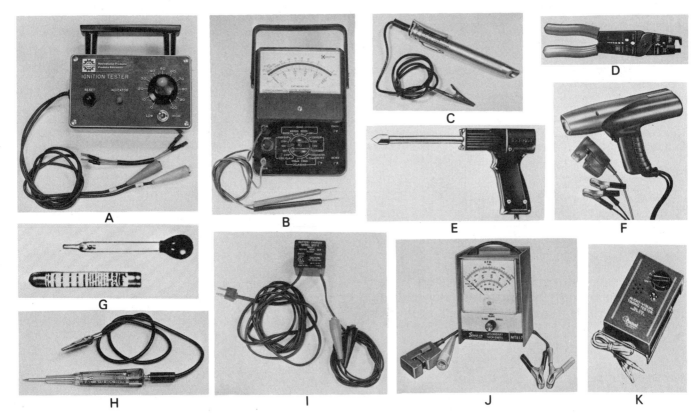

Fig. 2-47. Electrical testing and service tools: A—Ignition tester. B—VOM (volt-ohm-milliammeter). C—Continuity light. D—Wire crimp tool. E—Soldering iron. F—Timing light. G—Battery hydrometer. H—Low voltage test light. I—Battery charger. J—Dwell meter. K—Timing tester.

common variations of sockets used in motorcycle repair?
  a. 12-point.
  b. 8-point.
  c. Deep well.
  d. Standard (short).
  e. 6-point.
8. The purpose of an _____ is to move the ratchet away from the socket.
9. Pliers are useful for _____ or _____.
10. Allen wrenches are available in metric and conventional sizes. True or False?
11. List four types of hammers commonly found in a motorcycle shop.
12. Hacksaw and file teeth are designed to cut in only one direction. True or False?
13. Gasoline is acceptable as a parts cleaning solvent. True or False?

14. It is dangerous to wear _____ _____ or _____ when working in the shop.
15. Safety is dependent upon a _____ _____ attitude.

SUGGESTED ACTIVITIES

1. Acquire catalogs from major tool suppliers. Determine the type and prices of tools you would need to start your own tool set.
2. Research all available materials on tool safety and tool use. Use this information to begin a "safety notebook."
3. Using the service manual for your favorite motorcycle, make a list of the recommended uses of various types of pliers, sockets, wrenches, and hammers.

Other more specialized tools and equipment, like this engine stand, will be covered in later chapters, where they apply.

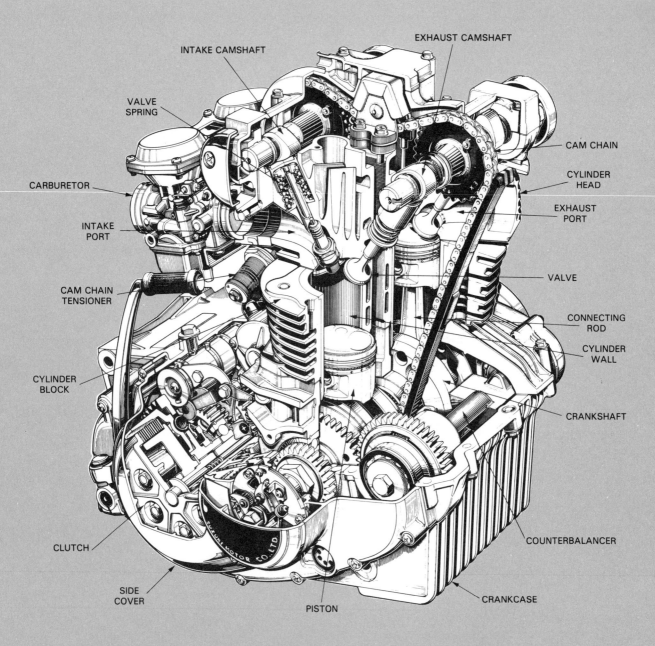

INTAKE CAMSHAFT

EXHAUST CAMSHAFT

VALVE SPRING

CAM CHAIN

CARBURETOR

CYLINDER HEAD

INTAKE PORT

EXHAUST PORT

CAM CHAIN TENSIONER

VALVE

CONNECTING ROD

CYLINDER WALL

CYLINDER BLOCK

CRANKSHAFT

CLUTCH

COUNTERBALANCER

SIDE COVER

CRANKCASE

PISTON

Study this cutaway view of a DOHC engine. Can you explain the basic function of each part?
(U.S. Suzuki Motor Corp.)

Chapter 3

MEASUREMENT AND PARTS CLEANING

After studying this chapter, you will be able to:
□ Select the proper cleaning method for the job.
□ Follow the safety rules critical to many cleaning operations.
□ Accurately measure motorcycle part wear using various types of measuring tools.

The first section of this chapter covers techniques for cleaning and inspecting motorcycle parts. You will learn safe and efficient methods for removing oil film, sludge, varnish, carbon, and corrosion. To prevent possible injury, safety rules are stressed with each type of cleaning method.

A good motorcycle mechanic realizes the importance of cleanliness when servicing or repairing a precision component. See Fig. 3-1. The slightest speck of dirt or metal can ruin or disable an engine, gearbox, or other complex and expensive assembly.

The second section of the chapter explains the use of precision measuring tools and equipment. It will include information on measuring with a micrometer, dial caliper, telescoping gauges, dial gauges, feeler gauges, pressure and vacuum gauges. Both the metric and conventional systems of measurement will be covered.

VISUAL INSPECTION AND CLEANING METHODS

It is general practice to always inspect motorcycle parts during disassembly and before reassembly. In the long run, close visual inspection for damage will save time and effort.

As one example, a piston with a cracked skirt (crack in lower, outer edge of piston) is very easy to overlook. The skirt should be cleaned and inspected closely. If the piston crack is NOT found, the engine may suffer serious damage when returned to service. The complete engine repair may have to be done over at the mechanic's or shop's expense.

METHODS OF CLEANING

Various types of deposits (carbon, varnish, sludge, dirt, grease, oil, rust, corrosion, and gum) are found in and on motorcycle parts. These deposits require several different cleaning techniques for removal. The common methods for cleaning motorcycle parts are:
1. Degreasing solvents.
2. Decarbonizing solvents.
3. Wire wheel.
4. Scraper.
5. Dry blasting.

Degreasing solvents

DEGREASING SOLVENTS are normally used for the removal of oil, sludge, or grease. They will NOT remove carbon deposits, corrosion, rust, and hard varnish. A degreasing tank is pictured in Fig. 3-2. Commercially prepared degreasing solvents are usually petroleum based (made from crude oil), but are chemically structured not to ignite and burn easily.

Fig. 3-1. Piston on left has heavy carbon deposits. Piston on right has been cleaned, inspected, measured, and is ready for installation.

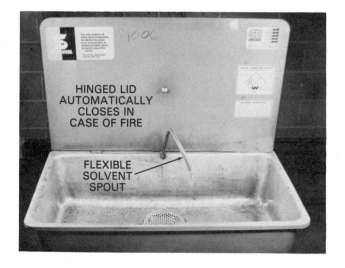

Fig. 3-2. Parts cleaning tank makes degreasing and cleaning a safe, simple task. Solvent is pumped from drum through flexible spout and then drains back into drum through filter.

CAUTION! Kerosene and gasoline must NEVER be used as a cleaning solvent. They are extremely flammable!

To use degreasing solvents, simply follow these steps:
1. Rinse and soak the parts for a few moments in the solvent. This is especially helpful on very dirty parts (heavy grease or sludge).
2. Wash and rub the parts using a cleaning brush and solvent, Fig. 3-3.
3. Dry the components using a blow gun and compressed air, Fig. 3-4. Make sure the gun is aimed away from your body and others. If compressed air is not available, a shop towel will work.

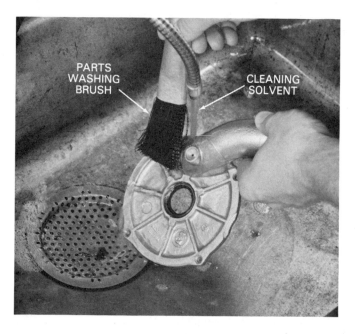

Fig. 3-3. Parts washing brush and solvent will quickly loosen and remove oily deposits.

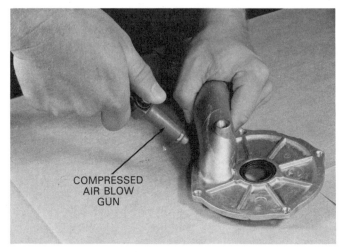

Fig. 3-4. Compressed air blow gun is used to dry parts after they have been cleaned in solvent. Wear safety glasses when using compressed air.

CAUTION! When using compressed air, wear safety glasses and use an OSHA (Occupational Safety and Health Administration) approved blow gun.

Decarbonizing solvents

DECARBONIZING SOLVENTS, sometimes called COLD SOAK CLEANERS, are specially formulated petroleum distillates. They loosen or soften carbon, gum, and varnish buildup on metal parts. See Fig. 3-5. Decarbonizing solvents are needed to remove stubborn or hard deposits, or those not easily removed with a scraper and degreasing solvents.

To use decarbonizing solvent, soak the parts for about fifteen to thirty minutes. Then, the parts must be washed in water to rinse off the powerful solvent.

CAUTION! Decarbonizing or cold soak cleaners are very strong! Always remember the following:
1. Decarbonizing solvents cause SEVERE BURNS. Use rubber gloves and safety glasses. If solvent comes into contact with your skin or eyes, follow the directions on the label of cleaner.
2. Decarbonizing solvents will remove paint and damage nonmetallic parts. Look at Fig. 3-6. Always remove any rubber or plastic components BEFORE submersing the main part in a decarbonizing cleaner.

Wire wheel (wire brush)

Deposits which are not removed by solvents (hard, thick carbon, rust, etc.) can usually be cleaned with a wire wheel. This is illustrated in Fig. 3-7. Since parts, especially soft aluminum parts, can be damaged by a wire wheel, use care and do not apply too much pressure.

CAUTION! When using a wire wheel, always wear SAFETY GLASSES and keep the tool rest and shield in place (close to the wire brush).

Common mistakes when using a wire wheel are:

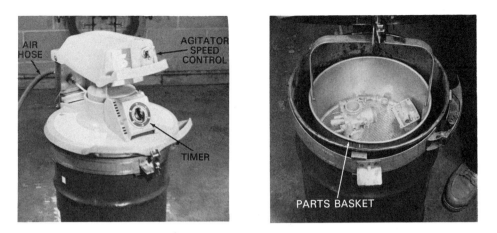

Fig. 3-5. Cold soak solvent is normally used for decarbonizing and carburetor cleaning. This cold soak cleaning tank uses an air driven agitator.

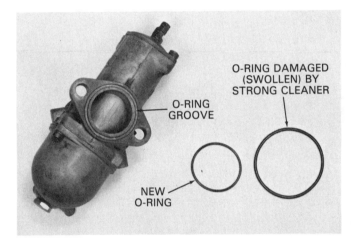

Fig. 3-6. Cold soak decarbonizing solvent will ruin rubber, plastic, and fiber parts. Notice how much O-ring on right expanded after exposure to cold soak or carburetor type cleaner.

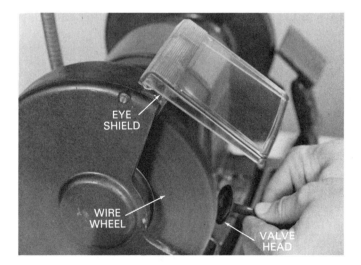

Fig. 3-7. A wire wheel is often used to clean carbon off of valve heads. To avoid catching the part in the brush, be careful to keep valve head at an angle to wire wheel. Always use the eye shield and safety glasses when operating wire wheel.

1. Damage to soft metal or aluminum parts (pistons, combustion chambers). Soft aluminum is easily marred by rubbing action of a wire wheel, Fig. 3-8.
2. Allowing parts to catch in the wheel. Part not held tightly. Part may be thrown and damaged or you could be injured.
3. Removal of metal plating by use of unnecessary brush pressure. Use only enough pressure to remove deposits.
4. Tool rest or safety shield NOT properly positioned—injury to face or eyes from flying debris. Refer to Fig. 3-9.

Scraper

A gasket scraper is used to remove gaskets, carbon, sludge, and sealing compounds from parts. For one example, look at Fig. 3-10.

When using a scraper, be careful not to slice into the metal or damage the part being cleaned. Even the slightest nick on a sealing surface can cause a leak. This is very critical on soft brass, copper, and aluminum parts.

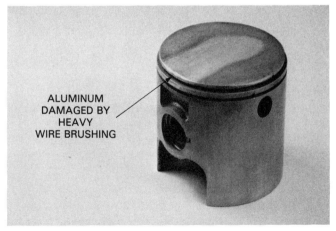

Fig. 3-8. This piston has been ruined by careless and excessive wire brushing.

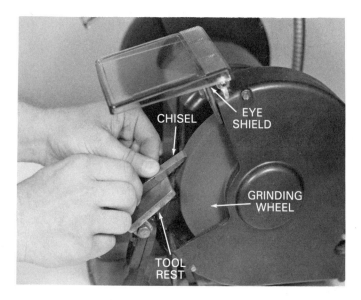

Fig. 3-9. Tool rest is used to support workpiece. Here tool rest helps to achieve proper angle while sharpening a chisel.

Fig. 3-10. When removing carbon from piston crown, use a dull scraper and be careful not to gouge aluminum. A sharp scraper is acceptable on harder metals.
(U.S. Suzuki Motor Corporation)

CAUTION! When using a hand scraper, scrape away from your body and always wear safety glasses.

Dry-blasting

DRY-BLAST CLEANING is the process of bombarding metal parts with glass shot (particles) to remove hard deposits. This method is quite different from sandblasting. Sandblasting is usually NOT acceptable for cleaning motorcycle parts because the sand will etch away the surface of the part being cleaned.

Fig. 3-11 shows a typical dry-blast cleaner. A dry-blast or glass-shot cleaner is useful for:
1. Removing hard carbon.
2. Removing rust and corrosion.
3. Cosmetic cleaning of engine cases, cylinder, and cylinder heads.

4. Surface preparation before painting.

A dry-blast cleaner is especially handy for cleaning hard to reach areas. It will clean in areas such as cylinder head cavities, cylinder ports, and between cylinder and case fins.

Obviously, the dry-blast cleaner is a great help to the mechanic. However, failure to remove all blasting grit can cause immediate damage to freshly assembled components. Proper preparation of parts BEFORE blasting and thorough cleaning AFTER blasting eliminates this problem.

To prepare parts for dry-blasting:
1. Remove all oil with solvent and thoroughly dry parts (includes threaded holes). Oil or grease will clog a dry-blaster.
2. Remove all ball, roller, and needle bearings.
3. Remove all seals.
4. Mask (tape over) any areas which may be damaged by dry-blast cleaning.

To remove grit after dry-blast cleaning:
1. Use compressed air for initial grit removal. Wear safety glasses!
2. Use solvent and a parts cleaning brush to remove grit.
3. Rinse parts in clean solvent and blow dry.
4. Use aerosol cleaner and compressed air to remove grit from all threaded holes.
5. Use thread chaser and blow out holes.

CAUTION! Do NOT use a tap to clean blasting material from threaded holes. The tap may jam into the bead blast substance, damaging the part or tap.

MEASUREMENT

Just about every aspect of motorcycle repair involves some type of measurement. A tune-up, engine overhaul, or even a simple chain adjustment requires measurement. There are two measuring systems—conventional (English) and metric (SI).

MEASURING SYSTEMS

You are probably more familiar with the CONVENTIONAL or English measuring system. It uses values like foot (ft), pound (lb), pounds per square inch (psi). The system used on most motorcycles is the METRIC SYSTEM, however. It has values such as centimetre (cm), kilogram (kg), kilopascal (kPa).

The metric system is a more consistent measuring system than our conventional system. The conventional system uses random number indexes. For example, it states that there are 12 inches in a foot and 3 feet in a yard. The average size for parts of the HUMAN BODY set the standards for the conventional measuring system.

The metric system uses more scientific multiples of ten to index all measurements. For example, 1000 millimetres equals 100 centimetres equals 10

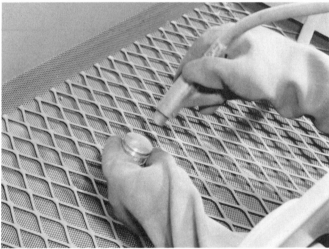

Fig. 3-11. Dry-blast cleaner is handy for removing hard deposits without eroding or damaging component. It is also useful for cleaning hard to reach areas.

decimeters equals 1 metre. Each of these numbers is equal and divisible by ten. This makes measurements with the metric system simpler and more consistent than with the conventional system.

Metric values

NOTE! Turn to pages 392 and 393 in this book. Study the charts showing metric values. Learn which metric values are equivalent to our conventional values.

Whether you are measuring distance, pressure, weight, or volume, it is sometimes necessary to change from conventional to metric or from metric to conventional. Conversion is normally done by using multipliers or a conversion chart. Multipliers are numbers that allow you to calculate an equal value in the other measuring system.

Again, turn to the rear of the text and study the conversion charts. They are very handy.

MEASURING TOOLS

Various types of measuring tools are frequently used in motorcycle mechanics. These include steel rulers, calipers, micrometers, pressure gauges. Selection of the correct measuring tool depends upon the available space and accuracy requirements. Proper tool use and selection is essential; it makes the job easier and more precise.

Yardstick (metrestick)

A STEEL YARDSTICK or METRESTICK can be used as a straightedge to check part alignment and for measurements not requiring extreme accuracy. As shown in Fig. 3-12, many have both conventional and metric scales. One very common use for a steel yardstick is to verify chain adjustment, as in Fig. 3-13.

Six inch scale (pocket rule)

Several types of six inch scales or rulers are available. Frequently termed a pocket scale, the most useful type has both conventional and metric scales. See Fig. 3-14.

A POCKET or SIX INCH SCALE is a very handy tool which can help the mechanic perform hundreds of different "rough" measurements on small parts.

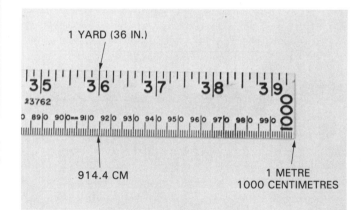

Fig. 3-12. A simple comparison of conventional and metric linear measurement is: 36 inches equals 914.4 centimetres.

Fig. 3-13. Chain and wheel alignment can be verified with a steel yardstick. Measure distance between axle center and swing arm pivot center on both sides of motorcycle. Measurement will be same if wheel is straight in frame.

53

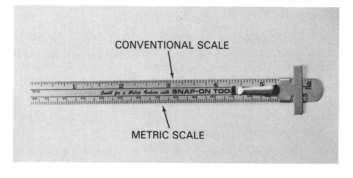

Fig. 3-14. This six inch pocket scale has both conventional and metric scales.

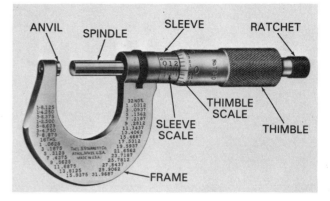

Fig. 3-16. Study names for basic parts of micrometer. (L.S. Starrett Company)

OUTSIDE MICROMETER

The OUTSIDE MICROMETER is one of the most important and frequently used precision measuring tools of the mechanic. It is used for the accurate measurement of numerous part dimensions. A metric outside micrometer is pictured in Fig. 3-15. Most outside micrometers are accurate to within .001 in. or 0.01 mm.

Reading a micrometer

Before reading a micrometer, you must first become familiar with the parts and scales of the micrometer. Fig. 3-16 illustrates the fundamental parts of a typical micrometer. Note the two scales used to make readings—the sleeve scale and the thimble scale.

The SLEEVE SCALE on a conventional micrometer is marked off in increments of .025 in. Each tenth of an inch (.100 in.) has a numeral.

The THIMBLE SCALE is marked off in .001 in. increments. Each full turn of the thimble moves the micrometer spindle .025 in. The edge of the thimble is used to indicate which sleeve marking to read. See Fig. 3-16. A horizontal reference line on the sleeve scale indicates which thimble number to read.

Adding the sleeve and thimble scales gives the final micrometer reading. Fig. 3-17 shows the basic pro-

Fig. 3-15. Outside micrometer shown here measures outside sizes with extreme accuracy.

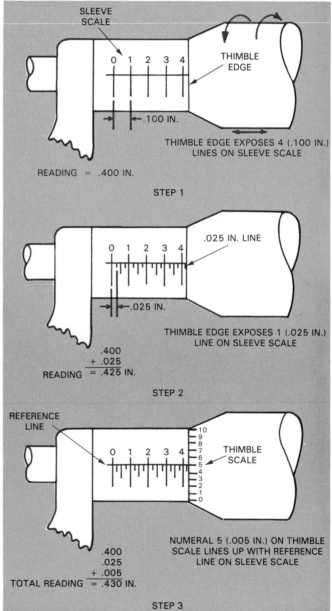

Fig. 3-17. Addition of steps 1, 2, and 3 give micrometer reading. First, take sleeve reading; second, thimble edge reading; finally, read thimble and add all three steps.

cedure for reading a micrometer.

First, read the largest sleeve number visible (each one equals .100). Second, count the visible sleeve marks past this number (each equals .025). Third, count the number of thimble marks past the sleeve reference line (each equals .001). If not perfectly aligned, round off your numbers. Finally, add the readings in steps 1, 2, and 3.

A metric micrometer is read the same way as a conventional micrometer, except the scale divisions are different. This is pointed out in Fig. 3-18.

For measurement of large diameters, larger micrometers are available. Conventional and metric micrometers come in various ranges, 0-1 in., 1-2 in., and up or 0-25 mm, 25-50 mm, and up. The micrometer size (2 in. for example) must be added to the micrometer reading (.236 in. for example) to determine the total measurement (2.236 in.).

Fig. 3-19 shows some practice or example micrometer readings. Cover the answer and try to find each micrometer reading without looking.

How to use outside micrometers

Accurate micrometer measurements require proper handling of a micrometer as well as the ability to correctly read the scales. It takes practice to get the feel for consistent readings.

Overtightening the micrometer or a loose fit on the part causes inaccurate readings. The part being measured must fit snugly between the anvil and spindle of the micrometer. Fig. 3-20 shows how to hold and adjust a micrometer. Grasp the frame in your palm and rotate the thimble with your thumb and fingers.

NOTE! Some micrometers are equipped with a ratchet type friction device to help obtain accurate and consistent readings.

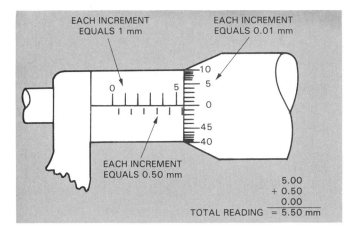

Fig. 3-18. Note scale divisions of a metric micrometer. They are given in millimetres (mm).

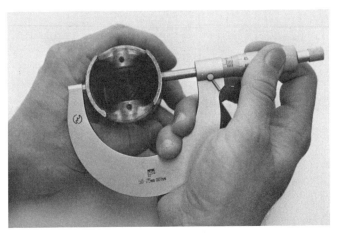

Fig. 3-20. Practice is required before you can make consistently accurate measurements. Hold tool as shown and gently screw thimble into part.

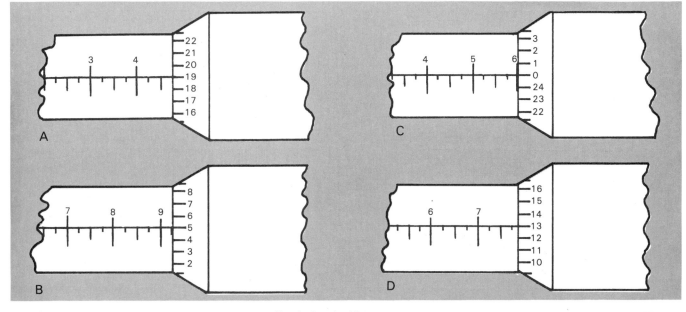

Fig. 3-19. Try to determine each micrometer reading before looking at answers (A = .469, B = .930, C = .600, D = .788).

Inside micrometer

The INSIDE MICROMETER works just like an outside micrometer. However, an anvil is NOT used. An inside micrometer will measure internal diameters and distances between surfaces. A typical example of inside micrometer use is shown in Fig. 3-21.

Depth micrometer

A DEPTH MICROMETER is used to measure the depth of a hole or recess in a part. See Fig. 3-22. The micrometer scale is read like other micrometer scales; however, it is adjusted in REVERSE, Fig. 3-23.

Dial caliper

A DIAL CALIPER is used to make inside, outside, and depth measurements. One is pictured in Fig. 3-24. Dial calipers are available with either metric or con-

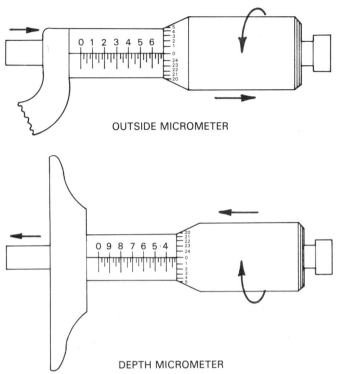

OUTSIDE MICROMETER

DEPTH MICROMETER

Fig. 3-23. A depth micrometer scale reads in reverse direction of an outside micrometer scale.

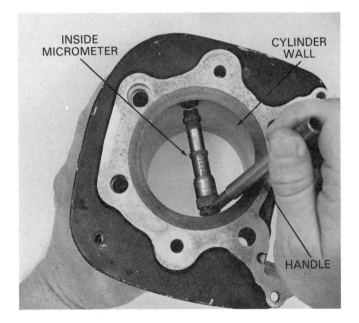

Fig. 3-21. Inside micrometer is useful for accurately measuring cylinder bore I.D. (inside diameter). A reading larger than specification would indicate cylinder wear and would require boring or sleeving.

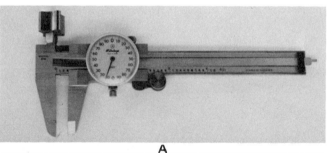

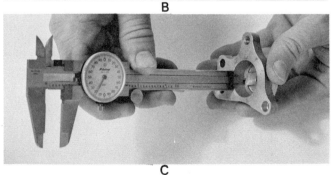

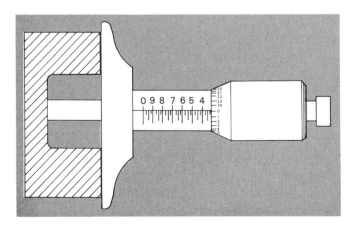

Fig. 3-22. This is a typical application for a depth micrometer.

Fig. 3-24. A dial caliper is capable of making inside, outside, and depth measurements: A—Inside diameter measurement. B—Outside diameter measurement. C—Depth measurement.

ventional scales. The large dial face is very easy to read.

Another type of caliper is the VERNIER CALIPER. This type of caliper is harder to read. For this reason, most mechanics elect to use a dial caliper.

CALIPERS are used for quick measurements requiring reasonable accuracy. They come in various shapes and sizes.

Telescoping gauge

A TELESCOPING GAUGE is a spring-loaded, T-shaped instrument used to duplicate inside diameters or distances. Two are shown in Fig. 3-25. A telescoping gauge by itself is of little use. As pictured in Fig. 3-26, it must be used with an OUTSIDE MICROMETER.

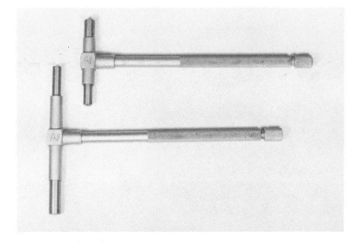

Fig. 3-25. Telescoping gauges are used only for duplicating inside diameters. They will fit into a small hole easily and still allow adjustment.

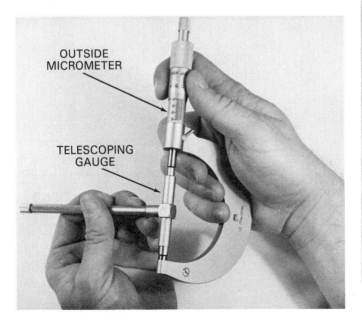

Fig. 3-26. Once a dimension has been duplicated by telescoping gauge, it is measured with an outside micrometer.

A telescoping gauge, like any precision measuring instrument, requires the proper feel and adjustment for accurate measurements. Fig. 3-27 shows the proper way to use a telescoping gauge.

Dial indicator

A DIAL INDICATOR, Fig. 3-28, is used for a variety of measurements. A dial indicator measures

Fig. 3-27. Accurate use of a telescoping gauge requires practice. This mechanic is measuring wear inside a transmission gear.

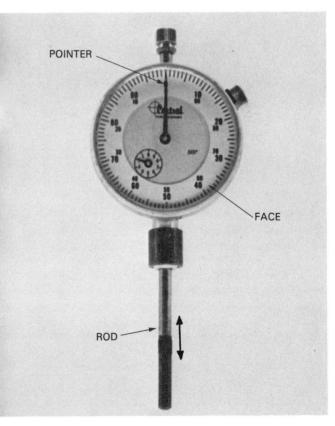

Fig. 3-28. Movement of indicator rod is transferred to indicator pointer. This is an English or conventional dial indicator. One full revolution of the gauge pointer equals .100 in. Each graduation equals .001 in.

movement. In the dial indicator, a vertical rod activates a circular scale pointer. Each scale graduation normally represents thousandths of an inch or hundredths of a millimeter. Common uses of a dial indicator are:

1. Measuring piston position for ignition timing.
2. Measuring shaft end play and runout.
3. Measuring gear backlash.
4. Crankshaft and wheel trueing.

A dial indicator must be set up or mounted parallel to the movement being measured, Fig. 3-29. If it is not positioned properly, false readings will result.

Dial bore gauge

A DIAL BORE GAUGE is a combination dial indicator and telescoping gauge. This is illustrated in Fig. 3-30. A dial bore gauge gives immediate measurement of an inside diameter. It is frequently used, for example, when measuring engine cylinder bore out-of-roundness and taper.

Feeler gauge (wire gauge)

A FEELER GAUGE is used to measure small clearances between parts, Fig. 3-31. It consists of a set of precision metal blades or wires of different thickness.

Feeler gauges usually come in sets ranging in size from around .001 in. to .025 in. (0.025 mm to 0.635 mm). Each blade size is often marked with both metric and conventional sizes.

A FLAT FEELER GAUGE, also called a strip or blade type feeler gauge, will accurately measure flat, parallel surfaces. Its use is illustrated in Fig. 3-32.

A WIRE GAUGE is similar to a flat feeler gauge

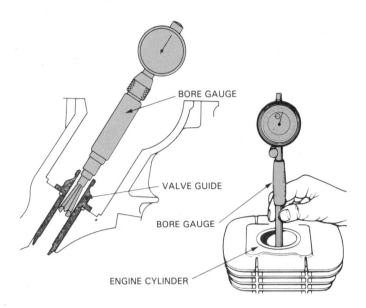

Fig. 3-30. A dial bore gauge is used for quick, accurate measurements of a tapered bore. When gauge is slowly moved from bottom to top of bore, movement of needle indicates taper and wear. (Yamaha Motor Corp., U.S.A. and U.S. Suzuki Motor Corp.)

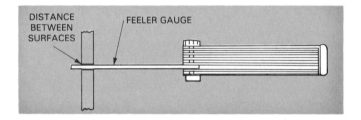

Fig. 3-31. Reasonably accurate measurements between surfaces can be quickly made with a feeler gauge.

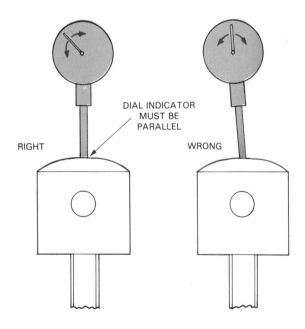

Fig. 3-29. To achieve accurate measurement, position dial indicator parallel to movement being measured. If not parallel, false readings will result.

Fig. 3-32. A flat feeler gauge is frequently used to check contact point gap.

but it has short wires of a precise diameter. See Fig. 3-33. A wire gauge is used to measure the clearance between irregular surfaces, like spark plug electrodes.

Plastigage

PLASTIGAGE is a disposable measuring device made of thin strips of a clay like substance. It is used to measure assembled clearances between plain bearings (rod bearings, main bearings, cam bearings). An example of how Plastigage will check bearing clearance is given in Fig. 3-34.

PRESSURE AND VACUUM MEASUREMENTS

Pressure and vacuum measurements frequently help the mechanic make accurate adjustments. They also aid in the diagnosis of many motorcycle problems.

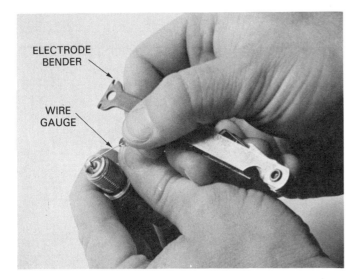

Fig. 3-33. A wire gauge will measure spark plug gap. Gap is adjusted by bending plug's ground electrode.

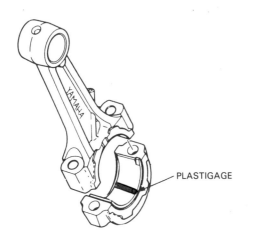

Fig. 3-34. A strip of Plastigage is placed on bearing. Then, the parts (connecting rod in this case) are assembled and torqued. After disassembly, width of the smashed Plastigage is compared to paper packaging scale. The Plastigage width indicates bearing clearance. (Yamaha Motor Corp., U.S.A.)

Typical applications for PRESSURE AND VACUUM MEASUREMENTS are:
1. Engine compression testing (check general engine condition).
2. Two-stroke cycle crankcase leak testing (check seals and gaskets).
3. Engine intake port vacuum measurement (carburetor adjustments and engine condition).
4. Fluid pressure testing (checking fuel and oil pressure).
5. Air pressure measurements (tire inflation).

Compression gauge

A COMPRESSION GAUGE measures the air pressure developed in an engine's combustion chamber on the compression stroke. See Fig. 3-35. This measurement quickly determines the mechanical condition of piston rings, cylinder walls, the head gasket, valves, camshaft, and the engine in general. The compression gauge reading should be within the factory specifications given in a service manual. If a low reading results, an engine problem exists.

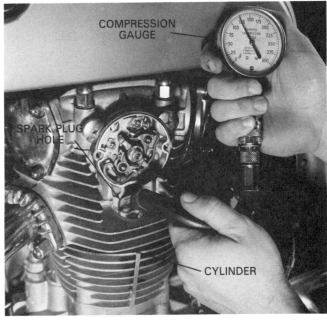

Fig. 3-35. Compression gauge indicates engine condition by measuring pressure on compression stroke. If pressure reading is lower than specs, engine rings, valves, or another component may be leaking. A high pressure reading indicates a carbon buildup in combustion chamber.

A compression gauge is screwed or held into the spark plug hole. The engine is then turned over while the throttle is held wide open. Continue cranking the engine until the pressure stops climbing. The gauge will read engine compression stroke pressure. A compression gauge may be used on either a two or four-stroke cycle engine.

A WET COMPRESSION TEST is used to determine exactly which parts inside a motorcycle engine might be causing low compression. First, perform a regular compression test. If compression is lower than specs, place about a teaspoon of motor oil in the low cylinder, Fig. 3-36. Then, repeat the test.

If the compression gauge reading GOES UP, the rings or cylinder are worn and leaking.

If the gauge reading STAYS THE SAME, then the valves or head gasket are probably at fault. The oil will temporarily seal any leakage past the piston rings. This permits problem isolation.

Two-stroke cycle leak tester

A two-stroke cycle leak test checks for leakage in the bottom-end and top-end of the engine. A source of pressure and vacuum is provided by a small pump and is monitored by a gauge. The procedure for this test is explained in the chapter on two-cycle engine overhaul.

Vacuum gauge

A VACUUM GAUGE is used to measure intake manifold vacuum (suction). See Fig. 3-37. The most common uses for this gauge are carburetor adjustment and to test for a vacuum leak at the carburetor or intake manifold. Vacuum readings lower than specifications point to a leak.

Fluid pressure gauge

A FLUID PRESSURE GAUGE can be used to measure fuel pressure or engine oil pressure. Sometimes, a vacuum gauge will also serve as a pressure

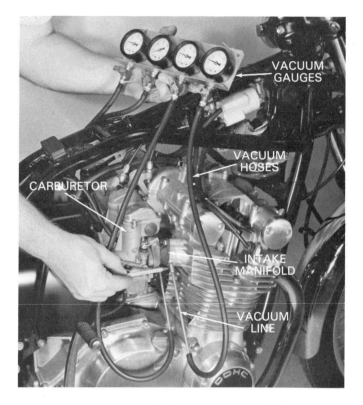

Fig. 3-37. Vacuum gauges connected to intake ports are used for making accurate throttle synchronization adjustments. They will also indicate vacuum leaks that would upset engine operation.

gauge. It can be connected to the pump output to measure pump pressure.

Tire gauge

You are probably familiar with a TIRE PRESSURE GAUGE, Fig. 3-38. It is commonly used to check air pressure in tires or air suspension units.

SPRING RATE MEASUREMENT

A SPRING TESTER is used to measure valve spring and clutch spring tension (pressure). Look at Fig. 3-39. When spring pressure, at a specified compressed height, is below specs, the spring has weakened. Quite often, the spring would be replaced. Sometimes, however, shims can be placed under the spring to increase tension to within factory specifications.

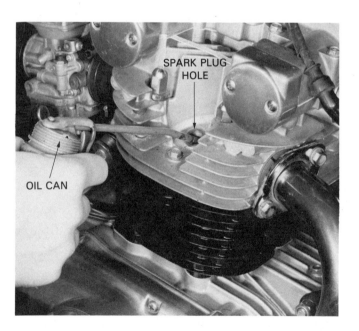

Fig. 3-36. If compression is low, squirt about a teaspoon of oil in each spark plug hole and check compression again. Oil will temporarily seal leaky rings. If compression is not improved, bad valves are probably the major cause of low compression. If compression improves significantly, piston rings may be worn.

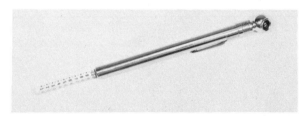

Fig. 3-38. Pencil type low pressure tire gauge is used for checking tire pressure on dirt bikes. Gauges with higher values are often needed for street bikes.

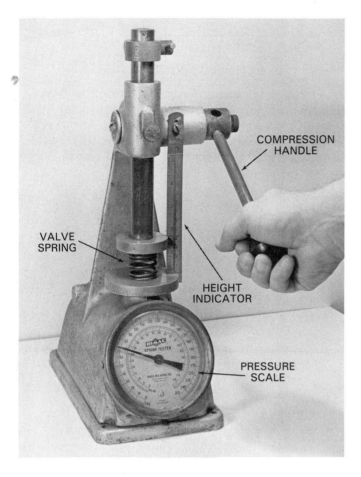

Fig. 3-39. A spring tester accurately measures spring pressure at a given height. Pressure reading is compared to factory specifications to determine spring condition.

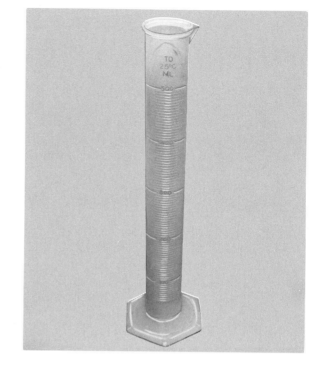

Fig. 3-40. Graduated cylinder will measure volumes in cubic centimetres or millilitres. Each line equals 5 cm³ or 5mL. Fluid level is matched to markings on cylinder to determine amount of fluid.

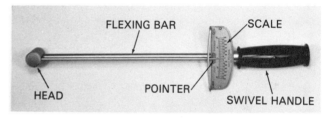

Fig. 3-41. A torque wrench is used to accurately tighten fasteners (head bolts, rod bolts). This torque wrench is incremented in both foot pounds and inch pounds.

FLUID VOLUME MEASUREMENT

Fluid volume measurement is necessary to accurately measure oil for forks, shock absorbers, gearboxes, primary chaincases, and fuel premixing.

A GRADUATED CYLINDER, baby bottle, or measuring cup can be used for accurate fluid volume measurement. Fig. 3-40 shows a graduated cylinder.

TORQUE MEASUREMENT

Tightening force or TORQUE MEASUREMENT is done with a TORQUE WRENCH, Fig. 3-41. Several types of torque wrenches are available in metric and conventional measuring systems. A 3/8 in. drive torque wrench is suitable for most motorcycle applications since bolt torques are relatively low.

KNOW THESE TERMS

Degreasing solvent, Decarbonizing solvent, Dry-blast cleaning, Conventional measuring system, Metric measuring system, Metrestick, Outside micrometer, Sleeve scale, Thimble scale, Depth micrometer, Dial caliper, Telescoping gauge, Dial indicator, Dial bore gauge, Feeler gauge, Plastigage, Compression gauge, Wet compression test, Two-stroke cycle leak test, Vacuum gauge, Pressure gauge, Spring tester, Graduated cylinder, Torque wrench.

REVIEW QUESTIONS—CHAPTER 3

1. Engine parts must be thoroughly _____ before they can be inspected and measured.
2. List three types of deposits found on engine parts.
3. What are two cautions to remember when working with decarbonizing solvents?
4. Sandblasting is an acceptable means of cleaning engine parts. True or False?
5. A measurement system which uses multiples of ten is called the _____ system.
6. The sleeve scale on a conventional (English) out-

side micrometer is marked off in increments of
_____.

7. What type of micrometer has a scale that reads in reverse?
8. A dial caliper is the most accurate measuring tool of the mechanic. True or False?
9. What measuring tool must be used in conjunction with a telescoping gauge?
    a. Inside micrometer.
    b. Outside micrometer.
    c. Dial indicator
    d. Metrestick.
10. List the four common uses for a dial indicator.
11. What two measurement tools are combined into a dial bore gauge?
12. What is the common conventional and metric range of a feeler gauge set?
13. The most common use of a vacuum gauge is for _____ _____ or _____.
14. What is the purpose of a torque wrench?
15. A_____ _____is commonly used to check and indicate engine condition. A

_____ _____ _____ will help isolate the engine problem.

SUGGESTED ACTIVITIES

1. Thoroughly clean the parts of an engine. Make a visual inspection of all parts and list any parts which need replacement.
2. Select appropriate engine parts and make practice measurements. Use each of the following precision measuring tools:
    a. Outside micrometer.
    b. Telescoping gauge.
    c. Dial caliper.
    d. Depth micrometer.
    e. Dial bore gauge.
    f. Plastigage.
3. A caliper makes inside, outside, and depth measurements. Compare caliper measurements to outside micrometer, telescoping gauge, and depth micrometer measurements on various parts.
4. Perform dry and wet compression tests on a motorcycle engine. Describe the results.

APPROXIMATE CONVERSIONS

MEASUREMENT		WHEN YOU KNOW:	YOU CAN FIND:	IF YOU MULTIPLY BY:
	Length	inch (in)	millimetre (mm)	25.4
		feet (ft)	metre (m)	.3
		yard (yd)	metre (m)	.9
		mile (mi)	kilometre (km)	1.6
		millimetre (mm)	inch (in)	.04
		centimetre (cm)	inch (in)	.39
		metre (m)	yard (yd)	1.09
		kilometre (km)	mile (mi)	.6
	Pressure	pounds per square inch (psi)	kilopascal (kPa)	6.89
		kilopascal (kPa)	pounds per square inch (psi)	.145
	Power	horsepower (hp)	kilowatt (kw)	.746
		kilowatt (kw)	horsepower (hp)	1.34
	Torque	pound-feet (lb-ft)	Newton-metre (N·m)	1.36
		Newton-metre (N·m)	pound-feet (lb-ft)	.74
	Volume	quart (qt)	litre (L)	.95
		litre (L)	quart (qt)	1.06
		cubic inch (in³)	litre (L)	.016
		litre (L)	cubic inch (in³)	61.02
	Mass	ounce (oz)	gram (g)	28.35
		gram (g)	ounce (oz)	.035
		pound (lb)	kilogram (kg)	.45
		kilogram (kg)	pound (lb)	2.20
	Speed	miles per hour (mph)	kilometres per hour (km/h)	1.61
		kilometres per hour (km/h)	miles per hour (mph)	.62

Chart gives most common metric-English and English-metric conversions. Study chart and make a few conversions.

Chapter 4

SPECIAL OPERATIONS

After studying this chapter, you will be able to:
- ☐ List safety rules for machining, cutting, drilling, welding, and other special operations.
- ☐ Correctly drill and deburr a hole.
- ☐ Repair damaged threads.
- ☐ Remove broken fasteners.
- ☐ Describe the use of a boring bar, lathe, mill, and other shop equipment.
- ☐ Explain basic welding techniques.

As a motorcycle mechanic, you will sometimes run into situations when special machining, cutting, welding, or other fabrication type operations must be performed. Adding accessory components, repairing damaged parts, and other unusual jobs require special skills, not covered in most service manuals. This chapter will introduce these special tools, equipment, and techniques.

CAUTION! All operations using power tools require safety glasses, protective clothing (no loose clothing or jewelry), correct operating procedures, and a safety conscious attitude.

DRILLING AND DEBURRING

DRILLING (machining a hole) is required during bracket fabrication, thread repairs, and many other instances where holes must be made in parts. A drill press or portable electric drill can be used with a variety of drill bits. Fig. 4-1 pictures a drill press, commonly used for drilling large holes. Fig. 4-2 shows a hand drill which is handy for making smaller holes. A set of drill bits is pictured in Fig. 4-3.

When using a drill, remember:
1. Always use a CENTER PUNCH to start the drill bit, Fig. 4-4.
2. Drill a PILOT HOLE if a large drill bit is to be used, Fig. 4-5.

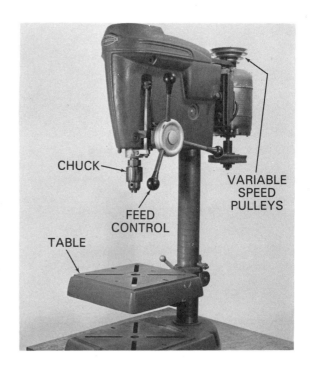

CHUCK

VARIABLE SPEED PULLEYS

FEED CONTROL

TABLE

Fig. 4-1. Always clamp part to table when using a drill press.

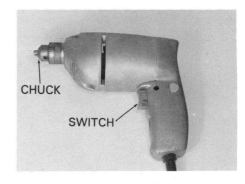

CHUCK

SWITCH

Fig. 4-2. A portable drill is handy when hole must be drilled in a part fastened to motorcycle.

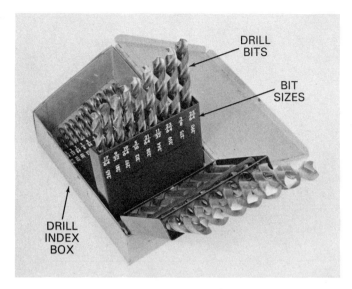

Fig. 4-3. To save time and effort, always store your drill bits in an index box.

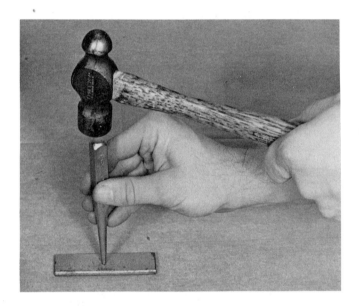

Fig. 4-4. A center punch aids in drill starting. Dimple formed by center punch guides tip of drill for initial cutting.

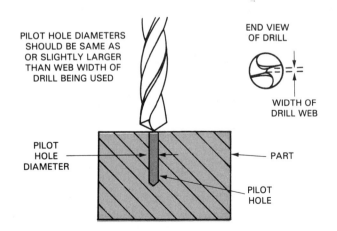

PILOT HOLE DIAMETERS SHOULD BE SAME AS OR SLIGHTLY LARGER THAN WEB WIDTH OF DRILL BEING USED

END VIEW OF DRILL

WIDTH OF DRILL WEB

PILOT HOLE DIAMETER

PART

PILOT HOLE

Fig. 4-5. Drill a pilot hole when finished hole diameter will be larger than 1/4 in. (6.35 mm).

3. Make sure the drill bit is TIGHT in the drill chuck, Fig. 4-6.
4. Use CUTTING FLUID (oil) on thick or hard metal, Fig. 4-7.
5. Do not spin the drill bit too fast or press too hard. Overheating will quickly soften and ruin the bit.

Drilling usually causes a BURR (rough edge) on both sides of the hole. A burr should be removed with

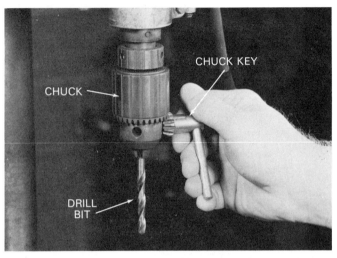

Fig. 4-6. A chuck holds and turns drill bit. Use chuck key to firmly tighten drill bit in chuck. Never leave key in chuck.

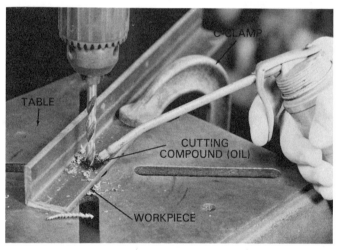

Fig. 4-7. Cutting oil is used to lubricate and cool drill bit. Workpiece should always be held firmly with c-clamps or in special drill press vise.

a deburring tool or countersink. Fig. 4-8 shows how a rough drilled hole can be cleaned up.

THREAD REPAIRS

THREAD REPAIRS are sometimes needed when threads have been stripped (broken out of hole or smashed) or when fasteners have been broken off inside a hole. For instance, look at Fig. 4-9. The broken

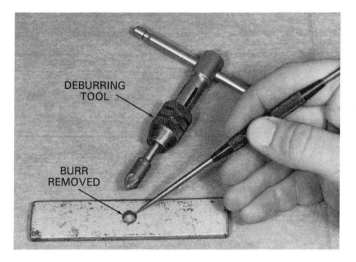

Fig. 4-8. A deburring tool was used to remove burr from drilled hole. Inserting and rotating tool will cut off any sharp edges.

Fig. 4-9. A typical broken fastener is shown. This one is in a hole which holds crankcases together. Broken bolt must be removed to salvage engine case.

bolt in this engine case would have to be removed very carefully, without part or internal thread damage.

There are a number of thread repairs that can be done quickly and inexpensively.

Minor thread repairs

MINOR THREAD REPAIRS can be made without complete thread replacement. When a thread has minor damage, such as flattening or misalignment from cross threading, it may NOT be necessary to totally replace the thread. Two useful tools for minor thread repairs are a thread file and thread chaser.

A THREAD FILE is used for external (bolt and stud) thread repairs. Shown in Fig. 4-10, it is simply rubbed parallel to the damaged threads to clean out the thread grooves.

A THREAD CHASER, Fig. 4-11, is used much like a tap which cuts internal threads. It is screwed into a threaded hole to cut away partially flattened threads.

Fig. 4-10. Thread file can be used to repair lightly damaged outside threads. Rub it parallel to threads for burr removal. Always select appropriate thread pitch (size).

Fig. 4-11. Thread chaser will repair lightly damaged inside threads. Avoid use of a tap in place of a thread chaser.

Major thread repairs

MAJOR THREAD REPAIRS must be performed when fasteners are broken off or threads are badly stripped.

Removing broken fasteners

Overtightening, corrosion, or extreme side loads (crash damage) can cause a fastener (bolt, screw, stud) to break off.

If the fastener is broken ABOVE the thread surface, locking pliers may be used to unscrew the fastener.

When a bolt is broken off FLUSH or BELOW the surface, it may be necessary to drill out the broken fastener and use an easy out (screw extractor). This is pictured in Fig. 4-12.

Accurate center punching and drilling is extremely important. Drilling the hole all the way through the fastener helps to relieve pressure and aids bolt removal.

Thread repair inserts

Sometimes, it is not possible to remove a broken fastener without thread damage. When this happens, a thread repair insert can be installed.

A THREAD REPAIR INSERT is a dependable and economical way to restore a severely stripped thread. Several types of thread repair inserts are available. Two are shown in Fig. 4-13.

Installation of a thread repair insert involves:
1. Drilling out the threaded hole.
2. Tapping the hole for the thread insert.
3. Installing the insert.

NOTE! Follow the instructions for the particular type of insert you are using. Procedures can vary.

Cutting new threads

Cutting new threads requires the use of a TAP for internal threads or a DIE for external threads. Tap and die sets, Fig. 4-14, are available in metric and conventional sizes.

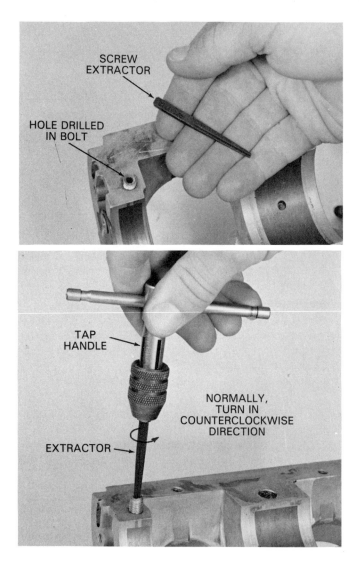

Fig. 4-12. This fastener is broken off flush with surface. It is easily removed by carefully drilling a hole in center of fastener and using an extractor. The extractor will unscrew broken section of bolt.

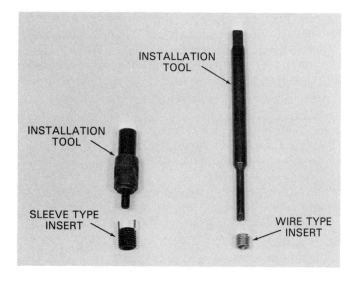

Fig. 4-13. Both of these are reliable thread repair devices. Sleeve type is easier to use but requires a much larger hole.

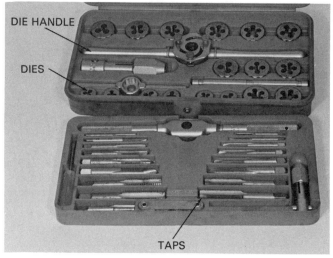

Fig. 4-14. Tap and die sets are available in conventional and metric sizes. Both are needed for motorcycle repair.

Dies are NOT frequently used in motorcycle repair since they cut external threads. External threads are found on bolts and studs which can be replaced easily.

Taps are often used for threading a new hole in parts being fabricated (brackets, accessory mounting) or preparing a hole for a thread repair insert.

The following procedure should be followed when tapping a new hole:

1. Drill a hole of the correct size. A tap drill chart will give the right size bit to use for a specific size tap. A tap-drill chart is located in the reference section of this book.
2. Lubricate the tap and hole with thread cutting fluid.
3. Start the tap squarely, Fig. 4-15.

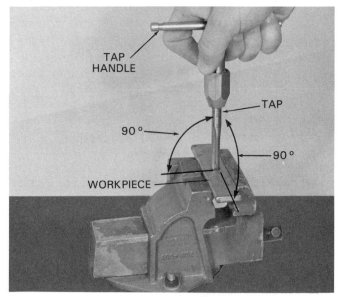

Fig. 4-15. For a straight and accurately tapped hole, tap must be started squarely. It is very easy to start it at an angle, ruining threads and possibly breaking the tap.

4. Back up (unscrew) the tap every one-half turn. This will clean cuttings out of the tap and prevent tap breakage. See Fig. 4-16.

MACHINING OPERATIONS

Major machining operations in a motorcycle shop may require the use of a boring bar, lathe, or vertical mill.

Boring bar

A BORING BAR is commonly used to machine worn engine cylinders to a larger diameter, Fig. 4-17.

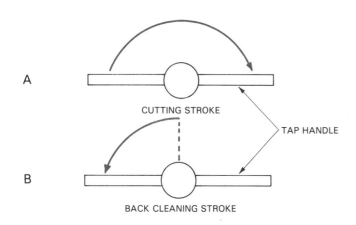

Fig. 4-16. After tap is started, tap must be back cleaned throughout threading process. A—Advance tap one-half turn at a time. B—After each half-turn of cutting, back clean tap by turning it counterclockwise one-fourth turn. Always use cutting oil to insure clean cutting and to lengthen tap life.

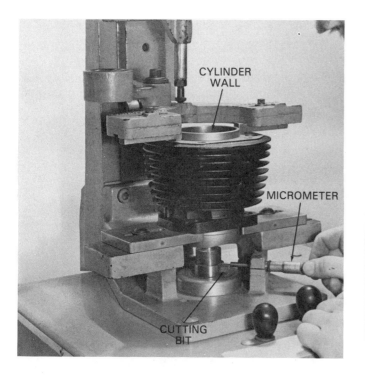

Fig. 4-17. Accurate positioning of boring bar cutting bit is done with built-in micrometer. Cutter feeds up through cylinder to true wall surface and allow for oversize piston.

The cylinder is held in position by a clamp. A cutting bit mounted on a rotating shaft machines (cuts) the cylinder bore. The amount of material removed is determined by the position of the cutting bit. A special micrometer is used to set the cutting bit for the desired size of cut.

Boring bar operating procedures vary from one brand to another. Important steps to remember with any boring bar are:
1. Double-check for accurate centering.
2. First, make a .001 in. (0.025 mm) cut to verify centering.
3. Do not take excessively large cuts (See bar instructions).
4. Always use a sharp cutter.

CAUTION! Make sure you have been fully trained before operating any type of machining equipment. They can be very dangerous if used improperly.

Lathe and vertical mill

A LATHE and VERTICAL MILL are expensive pieces of machining equipment. They are commonly found in specialized or high performance motorcycle machine shops. See Figs. 4-18 and 4-19. With these two tools, an experienced machinist can do many custom motorcycle machining operations, including fabrication of specialized parts.

Resurfacing parts

Resurfacing may be needed on a warped cylinder, cylinder head, or on damaged gasket surfaces. Minor resurfacing can usually be done on a FLAT PLATE covered with a piece of cutting paper. This is illustrated in Fig. 4-20. The part is rubbed on the cutting paper in a circular motion to remove high spots

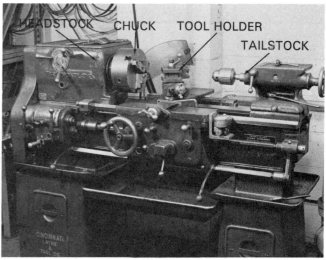

Fig. 4-18. A lathe is a machine tool used to accurately shape and size cylindrical components. Piece to be worked is mounted in rotating chuck. Cutting tool is mounted in movable tool holder.

Fig. 4-19. A vertical mill uses a rotating cutter to accurately remove metal.

Fig. 4-21. A bench grinder is a useful shop tool.

on the part. Badly nicked parts may also require draw filing.

Severely warped parts must be resurfaced by a machine shop. You would not be able to remove material accurately enough with a flat plate and cutting paper or by draw filing.

GRINDERS

Grinders are used for rough metal removal. Most shops have a BENCH GRINDER, Fig. 4-21. Some shops may also have a ROTARY GRINDER which is a handy tool for tight places, Fig. 4-22.

Avoid grinding aluminum or brass with abrasive stones. These soft materials will clog the stone.

WARNING! Improper use of a grinder can result in serious injury. Always wear eye protection and position the tool rest close to the stone.

Some other grinder rules to remember are:

1. When grinding small parts, hold them with locking pliers. This can help prevent serious hand injuries.
2. Use light pressure to avoid uneven stone wear, overheating, and catching.
3. Use water to keep parts cool during the grinding operation.
4. Do not grind near combustible materials. Check the area for flammable materials before grinding.

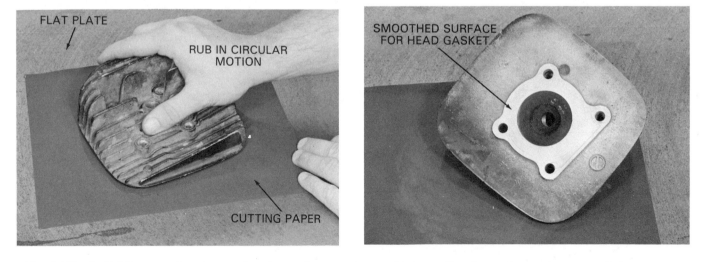

Fig. 4-20. A slightly warped or damaged gasket surface may be repaired on a flat plate using cutting paper. Rub part in a slow circular pattern. Solvent on both sides of cutting paper aids in both cutting and holding paper in place.

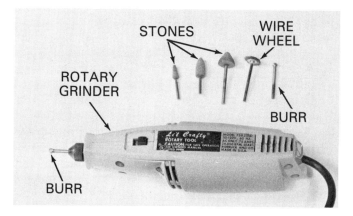

Fig. 4-22 A rotary grinder is used for light grinding, shaping, and polishing.

WELDING

WELDING uses extreme heat to melt and fuse metal parts together. High temperatures and a filler rod permanently connect the two parts. Welding is utilized in the repair of broken parts and fabrication of new parts. A gas flame or an electric arc can be used to produce sufficient heat for welding.

Common types of welding in motorcycle repair are: oxyacetylene (gas) welding, oxyacetylene brazing, and electric arc welding.

Oxyacetylene welding

OXYACETYLENE WELDING burns a mixture of oxygen and acetylene (flammable gas) to produce metal fusion. See Fig. 4-23. Filler rod is used to help fill the gap between the two parts.

Brazing

BRAZING is another form of oxyacetylene gas welding. It differs, however, from gas welding. Brazing uses less heat and a different filler rod (easier melting filler rod) than welding.

Gas welding causes a large area on the parts to be heated. As a result, it is not advisable to use gas welding for frame repair or when part warpage is critical. Oxyacetylene is very useful for exhaust system fabrication and repair, or heating metal parts for bending.

Electric arc welding

There are two types of electric arc welding common to motorcycle repair. These are AC (alternating current) or electric arc welding and heliarc welding.

ELECTRIC ARC WELDING uses a large electric current and electric arc to produce extreme heat. A steel filler rod, called an ELECTRODE, is melted into the joint. Fig. 4-24 illustrates arc welding.

Arc welding is frequently used for motorcycle frame repairs or when repairing other steel parts.

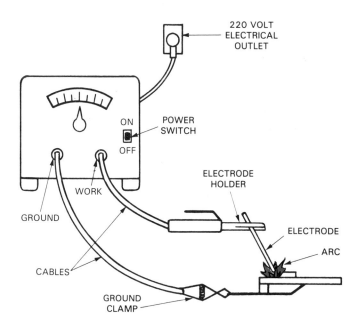

Fig. 4-24. Electric welder forces a very high current through cables, electrode, and workpiece. Since electrode is held away from metal parts, an electric arc jumps gap between electrode and part. Arc produces tremendous heat which melts both electrode and metal part.

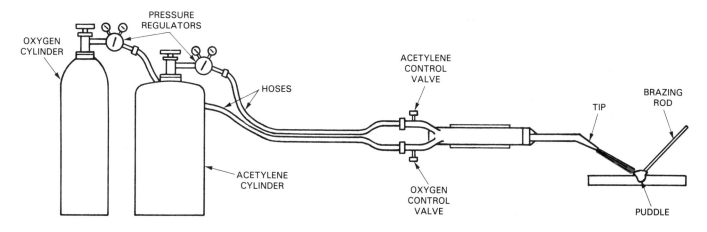

Fig. 4-23. Oxyacetylene torch burns a mixture of oxygen and acetylene to produce an intensely hot flame for welding, heating, and cutting.

Heat is concentrated in a small area which reduces part warpage.

HELIARC WELDING uses a DC (direct current) electric arc to produce heat. In addition, an inert gas such as helium is provided around the arc to prevent oxidation (contamination) during the welding process. This makes heliarc welding ideal for joining aluminum and magnesium as well as steel.

Welding and brazing require training, practice, and proper safety precautions. If at all possible, sign up for a welding course. Specialized training in welding will help you become a better motorcycle mechanic.

KNOW THESE TERMS

Pilot hole, Burr, Thread file, Thread chaser, Screw extractor, Thread repair insert, Tap, Die, Boring bar, Lathe, Vertical mill, Flat plat, Grinder, Oxyacetylene welding, Brazing, Electric arc welding.

REVIEW QUESTIONS—CHAPTER 4

1. List five important procedures to remember when drilling.
2. What is the difference between minor and major thread repairs?
3. An _____ _____ is used for removing fasteners broken off below the surface.
4. List the three steps for installing a thread repair insert.
5. What does a tap-drill chart tell you?
6. List four basic procedures to follow when operating a cylinder boring bar.
7. A _____ _____ is used for removing metal in tight places.
8. Grinding stones work well on brass and aluminum. True or False?
9. What is the difference between welding and brazing?
10. Oxyacetylene welding is NOT recommended for frame repair because a large area is heated during the welding process. True or False?

SUGGESTED ACTIVITIES

1. Obtain a small block of aluminum and a thread repair insert. Drill and tap the block for the insert. Follow the directions given by the insert manufacturer. Install the thread repair insert in the hole.
2. Check with local motorcycle dealers for the names and sources for several different brands of boring bars. Write to these manufacturers for catalogs and operating manuals. This literature can go into your "Useful Information" notebook.
3. For practice in external thread repair, damage the threads of a 12 mm bolt. Use a thread file to repair the damage.
4. Recondition the gasket surface of a cylinder head for a single cylinder engine. Use cutting paper on a flat plate.

Chapter 5

FOUR-STROKE CYCLE ENGINE

After studying this chapter, you will be able to:
□ Explain the operating principles of a four-stroke cycle engine.
□ List the functions of major four-stroke cycle engine parts.
□ Describe the construction and design aspects of four-stroke cycle engine components.
□ Explain the different classifications of four-stroke cycle engines.

This chapter explains the most common approaches used in the design and construction of modern four-stroke cycle motorcycle engines. Valve trains, cylinders, piston rings, bottom ends, and other important engine parts are discussed. This information will be very helpful in later text chapters when you are learning to diagnose, service, and repair engines.

Look at Fig. 5-1. It illustrates the fundamental parts of a four-stroke cycle engine. You should be able to describe the basic function of each of these components. If needed, review the material in Chapter 1 on engines.

VALVE TRAIN

Engine valves must be opened and closed precisely. Three common valve train types are used to operate the valves in four-stroke cycle motorcycle engines. In one of these designs, the camshaft or camshafts are located in the crankcase. In the other two designs, either single or double camshafts are positioned in the top of the cylinder head.

PUSH ROD OPERATED VALVES

Engines equipped with PUSH ROD OPERATED VALVES may have one or more camshafts located in the lower engine case. See Fig. 5-1. During engine

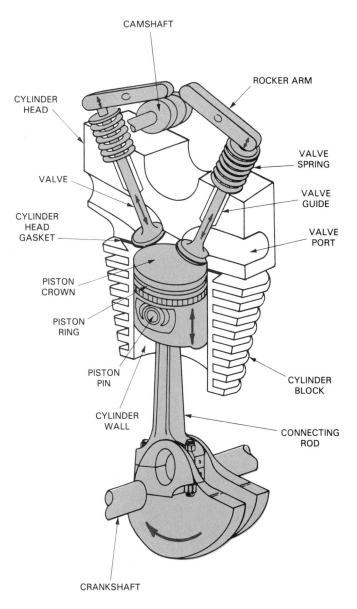

Fig. 5-1. Review the fundamental parts of this basic engine.

operation, the lobe on the rotating camshaft moves the lifter, push rod, and rocker arm. Then, the rocker arm can push the valve open, Fig. 5-2.

SINGLE OVERHEAD CAMSHAFT (SOHC)

A SINGLE OVERHEAD CAMSHAFT, abbreviated SOHC, has one camshaft mounted in the top of the cylinder head. The overhead camshaft design reduces reciprocating weight (weight of parts moving up and down) in the valve train by eliminating the need for lifters and push rods. Notice Fig. 5-3. The single overhead camshaft is located in the middle of the cylinder head. It directly operates cam followers, which are similar to rocker arms. The cam followers push on and open the valves.

DOUBLE OVERHEAD CAMSHAFTS (DOHC)

The DOUBLE OVERHEAD CAMSHAFT design further reduces valve train reciprocating weight by moving the camshafts closer to the valves. This is pictured in Fig. 5-4. A shim and shim bucket or a short follower are used between the cam lobe and valve stem.

CLOSING THE VALVES

VALVE SPRINGS are used to push the engine valves closed. When the cam lobe acts on the valve train, the valve is forced open, compressing the valve spring. Then, when the lobe rotates away from the

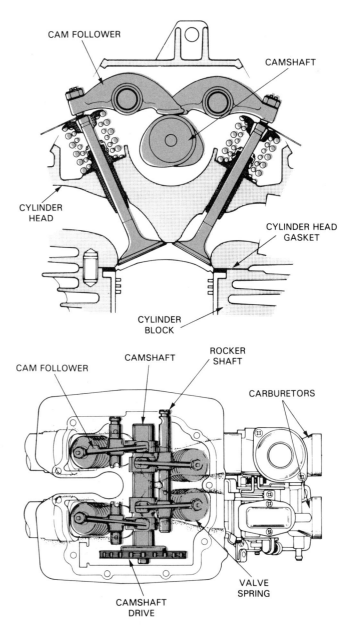

Fig. 5-3. A single overhead camshaft (SOHC) engine does not need push rods or lifters. Camshaft acts directly on cam followers. Followers push engine valves open. Top. Side view of SOHC engine. (Kawasaki) Bottom. Top view of another SOHC engine. (Yamaha)

valve train, the valve spring tension forces the valve closed. See Fig. 5-4.

Sufficient spring tension or pressure is needed to assure proper valve closing at high engine speeds. If the springs are too weak, valve float could occur. VALVE FLOAT results when the valve spring fails to close the valve at high engine RPM. Engine missing, power loss, and possibly valve and piston damage can result.

CAM LOBE DESIGN

CAMSHAFT LOBE DESIGN (contour or shape) determines when, how quickly, how long, and how

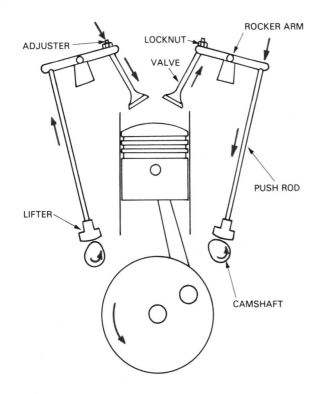

Fig. 5-2. Push rod equipped engines may use one or more camshafts located in crankcase. Note basic parts of this valve train.

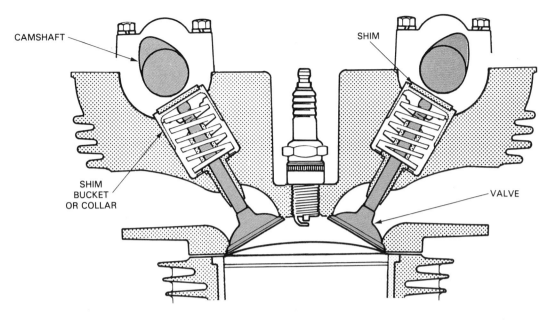

Fig. 5-4. Reciprocating weight is further reduced in dual or double overhead cam (DOHC) design by moving camshafts closer to valves. (Kawasaki Motors Corp., U.S.A.)

far a valve opens. Lobe profiles vary from engine to engine, as shown in Fig. 5-5.

Generally speaking, INCREASED camshaft LIFT (distance valve opens) and DURATION (length of time valve stays open) will raise the engine's power range (rpm at which maximum power is developed). However, increased cam lift and duration will normally REDUCE engine power at low to medium speeds and will increase roughness at idle. Stock cam profiles usually provide the best compromise between power, efficiency, and smoothness.

DRIVING THE CAMSHAFT

As discussed, a four-stroke cycle engine requires two revolutions of the crankshaft for each power stroke. Thus, the camshaft must rotate at one-half "crank" speed. Illustrated in Fig. 5-6, various methods will achieve this crank-to-cam reduction.

PISTONS, CYLINDERS, AND CRANKSHAFTS

The PISTON and CRANKSHAFT assemblies are often termed the engine's reciprocating assembly. The

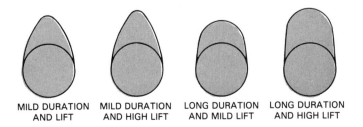

| MILD DURATION AND LIFT | MILD DURATION AND HIGH LIFT | LONG DURATION AND MILD LIFT | LONG DURATION AND HIGH LIFT |

Fig. 5-5. Numerous camshaft lobe profiles are used to vary valve lift and duration.

piston and rod reciprocate or move up and down in the CYLINDER. The crankshaft changes the piston's linear (straight line) motion into more usable rotary (spinning) motion.

It is very useful to understand how these parts vary from one engine to another. Though their basic purpose may remain the same, part construction and design characteristics can differ considerably.

SINGLE CYLINDER ENGINE

A SINGLE CYLINDER ENGINE consists of one piston, one cylinder, one connecting rod, and a crankshaft. The crankshaft assembly is supported by bearings resting in the crankcase, Fig. 5-7.

TWIN CYLINDER ENGINE

TWIN CYLINDER ENGINES are manufactured in three basic configurations: cylinders in-line, cylinders opposed, and cylinders in a "Vee."

In-line two cylinder engine

An IN-LINE TWO CYLINDER ENGINE may have two pistons moving up and down together, termed a 360° crankshaft. Or, the pistons may slide up and down alternately, called a 180° crankshaft. The crank is supported in MAIN BEARINGS in two or three places. Refer to Fig. 5-8.

Opposed-twin cylinder engine

In the OPPOSED-TWIN CYLINDER ENGINE, the cylinders lay horizontally at right angles to the motorcycle frame. This is pictured in Fig. 5-9. They lay in the same direction as the rider's foot pegs. With

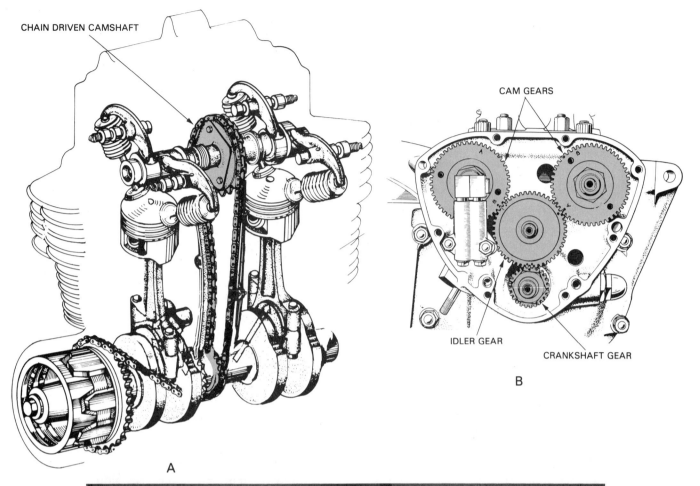

CHAIN DRIVEN CAMSHAFT

CAM GEARS

IDLER GEAR

CRANKSHAFT GEAR

A

B

CAM
SPROCKET

TENSIONER
PULLEY

CAM
SPROCKET

TIMING
BELT

TENSIONER
PULLEY

CRANKSHAFT
SPROCKET

C

Fig. 5-6. Camshafts may be driven by chains, gears, or belts. A—Chain and sprocket mechanism drive cams. B—Gears drive camshafts. C—Belt drives are sometimes used to drive camshafts. (Kawasaki and Triumph)

Four-Stroke Cycle Engine

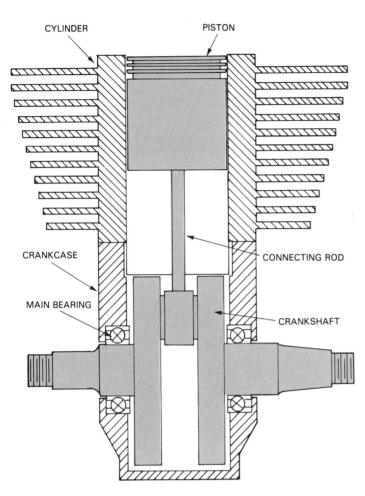

Fig. 5-7. Single cylinder, four-stroke cycle engine has one piston, one cylinder, one connecting rod, and a crankshaft supported by main bearings in crankcase.

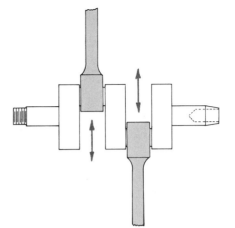

OPPOSED-TWIN CRANKSHAFT

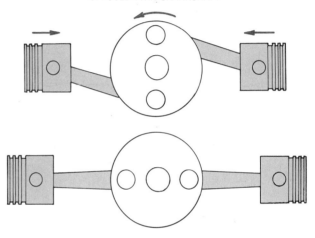

Fig. 5-9. Opposed-twin engine pistons move from TDC to BDC together.

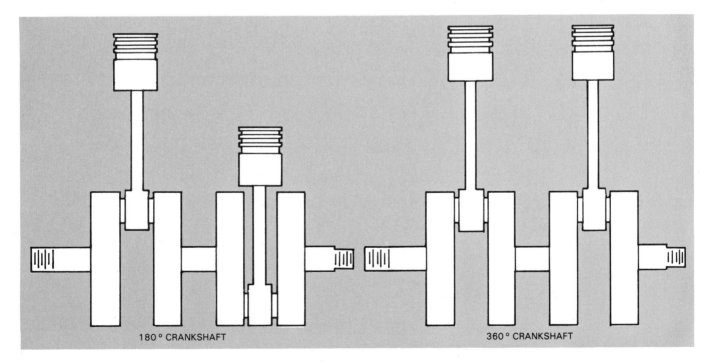

180° CRANKSHAFT

360° CRANKSHAFT

Fig. 5-8. Pistons in an in-line, twin cylinder engine may move up and down together (360° crankshaft) or alternately (180° crankshaft).

an opposed-twin, the pistons move to TDC (top dead center) and to BDC (bottom dead center) together.

V-twin cylinder engine

In a V-TWIN CYLINDER ENGINE configuration, the cylinders are at an angle to each other. The cylinders are positioned so that they form the letter "V" when viewed from the end of the crankshaft. See Fig. 5-10.

Crankshafts for most V-twins have a common crankpin for both connecting rods. There are two methods of mounting the rods on the crankpin. In one design, the connecting rods are SIDE-BY-SIDE, as in Fig. 5-11. In another design, the connecting rods are "SIAMESED" (overlapped), as in Fig. 5-12.

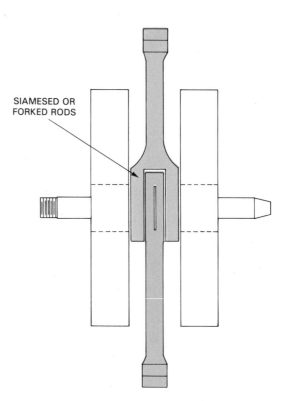

Fig. 5-12. Study construction of V-twin forked or siamesed rods.

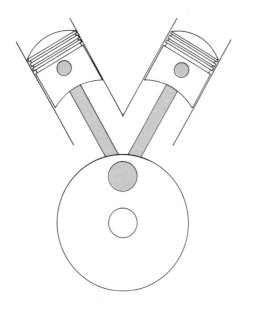

Fig. 5-10. V-twin engine cylinders are at an angle to each other.

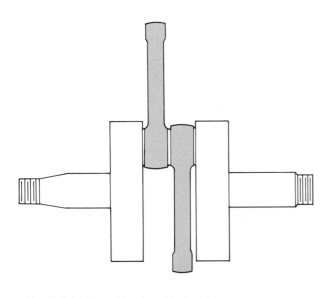

Fig. 5-11. Note V-twin, side-by-side rod with common crankpin.

MULTI-CYLINDER ENGINES

MULTI-CYLINDER ENGINES consist of either three, four, or six cylinders. Opposed and in-line engines commonly use three, four, or six cylinders, while V-type configurations normally have two, four, or six cylinders. See Fig. 5-13.

CYLINDER DESIGN AND CONSTRUCTION

Most modern four-stroke cycle motorcycle engine cylinders consist of a cast aluminum CYLINDER BLOCK with a cast iron LINER (sleeve). Some four-stroke motorcycle engines still use a one-piece cast iron cylinder block, however. Both designs are shown in Fig. 5-14.

Due to normal wear, the cylinder bore will become tapered and out-of-round, which reduces engine efficiency. A worn cylinder can cause blow-by, engine smoking, oil consumption, and spark plug fouling.

The cylinder is normally designed so that it can be BORED OUT (bore diameter increased by machining) to accept an oversized piston. This eliminates the need to replace the cylinder when it becomes worn. It also allows the mechanic to restore engine efficiency for minimum cost.

PISTON CONSTRUCTION

Four-stroke motorcycle pistons are either CAST (molten metal poured into mold) or FORGED (metal hammered into mold).

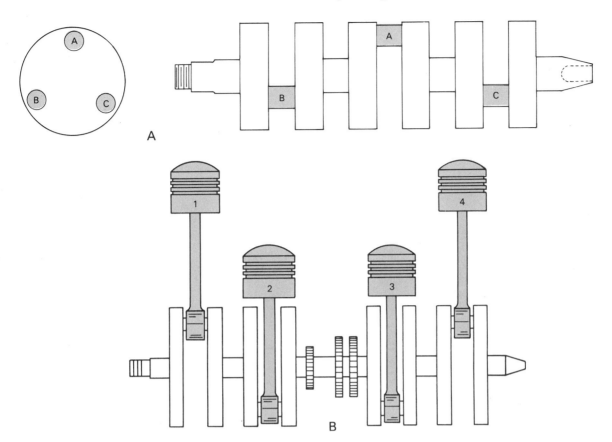

Fig. 5-13. A—Three cylinder crankshaft has its rod journals (A, B, C) spaced 120° apart. B—In-line, four-cylinder crankshaft. Pistons 1-4 and 2-3 move up and down together.

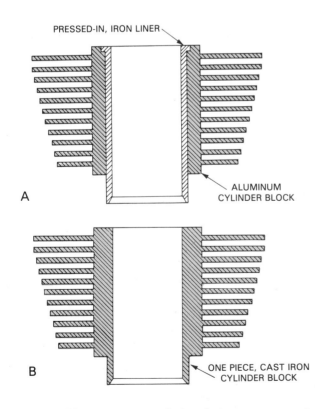

Fig. 5-14. A—Most common cylinder design uses a cast aluminum cylinder block with a pressed-in, iron liner (sleeve). B—One piece, cast iron cylinder block is also used, but less frequently.

The most common piston construction method uses high silicon content cast aluminum. The CAST PISTON is less expensive to produce, lighter in weight, and expands less than the forged piston.

The major advantage of the FORGED PISTON is superior strength and higher rpm capabilities. Due to the increased expansion characteristics, the forged piston requires more cylinder-to-piston clearance. It is suited to high performance applications.

PISTON DESIGN

A typical four-stroke cycle motorcycle piston consists of the crown, pin hole, land, groove, skirt, pin boss, circlip grooves, and oil holes. This is illustrated in Fig. 5-15.

Piston crown

The PISTON CROWN or top is directly exposed to the extreme heat and pressure caused by combustion. For this reason, it must be strong enough to withstand tremendous forces. The crown must have the ability to transfer extreme pressure and heat to the other parts of the piston. If not strong enough, the piston crown could overheat, melt, and BURN (hole pushed through partially melted piston top). In Fig. 5-15, note the thickness of the crown in relation to the rest of the piston.

77

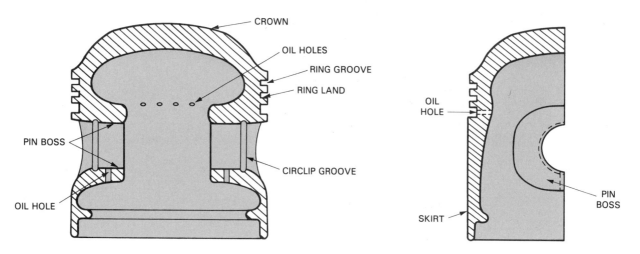

CROWN
OIL HOLES
RING GROOVE
RING LAND
PIN BOSS
CIRCLIP GROOVE
OIL HOLE
OIL HOLE
SKIRT
PIN BOSS

Fig. 5-15. A typical four-stroke cycle motorcycle piston. Study its parts.

Fig. 5-16 shows how the piston moves up to trap and compress the fuel mixture in the combustion chamber.

Piston taper

PISTON TAPER is produced by machining the top diameter of the piston smaller than the bottom. Due to the higher operating temperature and greater mass, the piston crown will expand more than the skirt area of the piston. To compensate for this uneven enlargement, a piston is usually tapered. See Fig. 5-17.

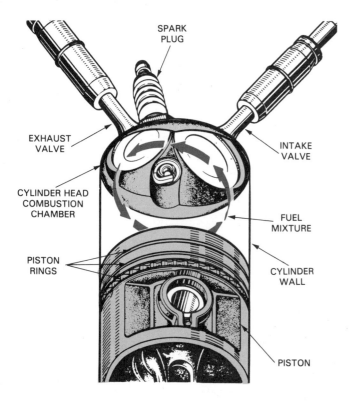

SPARK PLUG
EXHAUST VALVE
INTAKE VALVE
CYLINDER HEAD COMBUSTION CHAMBER
FUEL MIXTURE
PISTON RINGS
CYLINDER WALL
PISTON

Fig. 5-16. Piston moves up to compress fuel mixture inside cylinder head for combustion. Top of piston is exposed to burning fuel mixture. (U.S. Suzuki Motor Corp.)

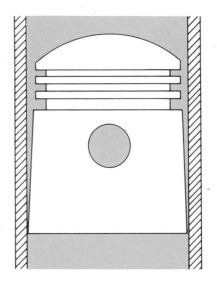

Fig. 5-17. Pistons are tapered to compensate for greater heat and expansion at crown.

Cam ground pistons

CAM GROUND PISTONS are machined out-of-round to provide dependable, quiet operation when the piston is both cold and hot. Cam grinding reduces piston clearance when the piston is cold. This prevents PISTON SLAP (knocking sound produced as cold piston rocks in cylinder). Cam grinding also assures proper piston clearance when the piston reaches full operating temperature.

A cam ground piston, when cold, will look oval shaped when viewed from the top, Fig. 5-18. The larger diameter is in a plane perpendicular to the piston pin. As the piston heats, the larger diameter will stay about the same size while the smaller diameter expands. The piston becomes almost ROUND at full operating temperature. See Fig. 5-19. This design allows for quieter operation. It also maintains minimum clearance for a lubricating film between the cylinder and piston skirt at all times.

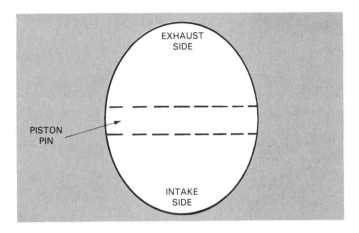

Fig. 5-18. A piston is usually oval shaped to help control direction of piston expansion. As heat expands piston, piston becomes almost round.

COMBUSTION CHAMBER DESIGN

A COMBUSTION CHAMBER includes the area in the cylinder head and the area above the piston where combustion occurs. A combustion chamber is normally designed to work with a specific piston crown and valve port shape. Both the cylinder head and the piston must work together to produce efficient combustion of the fuel mixture.

The HEMISPHERICAL (dome shaped) combustion chamber is a traditional design used in many four-stroke cycle motorcycles, Fig. 5-20. It provides a very smooth chamber wall, with very little surface area. This increases combustion efficiency.

In search of more performance, lower exhaust emissions, and better fuel economy, most manufacturers have changed to three-valve and four-valve chamber designs. See Fig. 5-21. The extra valve or valves increases the breathing efficiency of the engine and permits higher engine rpm and power levels. The additional valves can also improve efficiency by increasing swirl (mixing of fuel mixture) in the combustion chamber.

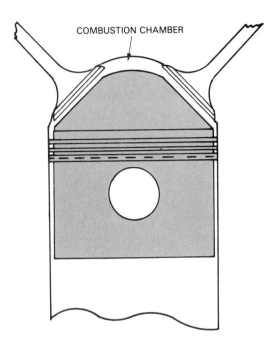

Fig. 5-20. A domed piston is normally used in conjunction with a hemispherical combustion chamber.

PISTON RING GROOVES

RING GROOVES are machined below the piston crown to accept the piston rings. These grooves are spaced to provide adequate strength to support the rings. These supporting areas between the grooves are called RING LANDS.

Four-stroke pistons usually have three ring grooves. The two upper ring grooves are for the COMPRESSION RINGS. The lower groove holds the OIL CONTROL RING.

PISTON RINGS

The PISTON RINGS seal the space between the piston and the cylinder wall. They keep combustion pressure from entering the crankcase. The rings also

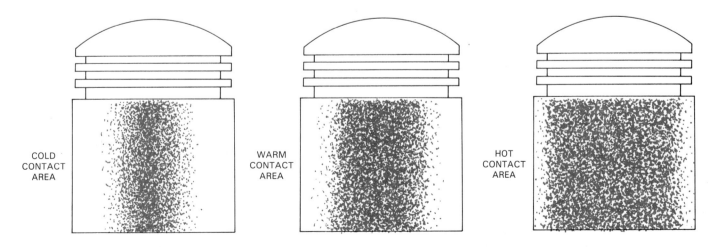

Fig. 5-19. Piston skirt contact area on cylinder changes with engine temperature.

amount of oil from reaching the scraper ring, compression ring, and combustion chamber.

Piston ring shape

Fig. 5-22 shows a cut view of a typical three ring set. The top compression ring is normally RECTANGULAR in cross section, with the inside, top edge chamfered (beveled). This chamfer causes combustion pressure to force the ring against the cylinder wall. Illustrated in Fig. 5-23, this helps the compression ring seal combustion pressure inside the combustion chamber.

The scraper ring is also rectangular shaped, but the bottom outside edge is usually STEPPED. This stepped area provides a scooping or scraping action which helps to control oiling. A typical scraper ring is

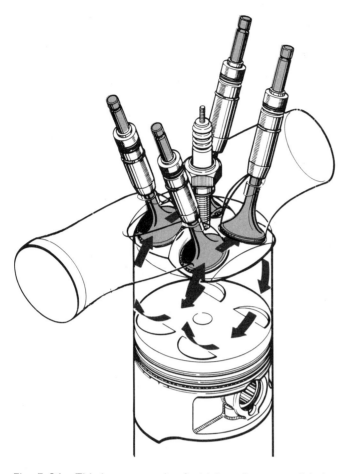

Fig. 5-21. This is an example of a high performance clyinder head which has a four-valve combustion chamber. (U.S. Suzuki Motor Corp.)

keep oil from entering the combustion chamber.

Piston rings are usually made of cast iron. In order to prolong ring and cylinder life, the top compression ring often has hard chrome plating on the sealing surface (edge which contacts cylinder wall). Good piston ring performance is essential to efficient and dependable engine operation.

Top ring

Each ring is designed to do a specific task. The TOP PISTON RING seals most of the combustion pressure. It also must withstand more heat and less lubrication than the other two rings.

Middle ring

The MIDDLE PISTON RING also acts as a compression ring, but it is shaped to help remove excess oil from the cylinder wall. This dual function ring is sometimes called a SCRAPER RING.

Bottom ring

The BOTTOM PISTON RING, termed the OIL CONTROL RING, has the primary function of removing oil from the cylinder wall each time the piston moves downward. This prevents an excessive

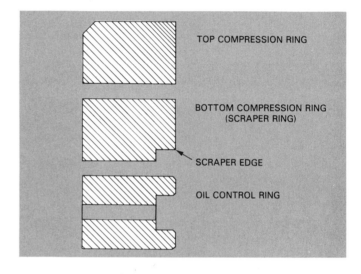

Fig. 5-22. This shows cross section of a typical three-ring set.

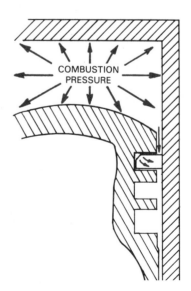

Fig. 5-23. Combustion pressure is used to force compression ring against cylinder wall and aid sealing action.

also shown in Fig. 5-22.

The oil control ring, Fig. 5-22, has two scraping surfaces and oil passage slots located in the back of the ring. Shown in Fig. 5-24, this allows oil, wiped from the cylinder wall, to return to the crankcase.

On some pistons, a three-piece oil ring is used. The three-piece ring consists of an expander ring which locates two thin, steel, oil control rings, Fig. 5-25.

FOUR CYCLE ENGINE BEARINGS

The purpose of a BEARING is to reduce friction while allowing movement between parts. The three basic types of bearings commonly used in the four-stroke cycle engine are ball bearings, roller bearings, and plain bearings. Refer to Fig. 5-26.

BALL BEARINGS provide the greatest reduction of friction. However, ball bearings cannot withstand heavy loading as well as ROLLER BEARINGS. Both ball bearings and roller bearings can survive with minimal lubrication. Yet, total lack of lubrication will destroy them.

A PLAIN BEARING, also termed a FRICTION BEARING, is capable of withstanding heavy loading, but it requires a lubricating oil film. Due to its larger surface area and its sliding action, the plain bearing usually does NOT reduce friction as efficiently as a

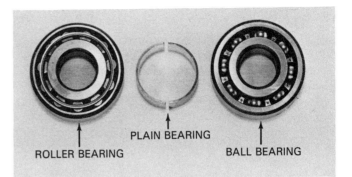

Fig. 5-26. Roller, plain, and ball bearings are used in four-stroke cycle engines.

ball or roller bearing.

As you will learn, engine design determines where each type of bearing should be utilized.

ENGINE CASE

The ENGINE CASE houses the engine crankshaft, bearings, gearbox, and related components. The cylinder block bolts to the case. In a few designs, the gearbox is located inside a separate case. Engine cases may be split horizontally or vertically.

NON-UNIT CONSTRUCTION

NON-UNIT CONSTRUCTION consists of separate engine and gearbox (transmission) assemblies. The gearbox can be removed from the engine as a single unit. Pictured in Fig. 5-27, this type arrangement can be found on a few large displacement bikes. With non-unit construction, the engine and gearbox are bolted solidly to the motorcycle frame. This provides proper engine to gearbox alignment and support.

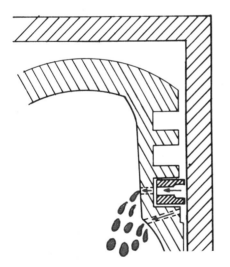

Fig. 5-24. Oil scraped from cylinder wall passes through small holes in piston and is returned to sump.

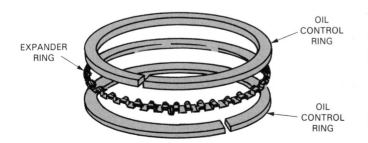

Fig. 5-25. Three-piece oil ring uses two, thin, steel rings with an expander ring located between and behind rings.

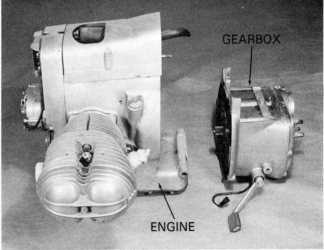

Fig. 5-27. A non-unit engine uses a separate gearbox case which can be removed from engine while still assembled.

UNIT CONSTRUCTION

UNIT CONSTRUCTION utilizes a single case or crankcase casting which contains the engine, primary drive, and gearbox. See Fig. 5-28. A SINGLE CASE assures proper alignment, lessens the possibility of oil leakage, and makes for a more compact, lighter assembly.

Unit construction has been a very common and popular design for many years.

VERTICAL AND HORIZONTAL SPLIT CRANKCASES

Most single cylinder four-stroke cycle motorcycle engine crankcases are SPLIT VERTICALLY, Fig. 5-29. However, motorcycle engines with two or more cylinders are normally SPLIT HORIZONTALLY, Fig. 5-30.

In converting reciprocating energy into rotating energy, the engine crankshaft is subjected to extreme vertical loading. The crankcases must provide a mounting place for the crankshaft main bearings and withstand these vertical loads. Since the vertical split case provides a solid, one-piece mounting for the main bearings, it can easily support the crankshaft and yet be lightweight.

Because horizontally split cases part at the crankshaft certerline, both the crankcase casting and the fasteners must be of very heavy construction. This is illustrated in Fig. 5-31.

Advantages of horizontal split cases are:
1. Easier teardown.
2. Less possibility of oil leakage.
3. Easier transmission servicing.
4. Lower production cost in multi-cylinder configurations.

FOUR CYCLE ENGINE COOLING

Modern motorcycle engines use two methods of cooling. The most common means is AIR COOLING, but LIQUID COOLING is becoming more popular.

In the combustion process, a great amount of heat is produced. Some of this heat is used for power production (piston movement). The remainder must be

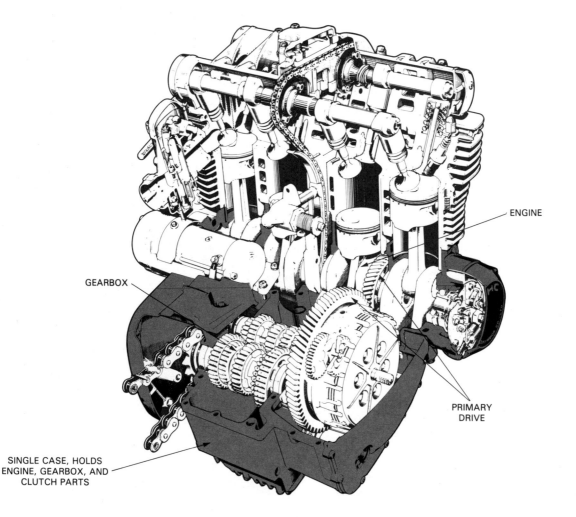

Fig. 5-28. Unit-construction engine uses same crankcase to house engine, primary drive, and gearbox.
(U.S. Suzuki Motor Corporation)

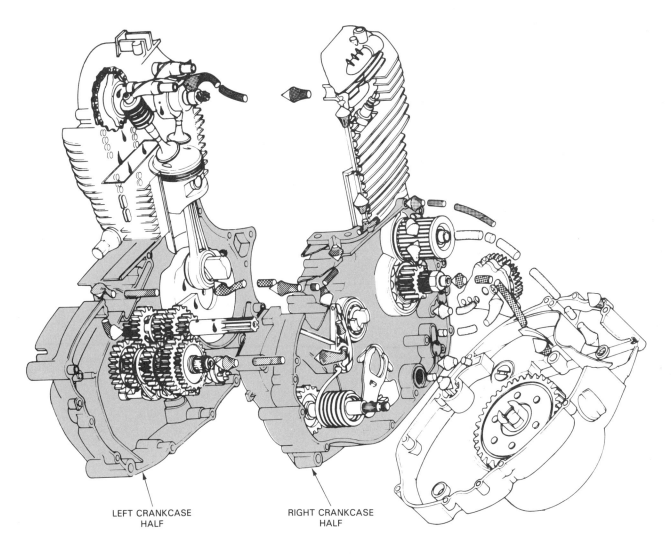

LEFT CRANKCASE
HALF

RIGHT CRANKCASE
HALF

Fig. 5-29. A typical four-stroke cycle, single cylinder engine normally has vertically split crankcases.
(Kawasaki Motors Corp., U.S.A.)

Fig. 5-30. Horizontally split crankcases are normally used in all current four-stroke cycle, multi-cylinder engines and a few single cylinder engines.

Fig. 5-31. Horizontally split crankcases must be heavily constructed to provide adequate support for crankshaft and gearbox shafts.

transferred away from the engine to prevent engine damage.

AIR COOLING

The AIR-COOLED ENGINE transfers heat directly into the air by means of cooling fins. COOLING FINS provide a larger surface area for exposure to outside air, Fig. 5-32. This allows for a greater transfer of heat.

Fins may be present on cylinders, cylinder heads and crankcases. They must be kept clean and not heavily coated with paint for proper heat transfer.

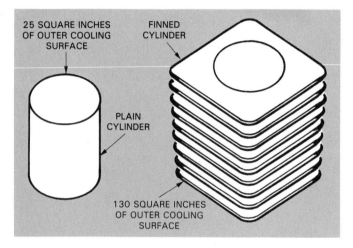

Fig. 5-32. Notice how cooling fins increase surface area on outside of cylinder. Large surface area is needed to transfer enough heat away from cylinder and into air.

LIQUID COOLING

The LIQUID-COOLED ENGINE transfers engine heat into COOLANT (water and antifreeze solution). The coolant circulates through cavities in the cylinder, head, and crankcase. The hot liquid coolant is then piped to a RADIATOR which efficiently transfers heat to the outside air. Operation of the liquid-cooling system is illustrated in Fig. 5-33.

The major advantage of a liquid-cooling system is that is maintains a more constant engine operating temperature than an air-cooled system. An air-cooled engine's operating temperature can rise and fall with changes in outside air temperature. Because of the more controlled operating temperature of the liquid-cooled engine, tighter (more precise) clearances between moving parts can be utilized. This results in quieter operation, improved efficiency, and longer engine life. However, a liquid-cooled engine costs more to manufacture, purchase, and maintain than an air-cooled engine.

Thermostat

A liquid-cooled engine's operating temperature is controlled by a thermostat. A THERMOSTAT is a temperature sensitive valve which controls coolant flow in the engine as coolant temperature changes. Thermostat construction is shown in Fig. 5-34.

When the engine is cold, the thermostat is closed. This prevents coolant flow through the radiator. As the engine warms up, the thermostat gradually opens, allowing the coolant to flow through the radiator and maintain a constant temperature. Refer to Fig. 5-33.

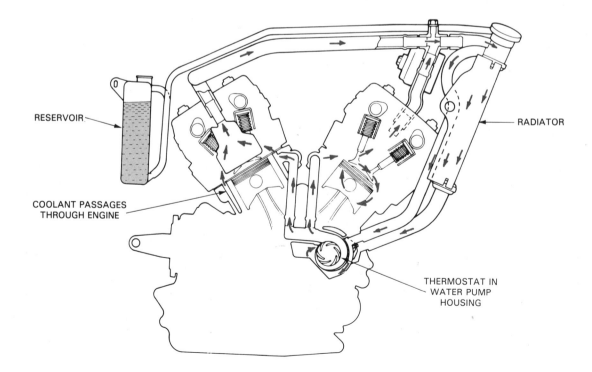

Fig. 5-33. Notice coolant flow through system. (Yamaha Motor Corp. U.S.A.)

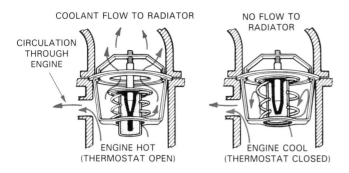

COOLANT FLOW TO RADIATOR

CIRCULATION THROUGH ENGINE

NO FLOW TO RADIATOR

ENGINE HOT (THERMOSTAT OPEN)

ENGINE COOL (THERMOSTAT CLOSED)

Fig. 5-34. With thermostat closed, no coolant flows through radiator. As engine and coolant warm up, thermostat opens to gradually allow circulation. (Mopar)

ENGINE LUBRICATION

The ENGINE LUBRICATION SYSTEM is designed to help reduce friction caused by engine parts rubbing against each other. Lubrication is accomplished by circulating engine oil to high friction points in the engine. The engine lubricating oil not only helps to reduce friction (lubricates), it also cleans, cools, and seals.

Thorough coverage of lubricating systems is included in Chapter 11 of this text.

KNOW THESE TERMS

SOHC, DOHC, Camshaft lift, Camshaft duration, Valve float, In-line engine, Opposed-twin engine, V-twin engine, Multi-cylinder engine, Cam ground piston, Hemispherical combustion chamber, Compression ring, Oil ring, Non-unit construction, Unit construction, Air cooling, Liquid cooling, Thermostat.

REVIEW QUESTIONS—CHAPTER 5

1. List the three types of valve operating mechanisms.
2. The camshaft is mounted inside the cylinder head in all three types of valve operating mechanisms. True or False?
3. The camshaft rotates at _____ crankshaft speed.
4. What are the three basic configurations of twin-cylinder engines?
5. Pistons in a twin-cylinder, in-line engine will move up and down together if a _____ crankshaft is used.
6. What are the two ways in which connecting rods are attached to the crankshaft in a V-twin engine?
7. An engine cylinder must always be replaced when worn out. True or False?
8. List the two types of piston construction and an advantage of each.
9. Why are some pistons oval shaped (cam ground)?
10. Name the three piston ring types.
11. Which piston ring serves a dual function?
12. Name three types of bearings commonly used in motorcycle engines.
13. Most modern motorcycle engines are termed non-unit construction. True or False?
14. Horizontally split cases provide for _____ transmission servicing.
15. What are the two methods of engine cooling?
16. In a liquid cooling system, the _____ transfers heat into the outside air.
    a. Cooling fins.
    b. Radiator.
    c. Thermostat.
    d. Fan.
17. List the four functions of engine oil.

SUGGESTED ACTIVITIES

1. Compare the valve train mechanisms of three different four-stroke cycle engines.
2. Using a repair manual:
   a. Find two V-twin motorcycles which use different crankshaft configurations.
   b. Find two V-twins which use the same type of crankshaft configuration.
3. List as many different ring shapes as you can find for four-stroke cycle engines. Use magazine articles, service manuals, and reference books.
4. Name several different non-unit construction type motorcycle engines.
5. Make a list of all current twin and multi-cylinder, four-stroke cycle motorcycle engines. Indicate whether a 180° or 360° crankshaft is used.

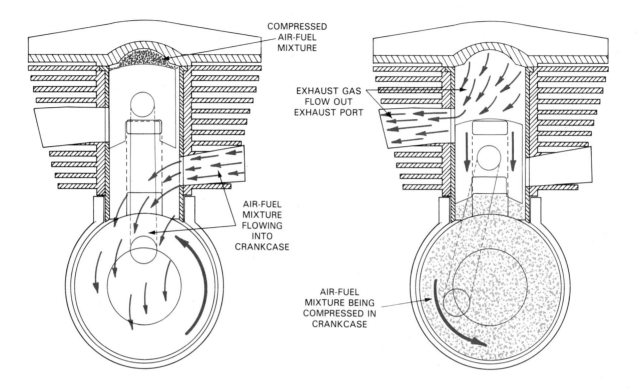

WHEN PISTON IS AT TDC, AIR-FUEL MIXTURE ABOVE PISTON IS COM-
PRESSED. COMPRESSION PREPARES MIXTURE FOR IGNITION. A NEW
CHARGE OF AIR-FUEL MIXTURE IS ALSO ENTERING CRANKCASE
THROUGH INTAKE PORT.

AFTER COMBUSTION, PISTON MOVES DOWN AND OPENS EXHAUST
PORT, ALLOWING EXHAUST GASES TO FLOW OUT OF CYLINDER.
DOWNWARD MOVEMENT OF PISTON CLOSES INTAKE PORT. FRESH AIR-
FUEL MIXTURE CHARGE IS BEING COMPRESSED IN CRANKCASE.

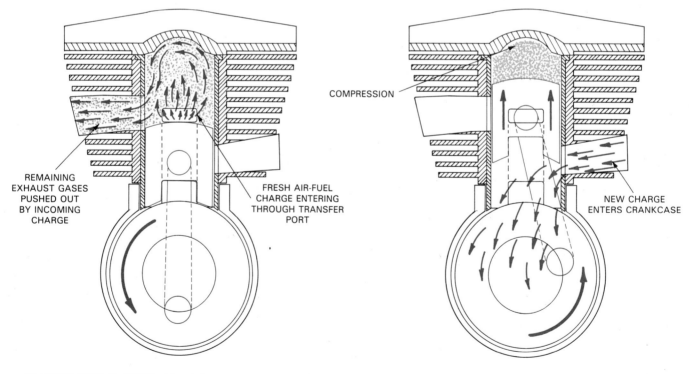

TRANSFER PORT IS OPENED AS PISTON CONTINUES DOWN. THIS
ALLOWS AIR-FUEL MIXTURE TO FLOW FROM CRANKCASE INTO
CYLINDER AREA ABOVE PISTON. SINCE EXHAUST PORT IS ALSO OPEN,
NEW CHARGE HELPS CLEAN LAST PART OF EXHAUST GASES OUT OF
CYLINDER.

AS PISTON MOVES BACK UP, AIR-FUEL CHARGE THAT WAS JUST
TRANSFERRED IS COMPRESSED. AT SAME TIME, PISTON SKIRT HAS
OPENED INTAKE PORT, ALLOWING A NEW CHARGE OF AIR-FUEL MIX-
TURE TO ENTER CRANKCASE.

Review the basic action of a two-stroke cycle engine.

Chapter 6

TWO-STROKE CYCLE ENGINE

After studying this chapter, you will be able to:
□ Explain two-stroke cycle engine operation.
□ Describe intake, exhaust, and transfer timing in regard to engine performance.
□ Explain how a two-stroke cycle engine crankcase is sealed.
□ Recall reed and rotary valve operating principles.
□ Name design variations in two-stroke cycle engine parts.
□ Describe construction differences in two-stroke cycle engines.

The simple two-stroke cycle engine discussed in Chapter 1 used the piston to regulate intake, transfer, and exhaust timing. More refined engine designs use other methods to control the movement of the air-fuel mixture through the engine.

In this chapter, we will discuss modern two-stroke cycle motorcycle engines. It is very important for you to understand how engine design effects engine performance and dependability. This knowledge will make you more prepared to correctly diagnose, service, and repair motorcycles.

INTAKE TIMING

INTAKE TIMING refers to the opening and closing of the intake port in relation to the position of the crankshaft and piston. The three methods used to control intake timing are the piston port, reed valve, and rotary valve.

PISTON PORT

A PISTON PORT type engine uses piston skirt length and intake port location to control intake timing. It is one of the simplest and least expensive two-stroke cycle engine designs. An example of a piston port configuration is shown in Fig. 6-1.

Placement of the port in the cylinder and the length of the piston skirt determines how early the intake port opens and how late it closes. See Fig. 6-2. More air and fuel can enter the crankcase if the intake port is left open for a longer period of time.

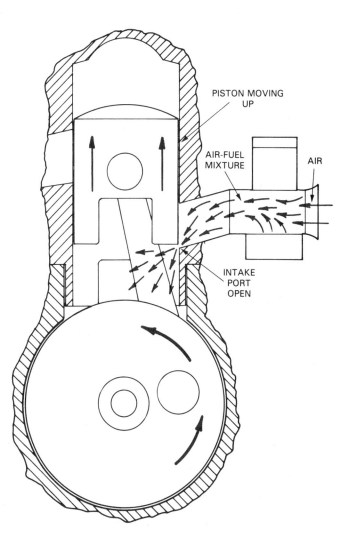

Fig. 6-1. As piston slides up in cylinder, intake port is opened and air-fuel mixture passes into crankcase.

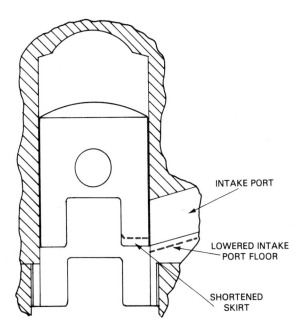

Fig. 6-2. Length of piston skirt and placement of intake port determines intake timing. A shorter intake skirt or lower port floor causes port to open earlier and close later.

Mild and radical timing

The power characteristics of the two-stroke cycle engine are greatly affected by intake timing. MILD TIMING (intake port open for moderate period of time) will provide good low end (low engine rpm) power and good midrange (medium engine rpm) power. RADICAL TIMING (intake port open long period of time) will give more top end (high rpm) power but will sacrifice some midrange and low end power.

High performance two-stroke cycle engines require radical timing. Radical intake timing allows a larger amount of air-fuel mixture to enter the crankcase.

If intake timing is too radical though, crankcase compression will overcome the inertia of the incoming intake charge. This will force some of the air-fuel mixture back out the intake port and carburetor before the intake port is closed.

A limitation upon piston port design is due to intake timing being SYMMETRICAL (same piston position over port both before and after TDC). Fig. 6-3 shows that an intake port which opens at 80

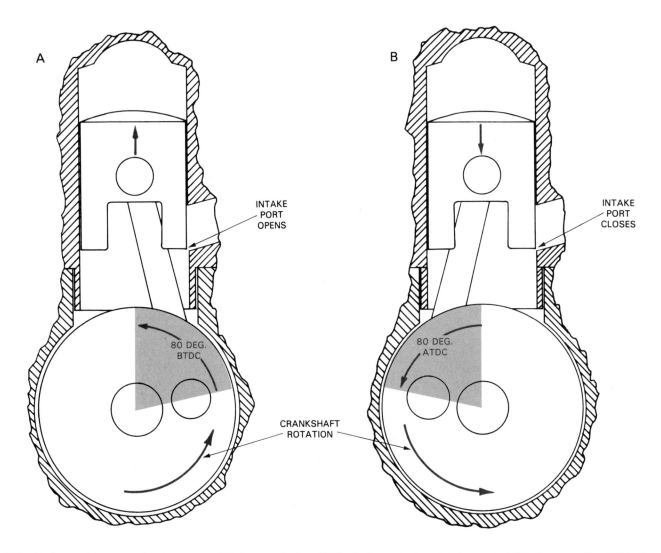

Fig. 6-3. If piston skirt opens intake port at 80 degrees before TDC, A, it must close intake port at 80 degrees after TDC, B.

degrees before TDC will always close at 80 degrees after TDC. This is undesirable because different intake timing is sometimes needed.

REED VALVE

The REED VALVE design eliminates STANDOFF (backward flow of intake charge) when used with the piston port design. An example of a reed valve is shown in Fig. 6-4. Operation of the reed valve is dependant on crankcase pressure and vacuum.

The reed valve may be used in conjunction with a piston controlled intake port to allow radical, NON-SYMMETRICAL TIMING without the disadvantage of excessive standoff or backflow. Fig. 6-5 shows reed placement in the intake port. This design provides non-symmetrical intake timing because:

1. The reed petals are opened by crankcase vacuum.
2. The reed petals are closed by crankcase pressure.

Reed valve operation

As crankcase vacuum develops, the REED PETALS, Fig. 6-6, A, are bent and lifted from the REED CAGE. This allows the air-fuel mixture to flow into the crankcase. Air-fuel mixture will continue to flow as long as there is enough vacuum to hold the reed petals open.

As the crankcase begins to pressurize, Fig. 6-6, B, the reed petals are forced closed. This prevents the flow of air-fuel mixture back out the intake port.

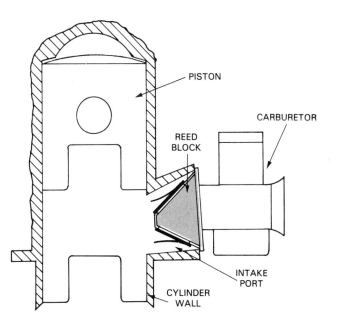

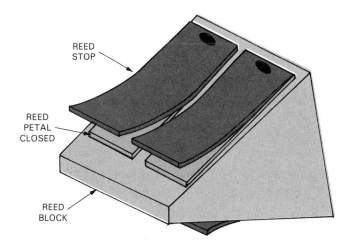

Fig. 6-4. Note basic parts of a reed valve. Reed petals move to operate valve.

Fig. 6-5. Reed assembly is mounted in intake port between carburetor and cylinder wall.

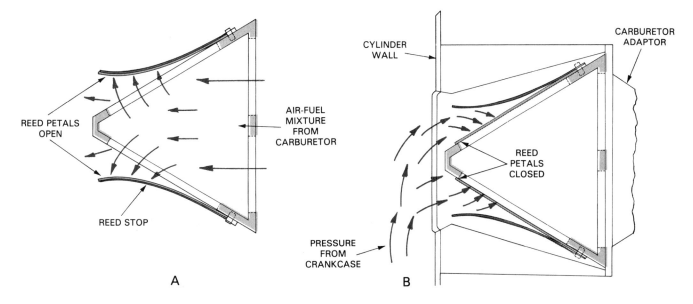

A

B

Fig. 6-6. A—As vacuum builds in crankcase, reed petals are pushed away from reed block. Air-fuel mixture flows into crankcase. Reed stops prevent over-flex and possible breakage of reed petals. B—As pressure builds in crankcase, reed petals are forced shut. This prevents air-fuel mixture from blowing backward through carburetor.

ROTARY VALVE

A ROTARY VALVE is a thin metal disc which opens and closes the engine's intake port. See Fig. 6-7. This method of intake timing has the most flexibility. The intake port on the side of the engine case is covered and uncovered by the spinning action of the disc. The rotary valve controls the flow of the fuel charge into the crankcase.

Rotary valve operation

The rotary valve is keyed or splined to the engine crankshaft. The valve is positioned between the carburetor and the crankcase. As the crankshaft and disc rotate, the cutaway portion of the disc opens the port, and the fuel mixture enters the engine. When the larger, uncut section of the disc moves in front of the port, the port is closed.

Since the disc can be changed quickly, intake timing can be altered easily. Fig. 6-8 shows two different disc configurations. Intake opening and closing can also be altered independently. Intake timing can be changed by using a disc with a larger or smaller cutout. In this way, the engine's power characteristics can be changed quickly and radically.

TRANSFER AND EXHAUST TIMING

The piston controls TRANSFER and EXHAUST TIMING in two-stroke cycle engines. It is important that intake, transfer, and exhaust timing work

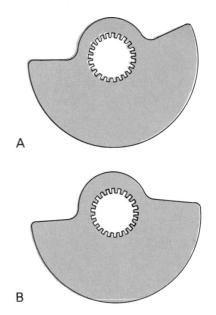

A

B

Fig. 6-8. Mild rotary valve, A, opens intake port later and closes it earlier than radical rotary valve, B.

together. An engine designed with mild intake timing will usually have mild transfer and mild exhaust timing. The same is true of radical timing.

Transfer and exhaust timing are usually determined by port height. This is illustrated in Fig. 6-9. A raised or heightened port will open earlier and close later.

A recent engine design allows for adjustable exhaust timing through the use of a centrifugal linkage, Fig. 6-10. The purpose of this design is to permit good torque in the middle rpm range and good horsepower at high rpm. As engine speed increases, the power valve is rotated, raising the height of the exhaust port.

CRANKCASE SEALING

A two-stroke cycle engine must produce sufficient vacuum and pressure in the crankcase. CRANKCASE VACUUM in used to draw the air-fuel mixture from the carburetor to the crankcase. CRANKCASE PRESSURE is used to transfer air-fuel mixture from the crankcase to the upper cylinder. In order to produce vacuum and pressure, the crankcase must be sealed.

A two-stroke cycle engine is sealed at:
1. Intake port (gasket or rubber flange between carburetor and cylinder, O-ring between rotary valve cover and crankcase).
2. Crankcase split line (gasket or chemical sealant).
3. Crankshaft seals (lip seal between crankshaft and crankcase).
4. Cylinder base (gasket between cylinder and crankcase).
5. Cylinder head (head gasket, spark plug gasket).

Leakage at any of these points will affect engine operation. See Fig. 6-11. To produce the proper

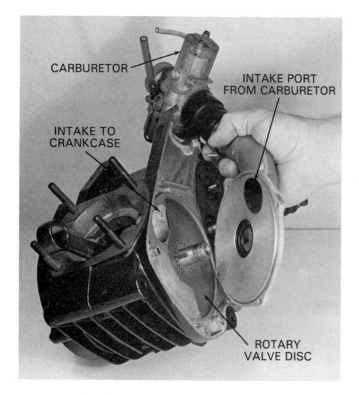

CARBURETOR

INTAKE PORT FROM CARBURETOR

INTAKE TO CRANKCASE

ROTARY VALVE DISC

Fig. 6-7. Rotary valve is a good way to control two-stroke cycle intake timing. Note basic parts.

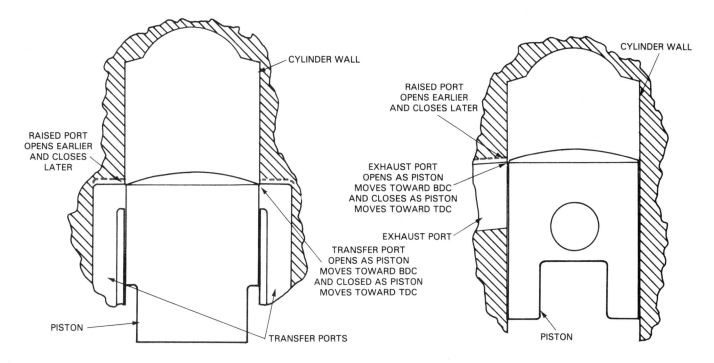

Fig. 6-9. Transfer and exhaust timing is determined by height of ports. As roof of port is raised, port is opened earlier and closed later by piston.

Fig. 6-10. Valve raises exhaust port as engine speed increases. (Yamaha Motor Corp., U.S.A.)

amount of vacuum and pressure, the piston, rings, and cylinder must also be in good condition.

CRANKSHAFT CONFIGURATIONS

In regard to cylinder and crankshaft configurations, common two-stroke cycle engine designs include single cylinder, twin-cylinder, and multi-cylinder engines.

SINGLE CYLINDER CRANKSHAFT

Two-stroke cycle, single cylinder crankshafts are normally made of several components pressed together. They are often termed BUILT-UP CRANKSHAFTS. One make of single cylinder crankshaft is shown in Fig. 6-12. It consists of:
1. Flywheels (provide inertia and hold crankpin).
2. Crankpin (fits into flywheels and supports rod).
3. Roller bearings and cage (reduces friction between rod and crankpin).
4. Connecting rod (fastens crankpin to piston pin).
5. Axle shaft (supports crank assembly in case and main bearings).
6. Thrust washers (limit rod side or thrust movement).

TWIN-CLYINDER CRANKSHAFT

A twin-cylinder, two-stroke cycle crankshaft is simply two single cylinder crankshafts constructed side-by-side. See Fig. 6-13. A centered pin connects the two inner flywheel halves together and is supported by a main bearing with seals on each side. The crankpins are located 180 degrees from each other.

MULTI-CYLINDER CRANKSHAFT

Multi-cylinder, two-stroke cycle crankshafts consist of three or four sets of flywheel assemblies connected together. Main bearings and seals separate each flywheel assembly and crankcase cavity. Fig. 6-14 shows a multi-cylinder crankshaft.

Three cylinder engine crankshafts have the

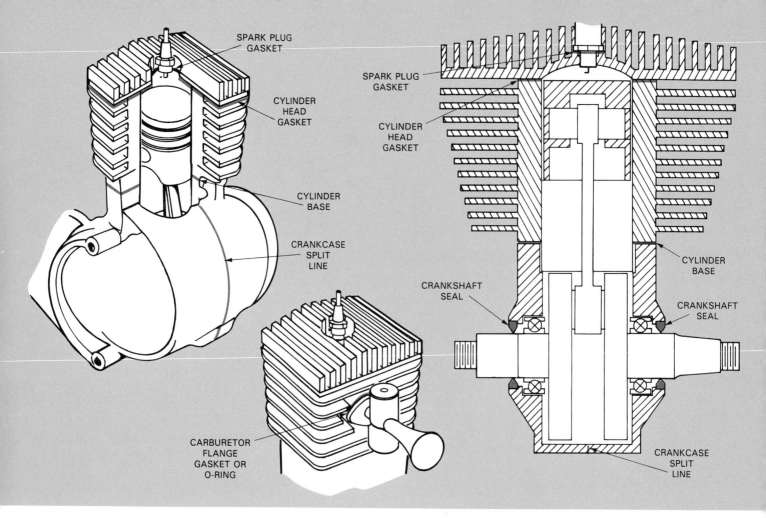

Fig. 6-11. Leakage at any of these points will cause poor engine operation.

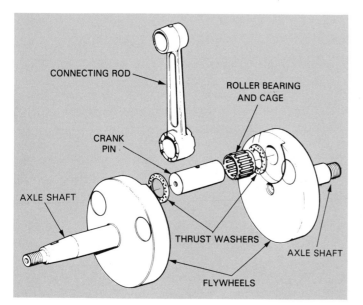

Fig. 6-12. An assembled crankshaft is made up of several components. Crankpin is pressed into one flywheel. Thrust washers, roller bearing, and connecting rod are installed on crankpin. Then, other flywheel is pressed on. (Kawasaki Motors Corp., U.S.A.)

crankpins positioned 120 degrees apart. Four cylinder engine crankshafts have the crankpins positioned 180 degrees apart.

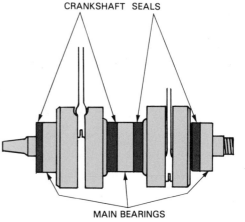

Fig. 6-13. Note construction of typical twin-cylinder, two-stroke cycle crankshaft.

PISTON AND RING DESIGN

Two-stroke cycle pistons differ in a number of ways from four-stroke cycle pistons. A two-stroke cycle piston often has:
1. Transfer cutouts below the piston pin boss.
2. Locating pins in the ring grooves.
3. Variations in intake skirt design.
4. No oil control ring.

92

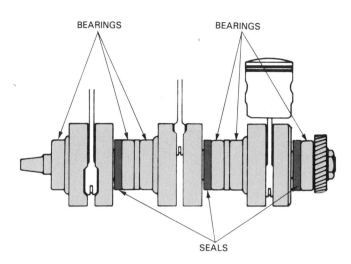

BEARINGS   BEARINGS

SEALS

Fig. 6-14. With three-cylinder crankshaft, main bearings and seals separate each flywheel assembly. (U.S. Suzuki Motor Corporation)

5. Needle bearings between the piston pin and rod small end.

TRANSFER CUTOUTS

With a two-stroke cycle engine, the skirt area below the piston pin boss is cut out to allow free air-fuel mixture flow into the transfer ports. This is termed a TRANSFER CUTOUT. When the piston is at BDC, the transfer cutout matches the transfer opening in the cylinder wall and crankcase, Fig. 6-15. As a result, fuel mixture can rapidly flow into the cylinder.

RING LOCATING PINS

In a two-stroke cycle engine, the piston rings must move past port openings in the cylinder. To prevent ring breakage, it is normally necessary to locate the

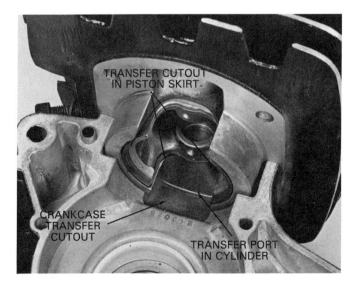

Fig. 6-15. Transfer cutouts in piston and crankcase match transfer port in cylinder.

ring end gaps AWAY from the port openings. This prevents the rings ends from protruding into and catching on the port edge. The ring could easily break on the port opening. Locating pins are positioned so that ring end gaps do NOT rotate in the cylinder and pass over the port, Fig. 6-16.

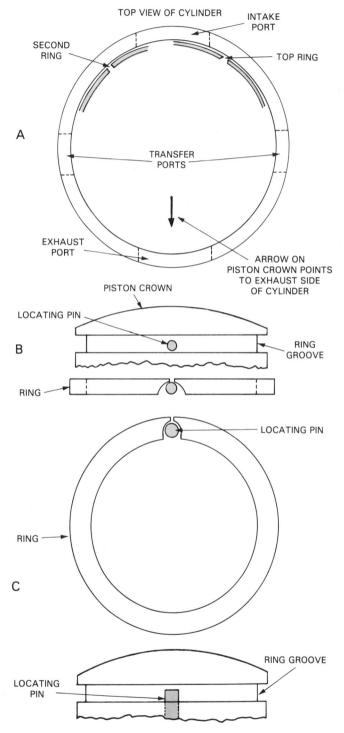

Fig. 6-16. Piston rings in a two-stroke cycle engine are normally located by pins. This prevents rings from rotating. If rings turned on piston, ring ends could get caught in port windows. A—Proper location of ring end gaps. B—Horizontal locating pin. C—Vertical locating pin.

INTAKE SKIRT

Two-stroke cycle piston skirts are not always shaped the same. Quite often, the intake and exhaust side of the piston will have different lengths. Intake skirts may be shortened, cutaway, or drilled to work properly with intake timing control. Common designs are shown in Fig. 6-17.

PISTON EXPANSION

To help control expansion and piston fit, two-stroke cycle pistons are cam ground (machined out-of-round) and tapered (machined to smaller diameter at top). Since the two-stroke cycle engine has a power stroke every revolution, the piston is subjected to much more heat than a four-stroke cycle piston. Thus, piston expansion can be a problem in a two-stroke engine.

PISTON RINGS

Two-stroke cycle engines are designed to use either one or two piston rings. No oil control ring is needed because lubrication is provided by the air-fuel mixture. For this reason, the rings are only required to seal compression, vacuum, and combustion pressures.

Shown in Fig. 6-18, the three basic ring designs used in two-stroke cycle engine are: conventional rectangular rings, dyke rings or L-rings, and keystone rings.

Rectangular ring

A two-stroke cycle rectangular ring is similar in design to a four-stroke cycle compression ring. The major difference is that the two-stroke cycle ring is locked in place by a pin in the piston ring groove. Also, rectangular rings may sometimes have a slight taper on their face.

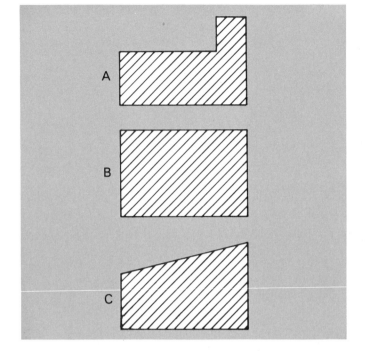

Fig. 6-18. Three common ring shapes used in two-stroke cycle engines: A—Dyke (L-shaped). B—Rectangular (conventional). C—Keystone.

Dyke ring (L-ring)

The DYKE RING, also termed an L-shaped ring, is designed to use combustion pressure to aid in sealing. Shown in Fig. 6-19, the L-shape allows combustion pressure to force the ring out against the cylinder wall. Because combustion pressure directly helps ring sealing, BLOW-BY (movement of pressure and gas between ring and cylinder wall) is held to a minimum.

Keystone ring

KEYSTONE RINGS also use combustion pressure to aid ring sealing. In this design, combustion

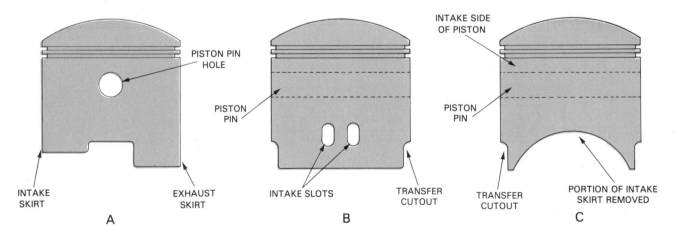

Fig. 6-17. Common piston skirt designs include: A—Intake skirt shorter than exhaust skirt (used in engines with piston controlled intake). B—Slots or holes in intake skirt (used with reed valve). C—Intake skirt with radius (used with reed valve).

pressure is trapped between the ring taper and ring groove, Fig. 6-20. Combustion pressure pushes the ring out against the cylinder wall. This action is especially desirable at high engine speeds when ring tension may not be strong enough to hold the ring outward.

CYLINDER CONSTRUCTION

Four methods of construction are used for two-stroke cycle cylinders:
1. Pressed-in sleeve.
2. Cast-in sleeve.
3. Coated bore.
4. Cast iron cylinder.
Each design has advantages and disadvantages de-

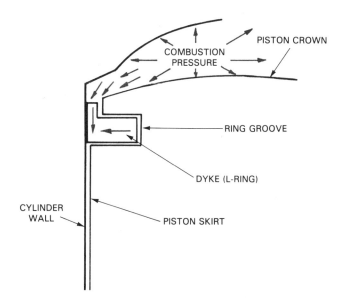

Fig. 6-19. Combustion pressure forces dyke (L-ring) against cylinder wall to increase sealing ability.

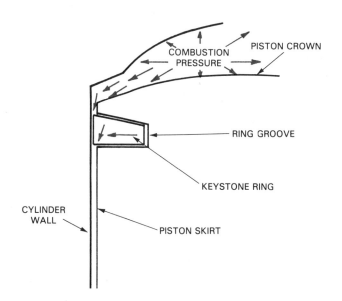

Fig. 6-20. Combustion pressure forces keystone ring against cylinder wall to increase sealing ability.

pending upon needs. It is important to understand these differences.

PRESSED-IN SLEEVE

The PRESSED-IN SLEEVE design for a two-cycle engine normally is made of a cast iron liner (sleeve) which is machined to fit tightly into an aluminum cylinder block. See Fig. 6-21. An interference fit (sleeve is slightly larger than hole in cylinder block) is used to lock the sleeve in place.

The major disadvantage of the pressed-in sleeve design is its manufacturing cost. The major advantage is that the sleeve can be resized (bored) when worn. It can also be replaced (resleeved) when the last overbore is used up. This avoids the need for expensive cylinder block replacement.

CAST-IN SLEEVE

A CAST-IN SLEEVE uses an iron liner cast into the cylinder block. This design is inexpensive to produce. When the last overbore is used up, however, the complete cylinder block must be replaced. Fig. 6-22 shows the cast-in sleeve design.

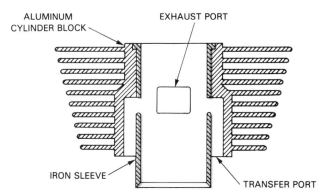

Fig. 6-21. Pressed-in sleeve method of cylinder construction often uses an iron sleeve pressed into an aluminum cylinder block.

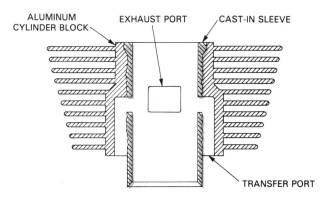

Fig. 6-22. Cast-in sleeve method of cylinder construction normally begins with an iron sleeve. Aluminum cylinder block is then cast around sleeve, making a one piece unit. Aluminum is lighter and dissipates heat better than iron.

COATED BORE

The COATED BORE type cylinder does NOT use any type of inserted liner, as shown in Fig. 6-23. Instead, a thin coating of chrome or iron is applied to provide a hard cylinder wall surface. This type of cylinder is expensive to produce and CANNOT be bored. However, superior heat dissipation, light weight, and relatively long cylinder life is provided by a coated bore design.

CAST IRON CYLINDER

Some small bore two-stroke cycle engines still use the solid CAST IRON CYLINDER assembly, Fig. 6-24. In this design, the bore is machined into a one-piece cylinder block. A cast iron cylinder generally is heavy and dissipates heat poorly. Yet, it is inexpensive and very dependable.

CYLINDER PORTS

We already know that the primary function of two-stroke cycle CYLINDER PORTS is to route the air-fuel mixture through the engine. They also allow exhaust gases to leave the engine cylinder. Since the piston and rings control opening and closing of the ports, port shape is important.

Piston rings pass the exhaust and transfer PORT WINDOWS (openings into cylinder) twice during

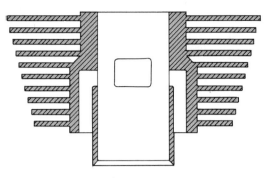

Fig. 6-24. This is an all cast iron cylinder block and cylinder bore.

each revolution of the engine. Since the rings press out against the cylinder wall, they have a tendency to expand into the port. If the port windows are not shaped properly, the rings can bulge into, catch, and break on the port edge, or wear out prematurely.

A number of port designs used to help eliminate this ring failure problem are the elliptical port, bridged port, and multiple ports.

Elliptical port shape

ELLIPTICAL PORT SHAPE allows a relatively large port opening without the danger of ring catching. Fig. 6-25 shows the advantage of elliptical shape over a rectangular port shape.

The curved sides of the elliptical port prevent the rings from catching on a horizontal or parallel edge. This port shape is most commonly seen in large exhaust ports.

Bridged port

The BRIDGED PORT design uses a vertical bridge (rib) across the middle of the port opening. As illustrated in Fig. 6-26, this supports the ring as it passes over the port window. It prevents the rings from bulging into the port and catching. A bridge allows the use of a large rectangular port without the danger of ring breakage.

Bridges are normally used on exhaust ports and

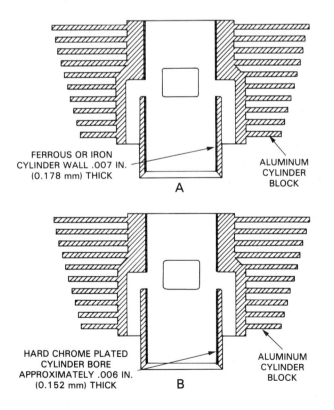

FERROUS OR IRON CYLINDER WALL .007 IN. (0.178 mm) THICK

ALUMINUM CYLINDER BLOCK

A

HARD CHROME PLATED CYLINDER BORE APPROXIMATELY .006 IN. (0.152 mm) THICK

ALUMINUM CYLINDER BLOCK

B

Fig. 6-23. A—Cylinder construction is similar to chromed cylinder except that iron is electrically bonded to aluminum cylinder block. B—In this method of cylinder construction, aluminum cylinder block is plated with a thin layer of chrome.

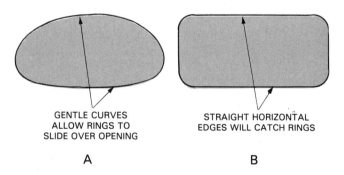

GENTLE CURVES ALLOW RINGS TO SLIDE OVER OPENING

STRAIGHT HORIZONTAL EDGES WILL CATCH RINGS

A

B

Fig. 6-25. Port shapes: A—Elliptical port shape permits large port window. B—Rectangular port could catch rings on its horizontal edges.

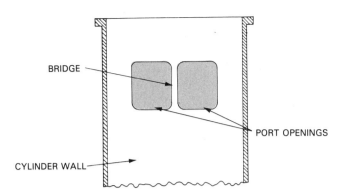

Fig. 6-26. Using a bridge in middle of a large rectangular port prevents rings from catching on horizontal port edges.

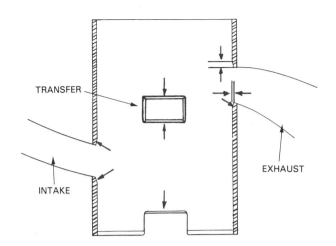

Fig. 6-28. Port edges are beveled (chamfered) to prevent rings from catching as they pass port openings.

piston controlled intake ports. This intake port design also prevents the piston skirt from swinging into and catching on the bottom of the port.

Multiple ports

MULTIPLE PORTS are mainly used as transfer ports, Fig. 6-27. Multiple ports are a number of small ports placed around the cylinder. This allows for a large total port area, even though the individual ports are small. A distinct advantage is that the incoming air-fuel charge can be better directed to help move exhaust gases out of the combustion chamber. Also, ring catching and breakage is avoided.

Many different combinations of port shapes are used. Regardless of shape, the ports must provide efficient filling of the crankcase and cylinder as well as SCAVENGING (cleaning) of the cylinder.

Another important method of increasing piston and ring life is shown in Fig. 6-28. Port edges are CHAMFERED (beveled) to keep the rings and piston from scuffing on the port. This must be done in all two-stroke cycle cylinders.

VERTICAL AND HORIZONTAL SPLIT CRANKCASES

Most single cylinder two-stroke cycle engines have VERTICALLY split crankcases. This is the least expensive design to produce. Fig. 6-29 shows a typical single cylinder vertically split two-stroke cycle engine.

Twin and multiple cylinder two-stroke cycle engines are normally split HORIZONTALLY, Fig. 6-30. Since each cylinder must have its own sealed crankcase, it would be impractical to use the vertical split design.

TWO-STROKE CYCLE ENGINE COOLING

Modern two-stroke cycle engines use liquid cooling as well as air cooling. Air cooling is more common than liquid cooling. Air and liquid cooling principles

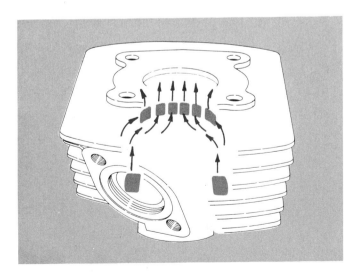

Fig. 6-27. This example of multiple transfer ports uses six small port windows. (U.S. Suzuki Motor Corporation)

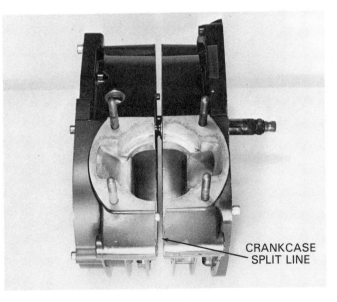

Fig. 6-29. Single cylinder cases are normally split or divided vertically in middle.

97

CRANKCASE
SPLIT LINE

Fig. 6-30. Horizontally split crankcases, like this twin, are divided horizontally through middle of crankshaft and gearbox shafts.

apply to both two-stroke and four-stroke cycle engines. For a review of cooling principles refer to Chapter 5, Four-stroke Cycle Engine.

In the two-stroke cycle engine, combustion takes place once during each crankshaft revolution. This produces heat each revolution and requires very efficient cooling. Because the four-stroke cycle engine has combustion every other revolution, combustion heat is produced less frequently. Cooling demands for a two-stroke cycle are generally more critical than with a four-stroke cycle engine.

A two-stroke cycle engine cooling system must be capable of dissipating a large amount of heat. This is clearly shown by comparing two and four-stroke cycle air-cooled cylinders. See Fig. 6-31. Notice the difference in cooling fin area. The heat dissipating surface is much larger on the two-stroke cycle cylinder.

Two and four-stroke cycle liquid cooling systems are very similar. Both types of engines (two and four-

stroke) benefit from liquid cooling in a number of ways. Quieter operation, stable operating temperature, and improved efficiency are some of the advantages of liquid cooling. Liquid cooling is ideal for small and medium displacement two-stroke cycle racing engines because it reduces the power loss caused by overheating. The added weight of liquid cooling is offset by its ability to reduce overheating. Fig. 6-32 shows two-stroke and four-stroke cycle, liquid-cooled engines.

ENGINE LUBRICATION

As with the four-stroke cycle engine, the two-stroke cycle engine must have lubrication to reduce friction. In the two-stroke cycle engine, lubricating oil is carried as part of the air-fuel mixture. Lubrication is provided as the air-fuel mixture moves through the inside of the engine.

There are a number of ways to provide lubrication to the two-stroke cycle engine. These will be discussed in Chapter 11, Lubrication Systems.

KNOW THESE TERMS

Intake timing, Piston port, Mild timing, Radical timing, Reed valve, Standoff, Reed petals, Reed cage, Rotary valve, Transfer timing, Exhaust timing, Built-up crankshaft, Multi-cylinder crankshaft, Transfer cutouts, Rectangular ring, Dyke ring, L-ring, Blow-by, Keystone ring, Pressed-in sleeve, Cast-in sleeve, Coated bore, Cylinder ports, Elliptical port, Bridged port, Multiple ports.

REVIEW QUESTIONS—CHAPTER 6

1. Name three methods used to control the intake timing of two-stroke cycle engines.
2. A two-stroke cycle engine which opens and closes

TWO-STROKE
CYLINDER
COOLING FINS

FOUR-STROKE
CYLINDER
COOLING FINS

Fig. 6-31. A two-stroke cycle engine requires much more cooling fin area than an equal displacement four-stroke cycle engine.

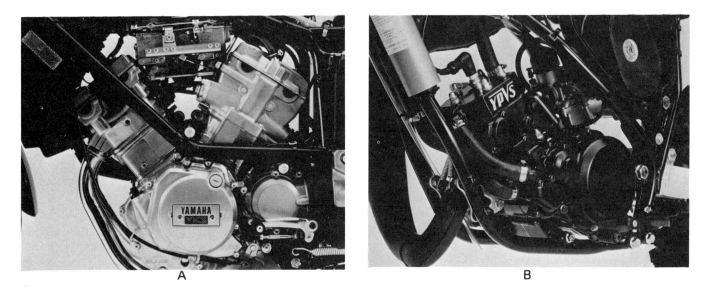

Fig. 6-32. Compare engine differences. A—Four-stroke cycle liquid-cooled engine. B—Two-stroke cycle liquid-cooled engine. Both engines lack cooling fins.   (Yamaha Motor Corp., U.S.A.)

its intake port at the same piston position before and after TDC has _____ port timing.
   a. Rotary.
   b. Unsymmetrical.
   c. Symmetrical.
   d. Reed.
3. The backward flow of the intake charge is called _____.
4. A _____ _____ helps to prevent standoff.
5. What makes a reed valve operate?
6. A _____ _____, keyed to the crankshaft, may be used to open and close the intake port.
7. List five areas where vacuum/pressure leakage may occur in a two-stroke cycle engine.
8. A crankshaft, made of several components pressed together, is called a _____ type crankshaft.
9. Name three differences betweeen two and four-stroke cycle pistons.
10. Two-stroke cycle pistons are NOT tapered or cam ground like four-stroke cycle pistons. True or False?
11. Two-stroke cycle pistons are subjected to more heat than four-stroke cycle pistons. True or False?
12. Combustion pressure never aids ring sealing. True or False?
13. List three common ring designs used in two-stroke cycle engines.
14. A _____ _____ type cylinder wall provides the most efficient type of engine cooling.

15. What are the three common port designs?
16. Twin and multi-cylinder, two-stroke cycle engines use _____ split crankcases.
   a. Opposed.
   b. Horizontally.
   c. Laterally.
   d. Vertically.
17. Internal components of a two-stroke cycle engine are lubricated by a mixture of _____, _____, and _____.

SUGGESTED ACTIVITIES

1. Compare intake configurations of common two-stroke cycle engines produced by different motorcycle manufacturers.
2. Contrast engine design differences between road bikes, trail bikes, motocross bikes, and trials bikes.
3. Check in manuals and determine the most popular type of two-stroke cycle piston ring (rectangular, dyke, keystone). Also, determine whether one or two rings are used in most two-stroke cycle engines.
4. Pick a popular two-stroke cycle motorcycle engine and use the shop manual to determine:
   a. Exhaust port configuration (shape).
   b. Transfer port configuration (shape and number of ports).
   c. Intake configuration (piston port, rotary valve, reed valve).
   d. Type of cylinder construction (coated bore, cast-in sleeve).

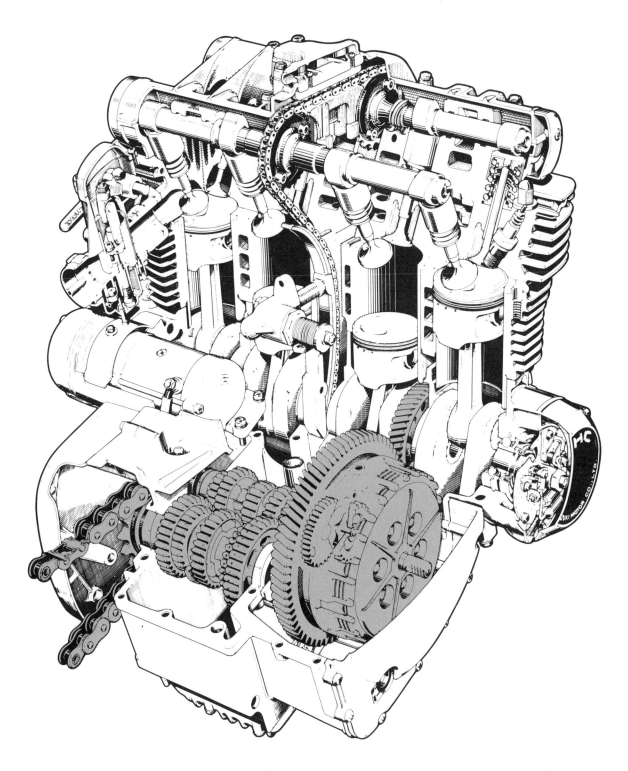

Primary drive and gearbox transfer power from engine crankshaft to final drive system.
(U.S. Suzuki Motor Corporation)

Chapter 7

PRIMARY DRIVE AND GEARBOX

After studying this chapter, you will be able to:
□ Define the major parts of a primary drive and gearbox.
□ Explain the operating principles of a primary drive, clutch, and gearbox.
□ List the different types of primary drives and clutches.
□ Trace power flow through a primary drive and gearbox.
□ Explain gearbox shift mechanisms.
□ Describe kickstart mechanisms.

Primary drive and gearbox (transmission) ratios are intended to make the best use of engine power and torque. In this chapter, you will study the various designs used for primary drives, clutches, and gearboxes. Many designs are used in motorcycles to achieve the desired gear reduction, speed, and multiplication of engine torque.

PRIMARY DRIVE

The PRIMARY DRIVE transfers engine power from the crankshaft to the clutch/gearbox assembly, Fig. 7-1. Primary drive reduction is accomplished by either a set of gears or by a chain and set of sprockets. A gear or sprocket mounted on the engine crankshaft turns a gear or sprocket on the clutch hub. Since the crankshaft gear is smaller than the clutch hub gear, GEAR REDUCTION (clutch turns slower than crank) and an increase in torque (turning force) is produced.

It is important for you to understand the different types of primary drives used on modern motorcycles.

PRIMARY GEAR DRIVE

The three common designs used for PRIMARY GEAR DRIVES are straight-cut gears, straight-cut offset gears, and helical gears. Each type has specific advantages and disadvantages.

Straight-cut gear drive

The STRAIGHT-CUT GEAR DRIVE uses conventional (non-angled) gear teeth to transmit power from the engine to the clutch. Refer to Fig. 7-1. Straight-cut gears must have a certain amount of backlash (clearance between teeth) in order to operate freely. Fig. 7-2 shows another view of straight-cut primary gears. With straight-cut teeth, backlash as well as the action produced by tooth engagement can cause a whining type noise during operation. Straight-cut gears, however, are inexpensive to manufacture.

Straight-cut offset gear drive

The STRAIGHT-CUT OFFSET GEAR DRIVE uses two straight-cut crankshaft gears and two straight-cut clutch gears mounted side by side. Each set of gears is staggered one-half tooth, as shown in Fig. 7-3. This eliminates backlash noise common to straight-cut gear teeth. Since the gear teeth engage alternately (one tooth after the other), backlash and gear noise is held to a minimum.

Helical gear drive

A HELICAL GEAR DRIVE uses angled gear teeth, Fig. 7-4. A helical primary drive also eliminates backlash noise since more than one tooth is engaged at all times. Angular sliding engagement of the gear teeth reduces the need for backlash. Unfortunately, this angular engagement also causes a side thrust, Fig. 7-5. The friction resulting from the side thrust may absorb a small amount of engine power.

Application of each type of primary gear drive is dependent upon manufacturing expenses, motorcycle use, acceptable gear noise, and power loss requirements.

101

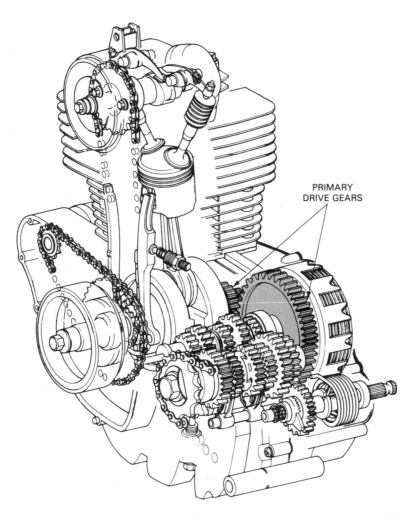

Fig. 7-1. Primary drive causes engine crankshaft to rotate clutch and gearbox. Either gears, as shown, or chain and sprockets may be used as primary drive.   (Kawasaki Motors Corp., U.S.A.)

Fig. 7-2. Backlash refers to free play between engaged gear teeth. Backlash is necessary for unrestricted movement of gears. Smaller primary gear on engine powers larger gear on clutch.

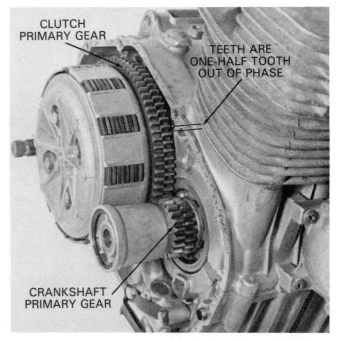

Fig. 7-3. Since gear teeth in straight-cut, offset primary drive do not mesh at same time, backlash noise is eliminated.

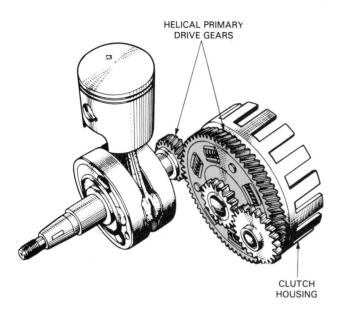

Fig. 7-4. Helical primary drive uses angled gear teeth for quiet operation. (U.S. Suzuki Motor Corporation)

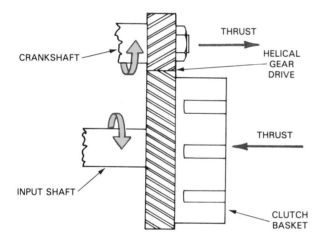

Fig. 7-5. Helical primary drive gears cause side thrust in one direction on crankshaft and opposite direction on clutch basket assembly.

PRIMARY CHAIN DRIVE

A typical PRIMARY CHAIN DRIVE normally consists of a crankshaft sprocket, primary drive chain, clutch sprocket, and chain tensioner. Fig. 7-6 shows one type of primary chain drive. A small sprocket drives the primary chain. The primary chain drives a larger sprocket on the clutch.

Depending upon the intended use, either single-row, double-row, triple-row, or a hy-vo chain may be employed. Fig. 7-7 illustrates triple-row and hy-vo type primary drive chain mechanisms.

To compensate for chain wear, a CHAIN TENSIONER is usually provided, Fig. 7-6. It presses lightly on the slack side of the chain to prevent chain slap (up and down movement and noise). The tensioner may be either manually or automatically adjusted.

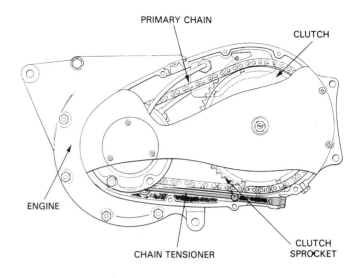

Fig. 7-6. Chain type primary drive is simple and efficient, but requires periodic chain adjustment. (Triumph Motorcycles [Meriden] Ltd.)

CLUTCHES

A CLUTCH is provided to connect and disconnect engine power to and from the gearbox. When the clutch lever is pulled (clutch disengaged), the primary drive continues to turn, but power is NOT transferred to the gearbox INPUT SHAFT. The clutch slips and the motorcycle does not move.

As the clutch lever is released (clutch engaged), the clutch gradually transfers power to the gearbox input shaft. Internal spring pressure and friction lock the clutch plates together. Engine power is then transferred into the gearbox and the motorcycle is propelled forward.

The relationship between the primary drive, clutch, and input shaft is shown in Fig. 7-8.

MULTI-PLATE CLUTCH

A typical MULTI-PLATE CLUTCH consists of:
1. Clutch basket (housing).
2. Clutch hub.
3. Clutch drive (friction) plates.
4. Clutch driven (steel) plates.
5. Clutch pressure plate.
6. Clutch springs.

The engine's primary chain or gear turns the CLUTCH HOUSING or BASKET. Clutch basket slots engage tabs on the friction drive plates. See Fig. 7-9. This causes the clutch housing and friction plates to rotate together.

The steel driven clutch plates have small inner teeth which engage with the outer teeth on the CLUTCH HUB. The driven plates are locked to the hub, but not to the basket. The clutch hub is connected to the transmission gearbox input shaft.

During clutch engagement, spring pressure forces the friction plates and steel driven plates together.

103

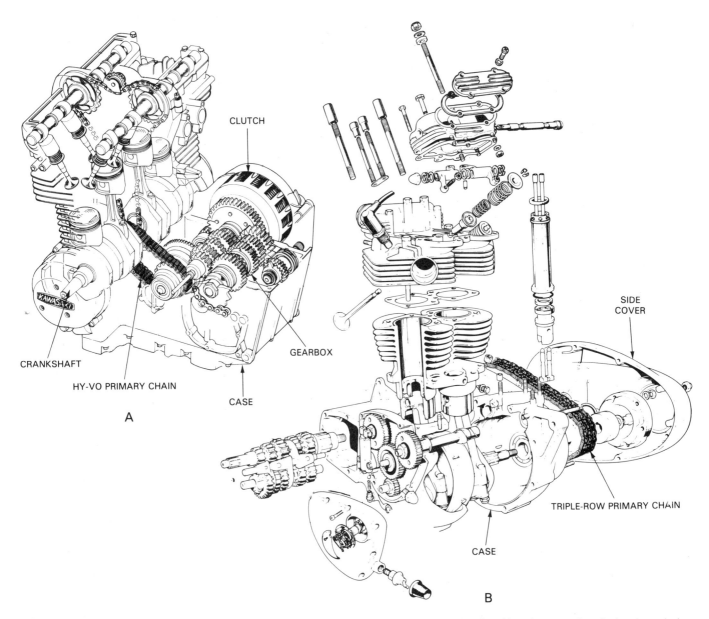

CLUTCH

CRANKSHAFT

HY-VO PRIMARY CHAIN

CASE

GEARBOX

A

SIDE COVER

TRIPLE-ROW PRIMARY CHAIN

CASE

B

Fig. 7-7. A—This engine uses a hy-vo type primary chain which is very strong and quiet. Note how engine design has chain coming off of middle of crankshaft. B—This engine uses a triple-row, roller type primary chain.
(Kawasaki Motors Corp., U.S.A.; Triumph Motorcycles [Meriden] Ltd.)

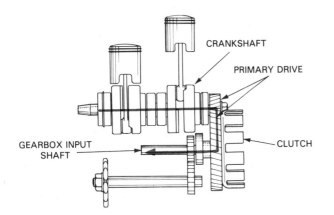

CRANKSHAFT

PRIMARY DRIVE

GEARBOX INPUT SHAFT

CLUTCH

Fig. 7-8. Power flows from crankshaft through primary drive chain to clutch, and from clutch to gearbox input shaft.
(U.S. Suzuki Motor Corp.)

Friction locks them tightly. Then, the clutch basket, drive plates, driven plates, clutch hub, and gearbox input shaft all spin together.

The clutch is released or disengaged when the clutch cable mechanism moves the clutch pressure plate away from the drive and driven plates. This relieves spring pressure holding the drive and driven clutch plates together, Fig. 7-10. The plates float away from each other and slip. Power is no longer transmitted into the transmission gearbox. Fig. 7-11 shows the flow of engine power through the clutch.

Multi-plate clutch action

A multi-plate clutch provides a very compact, yet high friction coupling between the engine and gear-

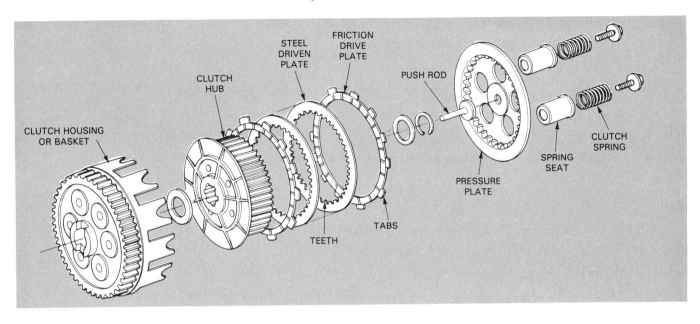

Fig. 7-9. Drive plate tabs fit into clutch basket slots. Driven plate teeth lock in hub teeth. When clutch is engaged, springs hold plates together and power flows from primary drive, through clutch, into gearbox. When rider pulls clutch lever, push rod compresses springs to separate clutch plates. Clutch basket and drive plates spin while driven plates and gearbox shaft remain stationary.   (Kawasaki Motors Corp., U.S.A.)

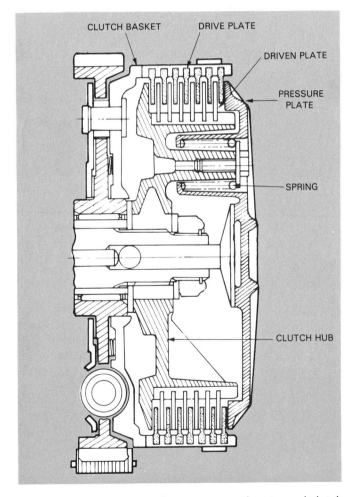

Fig. 7-10. Clutch springs force pressure plate toward clutch hub. This causes drive plates and driven plates to be locked tightly. Clutch would be engaged.
(Kawasaki Motors Corp., U.S.A.)

box. See Fig. 7-12. With multiple plates, the surface area, strength, and friction in the engaged clutch is increased.

Depending upon the size of the engine and weight of the motorcycle, four to eight sets of plates (four to

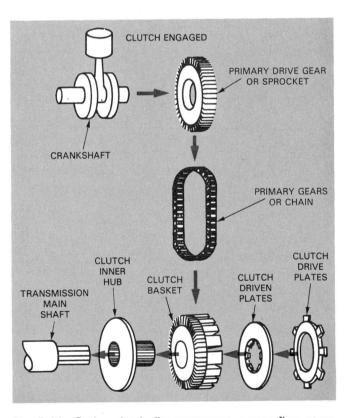

Fig. 7-11. During clutch disengagement, power flow stops at clutch drive plates. Drive and driven plates are separated and slip.

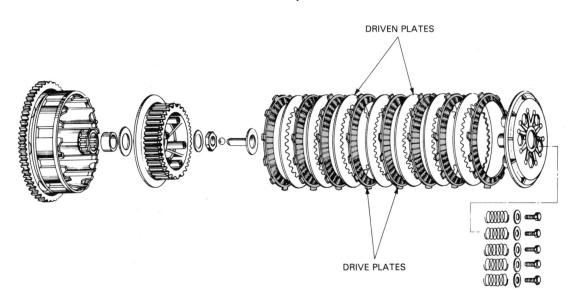

Fig. 7-12. This clutch uses eight drive plates and seven driven plates. Drive plates are made of friction material. Driven plates are steel. (Kawasaki Motors Corp., U.S.A.)

eight drive plates, four to eight driven plates) may be housed in the clutch basket.

Wet clutch

The discs of a WET CLUTCH operate in an oil bath (oil surrounds and covers discs). Most multi-plate clutches run in an oil bath. Wet clutches are used for several reasons.
1. Since the primary drive needs lubrication, it is less costly to use a wet clutch.
2. Debris (friction material, etc.) resulting from clutch wear can be drained with the oil or trapped by the oil filter.
3. Oil helps keep the clutch cool.

Dry clutch

A DRY CLUTCH is designed to run without an oil bath. This requires that the clutch is a sealed unit. Seals must be used to prevent the entry of oil into the clutch basket. Oil will cause clutch slippage and will ruin the clutch friction discs. Dry clutches can use either single plate or multiple plate construction.

CLUTCH SPRINGS

There are two basic types of springs used in motorcycle clutches: coil springs and diaphragm springs. Both types of springs press the clutch plates together to provide clutch engagement.

Coil springs

Some motorcycle clutches use from one to eight COIL SPRINGS to provide force against the clutch pressure plate.

On clutches using multi-coil springs, Fig. 7-13, it is important for spring pressure to be equal. Unequal spring pressure can cause clutch drag, clutch slippage,

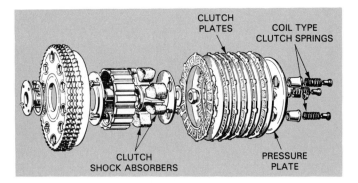

Fig. 7-13. Three springs are used in this clutch. As many as eight springs are used in some designs. Springs force pressure plate into clutch plates to lock clutch. (Triumph Motorcycles [Meriden] Ltd.)

chatter, vibration, and runout (wobble) of the pressure plate when disengaged.

On some designs, coil spring pressure is adjustable, Fig. 7-14. Most designs, however, do NOT allow adjustment. Balanced spring pressure is achieved by replacing the spring set.

Diaphragm springs

A DIAPHRAGM SPRING, Fig. 7-15, is a circular, conical disc made of spring steel. Partial flattening of the diaphragm against the pressure plate provides spring pressure, Fig. 7-16. The diaphragm spring is commonly used in the SINGLE PLATE DRY CLUTCH.

CLUTCH SHOCK ABSORBERS

Many manufacturers use a shock absorber in the primary drive or clutch. The purpose of the CLUTCH SHOCK ABSORBER is to smooth out

106

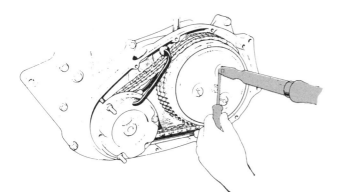

Fig. 7-14. In this design, spring pressure is adjustable. Fasteners can be tightened to increase pressure on clutch plates or loosened to lower pressure. Equal adjustment is critical. (Triumph Motorcycles [Meriden] Ltd.)

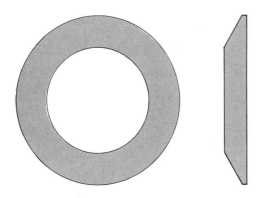

Fig. 7-15. A clutch diaphragm spring is a large flat washer made of spring steel and shaped with a curve.

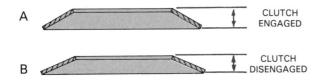

Fig. 7-16. A diaphragm clutch spring is a circular disc of spring steel with a slightly conical (curved) cross section. A—Spring pressure is provided by partially flattening spring. Spring is assembled between pressure plate and clutch disc. B—Disengagement is accomplished by forcing pressure plate against spring, flattening spring even more.

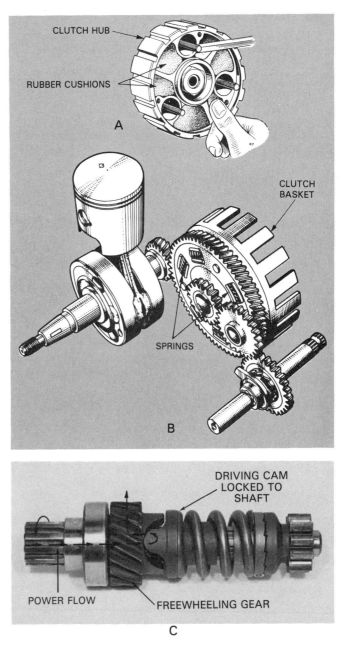

Fig. 7-17. Rubber cushions, springs, and compensators are used to absorb shock in primary drives. A—Clutch hub is mounted in rubber. B—Springs cushion blow of rapid clutch engagement. C—Freewheeling gear forced against driving cam absorbs shock and transfers power.
(Triumph Motorcycles [Meriden] Ltd.; U.S. Suzuki Motor Corp., U.S.A.)

power pulses and shock going into the gearbox. This reduces harsh impact of gearbox gear teeth as they strike each other during initial acceleration or when shifting gears.

Clutch shock absorbers also prevent damage to the primary drive, gearbox, and final drive due to sudden changes in throttle opening or clutch engagement. There are several ways to absorb shock in the primary drive and gearbox. Fig. 7-17 shows three of the most common designs.

It is also common to provide a shock absorber in the final drive. This type of shock absorber is covered in Chapter 21, Final Drive Systems.

AUTOMATIC CLUTCHES

There are two basic types of automatic clutches used on motorcycles. These are the centrifugal clutch and the hydraulic clutch.

Centrifugal clutch

A typical CENTRIFUGAL CLUTCH will engage and disengage automatically at a specific engine rpm. This is usually at an engine speed just above idle.

The clutch in Fig. 7-18 uses centrifugal force to cause clutch engagement. This clutch is mounted on the end of the crankshaft. When the engine is running, the clutch basket, pressure plate, and drive plates spin with the crankshaft.

As engine speed is increased from idle, centrifugal force causes the centrifugal rollers to fly outward against their cam ramps. The cam ramps force the rollers into the clutch, applying pressure to the primary drive plate. This locks the drive plates and driven plates together. As a result, the clutch hub and pinion gear turn with the crankshaft and drive the gearbox.

Hydraulic clutch

A HYDRAULIC CLUTCH uses hydraulic (oil) pressure to cause friction and clutch engagement which transfers power into the gearbox. Often called a torque converter, Fig. 7-19, it is a form of fluid coupling between the engine and transmission. A torque converter, like a centrifugal clutch, uses a spinning action and the resulting centrifugal force for engagement.

As the converter spins, fluid in the converter is thrown outward with considerable force. The pressurized fluid causes friction between the blades in the converter. When spinning fast enough, the converter locks and acts as an almost solid connection between the engine and gearbox. There is always a small amount of slippage between the stator and rotor.

CLUTCH RELEASE MECHANISMS

The function of the CLUTCH RELEASE MECHANISM is to move the pressure plate away from the clutch plates (clutch disengaged). A release mechanism may contact the pressure plate directly or it may use a push rod which passes through the gear-

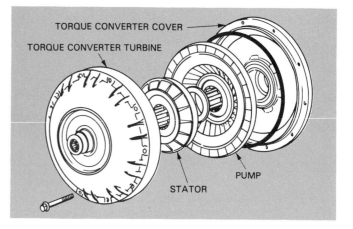

Fig. 7-19. A torque converter uses fluid between a turbine, stator, and pump to produce friction which connects engine power to gearbox. With enough speed, fluid flowing between blades causes converter to "lock up" and move motorcycle.

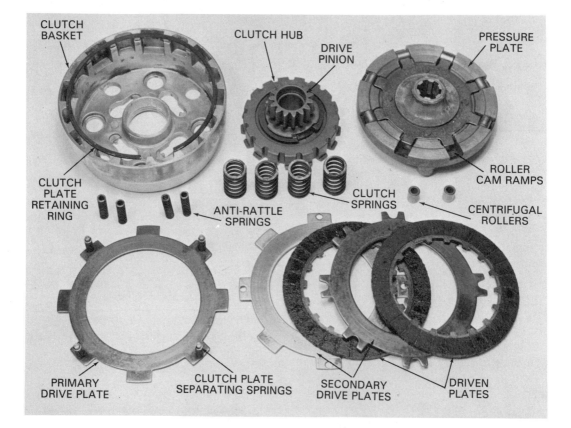

Fig. 7-18. Weights and cams provide pressure to engage centrifugal clutch as engine speed increases.

108

box input shaft, Fig. 7-20.

There are several methods used to actuate (release) the clutch pressure plate. The most common of these include the screw thread, ball and ramp, rack and pinion, and lever and pivot clutch release mechanisms.

Screw thread clutch release

The SCREW THREAD CLUTCH RELEASE mechanism normally uses a square cut, nylon thread to move the pressure plate for clutch disengagement. This is illustrated in Fig. 7-21.

Ball and ramp clutch release

The BALL AND RAMP CLUTCH RELEASE mechanism commonly uses three steel balls between two plates with stamped or machined ramps. See Fig. 7-22, A. One of the ramp plates is mounted solid. The other ramp plate is attached to the clutch cable by a lever. Rotation on the levered ramp plate causes the balls to climb the ramps and force the two plates apart, Fig. 7-22, B. As the plates are forced apart, the clutch is disengaged.

Rack and pinion clutch release

The RACK AND PINION CLUTCH RELEASE mechanism disengages the clutch with the use of a pinion gear and a rack gear, Fig. 7-23. The pinion gear is turned by a lever attached to the clutch cable. The teeth of the pinion gear engage the teeth of the rack gear. Rotation of the pinion gear moves the rack gear rod into the clutch and causes the clutch to disengage.

Lever and pivot clutch release

A LEVER AND PIVOT CLUTCH RELEASE uses a lever to achieve clutch disengagement. Look at Fig. 7-24. The lever is attached to the clutch cable and hand lever. When the cable pulls on the lever, the lever swivels on its pivot and pushes in on the push rod. The push rod then releases the pressure plate to disengage the clutch.

CLUTCH HAND LEVER

Almost all clutch release mechanisms are operated by a HAND LEVER mounted on the handle bar. Pulling the lever makes the clutch cable slide in its

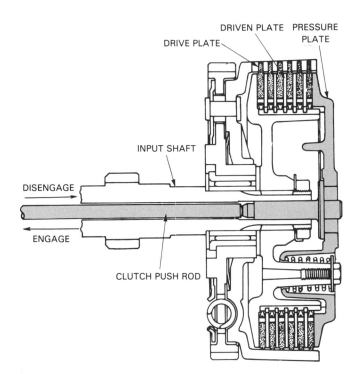

Fig. 7-20. Clutch push rod moves pressure plate away from drive plates. Then, driven plates disengage to release clutch. This allows rider to stop motorcycle with engine running and transmission in gear. (U.S. Suzuki Motor Corporation)

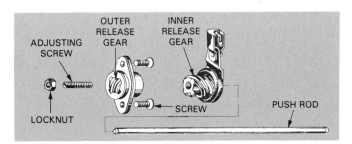

Fig. 7-21. Clutch cable is attached to inner release gear. When clutch lever is pulled, cable causes inner release gear to rotate in outer release gear. Rotation pushes inner gear into push rod which releases clutch pressure plate. An adjusting screw and locknut allow adjustment for free play. (Kawasaki Motors Corp., U.S.A.)

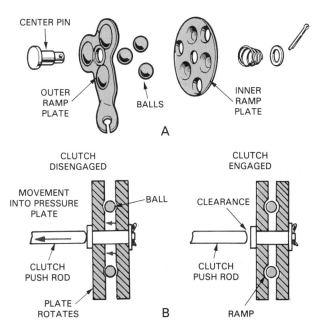

Fig. 7-22. A—Ball and ramp clutch release parts. B—Ball and ramp action. When outer ramp is rotated by clutch cable, balls climb ramps forcing plates apart. This movement is transferred to clutch pressure plate by clutch push rod. (Triumph Motorcycles [Meriden] Ltd.)

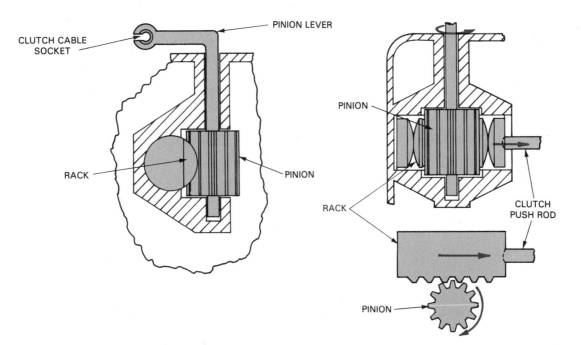

Fig. 7-23. In rack and pinion clutch release mechanism, pinion is rotated as clutch cable moves pinion lever. This rotation causes rack to disengage clutch by moving clutch push rod into pressure plate.

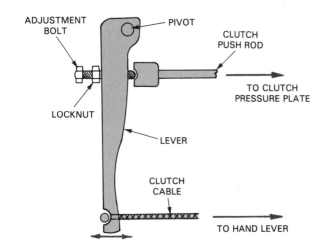

Fig. 7-24. When clutch handle is squeezed, cable, lever, and push rod movement force pressure plate away from plates in clutch. This causes clutch slippage and release.

housing, Fig. 7-25. Cable movement causes clutch release mechanism movement and clutch action.

Release mechanism adjustment

Clutch release mechanisms require adjustment for proper operation. Most release mechanisms require two adjustments: release mechanism free play, and cable free play.

All designs use a cable adjuster for cable free play. Most designs also have a screw and locknut located on the release mechanism, Fig. 7-26. Some play should be left in the clutch release mechanism. If not, clutch slippage and damage could result.

GEARBOX

A motorcycle GEARBOX (transmission) improves acceleration by allowing the rider to change the

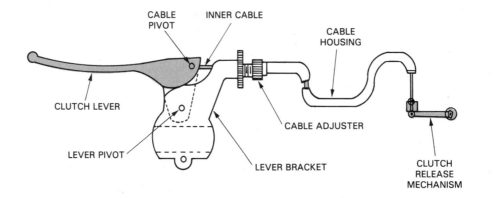

Fig. 7-25. When clutch lever is pulled, inner cable slides inside outer cable housing to provide movement of clutch release mechanism.

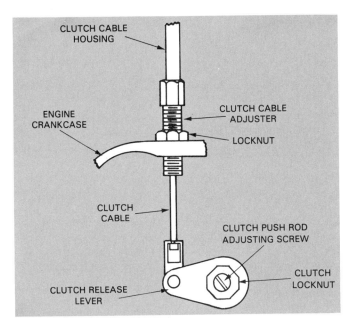

Fig. 7-26. A cable adjuster uses an adjusting screw and locknut to provide clutch adjustment. Screwing adjuster and cable housing away from release lever removes slack in cable.

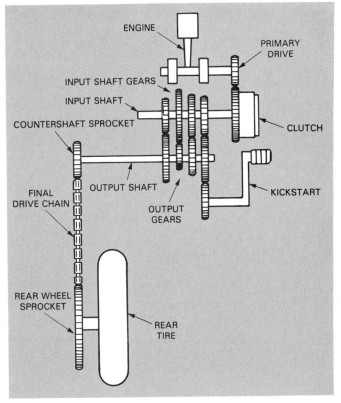

Fig. 7-27. This illustration shows main components of a motorcycle drive train. In particular, note two gearbox shafts.

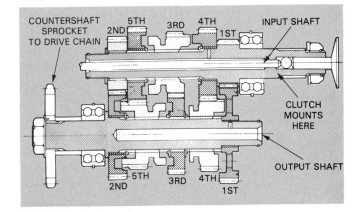

Fig. 7-28. Input shaft is turned by clutch. Power is transferred to output shaft when gears are engaged. A pair of gears must be used for each ratio. Countershaft sprocket is for chain to rear wheel. (Kawasaki Motors Corp., U.S.A.)

engine to rear wheel drive ratio. In lower gears, the gearbox ratio is increased to improve torque and acceleration. In high gear, the gear ratio is lowered to reduce engine speed, fuel consumption, engine noise, and engine wear.

GEARBOX SHAFTS

Motorcycle gearboxes commonly use two shafts: the input shaft (main shaft) and the output shaft (countershaft).

The input shaft and input shaft gears are powered by the clutch mechanism. See Fig. 7-27. The clutch is mounted on one end of the input shaft. Gears on the input shaft drive other gears on the OUTPUT SHAFT.

The transmission output shaft normally has a sprocket mounted on its outer end. This sprocket is commonly referred to as a COUNTERSHAFT SPROCKET. It is used to drive the chain going to the rear wheel. The countershaft sprocket normally mounts on the side of the engine which is opposite the clutch. On a shaft drive design, the gearbox output shaft powers the drive shaft.

MULTI-SPEED GEARBOXES

A MULTI-SPEED GEARBOX consists of two shafts and two or more gears on each shaft. Operation of a multi-speed gearbox is relatively simple if you have a basic understanding of the principles involved. A few basic multi-speed gearbox concepts are:

1. One pair of gears (one on each shaft) is used for each gearbox ratio, Fig. 7-28.

2. One gear may freewheel on its shaft while the other gear is locked to its shaft, Fig. 7-29.
3. The larger the gear (more teeth) on the input shaft, the lower the gear ratio. The largest gear on the input shaft is high gear, Fig. 7-30.
4. The smaller the gear (less teeth) on the input shaft, the higher the gear ratio. The smallest gear on the input shaft is first or low gear, Fig. 7-30.
5. Typically, all gear teeth are meshed at all times (constant mesh). However, only one gear on the

111

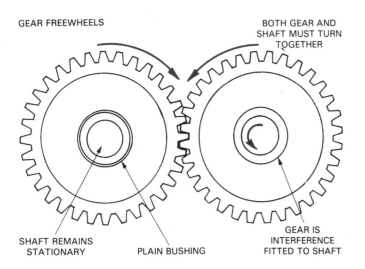

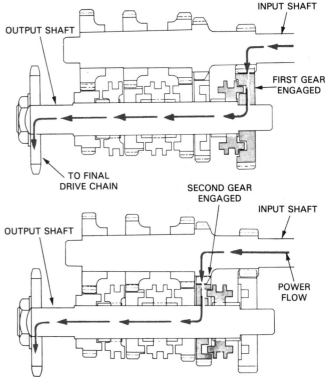

Fig. 7-29. Each pair of gears in gearbox (transmission) has one gear locked to shaft. Other gear freewheels on shaft until engaged.

input shaft and its output mate transfer power (are both locked) when a speed is selected, Fig. 7-31.

INTERNAL GEAR CHANGING

In order to change gearbox ratios, a SLIDING GEAR or SLIDING DOG, splined to the gearbox shaft, must be moved. The gear or dog must engage with the side of a freewheeling gear, Fig. 7-32. This engagement will cause the freewheeling gear to be locked to its shaft.

To move a sliding gear or dog, a SHIFTING FORK (part of the gear selector mechanism) is required. See Fig. 7-33. Most transmission gearboxes have two or three shifting forks.

Fig. 7-31. In a constant mesh gearbox, each gear is always meshed with its mate on other shaft. One pair of gears transfers power for each ratio. (U.S. Suzuki Motor Corp.)

Gear selector mechanisms

A GEAR SELECTOR MECHANISM changes up and down (vertical) movement of the gear change lever to sideways (horizontal) movement of the gears in the gearbox. There are two common types of gear selector mechanisms: drum type and cam plate type.

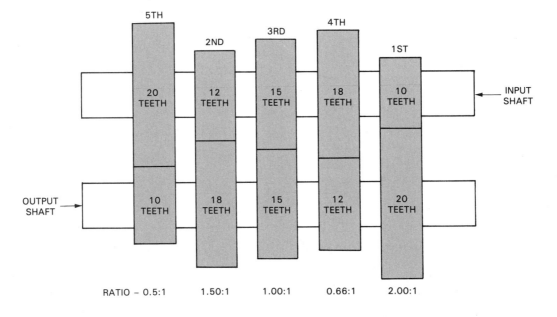

Fig. 7-30. Smallest gear (1st gear) on input shaft has highest ratio (2.00 to 1). Largest gear (5th gear) on input shaft has lowest ratio (0.5 to 1).

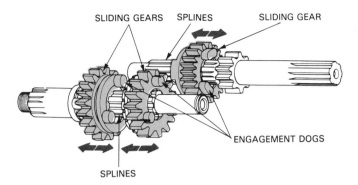

Fig. 7-32. Sliding gears are locked on shafts by splines. When they are moved sideways, engagement dogs mesh with engagement slots in freewheeling gear. This locks freewheeling gear to its shaft. (Kawasaki Motors Corp., U.S.A.)

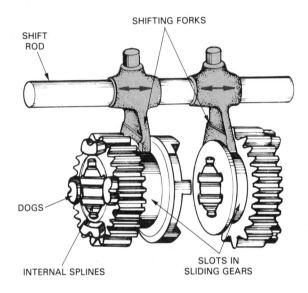

Fig. 7-33. Shifting forks fit into slots in sliding gears and control their side movement. As fork slides to one side, gears also slide. (Kawasaki Motors Corp., U.S.A.)

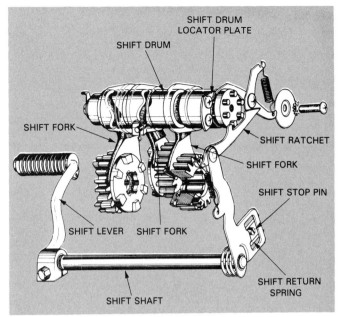

Fig. 7-34. In this gear selector mechanism, shift forks are located on shift drum rather than a separate shaft. Movement of shift linkage ratchets shift drum into new position, which moves forks. (Kawasaki Motors Corp., U.S.A.)

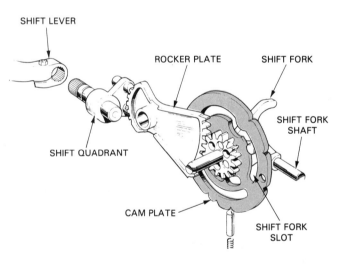

Fig. 7-35. Cam plate type shift mechanism uses a flat plate with slots that move shift forks. Slots force shift forks over to change gears. (Triumph Motorcycles [Meriden] Ltd.)

Drum gear selector

The most common type of gear selector mechanism is the DRUM TYPE. The parts which make up a drum gear selector mechanism are the shift lever, shift shaft, shift return spring, shift stop pin, shift ratchet, shift drum, shift fork, shift fork shaft, and shift drum locator plate. These components are illustrated in Fig. 7-34.

When your foot moves the gear shift lever, the shift drum and forks slide the gears sideways. This determines which gears are engaged in the gearbox.

Cam plate gear selector

A CAM PLATE GEAR SELECTOR mechanism uses a cam plate rather than a shifting drum to move the shifting forks. This type of shifting mechanism is shown in Fig. 7-35. When the shift lever is operated, movement of the cam plate forces the shift fork to slide on the fork shaft.

GEARBOX INDEXER

A GEARBOX INDEXER is used to precisely locate the shifting drum or cam plate into position for each gear and neutral. A spring-loaded arm and roller or a spring-loaded plunger is used to keep the transmission gears properly engaged with each other.

Fig. 7-36 shows how a shift drum or cam plate is located by its indexer. Accurate gear location is achieved by the indexer dropping into a dimple, recess, or gap between two pins on the shift drum.

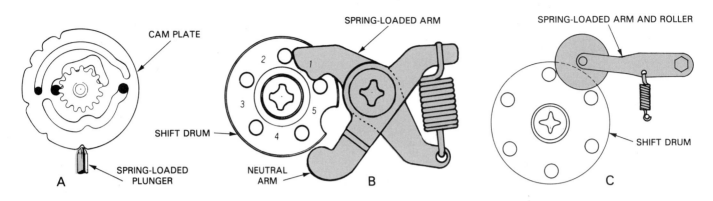

Fig. 7-36. Three common methods of indexing gearboxes. A—Spring-loaded plunger. B—Spring-loaded arm. C—Spring-loaded roller. (Triumph Motorcycles [Meriden] Ltd.; Kawasaki Motors Corp., U.S.A.)

The outside edge of the cam plate is notched for indexer engagement.

NEUTRAL INDICATOR SWITCH

Many drum type shift mechanisms have a NEUTRAL INDICATOR SWITCH which operates a neutral indicator light. This switch, Fig. 7-37, is normally located opposite the shift arm on the end of the shift drum. It illuminates a small instrument light when the transmission is in neutral.

When the shift drum is in the neutral position (between first and second gear) a tab or pin on the drum makes contact with a metal strip in the switch. This completes the circuit to the neutral indicator lamp. Fig. 7-38 shows how a neutral indicator switch operates.

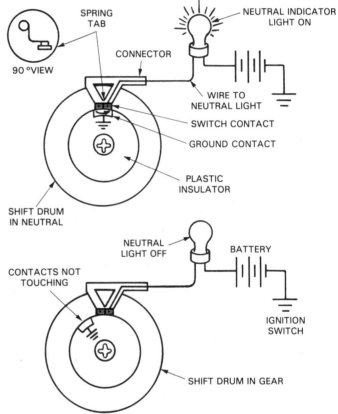

Fig. 7-38. When shift drum is in neutral, metal contacts on shift drum and neutral switch line up. This completes circuit to neutral light. When transmission is in gear, contacts do NOT line up and circuit to neutral light is broken.

SHIFT DRUM LOCATION DEVICES

As the shift drum rotates, it causes the shift forks to move sideways. Side loads are produced. This requires that the shift drum have very little end play.

For transmission shifts to be accurate (same amount of dog engagement with gear motion to the left or right), the shift drum must be precisely located. A shift drum location device serves this function.

Shown in Fig. 7-39, there are three common methods of locating shift drums:

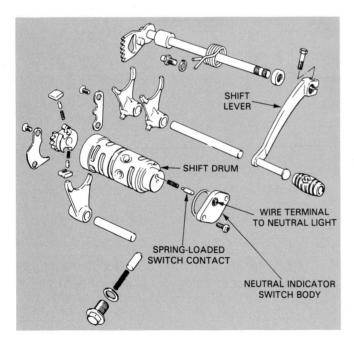

Fig. 7-37. Neutral indicator switch is usually located on end of shift drum, opposite shifting mechanism. With transmission shift lever in neutral, switch closes and neutral light glows. (U.S. Suzuki Motor Corporation)

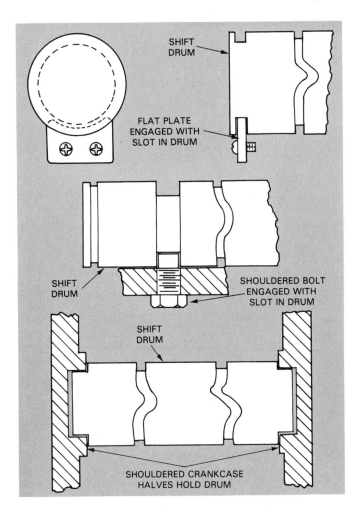

Fig. 7-39. These three methods are used to control shift drum location.

1. Flat plate engaged into a radial slot on the drum.
2. A shouldered bolt engaged in a radial slot on the drum.
3. Shouldered crankcase halves encasing the shift drum.

SHIFT STOPPER DEVICES

To prevent overshifting (movement past the desired gear), the gearbox may have a SHIFT STOPPER. A shift stopper functions by limiting shift linkage travel or shift drum rotation.

There are two types of shift stoppers: shift stopper pin and shift stopper linkage. Fig. 7-40 shows both types. Study their construction and operation.

GEARBOX TYPES

Modern motorcycle gearboxes use two means of gear engagement and two types of power flow through the gearbox. These methods of engagement and power flow should be understood.

Gear engagement and power flow

Gear engagement is normally accomplished by gear dogs, Fig. 7-41. Dogs are found on the sides of gears

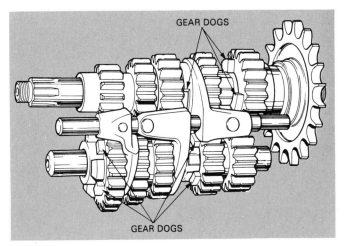

Fig. 7-41. When shift fork moves, it engages gear dogs on sides of neighboring gears. This locks the freewheeling gear to shaft and causes power transfer.
(Triumph Motorcycles [Meriden] Ltd.)

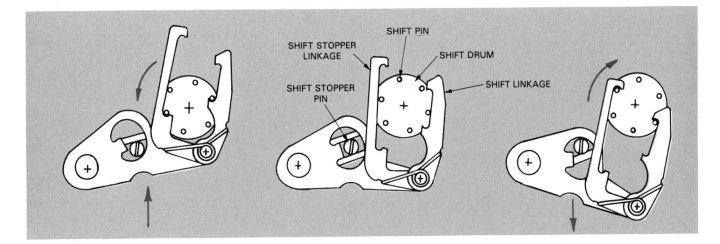

Fig. 7-40. In this design, both a shift stopper pin and shift stopper linkage are used. Shift stopper pin limits shift linkage travel. Shift stopper linkage prevents shift drum from rotating past desired position.   (Kawasaki Motors Corp., U.S.A.)

or on sliding dog assemblies. See Fig. 7-42. The function of both types of DOGS is to lock a freewheeling gear to its shaft and cause power flow.

Common gearbox designs use two methods of directing power through the gearbox: direct drive and indirect drive.

Direct drive gearbox

In most cases, the DIRECT DRIVE GEARBOX has the clutch and countershaft sprocket located on the same side of the engine. One is shown in Fig.7-43.

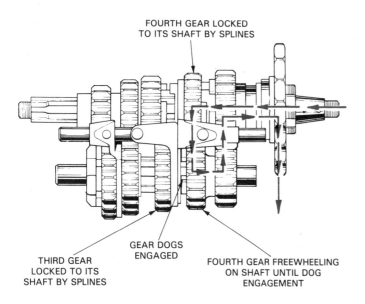

Fig. 7-42. Splined third gear has been moved by its shifting fork so that its dogs are engaged with dogs on freewheeling fourth gear. This locks freewheeling fourth gear and causes it to transfer power.   (Triumph Motorcycles [Meriden] Ltd.)

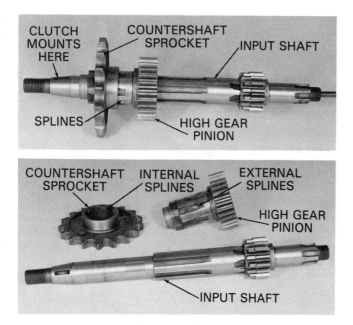

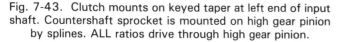

Fig. 7-43. Clutch mounts on keyed taper at left end of input shaft. Countershaft sprocket is mounted on high gear pinion by splines. ALL ratios drive through high gear pinion.

The gearbox INPUT SHAFT passes through the middle of the drive chain's countershaft sprocket. The countershaft sprocket is splined to the high gear pinion assembly.

The second shaft of the direct drive gearbox is called the LAYSHAFT, Fig. 7-44. All ratios in a direct drive gearbox end up driving the countershaft sprocket THROUGH HIGH GEAR.

Indirect drive

The clutch and countershaft sprocket are located on opposite sides of the engine with an INDIRECT DRIVE GEARBOX. This is illustrated in Fig. 7-45. Power enters the gearbox on one shaft (input shaft) and leaves the gearbox on the other shaft (output shaft), Fig. 7-46.

KICKSTART MECHANISMS

The purpose of a KICKSTART MECHANISM is to connect the kickstart lever to the engine crankshaft

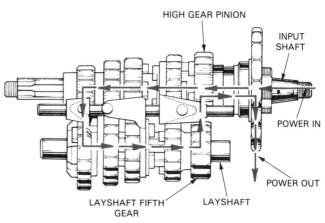

A

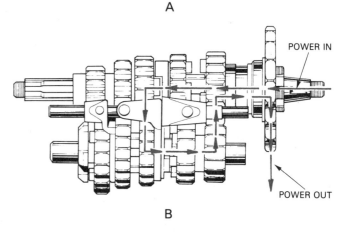

B

Fig. 7-44. Since countershaft sprocket is attached to high gear pinion in direct drive gearbox, all ratios must drive through high gear (fifth gear in example). Power comes through input shaft to selected gear. Then, power is transferred to the layshaft. Splined layshaft fifth gear transfers power to high gear pinion and countershaft sprocket in all gears except fifth. A—First gear. B—Third gear.
(Triumph Motorcycles [Meriden] Ltd.)

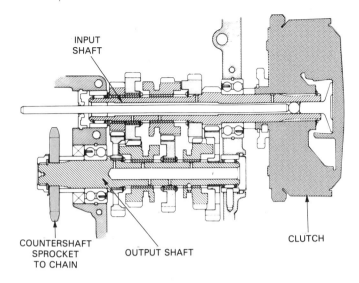

Fig. 7-45. Indirect drive gearbox has clutch and countershaft sprocket on opposite sides. Primary chain or gear is on one side and countershaft sprocket and chain to rear wheel is on other. (Kawasaki Motors Corp., U.S.A.)

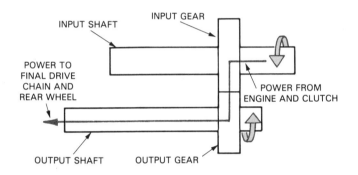

Fig. 7-46. With an indirect drive gearbox, power comes into gearbox on input shaft and leaves gearbox on output shaft. This is the most common gearbox design.

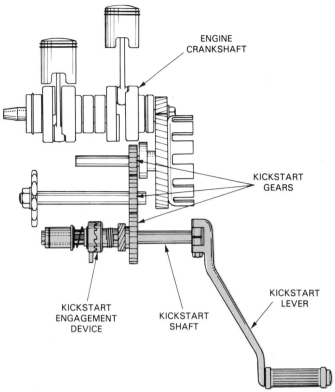

Fig. 7-47. This kickstart mechanism uses a lever, shaft, and set of gears to turn crankshaft for starting. (U.S. Suzuki Motor Corporation)

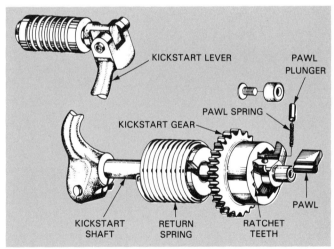

Fig. 7-48. Ratchet and pawl engagement device uses a spring-loaded pawl to lock kickstart gear to kickstart shaft. They lock on downward stroke of kickstart lever. As lever is released and spring returns assembly, pawl rides over ratchet teeth. (Kawasaki Motors Corp., U.S.A.)

so that the crankshaft can be turned over rapidly for starting. See Fig. 7-47. A kickstart mechanism uses an engagement device and a series of gears.

The kickstart engagement device must provide lockup for starting and disengagement when the engine begins to run on its own power. Since the kickstart lever is at the rear of the engine and a certain kickstart gear ratio is desired, a series of gears is used to provide adequate turning force.

The three types of KICKSTART ENGAGEMENT DEVICES are:
1. Ratchet and pawl, Fig. 7-48.
2. Cam-engaged radial ratchet, Fig. 7-49.
3. Threaded spindle, Fig. 7-50.

Primary and non-primary kickstarters

Most kickstart systems use the clutch outer hub for starting. This allows the engine to be started with the transmission in gear, but with the clutch disengaged. This is called PRIMARY KICKSTARTING.

A NON-PRIMARY KICKSTART system must use the gearbox input shaft and clutch assembly to start the engine. In this design, the engine CANNOT be started unless the gearbox is in neutral and the clutch is engaged. Fig. 7-51 shows kickstart system power flow for each design.

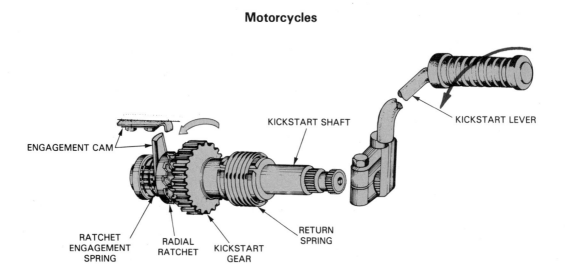

Fig. 7-49. This design uses a cam and radial ratchet to lock kickstart gear to shaft. Half of cam and ratchet are splined to shaft and spring-loaded. As lever is moved down, engagement cam releases allowing engagement spring to push splined half of ratchet into engagement. This locks kickstart gear to shaft and engine crankshaft rotates. (Kawasaki Motors Corp., U.S.A.)

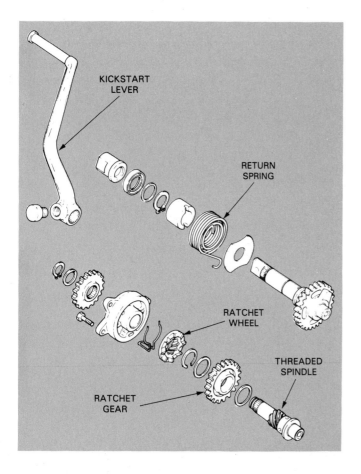

Fig. 7-50. Threaded spindle kickstart engages ratchet wheel with ratchet gear. When they lock together, engine rotates for starting. (Yamaha Motor Corp., U.S.A.)

TORQUE MULTIPLICATION AND REDUCTION RATIO

As discussed in Chapter 1, torque multiplication and reduction ratios are necessary to make the best use of engine power. There are three places for gear reduction to occur: primary drive (engine to transmission), gearbox (inside transmission), and final drive (transmission to rear wheel).

Primary and final drive ratios are fixed and can only be changed by parts replacement. The gearbox, however, permits the selection of various ratios.

OVERALL RATIO

The three ratios, (primary, gearbox, and final drive) are combined to give an OVERALL RATIO which is a comparison of crankshaft speed to rear wheel speed. This is illustrated in Fig. 7-52.

Because torque multiplication (power, speed, and acceleration) changes with reduction ratio, a typical gearbox should provide a wide range of torque multiplication. Fig. 7-53 shows overall reduction ratio and torque multiplication variance.

Internal gearbox ratios will vary depending upon engine power characteristics and intended use. A touring motorcycle will have a WIDE RATIO GEARBOX (wide ratio difference between gears). A motorcycle designed for motocross will have a CLOSE RATIO GEARBOX (close, evenly spaced ratios between gears).

KNOW THESE TERMS

Straight-cut gears, Straight-cut offset gears, Helical gears, Primary chain, Primary gears, Clutch, Clutch basket, Clutch hub, Driven plates, Drive plates, Dry clutch, Wet Clutch, Clutch shock absorber, Centrifugal clutch, Automatic clutch, Clutch release mechanism, Gearbox, Gearbox shafts, Gear selector mechanism, Neutral indicator switch, Direct drive gearbox, Indirect drive gearbox, Primary kickstart, Non-primary kickstart, Overall ratio.

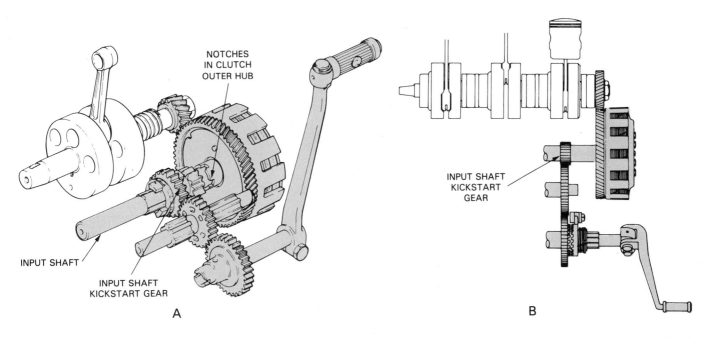

Fig. 7-51. A—Primary kickstart system. Input shaft kickstart gear freewheels on its shaft and is indexed into notches in back of outer clutch hub. This allows rider to kickstart engine with gearbox in gear and clutch disengaged. B—Non-primary kickstart system. Input shaft kickstart gear is locked to shaft. Kickstart system simply turns input shaft. This means that clutch must be engaged for kickstarter to turn crankshaft. (U.S. Suzuki Motor Corporation)

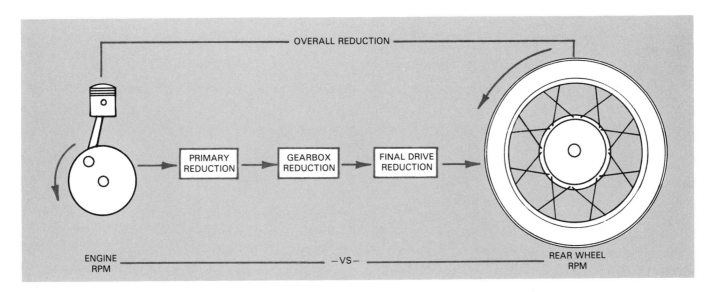

Fig. 7-52. Overall gear ratio is a comparison of crankshaft speed to rear wheel speed. Trace flow of engine power to rear wheel.

TRANSMISSION GEAR SELECTED	CRANKSHAFT SPEED (Revolutions Per Minute)	REAR WHEEL SPEED (Revolutions Per Minute)	OVERALL RATIO
1st	5,000 RPM	384.6 RPM	13:1
2nd	5,000 RPM	454.5 RPM	11:1
3rd	5,000 RPM	555.5 RPM	9:1
4th	5,000 RPM	666.6 RPM	7.50:1
5th	5,000 RPM	833.3 RPM	6:1

Fig. 7-53. This typical gearbox provides a variance of ratios from 13 to 1 in first gear to 6 to 1 in fifth gear. Notice how wheel speed increases while engine rpm stays constant.

REVIEW QUESTIONS—CHAPTER 7

1. List the three types of primary gear drives.
2. What is a disadvantage of the helical gear drive?
3. The purpose of a clutch is to _____ and _____ the engine and gearbox.
4. What drives the clutch basket?
5. What does the clutch hub drive?
6. Unequal clutch spring pressure can cause:
   a. Clutch slippage.
   b. Clutch drag.
   c. Pressure plate runout.
   d. All of the above.

7. The term "wet clutch" refers to a clutch which operates in an oil bath. True or False?

8. A clutch _____ _____ helps prevent damage to the gearbox and primary drive.

9. The function of a clutch release mechanism is to move the pressure plate _____ _____ the clutch plates.

10. List the four common types of clutch release mechanisms.

11. Which shaft in a gearbox is usually driven by the clutch?

12. What is the most common type of gear selector mechanism?

13. A gearbox _____ is used to precisely locate the shifting drum or cam plate.

14. Where is a neutral indicating switch normally mounted with a drum type shift mechanism?

15. Describe the function of a shift drum location device.

16. What component in a shifting mechanism prevents overshifting?

17. When speaking of power flow through the gearbox, direct drive and indirect drive are basically the same. True or False?

18. A motorcycle which can be kickstarted in gear with the clutch disengaged has a_____type kickstart system.

19. What three ratios are combined to give overall ratio.

20. What types of motorcycles use close ratio and wide ratio gearboxes?

SUGGESTED ACTIVITIES

1. Select three motorcycles. Then, using shop manuals, advertisements, and brochures, determine the specific design (type) used for the following items:
   a. Primary drive.
   b. Clutch.
   c. Clutch release mechanism.
   d. Gearbox (direct or indirect drive).
   e. Number of speeds and ratio for each gear.
   f. Shifting mechanism.
   g. Indexer.

2. Compare and analyze the design differences between the three motorcycles in activity one. Explain why one design might be used over another.

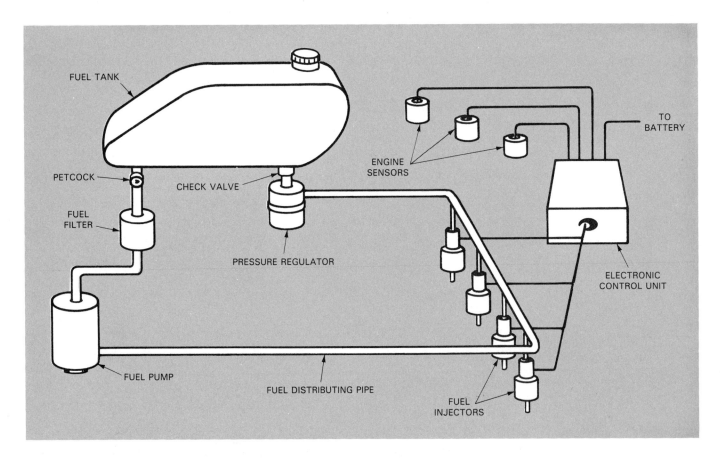

Electrical theory is very important to today's motorcycle mechanic. Even modern fuel injection systems, as shown, use electrical and electronic devices.

Chapter 8

ELECTRICAL THEORY AND SYSTEMS

After studying this chapter, you will be able to:
□ Explain the principles of electricity.
□ Describe a basic electric circuit.
□ Sketch different types of electrical circuits.
□ Connect a voltmeter, ohmmeter, and ammeter to a circuit.
□ Perform fundamental electrical tests.
□ Explain the operation of motorcycle electrical systems.

In this chapter, you will learn about basic electricity and how it is used in the modern motorcycle. Today's motorcycle electrical systems are relatively trouble free. However, when problems occur, the mechanic must be familiar with electrical theory, system design, system operation, and proper use of test equipment. This knowledge will enable a mechanic to quickly and accurately diagnose and repair electrical problems in a motorcycle.

ELECTRICAL THEORY

What is electricity? The answer to this question may seem complex. But actually, after you study the principles, electricity is easy to understand. Part of the problem is that you cannot see electricity. You can only see the results (light, heat, movement). For example, when you turn on your headlight, you can see the light bulb glow and feel it get warm. However, you cannot see what causes the bulb to function.

While electricity may seem to be a magical phenomenon, it follows specific laws of physics. A basic understanding of physics as it applies to electricity is the first step in understanding motorcycle electrical systems.

ELECTRICITY

Electricity, as used in the motorcycle electrical system, is dependent upon the flow of electric cur-

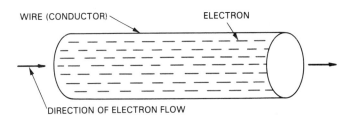

Fig. 8-1. Current flow is a movement of free electrons through a conductor. Free electrons are common in metals.

rent. ELECTRIC CURRENT is the flow or movement of electrons through a conductor, Fig. 8-1. A CONDUCTOR is any substance that will freely allow current flow (copper, steel, cast iron, and other metals). An INSULATOR is just the opposite. It is any substance that stops current flow (plastic, rubber, ceramic materials).

Current flow (electrical energy) is used to accomplish two basic functions:
1. Provide heat energy (arc at plug gap for example).
2. Provide mechanical energy (starting motor rotation for example).

ELECTRIC CURRENT

Motorcycle electrical systems use two types of electric current: direct current and alternating current. It is important for you to understand the differences between the two.

Direct current

In most motorcycle electrical systems, the battery supplies DIRECT CURRENT (DC) to power the system. According to ELECTRON FLOW THEORY, direct current flows from the negative terminal of the battery, through the circuit and returns to the positive terminal of the battery. This is illustrated in Fig. 8-2.

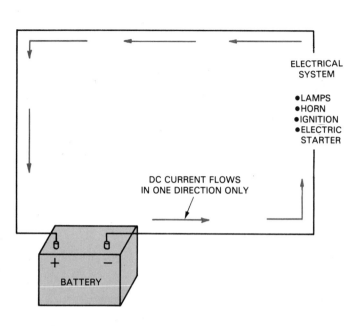

Fig. 8-2. A battery supplies direct current to electrical system. Current flows from negative (−) battery terminal through circuit and returns to positive (+) terminal.

The direction of DC current flow is only a theory. Concerning a motorcycle electrical system, the important thing to remember is that current flows through the circuit and battery.

Alternating current

Another type of electric current found in the motorcycle electrical system is ALTERNATING CURRENT (AC). A SINE WAVE, Fig. 8-3, represents the change in voltage and polarity (direction of current flow) which is associated with alternating current. Current flows one way and then the other. Another way to describe alternating current is shown in Fig. 8-4.

ELECTRICAL CIRCUITS

An ELECTRICAL CIRCUIT must have the following components:
1. A source of electricity (battery).
2. A load or resistance to current flow (bulb).
3. A means of connecting the source to the load (hot wire).
4. A means of connecting the load back to the source (ground).
Fig. 8-5, A, shows a typical electrical circuit. This can also be termed a "simple circuit."

Most motorcycle electrical circuits also have a FUSE to protect the circuit from excessive current and a SWITCH to provide a means of turning the circuit on and off. See Fig. 8-5, B.

An OPEN CIRCUIT contains a break or interruption (open switch, broken wire) in the circuit. Current

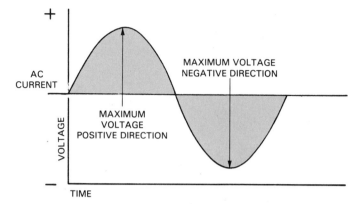

Fig. 8-3. A sine wave is a graphic description of alternating current. Peaks on positive and negative sides show maximum current flow in opposite directions.

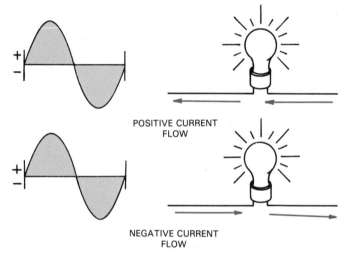

Fig. 8-4. As sine wave alternates from positive to negative, current flow reverses direction.

cannot flow in an open circuit. A CLOSED CIRCUIT is a complete circuit having a continuous path for current. When a switch is closed, current will flow through the circuit.

If a SHORT CIRCUIT develops (hot wire touches metal part or ground because of faulty insulation or component), the high current flow around the load melts the inside of the fuse. Shown in C of Fig. 8-5, the open fuse stops current flow and prevents a possible "electrical fire" (overheating and burning of wires).

The two basic types of electrical circuits used on motorcycles are the series circuit and the parallel circuit.

The SERIES CIRCUIT has all of the components connected one after the other with a single path for current flow. Fig. 8-6 shows this basic type of circuit. A series circuit operates like a cheap set of Christmas tree lights. If one bulb burns out (opens), all of the other bulbs stop functioning.

A PARALLEL CIRCUIT has a separate leg (path) for each component. See Fig. 8-7. If one bulb in a

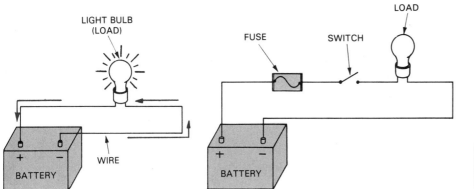

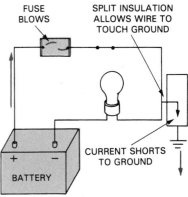

A—SIMPLE ELECTRICAL CIRCUIT CONSISTS OF A POWER SOURCE (BATTERY), A LOAD (LIGHT BULB), AND WIRE WHICH CONNECTS LOAD TO POWER SOURCE.

B—MOST CIRCUITS ARE OPENED AND CLOSED BY A SWITCH AND PROTECTED FROM OVERLOADING BY A FUSE.

C—BROKEN INSULATION ON WIRE HAS CONNECTED HOT WIRE DIRECTLY TO GROUND. WIRE COULD OVERHEAT AND BURN WITHOUT FUSE ACTION.

Fig. 8-5. Study the parts and action of each basic circuit. A—Simple circuit. B—Simple circuit with switch and fuse. C—Short circuit.

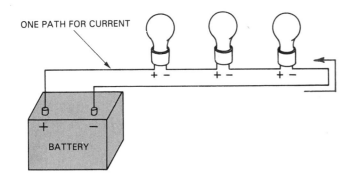

Fig. 8-6. In a series circuit, current must pass through each component in order to return to battery. If one component fails (opens), the entire circuit stops working.

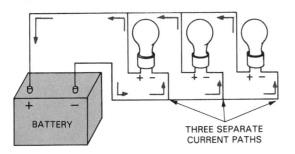

Fig. 8-7. In a parallel circuit, each component has its own current path. Failure of one component does not affect others.

parallel circuit burns out, the other bulbs still glow. They each have their own path for current flow.

Polarity

POLARITY refers to the positive and negative sides of the electrical system. Certain components must be connected with the proper polarity.

For example, a battery has a positive (+) and a negative (−) post. Generally, the positive side of the battery is referred to as the HOT SIDE, and the

negative as the GROUND SIDE.

The positive side of a circuit would include any point between the load (bulb) and battery positive. The negative side would be between the load and battery negative.

UNITS OF ELECTRICITY

The three fundamental units of electrical measurement are:
1. Voltage (V, E, or volts).
2. Amperage (I, A, or amps).
3. Resistance (R, Ω, or ohms).

Voltage (volts)

VOLTAGE can be described as the ELECTRICAL PRESSURE in a circuit. It is an indication of the amount of pushing force behind the current. This pressure is sometimes referred to as ELECTROMOTIVE FORCE (EMF). The unit of measurement for voltage is the VOLT, abbreviated V or E.

Amperage (amps)

The amount of current flow (the number of electrons flowing past a given point in a given time span) is called AMPERAGE. The unit of measurement for current flow is the AMP, abbreviated I or A.

Resistance (ohms)

Electrical RESISTANCE is the opposition to current flow in a circuit. High resistance would reduce current, Low resistance would increase current. Circuit resistance is measured in OHMS, abbreviated R or Ω.

A common analogy used to illustrate the three units of electricity is a water (hydraulic) circuit. See Fig. 8-8. Note that water pressure is comparable to voltage. Water flow is the same as electrical current. Resistance to water flow is like resistance to electrical current.

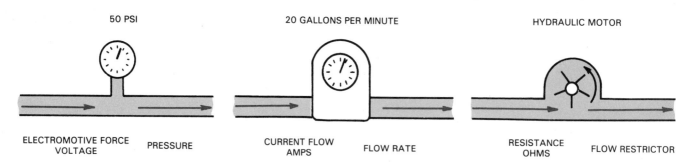

Fig. 8-8. A water or hydraulic system is sometimes used to explain electricity. Pressure can be compared to voltage. Flow past a point can be compared to electrical current. A hydraulic motor or turbine can be compared to an electrical component which causes resistance.

Ohm's Law

The mathematical relationship between voltage, resistance, and current can be expressed easily using OHM'S LAW. The following relationship exists:
1. Voltage = current × resistance.
2. Resistance = voltage ÷ current.
3. Current = voltage ÷ resistance.

For example, if a circuit in a 12V electrical system has 2 ohms of resistance, how much current would flow through the circuit? To find current, simply plug your values into the appropriate formula.

$$\text{Current} = \frac{\text{Voltage}}{\text{Resistance}}$$
$$= \frac{12}{2} = 6 \text{ amps in circuit.}$$

This example is given to show the relationship between these units of electricity. The formula can also be used to calculate voltage and resistance when the other two units are known.

Watts

Another unit of electrical measurement is the watt. A WATT is used to describe the amount of electrical work being done. The formula for watts is:

Watts = volts × amps.

Applying this to a motorcycle electrical system, how much wattage would be used if a 12V headlight drew 4 amps?

12 volts × 4 amps = 48 watts

MEASURING ELECTRICITY

Diagnosing electrical system problems requires the measurement of the three units of electricity:
1. A VOLTMETER is used to measure voltage (electrical pressure or volts).
2. An AMMETER is used to measure current (flow or amps).
3. An OHMMETER is used to measure resistance (opposition to current or ohms).

A VOM (volt-ohm-milliammeter) or multimeter contains all three meters (voltmeter, ohmmeter and ammeter) in one. It is commonly used by the motor-cycle mechanic. Meter hookup and use will be discussed later in this chapter.

SOURCES OF ELECTRICITY

There are three ways to provide electrical power for use in motorcycle electrical systems. These include a battery, alternator (AC generator), and a DC generator.

Battery

A BATTERY stores electricity and provides a steady supply of DC current for use in the electrical system. The battery will supply power for a considerable period of time, providing it is in good condition. As current is drawn from the battery, it becomes discharged. For this reason, a battery supported electrical system must provide a means of recharging the battery.

Battery operation

A motorcycle battery is made up of several two volt cells connected in series. This is illustrated in Fig. 8-9. A six volt battery has three cells and a twelve volt battery has six cells. Each CELL is made up of negative plates of sponge lead and positive plates of lead peroxide.

An ELECTROLYTE solution of dilute sulfuric acid (water and acid) is also contained in each cell. A chemical reaction between the plates and the electrolyte releases electricity. The battery discharges as current is used, Fig. 8-10. The charging system reverses this chemical reaction by supplying direct current to the battery, Fig. 8-11.

MAGNETIC FIELDS

Many electrical components rely on the principles of magnetism for operation. For this reason, you should have a basic understanding of magnetic fields before studying alternators, generators, regulators, relays, and starting motors.

A single bar magnet has a north and a south pole. Illustrated in Fig. 8-12, invisible lines of force, called

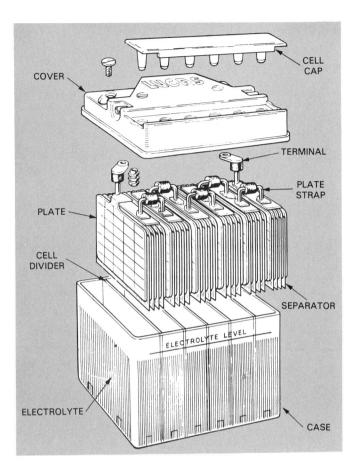

Fig. 8-9. Study the basic parts of a battery. A cell is made up of negative (sponge lead) plates, positive (lead peroxide) plates, and separators (insulators). Most batteries have six cells. Each cell fits into a different compartment in battery case. (Triumph Motorcycles (Meriden) Ltd.)

MAGNETIC LINES OF FORCE, extend out of each pole of the magnet. Like poles (N and N or S and S) REPEL each other. Unlike poles (N and S) AT-TRACT each other.

Magnetic lines of force can be used to produce movement or electricity. This is shown in Fig. 8-13. The attraction or repulstion of magnetic fields will cause motion, as in electric motors. If a wire cuts through a magnetic field, current will be induced in

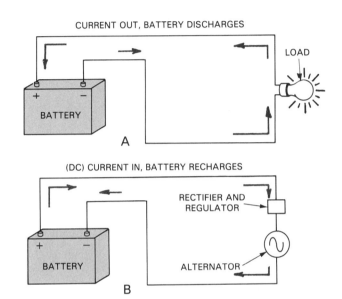

Fig. 8-11. A—Battery discharges as it supplies electricity to circuit load. B—Alternator replenishes battery as needed. In a properly functioning charging system, electricity is supplied as it is used, keeping battery charged at all times.

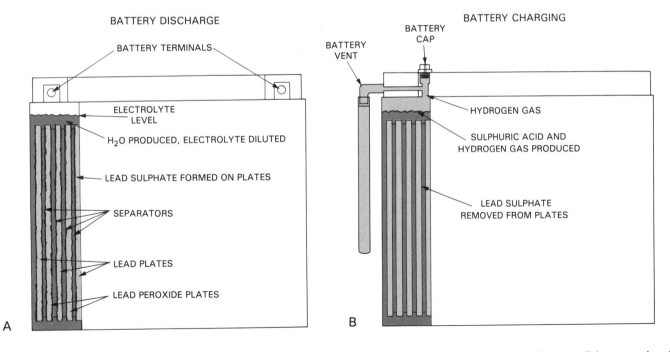

Fig. 8-10. A—Lead sulphate and water are by-products of chemical reaction that takes place as battery dishcarges. Lead sulphate is deposited on plates and water dilutes electrolyte. B—As battery is charged, lead sulphate is removed from plates, sulphuric acid and hydrogen gas are produced. Hydrogen gas is very explosive and must be vented.

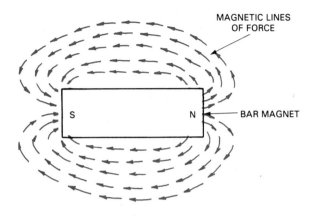

Fig. 8-12. Magnet has invisible lines of force extending from north pole to south pole.

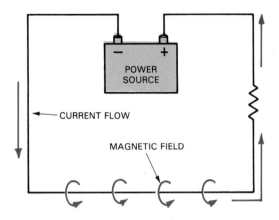

Fig. 8-14. When current flows through a wire, a magnetic field is formed around wire. This field is very useful.

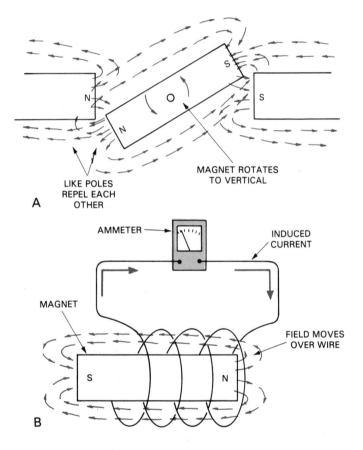

Fig. 8-13. A magnetic field can be used to produce movement or current flow. A—Like magnetic fields would cause center magnet to rotate into vertical position. B—When magnetic field is moved over wire, current would be induced in wire.

the wire. This is called INDUCTION, and it is used in generators and alternators.

On the other hand, when current flows through a wire, a MAGNETIC FIELD is formed, Fig. 8-14. If a wire is wrapped around a soft iron core, a stronger magnetic field will result when current flows through the wire. The windings around the iron core make an ELECTROMAGNET, Fig. 8-15. The electromagnet,

like a permanent magnet, can produce movement of ferrous metal objects.

ALTERNATOR

An ALTERNATOR is a true source and producer of electricity. It is capable of changing mechanical energy (rotating motion) into electrical energy. A motorcycle alternator, Fig. 8-16, is usually mounted on and driven by the engine crankshaft. Fig. 8-17 shows a simple alternator, Study its basic parts.

Refer to Fig. 8-18, A through H, as the operation of an alternator is expalined.

As the north pole approaches the coil, current begins to flow in the wire, A. As the north pole centers itself on the coil, current flow is at a maximum, B. As the north pole moves away from the

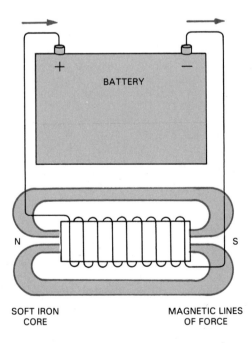

Fig. 8-15. When wire is wrapped around a soft iron core, current flowing through wire will cause a magnetic field in core. This creates an electromagnetic bar magnet (electromagnet).

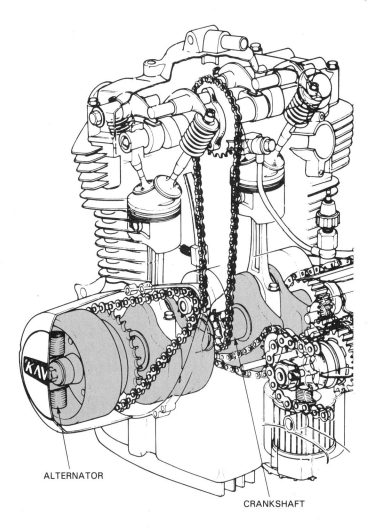

ALTERNATOR

CRANKSHAFT

Fig. 8-16. Alternator is mounted on end of crankshaft. Mechanical energy is converted to electrical energy as crankshaft spins alternator. (Kawasaki Motors Corp., U.S.A.)

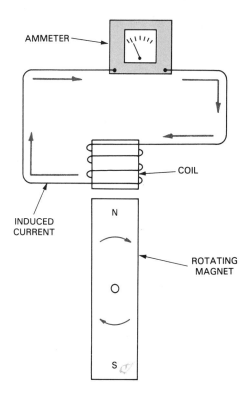

AMMETER

COIL

INDUCED CURRENT

N

ROTATING MAGNET

O

S

Fig. 8-17. A simple alternator can be made with a bar magnet and a coil of wire. Rotation of magnet induces current in coil. Current direction reverses as south pole approaches coil.

coil, current begins to drop off, C. At the 90 deg. position, current has stopped flowing completely, D.

As the south pole begins to approach the coil, current starts flowing in the opposite direction, Fig. 8-18, E. Movement of the south pole to the center position again causes maximum current flow, F. Movement away from the coil causes current to drop off, G.

As you can see, each 180 deg. movement of the magnet causes the current to reverse direction, H.

Three factors will increase the amount of current induced in our simple alternator:
1. A stronger magnetic field.
2. More windings on the coil.
3. Faster magnet rotating speeds.

DC GENERATOR

A DC generator works on the same principle as the alternator. Magnetism is used to induce current in the generator windings (ARMATURE). However, a GENERATOR differs from our simple alternator in three ways:

1. Electromagnets, instead of permanent magnets, are used to produce the magnetic field.
2. The coils (armature) rotate within the magnetic field.
3. Coil polarity is switched every 180 deg., causing current to flow through the coil in the same direction at all times.

Since current always flows in the same direction through the coil, generator output is direct current (DC). Fig. 8-19 shows how a simple generator operates. DC generators are rarely found in use on current motorcycles. However, some small dual-purpose dirt bikes use a DC generator for battery charging and electric starting.

ELECTRIC STARTING MOTOR

Motorcycle ELECTRIC STARTING MOTORS use direct current from the battery to rotate the engine crankshaft for starting. They are similar in construction to a DC generator. A DC motor uses electrical energy fed into the armature and field to magnetically force the armature to turn. This rotation creates mechanical energy. Fig. 8-20 illustrates DC motor operation.

A gear or chain drive and a simple clutch are normally used to engage and disengage the starter motor. Fig. 8-21 illustrates a starter and starter drive mechanism. Fig. 8-22 shows the starting motor and gears on an actual motorcycle.

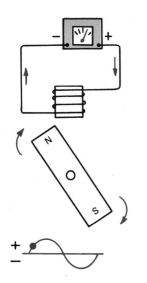

A—AS N POLE APPROACHES COIL, POSITIVE CURRENT FLOW BEGINS.

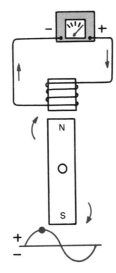

B—POSITIVE CURRENT FLOW IS AT MAXIMUM AS N POLE PASSES COIL.

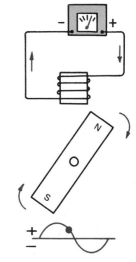

C—AS N POLE MOVES AWAY FROM COIL, POSITIVE CURRENT FLOW DROPS OFF.

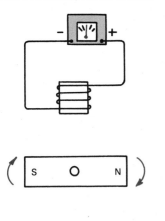

D—WHEN N AND S POLES ARE 90 DEG. FROM COIL, CURRENT FLOW STOPS.

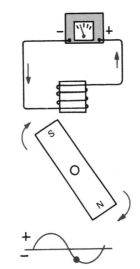

E—AS S POLE APPROACHES COIL, NEGATIVE CURRENT FLOW BEGINS.

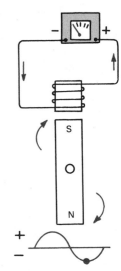
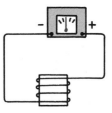

F—NEGATIVE CURRENT FLOW IS AT MAXIMUM AS S POLE PASSES COIL.

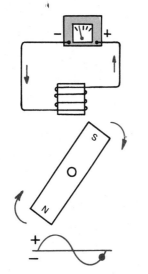

G—NEGATIVE CURRENT FLOW DROPS OFF AS S POLE MOVES AWAY FROM COIL.

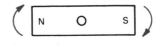

H—WHEN POLES ARE 90 DEG. FROM COIL, CURRENT FLOW STOPS AGAIN.

Fig. 8-18. Note action of meter and sine wave as magnet rotates.

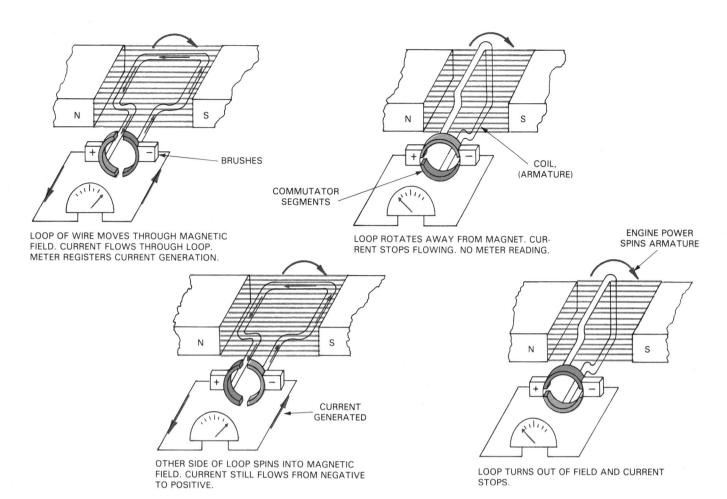

LOOP OF WIRE MOVES THROUGH MAGNETIC FIELD. CURRENT FLOWS THROUGH LOOP. METER REGISTERS CURRENT GENERATION.

LOOP ROTATES AWAY FROM MAGNET. CURRENT STOPS FLOWING. NO METER READING.

COIL, (ARMATURE)

COMMUTATOR SEGMENTS

BRUSHES

ENGINE POWER SPINS ARMATURE

OTHER SIDE OF LOOP SPINS INTO MAGNETIC FIELD. CURRENT STILL FLOWS FROM NEGATIVE TO POSITIVE.

CURRENT GENERATED

LOOP TURNS OUT OF FIELD AND CURRENT STOPS.

Fig. 8-19. Generators use a segmented commutator and brushes to switch polarity in coil (armature) every 180 deg. This causes current to always flow in same direction, producing direct current. Engine rotates loop or armature.

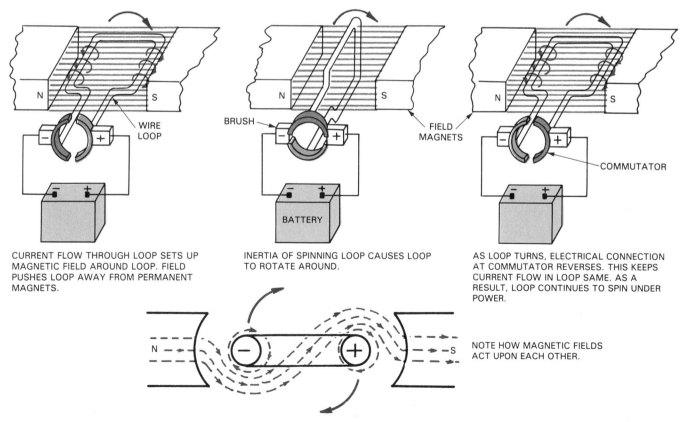

CURRENT FLOW THROUGH LOOP SETS UP MAGNETIC FIELD AROUND LOOP. FIELD PUSHES LOOP AWAY FROM PERMANENT MAGNETS.

INERTIA OF SPINNING LOOP CAUSES LOOP TO ROTATE AROUND.

AS LOOP TURNS, ELECTRICAL CONNECTION AT COMMUTATOR REVERSES. THIS KEEPS CURRENT FLOW IN LOOP SAME. AS A RESULT, LOOP CONTINUES TO SPIN UNDER POWER.

WIRE LOOP

BRUSH

FIELD MAGNETS

COMMUTATOR

BATTERY

NOTE HOW MAGNETIC FIELDS ACT UPON EACH OTHER.

Fig. 8-20. In many ways, a DC motor is similar to a DC generator. Instead of spinning the wire loop to induce current, motor connects loop to a source of electricity. This makes loop spin inside stationary magnetic field.

MOTORCYCLE CHARGING SYSTEMS

The most common motorcycle charging system uses an alternator to produce electrical power, Fig. 8-23. An alternator is capable of producing more low speed output than a DC generator. It will recharge the battery at low engine rpm.

Alternator and DC generator charging systems need a means of regulating battery charge rate. In addition, the alternator system must convert AC into DC for battery charging.

AC CHARGING SYSTEM

AC charging systems are classified into three categories:
1. Permanent magnet alternator.
2. Electromagnet alternator.
3. Magneto.
All three types of alternators normally use a rectifier and regulator. However, a magneto system may also use the battery as a form of regulator.

A RECTIFIER is normally a diode circuit connected to the output of the alternator to change AC into DC. A DIODE is an electronic component that only allows current flow in one direction. It blocks current flow in the other direction. With the diode circuit, the AC output of the alternator is rectified into DC for the electrical system of the motorcycle.

A REGULATOR controls the voltage and current output of an alternator or generator. Either contact points or an electronic circuit is used in the regulator. They sense charging system output and either shut off or increase the amount of current exciting the alternator or generator.

Permanent magnet alternator

Our simple alternator, shown in Fig. 8-17, was a permanent magnet type alternator. It differs from the type of alternator commonly used on a motorcycle.

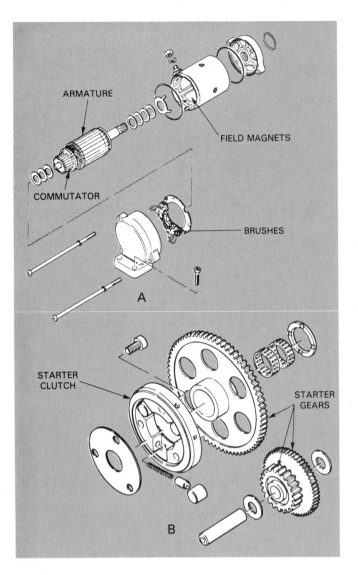

Fig. 8-21. A—Study parts of starter mechanism. B—Gears and a simple clutch are normally used to engage and disengage starter. (U.S. Suzuki Motor Corp.)

Fig. 8-22. Starter gears provide a gear reduction which increases turing force of electric motor.

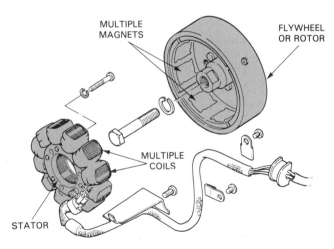

Fig. 8-23. Permanent magnet type alternator consists of stator and rotor. Stator has coils and rotor contains magnets. (U.S. Suzuki Motor Corporation)

Most motorcycle charging systems have an alternator with multiple magnets, multiple coils, and magnets cast within the rotor assembly. This is illustrated in Fig. 8-23.

Multiple coils and magnets are used to increase alternator output. In many systems, full output is NOT used most of the time. Sometimes, extra coils are wired into the circuit to increase output when the lights are switched on. This is called a DUAL-RATE CHARGING SYSTEM, Fig. 8-24.

Most permanent magnet alternators are SINGLE PHASE (type described above). However, some may be THREE PHASE. A three-phase alternator sine wave reverses direction more frequently, giving it a higher output, Fig. 8-25.

Electromagnet alternator

An ELECTROMAGNET ALTERNATOR has a FIELD COIL which produces magnetism by induction, Fig. 8-26. This design uses electric current, instead of permanent magnets, to produce magnetism. Stationary or rotating field coils may be used, as pictured in Figs. 8-27 and 8-28.

The advantage of this design is that alternator output can be precisely matched to battery demands. A disadvantage is, battery voltage is required for initial

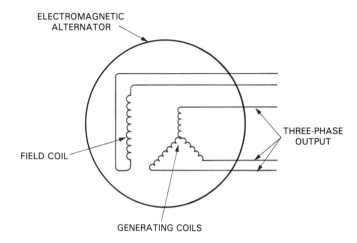

Fig. 8-26. In an electromagnet alternator, magnetism is produced by induction in field coil.

alternator output since the battery powers the electromagnet. A motorcycle with a fully dead battery cannot be push or kickstarted (no voltage for ignition system).

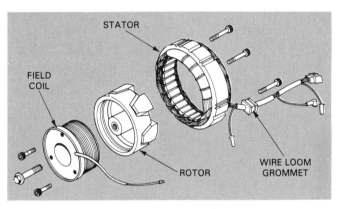

Fig. 8-27. In this stationary field coil alternator, magnetic field produced by field coil, makes rotor magnetic. Then, rotation of rotor induces current in stator windings.
(Kawasaki Motors Corp., U.S.A.)

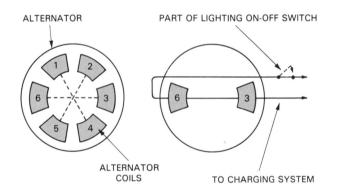

Fig. 8-24. In this dual-rate alternator, coils 1, 2, 4, and 5 operate all the time, but coils 3 and 6 are only operated when lights are switched ON.

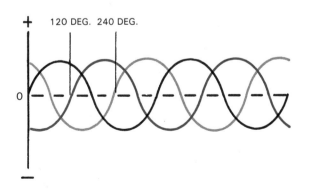

Fig. 8-25. A three-phase sine wave has voltage peaks occurring 120 deg. apart.

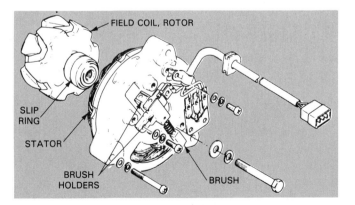

Fig. 8-28. With rotating field coil, current which energizes alternator field passes through brushes and slip rings.
(U.S. Suzuki Motor Corporation)

131

Electromagnet alternators are three phase, and are capable of high output. Electromagnet alternators are ideal for touring bikes because their high output provides enough current for a large number of electrical accessories.

Flywheel magneto

A FLYWHEEL MAGNETO ignition system, frequently used on dirt bikes, functions in the same manner as a permanent magnet alternator.

A true magneto is a self-contained ignition system. It is used to deliver high voltage to the spark plug. Because of the design of a flywheel magneto, it is also a convenient place to add extra coils for battery charging or direct AC lighting, Fig. 8-29. A charging/magneto system is combined into one assembly.

RECTIFIERS

Alternator equipped charging systems must include a rectifier to convert alternating current to direct current. SELENIUM PLATES or DIODES are used for this purpose. Pictured in Fig. 8-30, current will flow in only one direction through a selenium plate or diode.

There are two types of rectifiers: half-wave and full-wave.

Half-wave rectifiers

HALF-WAVE RECTIFIERS are used in magneto charging systems on many small, dual-purpose motorcycles. They change AC current into DC current. A half-wave rectifier only allows half of the alternator output to reach the battery. This is illustrated in Fig. 8-30.

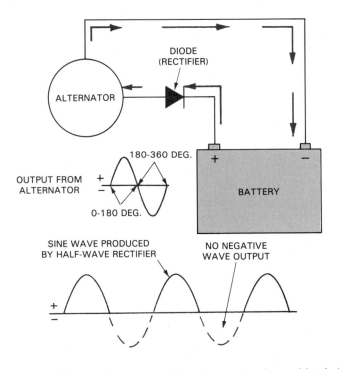

Fig. 8-30. A half-wave rectifier allows only the positive half (0-180 deg.) of sine wave to pass. Negative half (180-360 deg.) is not used. When current out of alternator reverses, diode blocks flow.

Full-wave rectifiers

FULL-WAVE RECTIFIERS are used to provide full alternator output conversion to DC for battery charging. Bridged diodes redirect the negative portion of the AC sine wave. See Fig. 8-31. Some older motorcycles used selenium plates.

VOLTAGE REGULATORS

A voltage regulator limits the charge rate and prevents battery overcharging. Regulators are classified in two categories: mechanical regulators and chemical regulators (solid state).

Mechanical regulator

A MECHANICAL REGULATOR is a device which uses one or more electromagnets and contact point sets to vary current flow through the alternator field coil (electromagnet alternator). This adjusts alternator output to match battery needs. Figs. 8-32 through 8-34 show a typical mechanical regulator and how it operates.

Electronic regulator

Electronic regulators are used in both electromagnet and permanent magnet charging systems. An ELECTRONIC REGULATOR is a solid state device which controls charging system output. An electronic regulator is a sealed unit which usually contains one or more zener diodes. A ZENER DIODE is a solid state device which limits charging voltage by

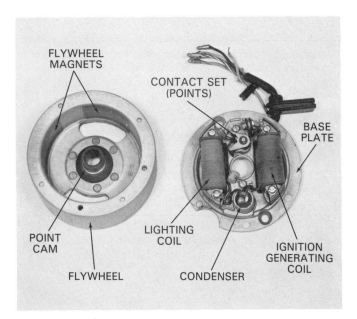

Fig. 8-29. A flywheel magneto may have extra coils for charging and lighting purposes. This magneto uses an extra coil for lighting.

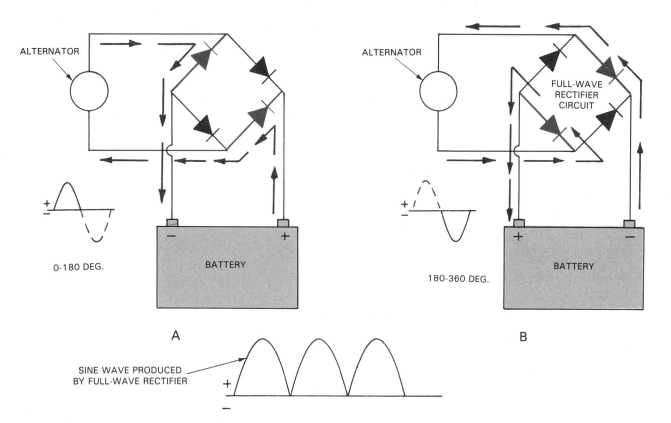

0-180 DEG.

SINE WAVE PRODUCED
BY FULL-WAVE RECTIFIER

180-360 DEG.

Fig. 8-31. A—Full-wave rectifier commonly has four diodes wired in a bridge. It uses both positive (0-180 deg.) and negative (180-360 deg.) alternator pulses for battery charging. B—Notice that during 180-360 deg. phase, diodes redirect current through battery in proper direction.

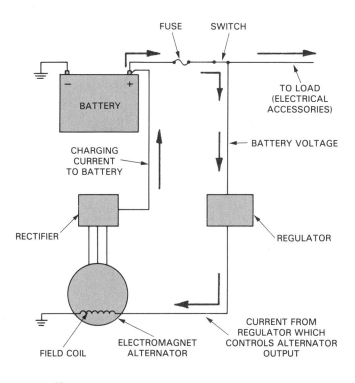

Fig. 8-32. This is a schematic showing placement of regulator in a typical three-phase charging system.

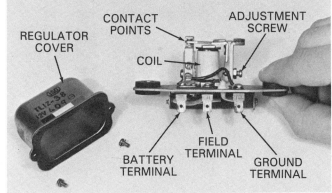

Fig. 8-33. Study basic parts of a mechanical (point type) charging system regulator.

output to battery needs by controlling alternator field voltage.

When an electronic regulator is used in a permanent magnet type charging system, it limits voltage delivered to the battery. The faster a permanent magnet alternator spins, the more voltage it produces. The electronic regulator must absorb excess voltage from the alternator to prevent battery overcharging. See Fig. 8-35.

Generator (DC) charging system

We already know that a DC generator produces direct current, therefore, a rectifier is not necessary. However, a regulator is needed in a DC generator

shunting excess voltage to ground. This is illustrated in Fig. 8-35.

When an electronic regulator is used in an electromagnet charging system, it serves the same function as a mechanical regulator. It matches alternator

133

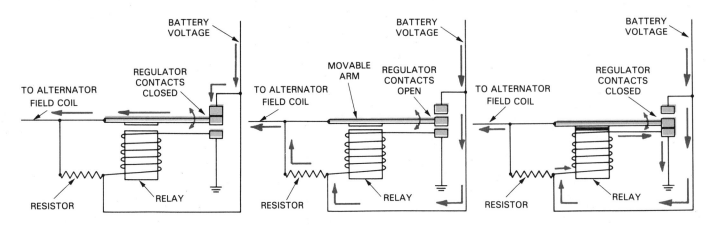

A—WITH LOW VOLTAGE, BATTERY VOLTAGE FLOWS DIRECTLY TO ALTERNATOR FIELD COIL SINCE VOLTAGE IS TOO LOW TO ENERGIZE REGULATOR FIELD COIL. SPRING HOLDS POINT ARM UP. THIS CAUSES MAXIMUM OUTPUT FROM ALTERNATOR TO BRING BATTERY CHARGE UP TO NORMAL.

B—WITH NORMAL VOLTAGE, BATTERY VOLTAGE IS HIGH ENOUGH TO PARTIALLY ENERGIZE REGULATOR RELAY. COIL MAGNETIC FIELD PULLS DOWNWARD ON POINT ARM. CURRENT MUST THEN FLOW THROUGH RESISTOR WHICH REDUCES CURRENT TO ALTERNATOR FIELD COIL.

C—WHEN VOLTAGE IS HIGH, BATTERY VOLTAGE IS HIGH ENOUGH TO FULLY ENERGIZE REGULATOR RELAY. THIS PULLS POINT ARM DOWN AND CURRENT FLOWS TO GROUND. NO CURRENT FLOWS TO ALTERNATOR FIELD COIL AND THERE IS NO ALTERNATOR OUTPUT.

Fig. 8-34. Study action of regulator points and how they change current flow.

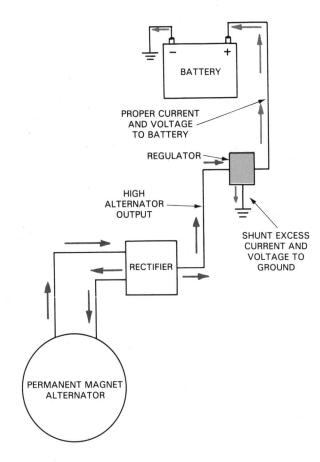

Fig. 8-35. In a charging system, which uses a permanent magnet alternator and electronic regulator, regulator shunts excess voltage and current to ground to prevent overcharging of battery.

charging system. Mechanical regulators are used with this type of charging system.

ELECTRICAL SCHEMATICS AND SYMBOLS

To become good at diagnosing and repairing motorcycle electrical systems, you must first learn

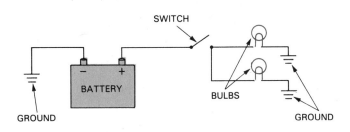

Fig. 8-36. This basic electrical schematic represents a battery powering two parallel light bulbs through a switch.

how to read electrical schematics (diagrams) and understand electrical symbols.

SCHEMATICS

A SCHEMATIC, sometimes called a WIRING DIAGRAM, is a drawing of a complete electrical system. Symbols are used to represent components in the system. Fig. 8-36 shows a very simple example of an electrical schematic. Fig. 8-37 gives some of the symbols commonly used in electrical schematics. Fig. 8-38 illustrates a complete electrical schematic. It shows every wire and electrical component on a particular motorcycle.

Next, we will discuss how to read and interpret electrical schematics. We will break the schematic down into its individual parts or circuits. This will help you to learn to use a schematic and service different electrical circuits.

MOTORCYCLE ACCESSORY SYSTEMS

The ACCESSORY SYSTEM is the grouping of circuits which make up the following:
1. Main lighting circuit.
2. Turn signal circuit.
3. Horn circuit.
4. Electric starter circuit.

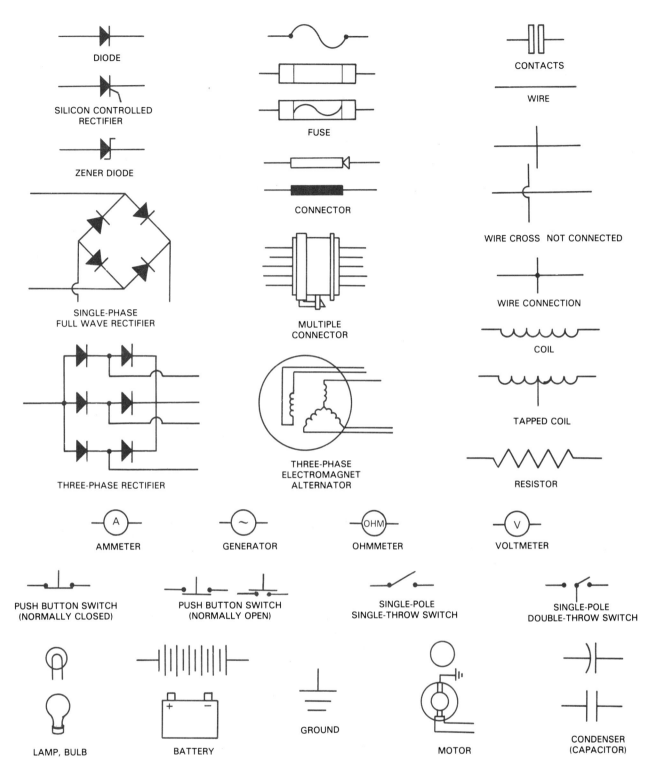

Fig. 8-37. Notice that more than one symbol may be used to represent some components. Good schematics have a key to explain switch operation and color coding.

5. Warning and indicator circuits.

The battery and ignition switch are usually used to supply and control power to these circuits.

Main lighting circuit

The MAIN LIGHTING CIRCUIT includes the headlight, taillight, stop light, wiring, and switches used to operate these bulbs. Study the components given in Fig. 8-39. Trace the wires back to the switches from the headlight and taillight bulbs.

Turn signal circuit

The TURN SIGNAL CIRCUIT normally includes four turn signal bulbs, indicators, flasher, switch,

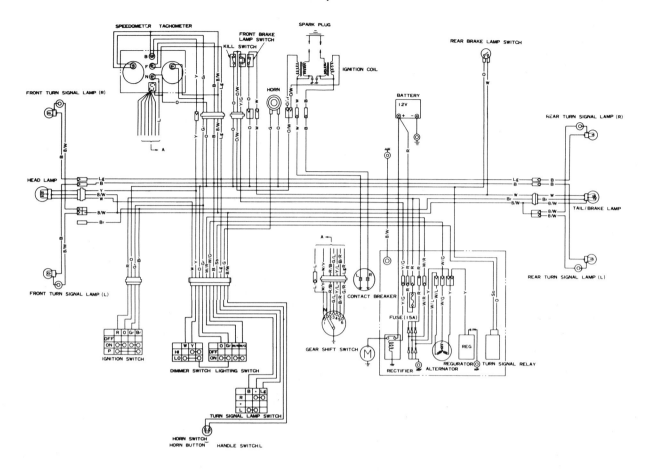

Fig. 8-38. This schematic is a representative example of today's motorcycle electrical system. To ease troubleshooting, color codes are provided on each wire. (U.S. Suzuki Motor Corporation)

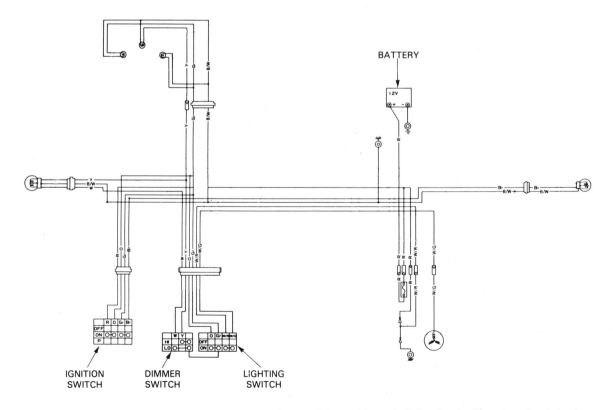

Fig. 8-39. Trace current flow from battery through each light in this main light circuit. Charging circuit is also given. (U.S. Suzuki Motor Corporation)

and wiring. The turn signal circuit is powered by the battery or alternator and controlled by the ignition switch and turn signal switch.

Flashing of the turn signal bulbs is controlled by a TURN SIGNAL FLASHER, Fig. 8-40. A bimetallic strip (two strips of dissimilar metals) in the flasher causes the circuit to open and close. As current flows through the bimetallic strip, it heats and expands, opening the circuit. As the strip cools, it contracts, closing the circuit again. See Fig. 8-41, A.

Notice that the flasher is placed before the turn signal switch in Fig. 8-41, B. This permits the flasher to perform its function while the switch selects which pair of bulbs (right or left) will flash.

Horn circuit

The HORN CIRCUIT consists of a horn button (switch), fuse, wires, ignition switch, and horn. One is

shown in Fig. 8-42. When the ignition switch is turned on, power is supplied to the horn. When the horn button is pushed, the circuit is completed to ground and the horn honks.

Electric starter circuit

The ELECTRIC STARTER CIRCUIT includes the starter motor, starter relay, starter switch, starter

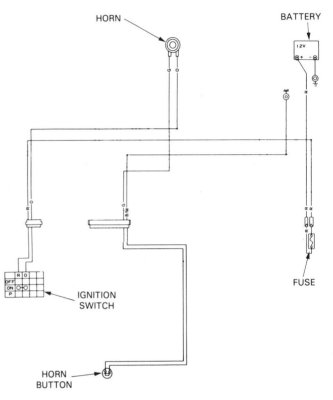

Fig. 8-42. Horn circuit is relatively simple. With ignition on, voltage is supplied to horn. When button is pushed, the circuit is completed to ground. (U.S. Suzuki Motor Corporation)

Fig. 8-40. Turn signal flasher uses a thin metallic strip to open and close power circuit to bulbs. Strip is enclosed in small metal housing.

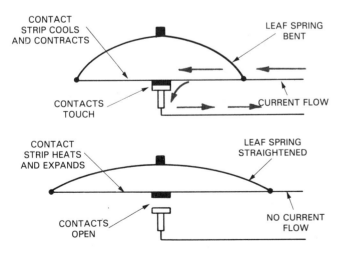

A—AS STRIP HEATS (EXPANDS) AND COOLS (CONTRACTS), POINTS OPEN AND CLOSE TO MAKE LIGHTS FLASH ON AND OFF.

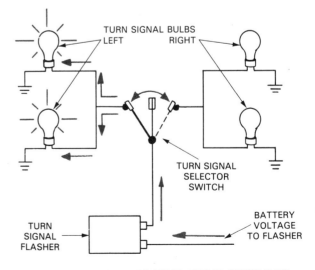

B—SHOWN IS A TYPICAL TURN SIGNAL CIRCUIT. NOTICE THAT FLASHER IS LOCATED IN CIRCUIT BEFORE SELECTOR SWITCH.

Fig. 8-41. Study flasher and turn signal operation.

cable, and starter wiring. These components are given in Fig. 8-43.

Because of the extremely high current draw of a starter motor, it is NOT connected directly to the starter button. Instead, the starter system is actually two circuits. A low current circuit (starter button circuit) activates a high current circuit (starter relay circuit).

The STARTER RELAY is a heavy duty magnetic switch operated by the starter button. The relay then connects the battery to the starter motor. See Fig. 8-44. A heavy cable connects the battery, relay, and starter. This is necessary because of the large current draw of the electric starter motor.

Warning and indicator circuits

Fig. 8-45 shows a typical circuit schematic for an oil pressure warning light. Study how the switch or sending unit operates the bulb. A temperature warn-

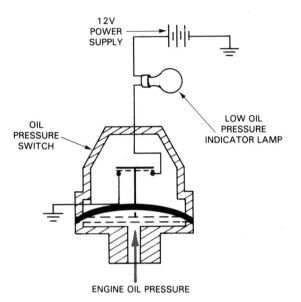

Fig. 8-45. This schematic represents an oil pressure warning light circuit. When oil pressure is low, switch completes circuit causing indicator bulb to light. Normal oil pressure pushes switch open to deactivate light.

ing circuit uses the same principle.

In working with the electrical systems of various motorcycles, you may also encounter:
1. An automatic turn signal canceller.
2. A headlight by-pass circuit activated by the starter button.
3. A solid state, automatic switching system for burned out bulbs.
4. Warning systems for battery condition, coolant temperature, fuel level, and inoperative bulbs.
5. A digital readout gear selection indicator.
6. LED (light emitting diode) instrumentation.

MAINTENANCE AND TESTING

Maintenance and testing of motorcycle electrical systems is not difficult. Most service manuals give adequate instructions for diagnosis and repair. Because there are so many different electrical systems with many different components, you should refer to a service manual when testing an electrical system.

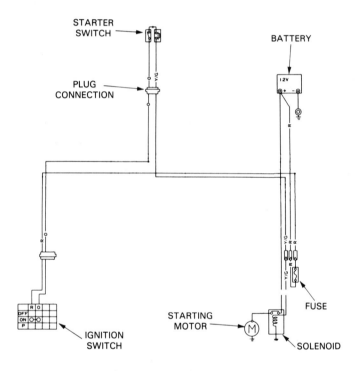

Fig. 8-43. In electric starter circuit, switch energizes solenoid. Solenoid then energizes starting motor to crank engine. (U.S. Suzuki Motor Corporation)

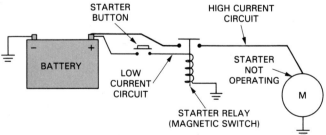

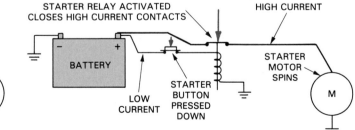

Fig. 8-44. A typical starter circuit actually consists of two circuits. A low current circuit is used to magnetically switch a high current circuit.

ELECTRICAL SYSTEM VISUAL INSPECTION

When electrical problems are experienced, visual inspection is the first step in making the repair. Check for:
1. Damaged insulation on wires.
2. Pinched wires.
3. Corroded connectors and bulb sockets.
4. Loose connectors.
5. Broken wires.
6. Improper connections (from previous repairs).

METER USE

An explanation of proper meter hookup is needed before actual testing. Improper meter connections may result in a damaged meter or circuit.

Voltmeter connection

Typical voltmeter connections are shown in Fig. 8-46. A voltmeter must be connected in PARALLEL, NOT in series. A voltmeter can also be used to check voltage at any point in a circuit, either a low or high reading may indicate circuit problems.

Ammeter connection

An ammeter is always connected in SERIES, as pictured in Fig. 8-47. Current must flow through both the circuit and the ammeter. A higher or lower than normal current reading would point to circuit problems.

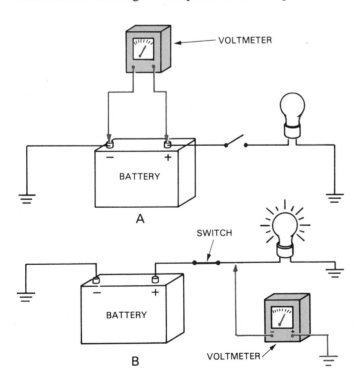

Fig. 8-46. A voltmeter is connected in parallel. A—Common voltmeter connection to measure battery voltage. Low battery voltage would indicate battery or charging system problem. B—Voltmeter will also check voltage in any part of circuit. A low voltage, in this example, might mean a bad (high resistance) switch or connection.

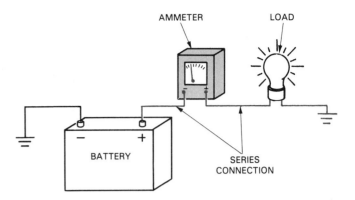

Fig. 8-47. Ammeter must always be connected in series. This connection would allow circuit current to flow directly through meter. In this example, ammeter would read current draw of light bulb.

Ohmmeter connection

An ohmmeter can be connected in either SERIES or PARALLEL, but it must NEVER be connected to voltage or current. An ohmmeter supplies its own power and could be damaged if connected to a live circuit. An ohmmeter can be used for:
1. Resistance testing.
2. Continuity testing (Electrical shorts and opens).
Fig. 8-48 shows common resistance and continuity tests made with an ohmmeter.

In the examples shown in Fig. 8-48, continuity (low resistance), lack of continuity (high resistance), or a specified resistance value is used to determine the condition of the component being tested. When testing continuity of a wire, no resistance is wanted. When testing continuity in a coil, a certain amount of resistance is common. Compare tested resistance to service manual specifications to determine circuit or component condition.

When testing diodes in a rectifier, readings of high resistance in one direction and low resistance in the other direction (changed polarity of meter connection to diode) normally indicates a good diode.

For proper test lead connections at the meter and proper meter setting, refer to the owner's manual provided with the meter. Also, refer to the motorcycle service manual for proper test connections and resistance values.

WARNING! Make sure your controls are set to the correct FUNCTION (volts, amps, or ohms) and RANGE (measuring value) before connecting the meter to a circuit. If set incorrectly, meter or circuit damage could occur.

Multimeter

A MULTIMETER combines the testing capabilities of a voltmeter, ammeter, and ohmmeter into one instrument, Fig. 8-49. By turning the control knob to the appropriate setting, almost any basic electrical measurement can be made.

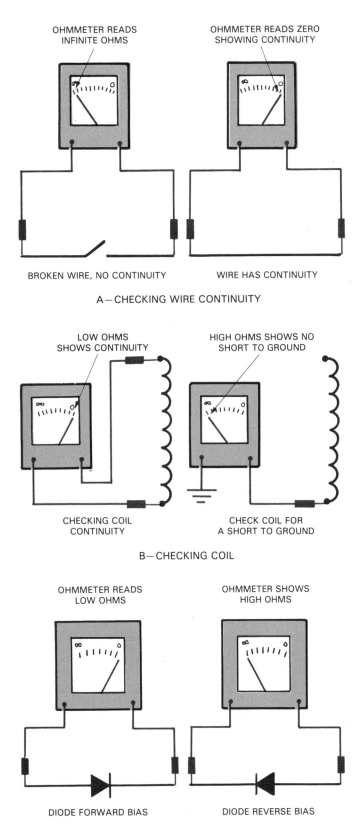

OHMMETER READS
INFINITE OHMS

OHMMETER READS ZERO
SHOWING CONTINUITY

BROKEN WIRE, NO CONTINUITY

WIRE HAS CONTINUITY

A—CHECKING WIRE CONTINUITY

LOW OHMS
SHOWS CONTINUITY

HIGH OHMS SHOWS NO
SHORT TO GROUND

CHECKING COIL
CONTINUITY

CHECK COIL FOR
A SHORT TO GROUND

B—CHECKING COIL

OHMMETER READS
LOW OHMS

OHMMETER SHOWS
HIGH OHMS

DIODE FORWARD BIAS

DIODE REVERSE BIAS

C—CHECKING DIODE

Fig. 8-48. Ohmmeter must never be connected to a source of electricity or it may be damaged. Note examples of ohmmeter use. A—A wire should have almost no resistance. B—Windings of coil should have low resistance and not be shorted to ground. C—A diode should have low resistance in one direction and high in other.

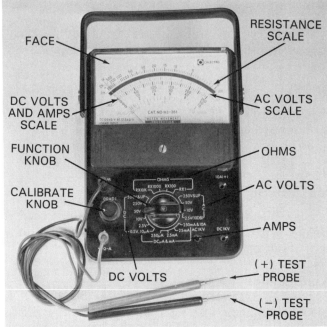

FACE

RESISTANCE
SCALE

DC VOLTS
AND AMPS
SCALE

AC VOLTS
SCALE

FUNCTION
KNOB

OHMS

CALIBRATE
KNOB

AC VOLTS

AMPS

DC VOLTS

(+) TEST
PROBE

(−) TEST
PROBE

Fig. 8-49. A typical multimeter will measure voltage, current flow, and resistance. Note various control settings and face scales on meter.

COMMON ELECTRICAL TESTS

The following tests are representative examples of common meter measurements used to check electrical components. These tests can be done on virtually any motorcycle. However, the points or locations of meter connections may vary. For this reason, refer to the proper service manual for correct meter connections and output specifications.

WARNING! When performing electrical tests, be careful NOT to touch "hot wires" on ground (metal parts of motorcycle connected to frame). Serious wiring and part damage could result.

Charging system voltage output

In this test, you measure the voltage output of the entire charging system (alternator, rectifier, voltage regulator, and interconnecting wires) with a voltmeter. The manual for one particular motorcycle states that system output should be 14.0 to 15.5V. If output is lower or higher, you must check the individual components in the system. Refer to Fig. 8-50.

Charging system current output

During a charging system current output test, you use an ammeter to measure charging system current (amperage). Again, this tests the performance of every component in the charging system. See Fig. 8-51. If output is NOT within specs, individual system components must be checked to find the source of the problem.

NOTE! For the two tests above, the battery must

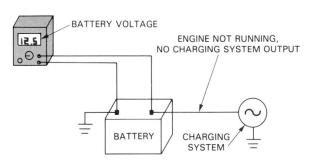

A—BATTERY VOLTAGE IS MEASURED TO CHECK BATTERY CONDITION AND ALLOW FOR METER INACCURACY.

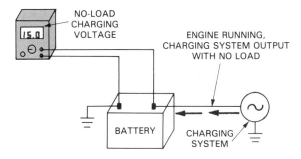

B—NO-LOAD TEST CHECKS ACTION OF VOLTAGE REGULATOR AND ALTERNATOR. VOLTAGE SHOULD INCREASE OVER BATTERY VOLTAGE BUT NOT BEYOND SPECS.

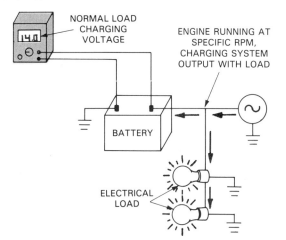

C—TURN ON HEADLIGHT HIGH BEAM AND TAILLIGHTS. THE VOLTAGE WILL DROP BUT SHOULD STAY ABOVE BATTERY VOLTAGE. IF VOLTAGE IS HIGHER THAN STEP A, CHARGING SYSTEM SHOULD BE RECHARGING BATTERY.

Fig. 8-50. Basic charging system output test involves taking battery voltage reading, no-load voltage reading, and voltage reading with load. Refer to a service manual and test equipment instructions for details.

be in good condition and fully charged to achieve accurate results.

Stator continuity

In this test, you check the condition of the alternator stator windings. In the first part of the test, Fig. 8-52, A, measure stator coil resistance and continuity. In the second part, Fig. 8-52, B, test for shorted or grounded stator coils.

Switch continuity

To check switch continuity, a battery test light is connected across the switch leads. See Fig. 8-53.

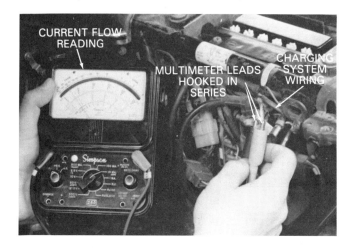

Fig. 8-51. A charging system current output test involves connecting an ammeter in series with charging system. Current flow at a stated rpm must agree with service manual specs.

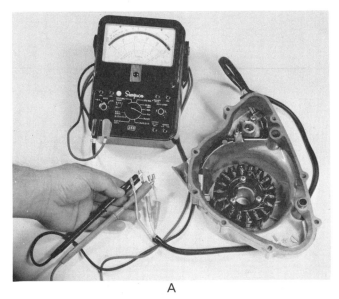

A

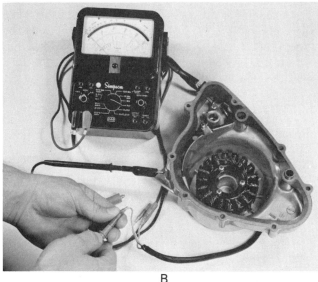

B

Fig. 8-52. An ohmmeter is commonly used to check stator coils. A—Checking coil resistance. Notice that there is only .6 ohms resistance. B—Checking for grounded coils. Infinite resistance is shown, indicating coils are not grounded. This stator is in good condition.

Fig. 8-53. A test light can be used to check switch continuity. In this example, mechanic is checking a brake light switch. Test light should glow when brake is applied.

When the switch is closed, the test light should glow. When the switch is opened, the test light should NOT glow. An ohmmeter can also be used to check switch operation.

Battery load test

The purpose of a BATTERY LOAD TEST is to determine battery capacity (strength) under high current draw conditions. A voltmeter is used to monitor voltage drop when the headlight and ignition is turned on to load the battery.

In the example shown in Fig. 8-54, minimum acceptable voltage is 10.5V. Follow manual instructions for proper meter connections and acceptable voltage drop. If battery voltage drops below specs, battery should be charged or replaced as needed.

BATTERY SERVICING

Battery service typically consists of:
1. Visual inspection, Fig. 8-55.
2. Cleaning battery terminals, Fig. 8-56.
3. Topping off cells with distilled water.
4. Charging the battery (when discharged).
5. Checking electrolyte specific gravity (state of charge).
6. Preparing a new battery for service.

DANGER! When working with a battery, wear eye protection. The acid in a battery can cause serious eye injury.

In the interest of safety, the first step for battery service is to remove the battery from the motorcycle. With the battery on a workbench, service procedures will be much more convenient.

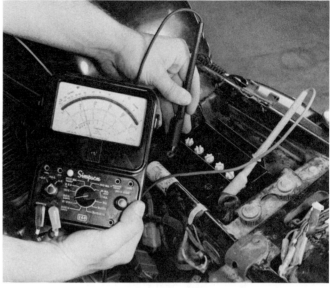

Fig. 8-54. In this test, voltmeter is reading battery voltage with ignition and headlight high beam on. Service manual normally calls for battery charging or replacement if voltage reads below 10.5 volts.

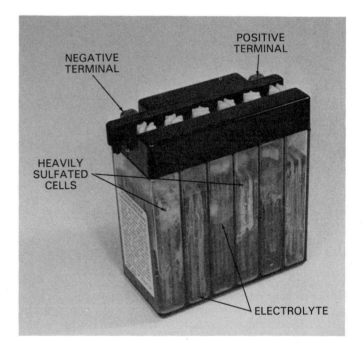

Fig. 8-55. Inspect battery for cracked case, terminal corrosion, terminal looseness, and sulfated cells. This battery is sulfated beyond recovery. Also, notice low electrolyte level.

Charging the battery

Before charging the battery, the electrolyte level must be checked. The battery should be filled to the proper level with distilled water if low. See Fig. 8-57.

CAUTION! Battery electrolyte is a corrosive acid and can cause skin burns or part damage. If spilled, neutralize with a solution of baking soda and water. Then, flush with water.

Leave each cell cap partially unscrewed to allow ad-

Fig. 8-56. Baking soda and an old tooth brush can be used to effectively clean corrosion from battery terminals. When performing battery service, place battery on a table or block of wood. Cold cement floor or metal bench can cause battery discharge.

Fig. 8-57. Battery cells should be serviced with distilled water. Tap water contains impurities that could reduce battery life.

ditional venting of gases when charging.

CAUTION! Batteries can explode! Keep sparks and flames away from a battery. Hydrogen gas, which is very explosive, is present around the top of a battery being charged or discharged.

To prevent sparks, make sure the battery charger is in the OFF position before connecting the charging leads. As shown in Fig. 8-58, connect the red lead (+) to the positive battery terminal. Connect the black lead (−) to the negative battery terminal.

Select the proper voltage setting on the charger (6 volts or 12 volts) and turn on the charger. MAXIMUM CHARGING RATE should not exceed one-tenth of the ampere-hour rating of the battery.

Example: 12 amp-hr battery = 12 × .10
= maximum 1.2 amps charge rate.

Check the output rating or setting on your battery charger so that you do not exceed the correct charging rate. Some battery chargers automatically adjust their output to meet battery needs.

Checking electrolyte specific gravity

SPECIFIC GRAVITY refers to the density of a liquid. For specific gravity testing, water is used as a standard. The specific gravity of WATER is 1.00. Since battery ELECTROLYTE is a dilute solution of sulphuric acid (sulphuric acid and water mixed), its specific gravity is higher than water.

Electrolyte in a FULLY CHARGED cell has a specific gravity of 1.260 to 1.280 (all cells must be equal). As a battery cell becomes discharged, the specific gravity drops since the electrolyte is more diluted. When specific gravity drops to 1.200, a battery is considered to be DISCHARGED. If only ONE CELL has low specific gravity, the low cell is bad and the battery must be replaced.

A HYDROMETER is used to check battery specific gravity, Fig. 8-59. Refer to the operating instructions for the type of hydrometer you are using.

Preparing a new battery for service

New batteries normally come with servicing instructions. Important considerations are:
1. Always remove the vent plug before filling the battery with electrolyte.
2. Fill each cell to the upper level mark with electrolyte.
3. Let the battery "soak-in" (sit filled with electrolyte) for a minimum of thirty minutes before charging.

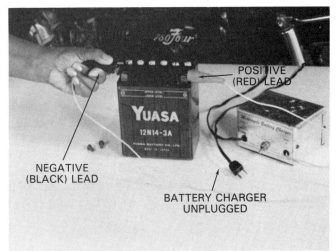

Fig. 8-58. Leave battery charger off or unplugged until charger leads are connected. Observe proper polarity when connecting battery charger leads to battery terminals (connect red to positive and black to negative). To prevent pressure buildup in battery, leave battery caps unscrewed.

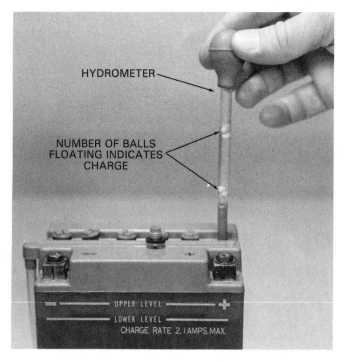

Fig. 8-59. A battery hydrometer is used to check electrolyte specific gravity and battery state of charge. When all cells are equally low, battery needs recharging. If only one cell is low, battery is usually bad.

4. Always charge the battery at least three hours at a rate recommended by the battery manufacturer.
5. After the proper specific gravity is reached, top off each cell with electrolyte to the fill marks.

Any time a battery is removed or installed, pay close attention to vent tube routing. Fig. 8-60 shows a rear fender information decal. Improper vent routing can allow acid to drip onto and damage motorcycle parts.

CAUTION! A kinked vent tube can cause battery explosion or acid leakage. Also, when installing a battery, hook up the ground lead last.

ELECTRICAL SYSTEM REPAIRS

Most electrical system components must be replaced if they are found to be faulty. However, it is common to repair or replace broken or damaged wires and connectors.

Solderless repairs

Solderless connectors are an acceptable means of splicing broken wires or replacing terminals. Refer to Fig. 8-61. They can be crimped or compressed around wire ends to make satisfactory connector ends for electrical connections.

Soldering

SOLDER is an alloy consisting of tin and lead which melts at a relatively low temperature. This is ideal for permanent connection of electrical wires or terminals.

Fig. 8-60. Proper battery vent tube routing is very important to prevent corrosion from battery vapors. This motorcycle has a tag that illustrates battery vent tube routing.

Proper soldering techniques require heating the components being soldered and correctly flowing solder into the connection. Pictured in Fig. 8-62, a soldering iron or gun is used for this purpose.

CAUTION! Use rosin core solder, NOT acid core solder for electrical repairs. Acid core solder will cause corrosion of wires and terminals.

KNOW THESE TERMS

Conductor, Insulator, DC, AC, Simple circuit, Short circuit, Open circuit, Series circuit, Parallel circuit, Voltage, Amperage, Ohms, Ohm's Law, Watt, VOM, Induction, Alternator, Generator, Starter motor, Rectifier, Regulator, Schematic, Accessory system, Battery load test, Specific gravity, Electrolyte, Rosin core solder.

REVIEW QUESTIONS—Chapter 8

1. Current flow is the movement of _____ through a conductor.
2. What are the two types of current used in motorcycle electrical systems?
3. Alternating current constantly changes its direction or _____.
4. List the four basic items needed to make a simple electrical circuit.
5. What are the three units of electricity?
6. What does a voltmeter, an ammeter, and an ohmmeter measure?
7. Describe the two types of plates and solution found in a typical motorcycle battery.
8. A six volt battery has _____ cells; a _____ volt battery has six cells.

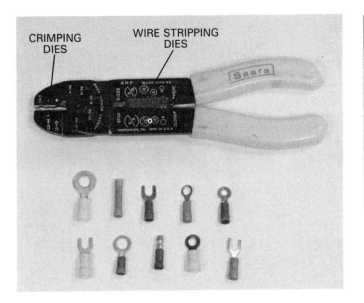

Fig. 8-61. Solderless connectors are available to suit most applications. Select appropriate connector for job. Always use a crimping tool to install solderless connectors.

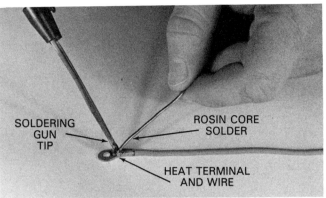

Fig. 8-62. When soldering electrical terminals, use radio-TV rosin core solder to prevent corrosion. To form a good solder joint, heat components enough so that solder melts and flows into joint.

9. Each _____ deg. of movement of an alternator magnet causes current to reverse direction.
10. List the three types of AC charging systems.
11. All alternators produce three-phase current. True or False?
12. An electromagnet alternator requires battery voltage to operate. True or False?
13. What is the purpose of a rectifier in an AC charging system?
14. Half-wave and full-wave rectifiers provide the same output. True or False?
15. What is the purpose of a regulator?
16. What are the five circuits which combine to make the accessory system?
17. Accessory system circuits are usually powered through the _____ switch.
18. Why are two circuits necessary for the electric starter system?
19. An ammeter is connected in _____, but a voltmeter is connected in _____.
20. An ohmmeter should never be connected into a _____ circuit.
21. Which side of the battery should be disconnected first?
22. What is the first step in battery servicing?
23. What is the maximum charge rate for battery charging?

24. Define "specific gravity."
25. The specific gravity of a fully charged battery is:
    a. 1.460 to 1.480.
    b. 1.200 to 1.210.
    c. 1.260 to 1.280.
    d. 1.000 to 1.200.

SUGGESTED ACTIVITIES

1. Select five motorcycles. Using your service manual, determine the following:
   a. What type of alternator is used.
   b. What type of rectifier is used.
   c. What type of regulator is used.
2. Using the wiring schematic from a current four-cylinder motorcycle, trace the following circuits:
   a. Electric starter circuit.
   b. Main lighting circuit.
   c. Turn signal circuit.
   d. Horn circuit.
3. Practice using a voltmeter, ammeter, and ohmmeter at various places in the electrical system of a motorcycle. Make a record of your tests and the results. Be sure to follow proper procedures.
4. Completely test a three-phase solid state rectifier, using an ohmmeter. Refer to your service manual and record your results.
5. Use a battery hydrometer to determine the condition of a motorcycle battery. If the battery needs charging, recheck it with the hydrometer after charging. Summarize your findings.

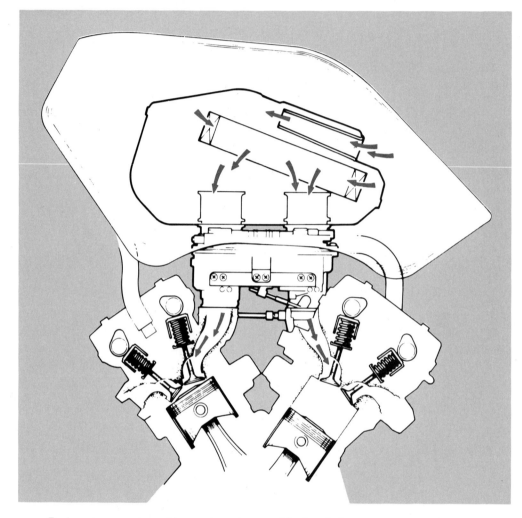

Fuel system must provide precise mixture of fuel and air to meet engine demands. (Yamaha Motors Corp., U.S.A.)

Chapter 9

FUEL SYSTEMS

After studying this chapter, you will be able to:
☐ Identify the parts of a fuel system.
☐ Explain the operating principles for each component of a fuel system.
☐ Describe basic carburetor circuits.
☐ List fundamental carburetor service and repair procedures.
☐ Explain the basic principles of electronic fuel injection.

This chapter introduces the most important parts of modern motorcycle fuel systems. Theory of operation, repair, and tuning will also be explained.

A fuel system that is NOT functioning properly can affect engine operation, and sometimes cause serious engine damage. While the fuel system appears quite simple, it performs the complex function of metering the right amounts of air and fuel to the engine. It must constantly change the air-fuel ratio with changes in engine temperature, speed, and power output.

FUNDAMENTAL FUEL SYSTEM PARTS

Before discussing fuel system theory, you should first become familiar with the major components of a fuel system. A typical motorcycle FUEL SYSTEM is made up of the following:
1. FUEL TANK to store supply of fuel.
2. FUEL PETCOCK to control the flow of fuel from the tank.
3. FUEL LINE to carry fuel from the tank to the carburetor.
4. FUEL PUMP to force fuel into the carburetor when gravity feed cannot be used.
5. FUEL FILTER to remove impurities from the fuel before the fuel enters the carburetor.
6. AIR FILTER to remove particles from the air entering the carburetor.
7. CARBURETOR to meter and mix the air and

fuel entering the engine.
8. INTAKE MANIFOLD to carry the fuel mixture from the carburetor to the engine intake port.
9. THROTTLE TWIST GRIP to allow the rider to control carburetor throttle opening and engine speed.
10. THROTTLE CABLE to connect the throttle twist grip to the carburetor butterfly or slide valve.

Fig. 9-1 shows a typical fuel system and the relationship of each component. Study this illustration closely. It is important that you understand these parts.

FUEL TANK

The FUEL TANK is a reservoir that safely stores a supply of gasoline. Fuel tanks can be made of steel, aluminum, plastic, or fiberglass. A gas cap fits on the top of the tank.

The GAS CAP may be a vented or non-vented type. If the gas cap is NOT vented, a vent hose is provided. Fuel tank venting is needed to prevent a build up of vacuum as fuel flows out of the tank. It also releases pressure as fuel temperature rises. Fig. 9-2 shows a typical fuel tank with two types of vented caps.

FUEL PETCOCK

A FUEL PETCOCK is an on/off valve attached to the bottom of the fuel tank. This provides a means of stopping fuel flow to the carburetor when the engine is not running. Fuel petcocks are either vacuum operated or manually operated.

Some motorcycles use two petcocks, one on each side of the fuel tank. Most motorcycles, however, use only one petcock. Fig. 9-3 shows manual and vacuum operated fuel petcocks.

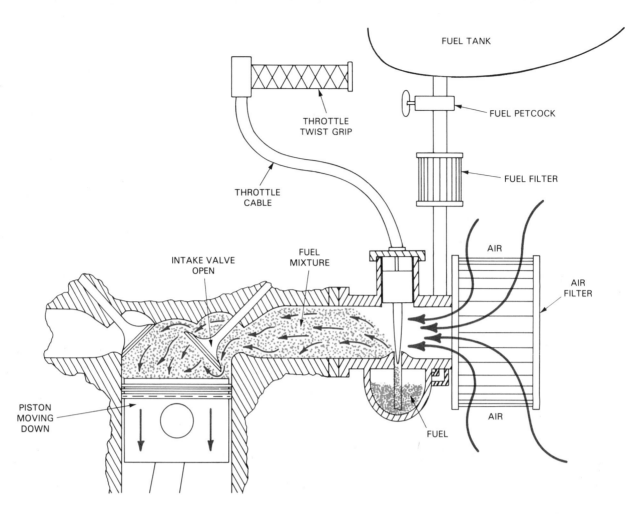

Fig. 9-1. Study part location of a basic motorcycle fuel system. This information will help you when each part is detailed in chapter.

Sediment bowl

Many petcocks incorporate a sediment bowl, Fig. 9-4. The SEDIMENT BOWL separates water and larger foreign materials (dirt, rust, scale) from the fuel before it enters the fuel line.

FUEL LINE

The FUEL LINE is a neoprene or plastic tube which carries fuel from the petcock to the carburetor.

It must be strong and flexible to withstand engine vibration. Small clamps are normally used to hold the fuel line on its fittings.

FUEL PUMP

A FUEL PUMP is required on motorcycles having the fuel tank located too low for gravity flow to feed fuel to the carburetor. The fuel pump supplies fuel under pressure (typically 4-8 psi or 28-55 kPa) to the

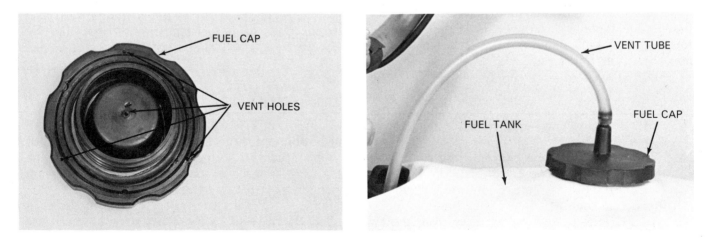

Fig. 9-2. An internally vented gas cap or a vent hose is used to prevent vacuum or pressure from building up in fuel tank.

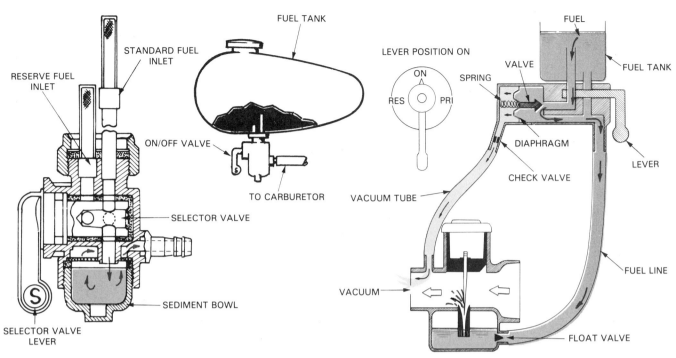

THIS MANUALLY OPERATED FUEL PETCOCK HAS THREE POSITION SELECTOR VALVE, PROVIDING RESERVE, STANDARD, AND OFF. IN STANDARD POSITION, FUEL ENTERS FROM APPROXIMATELY ONE INCH ABOVE BOTTOM OF TANK. RESERVE ALLOWS REMAINING FUEL FROM BOTTOM OF TANK TO ENTER FUEL LINE. (KAWASAKI MOTORS CORP., U.S.A.)

VACUUM OPERATED FUEL PETCOCK IS TURNED ON AND OFF BY INTAKE MANIFOLD OR CRANKCASE VACUUM. A PRIME POSITION IS PROVIDED TO ALLOW RAPID FILLING OF EMPTY FLOAT BOWLS. (U.S. SUZUKI MOTOR CORPORATION)

Fig. 9-3. Note differences between a manual and vacuum type fuel petcock.

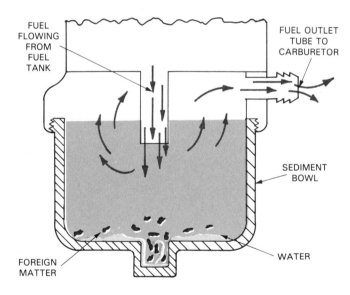

Fig. 9-4. Heavy particles (dirt, rust, scale) and water settle in bottom of fuel petcock sediment bowl. Clean fuel flows through sediment bowl before it reaches fuel outlet tube and fuel line.

carburetor. Fig. 9-5 shows a typical fuel pump.

A fuel pump is also used on all fuel injection systems. Fuel injection is covered later in this chapter.

FUEL FILTER

A FUEL FILTER is used to remove foreign matter from the gasoline before entry into the carburetor.

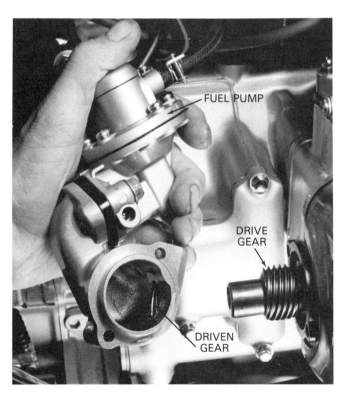

Fig. 9-5. This fuel pump is driven by engine camshaft.

Fuel filters can be located in three places: petcock filter, in-line filter, and fuel line banjo filter. An example of each filter type is shown in Fig. 9-6.

149

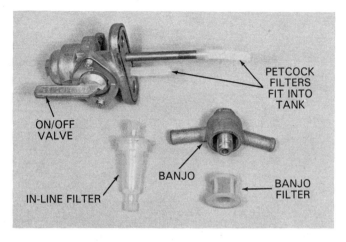

Fig. 9-6. These fuel filters use fine nylon mesh to trap contaminants.

AIR FILTER

An AIR FILTER prevents airborne dirt and foreign material from entering the carburetor throat and engine. Three types of filtering materials are used: paper, oiled foam, and oiled gauze.

Air filters and their mountings vary from motorcycle to motorcycle. In some applications, the air filter is attached directly to the carburetor. In most cases, however, the filter is enclosed in an air box connected to the carburetor with a rubber boot. This is illustrated in Fig. 9-7.

The AIR BOX provides a volume of still air for intake into the carburetors.

CARBURETOR

The CARBURETOR is the "heart" of the fuel system, Fig. 9-8. Its main function is to mix air and fuel and meter this mixture to the engine. The carburetor is one of the most important components in

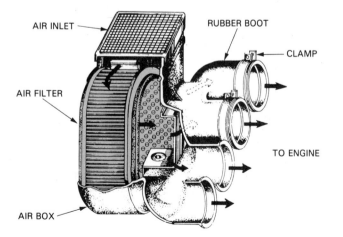

Fig. 9-7. Air filter is usually mounted inside an air box. This allows one filter element to filter air for more than one carburetor. Air box also helps protect filter from water and rapid contamination. (Kawasaki Motors Corp., U.S.A.)

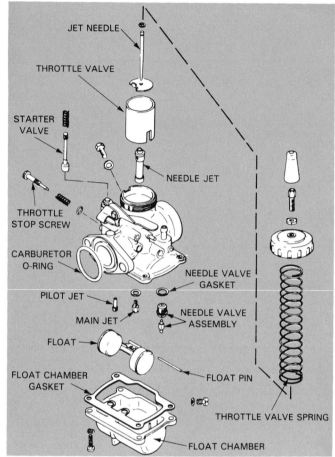

Fig. 9-8. Although motorcycle carburetor operation is quite simple, carburetors have many parts.
(U.S. Suzuki Motor Corp.)

the fuel system. It will be covered, in detail, later in this chapter.

INTAKE MANIFOLD

The INTAKE MANIFOLD provides a mounting place for the carburetor and directs the air-fuel mixture from the carburetor to the engine. Intake manifolds are made of aluminum, steel, or neoprene. Two intake manifold types are shown in Fig. 9-9.

THROTTLE TWIST GRIP

The THROTTLE TWIST GRIP is attached to the right handlebar and changes rotating movement of the grip to a push-pull movement of the throttle cable. This is accomplished with a drum inside the twist grip mechanism, Fig. 9-10.

Illustrated in Fig. 9-11, throttle twist grip rotation pulls on the throttle cable. In turn, the cable pulls on the carburetor throttle to increase engine speed and power. When the throttle twist grip is released, cable releases and carburetor throttle closes to reduce the flow of air and fuel into engine.

Some throttle twist grips use two cables. In one

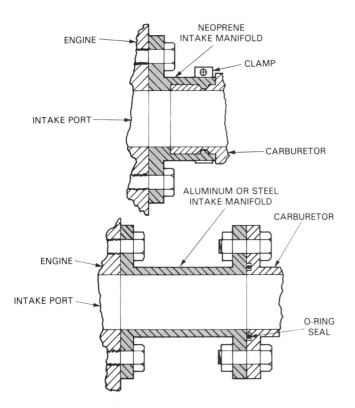

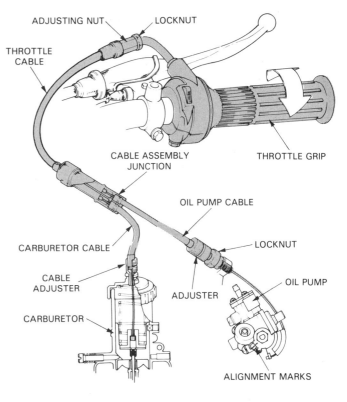

Fig. 9-9. Intake manifold carries air-fuel mixture from car-buretor to engine. Carburetor is bolted or clamped to intake manifold.

Fig. 9-11. This throttle cable has free-play adjusters at twist grip, carburetor, and oil pump.
(Kawasaki Motors Corp., U.S.A.)

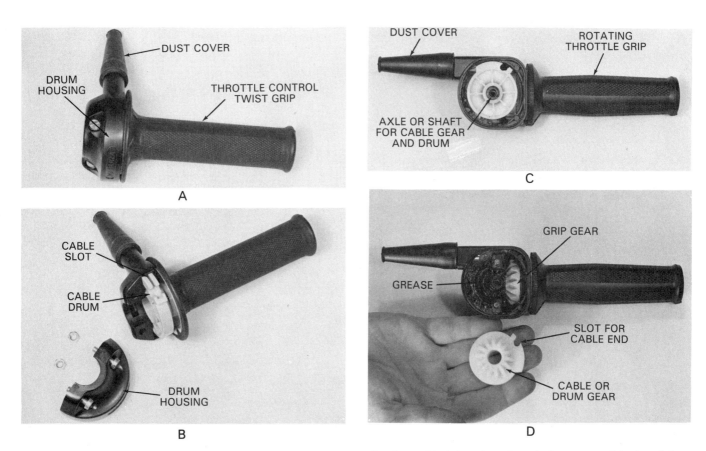

Fig. 9-10. Note two variations of drum type throttle twist grip. A—Assembled throttle twist grip fastens to right handlebar. B—This drum turns in the same direction as throttle twist grip. C—Another similar variation of drum type twist grip. D—Since drum does not turn in same direction as throttle twist grip, gear is used to transfer movement to drum.

type mechanism, both cables move in the same direction. In the other type, the cables move in opposite directions. With throttle twist grips where the cables move in opposite directions, positive throttle closing is assured at the carburetor.

THROTTLE CABLE

The THROTTLE CABLE connects to the twist grip at one end and to the carburetor or carburetor linkage at the other end. As the twist grip is rotated, the throttle cable changes the throttle opening at the carburetor. A means of adjusting cable free play is always provided. Fig. 9-11 shows a typical throttle cable mechanism.

POSITIVE CARBURETOR LINKAGES

POSITIVE CARBURETOR LINKAGES are used to operate throttles and chokes on some motorcycles. The purpose of a positive linkage is to:
1. Positively open and close a single throttle or choke.
2. Positively open and close more than one throttle or choke with a single cable or lever.

Positive carburetor linkages use two cables. One cable pulls the throttle OPEN and the other pulls it CLOSED.

The throttle cables are connected to opposite sides of a bell crank attached to a shaft. The shaft is connected to throttle slides or butterflies by throttle arms and connecting links. When the bell crank is turned by the throttle cable, the shaft, throttle arms, linkage,

and throttle slides or butterflies are moved in unison.

Figs. 9-12 and 9-13 show positive carburetor linkages. Study them closely.

CARBURETOR OPERATION

This section of the chapter explains carburetor operating principles. It is important for you to understand carburetors when studying tune-up, engine repair, and various other topics. Study this section carefully.

FUEL ATOMIZATION AND COMBUSTION

For efficient COMBUSTION (burning) to occur, gasoline must be mixed with air. In an open container of gasoline, the top surface is exposed to air. If ignited, the gasoline on top would burn, but very slowly since only a part of the gasoline is exposed to air, Fig. 9-14. If an equal amount of fuel was sprayed into the air and ignited, it would burn much more violently and rapidly. More of the gasoline is exposed to air, Fig. 9-14.

The function of the carburetor is to provide a finely ATOMIZED (broken up) mixture of air and fuel to the engine in correct proportions. The efficiency of an engine (fuel economy and performance) is closely related to proper fuel metering and atomization. Some carburetors atomize fuel better than others because of carburetor design differences.

In an engine cylinder, the finely atomized air-fuel mixture is compressed to provide even more violent combustion. Combustion is NOT an uncontrolled ex-

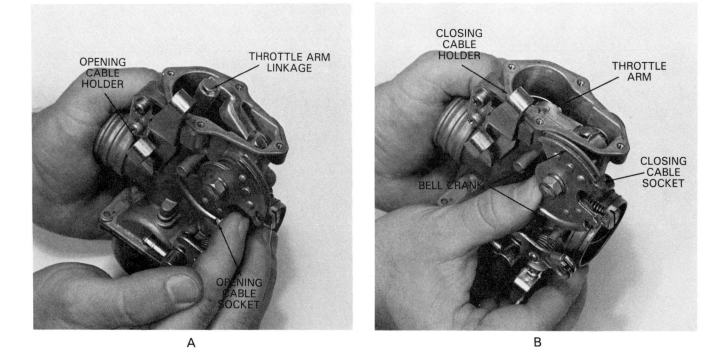

Fig. 9-12. This single carburetor uses a positive throttle linkage. A—Throttle is open. B—Throttle is closed.

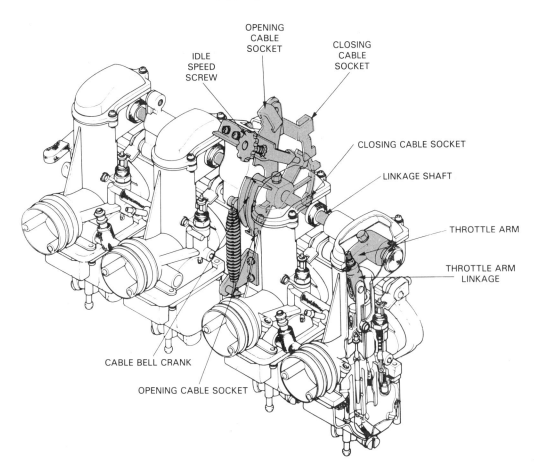

Fig. 9-13. Positive carburetor linkages use one cable to open throttles and another to close them. (Kawasaki Motors Corp., U.S.A.)

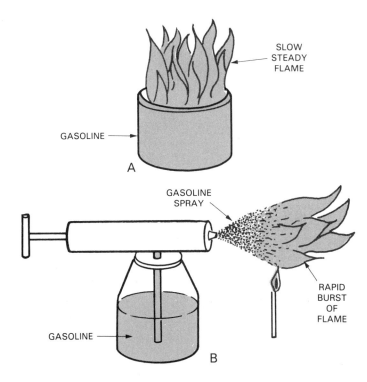

Fig. 9-14. Gasoline burns slowly unless mixed with air. A—Container of fuel burns slowly, small amount of fuel exposed to air. B—When sprayed into air, more fuel is exposed to air. Combustion is faster.

plosion. Instead, it is a very rapid, but controlled, burning of the air-fuel mixture. The heat causes expansion and pressure in the combustion chamber which forces the piston down with tremendous force. When the piston is forced down by combustion, the crankshaft spins, producing useful energy.

AIR-FUEL RATIO

Fuel atomization is not the only factor affecting engine performance and economy. The amount or proportion of air and fuel taken into the engine, termed AIR-FUEL RATIO, also affects performance and economy.

Generally speaking, an air-fuel ratio of 15:1 (15 parts air, 1 part fuel) is considered acceptable. However, at different engine speeds and loads, this ratio must be varied. The carburetor must vary this ratio. Fig. 9-15 shows how the air-fuel ratio is changed for different engine operating conditions.

Rich and lean fuel mixtures

As more fuel is mixed with air, the air-fuel ratio becomes RICH. As less fuel is mixed with the air, the air-fuel ratio becomes LEAN. The air-fuel ratio may be as rich as 3:1 for cold starting and as lean as 17:1 for cruising speeds.

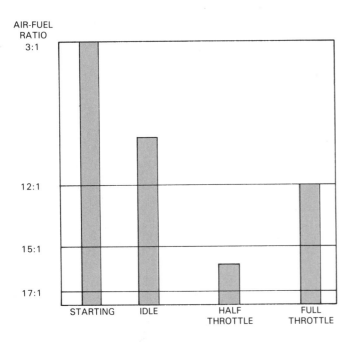

Fig. 9-15. This chart shows approximate air-fuel ratios needed under different engine operating conditions.

VENTURI PRINCIPLE

Carburetors rely on the VENTURI PRINCIPLE to draw fuel into the airstream. Look at Fig. 9-16. A VENTURI is a restriction formed in the carburetor throat that causes an increase in velocity and a decrease in pressure (vacuum increase) as air passes through.

A carburetor relies on this pressure difference to draw fuel into the airstream. Fig. 9-17 shows a simple carburetor using the venturi principle. Notice that atmospheric pressure is greater than venturi pressure, causing fuel to be drawn from the carburetor fuel reservoir into the airstream. The fuel is atomized into a fine mist as it enters the airstream.

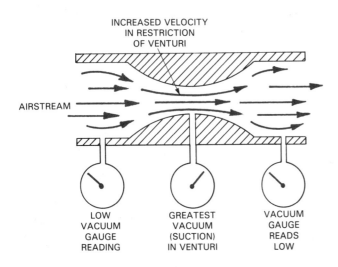

Fig. 9-16. As air passes through venturi, air speeds up, causing a vacuum (suction).

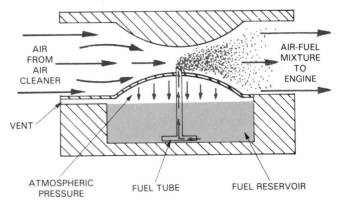
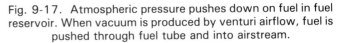

Fig. 9-17. Atmospheric pressure pushes down on fuel in fuel reservoir. When vacuum is produced by venturi airflow, fuel is pushed through fuel tube and into airstream.

COMMON CARBURETOR TYPES

Modern motorcycle engines commonly use three types of carburetors:
1. The slide controlled carburetor.
2. The vacuum controlled carburetor.
3. The butterfly controlled carburetor.

The major difference in these carburetor designs is in the way the venturi restriction is changed by the throttle. There are other carburetor designs, but these three are used as original equipment.

SLIDE CONTROLLED CARBURETOR

The SLIDE CONTROLLED CARBRETOR uses a round slide (piston) to alter the venturi restriction. Fig. 9-18 shows how the slide changes venturi size as it is raised. The slide is connected to the throttle twist grip by the throttle cable.

VACUUM CONTROLLED CARBURETOR

Intake manifold vacuuum, produced by the engine, operates the vacuum controlled carburetor. Engine vacuum changes with throttle opening and engine load. As the throttle is opened, vacuum decreases. As the throttle is closed, vacuum increases.

At the same time, as engine load is changed, vacuum also changes. More load decreases vacuum, and less load increases vacuum. For instance, as you begin to climb a hill, intake manifold vacuum will decrease (more load, less vacuum). As you crest the top of the hill and begin to go down the other side, there is less load on the engine, increasing vacuum.

If the throttle is snapped open, the velocity of the air passing through the venturi drops. This reduces vacuum in the venturi and starves the engine of fuel. As a result, the engine will hesitate or possibly even die because of an over-lean mixture. The vacuum controlled carburetor eliminates this type problem.

A VACUUM CONTROLLED CARBURETOR uses both a slide valve and butterfly valve to control

154

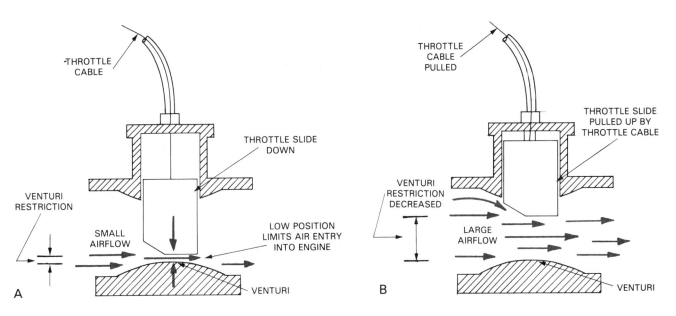

Fig. 9-18. As throttle slide is raised or lowered, venturi restriction is changed. A—Throttle slide is in a very low position allowing a small amount of air to pass through venturi. B—Slide is raised and causes much less restriction in venturi. This allows more air to flow for added power.

airflow through the venturi. Movement of the twist grip changes butterfly position. The slide is NOT connected to the throttle cable, but is controlled by changes in vacuum. Vacuum acting upon a piston or diaphragm causes the slide to raise or lower. Fig. 9-19 shows how this type carburetor operates.

BUTTERFLY CONTROLLED CARBURETOR

The BUTTERFLY CONTROLLED CARBURETOR uses only a flat circular disc (butterfly) pivoting in the carburetor throat to control airflow through the venturi. The throttle cable is connected directly to the butterfly by a lever on the outside of the carburetor. Fig. 9-20 shows how the butterfly carburetor controls the flow of air. When the butterfly is closed, airflow is limited, stopping venturi action. When opened, air and fuel flow increase for added engine power.

SLIDE CARBURETOR SYSTEMS (CIRCUITS)

To provide the proper air-fuel mixture at all throttle openings, several fuel metering systems, also called circuits, are used in the slide type carburetor. These systems include:
1. Float system.
2. Pilot system.

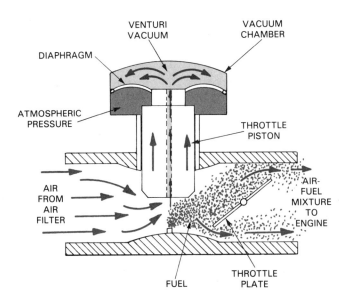

Fig. 9-19. In a vacuum controlled carburetor, atmospheric pressure below diaphragm pushes throttle piston up as vacuum increases above diaphragm.

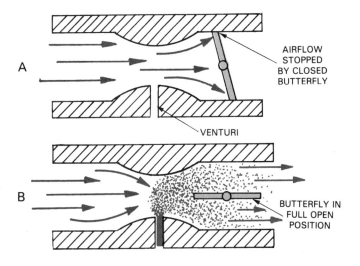

Fig. 9-20. Another way to control airflow through venturi is butterfly type throttle valve. A—Butterfly closed to restrict airflow and engine speed. B—Butterfly open to allow more air-fuel mixture to enter engine for increased power.

3. Slide cutaway system.
4. Needle system.
5. Main fuel system.
6. Accelerator pump system.
7. Starter system.

Float system

The FLOAT SYSTEM must maintain a constant level of fuel in the fuel reservoir (float bowl). This extra supply of fuel is needed for the fuel metering circuits. The float system is made up of:

1. Fuel reservoir or float bowl which stores fuel.
2. Float needle and seat to control entry of fuel into the bowl.
3. Float assembly that operates the needle valve.
4. Float pivot pin to allow float to swing up or down.
5. Overflow tube which routes excess fuel from bowl.
6. Float chamber vent that releases pressure and vacuum from float bowl.
7. Float primer button to feed fuel for easy starting.

Fig. 9-21 shows a typical float system. Study all of the basic components.

When the fuel petcock is turned ON, fuel flows past the opened FLOAT NEEDLE and SEAT. Fuel pours into the FLOAT BOWL, Fig. 9-22. As the fuel level rises in the float bowl, the FLOAT ASSEMBLY pushes the float needle against the seat which stops the flow of fuel into the bowl. See Fig. 9-23.

As fuel is used, the level in the float bowl drops, causing the float to drop. This opens the needle and seat. Float assembly action keeps a constant level of fuel in the bloat bowl.

An OVERFLOW TUBE is provided to prevent flooding of the float bowl in the event the float needle does NOT seat properly or the float sticks open.

Refer to Fig. 9-21.

The FLOAT BOWL VENT is needed to prevent a build up of vacuum or pressure in the carburetor bowl, Fig. 9-21. A vacuum build up could keep the fuel from entering the airstream. A pressure build up could keep the fuel from flowing into and filling the bowl.

Pilot system (idle circuit)

The PILOT SYSTEM or idle circuit meters air and fuel at idle and slightly above idle. It operates from idle to approximately one-eighth throttle opening. The pilot system consists of a pilot jet, pilot adjustment screw, and air and fuel passageways in the carburetor body.

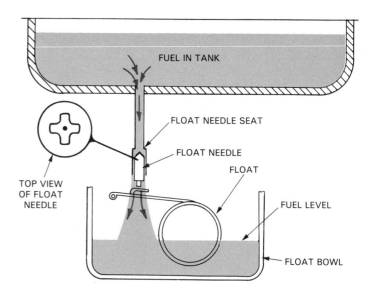

Fig. 9-22. When fuel level is low in float bowl, float is also lowered. This lets float needle drop away from its seat. Then, fuel refills bowl.

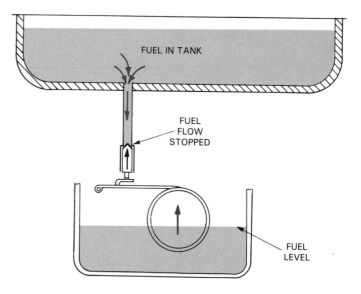

Fig. 9-23. As fuel level rises, float rises pushing float needle against its seat and stopping flow of fuel from tank.

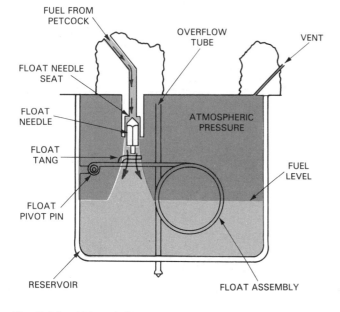

Fig. 9-21. Although float system is simple, it performs an important function by controlling fuel level in carburetor.

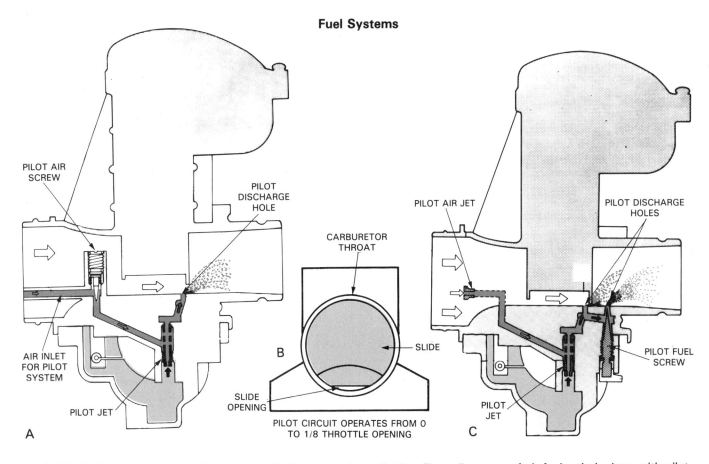

Fig. 9-24. A—In air screw type pilot system, fuel is metered by pilot jet. Fine adjustment of air-fuel ratio is done with pilot air screw. Pilot air screw controls amount of air mixed with fuel. B—Slide opening. C—In fuel screw type pilot system, fuel is metered by pilot jet. Air is metered by pilot air jet. Pilot fuel screw adjusts amount of air-fuel mixture discharged into airstream in throat of carburetor. (Kawasaki Motors Corp., U.S.A.)

The purpose of the PILOT JET is to meter the proper amount of fuel to a mixing chamber where the fuel is premixed with air. The PILOT ADJUSTMENT SCREW controls the amount of air or fuel bled (introduced) into the mixing chamber.

Once the air and fuel are mixed, the solution is fed to the carburetor throat through one or two discharge holes located in the venturi. Fig. 9-24 shows the two types of pilot circuits.

Slide cutaway system (off-idle circuit)

The SLIDE CUTAWAY SYSTEM, also called off-idle circuit, determines the air-fuel mixture from one-eighth to one-quarter throttle. The fuel for this circuit comes from the pilot circuit and the needle circuit. The air-fuel mixture is controlled by the cutaway on the throttle slide. See Fig. 9-25.

The front half (air cleaner side) of the slide bottom is cut at an angle. The height of this cutaway portion determines the amount of air that is mixed with fuel in the circuit. Fig. 9-26 shows the slide cutaway circuit in operation.

Needle system (midrange circuit)

The NEEDLE SYSTEM, also termed midrange circuit, controls the air-fuel mixture from one-quarter to three-quarter throttle opening. The two types of needle systems are the primary type and bleeder type.

The PRIMARY TYPE NEEDLE SYSTEM, shown in Fig. 9-27, consists of:
1. Needle jet to surround and work with jet needle.
2. Jet needle to regulate fuel flow by enlarging or reducing the opening in the needle jet.
3. Air jet to regulate airflow into the diffuser.
4. Diffuser to premix air and fuel.

The amount of fuel flowing through this circuit is determined by the clearance between the needle jet and the jet needle. The jet needle is tapered, allowing greater clearance at larger throttle openings, Fig. 9-28. As the needle is lifted out of its jet, fuel flow is

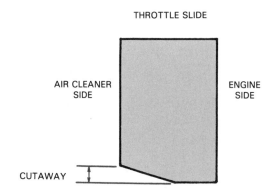

Fig. 9-25. In slide cutaway system, air-fuel ratio is controlled by height of slide cutaway.

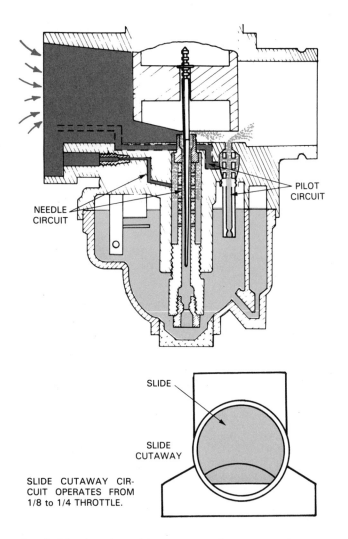

SLIDE CUTAWAY CIRCUIT OPERATES FROM 1/8 to 1/4 THROTTLE.

Fig. 9-26. A higher slide cutaway allows more air to pass, giving a leaner air-fuel ratio. A lower cutaway allows less air to pass, giving a richer air-fuel ratio. Fuel for slide cutaway system is drawn from pilot and needle systems. (Kawasaki Motors Corp., U.S.A.)

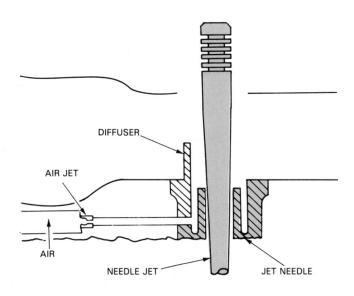

Fig. 9-27. Two major components in needle circuit are jet needle and needle jet.

increased. The amount of airflow is simply controlled by throttle slide position.

Primary needle system operation is shown in Fig. 9-29. The AIR JET provides for premixing of air and fuel in the DIFFUSER before the fuel reaches the diffuser outlet in the carburetor throat. This permits better atomization of the air-fuel mixture.

The BLEEDER TYPE NEEDLE (midrange) CIRCUIT uses the same components as the primary type needle circuit. The differences between the two circuits are:

1. The primary type needle circuit only meters fuel through the needle jet and jet needle, not air.
2. The bleeder type needle circuit meters an air-fuel froth (foam) through the needle jet and jet needle.

The bleeder type needle circuit can provide better fuel atomization since air and fuel are premixed in the needle jet rather than in the diffuser. See Fig. 9-30.

This is accomplished by directing air from the air jet into the body of the needle jet. Fuel and air are premixed here before being metered by the jet needle.

Fuel for the needle circuit (primary and bleeder types) passes through the main jet before it is metered by the needle jet and jet needle. However, since the main jet will allow more fuel to pass than the needle circuit uses, the main jet does not affect needle circuit operation.

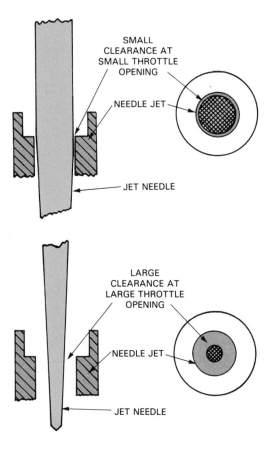

Fig. 9-28. As throttle is opened, tapered jet needle is lifted, creating more clearance between needle and jet. This allows more fuel to flow into throat and engine.

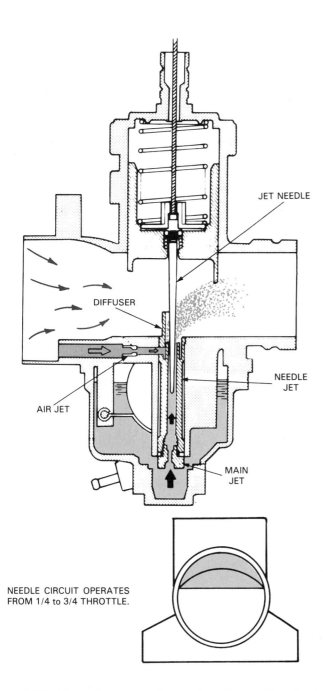

JET NEEDLE

DIFFUSER

NEEDLE JET

AIR JET

MAIN JET

NEEDLE CIRCUIT OPERATES FROM 1/4 to 3/4 THROTTLE.

Fig. 9-29. Venturi vacuum draws fuel for needle circuit through main jet and into needle jet. Clearance between needle jet and tapered jet needle meters fuel flow into venturi. Air jet mixes some air with fuel in diffuser before reaching venturi. This assists fuel atomization and combustion. (Kawasaki Motors Corp., U.S.A.)

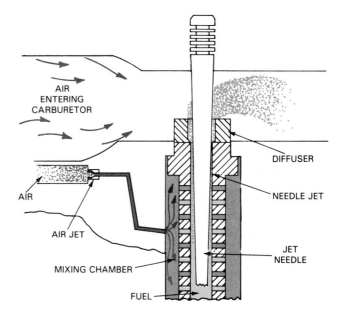

AIR ENTERING CARBURETOR

AIR

AIR JET

MIXING CHAMBER

FUEL

DIFFUSER

NEEDLE JET

JET NEEDLE

Fig. 9-30. In bleeder type needle circuit, perforations in walls of needle jet allow fuel to mix with air from air jet. Resulting air-fuel froth is then metered by needle jet and jet needle.

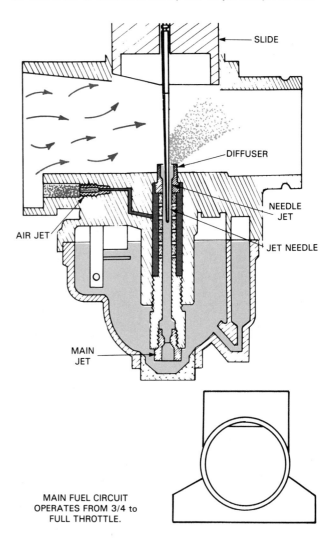

SLIDE

DIFFUSER

NEEDLE JET

JET NEEDLE

AIR JET

MAIN JET

MAIN FUEL CIRCUIT OPERATES FROM 3/4 to FULL THROTTLE.

Fig. 9-31. Main jet controls air-fuel ratio in main fuel circuit. Size of hole in jet meters maximum fuel flow. This is a bleeder type carburetor, so air-fuel froth is discharged into venturi. Notice, however, that main jet meters fuel only. (Kawasaki Motors Corp., U.S.A.)

Main fuel system (high speed circuit)

The MAIN FUEL SYSTEM, also called high speed circuit, controls the air-fuel mixture from three-quarter to full throttle opening. This circuit uses a single MAIN JET to meter fuel flow, Fig. 9-31.

Fuel for the main circuit is metered by the main jet. Fuel then passes through the needle jet and diffuser to reach the venturi. Even though fuel passes through the needle circuit, it does not alter the operation of the main circuit. This is because clearance between

159

the jet needle and needle jet at this throttle opening allows more fuel to pass than the main jet can supply. Therefore, the main jet alone controls fuel metering. The air jet provides premixing of air and fuel in the diffuser for the main circuit and the needle circuit.

Although operation of the four fuel metering systems (pilot, slide cutaway, needle, main) is controlled by throttle opening, there is some overlapping from one circuit to the next.

Accelerator pump system (acceleration circuit)

Some types of carburetors are equipped with an accelerator pump. The ACCELERATOR PUMP SYSTEM discharges a metered amount of fuel into the carburetor throat as the throttle is opened.

When the throttle is opened suddenly, vacuum drops in the venturi, causing a momentary reduction of fuel flow through the needle jet and main jet. Fuel starvation could result. The lean condition could cause the engine to hesitate or stumble momentarily.

The purpose of the accelerator pump is to prevent any hesitation by providing extra fuel during sudden opening of the throttle. Fig. 9-32 shows a typical accelerator pump circuit.

Fig. 9-33 illustrates how one accelerator pump can be used to feed several carburetors.

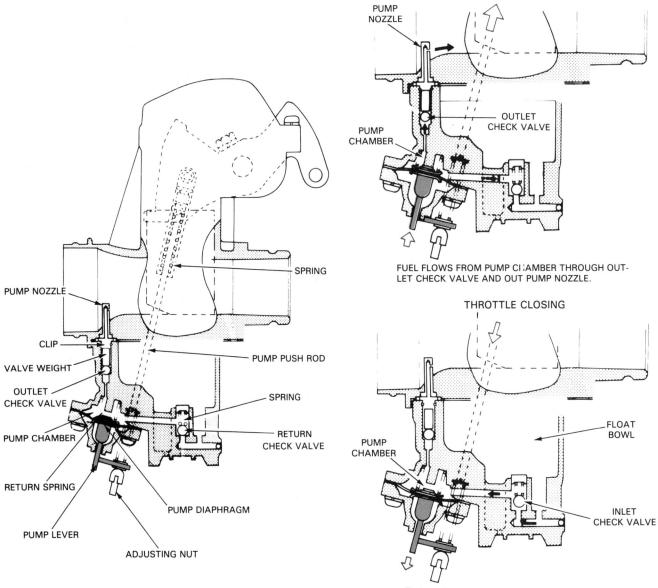

THROTTLE OPENING

FUEL FLOWS FROM PUMP CHAMBER THROUGH OUTLET CHECK VALVE AND OUT PUMP NOZZLE.

THROTTLE CLOSING

FUEL FLOWS FROM FLOAT BOWL THROUGH INLET CHECK VALVE AND INTO PUMP CHAMBER.

Fig. 9-32. In this accelerator pump system, opening of throttle lifts pump push rod and raises pump diaphragm in pump chamber. This forces fuel in pump chamber past outlet check valve and out pump nozzle. As throttle is closed, diaphragm lowers, drawing more fuel into pump chamber. (Kawasaki Motors Corp., U.S.A.)

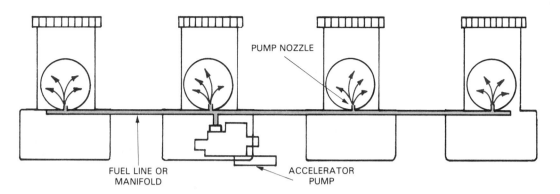

Fig. 9-33. When multiple carburetors are used, one accelerator pump usually supplies all carburetors.

Starter system

The STARTER SYSTEM provides an enriched mixture for cold engine starting and warm up. There are three basic methods used to provide a rich air-fuel mixture for cold starting:
1. Choke type system.
2. Tickler (primer) type system.
3. Enrichment type system.

Choke system

A CHOKE restricts the amount of air entering the carburetor. Shown in Fig. 9-34, it is a butterfly valve fitted in front of the venturi. Choke closing increases the vacuum in the venturi and causes more fuel to flow into the engine. At the same time, less air is allowed to enter the carburetor throat. This provides an extremely rich air-fuel mixture for cold starting.

Tickler system

The TICKLER SYSTEM provides a rich mixture by temporarily raising the float level. This is accomplished by depressing a spring-loaded rod which contacts the top of the float assembly. This causes a rich mixture because less vacuum is required to draw fuel into the venturi. Fig. 9-35 shows the operation of the tickler system.

Enrichment system

The ENRICHMENT SYSTEM is an air-fuel metering circuit separate from other carburetor circuits. Fuel for this circuit is drawn from the float bowl through an enrichment (starter) jet. Fig. 9-36 shows the enrichment circuit air and fuel passageways.

Air for the enrichment circuit is drawn into a drillway at the mouth of the carburetor. This drillway

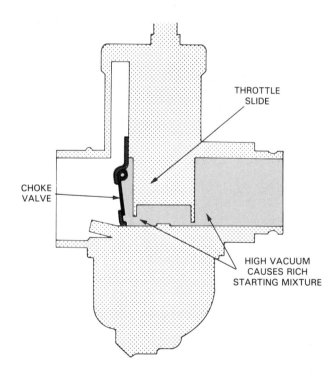

Fig. 9-34. Choke plate is lowered into throat of carburetor for cold starting. Spring-loaded relief valve allows a small amount of air into venturi. Blocking airflow in this manner increases venturi vacuum. Once engine is started, choke must be opened to prevent flooding. (Kawasaki Motors Corp., U.S.A.)

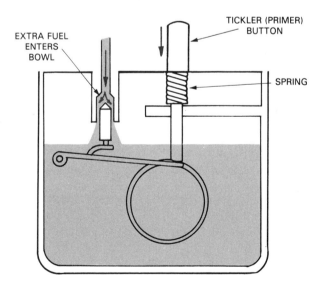

Fig. 9-35. In tickler system, tickler button is pushed down, lowering float and allowing extra fuel to flow into float bowl. This temporarily raises fuel level. A rich air-fuel ratio results since less vacuum is required to pull fuel into venturi.

161

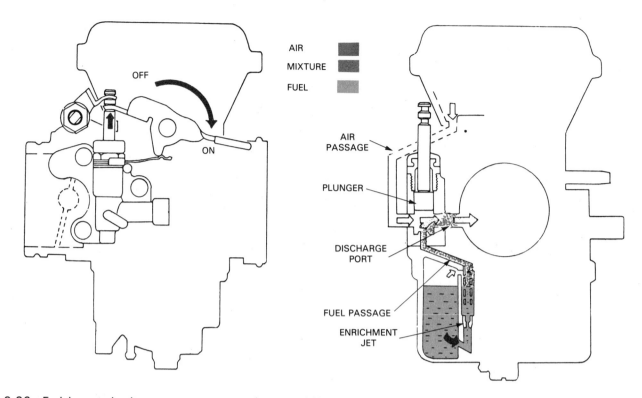

Fig. 9-36. Enrichment circuit acts as a separate carburetor within a carburetor, but is only used for cold starting and warm up. When lever is pushed down, a rich mixture enters engine. Plunger is lifted out of passage so that extra fuel can enter bore. (Yamaha Motor Corporation, U.S.A.)

bypasses the carburetor throat and venturi.

The enrichment circuit is controlled manually by a cable or linkage which operates a plunger. When the plunger is down, the enrichment circuit is blocked and does not operate. Fuel and air cannot flow through the circuit, Fig. 9-37. A normal air-fuel mixture is maintained.

When the plunger is raised, a rich air-fuel mixture is discharged from the enrichment port. This port is located directly behind the throttle slide, Fig. 9-38.

An enrichment circuit works best with the carburetor slide at IDLE (closed). High vacuum behind the closed slide can then easily draw air and fuel through the enrichment circuit.

VACUUM CARBURETOR SYSTEMS AND CIRCUITS

The fuel metering circuits in a VACUUM CARBURETOR, also called CV or constant velocity car-

Fig. 9-37. When plunger is down, air and fuel passages are blocked. Extra air and fuel does not enter carburetor barrel.

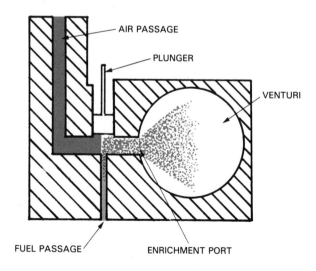

Fig. 9-38. When plunger is up, high vacuum behind throttle slide pulls air and fuel through passages and out enrichment port.

buretor, are similar to those of the slide type carburetor. The major differences are:

1. The vacuum carburetor uses a butterfly throttle valve.
2. Airflow through the venturi in a vacuum carburetor is controlled by a vacuum operated slide (piston).
3. The pilot adjustment screw on a vacuum carburetor always controls fuel rather than air.
4. A pilot bypass circuit controls off-idle air-fuel mixture.
5. A primary and secondary main fuel circuit is used on some vacuum carburetors.

Butterfly throttle

A vacuum carburetor uses a conventional butterfly throttle plate. This alone, however, does NOT control engine speed. The butterfly plate is only the primary means of controlling airflow through the carburetor.

Vacuum piston

The VACUUM PISTON controls venturi restriction. Its position is determined by vacuum in the venturi. The vacuum piston is not mechanically connected to the butterfly. Vacuum in the venturi causes a pressure difference between the top and bottom of the vacuum piston assembly. As venturi vacuum increases, the vacuum piston slides up.

There are two common types of vacuum pistons. One type uses a large diameter PISTON and CYLINDER. The other has a DIAPHRAGM attached to the top of the vacuum piston. Fig. 9-39 shows these two designs and how they operate.

Pilot bypass circuit

The piston in a vacuum carburetor does NOT use a cutaway. Instead, a pilot bypass circuit controls the off-idle air-fuel mixture. The fuel for this circuit is metered through the pilot jet and is controlled by the butterfly position.

When the butterfly is closed, the air-fuel mixture is controlled by the IDLE MIXTURE SCREW (pilot adjustment screw). As the throttle is opened, the bypass port is exposed to vacuum and fuel begins to flow. This is shown in Fig. 9-40.

On most CV (constant velocity) carburetors, the needle and main fuel circuits function in the same manner as on the slide type carburetor. However, some CV carburetors use primary and secondary main fuel circuits, Fig. 9-41. This type of carburetor does NOT provide for JET NEEDLE ADJUSTMENT (grooves at the top of needle). During the transition from pilot bypass to needle circuit operation, air-fuel ratio is controlled by the primary main jet.

As the throttle is opened from idle, vacuum increases. Fuel is first drawn through the primary main

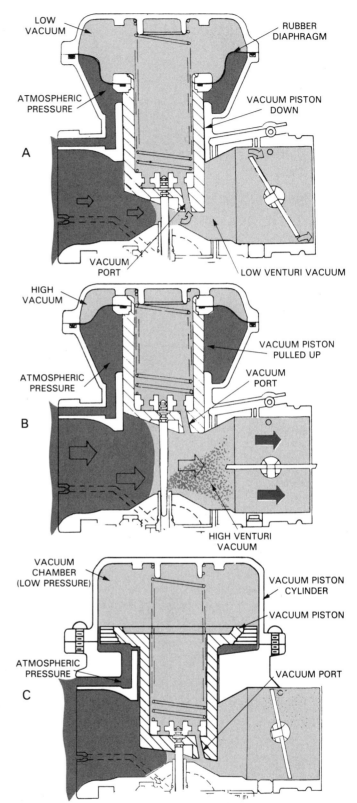

Fig. 9-39. Diaphragm and cylinder type vacuum pistons. A—With diaphragm type vacuum piston, lower side of diaphragm is exposed to atmospheric pressure. A vacuum port at base of vacuum piston admits venturi vacuum into chamber above diaphragm. B—As vacuum in venturi increases (pressure decrease), atmospheric pressure raises diaphragm and piston. C—In cylinder type vacuum piston, diaphragm is replaced by a vacuum cylinder and large diameter piston. (Yamaha Motor Corp., U.S.A.)

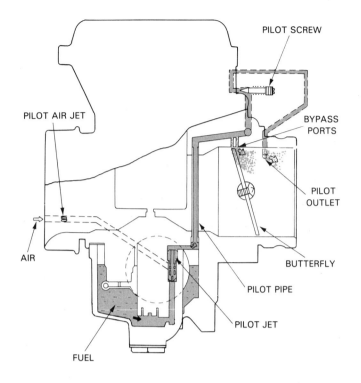

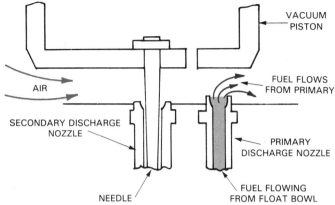

Fig. 9-42. Higher profile of primary discharge nozzle and its position relative to vacuum piston causes primary circuit to be affected by manifold vacuum. It begins discharging fuel before secondary circuit.

Fig. 9-40. At idle, butterfly is almost completely closed. Fuel is discharged only from pilot outlet. As throttle is opened, butterfly rotates exposing bypass ports, allowing them to discharge fuel. Pilot and bypass ports continue to discharge fuel as throttle is opened. (U.S. Suzuki Motor Corporation)

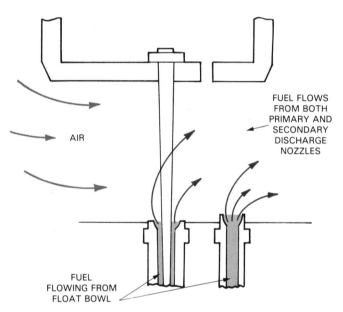

Fig. 9-43. As throttle is opened farther and vacuum increases, fuel is discharged from both primary and secondary circuits.

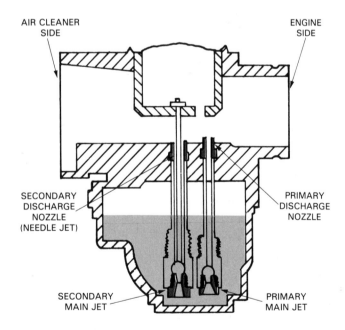

Fig. 9-41. Some CV carburetors use primary and secondary main fuel circuits.

BUTTERFLY CARBURETOR SYSTEMS

The BUTTERFLY CARBURETOR is a relatively simple, compact carburetor. It uses a BUTTERFLY VALVE (throttle plate) as the only means of controlling airflow through the venturi. A butterfly carburetor is illustrated in Fig. 9-44.

A float system, Fig. 9-45, similar to those used in the slide and CV type carburetors supplies fuel to the metering circuits.

A butterfly carburetor uses three basic systems or circuits to meter fuel:
1. Pilot system (slow circuit).
2. Main system (cruise circuit).
3. Accelerator pump system (acceleration circuit).

jet, Fig. 9-42. As the throttle continues to open and vacuum increases, fuel is also drawn through the secondary circuit, Fig. 9-43.

Note! A choke or enrichment circuit is normally used for cold starting in a vacuum type carburetor.

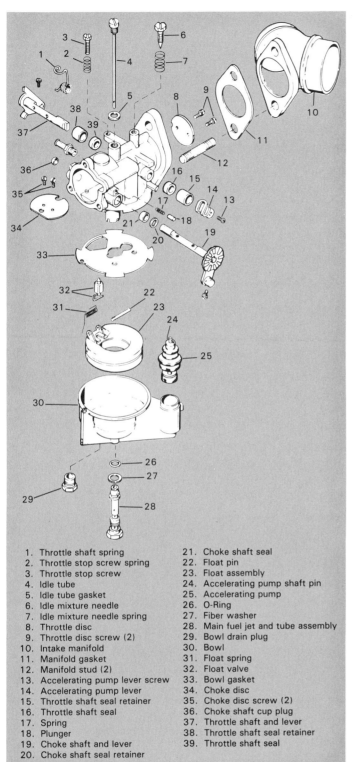

1. Throttle shaft spring	21. Choke shaft seal
2. Throttle stop screw spring	22. Float pin
3. Throttle stop screw	23. Float assembly
4. Idle tube	24. Accelerating pump shaft pin
5. Idle tube gasket	25. Accelerating pump
6. Idle mixture needle	26. O-Ring
7. Idle mixture needle spring	27. Fiber washer
8. Throttle disc	28. Main fuel jet and tube assembly
9. Throttle disc screw (2)	29. Bowl drain plug
10. Intake manifold	30. Bowl
11. Manifold gasket	31. Float spring
12. Manifold stud (2)	32. Float valve
13. Accelerating pump lever screw	33. Bowl gasket
14. Accelerating pump lever	34. Choke disc
15. Throttle shaft seal retainer	35. Choke disc screw (2)
16. Throttle shaft seal	36. Choke shaft cup plug
17. Spring	37. Throttle shaft and lever
18. Plunger	38. Throttle shaft seal retainer
19. Choke shaft and lever	39. Throttle shaft seal
20. Choke shaft seal retainer	

Fig. 9-44. This butterfly type carburetor is a compact and dependable design. (Harley-Davidson Motor Co., Inc.)

Pilot system (slow circuit)

The purpose of the PILOT SYSTEM is to meter fuel from idle to intermediate throttle opening. Fuel flows through the main jet and then into the pilot jet where it is metered and mixed with air from the pilot air jet. This makes an air-fuel froth. A passageway in the car-

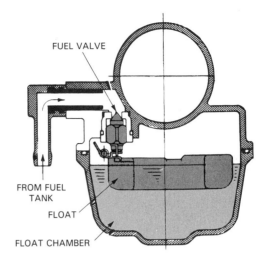

Fig. 9-45. Float system in butterfly carburetor is similar to ones used in slide and CV type carburetors. (Harley-Davidson Motor Co., Inc.)

buretor transfers this air-fuel froth to the idle discharge port and bypass discharge ports, Fig. 9-46.

In the pilot circuit, fuel is drawn through the main jet to the pilot jet. The pilot jet meters and mixes fuel with air in the pilot bleeder tube. The resulting air-fuel froth passes through a drilled passage in the carburetor body. The fuel then enters the bypass chamber and pilot discharge port, Fig. 9-46. A tapered needle (pilot mixture screw) partially blocks fuel flow through the pilot discharge port. As the pilot mixture screw is turned in or out, less or more fuel is allowed to pass into the airstream in the carburetor throat. This provides for adjustment of air-fuel ratio at idle.

As the throttle is opened, the bypass discharge ports are exposed to venturi vacuum and more fuel is

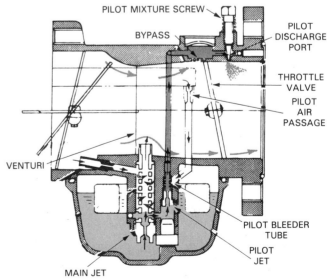

Fig. 9-46. Study parts and flow in a pilot system of butterfly type carburetor. (Harley-Davidson Motor Co., Inc.)

discharged into the airstream, Fig. 9-47. Pilot jet size determines the air-fuel ratio in the bypass stage.

Main system (cruising circuit)

The purpose of the MAIN SYSTEM is to meter fuel from intermediate to full throttle. Fuel flows from the float bowl through the main jet into a bleeder tube. The bleeder tube mixes the fuel with air from the main jet. This produces an air-fuel froth.

As the throttle plate is opened, engine speed increases (because of bypass circuit operation). Vacuum also increases in the venturi. When vacuum increases to a certain point, the air-fuel froth begins to discharge through the main fuel nozzle, Fig. 9-48.

The air-fuel ratio for the main system is controlled by MAIN JET SIZE.

Accelerator pump system (acceleration circuit)

The ACCELERATOR PUMP SYSTEM provides air-fuel mixture enrichment during rapid throttle opening. This compensates for the sudden drop in vacuum and resulting lean mixture caused by quick opening of the throttle. This circuit does NOT rely on vacuum for fuel delivery. Instead, it uses a diaphragm pump connected to the butterfly to force fuel into the venturi, Fig. 9-49.

Adjustment of the acceleration circuit is accomplished by changing the stroke of the pump.

The butterfly carburetor uses a choke plate to provide high vacuum for cold starting enrichment.

ELECTRONIC FUEL INJECTION

Electronic fuel injection is a recent development in motorcycle induction systems. Environmental Protection Agency (EPA) exhaust emissions regulations for motorcycles are not as stringent as those imposed on the automotive industry. However, many current motorcycles suffer from the effects of the lean air-fuel mixtures used to meet emission standards.

Generally, lean fuel mixtures burn cleaner than rich mixtures. Lean mixtures, however, tend to reduce engine power and smoothness.

Electronic fuel injection is an efficient way of eliminating the performance problems caused by lean carburetor settings. Fuel injection is capable of more precisely controlling the amount of fuel entering each cylinder.

ELECTRONIC FUEL INJECTION, abbreviated EFI, uses an electrically controlled fuel injector mounted in each intake port. See Fig. 9-50. The brain for this system is the electronic control box (computer) which decides how long to open the injectors based on information received from several monitoring devices.

For this explanation of EFI, a four-cylinder engine will be used as an example. Slight differences may be

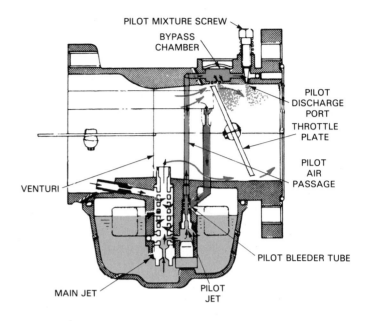

Fig. 9-47. Bypass consists of a small fuel chamber which is connected to carburetor throat by a series of tiny holes. It is actually part of pilot circuit. As throttle plate opens from idle, successive bypass discharge holes are exposed to vacuum and more fuel flows into carburetor throat. (Harley-Davidson Motor Co., Inc.)

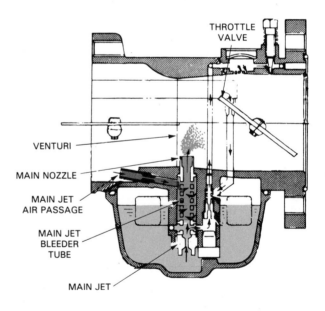

Fig. 9-48. Main fuel circuit operates when vacuum in venturi is high enough to draw fuel through main nozzle (intermediate to full throttle). (Harley-Davidson Motor Co., Inc.)

found in other systems, but operating principles are similar.

The VARIABLES MONITORED by the fuel injection system computer are:
1. Throttle position (for full throttle and idle enrichment).
2. Airflow.
3. Air temperature.
4. Engine rpm.

Fuel Systems

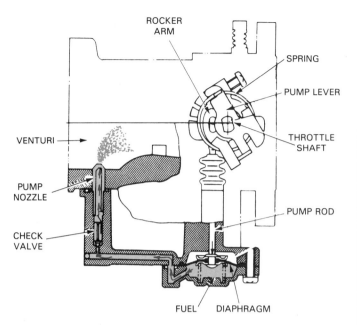

Fig. 9-49. Accelerator pump supplies a squirt of extra fuel to prevent a lean condition when throttle is snapped open. Lever attached to throttle shaft moves a diaphragm type pump as throttle is opened. Diaphragm pushes fuel through a drillway and check valve to pump nozzle where it is squirted into carburetor throat.   (Harley-Davidson Motor Co., Inc.)

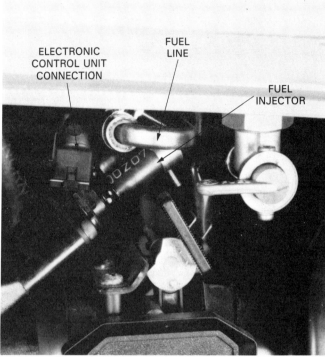

Fig. 9-50. An electronic fuel injection system squirts fuel directly into the engine's intake port under pressure. Fuel injector is an electric solenoid operated fuel valve. When electronic control unit (computer) sends current pulse to injector solenoid, injector opens and sprays fuel toward intake valve.

5. Engine temperature.

An electronic fuel injection system is made up of THREE SUBSYSTEMS:
1. Air system.
2. Fuel system.
3. Electronic control system.

These three systems work together to provide the engine with the proper air-fuel mixture under varying conditions. Refer to Fig. 9-51.

A complete diagram of an electronic fuel injection system is given in Fig. 9-52. Study how the sensors feed information to the computer and how computer controls opening of fuel injectors.

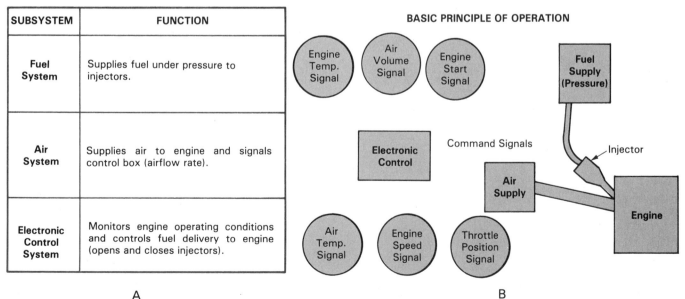

Fig. 9-51. In an EFI system, three systems work together to meet air-fuel needs of engine. A—Function of each system. B—Relationship of each system.

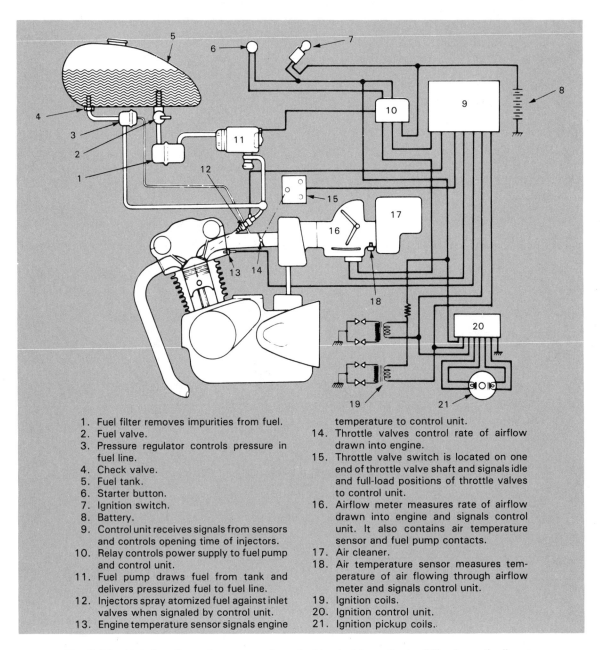

1. Fuel filter removes impurities from fuel.
2. Fuel valve.
3. Pressure regulator controls pressure in fuel line.
4. Check valve.
5. Fuel tank.
6. Starter button.
7. Ignition switch.
8. Battery.
9. Control unit receives signals from sensors and controls opening time of injectors.
10. Relay controls power supply to fuel pump and control unit.
11. Fuel pump draws fuel from tank and delivers pressurized fuel to fuel line.
12. Injectors spray atomized fuel against inlet valves when signaled by control unit.
13. Engine temperature sensor signals engine temperature to control unit.
14. Throttle valves control rate of airflow drawn into engine.
15. Throttle valve switch is located on one end of throttle valve shaft and signals idle and full-load positions of throttle valves to control unit.
16. Airflow meter measures rate of airflow drawn into engine and signals control unit. It also contains air temperature sensor and fuel pump contacts.
17. Air cleaner.
18. Air temperature sensor measures temperature of air flowing through airflow meter and signals control unit.
19. Ignition coils.
20. Ignition control unit.
21. Ignition pickup coils.

Fig. 9-52. Note locations of components and wiring in this particular EFI schematic diagram. (Kawasaki Motors Corp., U.S.A.)

EFI AIR SYSTEM

The EFI AIR SYSTEM resembles the air intake of a carbureted engine, with exception of the airflow meter, Fig. 9-53. The airflow meter consists of a flap located in the air passage. This flap swings open as air is drawn into the engine.

The AIRFLOW METER is actually part of the electronic control and air systems. A potentiometer (variable resistor) signals the position of the air flap to the control box. This tells the control box how much air is being drawn into the engine. A bypass passage helps control the air-fuel mixture at idle and at low engine speeds.

The THROTTLE VALVES are connected to the twist grip. They regulate the amount of air being drawn into the engine. The electronic fuel injection throttle valve serves the same function as the slide or butterfly in the constant velocity and butterfly type carburetor.

The remaining components, air box, and air cleaner, are similar to those found on a carbureted engine. However, the AIR BOX in the fuel injected engine also helps to stabilize air flap movement.

EFI FUEL SYSTEM

The EFI fuel system is somewhat different from the fuel system in a carbureted engine. Look at Fig. 9-54. The EFI FUEL SYSTEM uses an electric fuel pump, fuel filter, pressure regulator, high pressure lines, electrically activated fuel injectors and a conventional fuel tank.

The ELECTRIC FUEL PUMP is designed to provide an oversupply of fuel to the injectors at all times, Fig. 9-54. Excess fuel is returned to the fuel tank. This

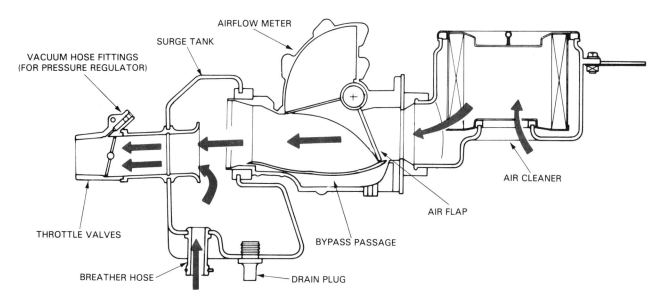

Fig. 9-53. Notice how similar this air intake system is to a carbureted engine. What differences do you see? (Kawasaki Motors Corp., U.S.A.)

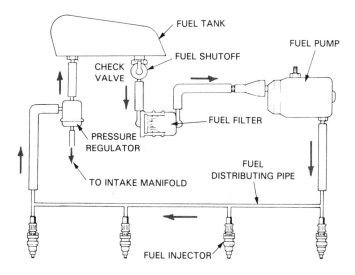

Fig. 9-54. Fuel pump and pressure regulator maintain constant fuel pressure above that of intake manifold vacuum. (Kawasaki Motors Corp., U.S.A.)

insures that there will always be enough fuel for any demand.

A PRESSURE REGULATOR is used to control fuel pressure at the injectors, Fig. 9-54. Proper pressure is maintained by intake manifold vacuum acting on the regulator diaphragm, Fig. 9-55. This maintains a constant pressure difference between the injector tip (intake manifold) and the fuel line.

The FUEL INJECTOR is the last component in the fuel system. Its function is to spray the proper amount of fuel into the intake port. Look at Fig. 9-56. The injector is a sealed unit which acts as an electrically controlled fuel valve. The fuel injector is normally closed. When an electric signal is received from the control unit, the injector opens, discharging fuel into the intake port. See Fig. 9-52.

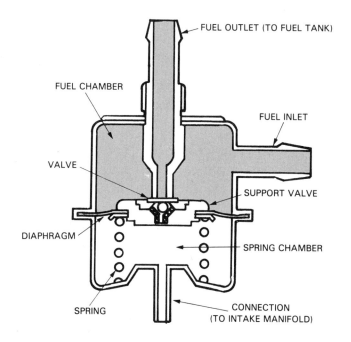

Fig. 9-55. Manifold vacuum acts on regulator diaphragm to maintain proper fuel pressure for fuel injection system. (Kawasaki Motors Corp., U.S.A.)

The air-fuel ratio is determined by the length of time the injector remains open. This is controlled by the electronic control system.

EFI ELECTRONIC CONTROL SYSTEM

The EFI ELECTRONIC CONTROL SYSTEM is the most complex part of the EFI system, Fig. 9-57. Its function is to monitor engine operating conditions and signal the injectors to open for the proper length of time.

The major component within the control system is

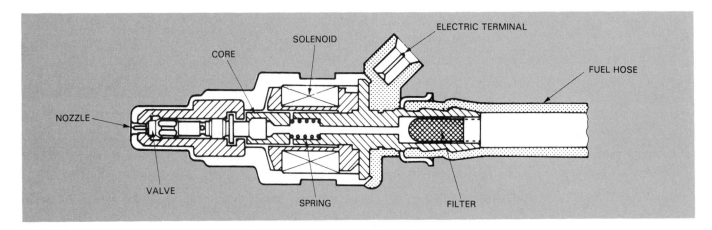

Fig. 9-56. Injector is opened when electric current is supplied to solenoid coil.
(Kawasaki Motors Corp., U.S.A.)

the MICROPROCESSOR (computer) which receives and processes information about engine operating conditions. This computer has complete control over fuel mixture delivery to the engine.

Once the electronic control system is activated through the starter relay, five conditions or variables are continuously monitored. These variables include airflow, engine speed, engine temperature, air temperature, and throttle position.

Airflow sensing

As described earlier, the function of the airflow meter is to monitor the amount of air entering the engine. This mixture adjustment is done electronically through the use of a potentiometer (pot). The potentiometer varies the circuit resistance and the electrical current flow to the control box as the air flap changes position. Movement of the air flap is translated into an electrical signal which indicates the amount of air entering the engine.

Engine speed sensing

The control box receives the engine speed signals from the ignition coils. This information is used to determine when to open the injectors. All the injectors are opened simultaneously every 360 deg. of crankshaft rotation. Therefore, fuel is injected into each intake port twice for each cycle of operation.

The length of time the injectors are open is determined by processing the information from all of the sensors.

Engine temperature sensing

The engine temperature sensor is mounted in the cylinder head and changes electrical resistance as the engine warms up. A cold engine requires a rich air-fuel ratio. Engine temperature signals are monitored by the control box and the air-fuel ratio is adjusted as needed.

Air temperature sensing

Air density changes with air temperature. Cool air is more dense than warm air. Since cooler, denser air has more oxygen, it requires more fuel to maintain the proper air-fuel ratio at any load or throttle opening. The air temperature sensor, mounted in the airflow meter housing, detects changes in air temperature and relays this information to the control box.

Throttle position sensing

The throttle position sensor, mounted on the end of the throttle shaft, tells the control box when the throttle valve is in the idle position or full throttle position. In both of these positions, the engine needs a richened air-fuel mixture. See Figs. 9-57 and 9-58.

COMPARISON OF FUEL INJECTION AND CARBURETION

After reading this description of EFI operation, you should be able to see some basic differences between an electronic fuel injection system and a carbureted fuel system.

The carbureted system mixes air and fuel using engine vacuum. It provides a predetermined air-fuel mixture to the engine. The EFI system monitors engine conditions and provides precise fuel delivery based on engine requirements.

As a result, an EFI system has the advantage of being able to make precise adjustments in the amount of fuel delivered to the engine. An electronic fuel injection system automatically compensates for varying engine operating conditions (riding in high altitudes, worn rings, changes in valve adjustment) that could alter the engine's air-fuel mixture ratio.

EFI SERVICE

Electronic fuel injection system service is somewhat different from carburetor service. Usually car-

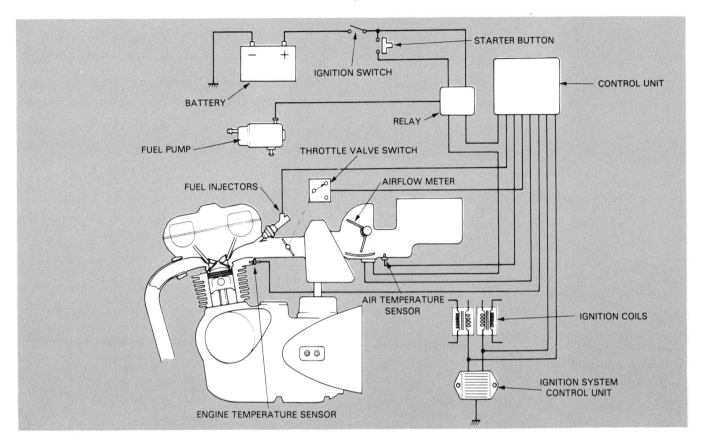

Fig. 9-57. Electronic control system monitors engine conditions and decides how long injectors should be opened. It also sends command pulses to injectors. (Kawasaki Motors Corp., U.S.A.)

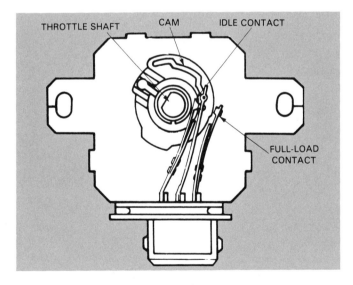

Fig. 9-58. Throttle position switch tells control box whether throttle is in idle or fully opened position by closing contacts. (Kawasaki Motors Corp., U.S.A.)

buretor service involves disassembly, cleaning, gasket replacement, and adjustment. EFI system service, however, typically consists of a visual inspection for air and fuel leaks, idle speed adjustment, throttle valve synchronization, and parts replacement. In addition, air and fuel filters and high pressure hoses are changed periodically.

The major components of the EFI system are NOT rebuildable and must be replaced if defective. Due to the complexity of the system, problem solving requires specific tests. These tests must be performed in the proper sequence with guidance from a factory service manual or troubleshooting guide.

CAUTION! Do not attempt to test the parts of an EFI system without following the specific procedures in a shop manual. The electronic system components can be damaged if tested improperly.

CARBURETOR ADJUSTMENT

To maintain the proper air-fuel mixture during the service life of the motorcycle, certain carburetor adjustments must be made. These common carburetor adjustments include:
1. Idle mixture.
2. Idle speed.
3. Multi-carburetor synchronization.
4. Float level.
5. Cable adjustment.

IDLE MIXTURE

Depending on carburetor type, IDLE MIXTURE is determined by either pilot jet size or an idle mixture screw setting. Under normal conditions, it is NOT necessary to change the pilot jet size. However, the air screw (slide type carburetor) or fuel screw (CV carburetor) may require occasional adjustment to improve idle smoothness.

Normally, turning a PILOT AIR SCREW clockwise (in) richens the idle mixture and turning it counterclockwise (out) leans the idle mixture. Turning a PILOT FUEL SCREW in leans the idle mixture and turning it out riches the idle mixture. Figs. 9-59 and 9-60 illustrate these adjustments.

IDLE SPEED

Engine IDLE SPEED is adjusted by means of a THROTTLE STOP screw. See Fig. 9-61. This screw

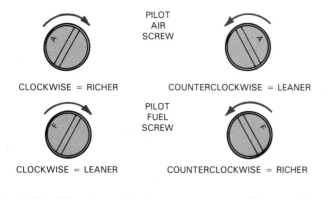

Fig. 9-59. Pilot air and fuel screws are turned in opposite directions to achieve same result.

Fig. 9-60. Turning a pilot air screw in (clockwise) richens air-fuel ratio since less air is admitted. Turning it out (counterclockwise) leans air-fuel ratio because more air is admitted.

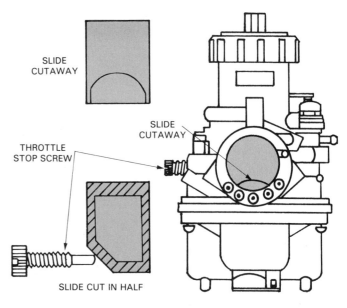

Fig. 9-61. A throttle stop screw is used to adjust idle speed by preventing slide or butterfly from closing completely. Stop screw may act directly on slide or on throttle linkage.

prevents the butterfly or throttle slide from closing completely. Engines with two or more cylinders may use a single stop screw which adjusts the position of the throttle linkage on all of the carburetors. This is shown in Fig. 9-62.

SYNCHRONIZATION

For maximum performance and smooth engine operation, all cylinders of an engine must work equally. If one carburetor has a larger throttle opening than another (twin or multi-cylinder engine), the cylinder with the larger opening is forced to work harder. This causes a rough running engine and possibly engine overheating.

Because cables can stretch and linkages can wear, it is necessary to periodically check and synchronize throttle openings on any engine using two or more carburetors.

Carburetor synchronization is checked using vacuum gauges. Visual inspection may also be used to verify synchronization. However, vacuum gauges are more accurate. Adjustment is accomplished by a cable adjuster or by linkage adjustment, Fig. 9-63.

Carburetor synchronization procedures are covered later in this chapter.

FLOAT LEVEL

FLOAT LEVEL refers to the level of fuel maintained in the float bowl. The proper level must be maintained for the carburetor to work properly. An improper carburetor float level can affect engine operation at any speed.

Changes in float level affect the air-fuel mixture. If

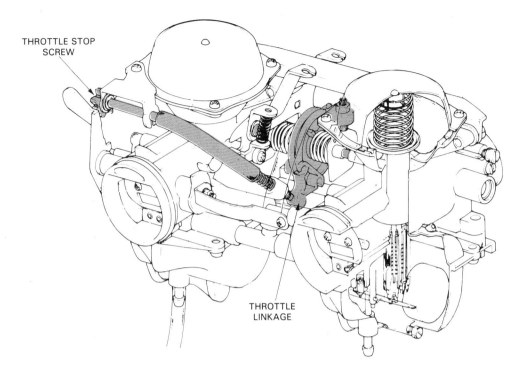

THROTTLE STOP
SCREW

THROTTLE
LINKAGE

Fig. 9-62. Engine idle speed is set by turning throttle stop screw attached to linkage. This opens or closes all carburetor throttles equally. (Kawasaki Motors Corp., U.S.A.)

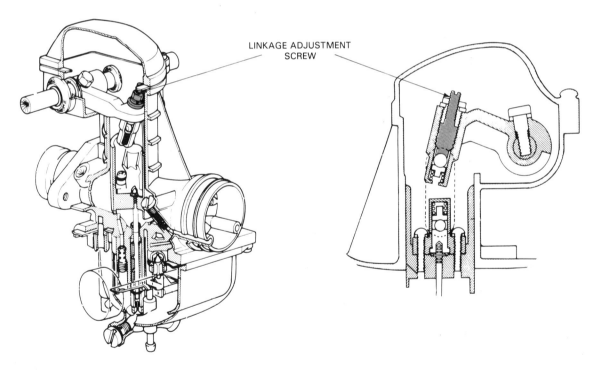

LINKAGE ADJUSTMENT
SCREW

Fig. 9-63. This is one type of linkage adjustment screw used to synchronize multiple carburetors. (Kawasaki Motors Corp., U.S.A.)

the float level is too low, more vacuum is required to draw fuel into the venturi. This produces a leaner mixture. Just the opposite, as the float level is raised, less vacuum is required, producing a richer mixture.

Manufacturer's specifications should be followed for float level settings. The float level can be checked in several ways. The most common method measures the distance from the carburetor base to the bottom of the float assembly with the float needle closed. This is illustrated in Fig. 9-64. The float level is adjusted by bending the tang on the float assembly. Look at Fig. 9-65.

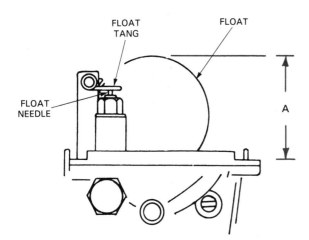

Fig. 9-64. Typically, to check float level, measure distance A with float tang just touching tip of float needle. Float level is high if measurement is less than specified in manual. Float level is low if measurement is larger than specified. (Yamaha Motor Corp., U.S.A.)

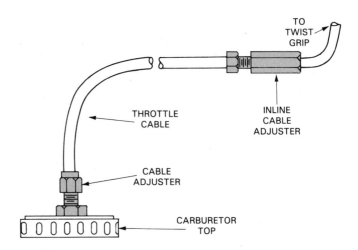

Fig. 9-66. Carburetor top cable adjuster and inline cable adjuster are two ways of adjusting throttle cable free play. Shortening outer cable housing increases cable free play.

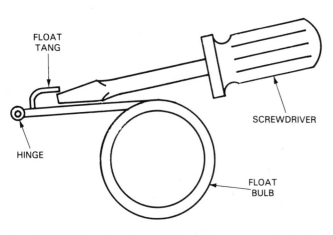

Fig. 9-65. If float level is too high, tang must usually be bent away from float. If float level is too low, bend tang carefully toward float. Slightest movement of tang makes a big difference in float level. Also, make sure float is not punctured and does not contain any fuel.

THROTTLE CABLE ADJUSTMENT

Proper throttle cable free play and synchronization is necessary for safe and smooth operation of the motorcycle engine.

Cable free play is adjusted at the top of the carburetor, at the throttle linkage, or by an inline cable adjuster. See Fig. 9-66. Free play is extremely important. A throttle with little or no free play can cause the engine to race when the handlebars are turned. The handlebar movement can strain and pull on the throttle cable causing the throttle to open. Manufacturer's specifications must be followed for throttle cable free play adjustment.

CARBURETOR JETTING

A carburetor jetting change will alter the air-fuel ratio in one or more of the carburetor circuits. Usual-ly jetting changes are used to compensate for changes in altitude or modifications to the engine.

At sea level, air is more dense than at higher altitudes. This requires larger jets so that more fuel will be mixed with the concentrated air. To achieve the proper air-fuel ratio at higher altitudes, smaller jets must be used. The air is thinner and requires less fuel.

Due to the many different designs of slide and CV carburetors, methods of changing jetting in individual circuits varies. For accurate information, refer to your service manual before making any jetting changes.

On many late model road bikes, provisions for making jetting changes in the idle and midrange circuits may be eliminated due to EPA regulations. It is common, however, for dirt bikes to require jetting changes.

With modifications to the air intake system, exhaust system, and engine, or if you live more than 1,000 feet (305 m) above sea level, jetting changes may be required. Use Fig. 9-67 and your service manual as a guide to change jetting in each of the carburetor circuits.

CAUTION! Because of federal emissions regulations, alterations affecting noise and pollution output levels are forbidden on late model motorcycles.

CARBURETOR REBUILDING

Usually, motorcycle carburetors require rebuilding because of a buildup of varnish and other deposits. This is generally the result of improper storage, as covered in Chapter 24. Occasionally carburetors need to be rebuilt as a result of normal wear. Improper air cleaner maintenance or removal of the air cleaner can accelerate wear. Carburetor rebuilding should also be done during an engine overhaul.

A typical carburetor rebuild consists of:

THROTTLE OPENING	CARBURETOR CIRCUIT	JETTING ADJUSTING PROCEDURE
Idle	Pilot circuit (CV and slide type carburetors)	1. Adjust air or fuel screw. 2. Install larger or smaller pilot jet (only if proper mixture cannot be attained by air or fuel screw adjustment).
Off-idle	Slide cutaway circuit (slide type carburetor)	1. Replace slide with one having higher or lower slide cutaway.
	Primary fuel circuit (CV carburetor)	1. Install larger or smaller primary jet.
	Bypass circuit (CV)	1. No adjustment available.
Midrange	Needle circuit (CV and slide type carburetors)	1. Adjust jet needle position by raising or lowering needle clip. 2. Install larger or smaller needle jet (only if proper mixture cannot be attained by needle clip adjustment).
Full throttle	Primary fuel circuit (CV carburetor)	1. Install larger or smaller primary jet.
	Main fuel circuit (CV and slide type carburetors)	1. Install larger or smaller main jet.

Fig. 9-67. Study procedures for adjusting carburetors. (Kawasaki Motors Corp., U.S.A.)

1. Carburetor removal.
2. Disassembly.
3. Cleaning.
4. Parts inspection and replacement.
5. Reassembly.
6. Float level adjustment.
7. Initial settings.
8. Carburetor installation.
9. Cable and linkage adjustments.
10. Final adjustments (engine at operating temperature).

CARBURETOR REMOVAL

Carburetors may be mounted to the engine in a number of ways. They may be mounted independently or together in a unit. A SLEEVE, SPIGOT, or FLANGE is used to attach the carburetor or carburetors to the engine. Refer to the proper service manual for correct carburetor removal procedures.

CARBURETOR DISASSEMBLY

Carburetors have a number of small parts that are easy to lose. Carburetor parts should always be placed in a shallow pan or container to prevent the loss of parts. See Fig. 9-68. Make sure you disassemble the carburetor with the proper tools to prevent damage to the carburetor body and other parts.

It is also important to note how the parts fit together. In particular, study the position of the needle clip and adjustment of the float. When more than one carburetor is disassembled, keep the parts for each carburetor separate.

If deposits (rust, dirt, water) are found in the float bowl, the fuel system may be contaminated. Replace all fuel filters. If needed, drain and flush the fuel system with clean fuel.

Make sure each carburetor is completely disassembled prior to cleaning, Fig. 9-69. This allows the solvent cleaner to reach all areas of the carburetor. It also prevents the accidental destruction of nylon, rubber, or fiber carburetor parts.

CARBURETOR CLEANING

Two types of carburetor cleaning solvents are available. One is the AEROSOL type which is used for external or light cleaning. This type is NOT adequate for carburetor rebuilding. The other type is a COLD SOAK cleaner which is ideal for thorough car-

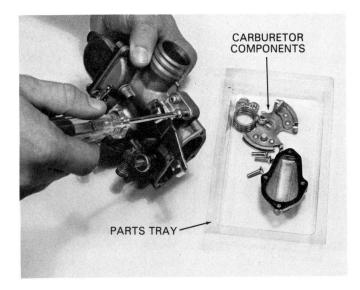

Fig. 9-68. Place disassembled carburetor parts in a clean, shallow pan to keep from losing small parts.

175

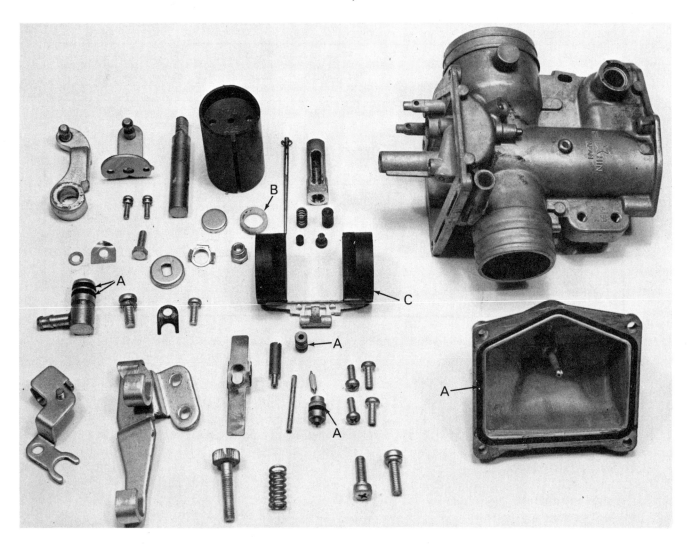

Fig. 9-69. Remove all rubber, fiber, and plastic parts before immersing carburetor in cleaner. A—Rubber O-rings. B—Plastic spacer ring. C—Plastic float assembly.

buretor cleaning. See Fig. 9-70. All metal carburetor parts are put in a basket and submerged in this type of cleaner.

Cold soak cleaner is VERY STRONG. It is important that:

1. No rubber, nylon, or fiber carburetor parts are put in cold soak cleaner.
2. Metal parts are not left in cold soak cleaner longer than 30 minutes.
3. Safety glasses and rubber gloves are worn to prevent burns.

When parts are removed from the cleaner, they should be thoroughly rinsed in warm water and dried with compressed air.

DANGER! If carburetor cleaner splashes into your eyes, seek medical attention. If it touches the skin, follow the directions given on the container.

PARTS INSPECTION AND REPLACEMENT

Once the carburetor body and parts are clean and dry, place them on a clean shop towel for inspection.

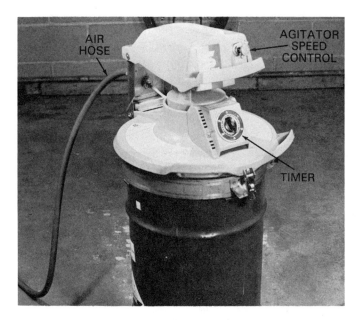

Fig. 9-70. Cold soak cleaner is commonly used during carburetor rebuilding.

The lack of a thorough inspection can nullify a carburetor rebuild.

Refer to the following list for proper carburetor parts inspection procedures.

1. Check jet orifices for obstructions.
2. Inspect float needle and seat for wear or pitting.
3. Check float assembly for holes, cracks, and proper seal.
4. Check carburetor body for varnish and corrosion.
5. Inspect all threads for damage.
6. Check carburetor mounting flange and float bowl seating surfaces for straightness.
7. Check the rubber tip on the enrichment plunger for damage.
8. Check carburetor slide for wear, damage, and freedom of movement through the length of the slide bore.

CARBURETOR REASSEMBLY

Carburetor reassembly is relatively simple, but must be done carefully. It is important to:

1. Use new gaskets and O-rings.
2. Make sure all jets and screws are properly tightened.
3. Check that the jet needle clip is seated properly and is in correct groove.
4. Make sure the pilot adjustment and throttle stop screws are installed in the proper holes.
5. Properly reassemble multiple carburetor linkage (linkage must work freely).

Most service manuals provide an exploded view of the complete carburetor. This helps ensure that the carburetor is reassembled correctly. A typical exploded view of a carburetor is shown in Fig. 9-71.

Initial settings

During reassembly, the float level should be checked and adjusted if necessary. The pilot adjustment screw should be set and multiple carburetor linkages visually synchronized. The shop manual gives specifications and procedures for initial settings or adjustments.

CARBURETOR INSTALLATION

To get the full benefit from a carburetor rebuild, proper installation is necessary. Mistakes during installation may result in air leaks, carburetor or manifold damage, and other problems. An AIR LEAK (vacuum leak) can cause a lean mixture, rough idle, and engine damage.

To avoid problems during carburetor installation:

1. Always use new carburetor mounting gaskets.
2. Check condition of O-rings and rubber flanges. Replace these parts if necessary.
3. Check the condition of the insulator block and replace if necessary.
4. Do not overtighten carburetor mounting bolts or

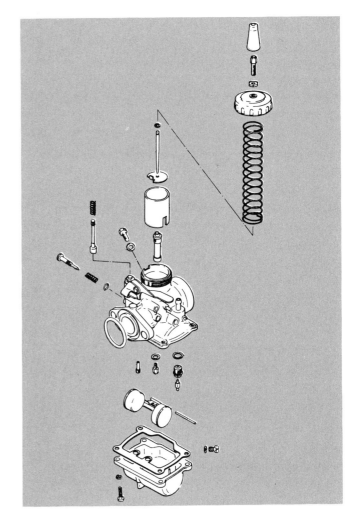

Fig. 9-71. A carburetor exploded view can be helpful during carburetor reassembly. It shows relative position of each part. (U.S. Suzuki Motor Corp.)

clamps.

5. Make sure carburetors are fully seated and straight in rubber mounting flanges.
6. Check throttle cable routing and freedom of operation.
7. Check and service air cleaner and air box.
8. Adjust cable free play.
9. Visually synchronize throttles on non-linkage type carburetors.
10. Check, clean, or replace fuel filter and petcock screen.

FINAL CARBURETOR ADJUSTMENT

The last carburetor adjustments are made with the engine operating. These include:

1. Throttle synchronization using vacuum gauges.
2. Final pilot screw adjustment.
3. Idle speed adjustment.

Using vacuum gauges for final synchronization

Use of a vacuum gauge is a positive way of comparing the throttle opening and airflow of two or more carburetors with the engine operating.

A vacuum gauge is connected between the throttle slide or plate and the intake valve on each cylinder. Look at Fig. 9-72. One gauge is required for each cylinder. Small changes in throttle opening will change the vacuum gauge reading, Fig. 9-73.

Proper throttle synchronization is achieved when all of the vacuum gauges read the same. If all readings are not the same, the linkage must be adjusted. Proper vacuum readings and procedures for linkage adjustment are outlined by the motorcycle manufacturer. Since linkage designs and vacuum specs vary, refer to your shop manual.

Basically, if one gauge reads lower than the others, its carburetor slide is open more than the others. You would need to lower the slide in that carburetor by adjusting its linkage. If one gauge reads higher than the others, its carburetor slide is closed more than the others and must be opened. Fig. 9-74 shows these two conditions. If two or more carburetors read the same,

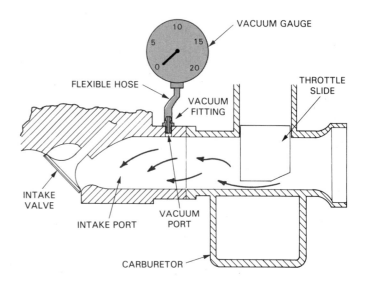

Fig. 9-72. A vacuum gauge is connected to intake tract between throttle slide or butterfly and intake valve. A vacuum port will be located in carburetor body or intake port.

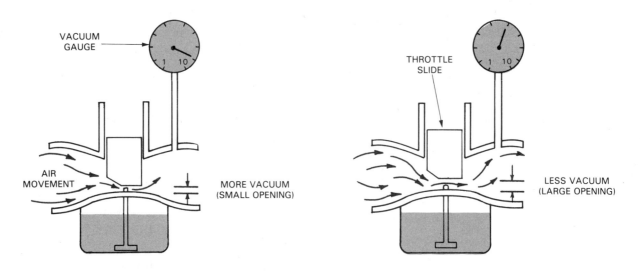

Fig. 9-73. Small changes in slide position (exaggerated in this illustration) will affect engine vacuum. Very slight changes in throttle slide position can be detected using a vacuum gauge.

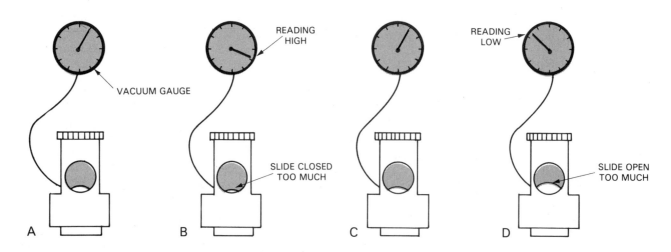

Fig. 9-74. In this example, vacuum readings on carburetors B and D show that adjustment is necessary. Throttle slide on carburetor B should be raised to lower vacuum. Throttle slide on carburetor D should be lowered to raise vacuum.

Fig. 9-75. Note location of pilot screw on this particular motorcycle.

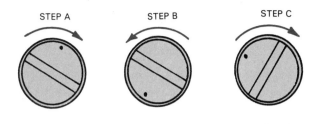

STEP A	STEP B	STEP C
IN (CLOCKWISE) UNTIL ENGINE FALTERS	OUT (COUNTERCLOCKWISE) UNTIL ENGINE FALTERS	IN 1/2 AMOUNT OF STEPS A AND B

Fig. 9-76. This is one way of adjusting pilot screws. Engine must be fully warmed and running for proper adjustment.

leave them alone and adjust the others.

NOTE! Idle speed should be reset after carburetor synchronization.

Final pilot adjustment

Some manufacturers recommend a specific pilot screw setting. For example, you may have to turn the pilot screw 3/4 to 1 turn out. During this adjustment, the engine does not have to be operating. See Fig. 9-75.

In other cases, an initial pilot setting is given and final adjustment is done with the engine running at operating temperature. To adjust with the engine running, turn the pilot screw in until engine rpm begins to drop. Then, turn the pilot screw back out until engine rpm begins to drop. The desired adjustment is HALFWAY between these two drop off points, Fig. 9-76.

Final idle speed adjustment

Manufacturer's specifications should be followed for idle speed adjustment.

Any twin or multi-cylinder engine which has individual throttle stop screws requires accurate adjustment of each stop screw. This is needed to insure a smooth idle. Twin or multi-cylinder engines that use positive linkage to operate the throttles will have a single idle adjustment screw.

CARBURETOR REBUILDING SUMMARY

Use the following summary when rebuilding a motorcycle carburetor. It will help you do a complete

and professional job.

1. Clean and degrease motorcycle.
2. Remove fuel tank (if necessary).
3. Drain fuel from carburetors.
4. Disconnect throttle cables.
5. Disconnect choke cables or linkage (if needed).
6. Remove air filters or air box (if necessary).
7. Loosen carburetor mounting hardware and remove carburetor.
8. Check condition of rubber mounting sleeves or insulator blocks.
9. Tape or plug off intake port.
10. Disassemble carburetor throttle linkage (if applicable).
11. Remove carbs from mounting block (if applicable).
12. Remove float bowls.
13. Check and record float level measurements.
14. Disassemble carburetors completely and record needle settings.
15. Remove all plastic, fiber, and rubber parts.
16. Soak metal parts in cold soak cleaner (30 minutes maximum). Use safety glasses and rubber gloves.
17. Wash parts in warm water and air dry thoroughly.
18. Organize all parts on a clean shop towel.
19. Inspect parts for wear, damage, and cleanliness.
20. Reassemble carburetors using new parts where necessary. Replace all gaskets and O-rings. Adjust needle position.
21. Adjust float level to specifications.
22. Remount carburetors on mounting block (if applicable).
23. Visually synchronize throttle linkage (multi-cylinder engines).
24. Set pilot adjustment screws (initial setting).
25. Set idle speed stop screws to lowest setting.
26. Remount carburetors on engine.
27. Install air cleaners or air box.
28. Connect throttle and choke cables.
29. Adjust cable free play.
30. Visually synchronize throttles (multi-cable designs).
31. Inspect fuel tank for rust, varnish, and foreign

32. Clean fuel tank (if needed).
33. Clean fuel petcock filter.
34. Install fuel tank.
35. Connect all fuel lines and vacuum lines (vacuum operated petcock).
36. Turn on fuel and check for leaks.
37. Install vacuum gauges (twin or multi-cylinder engines).
38. Start engine, warm up, and set idle speed.
39. Adjust pilot mixture.
40. Synchronize carburetors using vacuum gauges.
41. Reset idle speed.
42. Remove vacuum gauges.
43. Road test.

KNOW THESE TERMS

Petcock, Intake manifold, Throttle, Twist grip, Sediment bowl, Positive carburetor linkage, Atomization, Air-fuel ratio, Rich mixture, Lean mixture, Vacuum controlled carburetor, Butterfly carburetor, EFI, Airflow meter, Pressure regulator, Fuel injector, Microprocessor, Idle mixture, Synchronization, Jetting, Carburetor rebuild.

REVIEW QUESTIONS—Chapter 9

1. A fuel tank must be _____ to prevent a buildup of vacuum or pressure.
2. When is a fuel pump needed on a motorcycle?
3. Why are two throttle cables used on some twist grips?
4. Proper fuel atomization affects engine performance and _____.
5. What is a typical air-fuel ratio at cruising speeds?
6. What does a carburetor venturi do?
7. List the three common carburetor types.
8. Name the carburetor NOT using a throttle cable to directly operate the throttle slide.
9. List the seven systems or circuits of a slide carburetor.
10. The _____ circuit controls air-fuel mixture from 1/4 to 3/4 throttle.
11. The two types of needle circuits are the _____ and _____.
12. Which of the slide carburetor circuits is easiest to adjust?
13. Why is an accelerator pump sometimes necessary?
14. What are the three common types of starter systems?
15. Air for the enrichment circuit bypasses the carburetor throat and venturi. True or False?
16. The enrichment circuit works best when the throttle is open. True or False?
17. Which of the following is NOT monitored by the electronic fuel injection microprocessor?
    a. Airflow.
    b. Air temperature.
    c. Fuel pressure.
    d. Engine rpm.
    e. Engine temperature.
    f. Throttle position.
18. List the three subsystems of a fuel injection system.
19. What is an electronic fuel injector?
20. Explain the operation of the electronic control unit in an EFI system.
21. Turn a carburetor pilot air screw _____ to richen the mixture and _____ to lean the mixture.
22. Turn a carburetor pilot fuel screw _____ to richen the mixture and _____ to lean the mixture.
23. What measurement instrument is used to verify throttle synchronization?
24. Carburetor rebuilding should be done during an engine overhaul. True or False?
25. What must be done, in addition to carburetor rebuilding, if rust or water is present in the carburetor?
26. List three precautions when using a cold soak cleaner.
27. New gaskets should always be used when rebuilding a carburetor. True or False?
28. Improper carburetor installation can sometimes cause an _____ _____.
29. List the three final carburetor adjustments.
30. When one vacuum gauge reads low during synchronization, this indicates that the carburetor slide is too _____.
31. When one vacuum gauge reads too high during synchronization, this indicates that the carburetor slide is too _____.

SUGGESTED ACTIVITIES

1. Disassemble a slide type carburetor and a vacuum type carburetor. Make a list of the differences between the two.
2. List which make motorcycle uses each of the following types of carburetors:
    a. Slide type.
    b. CV with vacuum piston.
    c. CV with vacuum diaphragm.
    d. Butterfly type.
3. For each of the carburetors in the activity number two, determine the following:
    a. Type of pilot mixture adjustment (air screw or fuel screw).
    b. Type of needle circuit (bleeder or primary).
    c. Type of starter system.
    d. Is an accelerator pump used?
4. Complete a carburetor overhaul using the Carburetor Rebuilding Summary and a shop manual.
5. Synchronize a set of carburetors using specific service manual instructions.

Chapter 10

IGNITION SYSTEMS

After studying this chapter, you will be able to:
- ☐ Describe the operating principles of a basic ignition system.
- ☐ Explain the function of each major part of an ignition system.
- ☐ Define vacuum and centrifugal advance.
- ☐ Compare contact point, magneto, and electronic type ignition systems.

The efficient operation of a motorcycle engine requires a well maintained ignition system. Even when all other systems are in perfect working condition, a malfunctioning or imporperly adjusted ignition system can cause poor engine performance or even a mechanical breakdown.

This chapter discusses the operation and design of common motorcycle ignition systems. This is an important chapter because it prepares you for later textbook chapters on Tune-up and Troubleshooting. Before you can learn to perform diagnosis, service, and repair operations, you must have a complete understanding of how modern ignition systems operate. Study this material carefully!

IGNITION SYSTEM OPERATION

An ignition system is used to start controlled combustion (burning of air-fuel mixture) in the engine. It must produce a "hot" spark at just the exact moment, during the end of the compression stroke.

Most motorcycle ignition systems are powered by the battery. The ignition system must step up battery voltage (approximately 12 volts) to 20,000 volts or more. This high voltage is needed to "fire" the spark plug. An IGNITION COIL, Fig. 10-1, is a transformer used to provide this voltage increase.

A switching device driven by the crankshaft or camshaft is used to trigger the ignition coil at the proper time. See Fig. 10-2. Some systems have con-

tact points. More modern systems use a magnetic-electronic switching device.

Many dual-purpose and off-road motorcycles use the magneto or energy transfer system. In this system, the ignition is powered by the alternator. Fig. 10-3 il-

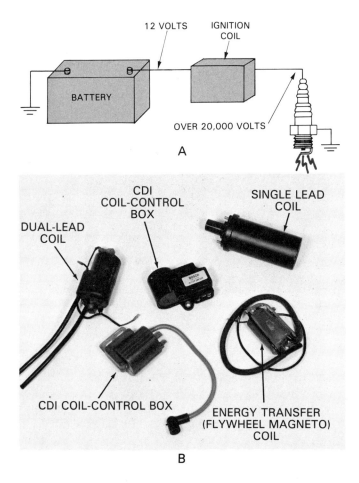

Fig. 10-1. An ignition coil steps up battery voltage from 12 volts to over 20,000 volts to fire spark plug. A—Basic action of coil. B—Different types of coils.

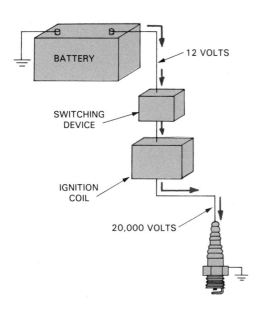

Fig. 10-2. Contact points or a magnetic trigger and electronic control box are used to operate ignition coil and fire spark plug.

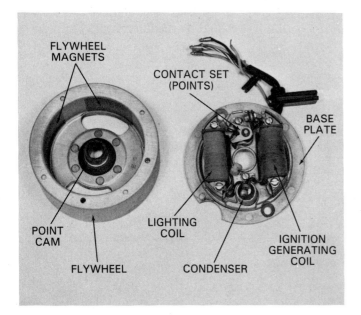

Fig. 10-3. A magneto ignition system is used on many small, dual-purpose motorcycles. If accessories are required, a battery is used along with magneto. A lighting circuit in magneto provides for battery recharging.

lustrates a typical magneto ignition system.

Normal engine operation requires the ignition system to produce an intense spark at the spark plug gap. It must overcome its own internal resistances as well as resistance caused by compression in the combustion chamber. Additional resistances to spark plug operation can be caused by:
1. Extremely rich or lean air-fuel mixtures.
2. Deposits on the spark plug (oil blow-by, low speed riding habits, contamainated fuel and air).

3. Increased engine load.
4. Excessive plug gap.

When the ignition system is functioning properly, it supplies enough voltage at the spark plug to overcome system and combustion chamber resistance. Recently, the job of the ignition system has become even more difficult because of lean air-fuel mixtures which are harder to ignite. Lean mixtures improve exhaust emission levels.

Two important factors in ignition system operation are intensity of the spark and timing of the spark.

SPARK INTENSITY

Proper combustion requires a "healthy" electric arc at the spark plug. SPARK INTENSITY refers to the amount of voltage and the duration of the spark at the spark plug. A satisfactory spark provides sufficient voltage for a long enough period of time to reliably ignite the air-fuel mixture.

Ignition system performance depends upon several components within the system. If any of these components are marginal, spark intensity and engine performance may deteriorate.

IGNITION TRIGGERING

In all ignition systems, the spark is triggered by a switching device. This switch may be a set of CONTACT POINTS or a magnetic-electronic device. See Fig. 10-4. This switching device determines the frequency of spark, depending on where it is located. These switching devices may be located:
1. On the end of the crankshaft (frequency of operation − 360 deg.).
2. On the end of a camshaft (frequency of operation − 720 deg.).
3. On a crankshaft driven idler (frequency of operation − 360 or 720 deg., depending on idler ratio).

A means of adjusting ignition timing is usually provided. The triggering device can be rotated in relation to the crankshaft, camshaft, or idler.

IGNITION TIMING

Since combustion is a controlled burning process rather than a rapid explosion, combustion must begin at the proper instant. It must begin near the end of the compression stroke, before TDC. Since combustion takes time for completion, ignition must occur so that maximum cylinder heat and pressure develops right after TDC. This is illustrated in Fig. 10-5.

In A, spark occurs with piston traveling up on the compression stroke. Then, in B, combustion has finally formed maximum heat and pressure to force piston down in cylinder for power stroke.

As engine speed increases, ignition timing must be advanced (occur earlier) because the piston will be moving faster. There would be less time for the air-fuel mixture to burn. See Fig. 10-6. This increase in

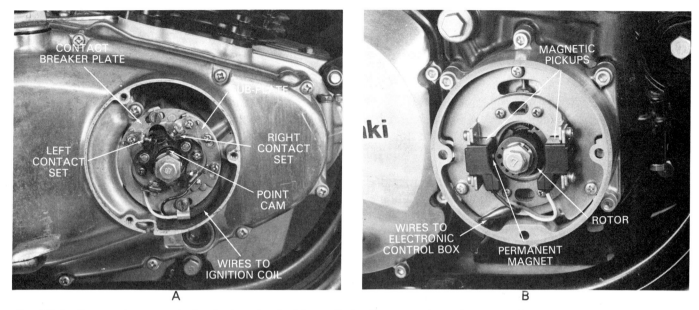

Fig. 10-4. Two common methods of triggering ignition coil. A—Contact points trigger coil directly by opening and closing. B—Magnetic trigger operates electronic unit. Control unit then interrupts current flow to ignition coil, which fires coil.

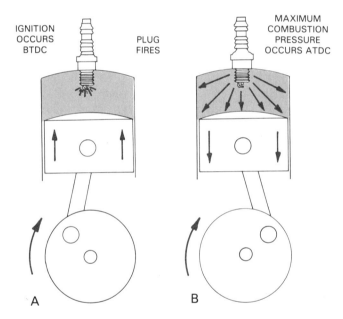

Fig. 10-5. Combustion must begin before TDC so that maximum heat and pressure develops just after TDC.

ENGINE SPEED	CRANKSHAFT DEG. REQUIRED TO ALLOW FOR COMBUSTION TIME LAPSE
3,000 rpm	25 deg.
6,000 rpm	35 deg.

Fig. 10-6. As engine speed increases, initial combustion must occur earlier.

Fig. 10-7. A centrifugal advance makes use of centrifugal force to advance ignition timing as engine rpm increases. Spring strength determines advance curve (amount of advance compared to engine speed). Stops determine maximum advance.

ignition spark lead or advance can be accomplished by:
1. Centrifugal advance.
2. Vacuum advance.
3. Electronic advance.

Centrifugal advance

A CENTRIFUGAL ADVANCE UNIT causes the spark to occur sooner as engine rpm increases. This improves engine efficiency and power. A centrifugal advance mechanism uses SPRING-LOADED WEIGHTS attached to the point cam or rotor, Fig. 10-7. As engine speed increases, the weights are

thrown outward by centrifugal force.

With a point type ignition, movement of the weights rotate the point cam so that the points open earlier. With an electronic type ignition, the movement of the weights act on the rotor (trigger wheel) to make the spark plug fire sooner. This gives the air-fuel mixture more time to burn at higher rpm.

Vacuum advance

A VACUUM ADVANCE UNIT advances or retards ignition timing in order to increase fuel economy. Vacuum produced in the carburetor controls movement of a vacuum diaphragm attached to the ignition base plate, Fig. 10-8.

Since engine vacuum is an indicator of engine load, vacuum can match ignition timing to the engine's needs. Under heavy loads, vacuum drops and timing is retarded. This prevents too much advance and possible detonation or spark knock. Then under moderate loads, engine vacuum increases. Suction pulls on the diaphragm and rotates the base plate. This advances the timing and improves engine efficiency.

Electronic advance

ELECTRONIC ADVANCE of ignition timing is found in magneto supported CDI (capacitor discharge ignition) systems and some transistorized ignition systems. Advance increases as rpm increases due to physical properties of magnetism and induction. Solid state devices may be used to modify or limit the advance curve. Operation of an electronic advance is covered later in this chapter.

FREQUENCY OF SPARK

FREQUENCY OF SPARK refers to the number of times a spark plug fires during one cycle of operation for any given cylinder. For example, in some engines, the spark plug fires once in every cycle while in others the spark plug fires twice. Ignition system design determines frequency of spark.

Four-stroke cycle

A four-stroke cycle engine requires an ignition spark for each cylinder every 720 deg. of crankshaft rotation. The spark must occur during the compression stroke. This is illustrated in Fig. 10-9.

Some twin and multi-cylinder engines use a single ignition system which fires two cylinders. As shown in Fig. 10-10, both spark plugs fire at the same time. One of the spark plugs initiates combustion and the

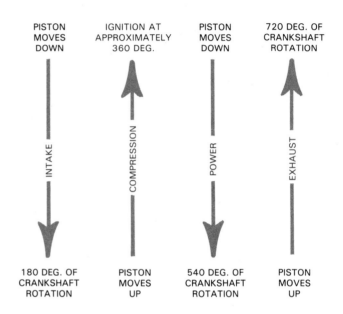

Fig. 10-9. Ignition spark required once every 720 deg. of crankshaft rotation with four-stroke cycle engine.

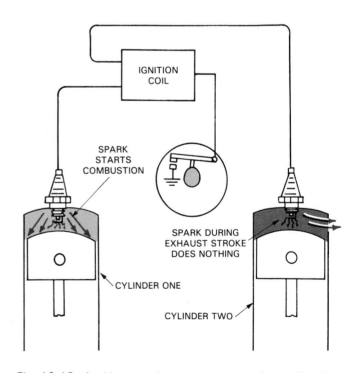

Fig. 10-10. In this example, one contact breaker and ignition coil fires spark plugs in both cylinders of two-cylinder engine. One cylinder is on compression stroke, other is on exhaust stroke.

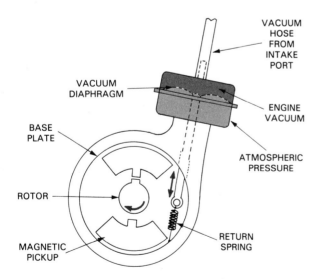

Fig. 10-8. Engine vacuum pulls on diaphragm to rotate and advance electronic pickup for increased efficiency. When engine load goes up, vacuum drops and spring retards timing to prevent spark knock.

other does nothing. It fires with the exhaust valve open, Fig. 10-11. This is done for purposes of economy, simplicity, and emission control.

Other engines may use a separate ignition system for each cylinder. Notice that in Fig. 10-12 each cylinder has its own breaker mechanism and ignition coil.

Two-stroke cycle

All two-stroke cycle engines require a separate ignition system for each cylinder. This is necessary

because each spark plug must fire once for every cycle of operation (360 deg.). See Fig. 10-13.

TYPES OF IGNITION SYSTEMS

Motorcycles use three basic types of ignition systems: battery and coil, flywheel magneto, and electronic. It is important that you understand the similarities and differences of each type.

BATTERY AND COIL IGNITION

The BATTERY AND COIL IGNITION SYSTEM is used on a majority of motorcycles. This is a relatively inexpensive and dependable system which has been in use for many years.

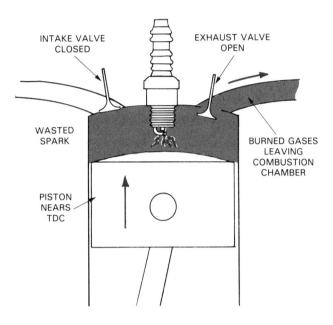

Fig. 10-11. When cylinder one is on compression stroke, cylinder two is on exhaust stroke. Since both spark plugs fire at same time, one makes power and two has a wasted spark at end of exhaust stroke. When two is on compression, one has wasted spark.

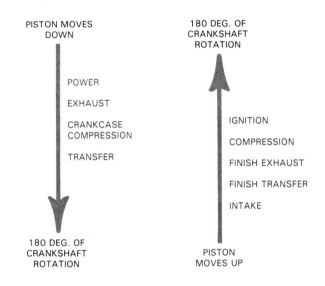

Fig. 10-13. Ignition spark required once every 360 deg. of crankshaft rotation with two-stroke cycle engine.

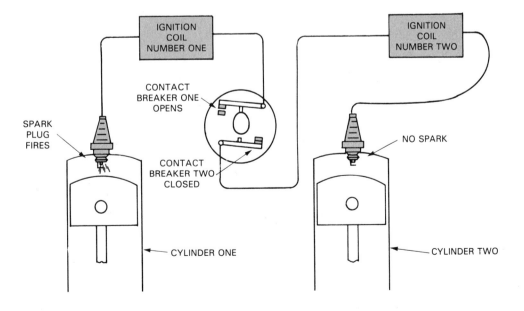

Fig. 10-12. Each cylinder has its own ignition coil and contact breaker which operate independently. Each plug fires on compression stroke to start combustion.

A battery and coil ignition system can be triggered either by contact points or by a magnetic-transistor triggering device. When a magnetic trigger is used, it is called a TRANSISTORIZED IGNITION SYSTEM. See Fig. 10-14.

A battery and coil ignition system is made up of two circuits: primary (low voltage) circuit and secondary (high voltage) circuit.

Before covering the details of these circuits, you must first have a better understanding of the operation of an ignition coil.

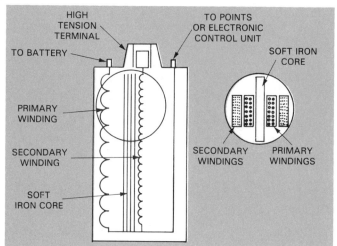

Fig. 10-15. An ignition coil consists of primary and secondary windings wrapped around a soft iron core. About 200 turns of coarse wire are used for primary windings. About 20,000 turns of fine wire are used for secondary windings

Fig. 10-14. When a magnetic trigger is used to fire a battery and coil ignition, it is called a transistor ignition.

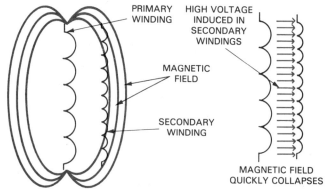

Fig. 10-16. Current flowing through primary windings of coil causes build up of magnetic field. As contact points or electronic circuit stops current, magnetic field collapses. This induces current and high voltage in secondary windings.

Ignition coil operation

The ignition coil is the "heart" of the ignition system. It is a simple step-up transformer. The ignition coil relies on induction to step up battery voltage (12 volts) to approximately 20,000 volts. An extremely high voltage is needed to make electricity jump the gap at the spark plug.

The ignition coil is made up of a primary winding and a secondary winding, as shown in Fig. 10-15. The SECONDARY WINDING is approximately 20,000 turns of fine wire wound around an iron core. The PRIMARY WINDING consists of approximately 200 turns of coarse wire wound around the secondary windings.

When current (battery voltage) flows through the coil primary windings, a magnetic field is built up. When the current flow through the primary windings is abruptly stopped, the magnetic field rapidly collapses. This collapse causes high voltage (15,000 to 20,000 volts) to be induced in the secondary windings, Fig. 10-16. This dramatic step-up in voltage results from the difference in the turns of wire in the primary and secondary. The high voltage then flows to the spark plug where it produces an electric arc to start combustion.

Ignition primary circuit

A basic battery and coil IGNITION PRIMARY CIRCUIT is made up of:
1. A battery.
2. An ignition switch.
3. A condenser.
4. Contact points.
5. Ignition coil primary windings.
6. Interconnecting circuit wiring.

See Fig. 10-17. All of the components using low voltage (battery voltage) are included in the ignition primary. The battery provides power to the primary circuit when the ignition switch is turned on.

The CONTACT POINTS make and break the primary circuit to fire the coil. Look at Fig. 10-18. When the contacts are closed, voltage flows through the coil primary windings, causing a magnetic field to build in the ignition coil. When the contacts open, current flow is stopped, collapsing the magnetic field

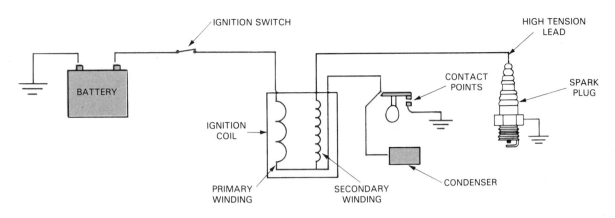

Fig. 10-17. This schematic represents a simple battery and coil ignition system. Wires and components in primary circuit are colored.

in the coil. The field cuts across the secondary windings to produce 20,000 volts for spark plug operation.

A CONDENSER is provided to minimize contact point arcing. It absorbs extra current flow to prevent point sparking and burning. Condenser operation can be broken down into two phases: initial breaking of the contact points and self-induced voltage surge.

As the contacts initially open, the condenser absorbs current which would otherwise try to jump across the opening contacts. As a result of the rapid collapse of the magnetic field and build up of secondary voltage, a high voltage is also induced in the primary windings. This high voltage also tries to arc across the contacts. When arcing occurs, contact surfaces are eroded and coil collapse is slowed. This reduces secondary voltage.

When the contacts close again, the condenser discharges and helps in rapid COIL BUILDUP. The condenser feeds stored electricity back into the system. Condenser operation is shown in Fig. 10-19.

Ignition secondary circuit

A basic battery and coil IGNITION SECONDARY CIRCUIT is made up of:

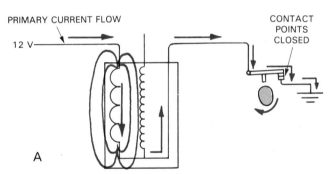

WITH CONTACT POINTS CLOSED, CURRENT THROUGH PRIMARY CIRCUIT CAUSES MAGNETIC FIELD BUILDUP IN PRIMARY COIL WINDINGS.

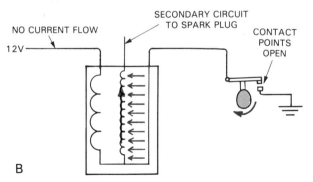

WHEN CONTACT POINTS OPEN, CURRENT FLOW IN CIRCUIT STOPS. THIS CAUSES MAGNETIC FIELD TO COLLAPSE, INDUCING CURRENT AND HIGH VOLTAGE IN SECONDARY CIRCUIT. HIGH VOLTAGE SHOOTS OUT COIL AND TO SPARK PLUG.

Fig. 10-18. Study basic ignition coil and primary circuit operation. A—Points closed. B—Points open.

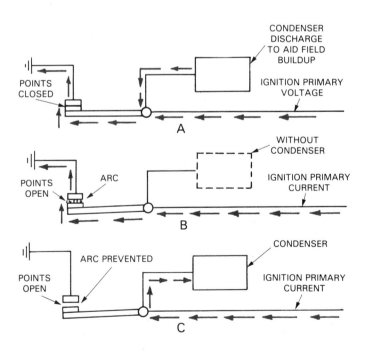

Fig. 10-19. Condenser action. A—Contact points are closed and primary circuit is completed to ground. Charged condenser feeds current into circuit. B—Without condenser, arc occurs at contacts as points open, which would burn contacts. C—Condenser absorbs and stores current to prevent point arcing and burning.

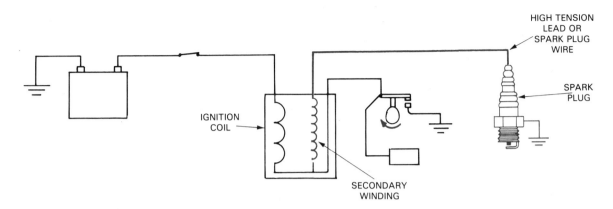

Fig. 10-20. Schematic shows all wiring and components of secondary circuit in red.

1. Ignition coil secondary windings.
2. Spark plug wire (high tension lead).
3. Spark plug terminal.
4. Spark plug.

The ignition secondary includes all of the components which operate on high coil output voltage. See Fig. 10-20. When the ignition coil voltage is stepped up, the spark plug wire (high tension wire) carries this voltage to the spark plug.

SPARK PLUG

The SPARK PLUG provides a spark gap in the combustion chamber of the engine. This gap is between a ground electrode and a center electrode. The center electrode is attached to the spark plug wire, Fig. 10-21. High voltage jumps between the two electrodes. The resulting heat ignites the air-fuel mixture in the combustion chamber.

TRANSISTORIZED (ELECTRONIC) IGNITION

A TRANSISTORIZED or ELECTRONIC IGNITION is a battery and coil ignition system which uses a magnetic triggering device and solid state control box. The magnetic triggering device and electronic control box replace the contact points. They operate the ignition primary circuit. The magnetic device (magnet and pickup coil unit) generates a small pulse of electrical current. This electrical pulse is used to trigger the electronic control box and ignition.

Fig. 10-22 shows both a contact point and a transistorized ignition system. Note the similarities and differences between the two types.

A typical transistorized ignition system consists of:
1. Rotor (trigger wheel).
2. Magnetic pickup (impulse generator).
3. Control box (electronic switching device).
4. Ignition coil (step-up transformer).
5. Interconnecting wiring (primary wire).
6. Spark plug wire (secondary wire).
7. Spark plug (device for igniting air-fuel mixture).
A transistor ignition system is pictured in Fig. 10-23. Note where the parts are located on the motorcycle.

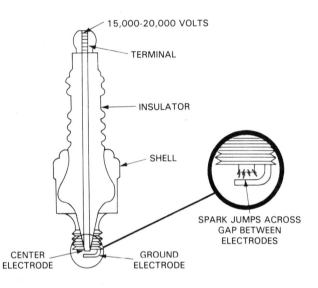

Fig. 10-21. Spark plug provides an electric arc between center electrode and ground electrode. This arc is used to ignite air-fuel mixture in combustion chamber.

Transistorized ignition operation

Power from the battery goes through the ignition switch to a solid state control box. Look at Fig. 10-24. An electric impulse from the rotor and magnetic pickup signals the control box to switch battery current on and off to the ignition coil primary windings. When current is switched off in the coil primary windings, the spark plug fires.

The rotor and magnetic pickup resemble a contact breaker plate and point cam, and are mounted similarly (on end of crankshaft or camshaft). The PICKUP ASSEMBLY consists of a small permanent magnet and coil. The ROTOR (trigger wheel) is used to cut the magnetic field of the pickup coil permanent magnet. This induces a tiny electrical current in the pickup coil windings. Fig. 10-25 shows how current is induced in a pickup coil. The control box uses this current pulse to operate the ignition coil. This type of rotor and pickup assembly is called a DARLINGTON GENERATOR.

Another type of magnetic trigger uses a Hall In-

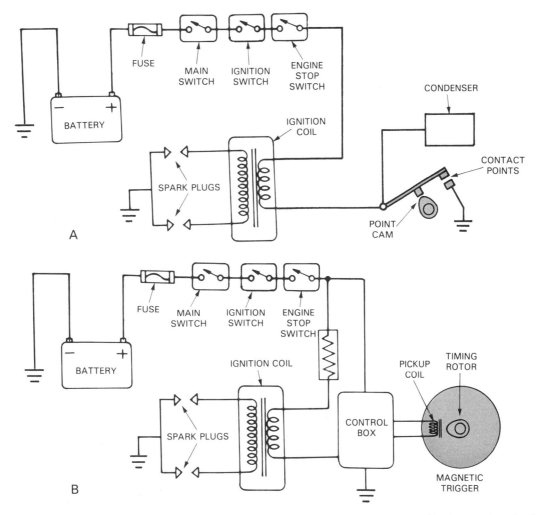

A

B

Fig. 10-22. Compare contact point and transistor type ignitions. A—Contact point ignition. B—In transistorized ignition, magnetic triggering device (pickup coil and timing rotor) generate small electrical pulse. Control box uses this pulse to switch primary current through ignition coil on and off. (Kawasaki Motors Corp., U.S.A.)

Fig. 10-23. These components make up a typical transistorized ignition system. Upper left. Note control box location. Fins help dissipate heat out of electronic circuit.

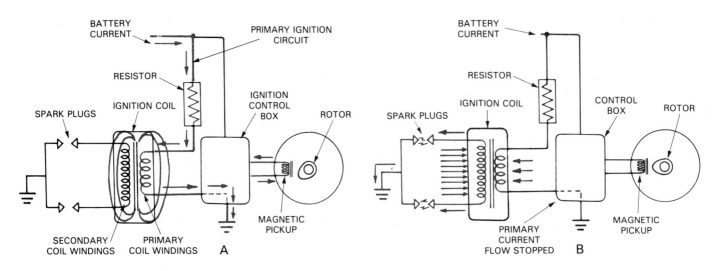

Fig. 10-24. A—With rotor away from magnetic pickup, current flows through coil primary and control box. Magnetic field builds in coil. B—As rotor moves past pickup, pulse from pickup coil causes control box to open primary circuit. Magnetic field in primary coil windings collapses and induces current in secondary which makes spark plugs fire. (Kawasaki Motors Corp., U.S.A.)

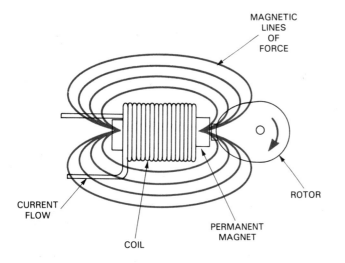

Fig. 10-25. Current is induced in magnetic pickup coil windings when rotor cuts magnetic lines of force.

tegrated Circuit (IC) to generate signal voltage. This type is called a HALL EFFECT TRANSISTORIZED IGNITION. A Hall IC diverts electric current when it is exposed to a magnetic field, Fig. 10-26. The diverted current is used to signal the control box.

The Hall IC and a permanent magnet are separated by a rotating disc, Fig. 10-27. The disc has a hole cut in it. The disc prevents the magnetic field from reaching the Hall IC until the hole, Hall IC, and magnet are aligned. At this point, current is diverted in the Hall IC and sent to the control box. The control box then triggers ignition, Fig. 10-28.

All motorcycle transistorized ignition systems work in basically the same way, however, there are variations in appearance and operation. We have covered two common methods of providing a signal voltage to the control box. Other ignition system variations include the different ways of controlling ignition ad-

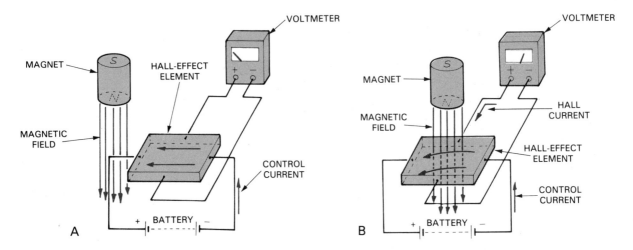

Fig. 10-26. Hall IC operation. A—Current from battery flows lengthwise through Hall-effect element. B—When Hall-effect element is exposed to a magnetic field, some current is diverted into separate circuit. Current then flows crosswise through element. This Hall current is used to signal electronic control box. (Kawasaki Motors Corp., U.S.A.)

Fig. 10-27. This six-cylinder engine uses three pickup (trigger) assemblies, each consisting of a permanent magnet and Hall IC. Timing holes in steel disc allow magnetic field from permanent magnet to reach Hall IC, triggering ignition.

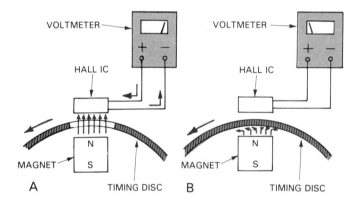

Fig. 10-28. A—When hole in timing rotor lines up with Hall IC and magent, Hall current is generated. B—Solid part of timing disc prevents magnetic field from reaching Hall IC and no Hall current is produced. (Kawasaki Motors Corp., U.S.A.)

vance and dwell. Ignition advance may be a centrifugal advance, vacuum advance, or electronic advance controlled by the control box. Dwell may be controlled by the type of signal from the pickup or electronically by the circuit in the control box.

FLYWHEEL MAGNETO IGNITION

The FLYWHEEL MAGNETO IGNITION SYSTEM uses alternating current rather than direct (battery) current, to power the ignition system. Shown in Fig. 10-29, a typical flywheel magneto ignition system is made up of:
1. A flywheel.

2. An ignition generating coil.
3. Contact points.
4. A condenser.
5. An ignition coil.

The current to power this type ignition system is produced by the FLYWHEEL MAGNETS. The magnets induce current in the IGNITION GENERATING COIL. This is illustrated in Fig. 10-30.

Two types of flywheel magneto ignition systems are used on motorcycles. One type produces a high secondary voltage as a result of the magnetic field COLLAPSE. The other uses a rapid BUILD UP (surge) of the magnetic field to induce high secondary voltage.

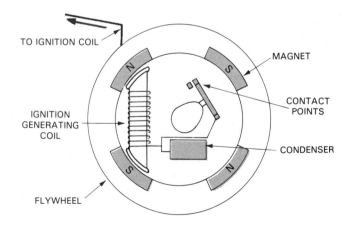

Fig. 10-29. A flywheel magneto is a simple and compact ignition system.

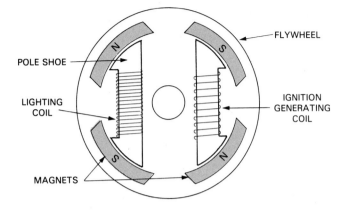

Fig. 10-30. In a flywheel magneto, current is induced in windings of ignition generating coil as flywheel magnets spin past pole shoes.

Field collapse magneto

A FIELD COLLAPSE MAGNETO ignition system works much like a battery and coil ignition system. The major difference is that alternating current is used instead of direct current. See Fig. 10-31.

Alternating current is produced in the ignition generating coil. This current causes a magnetic field to form around the ignition coil primary windings. When the contact points open, the field is abruptly collapsed and high voltage is induced in the secondary windings. This fires the spark plug.

Field buildup magneto

The FIELD BUILDUP MAGNETO ignition system makes use of rapid magnetic field buildup to induce high voltage in the secondary windings. See Fig. 10-32. The same components are used for this system as in the field collapse type magneto. The major difference is in the way the contacts are wired into the circuit.

In this system, closed contacts prevent primary current flow in the ignition coil. When the contacts open, current surges into the primary windings. This causes such a rapid magnetic field buildup that high voltage is induced in the ignition coil secondary windings. The contacts are timed to open just as maximum current is produced in the generating coil.

CAPACITOR DISCHARGE IGNITION (CDI)

A CAPACITOR DISCHARGE IGNITION, abbreviated CDI, is another form of electronic ignition system. It uses solid state components to control coil operation. Two possible advantages of a CDI are:
1. Low maintenance requirements (no moving parts to wear out).
2. Extremely high secondary voltage is available (25,000 to 45,000 volts).

One drawback of a CDI system is that most components are not repairable and they are costly to replace.

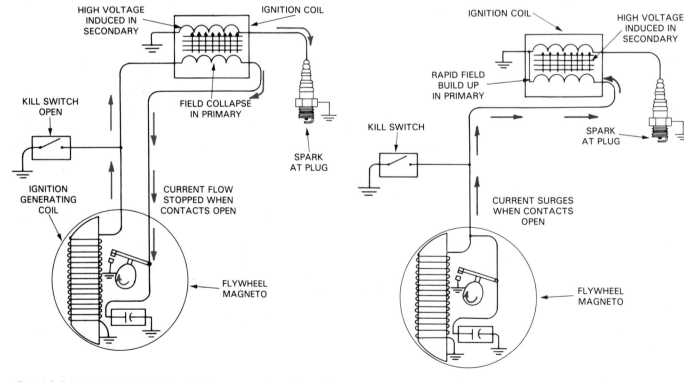

Fig. 10-31. In field collapse magneto, current produced in generating coil flows through primary coil windings, contacts, and condenser until contacts open. When contacts open, current flow stops and magnetic field collapses. This induces current in ignition coil secondary windings to spark plug.

Fig. 10-32. In field buildup magneto, current flow surges into primary coil windings when contact points open. This surge of current occurs so quickly that current is induced in secondary coil windings as magnetic field is building up.

High output from a CDI is possible because of the system's very high primary voltage (approximately 300 to 400 volts). This high primary voltage makes contact points impractical. Several hundred volts would quickly burn and ruin mechanical points.

Instead of contact points, electronic triggering and switching devices are used in the CDI ignition. A capacitor stores primary voltage, and an electronic control box (switch) releases this voltage to the ignition coil.

Coil induction in a CDI system works the same as the field buildup type magneto. They both use a primary voltage surge.

Magneto supported CDI

The most common CDI system in use today is the magneto supported CDI. This type is pictured in Fig. 10-33. The magneto supported CDI consists of:
1. Flywheel.
2. Base Plate.
3. Charging coil (exciter coil).
4. Trigger coil.
5. Electronic control box.
6. Interconnecting wiring.
7. Ignition coil.
8. High tension lead.
9. Spark plug.
10. Accessory coils (lighting or battery charging).

Magneto supported CDI operation

The magneto supported CDI is similar in appearance to a conventional flywheel magneto. Energy (AC current) to power the system is generated by the flywheel magnet and charging coil. This current is fed into an electronic control box which converts the AC to DC. The electric charge is stored in a capacitor in the control box, Fig. 10-34.

The rapid discharge of the capacitor into the primary windings of the ignition coil induces extremely high voltage (25,000 to 45,000 volts) in the second-

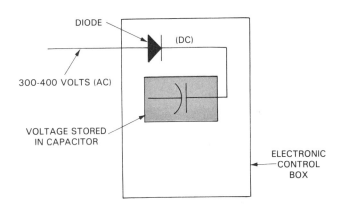

Fig. 10-34. High voltage from ignition generating coil is fed to electronic control box. It is converted to DC by diode and stored in capacitor.

Fig. 10-33. Magneto supported CDI systems are commonly used on off-road, two-stroke cycle motorcycles.

ary coil windings. This causes the spark plug to "fire." See Fig. 10-35.

Discharge of the capacitor is controlled by a thyristor or silicone controlled rectifier (SCR) in the control box. Look at Fig. 10-36. A THYRISTOR is a solid state electronic device which can control or SWITCH high voltages.

In a CDI, the thyristor is used to hold back the voltage in the charged capacitor. The thyristor releases the capacitor charge when signaled by a low voltage impulse of approximately 5 to 10 volts. This low voltage impulse is produced and timed by the trigger coil and flywheel magnets, Fig. 10-37.

Electronic advance

Since the CDI has no moving parts (contact points, point cam, centrifugal advance), ignition advance

Fig. 10-37. Trigger coil sends a low voltage impulse to control box when stepped magnet ends pass the trigger. Magnet ends are stepped in only one place on flywheel. Trigger coil and housing fit next to rotating magnets.

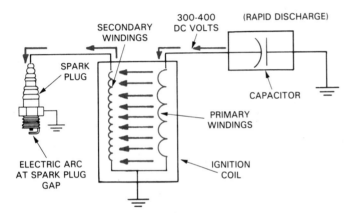

Fig. 10-35. Rapid discharge of CDI capacitor into primary coil windings causes an abrupt buildup of magnetic field. This induces high voltage in secondary windings. A "hot" spark shoots across gap at spark plug.

must be done electronically. The ELECTRONIC ADVANCE, common to a CDI ignition, is usually controlled by the properties of magnetism and induction between the trigger coil and flywheel magnets. Electronic advance is caused by the change in trigger coil VOLTAGE RISE TIME as engine speed increases. See Fig. 10-38.

The thyristor is designed to be activated at a predetermined voltage. For example, if a certain system requires seven volts to switch the thyristor, it will release the charge from the capacitor as soon as seven volts is reached. Look at Fig. 10-39.

Applying this to electronic advance, it is obvious that:

1. As engine speed increases, trigger coil voltage increases.
2. As trigger coil voltage increases, voltage rise time also increases.

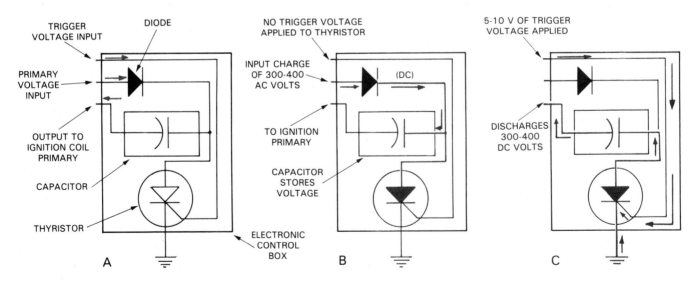

Fig. 10-36. A—Basic components of CDI electronic control box are a diode, capacitor, and thyristor. B—Capacitor is charged by rectified current from charging coil. Release of voltage from capacitor is controlled by thyristor. C—When low voltage from trigger coil is applied to thyristor, capacitor is connected to ground, causing capacitor to discharge into primary windings of ignition coil.

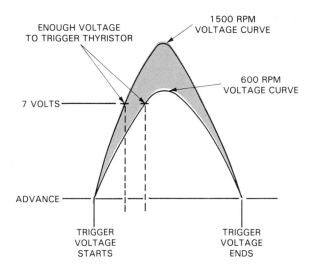

Fig. 10-38. A controlling factor in electronic advance is trigger coil voltage rise time. As engine speed increases, voltage curve becomes steeper. This principle is used to change ignition timing.

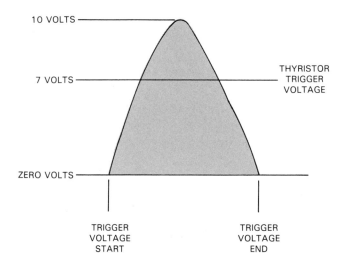

Fig. 10-39. Thyristor will allow capacitor to discharge when trigger voltage reaches a certain value (7 volts in this example). Higher voltage produced by trigger coil has no effect.

3. Trigger voltage is always generated in the same number of crankshaft degrees.
4. As engine speed increases, thyristor release voltage is reached earlier. This causes an advance of the ignition timing. Fig. 10-40 illustrates the factors which cause electronic ignition advance in a CDI ignition.

This type of electronic advance has some limitations. Most systems only produce a maximum of about six degrees of advance. Once maximum advance is reached, higher engine speed does not produce more advance.

Due to the limited advance in a CDI ignition, solid state devices may be used in the control box to change

the advance curve. The curve may be advanced beyond six degrees electronically. In other systems, the curve is designed to retard slightly at peak engine rpm to aid combustion.

Battery supported CDI

The BATTERY SUPPORTED CDI steps up battery voltage (12 volts) to 300 to 400 volts, which is necessary for CDI primary voltage operation. This voltage increase is accomplished by the CDI VOLTAGE AMPLIFIER-CONVERTER, Fig. 10-41. From this point on, the battery supported CDI works in the normal manner.

The battery supported CDI was commonly found on high performance two-stroke cycle road motorcycles. This type of motorcycle is no longer available in the United States, however.

Ignition summary

You are now familiar with several different types of motorcycle ignition systems. When a manufacturer is designing a motorcycle, the selection of the ignition system type is determined by a number of factors. Cost, service, maintenance, spark intensity, spark duration and advance curve requirements are all considered when selecting the ignition system design.

For example, the current popularity of transistorized ignition systems on four-stroke cycle "road bikes" is partially due to strict exhaust emission regulations. Extremely lean air-fuel mixtures are needed to lower exhaust emissions. Lean mixtures, however, are very difficult to ignite and burn. A very "hot" (high voltage) spark is needed.

Also, ignition timing must stay within specifications for extended periods of ignition system operation. A transistor ignition does not have contact

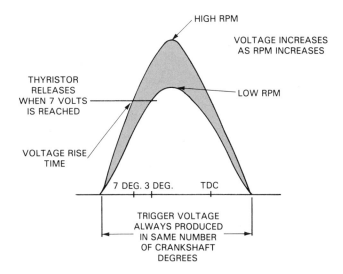

Fig. 10-40. Since trigger voltage is produced over same number of crankshaft degrees, regardless of engine speed, steeper voltage curve causes automatic advance. This happens because trigger voltage (7 volts) is reached more quickly.

195

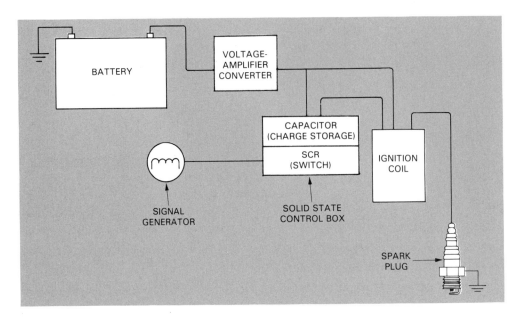

Fig. 10-41. Battery supported CDI uses a voltage amplifier-converter to increase battery voltage for use in primary ignition circuit. Signal generator and control box work in same manner as in magneto supported CDI. Generator triggers control box and control box triggers capacitor and ignition coil.

points which can wear and alter ignition timing. The transistor system can meet emission regulations better than a contact point type ignition.

The characteristics of a CDI (capacitor discharge ignition) make it very compatible with two-stroke cycle competition motorcycles. The high intensity spark of a CDI is capable of firing the spark plug at high speeds, even with the oil and air-fuel mixture in the combustion chamber.

KNOW THESE TERMS

Coil output voltage, Spark intensity, Ignition timing, Centrifugal advance, Vacuum advance, Electronic advance, Transistorized ignition system, Primary circuit, Secondary circuit, Ignition coil, Contact points, Condenser, Spark plug, Rotor, Magnetic pickup, Control box, Flywheel magneto ignition, Electronic advance, CDI.

REVIEW QUESTIONS — CHAPTER 10

1. The purpose of the ignition system is to:
   a. Charge the accessory system.
   b. Start controlled combustion.
   c. Cause detonation.
   d. None of the above.
2. What does the term spark intensity mean?
3. As engine speed increases, ignition must occur earlier because:
   a. Electricity does not travel as fast.
   b. Ignition does not occur earlier.
   c. There is less time for the air-fuel mixture to burn.
   d. The mixture will usually be richer.

4. A two-stroke cycle engine requires ignition every _____ deg. of crankshaft rotation.
5. List the three places where ignition switching devices may be located.
6. What is another name for a step-up transformer?
7. An ignition coil fires the spark plug when the contacts _____.
8. The main purpose of a condenser is to minimize contact point arcing. True or False?
9. A flywheel magneto operates only on direct current (DC). True or False?
10. What is another name for a magnetically triggered ignition system?
11. Electronic ignition systems may produce up to 80,000 volts for spark plug firing. True or False?
12. Name the two variations of a CDI system.
13. A battery and coil ignition system may be triggered by _____ _____ or a _____ triggering device.
14. What is a major advantage of a transistorized ignition system compared to a contact point type ignition?
15. List the three means of controlling transistorized ignition system advance.
16. During CDI operation, the rapid _____ of the capacitor into the _____ windings of the ignition coil causes a _____ which induces high voltage in the coil secondary.
17. In a CDI system, a thyristor or SCR steps up capacitor voltage. True or False?
18. What controls electronic ignition advance in a CDI system?
19. A transistorized ignition system usually requires less maintenance and adjustment than a contact

point type ignition system. True or False?
20. A high voltage is induced in the secondary windings of an ignition coil because:
    a. The primary and secondary winding ratio is approximately 1:1.
    b. Current flow through the primary coil windings continues when spark plug fires.
    c. The magnetic field in the primary coil windings is collapsed across secondary.
    d. All of the above.
    e. None of the above.

SUGGESTED ACTIVITIES

1. Select a motorcycle with a battery and coil ignition system. Using the wiring schematic, trace the complete primary and secondary ignition circuits, and label all the components. Do this on both a contact point and a transistorized ignition system.
2. Select a motorcycle with a flywheel magneto. Using the wiring schematic, trace the complete primary and secondary circuits, and label all components. Determine whether the system uses field collapse or field build up to induce high voltage.
3. Select a motorcycle with a battery supported CDI, and one with a magneto supported CDI. Using the ignition wiring schematic, trace current flow through these systems, and label all the components.
4. On a workbench, connect an ignition coil to a battery and to a spark plug. Make and break the primary while observing coil action.

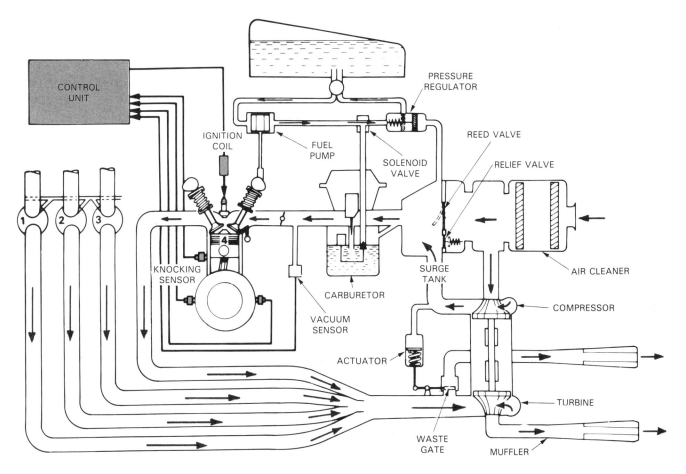

This turbocharged engine uses an electronic control unit. Engine sensors feed information to control unit. Unit can then operate ignition system for maximum efficiency. (Yamaha Motor Corp., U.S.A.)

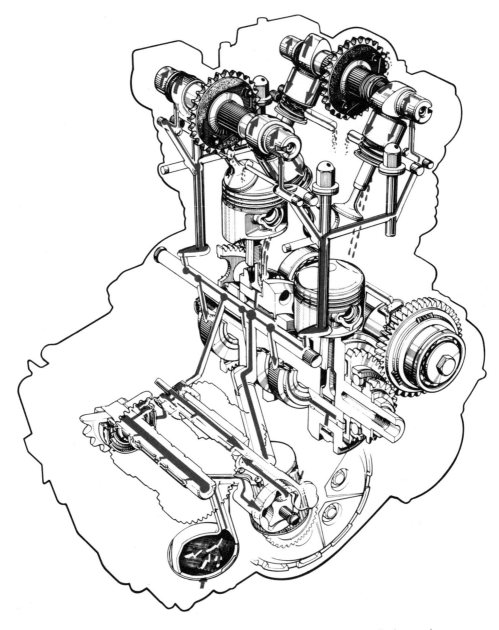

Trace oil flow through lubrication system on this two-cylinder engine.
(U.S. Suzuki Motor Corporation.)

Chapter 11

LUBRICATION SYSTEMS

After studying this chapter, you will be able to:
- List the basic functions, types, and characteristics of motor oil.
- Compare two-stroke and four-stroke cycle engine lubrication systems.
- Describe gearbox lubrication.
- Identify the major parts of motorcycle lubrication systems.
- Perform basic service operations on motorcycle lubrication systems.

This chapter introduces modern motorcycle lubrication systems. Both the two-stroke and the four-stroke cycle lubrication system will be covered. The chapter also explains oil classifications, ratings, and operating characteristics.

The importance of an engine lubrication system and quality lubricants cannot be overemphasized. Without proper lubrication, the moving parts inside an engine can get hot enough to melt. The parts can score or even lock together in a matter of minutes. This heat build up is caused by friction, one of an engine's worst enemies.

FRICTION

FRICTION is the resistance to movement between two touching parts. A LUBRICANT is used to reduce friction and part wear.

A motorcycle LUBRICATION SYSTEM is designed to provide an adequate supply of lubricant (oil) to points of high friction. Oil must be pumped or sprayed onto moving engine and gearbox parts. This reduces friction and prevents rapid part wear and damage.

OIL

Lubricating OIL has four basic functions:
1. Lubricate (reduce friction between moving parts).
2. Clean (carry contaminates to filter).
3. Cool (help dissipate heat).
4. Seal (prevent leakage past rings and seals).

Lubricating action

The internal combustion engine consists of many moving parts that rub against each other. As a result, a certain amount of friction and heat is always present in an engine. It is the oil's job to reduce this friction. Oil must provide a THIN FILM between all moving parts to prevent metal-to-metal contact. Fig. 11-1 illustrates dry friction and friction after lubrication.

Cleaning action

While the oil is lubricating parts (preventing metal-to-metal contact), it is also cleaning the engine. Combustion and normal wear of engine parts produce tiny metalic particles, carbon particles and other contaminants. The oil must be able to keep these particles and contaminants in suspension (floating). Then, the contaminants can be trapped in the oil filter and removed from the engine by changing the oil and filter.

The oil must also be able to NEUTRALIZE

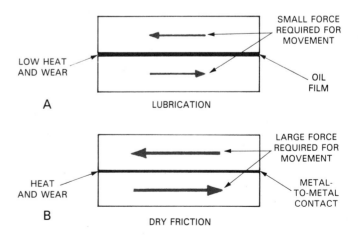

Fig. 11-1. A—Surfaces are separated by an oil film. This prevents metal-to-metal contact and reduces friction. B—Unlubricated surfaces are in contact. Movement can cause friction, heat, galling, and wear.

ACIDS and DISSOLVE VARNISH formed during the combustion process. An oil which has these cleaning qualities is called a DETERGENT OIL. Detergent oil is normally recommended by motorcycle manufacturers.

Cooling action

In addition to lubricating and cleaning, oil helps to cool the engine. Oil transfers heat between parts, absorbs heat, and carries the heat to a cooler part of the engine. Shown in Fig. 11-2, heat is dissipated into the oil film and then into the cooling fins or an oil cooler. An oil cooler resembles a small radiator.

Sealing action

Another function of oil is to help the piston rings seal compression and combustion pressure. The thin oil film between the piston rings and cylinder wall is essential for proper ring sealing. See Fig. 11-3. Oil between a piston ring and ring groove also aids in preventing pressure leakage.

TYPES AND USES OF OIL

There is a large selection of lubricating oils suitable for use in a modern motorcycle engine. Specialized oils have been developed to meet specific needs. A list of the basic types of motorcycle oils includes:

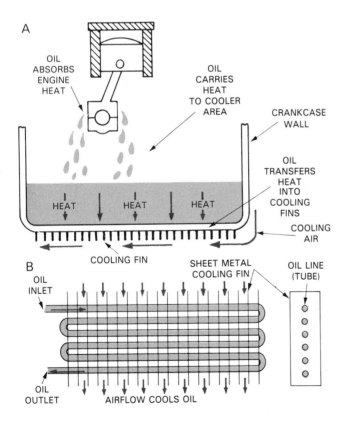

Fig. 11-2. A—Oil is cooled by fins on crankcase. B—Oil flows through a finned radiator (oil cooler) to reduce oil temperature. Both methods transfer engine heat into surrounding air.

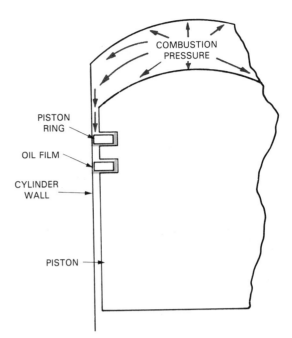

Fig. 11-3. A thin film of oil is required between piston rings and cylinder wall to seal combustion pressure. Without this sealing action, combustion pressure would blow past rings, reducing engine power and efficiency.

1. Four-stroke cycle engine oil (petroleum based, derived from crude oil).
2. Two-stroke cycle engine oil (petroleum based, also derived from crude oil).
3. Synthetic four-stroke cycle engine oil (manufactured chemically, not made from crude oil).
4. Synthetic two-stroke cycle engine oil (manufactured chemically, not made from crude oil).
5. Gear oil (petroleum based, made from crude oil).
6. Two-stroke cycle racing castor oil (vegetable oil derived from castor bean).

Additives

ADDITIVES are carefully selected and used in the manufacture of oils to improve the oil's operating qualities. Some desirable characteristics that result from the proper use of oil additives are:
1. High film strength.
2. Control of viscosity (thickness) at different temperatures.
3. Resistance to foaming.
4. Resistance to oxidation.
5. Ability to keep contaminants in suspension.
6. Ability to burn cleanly (two-stroke cycle engine).

Film strength

FILM STRENGTH is the ability of an oil to remain between two lubricated parts, preventing metal-to-metal contact. Since extremely heavy loads are exerted on bearing surfaces, film strength is very important. Film strength is closely related to viscosity

200

(thickness). Additives that help to increase film strength are used in quality oils.

Viscosity and temperature

VISCOSITY refers to the thickness of an oil and is determined by the rate of oil flow under controlled conditions. Generally, high viscosity oils have high film strengths.

Temperature plays an important role in changing oil viscosity. As oil heats up in an engine, it gets thinner and flows more freely. As oil is chilled (cold weather), it thickens and resists flow. Ideally, oil should flow as if it were thin and lubricate as if it were thick. Discussed later, the proper combination of additives during the manufacturer of oil can provide this desirable characteristic.

Foaming

As oil sprays around the inside of an engine crankcase, the oil comes into contact with fast moving parts (crankshaft, connecting rods, piston). Air is also present in the crankcase and can be mixed with the oil. This can cause the oil to become saturated with air bubbles, a condition called FOAMING.

Foaming is very undesirable because the oil's ability to lubricate and cool is greatly reduced. Foaming can also speed oil oxidation. Additives that help control foaming are normally added to motorcycle oils.

Oxidation

As oil is used, it oxidizes (combines with oxygen) and picks up contaminants (rust, combustion by-products, condensed water, and acids). OXIDATION increases drastically with higher temperatures and results in the formation of sludge and varnish. Since air cooled motorcycle engines run very hot, oil oxidation can be a serious problem.

Although effective oxidation inhibitors are used in motorcycle oils, extreme temperatures still pose a problem. The only effective remedy for oil oxidation is regular oil changing.

Detergents

As mentioned, by-products of incomplete combustion and oil breakdown (oxidation) at high temperatures produce varnish and sludge. DETERGENT additives in oil prevent the build up of these deposits in an engine.

Detergent additives keep the unwanted products suspended in the oil so they may be drained during an oil change. Detergents also keep metal particles in suspension. One reason oil gets dirty so quickly is because the detergents are doing their job.

Two-stroke cycle oil additives

Two-stroke cycle lubricating oil is burned during combustion. The oil is mixed with gasoline before it reaches and lubricates the internal parts of the engine.

Special additives are present in two-stroke cycle oils to accommodate these conditions.

Two-stroke cycle oils must provide sufficient lubrication in a diluted state. They must also burn cleanly to prevent spark plug fouling, excessive carbon buildup, and air pollution.

API AND SAE OIL CLASSIFICATIONS

As internal combustion engines became more sophisticated, the operating requirements of engine oil increased tremendously. Petroleum engineers and researchers have constantly worked to improve lubricating oils. As a result, a system was needed to test, standardize, and classify lubricating oils.

The American Petroleum Institute (API) and Society of Automotive Engineers (SAE) are the organizations responsible for the testing and classification of oils. They have classified oil in terms of viscosity and intended use.

Oil use classification

A double letter code is used to classify oils for specific uses. All oils for use in gasoline engines have a code beginning with the letter S.

The lowest grade of oil for use in the gasoline engine is classified as SA. This is a straight petroleum based oil with no additives. It is NOT suitable for use in a motorcycle.

The highest quality oil is rated SF and is recommended for all four-stroke cycle motorcycle engines. SE rated oil may also be recommended for four-stroke cycle motorcycle engines. Oils which are classified SB, SC, SD are NOT suitable for use in motorcycle engines.

Viscosity rating system

A VISCOSITY RATING SYSTEM or numbering system identifies the thickness of oil—the larger the number, the thicker the oil. For instance, a 40 weight oil is thicker and will pour slower than 30, 20, or 10 weight oil. Look at Fig. 11-4. The viscosity rating is normally printed on top of the oil can in large numbers.

As mentioned, engine oil tends to thicken when a motorcycle sits in cold weather. This could make the engine hard to kick over and start. After starting, when the engine heats to full operating temperature, the oil thins, losing some of its film strength.

To solve this problem, a MULTI-GRADE OIL, also called multi-weight or multi-viscosity oil, was developed. It operates with the characteristics of a light oil (10 or 20 weight) when cold to allow easy starting. Then, when heated to engine operating temperature, it serves as thick oil (30 or 40 weight) to provide adequate film strength and protection. See Fig. 11-4. Multi-grade oil has the advantages of both high and low viscosity oils.

Always follow manufacturer specifications for oil

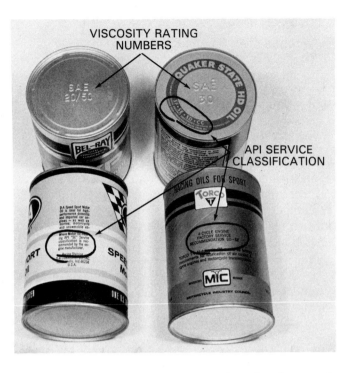

Fig. 11-4. Oil viscosity rating is stamped or printed on top of can. API service classification is located either on top or side of can.

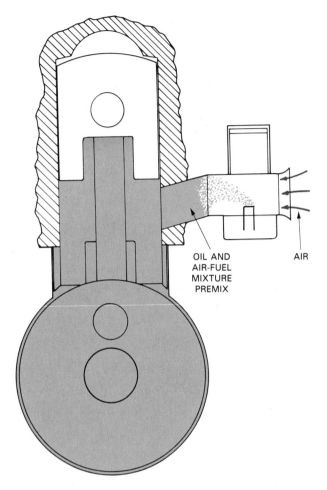

Fig. 11-5. In a premix two-stroke cycle engine, oil is carried in air-fuel mixture, providing lubrication for internal engine parts.

viscosity. They are listed in owner's manuals and service manuals.

TWO-STROKE CYCLE ENGINE LUBRICATION

In the two-stroke cycle engine, lubricating oil passes through the engine with the air-fuel mixture. Two methods are used to provide lubrication; premixed fuel and oil, and oil injection.

PREMIX LUBRICATION

The PREMIX LUBRICATION of a two-stroke cycle engine uses a specified ratio of fuel and oil mixed together in the fuel tank. The ratio may vary from 20:1 (20 parts fuel, one part oil) to 50:1 (50 parts fuel, one part oil) depending upon manufacturer recommendations, type of oil, and type of use.

Lubrication is provided by an oil mist as the engine operates and slings oil around inside the crankcase. This type lubrication is shown in Fig. 11-5.

OIL INJECTION LUBRICATION

Two-stroke cycle OIL INJECTION LUBRICATION uses a small pump to force oil into the engine depending upon throttle setting and engine rpm (speed). See Fig. 11-6. In this system, oil is stored in a separate reservoir (oil injection tank) and gasoline is stored in the fuel tank. The oil injection system automatically meters the correct amount of oil into the gasoline entering the engine.

Manifold injection

Oil fed directly to the intake port is referred to as MANIFOLD INJECTION, Fig. 11-7. The same type lubrication is provided as with the premix system. Oil is mixed with the air-fuel mixture BEFORE entering the crankcase. The advantage of manifold injection is that it is not necessary to hand mix oil and gasoline each time the fuel tank is filled.

Direct bearing injection

DIRECT BEARING INJECTION provides undiluted oil directly to the main bearings and connecting rod of the engine. Oil used to lubricate the main bearings is thrown off and fed to the connecting rod by an oil slinger. Fig. 11-8 illustrates this system.

Direct bearing injection provides superior lubrication and protection of engine bearings, giving longer engine life. Some engines use both direct bearing and manifold injection lubrication.

Because oil consumption is controlled by engine speed and load, an oil injection system usually uses less oil than the premix system. A typical injection system provides a 100:1 fuel-oil ratio at idle and a 20:1 fuel-oil ratio at full throttle. A typical premix

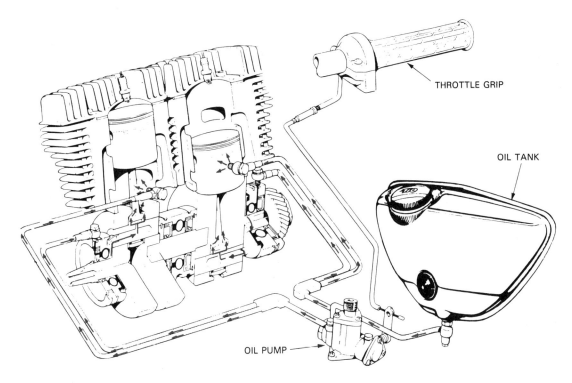

Fig. 11-6. With a two-stroke cycle oil injection system, oil pump output is controlled by throttle position and engine rpm. (U.S. Suzuki Motor Corporation)

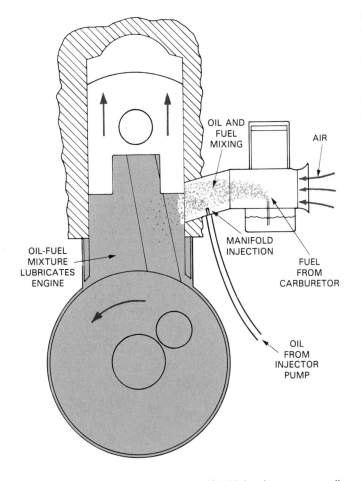

Fig. 11-7. In two-stroke cycle manifold injection system, oil is discharged into intake manifold. It then mixes with incoming air-fuel mixture.

system provides a 20:1 fuel-oil ratio at all engine speeds.

OIL INJECTION SYSTEM MAINTENANCE

Since proper oiling is extremely important to engine life, you should check a two-stroke cycle oil injection system periodically.

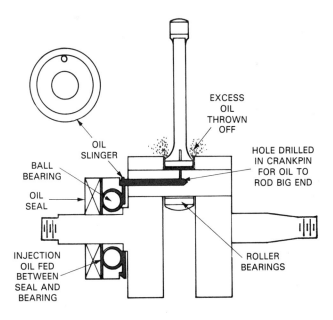

Fig. 11-8. In a direct bearing injection system, oil is fed directly to crankshaft main bearing. As oil is thrown out of main bearing, it is trapped by oil slinger. Slinger feeds oil into hollow crankpin. This provides lubrication for connecting rod bearing.

Oil pump adjustment

The two-stroke cycle oil injection pump is a metering device which controls oil flow to the engine. Its output is controlled by engine rpm and throttle position.

The THROTTLE CABLE is connected to the oil pump and carburetor by a junction block, Fig. 11-9. Due to normal wear and stretch, cable adjustment is a required and critical maintenance procedure. Cable adjustment consists of aligning a reference mark on the oil pump lever with a stationary mark (usually on oil pump housing) at a certain throttle position. See Fig. 11-9. Another method of adjustment requires measuring linkage free play at the pump with the throttle full open.

Oil pump cable adjustment is accomplished by turning an adjuster which varies the length of the outer oil pump cable housing. Oil pump adjustment is very important and is detailed in the service manual.

Oil pump bleeding

OIL PUMP BLEEDING is required whenever AIR enters the feed line or oil pump. Air in the system can cause oil pump CAVITATION (air bubbles displace oil). Any air in the system will interrupt the flow of oil and may cause serious damage to the engine.

Air can enter the oil supply line in a number of ways:

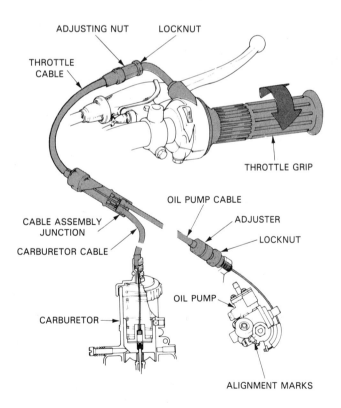

Fig. 11-9. Turning throttle grip opens carburetor throat and increases oil pump output. As engine speed increases, oil injection output is also increased to maintain correct fuel-oil mixture. (Kawasaki Motors Corp., U.S.A.)

1. Loose oil line.
2. Empty oil tank.
3. Hole in oil line.
4. Disconnecting oil line and not bleeding pump.
5. Plugged oil tank vent.

Most oil injection pumps have a BLEED SCREW in the pump body (housing), Fig. 11-10. Loosening the bleed screw allows gravity flow of oil to force the air out of the supply line and pump.

Some oil injection pumps do not have a bleed screw. In this case, the oil line must be loosened at the pump to PURGE (remove) the air.

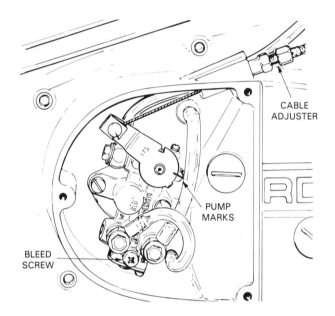

Fig. 11-10. Two-stroke cycle cable adjuster must be turned until marks on oil pump arm and body line up. Service manual explains proper throttle position for oil injection pump adjustment. Loosening bleed screw allows air to be removed from pump and supply line. (Bombardier Ltd., Owner of the trademark CAN-AM)

Oil tank vent

For oil to flow to the pump, the oil tank must be VENTED. Two methods are used to vent the oil tank. One uses a small vent hole in the tank cap, Fig. 11-11. The other uses a vent line attached to the top of the oil tank.

A clogged oil tank vent (dirt filled cap vent, kinked vent line) can allow a vacuum to build in the oil tank. The vacuum could then stop the flow of oil out of the tank and cause serious engine damage.

Check valves and oil feed lines

CHECK VALVES are sometimes used in oil feed lines to allow oil flow in only one direction (towards the engine), Fig. 11-12. If dirt gets caught in the check valve, oil can flow in both directions within the feed line. This might allow oil to cycle back and forth in the line without entering the engine. Severe engine damage could result because of oil starvation. A stuck

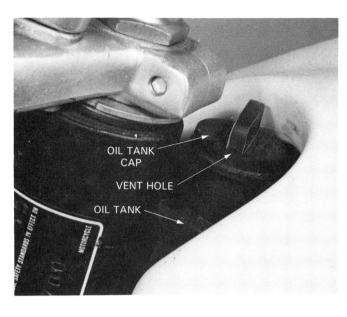

Fig. 11-11. This motorcycle uses large frame tube as an injection oil tank. Venting is provided by a hole in cap.

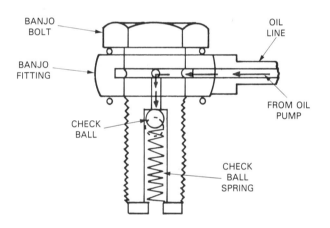

Fig. 11-12. A check valve allows oil to flow only in one direction. In this example, check valve is part of banjo bolt fitting that attaches oil line to engine.

open check valve can also cause unwanted gravity flow of oil into the engine when the engine is not running. A check valve should only pass oil when pressure unseats the check valve ball.

Oil injection filters

Oil injection systems are provided with either an IN-LINE or an IN-TANK OIL FILTER. Both of these types should be checked or cleaned periodically, or when an oil supply problem exists.

Oil injection pump output

Some manufacturers give specifications for checking injection pump output. If an oil supply problem is suspected, pump output should be measured.

Oil pump testing consists of running the engine on premix and measuring the injection pump output at a

given rpm for a specified time. If not within factory specifications, repairs are needed.

PRIMARY AND GEARBOX LUBRICATION

Since the two-stroke cycle crankcase must be sealed another means of lubrication is necessary for the primary drive and gearbox. An OIL BATH is commonly used for primary and gearbox lubrication in a two-stroke engine, Fig. 11-13. Special motorcycle GEAR OILS are recommended. The amount and type of oil for the primary and gearbox is specified in the motorcycle's service manual.

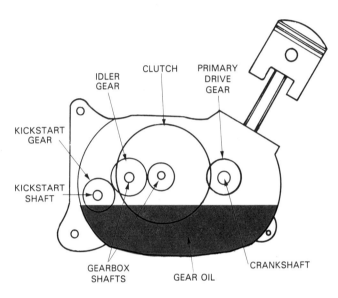

Fig. 11-13. Primary drive oil bath lubrication. Lubrication is provided by gear movement through oil. Oil is splashed around in case to protect parts.

FOUR-STROKE CYCLE LUBRICATION

Four-stroke cycle lubrication differs greatly from two-stroke cycle lubrication. Rather than burning the oil during combustion, the four-stroke cycle engine reuses its lubricating oil. An OIL PUMP constantly circulates the same oil throughout the parts of a four-stroke cycle engine. Refer to Fig. 11-14.

There are three common types of four-stroke cycle lubrication systems: dry sump, wet sump, and common sump.

The word SUMP refers to the lowest portion of the crankcase cavity. It is the area where oil collects in the bottom of the engine.

DRY SUMP LUBRICATION

A typical DRY SUMP lubrication system, Fig. 11-14, consists of:
1. Oil tank.
2. Oil feed line.

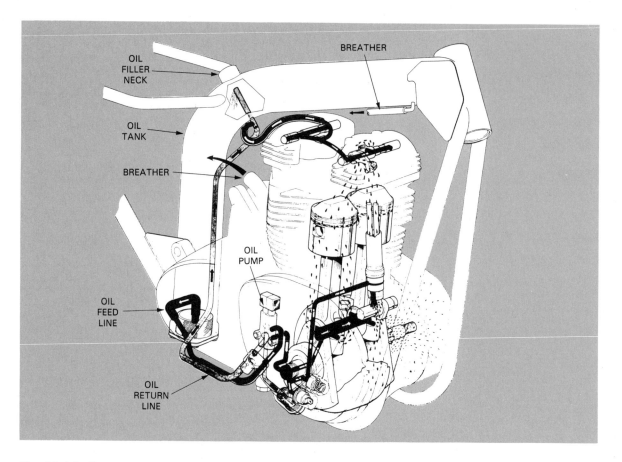

Fig. 11-14. Dry sump lubrication system uses an oil tank separate from engine. Oil pump supplies oil under pressure to engine and returns oil to oil tank. Trace flow from tank, through engine, and back to tank. (Triumph Motorcycles [Meriden] Ltd.)

3. Oil pump (two-sided pump with oil pressure feed and oil return).
4. Oil return line.

Oil is gravity fed to the pressure feed side of the oil pump from a remote oil tank. Then, the pump forces oil through oil passages in the engine under pressure. This lubricates moving engine parts, which would otherwise be damaged by friction.

Oil that is thrown off pressure fed parts lubricates other engine components by a splash or vapor method. Excess oil in the sump is returned to the oil tank by the return side of the oil pump.

WET SUMP LUBRICATION

WET SUMP LUBRICATION differs from dry sump in two ways:
1. Oil is stored in the sump, NOT in an external tank.
2. The oil pump does NOT have a return side.

The wet sump oil pump supplies oil under pressure in the same manner as the dry sump lubrication system. It pressure feeds oil to all high friction areas (rod and main bearing, cam bearings) in the engine. The oil pump, however, draws oil from the sump rather than from a remote tank. Oil that is pressure fed and thrown off drains back to the sump where it is again picked up and circulated by the oil pump.

Since there are less components involved and no external oil lines, the wet sump system is usually simpler

and less prone to leakage than a dry sump type lubrication system.

COMMON SUMP LUBRICATION

COMMON SUMP LUBRICATION is a design which uses engine oil to also lubricate the gearbox and primary drive. This is only used on four-stroke cycle motorcycle engines. A typical common sump system is shown in Fig. 11-15. As you can see, oil is fed or pumped to both the engine and transmission.

The common sump system is normally used with a wet sump type engine lubrication system. However, some dry sump oiling systems also use a common sump. Compare Figs. 11-14 and 11-15.

Separate gearbox lubrication

Motorcycles not having a common sump design use a sealed gearbox. The gearbox has its own oil supply. Transmission oil simply splashes around and lubricates the gears. Most dry sump systems use this method of gearbox lubrication.

OIL PUMP TYPES

Four-stroke cycle motorcycle engines use three basic oil pump designs: gear, plunger, and rotor. It is important that you fully understand the operation of each type.

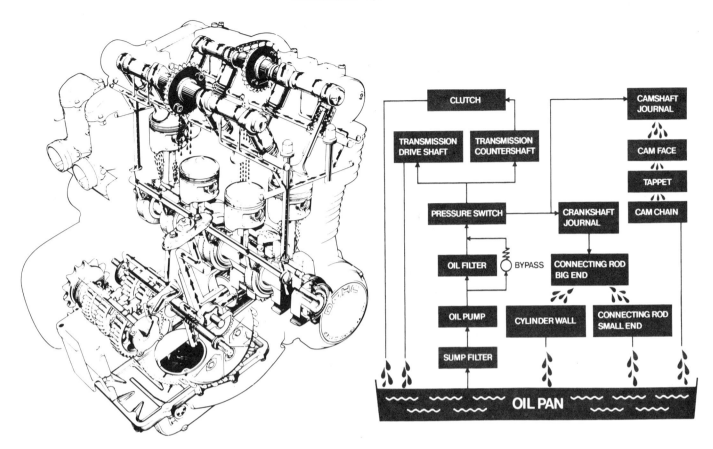

Fig. 11-15. Common sump lubrication system uses same oil to lubricate engine as well as gearbox (transmission). Follow oil flow through system. (U.S. Suzuki Motor Corporation)

Gear type oil pumps

A GEAR OIL PUMP consists of a housing, drive gear, and driven gear. Refer to Fig. 11-16. The teeth of the gears move oil as they rotate. Oil is picked up at one side of the oil pump and forced to the other side by the gear teeth. Gear type oil pumps generally produce moderate volume and pressure.

Plunger type oil pumps

A PLUNGER OIL PUMP consists of a piston, cylinder, and set of check valves. Look at Fig. 11-17.

As the piston moves up in the cylinder, oil is drawn in past the inlet check ball. As the piston moves back down in the cylinder, the inlet check ball closes. Oil is then forced past the outlet check ball under pressure.

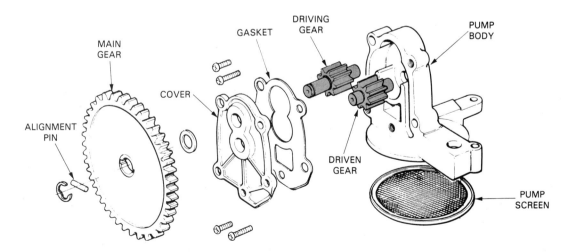

Fig. 11-16. Gear type oil pump is a common design. Gear teeth trap oil and produce oil pressure for engine lubrication system. (Kawasaki Motors Corp., U.S.A.)

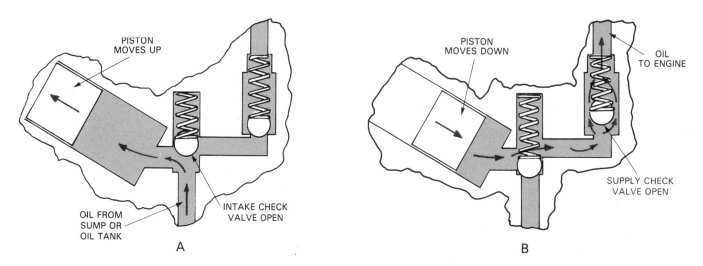

Fig. 11-17. Plunger or piston type oil pump. A—Piston moves up. Oil is drawn past intake check valve to fill cylinder. B—Piston moves down. Intake check valve closes and supply check valve opens. This allows oil to flow to engine under pressure.

Generally, the plunger pump is capable of high pressure but produces low volume.

Rotor type oil pumps

A ROTOR OIL PUMP, also called TROCHOID oil pump, consists of a drive shaft, housing, inner rotor, and outer rotor. See Fig. 11-18.

The drive shaft is attached to the inner rotor and is free to spin in the housing. The drive shaft and inner rotor are offset in the housing. The outer rotor is free to turn in the housing and is driven by the inner rotor.

The relationship of the impellers of the inner rotor and the depressions of the outer rotor constantly change as the pump turns. See Fig. 11-18. As the inner rotor "walks" around the inside of the outer rotor, oil is constantly being picked up from the inlet side, transferred, and pumped through the outlet side. Oil is squeezed between the two (inner and outer) rotors to produce pressure. Generally, the rotor type

oil pump is capable of high volume and high pressure. It is the most widely used type oil pump.

CHECK VALVES

A CHECK VALVE is a device which allows oil flow in only one direction. Spring-loaded balls or pistons provide this control. Fig. 11-19 shows both types of check valves.

In the four-stroke cycle motorcycle engine, check valves perform three functions:
1. In the plunger type pump, check valves are necessary to prevent oil cycling (same oil moving back and forth in pump).
2. In the dry sump system, check valves prevent oil from draining from the tank into the sump.
3. A check valve on the output side of the oil pump prevents oil from draining out of the engine oil passages and back through the pump.

Check valves are relatively trouble free. Malfunc-

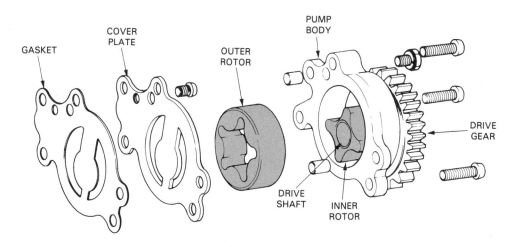

Fig. 11-18. Rotor type oil pump is another common design. Basically, it squeezes oil between inner and outer rotors to produce pressure and flow. (Kawasaki Motors Corp., U.S.A.)

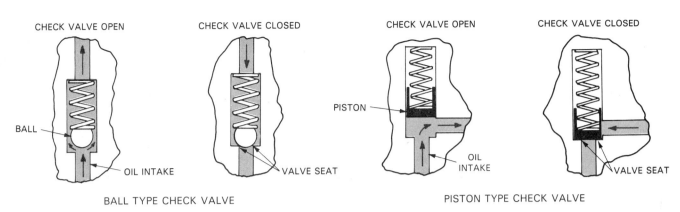

CHECK VALVE OPEN   CHECK VALVE CLOSED   CHECK VALVE OPEN   CHECK VALVE CLOSED

BALL   OIL INTAKE   VALVE SEAT   PISTON   OIL INTAKE   VALVE SEAT

BALL TYPE CHECK VALVE   PISTON TYPE CHECK VALVE

Fig. 11-19. Check valves control direction of oil flow. Oil pressure at intake side of valve forces ball or piston away from seat. This allows oil to flow through valve. When there is not pressure at intake side of valve, ball or piston is returned to its seat by spring pressure. This prevents oil from flowing through valve in opposite direction.

tions may occur if foreign material is present in the valve. The check valve could stick open or closed.

RELIEF VALVES

A RELIEF VALVE is a device used to control maximum oil pressure. If oil pressure becomes too high, the spring-loaded relief valve opens. This allows excess oil to bleed off into the sump. Since oil pressure increases with engine speed, a relief valve is needed to maintain constant oil pressure. Fig. 11-20 illustrates a typical oil pressure relief valve.

A relief valve is similar in appearance to a check valve. The spring in the relief valve, however, is much stiffer. Since spring tension directly controls oil pressure, it is vital to the life of the engine. A weak spring or stuck piston can reduce oil pressure and cause serious engine damage.

OIL FILTERS

The function of an OIL FILTER is to remove foreign material from the oil and prevent its recirculation through the engine. Two common filter designs are used: centrifugal and element.

Centrifugal oil filters

One method of oil filtration is the CENTRIFUGAL OIL FILTER or SLINGER. One is shown in Fig. 11-21.

It uses centrifugal force to remove foreign material

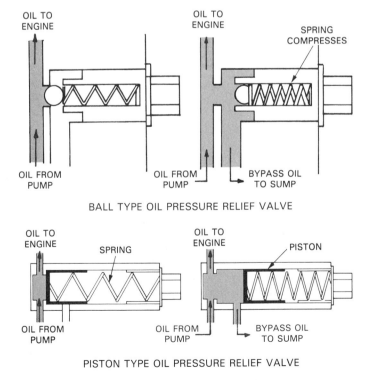

Fig. 11-20. Study action of oil pressure relief valves. Both ball and piston types use same principles.

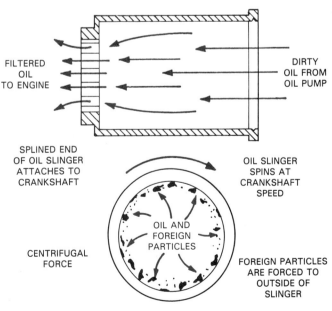

Fig. 11-21. Spinning action forces oil contaminants to fly outward and remain in filter.

209

from the oil. As the slinger spins, foreign particles (particles heavier than oil) are thrown to the outside and held there. Oil slingers are attached to the engine crankshaft so they turn at relatively high speeds.

Element oil filters

A very efficient method used to filter engine oil is the pleated paper oil filter element, Fig. 11-22. Oil is circulated through the filtering material (element) where foreign particles are trapped before they can reach the engine.

Generally, ELEMENT FILTERS are more efficient and easier to service than centrifugal filters. If an oil filter element becomes clogged and hinders oil flow, a BYPASS VALVE is normally provided, Fig. 11-23. It lets oil flow around the clogged filter element and to the engine parts.

LUBRICATION SYSTEM MAINTENANCE

Proper maintenance and servicing of the lubrication system is very important. Basic LUBRICATION SYSTEM MAINTENANCE includes:
1. Checking oil levels.
2. Inspecting for leaks.
3. Changing oil and filters at proper intervals (cleaning centrifugal filters).
4. Periodic checking of oil pressure.

Changing oil and filter

When changing the oil and filter, the engine should be at operating temperature, Fig. 11-24. Oil drains more quickly when it is hot. The hot oil will also carry out any foreign material and contaminants not trapped by the filter.

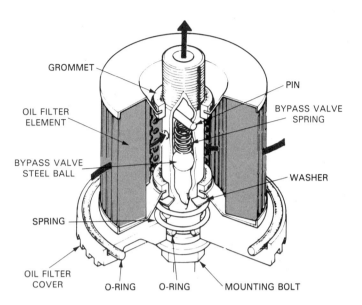

Fig. 11-23. Oil filter bypass valve allows oil to flow even if filter is clogged. (Kawasaki Motors Corp., U.S.A.)

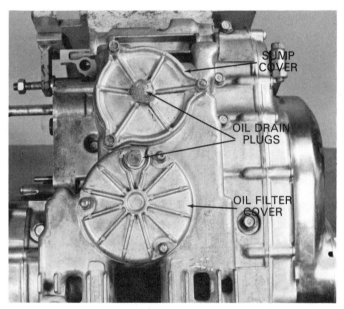

Fig. 11-24. Note shape and location of oil drain plugs and filter on bottom of this particular engine.

The service manual outlines proper procedures for oil and filter service. Oil and filter change intervals should be considered maximum. Contaminated oil can increase engine part wear tremendously. Refer to Fig. 11-15.

When refilling the engine with motor oil, make sure you use the manufacturer recommended type and amount of oil. Look at Fig. 11-26.

KNOW THESE TERMS

Friction, Four-stroke cycle motor oil, Two-stroke cycle motor oil, Synthetic oil, Gear oil, Oil additive,

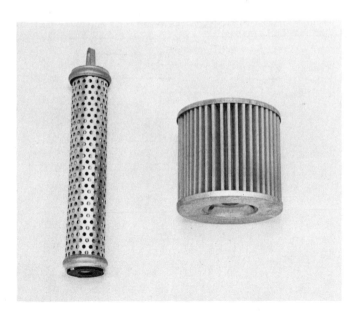

Fig. 11-22. Pleated paper oil filters, like these, are easy to change and provide good filtering. Pleats increase element surface area and filter life.

Fig. 11-25. Drain oil after warming engine to operating temperature. This will help suspend and drain deposits.

Fig. 11-26. When changing engine oil, be sure to remove all drain plugs after oil is warm. Refill with proper quantity of recommended oil. Refer to manual for oil viscosity, service ratings, and quantity.

Film strength, Viscosity, Foaming, Oxidation, Detergents, API, SAE, Multi-weight oil, Premix lubrication, Oil injection, Oil pump bleeding, Dry sump lubrication, Wet sump lubrication, Common sump lubrication, Gear pump, Plunger pump, Rotor pump, Check valve, Relief valve, Oil filter.

REVIEW QUESTIONS — CHAPTER 11

1. The main purpose of a lubricant is to help reduce friction. True or False?
2. List the four functions of oil.
3. A _____ oil has the ability to dissolve varnish and neutralize acids.
4. Describe the two ways that a lubricant helps to cool an engine.
5. List three characteristics which result from the proper use of additives during the manufacture of lubricating oils.
6. Define "film strength."
7. Define "viscosity."
8. A multi-grade oil always has low film strength. True or False?
9. Foaming of engine oil _____ lubrication efficiency.
10. As oil temperature rises, oxidation tends to _____ (increase, decrease).
11. A detergent oil holds unwanted products from _____ in suspension so they may be caught in the _____ and drained during an oil change.
12. What two important characteristics must a two-stroke cycle oil have?
13. What does the "S" in SE and SF mean?
14. List two methods of lubrication for two-stroke cycle engines.
15. Direct bearing injection provides better lubrication than:

a. Indirect injection.
b. Exhaust injection.
c. Manifold injection.
d. Cylinder injection.
16. Injection system oil consumption is controlled by engine _____ and _____.
17. What is meant by the term cavitation?
18. Check valves are never used in oil injection systems. True or False?
19. List three types of four-stroke cycle engine lurication system designs.
20. Three types of four-stroke cycle oil pumps are _____, _____, and _____.
21. A rotor type oil pump provides oil at _____ pressure and _____ volume.
22. A check valve provides the same function as a relief valve. True or False?
23. Why should engine oil be drained when at operating temperature?

SUGGESTED ACTIVITIES

1. List the different types of lubrication systems used for two-stroke cycle motorcycle engines. Determine the advantages and disadvantages of each.
2. Make drawings and trace the flow of oil through a wet sump, dry sump, and common sump type four-stroke cycle engines.
3. Select five brands of two and four-stroke cycle motor oil and list the following:
a. SAE viscosity rating.
b. API use classification.
c. Base oil (petroleum, synthetic, vegetable).
d. Cost.
4. Choose three different motorcycles and list the oils you would use to lubricate the engine, gearbox, and primary drive. Base your answers on what you learned from Activity number 3 and a service manual.

5. Interview dealers, mechanics, and racers in your area to determine which lubricants they prefer for different uses and why.
6. Pick a specific type of riding condition (road, trail, motocross, dirt track, racing) and determine the range of suitable lubricants for that type of riding.
7. Choose five two-stroke engines and determine which type of engine lubrication system is used (direct bearing injection, manifold injection, or premix).
8. Choose five four-stroke cycle engines. Use service and owner's manuals to list and compare the following information:
   a. Type of lubrication system.
   b. Recommended engine and gearbox lubricants.
   c. Engine and gearbox oil quantities.
   d. Type of oil pump and system pressure.
   e. Type of oil filter.
   f. Specified oil and filter change interval.

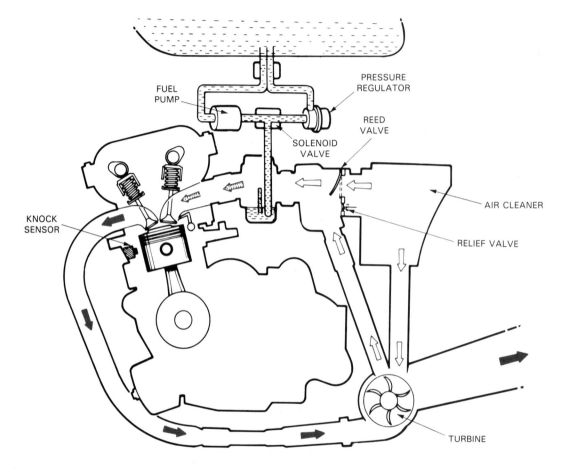

Layout of a turbocharged engine. Turbo uses exhaust gases to spin turbine. Turbo then forces air into engine under pressure for more power output. (Yamaha Motor Corp., U.S.A.)

Chapter 12

TUNE-UP AND GENERAL SERVICE

After studying this chapter, you will be able to:
□ Describe common motorcycle ignition system adjustments.
□ Adjust ignition timing.
□ Describe engine valve and cam chain adjustment.
□ Perform basic carburetor adjustments.
□ List the steps for a complete motorcycle tune-up.
□ Service a motorcycle.

This chapter outlines the basic procedures for engine tune-up and general servicing of a motorcycle. Tune-up and general service are generally considered separate operations. Yet, they are usually done at the same time. A complete tune-up involves the adjustment of the ignition system, fuel system, and valve train. It also includes the inspection, replacement, adjustment, or lubrication of any other component that requires periodic service.

NOTE! Many of the previous textbook chapters gave information essential to the complete understanding of tune-up procedures. Make sure you have studied the earlier material on engines, ignition systems, electrical systems, measurement, and tools before beginning this chapter.

MEASURING ENGINE COMPRESSION

Always make sure an engine is in good mechanical condition before attempting a tune-up. First, perform a COMPRESSION TEST to check the engine top-end (rings, valves, pistons, head gasket). See Fig. 12-1. If an engine has low compression and is in poor condition (worn rings, burned valves, blown head gasket), you would be wasting time by trying to tune the engine. Any mechanical problem must be repaired before the tune-up.

Fig. 12-1. A screw-in type compression gauge is easy to use. Crank engine and check compression in all cylinders. Refer to a service manual for acceptable pressure values and variation between cylinders. If compression is not up to specs, repair engine before tune-up.

IGNITION SYSTEM TUNE-UP

Exact ignition system tune-up procedures vary depending upon the particular system being serviced. However, you should be able to relate the general information in this section of the chapter to the specific information in a service manual. This will give you the skills needed to properly tune a motorcycle ignition system.

CONTACT POINT IGNITION SYSTEM SERVICING

Any ignition system using contact points requires:
1. Inspection of contact points.
2. Replacement of contact points if worn.
3. Cleaning of contact surfaces.
4. Contact point lubrication.
5. Auto advance inspection and lubrication.
6. Point gap or dwell adjustment.
7. Ignition timing adjustment.

Inspection of contact points

Inspect the contact points for evidence of pitting or erosion, Fig. 12-2. Contact points which still have flat surfaces can sometimes be refinished with a flexstone. Refer to your service manual. Some manufacturers recommend contact point replacement rather than refinishing. Contacts that are heavily pitted or eroded must always be replaced.

Heavy contact pitting or erosion usually indicates the need for condenser replacement. The condenser helps protect the points from arcing.

Replacement of contact points

Both the movable and ground contacts must be replaced as a set. During contact point replacement, it is important to make sure that the new, replacement contacts are the same as the old ones being replaced.

Some contact sets must be disassembled during installation. Make sure the contact return spring and fiber washers are installed in the proper order, Fig. 12-2. Failure to properly insulate the contact spring or wire from ground will cause the contact set to be per-

manently grounded. This will keep the ignition system from functioning.

After contact installation, make sure the contact wires are properly routed. Also, check that the contact surfaces are parallel. See Fig. 12-3.

Cleaning contact point surfaces

Whether the contact points are refinished or replaced, the surfaces must be thoroughly cleaned. Refinishing of contact surfaces leaves residue. New contacts commonly have a protective coating that must also be removed. Aerosol contact cleaner may be used for contact cleaning. Look at Fig. 12-4.

Contact point lubrication

Contact point rubbing blocks and point cams must be lubricated to prevent wear. Illustrated in Fig. 12-5, this prevents premature rubbing block wear. Rubbing block wear reduces point gap and retards ignition timing. A special point cam grease should be used to lubricate the point cam and rubbing block.

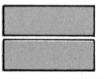

CONTACT SURFACES PARALLEL, LARGE CONDUCTING AREA

CONTACT SURFACES NOT PARALLEL, SMALL CONDUCTING AREA

Fig. 12-3. Contact point surfaces should be parallel for best performance. After installing new contacts, check to see that surfaces are parallel and adjust by carefully bending stationary contact base.

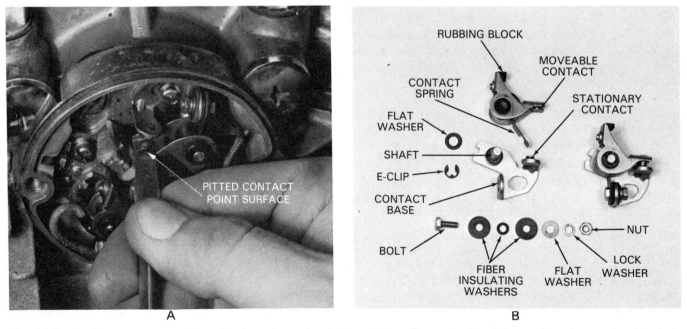

A

B

Fig. 12-2. A—Inspect contact points closely to determine their condition. Contact point pitting and erosion can be detected visually. B—Note parts of points. A weakened point spring can cause high speed missing. Burned points or worn point shaft and bushing can alter engine performance. A missing or broken fiber washer can short points, keeping engine from running.

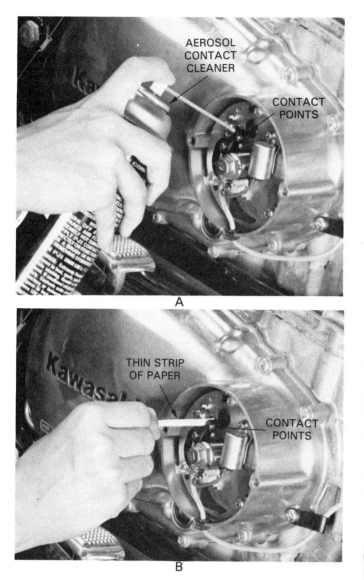

Fig. 12-4. A—Use aerosol contact cleaner to remove oil film and grit. B—Use a thin strip of paper to assure cleaning and drying of contact surfaces. This method is good for both new and old contact sets.

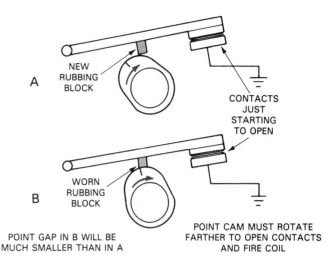

Fig. 12-5. Wear of contact point rubbing block retards ignition timing. As gap decreases, both dwell and retard increase. Lubricant rubbing block to help prevent this problem.

Fig. 12-6. A light application of an aerosol lubricant is an acceptable method of lubricating an ignition system auto advance unit.

Auto (centrifugal) advance lubrication

When lubrication of the contact breaker rubbing blocks and point cam is being performed, it is good idea to also check and lubricate the auto or centrifugal advance unit.

Make sure the auto advance unit operates freely and inspect for evidence of moisture or corrosion. Fig. 12-6 illustrates proper lubrication of the ignition system auto advance unit.

Contact point gap adjustment

CONTACT POINT GAP is the amount of clearance between the contact surfaces when they are wide open. Most contact point cams have an index mark to indicate the position of the widest opening, Fig. 12-7. Rotate the engine until the cam lobe mark is aligned with the point rubbing block.

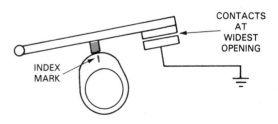

Fig. 12-7. When index mark on point cam lines up with contact rubbing block, contacts should be at their widest opening. They are then ready to be gapped with a feeler gauge.

Contact point gap determines the amount of time for coil build-up (current flow into coil). DWELL is the amount of time in crankshaft degrees that the contacts are closed. See Fig. 12-8. A special dwell meter must be used to set point dwell in degrees.

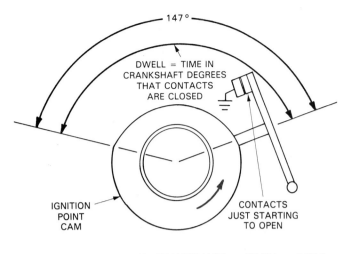

POINT CAM MOUNTED ON CRANKSHAFT   DWELL = 147°
POINT CAM MOUNTED ON CAMSHAFT   DWELL = 294°

Fig. 12-8. Point cam profile and contact gap determines ignition dwell.

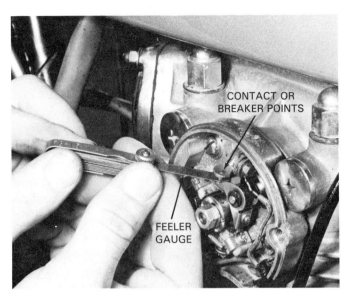

Fig. 12-10. A feeler gauge can be used to measure and verify contact point gap with reasonable accuracy.

It is important to understand the relationship between dwell and point gap. As point gap increases, dwell decreases. As point gap decreases, dwell increases. Fig. 12-9 illustrates this relationship.

Contact point gap is adjusted in one of two ways:
1. Using a feeler gauge (static), Fig. 12-10.
2. Using a dwell meter (dynamic), Fig. 12-11.

A range is usually given for acceptable contact point gap and dwell. Follow the directions in your service manual for contact point gap adjustment. Specifications vary.

IGNITION TIMING ADJUSTMENT

IGNITION TIMING refers to the position of the crankshaft and piston when the spark occurs. As

mentioned earlier, timing of the spark is critical to engine efficiency, performance, and service life. Ignition timing is checked by using markings on the engine or by measuring piston position. Usually, timing marks are provided to simplify adjustment. Look at Fig. 12-12.

Three methods are used to alter ignition timing:
1. Rotation of the ignition base plate.
2. Movement of a breaker subplate mounted on the base plate. This is illustrated in Fig. 12-13.
3. Changing contact point breaker gap.

Some flywheel magnetos use point gap as the only means of adjusting ignition timing. Refer to Fig. 12-14. On engines using this design, widen the point

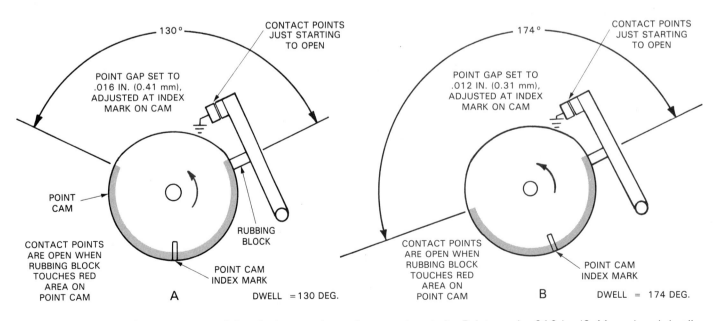

Fig. 12-9. Dwell refers to amount of time in degrees that points are closed. A—Point gap is .016 in. (0.41 mm) and dwell is 130 deg. B—Point gap has been reduced to .012 in. (0.31 mm). This causes points to open later and close sooner, increasing dwell. When point gap is increased, dwell is reduced. When gap is reduced, dwell is increased.

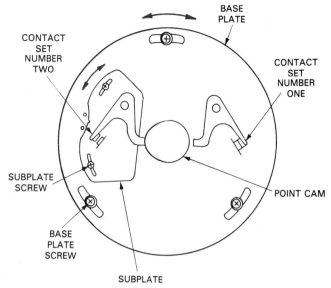

Fig. 12-13. In this example, ignition timing is adjusted by rotating base plate to time number one contact set, and subplate to time number two contact set.

Fig. 12-11. A dwell meter is used to verify contact point dwell in degrees, which in turn indicates contact point gap. To set dwell, idle engine slowly. Open or close points until meter reads within specs.

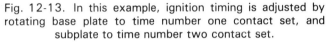

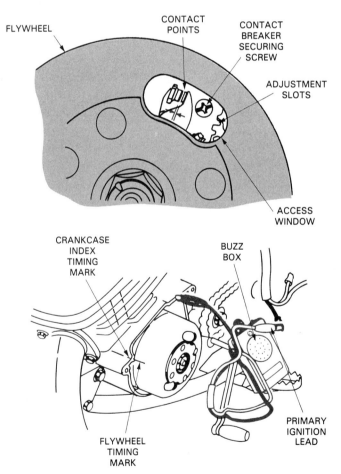

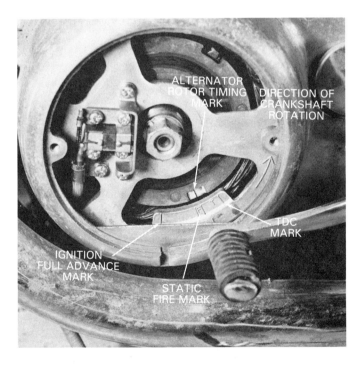

Fig. 12-12. Permanent engine timing marks allow positioning of crankshaft for ignition timing check. This engine has three marks: full advance mark, F mark, and T mark. Full advance mark must align at certain rpm. F mark (static fire) must align at idle. T mark (TDC) is used for valve and cam timing adjustment.

Fig. 12-14. In most flywheel magnetos, timing is adjusted by changing point gap. Timing is checked with a buzz box or a test light. If timing is too retarded, widen point gap. If timing is too advanced, reduce point gap. If proper timing cannot be achieved, contact points are worn and must be replaced.
(U.S. Suzuki Motor Corporation)

gap to advance the ignition timing. Close the contact points to retard the ignition timing.

Other engines do not have timing marks and usually require a dial indicator to measure piston position. Look at Fig. 12-15. The dial indicator takes the place of the permanent timing marks. The contact points must begin to open at a specific piston position or dial indicator reading. Service manual specs are given in piston position or crankshaft degrees before top dead center (BTDC), when the contacts should open.

Actual timing adjustment can be done in two ways:
1. Static (at rest).
2. Dynamic (when operating).

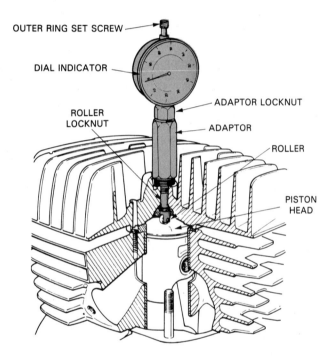

Fig. 12-15. On some engines, a dial indicator is used to measure piston position for ignition timing or timing mark verification. (Bombardier Ltd., Owner of trademark CAN-AM)

Static timing adjustment

STATIC IGNITION TIMING adjustment is done without the engine running and with the ignition switch in the OFF position. A buzz box, continuity light, or ohmmeter is used to indicate when the contact points just begin to open. Fig. 12-16 illustrates static ignition timing adjustment using these test instruments.

One lead of the ohmmeter, buzz box, or continuity light is connected to ground. The other lead is connected to the movable (hot) side of the contact breaker.

When the contacts are closed, current will flow from one lead, through the points, into the other lead. This completes the circuit. When the contacts just open, the circuit is broken. The ohmmeter needle will deflect; the buzz box tone will stop or change

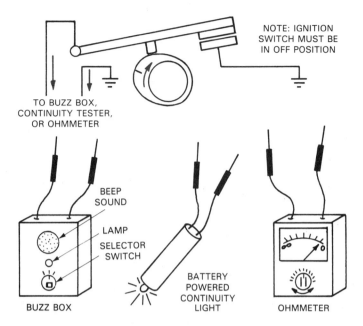

Fig. 12-16. Three methods of determining static timing (contacts begin to open) are shown. A—Buzz box makes a noise to indicate closed points. B—Test light glows. C—Ohmmeter needle deflection shows whether points are opened or closed.

pitch; the continuity light will go out.

Remember, contact opening, not closing, causes the spark to occur.

Static timing is simply the matching of contact initial opening to the engine timing mark or dial indicator position. It is especially useful for initial timing adjustment of an engine after major repairs.

If the timing marks do not line up correctly, ignition timing is either advanced or retarded, Fig. 12-17. To adjust incorrect ignition timing:
1. Advanced timing: Rotate the ignition base plate the same direction the point cam rotates to retard the timing.
2. Retarded timing: Rotate the ignition base plate in the opposite direction of point cam rotation to advance the timing.

Dynamic timing adjustment

DYNAMIC IGNITION TIMING is the most accurate method of verifying and adjusting ignition timing. A strobe light (timing light) triggered by the secondary ignition circuit (spark plug wire) is used to check dynamic timing. Look at Fig. 12-18.

A strobe timing light is connected to the positive and negative sides of the battery, and to one spark plug wire. Most modern timing lights use an induction type pickup. It clips around the spark plug wire. Older non-inductive timing lights must be connected using a special adapter.

Dynamic timing is more accurate than static timing because:
1. The strobe light is triggered by actual ignition operation.
2. Proper ignition advance at a recommended engine rpm can be verified.

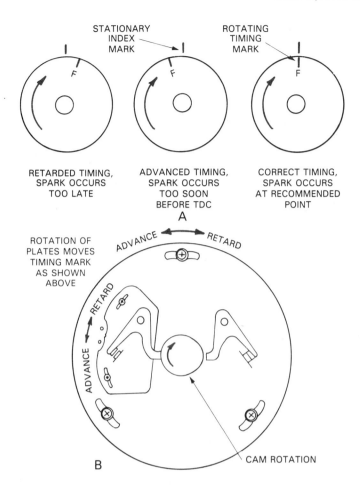

Fig. 12-17. A—Position of rotating timing mark and stationary index mark indicates timing. B—Point cam rotates clockwise. To advance timing, rotate base or subplate in opposite direction of cam rotation. To retard timing, rotate plates in same direction as cam rotation.

Fig. 12-18. A strobe light makes spinning ignition timing marks visible while engine is running. One lead connects to specified spark plug wire and others to battery or 12V source.

Adjustment of ignition timing by the static method does not guarantee perfect timing. Wear in the auto advance unit or point cam and shaft cannot accurately be accounted for by the static adjustment method. Movement of the centrifugal advance unit to the full advance position at a specified rpm can only be verified by the dynamic method of ignition timing.

NOTE! When contact points are replaced or when contact gap is adjusted, ignition timing will be changed. Timing adjustment is required whenever point gap is altered. Static timing should be done first. This insures that ignition timing is reasonably close. Dynamic timing should then be done as a final verification. Adjustments for correcting dynamic timing are the same as for static timing. Refer back to Fig. 12-17.

When rotating the base plate (engine running), leave the base plate screws snugged lightly. Move the base plate a little at a time and check timing after each movement. When correct timing is achieved, recheck timing after the base plate screws have been tightened.

When adjusting the base plate on engines which drive the point cam off the camshaft, rotate the base plate a very small amount. The amount of base plate rotation will be doubled at the crankshaft.

ELECTRONIC IGNITION SYSTEM SERVICING

Some electronic ignition systems (including transistorized) cannot be adjusted. Adjustment could upset engine operation and cause problems with exhaust emission requirements. With these systems, no slots are provided for rotation of the base plate or movement of the magnetic pickup. The timing marks are simply used to check system condition and operation. Look at Fig. 12-19.

With electronic ignition systems having provisions for adjustment, ignition timing is adjusted in a similar manner to the contact point type system. The base plate is rotated to change timing. Figs. 12-20 and 12-21 show typical electronic ignition timing adjustment.

Air gap adjustment

Another adjustment which may be necessary on an electronic ignition is the air gap adjustment. In order for a magnetic trigger to operate properly, a certain AIR GAP must be maintained between the pickup coil and rotor. This air gap is checked with a feeler gauge, and is usually adjusted by moving the pickup

Fig. 12-19. This transistorized or electronic ignition system does not provide for ignition timing adjustment. However, timing marks are used to verify ignition timing, ignition advance, and system condition.

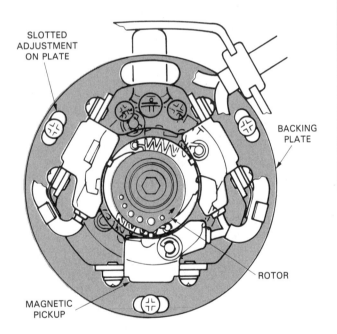

Fig. 12-20. Some electronic ignition systems provide for ignition timing adjustment. Rotation of backing plate changes timing. (Kawasaki Motors Corp., U.S.A.)

assembly. See Fig. 12-22.

Refer to the service manual for proper air gap adjustment procedures and specifications.

ENGINE AND CARBURETOR TUNE-UP

It was mentioned earlier that the valve train and carburetor must also be adjusted during a tune-up. The necessary adjustments typically include:
1. Valve clearance adjustment.
2. Cam chain adjustment.

Fig. 12-21. This type electronic ignition can also be timed by turning plate that holds trigger coil.

Fig. 12-22. A feeler gauge is used to check air gap between rotor and magnetic pickup of electronic ignition.

3. Carburetor pilot circuit adjustment.
4. Carburetor synchronization.
5. Idle speed adjustment.

VALVE CLEARANCE ADJUSTMENT

Correct valve clearance adjustment helps assure long valve train service life. When valve clearance is too tight, valves can overheat. This can cause the valve faces and seats to burn. Loss of compression and accelerated cam and follower wear may also result from inadequate valve clearance. When valve clearance is too loose, valve train life is shortened because of the pounding or hammering effect between parts.

Several methods of adjustment are used to compensate for changes in valve clearance caused by normal wear:

1. Screw type adjusters on cam followers or rocker arms, Fig. 12-23.
2. Adjustable push rods, Fig. 12-24.
3. Shim type adjusters, Fig. 12-25.

CAM CHAIN ADJUSTMENT

Cam chain adjustment is needed to take up excess slack as the chain and sprockets wear. A loose chain

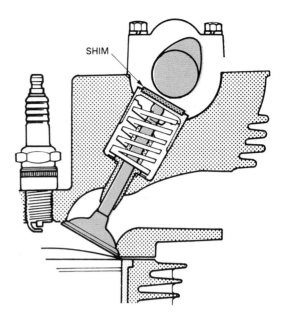

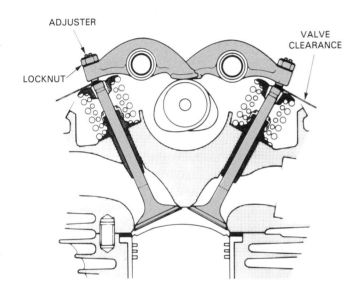

Fig. 12-25. Clearance is adjusted by changing valve shim thickness with this engine design.
(Kawasaki Motors Corp., U.S.A.)

wears prematurely and can cause improper valve timing, chain guide damage, and an annoying chain slap noise.

A manual chain tensioner, Fig. 12-26, or automatic cam chain tensioner, Fig. 12-27, is provided for chain adjustment. On some engines, the chain is adjusted with the crankshaft in a specified position and with

Fig. 12-23. Screw and nut type adjuster provides a quick and easy means of valve adjustment. A feeler gauge will measure valve clearance when valve is closed.
(Kawasaki Motors Corp., U.S.A.)

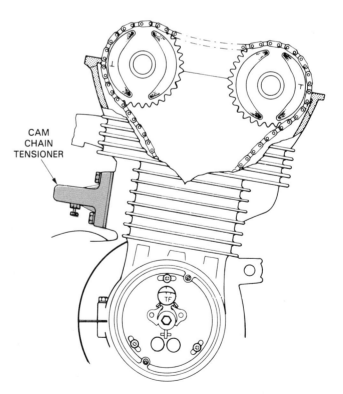

Fig. 12-24. With adjustable push rods, valve clearance is reduced by lengthening push rod. Clearance is increased by shortening push rod. This is done by means of a threaded adjuster and locknut at tappet end of push rod.

Fig. 12-26. A manual type chain tensioner uses a bolt and locknut to hold tensioner in position after adjustment.
(Kawasaki Motors Corp., U.S.A.)

Fig. 12-27. An automatic cam chain tensioner compensates for chain wear as engine runs.

Fig. 12-28. Use a screwdriver to adjust pilot air screw while following specific service manual procedures.

the engine stopped. Other engines require the engine to either be kicked over or running while tension is adjusted. Always follow the service manual since adjustment procedures vary.

CARBURETOR PILOT CIRCUIT ADJUSTMENT

Pilot circuit adjustment is a very fine adjustment of the carburetor's air-fuel mixture at idle and slightly above. Adjustment of the carburetor pilot circuit is usually required during a tune-up to achieve a proper air-fuel mixture. The fuel mixture can be affected as a result of the tune-up.

Some of the tune-up procedures which can cause a need for carburetor adjustment are:
1. Installing a new air filter.
2. Replacing spark plugs.
3. Adjusting point gap and ignition timing.
4. Adjusting valve clearance.

Pilot screws are easily located on the carburetor. Your manual will give the proper initial pilot screw settings. For final adjustment, make sure the engine is completely warm. See Fig. 12-28.

CARBURETOR SYNCHRONIZATION

Carburetor synchronization is the adjustment of the throttles to achieve equal air-fuel delivery to each engine cylinder. VACUUM GAUGES are used to monitor intake manifold vacuum for each cylinder. When the vacuum gauges all read the same, the carburetors are properly synchronized.

Like the pilot circuit, carburetor synchronization is affected by other tune-up operations, especially valve clearance. Fig. 12-29 illustrates typical carburetor synchronization.

Refer to your service manual since adjustment procedures and recommended vacuum settings vary.

IDLE SPEED ADJUSTMENT

The final carburetor adjustment normally required is the idle speed adjustment. Most modern motorcycles with two or more cylinders have a single idle adjustment screw, Fig. 12-30. It is easy to get at and does not require the use of tools.

Recommended idle speeds range from about 800 to 1100 rpm. Follow the recommendation of the service manual for an exact idle speed.

NOTE! Correct procedures for all carburetor adjustments are covered in Chapter 9, Fuel Systems. If needed, refer to this chapter for a quick review.

TUNE-UP AND GENERAL SERVICING SUMMARY

The following is a summary of the most important steps for completing the thorough tune-up and servicing of a motorcycle.

Remember to always use the instructions in a service manual. The slightest mistake could upset engine performance, motorcycle safety, or result in serious part damage.
1. Test compression in each cylinder, Fig. 12-31.
2. Adjust valves, Figs. 12-32 through 12-36.
3. Adjust cam chain.
4. Clean or replace contact breakers. Adjust gap.
5. Clean and lubricate contact breaker cam and rubbing block.
6. Check electronic ignition trigger (pickup) clearance.
7. Clean or replace air filter, Figs. 12-37 and 12-38.
8. Clean fuel sediment bowl and screen, Figs. 12-39 and 12-40.
9. Gap and install new spark plugs, Figs. 12-41 and 12-42.

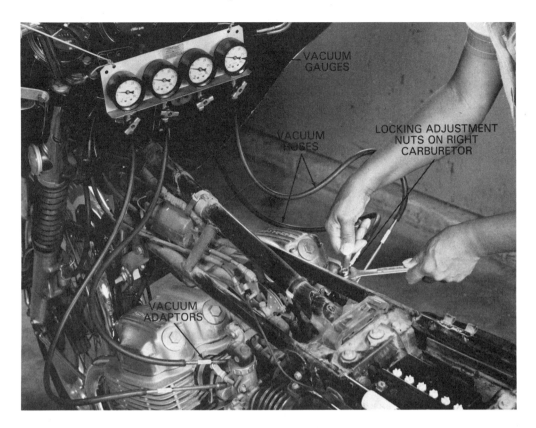

Fig. 12-29. Mechanic has locked adjustment nuts on right carburetor. Notice that all vacuum gauges are reading same, about 7 1/2 in. of vacuum. This shows that all carburetor throttles are adjusted properly.

Fig. 12-30. Most motorcycles using a multiple carburetor throttle linkage have a single screw for idle speed adjustment. This screw adjusts position of throttle linkage and engine rpm.

Fig. 12-31. Measure engine compression before attempting a tune-up. If pressure reading in any cylinder is below specs, repairs are usually needed.

10. Adjust carburetor mixture.
11. Adjust and lubricate throttle cables.
12. Adjust and lubricate oil injector cable (two-stroke cycle engine), Fig. 12-43.
13. Check and refill oil injection tank (two-stroke cycle engine).
14. Check battery electrolyte level, Fig. 12-44.
15. Check battery state of charge with hydrometer.

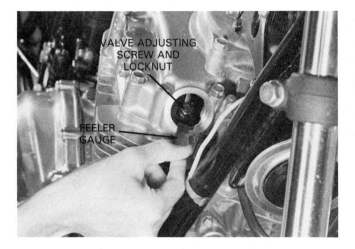

Fig. 12-32. With adjusting screw and nut type valve adjuster, check clearance with feeler gauge. Valve should be fully closed.

Fig. 12-33. If valve clearance is not within specs, turn adjusting screw in or out as needed. Tighten locknut and recheck valve clearance.

Fig. 12-34. When a shim type valve adjuster is used, valve clearance is also measured with a feeler gauge. Cam should be on base circle or in position described in manual.

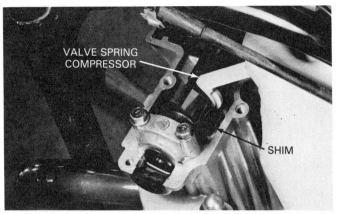

Fig. 12-35. If valve adjuster shim thickness must be changed, a valve spring compressing tool is required. Push down on spring. Slide out old shim and install shim of correct thickness.

Fig. 12-36. To adjust valves on engine with adjustable push rods, loosen locknut and shorten or lengthen push rod as needed. Exact procedures for adjustment and specifications vary with engine design. Refer to a service manual for complete details on the particular engine.

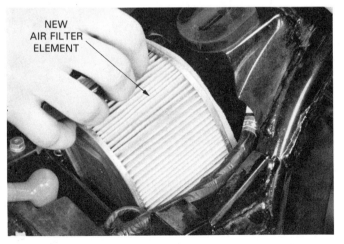

Fig. 12-37. Many air filter elements can be cleaned with solvent, soap and water, or low pressure compressed air. Be sure to check your manual for proper cleaning procedures. Compressed air will destroy some filters.

Fig. 12-38. Paper, foam, and gauze are three common materials used in motorcycle air filters.

16. Check battery terminals for corrosion, grease if necessary.
17. Check liquid cooling system level. If low, check for leaks, Figs. 12-45 and 12-46.
18. Check ignition dwell.
19. Check and adjust ignition timing.
20. Synchronize carburetors.
21. Readjust mixture screws if necessary.
22. Change oil and filter (engine, primary, and gearbox).
23. Check and grease swing arm pivot, Fig. 12-47.

Fig. 12-39. When a sediment bowl is used in petcock, unscrew it so bowl and screen can be cleaned.

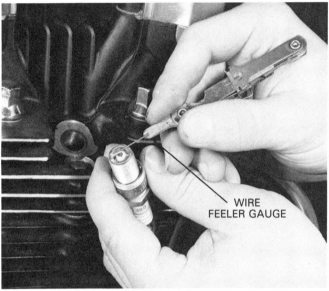

Fig. 12-41. Always use a wire type feeler gauge for spark plug gap measurement. Set to manual specifications.

Fig. 12-40. After cleaning sediment bowl screen, replace O-ring if it shows any signs of deterioration. The O-ring should not be hardened, cracked, or smashed.

Fig. 12-42. A torque wrench is most accurate way to properly tighten a spark plug. Remember! Spark plug torque is very low. Another method is to tighten 1/2 to 3/4 turn after plug gasket is just seated (new gaskets only).

24. Lubricate control levers, control rod ends, and all pivots.
25. Check, lubricate, and adjust the drive chain, Fig. 12-48.
26. Check oil level in rear drive unit (shaft type drive).
27. Lubricate and adjust primary chain.
28. Lubricate and adjust clutch release and cable, Figs. 12-49 through 12-51.
29. Check steering head bearings for looseness. Adjust if necessary, Fig. 12-52.
30. Change fork oil, if needed.

Fig. 12-43. Injection oil pump output is determined by oil pump arm position. Oil pump arm is adjusted by tightening or loosening cable. Index marks are usually provided to insure proper adjustment. Refer to your manual for index mark locations and adjustment procedures.

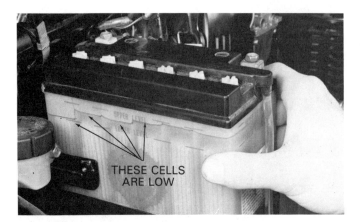

Fig. 12-44. It may be necessary to remove battery to check electrolyte level. This battery needs distilled water added.

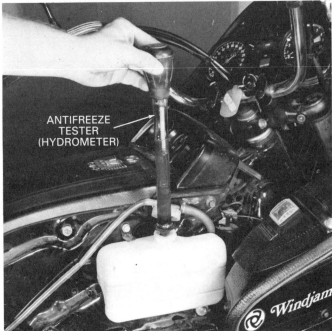

Fig. 12-46. Antifreeze tester or hydrometer will check concentration of water compared to antifreeze. Refer to your service manual for information on antifreeze type and mixture percentage.

Fig. 12-45. Liquid cooling systems should be checked visually for external leaks (hoses, radiator), especially if coolant level is low in reservoir. If coolant must be added, use distilled water and approved antifreeze.

Fig. 12-47. Grease swing arm pivot if grease fittings are provided.

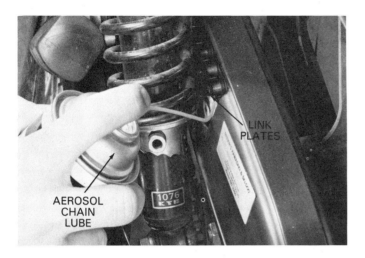

Fig. 12-48. Apply chain lube between link plates while rotating rear wheel.

31. Check operation of forks and shocks.
32. Check brake wear indicators. Adjust brakes, Figs. 12-53 and 12-54.
33. Check brake light switch operation. Adjust if needed, Fig. 12-55.
34. Check brake fluid level. Add if low and check for leakage.
35. Check tire condition and pressure.
36. Check spokes and wheel runout. Tighten any loose spokes, Figs. 12-56 and 12-57.
37. Check lights, horn, electric starter, warning lights, buzzers, and kill switch. Replace burned out bulbs.
38. Check important nuts and bolts for tightness. Replace any missing fasteners, Fig. 12-58.

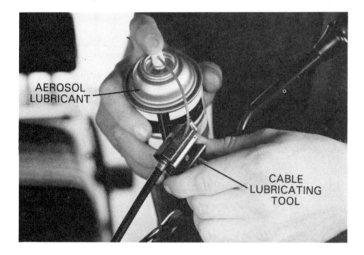

Fig. 12-49. A cable lubricating tool will aid and speed up cable lubrication.

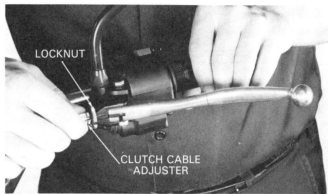

Fig. 12-51. After adjusting clutch release mechanism, set clutch cable free play.

Fig. 12-50. Clutch adjustment is done in three steps: Loosen cable tension, adjust clutch release mechanism, and adjust cable free play. Mechanic is adjusting clutch release in this photo.

Fig. 12-52. A quick check to detect steering head looseness is done by gripping lower fork legs and applying forward and aft pressure. Front wheel should be off ground. Use center stand and weight on rear of motorcycle.

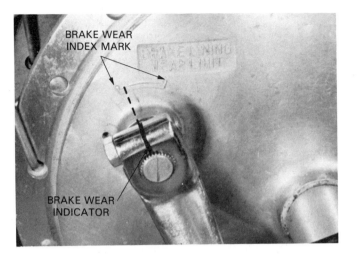

Fig. 12-53. On drum brakes, a wear limit indicator and index mark may be used to show when brake linings are becoming badly worn.

Fig. 12-54. Disc brake pads sometimes use a groove around friction material to indicate maximum wear. If worn down to groove, replace pads.

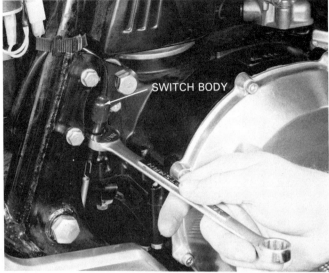

Fig. 12-55. Adjustment of brake light switch is usually done by moving switch body up or down (special adjuster nut is rotated). Adjust brake light switch using manual specs and double-check that it operates properly.

Fig. 12-56. A quick check for excessive wheel runout can be made using any aerosol can and spray tube as an indicator. A dial indicator should be used to measure exact wheel runout. If runout exceeds about .040 in. (1 mm), remove and true rim.

39. Road test while checking for leaks, proper handling, braking, and engine performance.

KNOW THESE TERMS

Contact point gap, Point cam index mark, Dwell, Static timing, Dynamic timing, Advanced timing, Retarded timing, Strobe or timing light, Electronic ignition air gap, Valve clearance, Carburetor synchronization, Compression test, Cam chain adjustment, General service, Tune-up.

REVIEW QUESTIONS—CHAPTER 12

1. Define the term tune-up.
2. What is the first step of any tune-up?
3. Heavy contact pitting indicates fouled spark plugs. True or False?
4. Where is lubrication required on breaker point ignition systems?
5. What is ignition dwell?
6. What are two ways of determining contact point gap?
7. Static timing is accomplished with the engine run-

Fig. 12-57. Tightening a few loose spokes should not affect wheel runout. If extensive tightening is required, it might be necessary to remove wheel and tire assembly to true wheel.

ning. True or False?
8. Give two reasons why dynamic timing is more accurate than static timing.
9. List four of the valve train and carburetor adjustments that are done during a tune-up.

10. Always replace both the movable and stationary contacts as a complete set. True or False?
11. What can happen if the contact spring and fiber washers are NOT installed correctly?
12. If contact rubbing blocks are NOT properly lubricated, which of the following can result?
    a. Premature rubbing block wear.
    b. Reduced point gap.
    c. Increased dwell.
    d. Retarded ignition timing.
    e. All of the above.
    f. None of the above.
13. List three ways of altering ignition timing for adjustment purposes.
14. A buzzbox, continuity light, or _____ can be used to check static ignition timing.
15. Valve clearance which is too tight can cause _____.
16. List three methods used for valve clearance adjustment.
17. Carburetor pilot circuit adjustment is NOT affected by valve clearance. True or False?
18. Vacuum gauges are frequently used for _____ _____.

Fig. 12-58. It is important to check all external mounting fasteners for tightness. This job only takes a few minutes and can help you avoid embarrassment and danger caused by loose parts. Make sure you replace any missing, striped, or broken fasteners.

SUGGESTED ACTIVITIES

1. Perform a compression test. Refer to shop manual specifications to see if the engine top end is in good condition. Do this on several different makes of engines.
2. Replace contact points. Make the following adjustments and checks:
   a. Contact point gap with a feeler gauge.
   b. Dwell with a dwell meter.
   c. Static ignition timing.
   d. Dynamic ignition timing.
3. Check and adjust valve clearance on motorcycles which use two different adjustment methods.
4. Using vacuum gauges, synchronize the carburetors on a motorcycle.

Before studying Chapter 13, see how many bolts and parts you can find that must be removed to allow engine removal.

Chapter 13

ENGINE REMOVAL

After studying this chapter, you will be able to:
☐ Prepare a motorcycle for engine removal.
☐ Disconnect the electrical system, control cables, and other parts fastened to the frame.
☐ Remove engine mounting bolts while securing engine.
☐ Remove and mount engine on stand or box.
☐ Summarize the basic steps for engine removal.

In this chapter, we will discuss the procedures for proper and safe engine removal from a motorcycle frame. This is a very common operation that requires considerable skill.

Before unbolting the engine, you must know exactly what is wrong. Find out whether or not the engine can be repaired while still in the frame. It may be possible to fix the engine without removal.

Engine removal may be needed for:
1. Complete engine overhaul.
2. Top-end overhaul.
3. Bottom-end repairs.
4. Gearbox repair.
5. Exterior damage (crash related).

CLEAN THE MOTORCYCLE

Before beginning work, it is important to clean the engine and motorcycle thoroughly. This makes engine removal and disassembly a much cleaner and safer job. Shown in Fig. 13-1, engine degreaser and a pressure washer or hose makes cleaning easy.

Remember! The smallest particle of dirt can easily ruin engine bearings, cylinders, oil pumps, and the job.

READ THE SERVICE MANUAL

A few minutes spent reading the service manual prior to engine removal will save time and aggravation. Several service manuals are pictured in Fig. 13-2.

Fig. 13-1. Degreasing and pressure washing makes engine removal more enjoyable and less messy. External cleaning only takes a few minutes.

Fig. 13-2. A service manual is an absolute necessity. It provides you with clearances, specifications, and procedures. A manual will help you perform competent service and repair work.

231

The service manual gives information on:
1. Which way the engine comes out of the frame.
2. The location of engine mounting bolts.
3. Which cables, linkages, and electrical wires must be disconnected.
4. Whether or not the carburetors must be removed.
5. The procedure for disconnecting the final drive.

For example, avoid lifting the engine halfway out of the frame and realizing that something is still connected. This wasteful mistake would be a result of not reading the service manual.

DRAIN FLUIDS

Normally, it is much easier to drain all oils (engine and transmission) before the engine is removed, Fig. 13-3. Dry sump lubrication systems must be drained and disconnected before the engine can be removed. On two-stroke cycle engines using oil injection, the feed line must be disconnected and plugged.

DISCONNECT ELECTRICAL SYSTEM

Always remove the battery during engine removal. This prevents accidental shorting of the battery leads, damage to the electrical system, and possibly an electrical fire. Fig. 13-4 illustrates proper battery removal.

Electrical disconnects

There are three types of wire disconnects used in motorcycle electrical systems:
1. Master plug (many wires in a single keyed plug).
2. Individual male-female connectors (bullet or spade types).
3. Eyelet and forked connectors (connected by bolt or screw).

Fig. 13-4. When removing a battery, always disconnect ground side first. If you were to disconnect hot side first, screwdriver or wrench might tough frame. This would cause a short circuit. A spark could then ignite battery gas, blowing battery apart.

Fig. 13-5 shows the three types of electrical connectors. Study their shape and how they fit together.

Color coding of electrical wires

All motorcycle manufacturers COLOR CODE electrical wires. The wire has the same color pattern before and after a plug socket. This makes proper wire connection easy. Fig. 13-6 illustrates typical wire color coding.

On older motorcycles, the color coding may be faded. On some motorcycles, coded wires may have been replaced. When wires are not properly coded or if they are faded, LABEL EACH WIRE as it is disconnected. This insures proper connection during reassembly.

Fig. 13-3. Engine oil should be drained prior to engine removal.

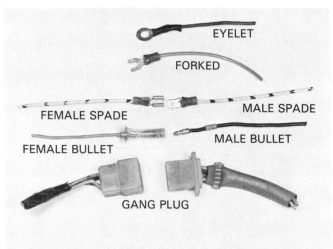

Fig. 13-5. These are common types of connectors used in motorcycle electrical systems.

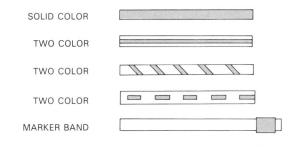

Fig. 13-6. Color coding is used to identify individual wires in electrical system.

DISCONNECT CONTROL CABLES

Control cable disconnection varies from one motorcycle to the next. Look at Fig. 13-7. Cables which may require disconnection for engine removal are:
1. Clutch cable.
2. Tachometer cable.
3. Throttle cables.
4. Oil injection pump cable (two-stroke cycle engine).
5. Enrichment-choke cables.
6. Compression release cable.
7. Rear brake cable (certain motorcycles).

REMOVE CARBURETORS

Carburetor removal is usually necessary during engine removal. The service manual lists exact procedures for carburetor removal. The carburetors could be damaged if left installed during engine removal, Fig. 13-8.

It is important to drain the fuel from the float bowls and store the carburetors properly. This reduces the risk of fire or damage to the carburetors, motorcycle, shop area, or yourself.

Fig. 13-8. On this motorcycle, air box must be removed in order to remove carburetors.

When the engine is being removed for a complete overhaul, the carburetors should be rebuilt. Chapter 9 outlines procedures for carburetor rebuilding.

DISCONNECT FINAL DRIVE

On a motorcycle using a chain type final drive, the chain should be removed, cleaned, inspected, lubricated, and stored. Refer to Fig. 13-7.

On motorcycles using shaft drive, refer to the service manual for proper disconnection methods. Procedures vary from motorcycle to motorcycle.

REMOVE ENGINE MOUNTING BOLTS

Carelessness in removing engine mounting bolts can result in injury. Make sure the engine is properly

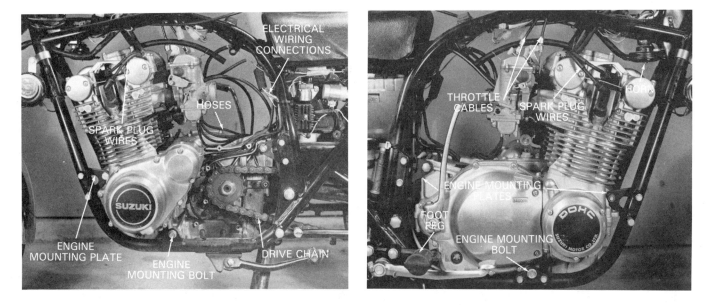

Fig. 13-7. Note typical components that must be disconnected for engine removal.

braced before bolts are removed. See Fig. 13-9. Not only can engines be very heavy, they can be clumsy.

NOTE! You may have to LIFT the engine slightly to ease removal of the last mounting bolt, Fig. 13-10.

Make a note showing the location and position of ground wires, spacers, and mounting brackets. These components will be replaced on the frame after the engine is removed. This will help avoid reassembly confusion and loss of parts.

LIFT ENGINE OUT OF FRAME

Some engines will only come out of the frame in one direction. Components may block removal on the right or left side of the frame. Make sure you know the correct removal direction.

Double-check that all parts (wires, cables, hoses, exhaust system), fastened between the engine and frame are disconnected. Also, make sure everything is out of the way that might block engine removal. Parts can be damaged very easily when lifting a heavy motorcycle engine out of the frame.

The service manual will explain how the engine should be lifted, turned, tipped, and taken out of the motorcycle.

Follow safety rules

To keep engine removal a safe operation:
1. The use of a jack may be necessary.
2. Two people may be required to remove heavy or awkward engines.
3. All tools should be picked up.

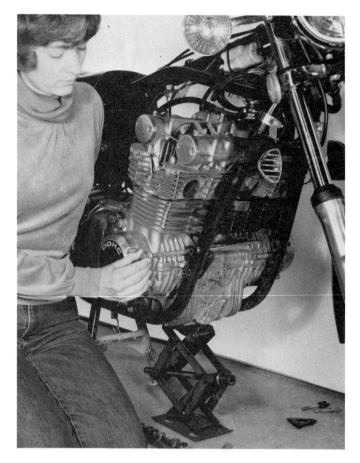

Fig. 13-10. You may need to use a jack to lift and support a heavy engine while removing mounting bolts.

4. Oil or fuel spills should be wiped up immediately.
5. An engine box or stand should be readied.

ORGANIZE PARTS

Once the engine is out of the frame, install it on a stand or engine box, as in Fig. 13-11. All mounting bolts and hardware should be reinstalled on the frame in their proper locations.

At this time, the frame can be more thoroughly cleaned. The paint can be touched up. Then, the frame should be stored out of the way.

ENGINE REMOVAL SUMMARY

Using the following engine removal summary as a guide will help you carry out engine removal in the proper sequence.
1. Clean and degrease motorcycle exterior.
2. Check service manual for:
   a. Direction of engine removal.
   b. Mounting bolt locations.
   c. Sequence for disassembly (specific).
3. Drain fluids.
4. Remove battery.
5. Disconnect engine electrical connectors.
6. Remove carburetors.

Fig. 13-9. A sturdy, secure engine brace should be used while removing engine mounting bolts. If not, engine case damage or bodily injury could result.

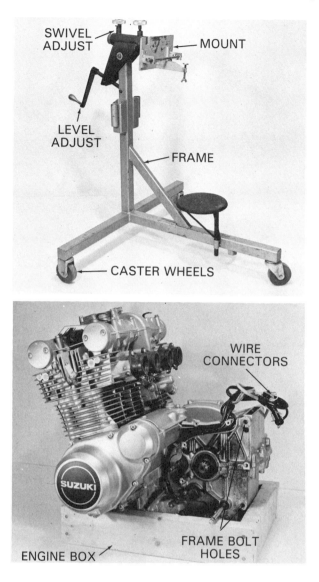

SWIVEL ADJUST — MOUNT

LEVEL ADJUST

— FRAME

— CASTER WHEELS

WIRE CONNECTORS

SUZUKI

ENGINE BOX

FRAME BOLT HOLES

Fig. 13-11. For safety and convenience, engine should be installed on an engine stand or box as soon as it has been removed from frame.

a. Drail fuel.
b. Store properly.
7. Disconnect control cables.
8. Disconnect exhaust system and store system properly.

9. Disconnect final drive
10. Brace engine and remove mounting bolts.
11. Clean work area.
12. Prepare engine box or stand.
13. Lift engine out of frame and install on engine box or stand.
14. Replace mounting bolts and brackets on frame.
15. Clean and touch up paint on frame.

KNOW THESE TERMS

Master plug, Wire connectors, Eyelet connectors, Wire color coding, Engine mounting bolts, Engine removal direction, Engine stand, Engine box.

REVIEW QUESTIONS—CHAPTER 13

1. It is a waste of time to clean the engine before it is removed from the frame. True or False?
2. All engines can be removed from either side of the frame. True or False?
3. The main reason for removing a battery during engine removal is to prevent _____.
4. Name three types of electrical connectors which may have to be disconnected during engine removal.
5. The _____ side of the battery should always be disconnected first.
6. After removing an engine, it should be mounted on a _____ or _____.
7. List three safety rules for engine removal.

SUGGESTED ACTIVITIES

1. Construct an engine box or stand.
2. Remove a two-stroke cycle engine from a motorcycle.
3. Remove a four-stroke cycle engine from the frame.
4. Locate all of the engine mounting bolts on various motorcycles.
5. Make a general list of the wires, cables, hoses, brackets, and other parts that must be unfastened before engine removal. Place this list in the useful information section of your notebook.

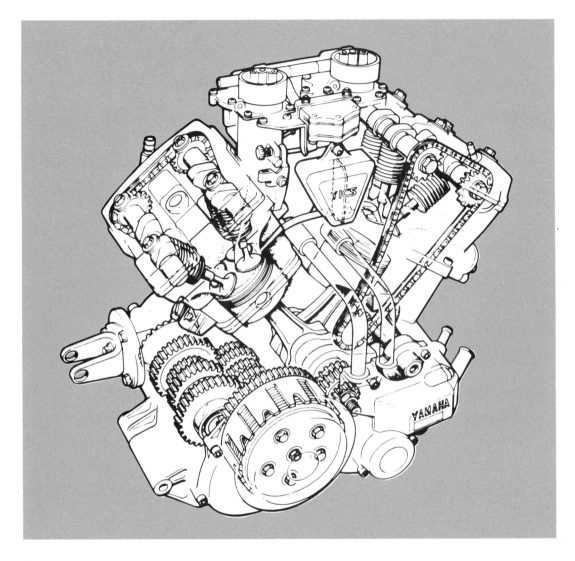

Cutaway view of high performance four-valve per cylinder engine. Can you identify all of the parts?
(Yamaha Motor Corporation, U.S.A.)

Chapter 14

ENGINE, PRIMARY DRIVE, AND GEARBOX DISASSEMBLY

After studying this chapter, you will be able to:
□ Use the specific instructions in a shop manual to disassemble an engine, primary drive, and gearbox.
□ Organize wires, shims, and other parts properly during dissasembly.
□ Explain the use of special holding and pulling devices.
□ Describe the use of heat to aid disassembly.
□ List typical problems encountered during engine, primary drive, and gearbox disassembly.

This chapter discusses the importance of organization and correct procedures during the disassembly of a motorcycle engine, primary drive, and gearbox. It also covers special disassembly methods and problems. The information in this chapter is very important. Study carefully!

ORGANIZE YOUR WORK AREA

Always organize your work area before starting to work. Proper organization of the work area, tools, and disassembled parts is essential. A little extra effort and care during teardown can help avoid problems later. The slightest mistake upon reassembly (wrong bolt, shim, spring, or tool) can cause severe engine, primary drive, or gearbox damage. You might have to do the repair over again, at your expense.

A professional, high quality repair is much easier to do in a clean, orderly work area. Your work area should also have sufficient lighting and ventilation.

Remember! The condition of your work area reflects upon your work habits and mechanical ability. A SLOPPY WORK AREA indicates a sloppy worker!

Shop manual

Before beginning disassembly, read the proper sections of a shop manual for the particular motorcycle being repaired. This will enable you to gather many of the necessary tools and preview general disassembly procedures.

Engine stand

To steady the engine and allow easy access to different areas of the engine, an engine stand is very helpful. It allows the engine to be rotated and held in various positions while working. Fig. 14-1 shows a motorcycle engine mounted on an engine stand.

If an engine stand is not available, a homemade engine box should be used. An engine box was shown in Fig. 13-11.

Tools and equipment

To prevent part damage during disassembly, you must use the proper hand tools and special tools. Correct tool selection and use will also save time and effort. Fig. 14-2 shows an impact driver, commonly needed to loosen Phillips head fasteners. Fig. 14-3 shows a valve spring compressor.

An unprofessional mechanic might be able to take an engine apart with a monkey wrench, a hammer, and a chisel. However, would you want this mechanic to work on your motorcycle? It is extremely important to select the correct tools for the job at hand.

If needed, review Chapter 2, Tools and Safety. This will help you with the rest of the information in this chapter.

Storage containers

During engine disassembly, it is important to keep groups of related parts together. This may be done by

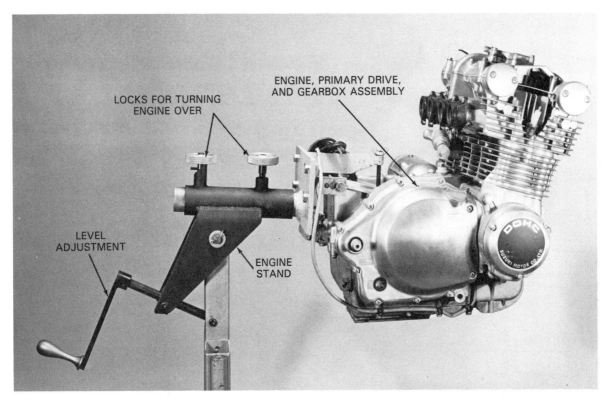

Fig. 14-1. An engine stand is very useful for engine disassembly. It lets engine swivel into various positions for easy repair. Stand and engine will also roll easily to other locations in shop.

Fig. 14-2. An impact driver provides inward pressure and torque to loosen stubborn fasteners without damaging them. When driver is hit with hammer, driver rotates with tremendous force.

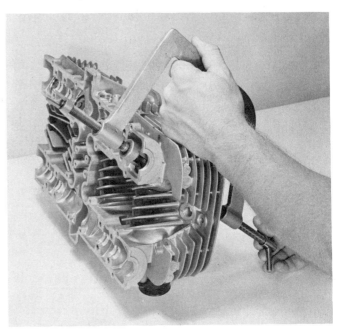

Fig. 14-3. A valve spring compressor is just one type of special tool. It is needed for cylinder head disassembly and reassembly.

by using plastic bags, plastic containers, small metal pans, cans, and cardboard boxes. See Fig. 14-4. Orderly part and bolt storage saves time and effort during reassembly.

Tags and markings

When disassembling an engine for the first time, you should place TAGS or MARKINGS on some parts to aid reassembly. Mark any part that could get mixed up. Never rely solely on memory when working on an unfamiliar engine assembly. For example, if two wires are crossed during reassembly, part damage could result. Place tags on wires noting their location or connection point.

Fig. 14-4. Use cardboard boxes, plastic bags, and pans to keep groups of engine parts separated. This procedure takes little time but can save much time when reassembling engine.

Engine fasteners

The assorted bolts, nuts, screws, and other fasteners that secure engine parts vary in size, length, and shape. These fasteners should be kept organized. If bolt lengths are mixed up, for example, thread or part damage can occur. Two methods are commonly used to keep fasteners organized:
1. Draw a picture illustrating the position of each screw or bolt (measure length of each).
2. Make a pattern board of screw and bolt locations as in Fig. 14-5.

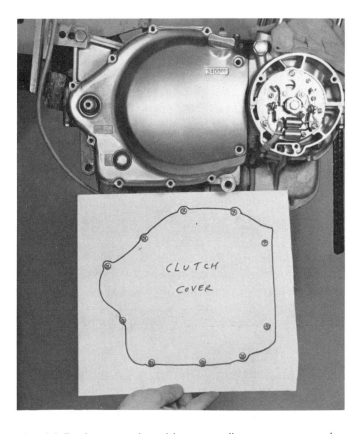

Fig. 14-5. A pattern board is an excellent way to organize fasteners. Fasteners fit into board as they would into cover. This assures that different screw or bolt lengths will be installed in proper holes upon reassembly.

Mating parts

Because mating parts rub against each other during engine operation, they develop certain wear patterns. If mating parts are to be reused, they must be assembled in the exact same position during reassembly. This eliminates the development of a new and different wear pattern. Failure to properly organize and tag mating parts during engine disassembly may lead to premature wear, leakage, and excessive clearance between parts.

A typical motorcycle engine has many mating parts. Some of these are:
1. Cylinder wall and its piston.
2. Valve stem and its guide.
3. Cam follower and its cam lobe.
4. Cam follower and its shaft.
5. Tappet, with its push rod, rocker arm, and rocker shaft.
6. Piston, piston pin, and connecting rod.
7. Rod bearing, connecting rod, and journal.
8. Main bearing and its journal.
9. Roller bearing and its outer race (two-piece type).
10. Shim bucket and its bore.
11. Cam bearing and its journal.

This is only a small representative list of mating parts. There are many other mating parts in an engine. Keep them organized and paired for reassembly!

Shims and washers

SHIMS and THRUST WASHERS are used to properly locate, align, or provide clearance for certain engine parts. These shims and washers may have the same inside and outside diameters but different thicknesses. Failure to locate even one shim or washer in its correct position can cause premature wear, misalignment, and engine failure. Too much or too little end play can result if a shim is located incorrectly.

Remember! Careful observation, marking, and tagging during disassembly assures proper location of shims and washers during reassembly.

Tape, wire tags, string tags, and labeled plastic bags are helpful for organizing shims and washers.

239

Fig. 14-6 illustrates how valve components (valves, springs, keepers) are marked and bagged for quick and precise assembly.

DIVIDING THE ENGINE

The engine should be taken apart and organized into five groups:
1. Top end.
2. Left side.
3. Right side.
4. Lower end.
5. Gearbox.

Fig. 14-7 shows these divisions. Separating the parts of the engine in this manner will make the job much easier.

Engine top end

The top end of an engine consists of the parts from the cylinder base up. This typically includes the pistons, piston pins, cylinder head, and valve components. See Fig. 14-7.

Engine left and right side

Depending upon design, some of the parts you may encounter on the left and right of an engine are:
1. Primary drive (gear or chain type).
2. Clutch.
3. Alternator.
4. Magneto.
5. Cam gears and chains.
6. Countershaft sprocket.
7. Battery and coil ignition breaker plate.
8. Capacitor discharge ignition rotor and coils.

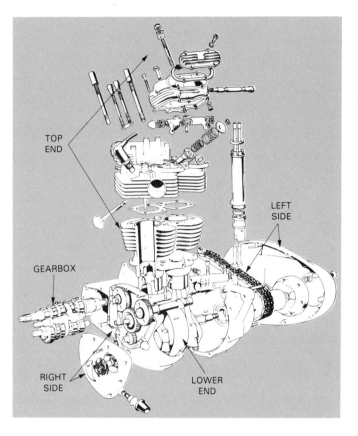

Fig. 14-7. Engine disassembly, inspection, and reassembly is made easier when engine is divided into groups. Study parts within each grouping.
(Triumph Motorcycles [Meriden] Ltd.)

9. Kickstart mechanism.
10. Rotary valve and carburetor.

It is very important to keep left side parts separate from right side parts. These parts vary from engine to engine. They can cause confusion, frustration, and time loss if not organized.

Removal of left and right side parts allows access to the crankcase of the engine.

NOTE! On horizontally opposed or transverse V-type engines, the left and right sides are called "front" and "rear."

Engine lower end (bottom end)

The lower end or bottom end of an engine is the group of components contained within the crankcase (crankshaft, connecting rods, main bearings), excluding the gearbox.

Gearbox (transmission)

The gear change mechanism, shafts, and gears make up the gearbox division of the engine. There are two types of gearbox divisions—unit and non-unit types.

With non-unit types, the gearbox division includes a gearbox case that is separate from the engine. One is shown in Fig. 14-8. With UNIT CONSTRUCTION ENGINES, the gearbox is housed within the

Fig. 14-6. It is important to keep mating components matched. Numbering or labeling makes this easy. Notice that valve seats and plastic bags have been numbered with a marker.

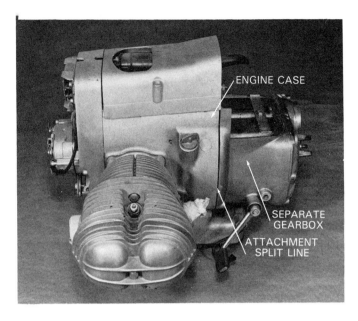

Fig. 14-8. A separate gearbox or transmission case is bolted to engine on a non-unit design.

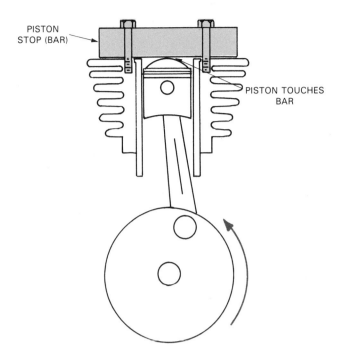

Fig. 14-9. Bolting a piston stop bar or plate across top of cylinder is one way to prevent crankshaft movement. It lets various bolts and nuts be loosened without engine crankshaft rotation.

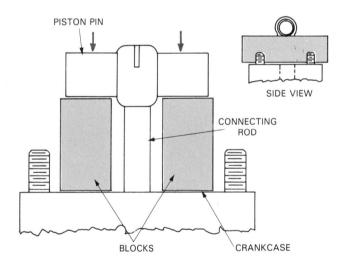

Fig. 14-10. Piston pin blocks placed across top of crankcase provide a positive crankshaft stop. This keeps engine from turning during disassembly and reassembly.

crankcase assembly. The engine crankcase must be split in order to reach the gearbox. Most motorcycles use unit type construction.

HOLDERS AND PULLERS

Holders and pullers are required to properly disassemble an engine. An ENGINE HOLDER is a device for preventing engine, clutch, and gearbox rotation while loosening nuts or bolts. A PULLER is a device for removing tight fitting or interference fitted parts (pulley, gears, housings) from shafts.

Engine holders

There are a number of ways to keep the engine crankshaft, clutch, and gearbox from rotating during engine disassembly. The most common methods used are:

1. A bar or plate bolted across the cylinder top to stop piston movement, Fig. 14-9.
2. Blocks fitted under piston pin to limit rod and crankshaft movement, Fig. 14-10.
3. A clutch holder made by welding a handle on clutch plates (may be constructed or a factory special tool), Fig. 14-11.
4. Special locking pliers for holding the clutch center hub, Fig. 14-12.
5. Clamp pliers or a chain wrench to hold the gearbox output sprocket, Fig. 14-13.

Many service manuals do not cover proper methods of locking (preventing rotation) of an engine during disassembly. Proper use of one or more of the above methods makes disassembly easy. However, improper locking techniques usually lead to broken or damaged parts.

Pullers

Manufacturers produce various types of special pullers needed during engine disassembly. Components which may require the use of pullers are:

1. Alternator rotor.
2. Cam gears.
3. Primary drive sprocket or gear.
4. Clutch hub.
5. Crankshaft (from one crankcase half).
6. Gearbox output sprocket.

241

Fig. 14-11. This factory clutch holder is made from one drive plate and one driven plate with a handle attached. Tool can be welded together easily. Tool holds clutch hub while fasteners are removed.

Fig. 14-12. These locking pliers grip clutch hub firmly. They allow you to loosen or tighten clutch hub nut. Overtightening of pliers, though, could damage clutch basket.

7. Piston pin.

Puller designs vary as much as engine designs. See Fig. 14-14. Pullers come in various configurations and sizes. The basic types of special pullers are:
1. Bolt type puller.
2. Double-threaded type puller.
3. Slide hammer type puller.
4. Bar type puller.

Most service manuals list the special tools required for an engine overhaul. It is extremely important to use these tools when needed.

Some accessory manufacturers produce special pullers and other tools which have universal applications. When your tool budget is limited, universal type tools should be purchased. They can be used for varying operations and on different motorcycle types.

Fig. 14-13. A pair of clamp pliers can be used to safely hold countershaft sprocket while loosening sprocket nut.

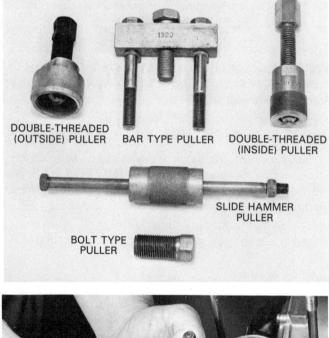

Fig. 14-14. Special pullers are essential in many situations. These are the most common types of pullers used in motorcycle repair.

USING HEAT TO AID DISASSEMBLY

Heating a part causes the part to expand. Engine parts made of different metals will expand at dif-

242

ferent rates. This principle aids engine disassembly and reassembly.

A steel part surrounded by an aluminum part is a good example of heat expansion rates of different metals. As both parts are heated, the aluminum expands more than the steel. This causes clearance between the parts and allows the steel part to be removed easily from the aluminum part. Fig. 14-15 illustrates this principle.

The use of heat on the following parts is common during engine disassembly and reassembly:
1. Valve guides.
2. Piston pins.
3. Bushings mounted in crankcase.
4. Tight fitting bearings in crankcase (vertical-split crankcases).
5. Cylinder sleeves.
6. Transmission gears (press-fit type).

Three acceptable methods of heating parts are a torch (propane), hot plate, and oven.

The oven is usually the best method of heating parts. It provides an accurate method of heat control. A torch or hot plate can cause uneven heating and part damage (cracking, warping, melting).

Heat use warnings

Some rules to remember when using heat are:
1. Do NOT exceed 275°F (135°C) except for valve guide or sleeve removal.
2. Do NOT heat engine parts to the point of discoloration.
3. When using a torch, keep it moving. DO NOT heat one area too much.
4. When removing crankcase bearings, use an oven. Heat the whole crankcase, NOT just the area around the bearing.
5. When heating pistons, heat the crown, NOT the

skirt or pin boss.
6. Use insulated gloves or hot pads when handling heated parts.
7. Work only in a well ventilated area. Make sure gasoline or paint fumes are NOT present.

Parts can sometimes be overheated, causing warpage, softening and discoloration. Your service manual outlines more precise use of heat for particular engine disassembly and assembly procedures.

SEQUENCE OF DISASSEMBLY

The sequence of disassembly is determined by engine design and the type of overhaul being done. Most engines can be disassembled in any sequence, however, following the recommended sequence usually makes the job easier. The motorcycle's service manual gives the proper disassembly sequence for each job.

TWO-STROKE CYCLE LEAK TEST

Before disassembling a two-stroke cycle engine, it is advisable to perform a crankcase leak test. This is especially important on multi-cylinder, two-stroke cycle engines. A visual inspection of the inner seals requires crankshaft disassembly. A leak test determines seal condition before disassembly.

A two-stroke cycle engine CRANKCASE LEAK TEST consists of:
1. Sealing the intake and exhaust ports.
2. Positioning the piston at BDC (bottom dead center).
3. Pressurizing the crankcase to 6 psi (4l kPa).
4. Monitoring the pressure gauge while using a soap and water solution to find any crankcase leaks.

Fig. 14-16 illustrates the procedure for a two-stroke cycle leak test.

TYPICAL ENGINE DISASSEMBLY PROBLEMS

Various problems may be encountered during engine disassembly. Your ability and patience in dealing with these problems will make the difference between an easy job and one that results in broken engine parts.

A number of minor difficulties can cause problems during engine disassembly. These include tightly bonded gaskets that will not separate or an interference fit component that will not slide free.

The following list outlines some of the more common problems that you could encounter during engine disassembly.

CYLINDER HEAD AND CYLINDER BLOCK REMOVAL PROBLEMS
1. Tightly bonded gaskets.
2. Corroded or damaged locating dowels.
3. Missing fasteners.
4. Stripped bolt heads and threads.

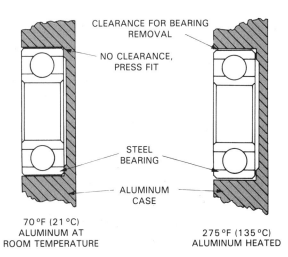

Fig. 14-15. Using heat during assembly and disassembly can make bearing installation and removal easy. This is because heat causes one metal part (housing) to expand at a faster rate than the other (bearing).

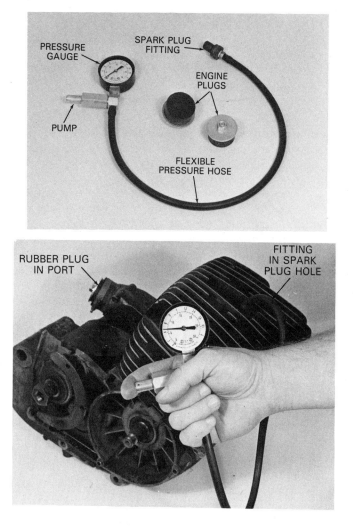

Fig. 14-17. Multi-cylinder heads are frequently bonded to cylinder block by gasket material. A plastic hammer may be used to break head loose. Only hammer on reinforced area. Cooling fins will break off easily.

4. Fasteners still installed (hidden by grease or mud).

The remedy for many of these problems is self-explanatory. You would need to hammer or pry in the right place on the parts. A puller or heat may also be needed to free the parts. In any case, use the right tools and procedures. The information in this chapter and a service manual will guide you through most disassembly problems.

Figs. 14-17, 14-18, and 14-19 give examples of very common procedures that solve typical engine disassembly problems.

Fig. 14-16. This two-stroke leak tester uses a spark plug adaptor to pressurize crankcase. Expanding rubber plugs seal intake and exhaust ports. If everything is in good shape, engine should hold six psi (41 kPa) pressure for six minutes.

WRIST PIN REMOVAL PROBLEMS
1. Interference fit between wrist pin and piston boss.
2. Varnish formed on wrist pin.
3. Peened edge (burred edge) next to wrist pin circlip.

CYLINDER HEAD DISASSEMBLY PROBLEMS
1. Stuck (wedged) valve spring collars and keepers.
2. Mushroomed valve stems.
3. Lip formed just above keeper groove on valve stems.

PRIMARY DRIVE DISASSEMBLY PROBLEMS
1. Difficulty holding clutch hub and primary drive gear when loosening center nuts.

FLYWHEEL REMOVAL PROBLEMS
1. Extremely tight interference fit on crankshaft.
2. Corroded or damaged surfaces.

CRANKCASE SEPARATION PROBLEMS
1. Binding of shaft ends in cases by trying to separate cases unevenly (vertical-split cases).
2. Extremely tight interference fit between crankshaft and main bearings (vertical-split cases).
3. Corroded case locating dowels.

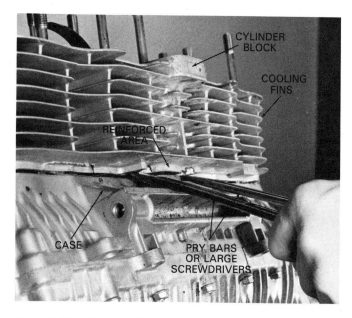

Fig. 14-18. Pry bars, if used carefully, will release cylinder block from crankcase. Do not pry on fins, only bossed area. On some engines, special areas are provided for hammering and prying. Refer to a service manual for location of these areas.

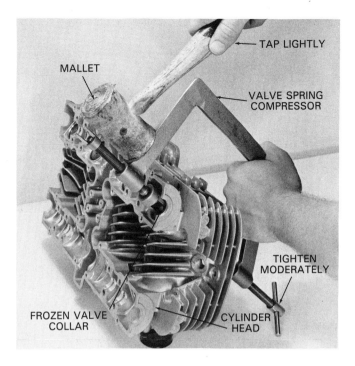

MALLET

TAP LIGHTLY

VALVE SPRING COMPRESSOR

TIGHTEN MODERATELY

FROZEN VALVE COLLAR

CYLINDER HEAD

Fig. 14-19. Avoid overtightening valve spring compressor. It could slip off and damage parts. When keepers are wedged, use light taps from a mallet on compressor. This will cause parts to pop free with minimum strain on compressor.

KNOW THESE TERMS

Engine stand, Engine box, Valve spring compressor, Tags, Markings, Mating parts, Shims, Engine top end, Engine lower end, Engine holder, Puller, Heat expansion, Oven, Crankcase leak test.

REVIEW QUESTIONS—CHAPTER 14

1. You should review a _____ before starting disassembly of an unfamiliar engine.
2. It is important to _____ or _____ certain engine parts to prevent mating parts from getting mixed up.
3. List the five common divisions or sections of an engine.
4. Shims and thrust washers:
   a. Are always interchangeable.
   b. Are only available in one standard size.
   c. Vary in size and thickness.
   d. Vary in size, but not thickness.
5. Why should engine left and right side parts be kept separate?
6. A valve spring is part of which engine division?
7. Most motorcycle engines do NOT require crankcase splitting to reach the gearbox. True or False?
8. A holder and puller perform the same function. True or False?
9. Heat is used to _____ engine parts for easier disassembly.
10. When heating most engine parts, you should not exceed _____°F or _____°C.
11. During a two-stroke cycle engine leak test, you should use how much air pressure?
12. Which of the following is NOT a problem related to cylinder head removal?
    a. Tightly bonded gaskets.
    b. Corroded or damaged locating dowels.
    c. Stripped bolt heads and threads.
    d. Varnish on wrist pins.

SUGGESTED ACTIVITIES

1. Make engine fastener pattern boards for the following areas:
   a. Left side engine covers.
   b. Right side engine covers.
   c. Cylinder head and cam cover (if applicable).
2. Using this chapter's list of items, determine how many mating parts your engine has in each area.
3. Perform a two-stroke cycle leak test.
4. Fabricate a clutch hub holder.
5. Disassemble an engine. Keep a record of problems you encounter during disassembly and their solutions. Use this information for your notebook of "Useful Information."
6. Mount an engine on an engine stand.

As you will learn, two-stroke cycle engines normally require more frequent service than four-stroke cycle engines. This off-road bike has a two-stroke cycle engine capable of producing considerable power for its size.   (Yamaha Motor Corp., U.S.A.)

Chapter 15

TWO-STROKE CYCLE ENGINE OVERHAUL

After studying this chapter, you will be able to:
- [ ] Describe two-stroke cycle engine top end service.
- [ ] Measure two-stroke cycle engine parts wear.
- [ ] Explain two-stroke cycle engine bottom end service.
- [ ] Summarize crankshaft reconditioning.
- [ ] Diagnose common two-stroke cycle engine problems.
- [ ] Outline two-stroke cycle engine reassembly.
- [ ] Summarize the procedures for installing an engine in the motorcycle frame.
- [ ] Describe initial engine starting and break-in procedures.

This chapter discusses the most important steps for overhauling a two-stroke cycle engine. Engine parts inspection, reconditioning, diagnosis, and reassemby are covered. This is an important chapter that explains many basic procedures. If you study carefully, you should be able to relate these procedures to all makes and models of two-stroke cycle engines. With the aid of a service manual, you will be prepared to overhaul most two-stroke cycle engines.

ENGINE TOP END SERVICE

The basic parts included in a two-stroke cycle engine TOP END are the piston, rings, cylinder, piston pin, reed valve, head gasket, and cylinder head. A two-stroke cycle engine top end requires more frequent service and repair than a four-stroke cycle engine. This is because:
1. The two-stroke cycle engine's piston rings pass over port openings in the cylinder.
2. The two-stroke cycle engine's oil is diluted with fuel.
3. The temperatures in a two-stroke cycle engine are higher.

PISTON AND CYLINDER INSPECTION

The piston and cylinder must be inspected and measured closely during an overhaul. Inspect the piston for scoring, galling (seizure), evidence of foreign material, and crown damage.

Piston damage

Fig. 15-1 shows common types of piston damage. PISTON SCORING may be caused by dirt particles entering the engine (missing air filter, for example). PISTON GALLING can be caused by excessive heat and poor lubrication. PISTON CROWN DAMAGE can be the result of a lean fuel mixture (too much air in relation to fuel), improper spark timing, or part breakage.

Always use the type of piston damage to find and correct the source of the problem.

Cylinder problems

Inspect the cylinder for scoring, rust, a ridge (lip around top of cylinder), and obvious damage caused by foreign material. CYLINDER RUST can be present after periods of storage and water condensation. A RIDGE or lip at the top of the cylinder is due to wear. The ring does not rub on and wear the extreme top portion of the cylinder. The unworn portion forms the ring ridge in the cylinder. CYLINDER

Fig. 15-1. Typical forms of piston damage. A—Seizure. B—Crown damage.

SCORING, as with piston scoring, is caused by dirt or foreign matter entry into the engine.

PISTON AND CYLINDER MEASUREMENT

Piston and cylinder measurement is used to determine:
1. Piston skirt and ring land wear (wear on thrust surfaces and in ring grooves of piston).
2. Piston ring end gap and tension (fit of new ring in cylinder).
3. Cylinder taper (wear difference at top and bottom of cylinder).
4. Cylinder out-of-roundness (diameter difference in cylinder).
5. Piston-to-cylinder clearance (play between piston and cylinder wall).

Piston skirt and ring land wear

PISTON SKIRT WEAR is checked by measuring the piston skirt diameter with a micrometer. This operation is illustrated in Fig. 15-2. Most service manuals give upper and lower limits (specifications) for piston diameter. However, some manuals only give piston-to-cylinder clearance specifications. This requires measurement of both the piston and cylinder. Then, the clearance is calculated.

Piston RING LAND WEAR is determined by measuring side clearance between the piston ring and the ring land with a feeler gauge. Fig. 15-3 shows how to measure ring land wear.

Piston ring end gap and free gap

PISTON RING FIT is checked by measuring piston ring end gap and piston ring free gap.

Measurement of PISTON RING END GAP indicates the size of the piston ring. An end gap that is too small could cause ring seizure when the ring heats up and expands during engine operation. It could jam out against the cylinder wall and cause excessive friction and heat. The ring and cylinder wall surfaces could overheat and seize. A ring gap that is too large

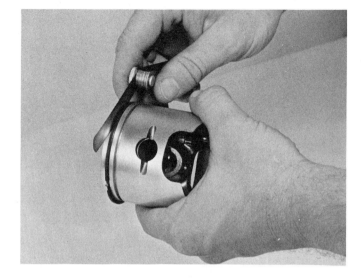

Fig. 15-3. Use a feeler gauge to measure piston ring-to-land clearance. Largest feeler gauge thickness that fits indicates clearance.

could cause blow-by (combustion pressure leaking past rings). Always check ring end gap carefully, as in Fig. 15-4.

Measurement of PISTON RING FREE GAP indicates the amount of ring tension. As free gap decreases, tension also decreases. A ring which has excessive end gap or insufficient free gap may not seal properly and should not be used. Refer to Fig. 15-5.

Cylinder taper

CYLINDER TAPER is wear that causes the top of the cylinder to be worn larger than the bottom. This is illustrated in Fig. 15-6. If the cylinder bore is tapered, two undesirable conditions result:
1. Piston-to-cylinder clearance changes as the piston

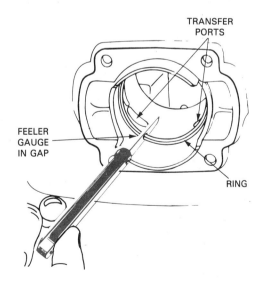

Fig. 15-4. Ring end gap is distance between ends of ring when ring is installed squarely in cylinder. End gap is measured with a feeler gauge.
(Bombardier Ltd., Owner of the trademark CAN-AM)

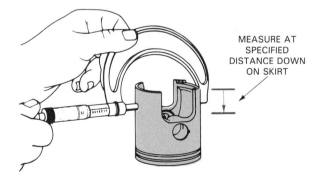

Fig. 15-2. Piston skirt must be measured 90 deg. from wrist pin. Make sure to measure at proper distance from bottom of skirt. Check your manual for details.
(Bombardier Ltd., Owner of the trademark CAN-AM)

Fig. 15-5. Ring free gap is distance between ends of ring. Free gap is measured with a caliper without forcing ring open.

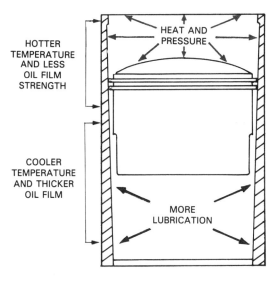

Fig. 15-7. Difference in heat, pressure, and lubrication at top and bottom of cylinder causes cylinder taper.

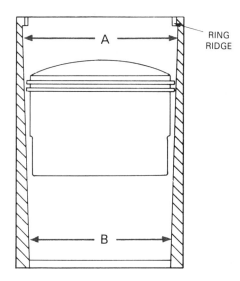

Fig. 15-6. Cylinder taper is result of normal wear. Cylinder becomes larger at top than at bottom.

moves from TDC to BDC.
2. Ring end gap and tension change as the ring moves up and down in the cylinder.

A tapered cylinder accelerates ring wear, leading to blow-by. It causes the ring to rapidly retract and expand to match the changing cylinder diameter.

Combustion pressure and heat are greatest at the top of the cylinder. There is also less lubrication at the top of the cylinder. As a result, taper occurs as in Fig. 15-7. A ridge at the top of the cylinder is a visual indication of cylinder taper.

Measurement of cylinder taper is done with a telescoping gauge and an outside micrometer. Fig. 15-8 shows this procedure. The service manual gives wear limits and specific directions for checking cylinder taper. Cylinder taper equals top cylinder diameter minus bottom cylinder diameter.

Cylinder out-of-roundness

CYLINDER OUT-OF-ROUNDNESS is a type of wear which causes the cylinder to become oval or egg-

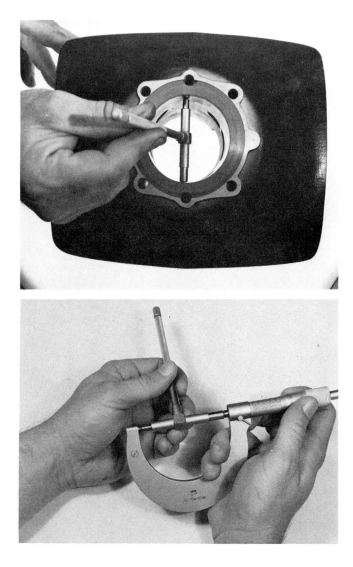

Fig. 15-8. A telescoping gauge and micrometer are used to measure cylinder taper. Adjust gauge to cylinder diameter. Then, measure gauge with micrometer. Difference in measurements at top and bottom of cylinder shows taper.

shaped, as in Fig. 15-9. As a cylinder becomes out-of-round, piston clearance increases. Since new piston rings are designed to seal a round bore, out-of-roundness can also cause blow-by if not corrected.

Out-of-roundness normally occurs at the front and back of the cylinder, opposite the piston pin centerline. Because of piston thrust, wear is more pronounced on the cylinder surfaces shown in Fig. 15-10.

Measurement for cylinder out-of-roundness is similar to measurement of cylinder taper. Fig. 15-11 shows which areas in a cylinder should be measured to determine cylinder out-of-roundness. Check in your service manual for specific wear limits.

Piston-to-cylinder clearance

PISTON-TO-CYLINDER CLEARANCE is determined by comparing piston diameter to cylinder bore diameter. Measure the diameter of the piston skirt with an outside micrometer. Then, measure the inside diameter of the cylinder at its largest point with a telescoping gauge and micrometer. The difference between the two measurements equals piston-to-cylinder clearance.

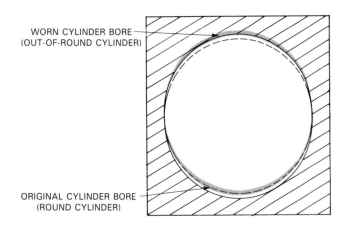

Fig. 15-9. Normal wear causes cylinders to become out-of-round.

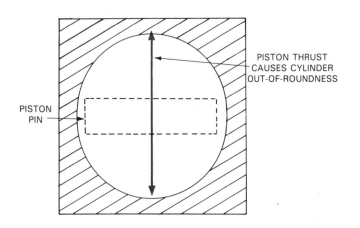

Fig. 15-10. Cylinder out-of-roundness is caused by piston thrust.

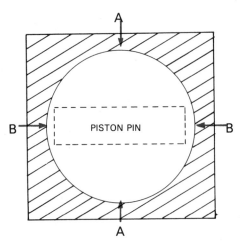

Fig. 15-11. To check for cylinder out-of-roundness, measure cylinder across A and B. Difference between measurements equals out-of-roundness.

Cylinder bore diameter − Piston skirt diameter = Piston clearance.

Incorrect piston-to-cylinder clearance can cause:
1. Piston seizure (piston overheats and locks in cylinder).
2. Piston galling (piston overheats scoring piston and cylinder).
3. Piston slap (knocking sound caused by worn piston and cylinder).
4. Blow-by (overheating and power loss).
5. Piston skirt breakage (excessive piston-to-cylinder clearance allows piston "rocking" to break skirt).

DECARBONIZING

Since two-stroke cycle engines burn oil with the air-fuel mixture, some carbon buildup in the top end is normal. Two-stroke cycle top end decarbonizing (removal of carbon buildup) is often considered part of a major tune-up and top end overhaul. Carbon deposits are found on the piston crown, in piston ring grooves, combustion chambers, and in the exhaust ports.

Carbon is commonly removed by scraping, soaking in decarbonizing solvent, dry blasting, and wire brushing. Be careful not to damage or scratch parts while removing hard carbon. Fig. 15-12 shows one method for removing carbon from piston ring grooves. Soft aluminum parts must be cleaned very carefully. They can be scratched and damaged easily.

PARTS REPLACEMENT AND RECONDITIONING

Once parts have been cleaned, inspected, and measured, you can begin reconditioning and replacement of parts.

A two-stroke cycle engine, which has minimal wear, can usually be reconditioned by DEGLAZING (honing) the cylinder and installing a new piston ring. The cylinder must be deglazed or honed to provide a textured surface which helps seat and seal the new

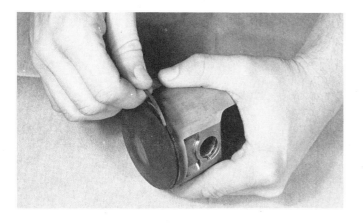

Fig. 15-12. An old piston ring can be used to scrape carbon from inside ring grooves.

ring. Fig. 15-13 demonstrates how to deglaze a two-stroke cycle motorcycle cylinder.

CAUTION! Be careful not to pull the spinning hone out of the cylinder while honing. The honing stones could break and fly out with considerable force.

After cylinder deglazing, wash the cylinder with soap and water. Then, wipe the cylinder out with a clean rag soaked in oil. Soap and water as well as oil are needed to remove the heavy deglazing grit from the surface of the cylinder. Degreasing solvents will NOT do an effective cleaning job. They are too light and runny to pick up heavier grit particles. Improper cleaning of a cylinder after deglazing will cause rapid wear of the piston, cylinder, and ring. Short engine life can result.

Ring replacement alone, without boring and piston replacement, is allowable when the piston and cylinder are both within wear limits. If the cylinder is within wear limits (acceptable taper, out-of-roundness), but the piston is undersize (worn), a new piston and ring can be installed. This should achieve proper piston-to-cylinder clearance.

REMEMBER! Deglazing is required any time a new ring is being installed.

Cylinder boring

When the cylinder is worn beyond specifications (excessive taper, out-of-roundness, or scoring), the cylinder must be BORED (machined larger). Then, the cylinder can be fitted with an oversize piston and oversize rings.

After boring, the finish of the cylinder wall is rough and the port edges are sharp. You must chamfer the port edges as in Fig. 15-14. Also, hone the cylinder to final size and smoothness.

WARNING! Be extremely careful when chamfering cylinder ports. The slightest slip and nick in the cylinder wall could ruin the cylinder.

Honing to achieve final sizing of the cylinder is different from deglazing the cylinder. Deglazing is done

Fig. 15-13. Top—Surface texture of worn cylinder bore is smooth and shiny. New rings would not seat and seal properly. Middle—Cylinder hone is used to deglaze cylinder bore. Pull drill back and forth in cylinder to form correct honing pattern. Bottom—Proper deglazing results in a crosshatch pattern which causes controlled wear of new piston rings for proper ring seating.

to achieve a textured crosshatch pattern. It removes a MINIMUM amount of material from the cylinder wall.

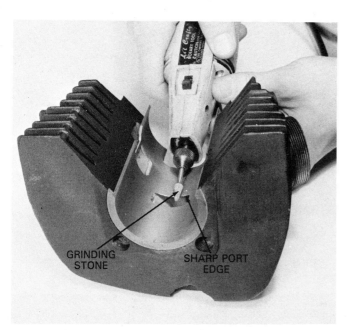

Fig. 15-14. Proper port chamfering is extremely important. A rotary grinder or small file can be used to chamfer ports. Be careful not to scratch or grind cylinder wall. Chamfer all horizontal edges, including transfer cutout at base of cylinder.

FINAL SIZING of the cylinder by honing is required for three reasons:
1. To remove rough boring marks.
2. To achieve accurate final sizing.
3. To obtain desired crosshatch and texture.

The service manual lists the number of overbore sizes available and gives proper piston-to-cylinder clearances.

Cylinders which use a coated bore CANNOT be fitted with oversize pistons. When these cylinders are worn out or damaged, they must be replaced.

Cylinders which use a cast-in sleeve must be replaced after the largest overbore has been used. Cylinders which have a pressed-in sleeve can be reconditioned over and over. After installing a new sleeve (liner) in the cylinder, the liner can be bored to original standard bore size.

The procedures for boring a cylinder were outlined in Chapter 4, Special Operations. Refer to this chapter if needed.

ENGINE LOWER END SERVICE

Inspection and service of a two-stroke cycle engine lower end includes:
1. Measuring connecting rod bearing clearance.
2. Checking connecting rod thrust washers and side play.
3. Checking main bearing condition.
4. Checking the condition and cleanliness of the crankwheels.
5. Reconditioning and trueing of crankshaft.

CONNECTING ROD BIG END BEARING CLEARANCE

The proper procedure for measuring connecting rod bearing clearance is outlined in your service manual. Typical procedures include:
1. Measuring CONNECTING ROD TIP, Fig. 15-15.
2. Checking for ROD BEARING RADIAL PLAY, Fig. 15-16.

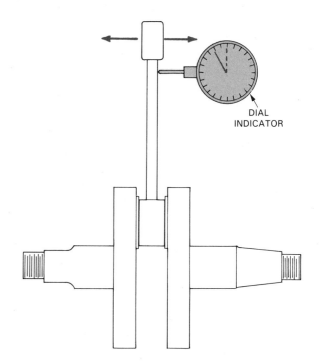

Fig. 15-15. Connecting rod tip is one way of checking crankpin bearing and big end condition. As shown, a dial indicator is used to measure connecting rod tip. Excessive tip indicates excessive wear.

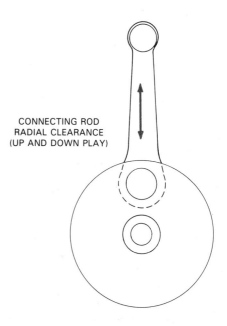

Fig. 15-16. If radial clearance can be felt, crankshaft must be rebuilt because of wear.

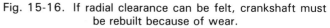

NOTE! The rod bearing and crankshaft must be free of oil for accurate measurement of connecting rod play.

CONNECTING ROD SIDE PLAY

Connecting rod side play is checked with a feeler gauge. This is illustrated in Fig. 15-17.

Most crankshafts use thrust washers to center the connecting rod on the crankpin. If the thrust washers are grooved or scored, as in Fig. 15-18, a feeler gauge may NOT give an accurate measurement of side play. Visual inspection is needed to check the condition of the thrust washers.

Some two-stroke cycle connecting rods are centered by the small end (piston end) of the rod. In this design, the piston pin boss or thrust washers on the pin provide connecting rod centering. See Fig. 15-19.

If rod side play or big end bearing clearance does not meet service manual specifications, the crankshaft must be disassembled for reconditioning.

MAIN BEARINGS

Main bearings should be checked for lateral and radial play, Fig. 15-20. Before checking the main

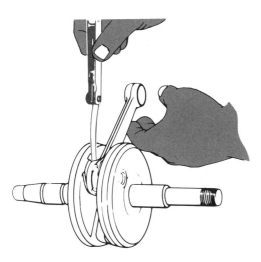

Fig. 15-17. Connecting rod side play is measured with a feeler gauge.
(Bombardier Ltd., Owner of the trademark CAN-AM)

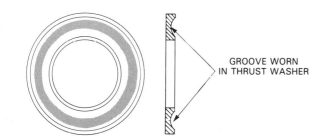

Fig. 15-18. Worn crankshaft thrust washers can have a wear groove where they contact connecting rod. Feeler gauge reading for clearance may not detect these grooves.

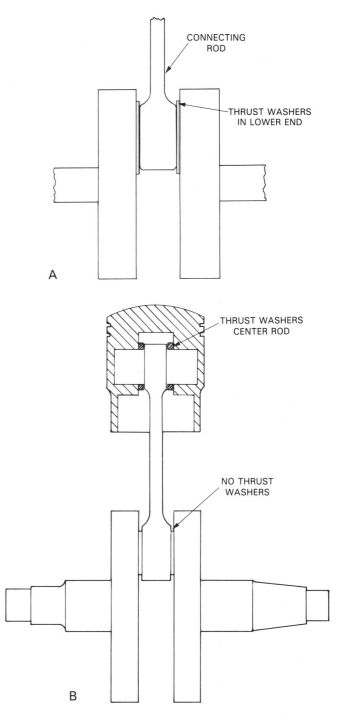

Fig. 15-19. Connecting rods are centered on crankshaft by thrust washers. A—Usually thrust washers are located on crankpin. B—Some designs have thrust washers on piston pin.

bearings for looseness, wash them in solvent. Then, dry the bearings thoroughly.

CAUTION! Do not spin bearings with compressed air when drying. This can cause permanent bearing damage or the bearing could fly apart with lethal force.

If lateral and radial play is within service limits, visually inspect the balls, races, and cages for evidence of pitting, chipping, discoloration, or signs of overheating. Replace the bearings as needed.

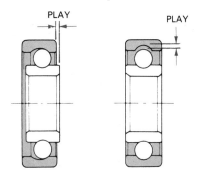

Fig. 15-20. Bearings must be replaced if axial or radial play is excessive. (U.S. Suzuki Motor Corporation)

The oil slinger is mounted behind one of the main bearings on oil injection engines. Any contamination or dirt passing through the engine is often trapped in the channel of the OIL SLINGER, Fig. 15-21. It is extremely important to thoroughly clean the oil slinger during an overhaul.

The service manual details proper procedures for main bearing removal and installation.

CRANKSHAFT WHEEL AND AXLE CONDITION

Crankshaft wheels (crankwheels) and axles must be thoroughly cleaned and inspected during an overhaul.

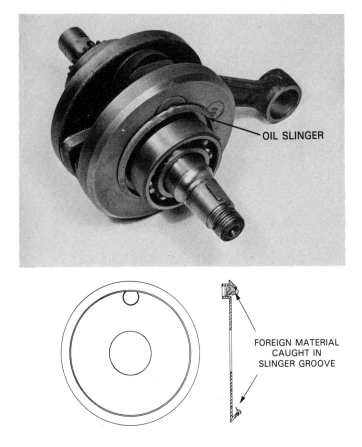

Fig. 15-21. Foreign material is often caught and held in oil slinger groove. Slinger must be cleaned thoroughly.

Refer to Fig. 15-22. The following list outlines the areas of the crankshaft wheels and axles that require special attention:

1. Clean all foreign material from balancing holes and counterweights.
2. Inspect lip seal contact surface on axles for grooving.
3. Inspect all threads, keyways, and tapers for damage.
4. Check all parts for cracks.

CRANKSHAFT RECONDITIONING

CRANKSHAFT RECONDITIONING involves the installation of a CONNECTING ROD KIT (connecting rod, thrust washers, bearing, and crankpin). As shown in Fig. 15-23, replacement of these com-

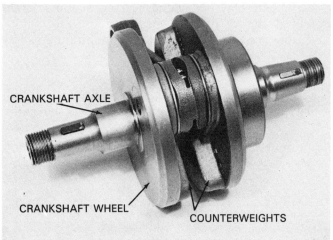

Fig. 15-22. Clean and inspect crankshaft thoroughly during an overhaul.

Fig. 15-23. A hydraulic press and special tools are needed to recondition a motorcycle crankshaft.

ponents requires special tools and equipment, such as:
1. Hydraulic press.
2. Crankshaft wheel splitting plates and cylinder.
3. Push pins.
4. Crankshaft trueing stand.
5. Lead or brass hammer.

Crankshaft width measurement

Crankshaft width must be measured BEFORE the crankshaft is pushed apart. This is demonstrated in Fig. 15-24.

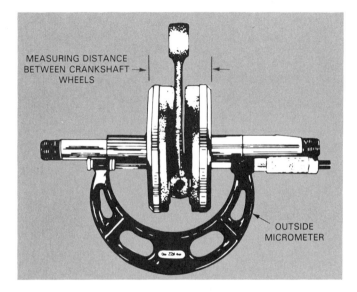

Fig. 15-24. Measuring crankshaft width before disassembly is helpful in achieving proper end play, when crankshaft is reassembled.
(Bombardier Ltd., Owner of the trademark CAN-AM)

The crankshaft width measurement is used in two ways:
1. In engines using the connecting rod small end for connecting rod centering, crankshaft width must be the same before and after crankshaft reconditioning. The same crankshaft width will help maintain proper crankshaft end play.
2. In engines using thrust washers to center the connecting rod, crankshaft width may vary, as rod side play must be correct. In this case, this measurement is helpful in indicating changes in crankshaft shimming for end play.

Crankshaft disassembly

Crankshaft disassembly requires removal of the crankpin and rod assembly from the crankwheels. To make the crankshaft rigid, an extremely tight interference fit is used between the crankpin and crankwheels. On larger engines, as much as forty tons of force may be needed to push the crankshaft apart. Fig. 15-25 shows the general procedures for crankshaft disassembly.

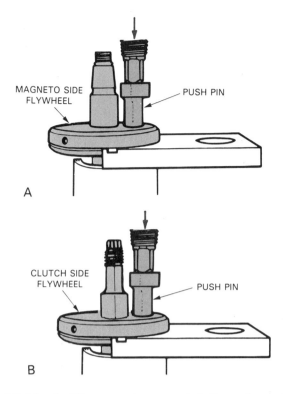

B

Fig. 15-25. A—When pressing a crankshaft apart, crankpin is pushed out of one flywheel first. Then, connecting rod, roller bearing, and thrust washers are removed. B—Finally, crankpin is pressed out of other flywheel.
(Bombardier Ltd., Owner of the trademark CAN-AM)

DANGER! Be careful when using a press to disassemble or reassemble a crankshaft. The tremendous force could cause parts to fly out and cause injury. Wear eye protection!

Crankshaft assembly

Before assembling the crankshaft with a new rod kit, check the pin holes in the crankwheels for burrs and sharp edges. Then, press the pin all the way into one of the crankwheels. On engines using oil injection, make sure the oil hole in the crankpin is in the proper position, Fig. 15-26.

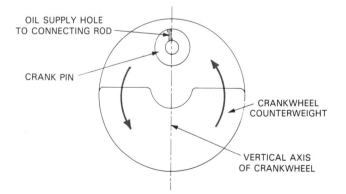

Fig. 15-26. Connecting rod oil supply hole in crankpin must be positioned slightly forward of vertical axis of crankwheel. Make sure oil hole is positioned properly before pressing crankpin into first flywheel.

The connecting rod and bearings should be greased and positioned over the crankpin. Use petroleum jelly to hold the bearings in place. Make sure one thrust washer is placed on each side of the connecting rod.

To aid alignment and make crankshaft trueing easier, line up the wheels before pressing the crankshaft together. Fig. 15-27 illustrates initial alignment of the crankwheels.

The crankshaft is now ready to be pressed together. Check and correct alignment as the wheels are initially pressed together. To achieve proper side play on the connecting rod, use a feeler gauge of the proper thickness between the thrust washer and rod. Be careful not to pinch the feeler gauge.

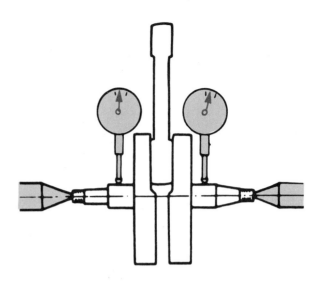

Fig. 15-28. Crankshaft alignment is checked using a trueing stand and two dial indicators. Indicator readings show runout as crankshaft is turned on stand.
(Bombardier Ltd., Owner of the trademark CAN-AM)

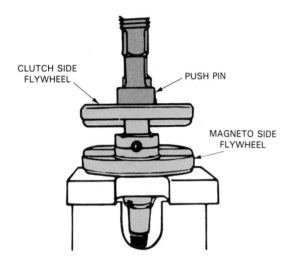

Fig. 15-27. Accurate initial flywheel alignment can make crankshaft trueing much easier and faster. It is more difficult to move flywheels after crankshaft is pressed all the way together.
(Bombardier Ltd., Owner of the trademark CAN-AM)

Crankshaft trueing

CRANKSHAFT TRUEING is the accurate aligning of the crankshaft axle shafts. A crankshaft trueing stand is used to determine and measure crankshaft runout, Fig. 15-28. The axles must be aligned both vertically and horizontally. See Fig. 15-29.

A VISE or WEDGE is used to correct crankshaft vertical runout, as in Fig. 15-30. A LEAD or BRASS HAMMER is used to correct horizontal runout, as in Fig. 15-31. Careful observation and placement of the DIAL INDICATORS will let you determine the type of runout and appropriate procedure for correction.

Fig. 15-32 illustrates typical misalignment and dial indicator movement during crankshaft trueing. Usually, several corrections for vertical and horizontal runout are necessary. PATIENCE and ACCURACY are absolutely essential during crankshaft trueing.

Specifications for maximum runout are found in your service manual. Ideally, always try to achieve zero runout.

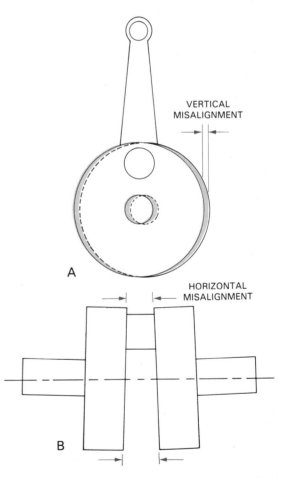

Fig. 15-29. Crankshaft axles must be aligned perfectly. A-Vertically out of alignment. B—Horizontally out of alignment.

Multi-cylinder crankshafts

Multi-cylinder crankshafts require more equipment and skill for crankshaft reconditioning. Reconditioning multiple cylinder type crankshafts should be left to a specialist.

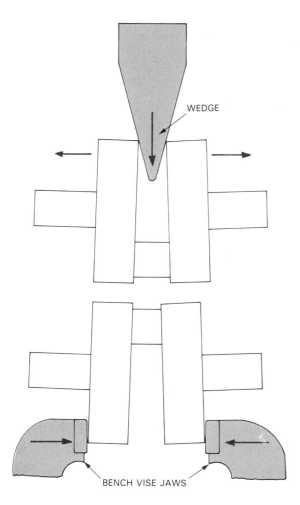

Fig. 15-30. Wedge or vise may be used to correct horizontal misalignment of crankshaft.

Replacement parts are not available for some multi-cylinder crankshafts. In this case, the complete crankshaft assembly must be replaced as one unit.

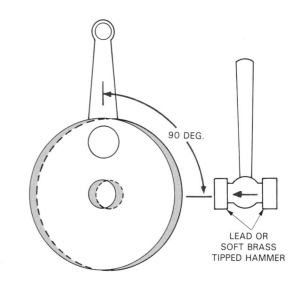

Fig. 15-31. Lead or brass hammer blows should be used to correct horizontal misalignment of crankshaft.

ENGINE DIAGNOSIS

Far too many motorcycle engines are disassembled, repaired, and reassembled without regard to the cause of the failure. DIAGNOSIS of a problem is perhaps the most important aspect of service. If the cause of a failure is NOT properly diagnosed, it can only be corrected by chance and may not be corrected at all. The engine overhaul might fail after only a short period of operation.

A typical example would be a two-stroke cycle engine with a hole in the top of the piston. Obviously the engine will not run with a burned piston. However, if the mechanic bores the cylinder and installs a new piston, the engine will again run. But more than likely, the new piston will soon fail and look just like the old one.

The hole in the piston was caused by a problem—

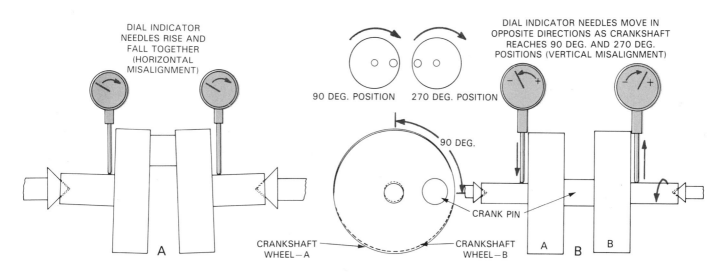

Fig. 15-32. A—When crankshaft axles are misaligned horizontally, dial indicators rise and fall together. B—When crankshaft axles are misaligned vertically, dial indicators move in opposite directions.

lean mixture, wrong spark plug, improper ignition timing, or abuse. The mechanic (you) must determine which of several possible problems is responsible for the mechanical failure.

Typical problems which occur in two-stroke cycle engines are:
1. Normal part wear.
2. Lubrication failure.
3. Damage caused by foreign material.
4. Damage caused by overheating.
5. Damage from an incorrect adjustment.

NORMAL WEAR

Normal wear is usually an easy problem to diagnose. A problem resulting from normal wear does not always cause the engine to fail. Usually, normal wear causes the engine to be noisy, smoke excessively, and perform poorly. Normal wear is easily diagnosed during top end disassembly and measurement.

A common condition resulting from normal engine wear is blow-by. Blow-by is the escape of the combustion gasses past the piston rings, Fig. 15-33. BLOW-BY is caused by excessive clearance between the piston and cylinder or by worn piston rings. Either problem can prevent the ring from sealing properly.

Excessive blow-by can become a serious problem, causing:
1. Overheating of the piston.
2. Removal of the lubricating film between the piston and cylinder wall.
3. Poor engine performance.

If conditions causing blow-by are not corrected during the overhaul, piston seizure can result.

Regular top end service is necessary to maintain good performance in a two-stroke cycle engine. However, you may be required to repair a badly neglected engine. For example, the engine might have such extreme wear that the piston skirt has cracked and broken, as in Fig. 15-34. This problem is usually a result of excessive clearance between the piston and cylinder wall.

LUBRICATION FAILURE

A LUBRICATION FAILURE is also an easy problem to diagnose. Without lubrication, engine components will generally have a dry, dull, burned appearance, as in Fig. 15-35. Lubrication failures are generally caused by:
1. Improper oil premix ratio.
2. Improper type of oil.
3. Improper oil injection system adjustment and service.
4. Running out of injection oil.
5. Injection pump failure.

If signs of lubrication failure are found, always check all five of these possible causes. Any one of

Fig. 15-33. Blow-by is caused by poor sealing of piston ring or rings. Dark area at top of this piston's skirt indicates blow-by. This discoloration is burned on oil and may range from carmel color to brownish black.

Fig. 15-34. Extreme wear of cylinder and piston resulted in piston rocking or slapping so severely that skirt broke off.

Fig. 15-35. Damage on this piston was caused by running engine with oil injection tank empty.

them could ruin the freshly rebuilt engine in a matter of minutes.

FOREIGN MATERIAL DAMAGE

The most common foreign materials found in a two-stroke cycle engine are dust, dirt, sand, mud, and broken parts.

Some types of foreign material (dust, dirt, sand, and mud) enter through a dirty air cleaner or they may bypass the air cleaner (loose rubber connector boot, air box, or cylinder). Foreign material causes rapid wear of bearings, pistons, cylinders, and rings. Fig. 15-36 shows typical foreign material damage.

OVERHEATING

OVERHEATING is the most common cause of serious damage to a two-stroke cycle engine. Since there are many causes of overheating, accurate diagnosis is sometimes difficult.

Some causes of engine overheating damage are:
1. Carburetion or fuel problem.
2. Incorrect ignition timing.
3. Incorrect spark plug heat range.
4. Excessive carbon buildup.
5. Detonation or preignition.
6. Air leaks.
7. Lubrication failure.
8. Excessive piston clearance.

If normal wear is NOT the problem, overheating can usually be broken down into two basic areas, ignition system problems and fuel system problems.

Ignition system problems

Overheating caused by the ignition system is usually the result of incorrect ignition timing or a wrong spark plug heat range. Ignition related overheating may cause seizure or erosion of the piston crown or a hole to be burned in the piston. These problems are shown in Fig. 15-37. The severity of damage is determined by:
1. The length of time the engine is operated while overheated.
2. The amount of error in ignition timing or plug heat range.

A

B

Fig. 15-36. A—Dull scratched appearance of piston was caused by dirt that passed through a dirty air cleaner. B—Piston has been severely damaged by a broken ring.

A

B

Fig. 15-37. These pistons show results of severe ignition related overheating. A—Ignition timing was too advanced. B—Too hot a spark plug burned hole in piston.

Again, always correct the cause of any overheating problem before reassembly and engine starting.

Fuel system problems

Damage caused by fuel system problems often appears to be damage caused by the ignition system. PISTON SEIZURE is one of the most common forms of damage that might be caused by the fuel system. Fuel system related overheating can usually be detected before severe damage has occurred. Some of the causes of fuel system overheating are:

1. Improper carburetor jetting.
2. Clogged carburetor jets.
3. Contaminated or low octane fuel.
4. Improper carburetor float level.
5. Clogged fuel filter.
6. Clogged fuel tank vent.
7. Air leak (crankcase or intake manifold).

Diagnosis of overheating

Ignition system and fuel system-caused overheating will usually cause piston seizure.

Extreme cases of ignition system-caused overheating usually lead to piston crown erosion in a small area (hole in piston). The remainder of the crown will usually maintain a normal appearance.

During fuel system-caused overheating, the piston crown usually has a uniform but lighter than normal color. Because there is no erosion of the piston crown, the spark plug will read (indicate upon visual inspection) a lean mixture (light gray to white plug insulator).

Detonation and preignition

Extreme damage such as a hole burned in a piston or an eroded piston crown normally results from detonation and/or preignition. These problems occur when combustion chamber temperatures are high enough to produce uncontrolled combustion.

Under normal conditions the air-fuel mixture burns at a rapid but controlled rate. During detonation and preignition, this rate is greatly increased, causing damage to engine components. The fuel mixture almost explodes.

The two most common causes of DETONATION are excessive compression ratio and low octane fuel. As the air-fuel mixture begins to burn after normal ignition, pressure and temperature rise to a point where the unburned air-fuel mixture at the outside edge of the combustion chamber ignites. See Fig. 15-38, A. Because combustion is occurring in two areas of the combustion chamber at once, the air-fuel mixture burns almost explosively. The collision of the two flame fronts causes a pinging noise or knock.

PREIGNITION occurs when a "hot spot" (overheated surface) in the combustion chamber ignites the air-fuel mixture before the spark plug fires. Usually, a carbon flake, gasket protruding into the combustion chamber, or excessively high spark plug heat range cause this premature igniting of the air-fuel mixture. Preignition may also cause an audible ping or knock, as the two flame fronts collide, Fig. 15-38, B.

Both fuel system and ignition system problems can produce detonation and preignition damage.

ENGINE REASSEMBLY

All the time and effort invested in cleaning, measuring, reconditioning, and diagnosing is WASTED if the engine is not assembled properly. The recommended sequence and specific procedures

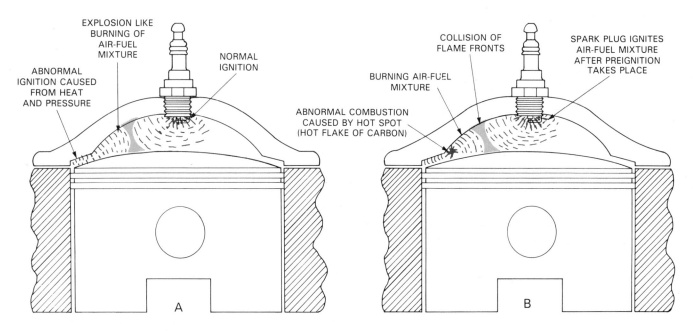

Fig. 15-38. A—Detonation occurs after normal ignition. B—Preignition occurs before spark plug fires.

for engine reassembly are found in your service manual. However, there are a number of important general procedures to keep in mind.

CRANKSHAFT AND GEARBOX SHAFT END PLAY

To allow for expansion and freedom of movement at operating temperatures, it is important to check CRANKSHAFT and GEARBOX SHAFT END PLAY. There are two methods used to measure end play. If the components are free to float from side to side, a dial indicator may be used to check end play. Another method for checking end play requires a parallel bar and vernier caliper. Fig. 15-39 shows a vernier caliper being used to measure crankcase width.

LIP SEAL INSTALLATION

Proper lip seal installation is extremely important. A serious leak can result from faulty lip seal installation techniques, Fig. 15-40. Leaking seals can cause loss of gear oil or crankcase compression and vacuum.

The most critical seals are those which seal the crankcase and crankshaft. A mistake in the installation of one of these seals can ruin an engine. When installing lip seals, remember to:

1. Remove burrs and sharp edges that might damage the outside diameter of the seal.

2. Position the seal in the proper direction, as shown in Fig. 15-41.
3. Install the seal straight and to the proper depth.
4. Use grease to lubricate the sealing lip, Fig. 15-41.

OIL AND GREASE TYPES

Engine components must be lubricated during assembly. This assures proper lubrication and prevents possible damage when the engine is first started after reassembly. Failure to lubricate components during assembly can result in immediate part damage.

Generally, use the same lubricant for engine

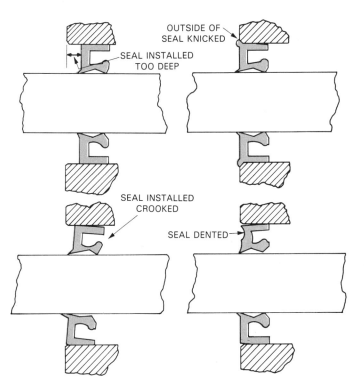

Fig. 15-40. Improper seal installation can cause engine damage by allowing oil leakage at gearbox output shaft, shift shaft, or vacuum and pressure leakage at crankshaft.

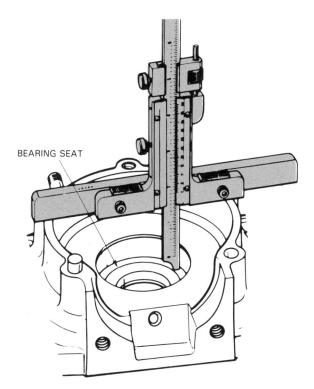

Fig. 15-39. A depth micrometer or vernier caliper and parallel bar will measure crankcase width to determine shimming for proper crankshaft end play.
(Bombardier Ltd., Owner of the trademark CAN-AM)

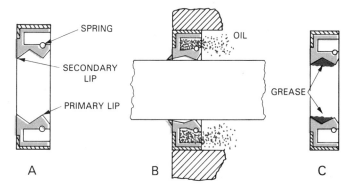

Fig. 15-41. A—Note parts of seal. B—Oil seals must be installed with primary lip toward oil. C—Seals must be packed with grease to lubricate seal lips.

assembly as will be used during engine operation. Lubricate two-stroke cycle engine components with two-stroke cycle oil. Lubricate primary and gearbox components with the proper gear lubricant. However, grease can be used on a number of parts during engine assembly:

1. On seals (all purpose grease).
2. On rollers during crankshaft assembly (petroleum jelly).
3. To locate shims or hold parts in position (all purpose grease).

CHECKING FOR BINDING AFTER EACH INSTALLATION

All rotating parts are susceptible to binding if installed improperly. Check for free movement after installing shafts, the shift drum, and crankshaft. A check for BINDING should be made as parts are assembled and after the crankcases are torqued. Also, make sure the gearbox shifts smoothly through each gear.

GASKET SEALERS

Machined surfaces not using a gasket must always be sealed with silicone sealer or an approved liquid gasket. Modern paper type gasket materials do NOT require any type of gasket sealer. In many cases, the use of grease or gasket cement to locate or hold a gasket in place is helpful. Refer to your service manual for the proper type gasket sealing compounds and where they should be used.

ROTARY VALVE TIMING

Two-stroke cycle engines which use a rotary valve for intake timing require specific positioning (timing) of the valve during reassembly. Timing marks, keyways, or locating pins are used to index the rotary valve in the proper position. Fig. 15-42 illustrates a typical rotary valve timing procedure.

TOP END REASSEMBLY

A two-stroke cycle engine top end is relatively simple to reassemble. However, minor mistakes during assembly can cause serious damage. Important steps to follow during the reassembly of any two-stroke cycle engine are:

1. All gasket surfaces must be clean.
2. Use new gaskets and new piston pin circlips.
3. Face the piston in the proper direction, Fig. 15-43.
4. Check that circlips are installed and seated properly, Fig. 15-44.
5. Generously lubricate piston, pin and pin bearing, piston rings, and cylinder.
6. Check that piston rings are installed properly in grooves and indexed in locating pins, Fig. 15-45.
7. Carefully install cylinder over piston, Fig. 15-46.

Fig. 15-42. Typical rotary valve timing. Position piston at TDC. Then, align valve edge (or rotary valve mark) with index mark.

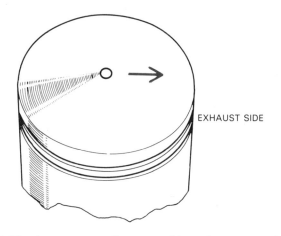

Fig. 15-43. An arrow usually stamped into piston crown indicates piston installation direction. (U.S. Suzuki Motor Corporation)

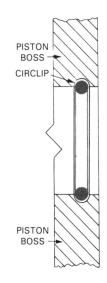

Fig. 15-44. Piston pin circlips are installed with needle nose pliers. Make sure circlip is fully seated.

262

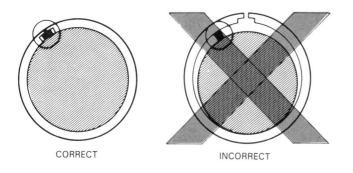

Fig. 15-45. Two-stroke cycle piston rings must be properly indexed with ring locating pins.
(U.S. Suzuki Motor Corporation)

8. Torque cylinder and cylinder head bolts to specifications in proper sequence, Fig. 15-47.

Torque sequence

Due to the size of cylinders, cylinder heads, and crankcases, torque patterns must be utilized to prevent warping. Generally, a TORQUE PATTERN (sequence) follows a crisscross pattern from the center to the outside of the part. This sequence is repeated in small graduations until the final torque is achieved. Fig. 15-48 shows a typical torque sequence. It assures an even clamping action. For specific torque sequences and torque values, refer to the proper service manual.

Crankcase leak test

To make sure that all seals and gaskets are properly installed, you should perform a two-stroke cycle engine leak test. Refer to Chapter 14 for leak test procedures.

Fig. 15-46. Make sure ring end gaps are properly engaged with ring locating pins when installing cylinder. Do not force cylinder over piston or part damage may result.

Fig. 15-47. Torque cylinder and head to factory specs. Use proper crisscross torque sequence. Tighten in two or three stages, as described in service manual.

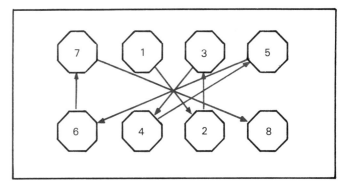

Fig. 15-48. A typical torque pattern crisscross from center to outside.

Ignition timing

The last adjustment to be made before installing the engine in the frame is STATIC IGNITION TIMING. This insures that the ignition timing will be close enough for initial engine starting.

Final DYNAMIC IGNITION TIMING must be done with the engine running, using a strobe (timing) light. Refer to a service manual and Chapter 10, Ignition Systems, for proper static and dynamic timing procedures.

ENGINE REASSEMBLY SUMMARY

The following list summarizes some of the important aspects of two-stroke cycle engine reassembly. Use your service manual for specific step-by-step instructions and to select the proper tools.

1. Lubricate moving engine components, Fig. 15-49.
2. Use new gaskets, seals, and O-rings.
3. Check crankshaft and gearbox end play.
4. Install lip seals properly.
5. Install bearing locating half rings, dowel pins, and plates properly, Fig. 15-50.
6. Do not forget to install crankcase dowel pins.

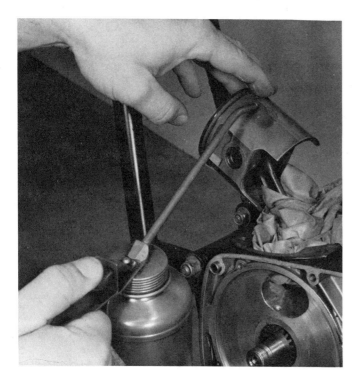

Fig. 15-49. Thoroughly lubricate all moving parts with two-stroke cycle oil.

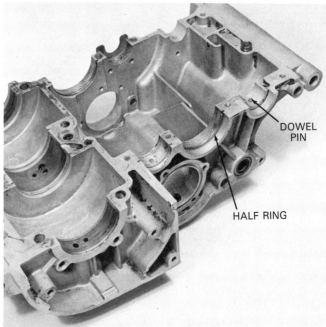

Fig. 15-50. Double-check installation of bearing locating half rings, dowel pins, and plates.

7. Position crankshaft spacers and shims correctly.
8. Install oil slinger properly.
9. Make sure crankshaft bearings are installed in proper direction and are fully seated on crankshaft or in case.
10. Properly assemble the gearbox. See gearbox assembly summary.
11. Check that crankcase fasteners of different lengths are in proper locations.
12. Check for binding after each installation.
13. Properly apply sealing compounds.
14. Check rotary valve timing.
15. Check for proper clutch and primary drive assembly. See clutch and primary drive assembly summary.
16. Make sure piston is facing correct direction and that circlips are installed properly.
17. Check that piston ring direction and positioning are correct.
18. Carefully install cylinder.
19. Use proper torque values and sequence.
20. Properly install oil injection pump and lines.
21. Perform a crankcase leak test.
22. Carefully install ignition components.
23. Check and adjust static ignition timing. This is shown in Fig. 15-51.

INSTALLING ENGINE IN FRAME

Before attempting to install the engine, locate and organize all engine mounting fasteners and brackets. Make sure the frame is clean. Loosen or remove any components which might hamper engine installation (fuel tank, brake pedal). Refer to the proper service manual for detailed engine installation instructions.

The following summary will help insure that nothing is overlooked after engine installation:
1. Properly tighten engine mounting bolts.
2. Check routing and secure connection of cables, fluid lines, and wires.
3. Install the carburetor and adjust throttle cable freeplay. Synchronize if engine has multiple carburetors.
4. Install the exhaust system.
5. Adjust the clutch.
6. Adjust oil pump cable.
7. Install and adjust the drive chain.
8. If air is present in the oil feed lines, use a clean oil can to inject oil into the lines until all air is removed. This will bleed the lines.

INITIAL ENGINE STARTING AND RUNNING

Before attempting to start the engine, the following summary should be reviewed:
1. Service the clutch and gearbox with the recommended lubricant.
2. Service the injection oil tank (clean the filter and fill with the recommended lubricant).
3. Fill injection oil lines and bleed injection pump.
4. Clean fuel petcock and sediment bowl.
5. If premix lubricant is used, fill the fuel tank with the recommended fuel-oil mixture.
6. Service the air filter.

After the engine has been started, complete the

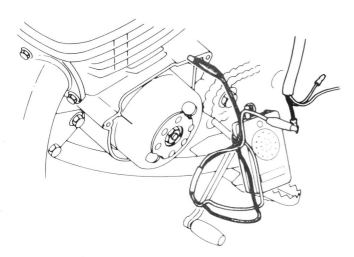

Fig. 15-51. Use an ignition timing tester to check and adjust static ignition timing. (U.S. Suzuki Motor Corporation)

following:
1. Check oil pump operation.
2. Check ignition timing with a strobe light.
3. Check for unusual noises and overheating.
4. Check for leaks.
5. Adjust carburetors.
6. Road test.
7. Retorque cylinder head, after the engine has cooled.

Because a freshly overhauled engine is "tight" (high friction between new parts), it is necessary to follow careful break-in procedures. During break-in, avoid overloading, high engine speeds, and overheating the engine. It is also important to monitor engine operation and performance, and make adjustments as necessary. Typical break-in period is three hours for an off-road bike and three hundred miles for a road bike.

KNOW THESE TERMS

Piston galling, Piston scoring, Cylinder scoring, Piston skirt wear, Piston ring end gap and free gap, Cylinder taper, Cylinder out-of-roundness, Piston-to-cylinder clearance, Cylinder boring, Connecting rod big end clearance, Connecting rod side play, Crankshaft trueing, Blow-by, Detonation, Preignition, Crankshaft and gearbox shaft end play, Torque pattern, Engine break-in.

REVIEW QUESTIONS—CHAPTER 15

1. List some of the problems to look for during piston and cylinder inspection.
2. A piston ring which has excessive _____ gap and insufficient _____ gap must be replaced.
3. Cylinder _____ will cause a ring to change its end gap and tension as it moves up and down in the cylinder bore.
4. Out-of-roundness of the cylinder bore affects

ring sealing. What can this condition cause?
5. List three problems resulting from incorrect piston-to-cylinder clearance.
6. It is necessary to _____ a cylinder before installing a new ring. This provides controlled ring break-in.
7. A ring end gap clearance that is too small can cause _____. A ring with too much ring end gap can cause _____.
8. List the three reasons why honing is necessary after cylinder boring.
9. Connecting rod side play can ALWAYS be accurately measured with a feeler gauge. True or False?
10. Crankshaft main bearings should be checked for both lateral and _____ play.
11. It is always a good idea to measure crankshaft _____ before pushing a crankshaft apart.
12. Draw a simple picture of:
   a. Crankshaft vertical runout.
   b. Crankshaft horizontal runout.
13. Some multi-cylinder crankshafts must be replaced since replacement parts (rod kit) are not always available. True or False?
14. Define the term "blow-by."
15. Blow-by can cause piston _____.
   a. Overcooling.
   b. Seizure.
   c. Explosion.
   d. Knurling.
16. Describe the condition and appearance of engine parts that have suffered a lubrication failure.
17. Where does foreign material enter a two-stroke cycle engine?
18. List three of the common causes of engine overheating.
19. Incorrect ignition _____ and/or the wrong spark plug _____ _____ can cause a hole to be burned in the piston crown.
20. An improperly installed seal can cause the loss of:
   a. Gear oil.
   b. Crankcase compression.
   c. Crankcase vacuum.
   d. All of the above.
   e. None of the above.
21. What kind of oil is used to lubricate engine parts during engine assembly?
22. A crankcase leak test should be done only when a problem is suspected. True or False?
23. What are four important considerations during engine break-in?

SUGGESTED ACTIVITIES

1. Design your own two-stroke cycle engine measurement and inspection checklist. Refer to this chapter and manufacturer's service manuals for guidance in compiling and organizing the checklist. Use your checklist while completing the

following activities.

2. Disassemble and inspect a two-stoke cycle engine top end. Use this chapter and your service manual to determine the necessary repairs.
3. Rebuild and true a two-stroke cycle engine crankshaft.
4. Visit a local motorcycle dealership and try to acquire some damaged two-stroke cycle engine parts. Using the diagnosis section, try to determine the cause of each engine failure.
5. Using what you have learned and the proper service manual, reassemble a two-stroke cycle engine and install it in the frame.
6. Before starting the engine, refer to the "Initial Starting and Running" summary in this chapter. Complete this checklist.

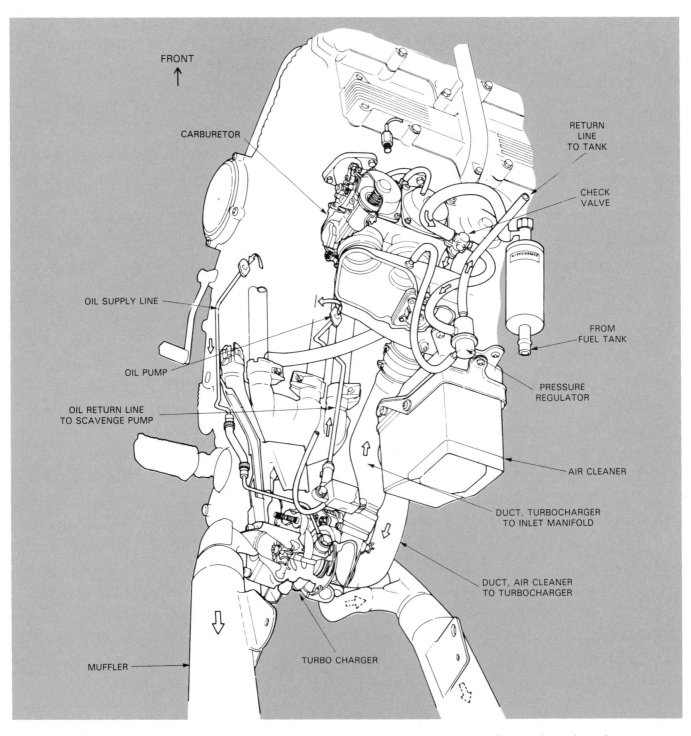

Cutaway view shows parts of fuel, exhaust, and turbocharging system on modern four-stroke cycle engine.
(Yamaha Motor Corp., U.S.A.)

Chapter 16

FOUR-STROKE CYCLE ENGINE OVERHAUL

After studying this chapter, you will be able to:
☐ Inspect the parts of a four-stroke cycle engine for signs of wear or damage.
☐ Measure four-stroke cycle engine part wear.
☐ Explain how to recondition a four-stroke cycle engine top end.
☐ Diagnose four-stroke cycle engine failures.
☐ Explain how to recondition the lower end of a four-stroke cycle engine.
☐ Summarize four-stroke cycle engine reassembly.
☐ Describe engine installation, initial starting, and break-in procedures.

The purpose of this chapter is to help you become familiar with the proper methods of performing a four-stroke cycle engine overhaul. Top and lower end reconditioning, reassembly, and initial starting are covered.

NOTE! Several other textbook chapters give information relating to the overhaul of a four-stroke cycle engine. Use the index to locate this added information as needed.

ENGINE TOP END SERVICE

Four-stroke cycle engine TOP END PARTS include: piston, rings, piston pin, circlips, cylinder, cylinder head, valves, valve springs, camshafts, push rods, cam sprockets, cam chain tensioner and guides, cam followers or rocker arms, head gasket, cylinder base gasket, and intake manifold.

The condition of the top end of a four-stroke cycle engine is a critical factor in determining engine performance. The top end parts control the movement of the air-fuel mixture through the combustion chamber. These parts are also responsible for sealing the energy produced by combustion. Obviously, leaky valves or piston rings greatly reduce engine efficiency and power.

CLEANING AND DECARBONIZING

Cleaning and decarbonizing is a similar process for two and four-stroke cycle engines. The main difference is that the four-stroke cycle engine has a few more parts to be decarbonized. Refer to Chapter 3, Measurement and Parts Cleaning, for a review of cleaning and decarbonizing.

TOP END INSPECTION AND MEASUREMENT

Valve train components are exposed to high temperatures, heavy loads, and high speeds. Because of these severe conditions, valve train components usually wear more rapidly than other engine components. This is especially true if the lubrication system is not functioning properly. See Fig. 16-1.

The following components make up the valve train,

Fig. 16-1. Notice how cam lobes, cam journals, and cam follower were badly damaged by lubrication system failure.

and they require a thorough visual inspection during top end repairs:

1. Camshafts and bearings.
2. Cam followers, rocker arms, and shafts.
3. Push rods and lifters.
4. Cam sprockets, timing chain, drive gears, or belts.
5. Valve springs, collars, and keepers.
6. Valve stems, guides, and seals.
7. Valve seats and faces.

Inspecting camshafts and bearings

Inspect the camshafts and bearings for any signs of abnormal wear. Many manufacturers give specifications for:

1. Base circle diameter, Fig. 16-2.
2. Cam lobe height, Fig. 16-3.
3. Bearing journal diameter.
4. Shaft runout, Fig. 16-4.
5. Bearing inside diameter.
6. Journal-to-bearing clearance, Fig. 16-5.
7. Camshaft end play, Fig. 16-6.

Some valve train designs use needle bearings or ball bearings to support the camshaft. When measuring a design of this type, check for excessive lateral play, radial play, and smooth bearing operation. Also, look for pitting of the bearings.

Cam followers, rocker arms, and shafts

Cam followers and rocker arms wear in three places:

1. At the valve end.
2. At the camshaft end (follower) or push rod end (rocker).
3. Where the rocker shaft passes through the follower or rocker. See Fig. 16-7, A.

Check these high wear points closely. Any area worn excessively will require part replacement.

Inspection of followers, rocker arms, and shaft includes:

1. Visual inspection for galling, flaking, or pitting.
2. Measurement of rocker and follower shaft bore diameter, Fig. 16-7, B.

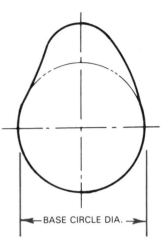

Fig. 16-2. Use an outside micrometer to measure camshaft base circle diameter. (Kawasaki Motors Corp., U.S.A.)

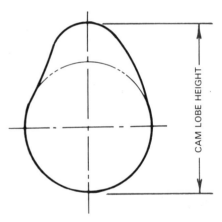

Fig. 16-3. Use an outside micrometer to measure cam lobe height. Check all lobe heights because wear can vary. (Kawasaki Motors Corp., U.S.A.)

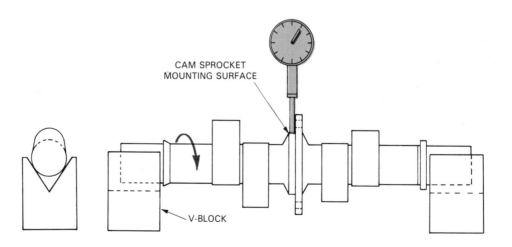

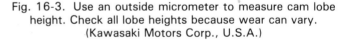

Fig. 16-4. Use a dial indicator to detect camshaft runout. Make sure indicator rides on machined surface of cam as shown.

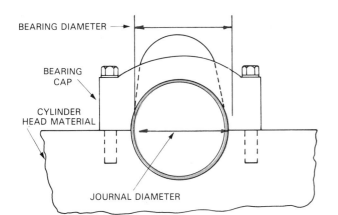

Fig. 16-5. Camshaft journal-to-bearing clearance can be measured with Plastigage or a telescoping gauge and outside micrometer. When using a micrometer, subtract journal diameter from bearing diameter to get clearance.

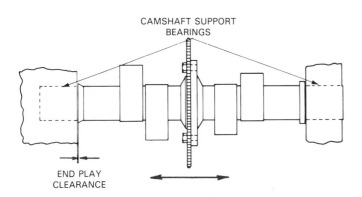

Fig. 16-6. Camshaft end play can be checked with a feeler gauge. Thickest blade that fits between camshaft flange and support bearing shows cam end play.

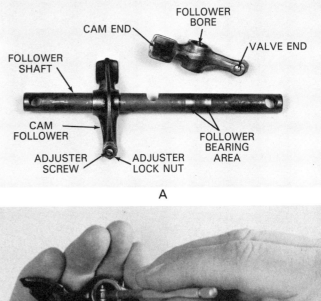

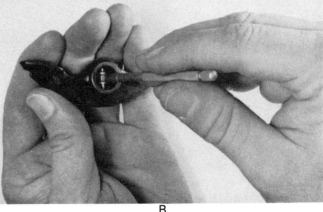

Fig. 16-7. A—Cam followers wear where contact is made with cam, valve, and shaft. Followers also wear shafts. B—An easy way to measure follower or rocker bore wear is with a telescoping gauge and outside micrometer. After fitting telescoping gauge in bore, measure it with an outside micrometer.

3. Measurement of shaft diameter.

Excessive wear or clearance usually causes valve train noise, increased oil consumption (oil drains down through guides), and reduced performance.

Most DOHC engines use shims and buckets for valve operation and adjustment. Wear in this design is unusual. However, bucket diameter and bucket bore diameter, should be measured and compared to specs. Look at Fig. 16-8.

Push rods and lifters

In push rod engines, the lifters may be located in the base of the cylinder or in the crankcase. The camshafts are always located in the crankcase. See Fig. 16-9. Push rods and lifters must be inspected for:
1. Galling, flaking, or pitting.
2. Excessive clearance between lifter and lifter bore.
3. Straightness of push rods.
4. Loosening of push rod ends.

Chain type cam drive

The most common method of driving the camshaft is with a chain and sprockets. While this is a depend-able design, engines with high mileage, or engines which have not been properly maintained, will often have a worn cam chain and sprockets. This can cause slack in the cam chain which may upset valve timing, engine performance, and cause chain noise.

Visual inspection for cam chain play or slack and evidence of sprocket tooth wear (sharpening) is required. Some manufacturers give specifications for the maximum distance between a certain number of chain links (pins) for determining chain wear. In any case, if excessive timing chain wear or slack is present, refer to your service manual for exact specifications.

Common timing chain designs use a one piece chain. The cost or price of purchasing a new cam chain is nothing compared to the labor time in doing major engine repairs. For this reason, an old cam chain is normally replaced during an overhaul.

Most all chain drive cams require a tensioner and one or more guides, as shown in Fig. 16-10. These may be rollers, sprockets, or blades. Each must be checked for wear and deterioration. A loose or badly worn chain can damage (crack or break) the tensioner.

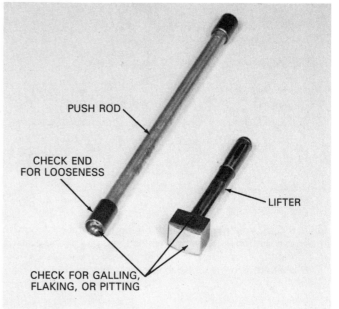

Fig. 16-9. Inspect push rods and lifters for galling, flaking, pitting, excessive clearance, straightness of pushrods, and loosening of ends.

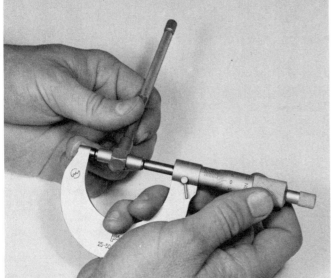

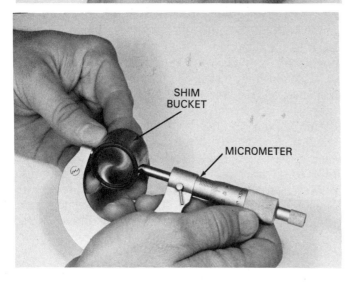

Fig. 16-8. A telescoping gauge and micrometer are used to check shim bucket-to-bucket bore clearance. Subtract bucket diameter from bucket bore diameter to determine clearance. Acceptable bucket and bore sizes as well as clearance are found in service manual.

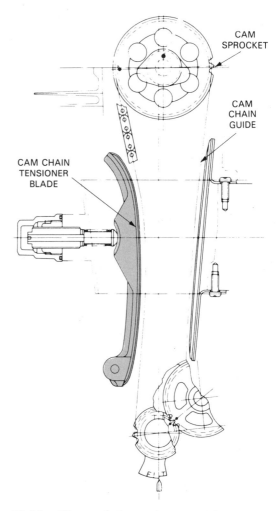

Fig. 16-10. All cam chain tensioners, guides, and sprockets must be checked for wear or deterioration. (Yamaha Motor Corporation, U.S.A.)

Gear type cam drive

Only a few manufacturers still use a gear type camshaft drive, although it is extremely dependable. Some designs use an idler gear to drive the cams. Wear of the idler gear shaft and bushing is fairly common. Gear tooth wear, though, is rarely seen.

Belt type cam drive

A belt cam drive is another extremely dependable and maintenance free design, Fig. 16-11. Replacement because of wear is uncommon. In some cases, however, crash or oil leak damage may require belt replacement.

Valve springs, collars, and keepers

Inspection of valve springs during an overhaul consists of checking for:
1. Valve spring squareness.
2. Rust or corrosion.
3. Spring free length.
4. Spring pressure.

Fig. 16-12 shows proper valve spring inspection. Collars and keepers usually do not wear. However, they must be inspected for cracks or damage caused by valve spring failure or excessive engine speeds.

Valve stems, guides, and seals

Valve stems and guides must be measured to check for wear and valve-to-guide clearance. Excessive clearance may interfere with the sealing ability and life of the valve face and seat. If a valve can be wiggled sideways in its guide, measure the side play and

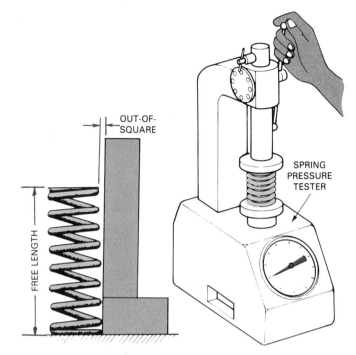

Fig. 16-12. Valve spring condition is checked by measuring spring squareness, free length, and pressure. To measure spring pressure, compress spring to given height and read scale. Spring pressure should be within factory ratings. (Kawasaki Motors Corp., U.S.A.)

compare to specifications. See Fig. 16-13, A.

Valve stems should also be checked for physical damage (cracks, bends, scarring), Fig. 16-13, B. Inspection of valve stem seals is not needed. New valve stem seals are ALWAYS installed whenever a cylinder head is disassembled.

Fig. 16-11. This engine design uses a toothed rubber belt to drive camshaft.

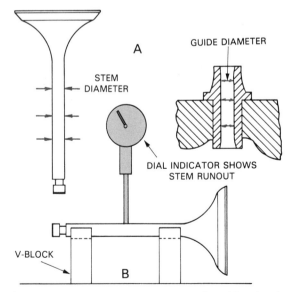

Fig. 16-13. A—Measure valve stems and guides in three places using an outside micrometer and small hole gauge. Measure valve guides in all directions to find greatest amount of wear. B—Dial indicator can be used to check valve stem runout. A valve with stem runout must be replaced. (Kawasaki Motors Corp., U.S.A.)

Valve seat and face inspection

Inspect the valve seat and face for burning, pitting, and other signs of damage. See Fig. 16-14. Also check for valve face runout, as in Fig. 16-15. The service manual gives specifications and proper procedures for carrying out more detailed valve train inspection.

Inspecting cylinder head for warpage

The cylinder head can be checked for warpage (head gasket surface not flat) by using a feeler gauge and a straightedge or surface plate. This is pictured in Fig. 16-16. For cylinder head resurfacing procedures, refer to Chapter 4, Special Operations.

RECONDITIONING THE CYLINDER HEAD ASSEMBLY

Reconditioning the cylinder head assembly typically consists of:
1. Valve guide replacement.

Fig. 16-14. Pitting or burning of valve seat is easily recognizable and requires seat reconditioning or replacement.

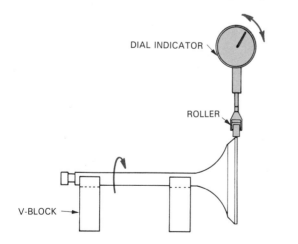

Fig. 16-15. Valve head runout is measured with a dial indicator.

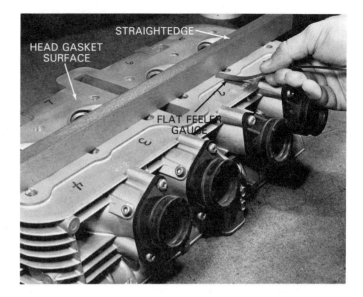

Fig. 16-16. Cylinder head warpage can be detected with a feeler gauge and straightedge. This method works well on multi-cylinder engines. If gauge slides under straightedge, head may need resurfacing or replacement. Check your manual.

2. Resurfacing valve face, tip, and seat.
3. Checking valve spring installed height.
4. Thorough parts cleaning.

Valve guide service

When a valve guide is worn beyond specifications, a new one must be installed and reamed to size. Valve guide replacement is a relatively simple operation if done correctly:
1. Heat the cylinder head in an oven as described in the service manual. An oven provides even heating to prevent warping.
2. Drive the old guides out using the proper valve guide drift. This is illustrated in Fig. 16-17, A.
3. After the head cools, remove any carbon or sharp edges in the guide bores.
4. Chill (shrink) the new guides in a freezer.
5. Reheat cylinder head.
6. Install the chilled guides using a hammer and the proper drift, Fig. 16-17, B.
7. Finally, ream the guides to size after the head cools down, Fig. 16-17, C.

Valve and seat refacing

Valves, which can be reconditioned, are refaced in a valve grinding machine. Refer to Fig. 16-18. The valve face should be ground until all dark spots, grooves, and pits are removed.

The service manual often gives specifications for VALVE MARGIN THICKNESS (flat edge between valve face and valve head). Look at Fig. 16-19. If the valve margin is too thin after grinding, a new valve must be used. A thin, sharp margin will not dissipate heat properly and can burn or fail quickly.

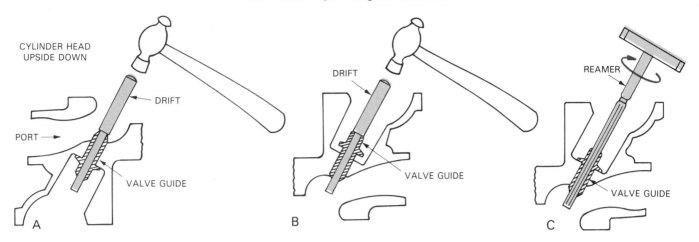

Fig. 16-17. A—Valve guide drift is used to remove and install valve guides. B—Installing new guide. C—Valve guide reamer is used to properly size valve guide after installation. Guides must be serviced before valve seats.

Fig. 16-18. A valve grinding machine reconditions valves by resurfacing face area.

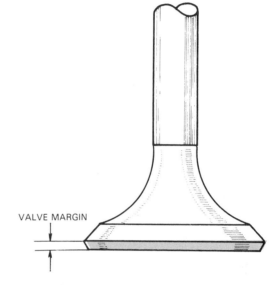

Fig. 16-19. After grinding valve, inspect margin. Margin should be within specifications or valve must be replaced. A sharp margin cannot handle combustion heat and will burn easily. (Kawasaki Motors Corp., U.S.A.)

Valve refacing machines have adjustments for different VALVE FACE ANGLES (angle between valve face and head). Select the proper angle in accordance with the motorcycle manufacturer specifications. With most motorcycles, 30 and 45 deg. valve face angles are used.

Sometimes, an INTERFERENCE ANGLE (one degree difference between valve face and seat angles)

is used to speed valve break-in and sealing. Look at Fig. 16-20.

Valve seat refacing is one of the most critical aspects of a valve job. Four important considerations for seat grinding are:

VALVE SEAT CONCENTRICITY: The valve seat must be uniform width and be located an equal distance around the valve guide bore, Fig. 16-21.

VALVE SEAT SURFACE FINISH (smoothness): The finish of the valve seat must be smooth and even to permit positive sealing.

VALVE SEAT WIDTH: The valve seat must be wide enough to prevent overheating and cupping, but not wide enough to trap carbon, Fig. 16-22.

VALVE SEAT-TO-VALVE CONTACT: The valve seat must touch the center of the valve face, as shown in Fig. 16-23.

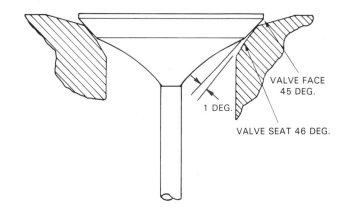

Fig. 16-20. One degree interference angle assures good sealing. A slight wedging action between valve and seat creates a positive seal.

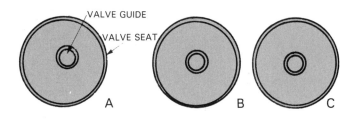

Fig. 16-21. A—Valve seat is not concentric with valve guide. B—Valve seat varies in width. These conditions can occur when valve guide is worn and when resurfacing equipment is worn or used improperly. C—Proper valve seat concentricity and width.

A valve seat refacing operation sometimes requires the use of cutters or stones of three different angles. Although the specific angles may vary, common stone or cutter angles are 15 (or 30) deg., 45 deg., and 60 deg. The 45 deg. cutter or stone is used for resurfacing the actual valve seat area. The 15 (or 30) deg. and 60 deg. cutters or stones are used to adjust valve seat width and position. Fig. 16-24 shows where seat material is removed when using these cutters.

During VALVE SEAT REFACING, the following sequence should be followed:
1. Make sure each valve and seat is properly numbered and kept in order, Fig. 16-25.

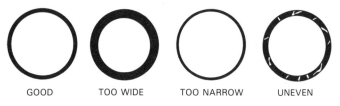

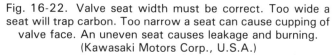

Fig. 16-22. Valve seat width must be correct. Too wide a seat will trap carbon. Too narrow a seat can cause cupping of valve face. An uneven seat causes leakage and burning. (Kawasaki Motors Corp., U.S.A.)

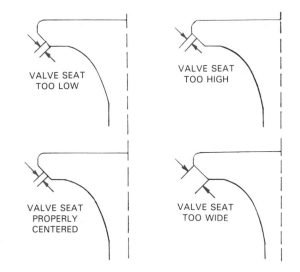

Fig. 16-23. If 45 deg. valve seat is too wide, use 30 deg. and 60 deg. cutters to narrow and center seat. If 45 deg. valve seat is too high, use 30 deg. cutter to lower seat. If 45 deg. valve seat is too low, use 60 deg. cutter to raise seat. (Yamaha Motor Corporation, U.S.A.)

2. Install the cutter pilot in the valve guide, Fig. 16-26. Check that it is the right diameter and is tight in the guide.
3. Cut the 45 deg. angle as shown in Fig. 16-27.
4. Visually inspect the seat for even width, Fig. 16-28.
   If seat width and concentricity are correct, skip steps 5 and 6, and continue with step 7.
5. Paint seat with dye and cut the 15 deg. angle until

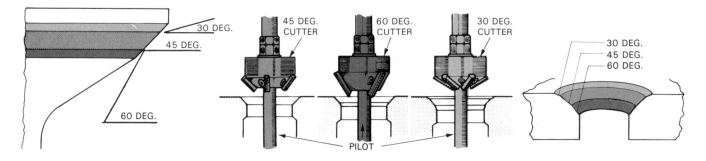

Fig. 16-24. A 45 deg. cutter resurfaces valve seat. A 60 deg. cutter narrows valve seat from botton. A 30 deg. cutter narrows valve seat from top. (Kawasaki Motors Corp., U.S.A.)

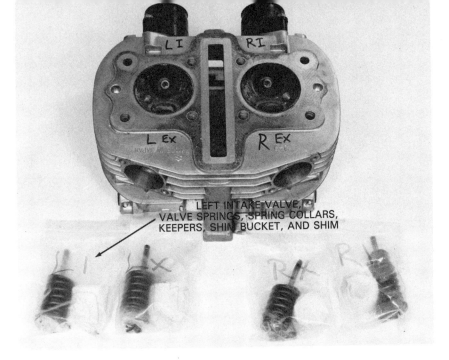

Fig. 16-25. Labeled bags will help you keep parts segregated during cylinder head reconditioning.

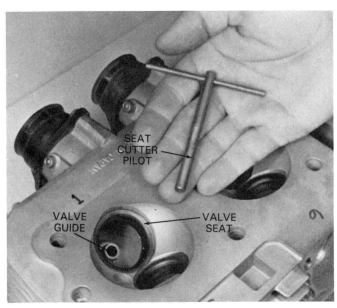

Fig. 16-26. Valve cutter pilot must fit snugly in valve guide to accurately center cutter. Remove handle after installing pilot.

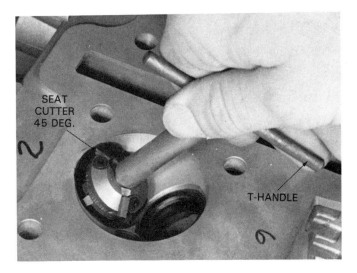

Fig. 16-27. Use light even pressure when cutting valve seat. Cut until all pitting is removed and no further.

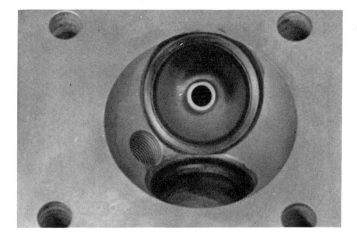

Fig. 16-28. After cutting valve seat (45 deg.), visually check seat for even width.

contact is made all the way around the seat. Refer to Fig. 16-29.

6. Cut the 60 deg. angle until contact is made all the way around seat. See Fig. 16-30.
7. Check seat width and contact position on valve face, Fig. 16-31.
8. Adjust seat width and contact position with appropriate cutters. With a 45 deg. angle seat, the following rules apply:

   a. The 15 deg. cutter NARROWS the seat and

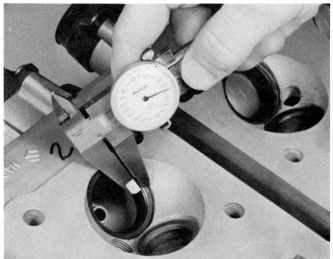

MEASURE SEAT WIDTH (45 DEG. AREA) WITH A DIAL CALIPER. COMPARE YOUR MEASUREMENT TO MANUAL SPECS.

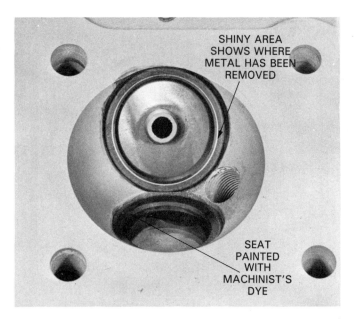

Fig. 16-29. Paint valve seat with machinists' dye so your 15 deg. and 60 deg. cuts stand out. Usually very little metal will have to be removed with 15 deg. cutter. Be very careful to remove only enough metal so that contact is made all the way around.

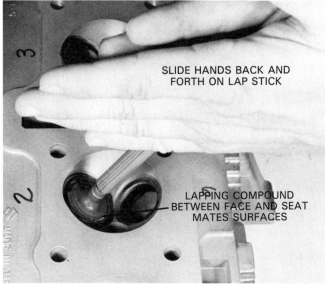

USE A COMMERCIAL LAPPING COMPOUND (ABRASIVE PASTE) AND HAND LAP STICK TO SMOOTH AND DOUBLE-CHECK VALVE AND SEAT CONTACT. BE CAREFUL NOT TO GET ANY LAPPING COMPOUND ON VALVE STEM OR GUIDE. IT WILL CAUSE RAPID WEAR.

Fig. 16-30. Use same caution and care with 60 deg. cutter. Removal of too much metal can ruin your valve job.

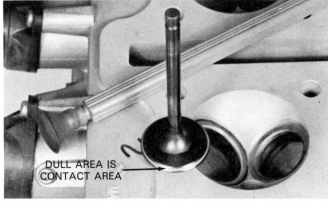

AFTER CLEANING ALL LAPPING COMPOUND FROM VALVE FACE AND SEAT, VISUALLY CHECK SEAT CONTACT ON VALVE FACE. IT MUST BE CENTERED ON VALVE FACE. IF NOT, MOVE SEAT USING YOUR 15 AND 60 DEG. CUTTERS.

Fig. 16-31. Checking valve face contact on seat.

moves the contact position DOWN on the valve face.

   b. The 60 deg. cutter NARROWS the seat and moves the contact position UP on the valve face.

   c. The 45 deg. cutter WIDENS the seat.

9. Lap the valve and seat. Then, recheck the seat width and contact position.

Valve spring installed height

Valve spring installed height adjustment is necessary because material removed from the valve face and seat during reconditioning causes the valve to move deeper into the head. This increases the amount of stem sticking through the head, Fig. 16-32.

VALVE SPRING INSTALLED HEIGHT determines valve seat pressure and valve spring tension throughout valve travel. Installed height is adjusted with valve spring shims. As in Fig. 16-33, shims increase spring tension. The service manual gives specifications and proper procedures for carrying out spring shimming.

CYLINDER HEAD RESSEMBLY

Your manual probably says, "Reassemble the cylinder head in the reverse order of disassembly." Although this is true, some important procedures to remember are:

1. Thoroughly clean all parts to remove lapping compound, grit, and metal filings.

2. Install lower valve spring collars before installing the valve stem seals. On some engines, the collars will not fit over the stem seals.

3. Lubricate the valve stems and guides with motor oil or assembly lube.

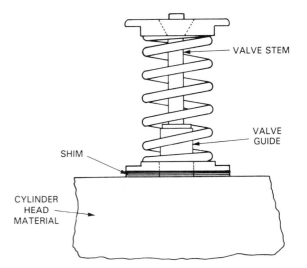

Fig. 16-33. Valve spring shims shorten valve spring to compensate for material removed during valve job. They return spring tension to normal (inner spring only shown).

4. Install progressively wound valve springs with the tight coils toward the bottom collar, Fig. 16-34.

5. Use a valve spring compressor to assemble upper spring collar and keepers, Fig. 16-35.

6. To insure proper seating of the valve spring keepers, lightly tap the end of the valve stem with a plastic hammer, Fig. 16-36.

7. After reassembly, use solvent to leak test each valve, Fig. 16-37.

8. After the reconditioning process, wrap the head in plastic or put it in a sealed box. This will prevent contamination while finishing the engine overhaul.

PISTON AND CYLINDER INSPECTION AND SERVICE

Due to the extreme temperatures, friction, and loads placed on pistons and cylinders, thorough inspection for wear, cracks, and damage is very critical. If the slightest problem is overlooked, the overhaul can fail in a short period of time.

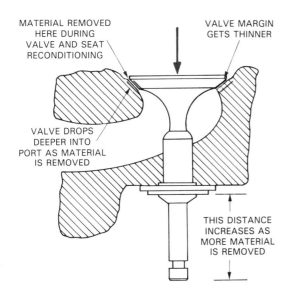

Fig. 16-32. Effects of removal of material during a valve job are shown. Valve and seat grinding sinks valve into cylinder head.

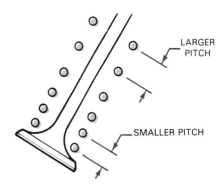

Fig. 16-34. Tightest coils of progressive wound valve springs must be installed towards cylinder head. (Yamaha Motor Corporation, U.S.A.)

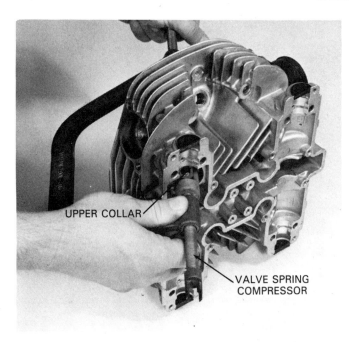

Fig. 16-35. A valve spring compressor compresses valve springs by pushing top collar down so keepers can be installed.

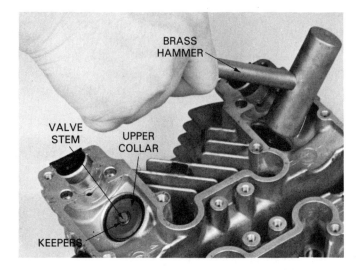

Fig. 16-36. Using a soft faced hammer (plastic or brass), tap each valve stem to insure firm seating of keepers in upper collar.

Fig. 16-37. After head is assembled, check each valve and seat for leakage by pouring solvent into each port. Any weeping (leakage) around valve head indicates a poor seal. Check for dirt, hand lap, or regrind as needed.

Checking cylinder wear

The cylinder must be inspected for excessive taper, out-of-roundness, a ridge, and cylinder damage (galling, cracks) caused by other broken parts. Look at Fig. 16-38.

Measurement of a four-stroke cycle cylinder is done in the same manner as for a two-stroke cycle cylinder. Important procedures to remember are:
1. Measure the cylinder at top, middle, and bottom.
2. Make all three measurements front-to-back and side-to-side in the bore.
3. Record all your measurements, Fig. 16-39.

Piston measurement and inspection

Inspect the pistons for damage (seizure, cracks, groove and land wear). See Fig. 16-40. Also, measure skirt diameter, as in Fig. 16-41.

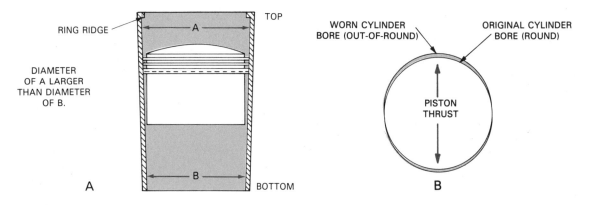

Fig. 16-38. A—Cylinder taper and ridge results from normal wear. A ridge is formed at end of ring travel. Cylinder also becomes larger at top than at bottom. There is less lubrication at top of cylinder. B—Cylinder out-of-roundness is caused by thrust of piston.

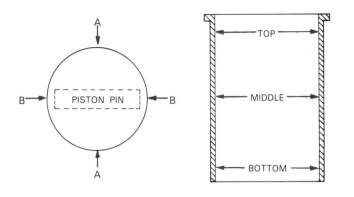

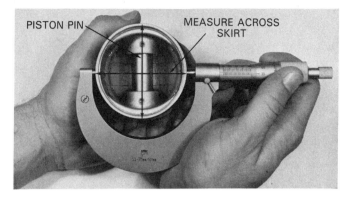

Fig. 16-39. To effectively measure a cylinder for taper and out-of-roundness, measurements must be taken front-to-back and side-to-side at top, middle, and bottom of cylinder. This is a total of six measurements.

Fig. 16-41. Piston skirt diameter and wear is accurately measured using an outside micrometer. Measure perpendicular to piston pin as shown.

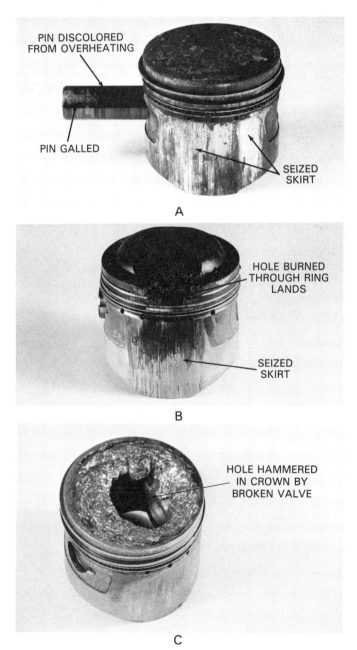

Fig. 16-40. Typical four-stroke cycle piston damage. A and B—Seizure. B—Burned hole. C—Hammered hole (broken valve).

Subtract the skirt diameter from the largest diameter of the cylinder to get PISTON CLEARANCE. This is shown in Fig. 16-42. Wear limits are given in the service manual.

Another important measurement made on a four-stroke cycle piston is RING-TO-GROOVE CLEARANCE (play between ring and piston ring groove). Shown in Fig. 16-43, find a feeler gauge blade that fits snugly between the piston ring and piston ring groove. Compare the gauge size to specifications. If the clearance is too large, the piston should be replaced.

Example:

Cylinder diameter	= 2.558 in.
Piston diameter	= 2.553 in.
Piston clearance	= .005 in.

Fig. 16-42. To get piston clearance, subtract piston diameter from cylinder diameter.

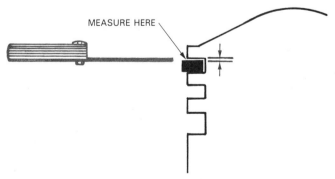

Fig. 16-43. Ring-to-ring groove clearance is measured with a feeler gauge. Largest gauge that will fit between ring and groove equals clearance.

Piston ring end gap measurement

PISTON RING END GAP should be measured with the rings installed squarely into the cylinder. Measure the ring end gap with a feeler gauge, as in Fig. 16-44. If gap is too small, ring end must be filed. Rings must be replaced if end gap is excessive. After ring end gap has been checked and adjusted, place them in a labeled bag so that each set of rings stays with the proper cylinder and piston.

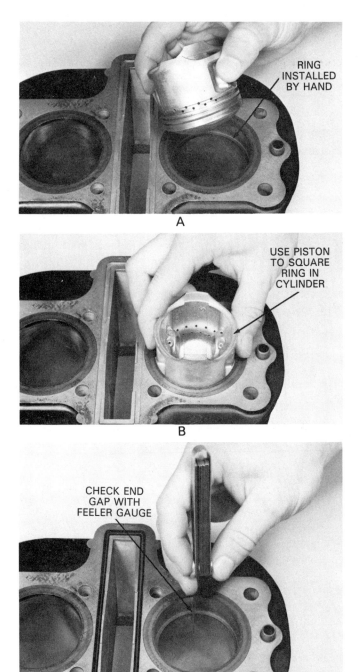

Fig. 16-44. Before end gap can be measured, ring must be installed squarely in cylinder. A—After slipping ring into cylinder, use piston to push ring a little farther into cylinder. B—This will insure that ring is square in cylinder. C—End gap can be accurately measured with a feeler gauge.

Wrist pin and small end bearing measurement

Measure the wrist pin diameter and inspect the pin for discoloration (overheating) and surface damage. Measure the bore diameter of the connecting rod small end and subtract wrist pin diameter to determine clearance. Fig. 16-45 illustrates how to make these measurements. If clearance is excessive but wrist pin diameter is correct, the connecting rod must be replaced or reconditioned.

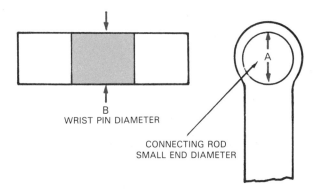

Fig. 16-45. Use a telescoping gauge and outside micrometer to measure piston pin and connecting rod. Subtract measurement B from measurement A to find piston pin clearance. Compare this value to specifications.

Reconditioning the cylinder

If the cylinder is worn beyond service limits, it must be bored to the next oversize. Cylinder boring procedures are covered in Chapter 4, Special Operations.

When a cylinder is bored to fit an oversize piston, the end gap of the new rings must be checked and adjusted. If the cylinder is within service limits, it must be deglazed to aid in seating the new piston rings. Fig. 16-46 illustrates cylinder deglazing.

A cylinder which has been honed or deglazed must be washed in warm soapy water to remove grit and metal particles. After washing, wipe with an oiled rag. Dry the cylinder and recoat the bore with oil to prevent rust. If new rings are being installed, the end gap should be checked after cylinder deglazing, refer back to Fig. 16-44.

ENGINE LOWER END SERVICE

The four-stroke cycle engine lower end is made up of all the components from the cylinder base down. This includes the crankshaft, connecting rod, main bearings, connecting rod bearings, engine balancers, cam chain, oil pump, and crankcases.

Some four-stroke crankshafts can be reconditioned when worn or damaged, while others cannot. An example of a crankshaft which cannot be reconditioned is a multi-cylinder assembled crankshaft. Damage or wear to this type of crankshaft requires replacement of the complete crankshaft assembly. Your service manual will tell you the appropriate reconditioning procedure for particular crankshafts.

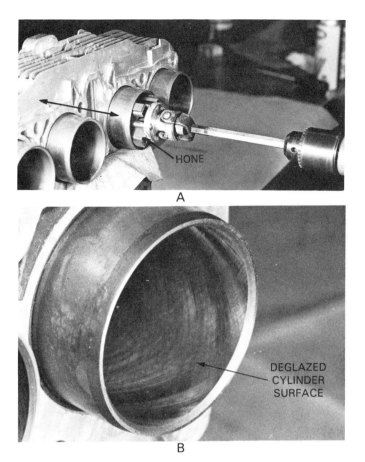

Fig. 16-46. A—Hone is used to deglaze cylinder walls. B—Correct texture is achieved with proper hone speed and stroke action.

INSPECTION AND MEASUREMENT OF BEARINGS

The four types of bearings found in the four-stroke cycle engine are roller, ball, plain, and needle types. All types of bearings should be checked visually for discoloration, scoring, flaking, or disintegration. Roller, ball, and needle bearings should be checked for radial play, Fig. 16-47. Ball bearings must also be checked for lateral play, Fig. 16-48.

Plain bearing (bushings, split type bearings) clearance can be measured in two ways:
1. With the use of precision measuring equipment.
2. With the use of Plastigage (split bearings only), as in Fig. 16-49.

CHECKING OIL PUMP CONDITION

An important step during any engine overhaul is the inspection of the oil pump. The most carefully done engine overhaul can quickly self-destruct and turn into "junk" if the oil pump is not functioning properly. Oil pumps should be visually inspected and measured to check clearances.

Rotor and gear type pumps are measured with a feeler gauge. Measure in the areas shown in Fig. 16-50. Piston type pumps are measured with a

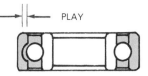

Fig. 16-47. Radial (up and down) play must be checked in roller, ball, and needle bearings. If not within specs, replace bearing. (U.S. Suzuki Motor Corporation)

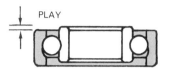

Fig. 16-48. Lateral (side-to-side) play must be checked in ball bearings. Wiggle sideways and compare to specs. Replace bearings if too loose. (U.S. Suzuki Motor Corporation)

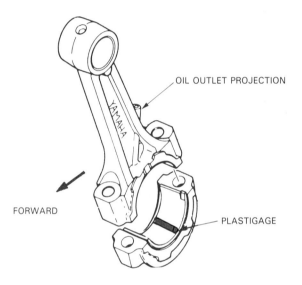

Fig. 16-49. Plastigage can be used to check clearance on any split bearing (crankshaft, camshaft). Crush Plastigage between rod bearing and crank. Then compare width of Plastigage to scale provided. Small bearing clearance is indicated by wide Plastigage. If smashed Plastigage is still narrow, larger clearance is indicated. (Yamaha Motor Corp., U.S.A.)

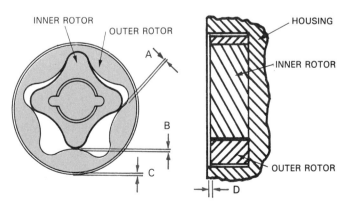

Fig. 16-50. When checking condition of a rotor type oil pump, clearance must be measured at A, B, C, and D. Use a flat feeler gauge. (Yamaha Motor Corp., U.S.A.)

micrometer and telescoping gauge or small hole gauge. See Fig. 16-51.

An oil pump should always be inspected and measured, whether lubrication problems are evident or not. The slightest wear or damage would require a new oil pump.

CLEANING OIL PASSAGES AND LOWER END FILTERS

All oil passageways, orifices, check valves, relief valves, screen type filters, and the oil tank should be thoroughly cleaned during an overhaul. Sludge traps and centrifugal filters should also be cleaned. Extreme care should be taken in cleaning these components since the deposits in them are very dense and difficult to remove. The oil filter element must also be replaced during an overhaul.

DIAGNOSIS OF OIL SYSTEM PROBLEMS

No matter how carefully an overhaul is done, overlooking a simple problem in the lubrication system can cause rapid engine failure. Dry, seized, or burned engine components indicate a lubrication system problem.

The following questions will give you guidance in diagnosing lubrication system problems:
1. Was the oil pump mounted securely?
2. Were gaskets and O-rings, which seal oil pressure, properly installed.
3. Were check balls and relief valves free of debris and in good working order?
4. Were oil passageways and orifices clogged or restricted?
5. Were external oil lines damaged, leaking, and con-

nected properly?
6. Were oil filters and screens clogged or blocked?
7. Was engine oil contaminated or diluted?
8. Was there sufficient oil in the engine?

CAMSHAFT INSPECTION AND MEASUREMENT (PUSH ROD ENGINES)

In the push rod engine, the camshaft or camshafts are located in the crankcase. Inspect and measure this type camshaft as you would with an overhead camshaft engine. See Fig. 16-52.

ENGINE BALANCER INSPECTION

Some engines are equipped with chain or gear driven balancers. Check for wear of the chain and sprocket or gears, as well as balancer shaft bearings and cushion. Typical balancer system inspection

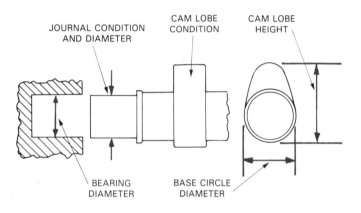

Fig. 16-52. Typical inspection and measurement points for a camshaft in a push rod engine.

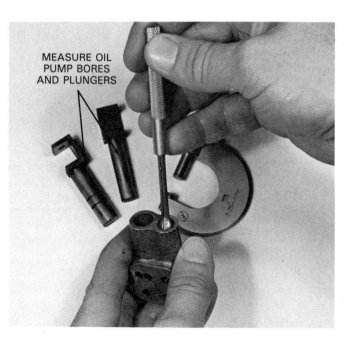

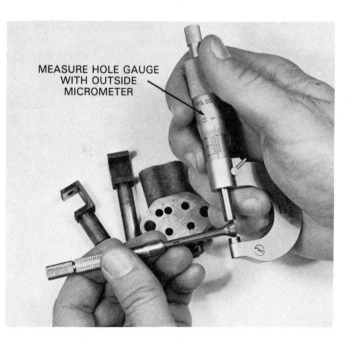

Fig. 16-51. A small hole gauge and outside micrometer will accurately measure clearance in a piston type oil pump.

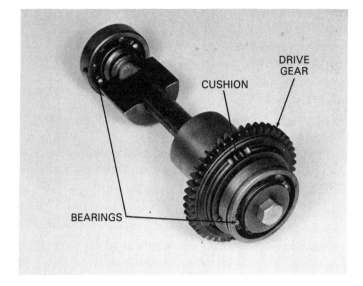

Fig. 16-53. Components on balancer which must be inspected include bearings, drive gear, and cushion.

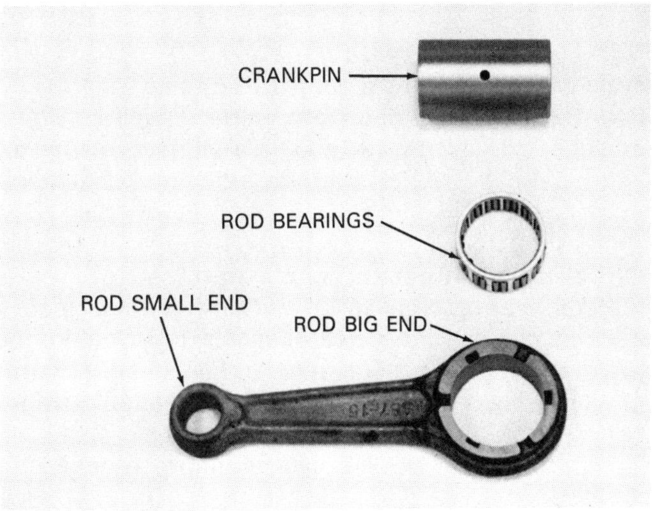

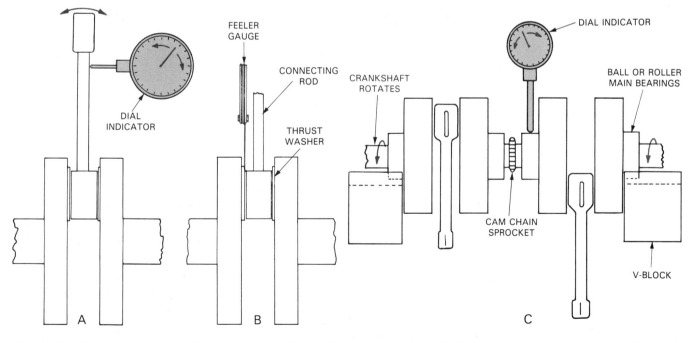

Fig. 16-55. A typical rod kit for a four-stroke cycle engine using an assembled type crankshaft. It allows engine rebuilding at a minimum cost.

points are shown in Fig. 16-53. Refer to your service manual for proper procedures since there are many variations in design.

CRANKSHAFT MEASUREMENT AND RECONDITIONING

Four-stroke cycle motorcycle engines use two types of crankshafts, assembled crankshaft and one-piece crankshaft. Both types require thorough inspection and measurement for wear. Depending on parts availability and how the crankshaft is designed, you may be able to recondition some types.

Assembled crankshaft

An assembled four-stroke cycle crankshaft is checked for wear in the same manner as a two-stroke cycle crankshaft. Make sure the crankshaft has been thoroughly cleaned and is free of oil. An oil film left on bearings (connecting rod roller bearing) makes wear difficult to detect. Fig. 16-54 illustrates typical assembled crankshaft measurement. Your manual will outline crankshaft inspection procedures for the specific engine type.

Rod kits (rebuild parts) are available for some four-stroke cycle engines which use assembled crankshafts. A typical rod kit is pictured in Fig. 16-55. Four-stroke

Fig. 16-54. Measuring an assembled type crankshaft. A—Measurement of rod tip determines wear of crankpin, bearing, and rod big end. B—A feeler gauge inserted between rod and thrust washer measures rod side play. C—Measurement of crankshaft deflection is accomplished by supporting crankshaft by its outside ball or roller main bearings. Measure runout in center main bearings while rotating crankshaft.

cycle crankshafts are rebuilt in the same manner as two-stroke cycle engine crankshafts. The crankshaft must be disassembled and reassembled using a hydraulic press. After assembly, the crank assembly must be trued.

One-piece plain bearing crankshaft

Plain bearing crankshaft journals (rod and main) must be measured to check diameter, taper, and out-of-roundness. This is illustrated in Fig. 16-56. A worn plain bearing type crankshaft may be reconditioned in two ways:

1. Insert bearing replacement (minor reconditioning).
2. Grinding journals for undersize bearings (major reconditioning.).

Minor crankshaft reconditioning

When crankshaft journals measure within service limits and have a smooth surface, they may be polished with crocus cloth. In most instances, a new set of standard insert bearings will recondition the crank-rod assembly. A check of bearing clearance will usually show clearance to be within specs. See Fig. 16-57.

Some designs allow for minute adjustment of clearance. Bearing inserts are classified and coded in several increments within a .002 in. (0.05 mm) range. Your service manual explains this operation if applicable.

Major crankshaft reconditioning

Major crankshaft reconditioning consists of re-grinding rod or main journals to a smaller diameter and fitting undersize bearings. Crankshaft grinding must be done by a specialist. Many automotive machine shops can handle this operation. Some modern plain bearing type crankshafts cannot be reground when they are outside of wear limits. Refer to the shop manual if in doubt.

CONNECTING ROD RECONDITIONING (PLAIN BEARING TYPE)

With severe four-stroke cycle engine lower end failures, the connecting rod can be damaged. A broken connecting rod is quite obvious. A bent connecting rod may or may not be obvious, depending on how badly it is bent. If you notice uneven wear on the sides of the piston or angled wear marks on the skirt, check for a bent rod. Look at Fig. 16-58.

A different type of damage which is not obvious occurs when bearings and rod journals are worn ex-

A

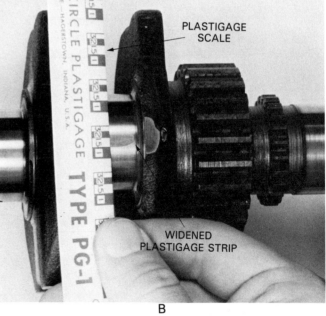

B

Fig. 16-57. A—To check rod bearing clearance, lay a strip of Plastigage on crankshaft journal. Carefully install and torque rod. This squeezes Plastigage into a wider strip. B—Plastigage scale is then used to measure width of strip. In this example, rod bearing clearance is .0015 in.

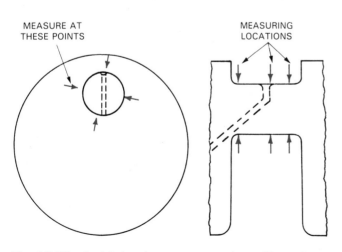

Fig. 16-56. A plain bearing type connecting rod journal must be measured in areas shown to detect taper and out-of-roundness.

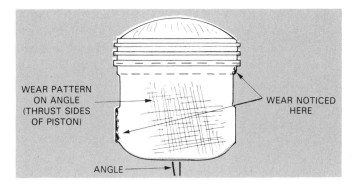

Fig. 16-58. A bent connecting rod may cause sides of piston to be worn unevenly (wear at top on one side and bottom on other side). An angled wear pattern on piston skirt may also be evident.

cessively. In this situation, extreme stresses may cause the big end of the connecting rod to become oval shaped, as in Fig. 16-59. It is a good idea to measure the connecting rod for this condition during an overhaul. Use a telescoping gauge and a micrometer to measure vertically and horizontally in the connecting rod big end.

Depending upon costs and type of connecting rod problem, you may either replace the old rod or have it reconditioned by a machine shop. Refer to a manual for specific directions and specs.

ENGINE MEASUREMENT AND INSPECTION SUMMARY

At this point, you are very much aware of the quantity of information you must gather and put to use while completing a four-stroke cycle engine overhaul. The following list of procedures should be used as a guide. Use it with your service manual as needed for the specific engine being repaired.

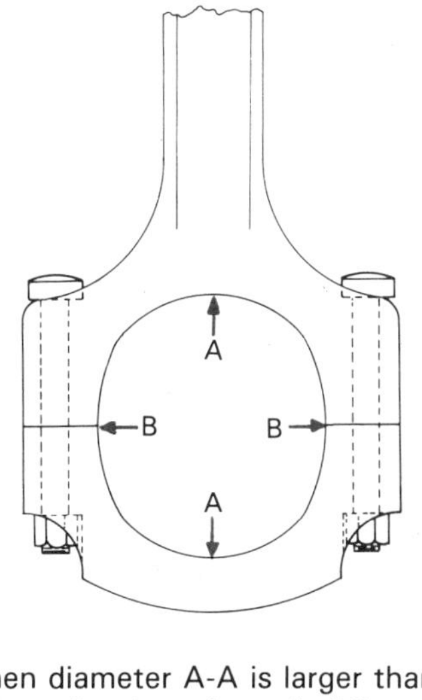

Fig. 16-59. When diameter A-A is larger than B-B, connecting rod is oval shaped and requires rebuilding or replacement. Oval shape can be detected by measuring a torqued rod and cap with an outside micrometer and telescoping gauge.

TOP END COMPONENTS

1. Measure rocker (follower) shaft diameter.
2. Measure rocker (follower) inside diameter.
3. Check for camshaft runout.
4. Measure camshaft bearing bore diameter.
5. Check camshaft journal diameter.
6. Measure camshaft lobe wear.
7. Use Plastigage to measure camshaft bearing clearance.
8. Check camshaft end play.
9. Measure shim bucket and shim bore diameters.
10. Check valve stem diameter, valve margin thickness, and stem runout.
11. Measure valve guide wear.
12. Measure valve spring free and installed heights.
13. Make sure cylinder head surface and top of cylinder block are straight.
14. Measure cylinder bore diameter, out-of-roundness, and taper.
15. Check piston diameter, wrist pin diameter, ring end gap, ring side clearance, and piston clearance in cylinder.
16. Measure tappet bore and stem diameters.

BOTTOM END COMPONENTS

1. Check for crankshaft runout.
2. Measure main bearing journal diameter, journal out-of-roundness, and clearance.
3. Check connecting rod journal diameter, out-of-roundness, and bearing clearance.
4. Check main and connecting rod bearing looseness (ball-roller types).
5. Measure cam chain length.
6. Measure crankshaft end play.

OIL PUMP

1. Measure shaft diameter and body inside diameter.
2. Check gear-rotor side play.
3. Measure plunger diameter and plunger body diameter.
4. Check plunger clearance.
5. Inspect drive gear or block for wear.

GENERAL INSPECTION

1. Inspect for damaged surfaces (corrosion, scoring, discoloration, grooving).
2. Check for frozen or stiff moving parts (lack of lubrication, excessive heat, insufficient clearance, foreign material).
3. Watch for broken parts (cracks, chips, bits of material in engine).
4. Measure warpage (distortion of part due to overheating, improper installation, excessive wear).
5. Make sure no parts are missing because of improper assembly (usually small part, spring, clip, spacer, lock tab).

VISUAL INSPECTION LOCATIONS

1. Inspect cam followers and cam lobe surface condition.
2. Check tappet surface condition.
3. Inspect cylinder bores for a ridge.
4. Check valve faces for grooving or pitting.
5. Inspect valve step tips for wear.
6. Make sure cam chain tensioner is not damaged.
7. Check piston skirts to detect blow-by discoloration.
8. Check all seal lips for sharpness and surfaces that seals ride on for grooving.
9. Inspect all plain bearings, bushings, and journals for smoothness.

FOUR-STROKE CYCLE ENGINE REASSEMBLY

Engine reassembly is a relatively simple operation, but it must be done with great care. Failure to keep parts clean or properly organized can prevent you from doing a professional overhaul. Many of the steps of two-stroke cycle engine assembly (Chapter 15) also apply to four-stroke cycle engine assembly.

PLAIN BEARING INSTALLATION

On engines using plain bearings for crankshaft main bearings or connecting rods, care during assembly must be emphasized. To insure proper installation of plain bearings:

1. Make sure the bearing seating surfaces on the engine and back side of the bearing are perfectly clean. Do NOT touch the bearing surface. It is easily damaged. The acid on your fingers can even etch the surface. If dirt is present on the bearing, wash in solvent and blow dry.
2. Install the bearing shells with the locating tabs properly indexed and with each bearing in its proper location, Fig. 16-60. Refer to the service manual for bearing identification.
3. Use Plastigage to determine bearing clearance. Refer to the service manual for proper clearance. If clearance is incorrect, the manual will explain proper corrective action.
4. Carefully remove Plastigage residue from bearing shells and crankshaft.
5. Lubricate crankshaft and bearing shells.
6. Make sure the connecting rod is installed facing the proper direction. The cap and rod index marks must be correctly aligned. Torque the rod bolts to specs. See Fig. 16-61.

Final assembly of the main bearings is completed when the crankcase halves are bolted together.

CRANKSHAFT AND GEARBOX SHAFT INSTALLATION

The crankshaft and gearbox shafts must be located properly during lower end assembly. Half rings and

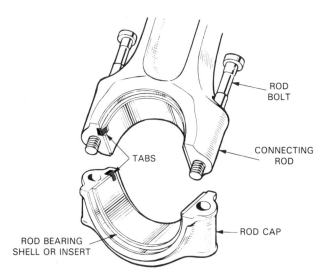

Fig. 16-60. Insert bearing tabs must be indexed and bearing shells must be fully seated. (Triumph Motorcycles [Meriden] Ltd.)

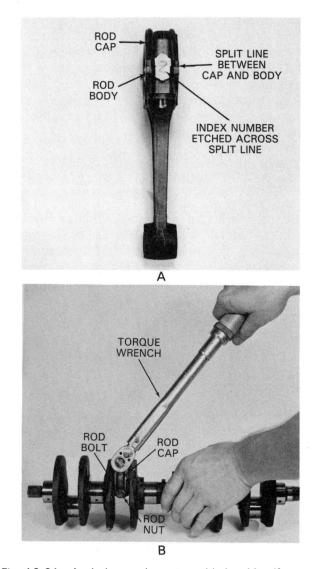

Fig. 16-61. A—Index marks are provided to identify proper direction of rod cap installation. B—Using a torque wrench, tighten each rod nut a little at a time until proper torque is reached.

dowel pins indexed into bearings provide correct location, Fig. 16-62. On engines using internal primary drive (gear or chain), the primary drive must be assembled in conjunction with the crankshaft, Fig. 16-63. Four-stroke cycle engines, which use vertically split crankcases, may require measurement and adjustment of crankshaft and gearbox end play.

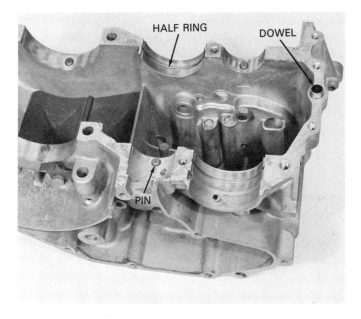

Fig. 16-62. Typical crankcase locating devices are: dowels, pins, and half rings. Always make sure they are in place and undamaged before assembly.

Fig. 16-63. In this internal primary drive, crankshaft, primary chain, and jackshaft are installed together.

OIL AND GREASE USE

Engine components must be lubricated during assembly. This insures proper lubrication when the engine runs for the first time. Failure to lubricate components during assembly can result in immediate part damage.

Special assembly lubricants are available and should be used where recommended by the motorcycle manufacturer. Lubrication with a good four-stroke motorcycle OIL is usually acceptable.

GREASE is used for lubrication of seal lips. Thick grease will also hold parts (valve keepers, thrust washers, or gaskets) in position during assembly.

CHECKING FOR BINDING AFTER EACH INSTALLATION

All rotating parts are susceptible to binding if installed improperly or if damaged. Check for free movement after installation of shafts, shift drum, connecting rods, and crankshaft. Check for binding as parts are assembled and after the crankcases are torqued. Also, be sure the gearbox shifts smoothly through each gear ratio.

SEALING COMPOUNDS

Machined surfaces which do not use a gasket must always be sealed with silicone sealer or an approved liquid gasket. CAUTION! Do not use an excessive amount of silicone sealer. Sealer can block oil passages if it squeezes out when fasteners are tightened.

Refer to your service manual for the proper type sealing compounds and where they should be used.

TIMING OF ENGINE BALANCERS

In order to reduce engine vibration, engine balancers must be timed with the crankshaft. Timing marks are provided to allow for easy and precise timing. Fig. 16-64 illustrates timing of a typical engine balancer.

Fig. 16-64. An engine balancer must be timed to work properly. This gear driven balancer has punch marks which must be aligned for proper timing.

Reference or timing marks may be found on gears, sprockets, or balancer weights. Always refer to your service manual for specific timing procedure.

TORQUE SEQUENCE AND VALUE

Due to the size of cylinder, cylinder head, and crankcase castings, a proper TORQUE PATTERN (fastener tightening sequence) must be used to prevent warpage. Generally, a torque pattern follows a crisscross pattern from the center to the outside of the part. However, due to the complex design of modern engine castings, torque patterns vary.

For convenience, some current four-stroke engines have torque sequence numbers cast into the cylinder head or crankcase, Fig. 16-65. This sequence must always be followed. If numbers are not present, refer to your manual for a proper torque sequence.

The other important aspect of torquing engine components is the final torque value (amount of torque applied). Proper torquing is not achieved in

one torque sequence. Gradual tightening of fasteners in THREE or FOUR STAGES (approximately 1/2 torque, 3/4 torque, and full torque twice) is necessary. Again, refer to the service manual for details.

PISTON RING INSTALLATION

The importance of piston ring installation is sometimes overlooked. Piston rings which are installed incorrectly can cause a loss of compression, oil consumption, or cylinder damage. Critical considerations during piston ring installation are:

1. Piston rings must be located in the proper grooves (chrome ring in top groove, scraper ring in middle groove, oil ring in bottom groove).
2. Piston rings should be installed with the right side up. As shown in Fig. 16-66, markings are usually provided on the top of the ring.
3. Use a ring expander, to prevent breakage during installation. Look at Fig. 16-67. Rings can also be installed without a ring expander if care is exercised, Fig. 16-68. Segmented oil rings must be installed by hand. See Fig. 16-69.
4. Install the oil ring first, then the middle ring, then the top ring.

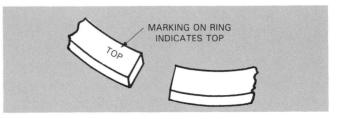

Fig. 16-66. Rings with markings must be installed with mark up. Markings you may encounter are: N, .5 and 1.0 for oversize metric, or .010, .020 for oversize English.

Fig. 16-65. Torque sequence numbers are sometimes cast into crankcases and cylinder heads.

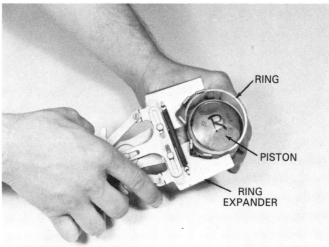

Fig. 16-67 A ring expander makes piston ring installation in piston grooves easy.

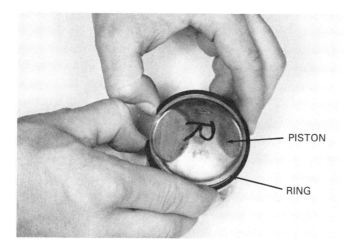

Fig. 16-68. Piston rings can be installed by hand. Be careful not to overexpand and break rings.

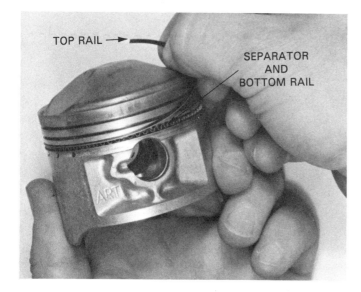

Fig. 16-69. When installing segmented oil rings, install separator first, then bottom rail, and top rail. Be sure separator ends are butted together, not overlapped.

PISTON INSTALLATION

During piston installation, piston direction is important because of offset wrist pins or different size valve pocket cutouts. Pictured in Fig. 16-70, an arrow is usually cast or stamped into the piston crown to indicate piston direction. This arrow usually points toward the front of the engine. Refer to your service manual for proper piston direction.

Some simple but important tips for piston installation are:
1. Install a new cylinder base gasket.
2. Cover the crankcase opening with clean shop towels. This will prevent an accidentally dropped part (circlip for example) from entering the engine. In many cases, complete engine disassembly will be required to recover anything dropped into the crankcase.

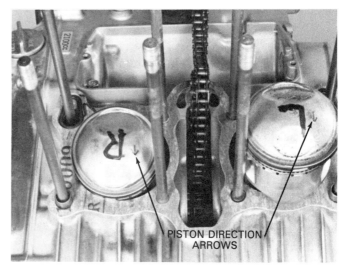

Fig. 16-70. Piston installation direction arrows point toward front (exhaust) on this engine.

3. Always install one circlip in the piston while still on the bench. This leaves only one circlip to be installed while over the crankcase.
4. Install the pin through one side of the piston before placing the piston over the connecting rod. Most piston pins are slip fit into the pin boss. If the pin does not slip freely into place, it may be necessary to heat the piston for installation. Refer to Fig. 16-71.
5. Install the remaining circlip and make sure all circlips are fully seated in their grooves. Refer to Fig. 16-72.

CYLINDER INSTALLATION

Cylinder installation procedures vary from engine to engine. Important considerations which apply to most engines are:
1. Install locating dowel pins and O-rings in the

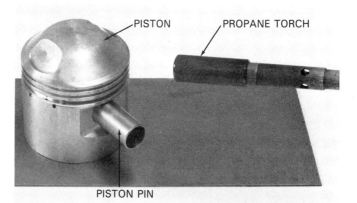

Fig. 16-71. A propane torch can be used to warm piston so piston pin will move freely into place. Be careful not to overheat piston.

Fig. 16-72. Make sure circlips are fully seated in their grooves. A shop towel covering crankcase opening will prevent dropped circlip from entering engine lower end.

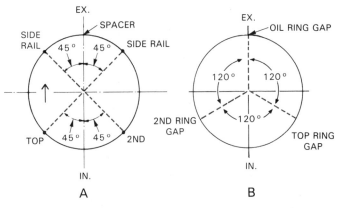

Fig. 16-74. A—Proper ring end-gap position with a three-piece oil ring. B—Proper ring end-gap for a one-piece oil ring.

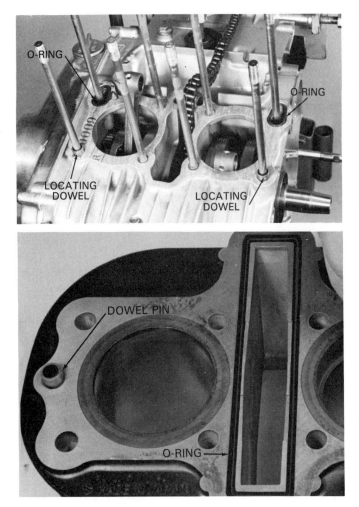

Fig. 16-73. Do not forget to install all locating dowels and O-rings in crankcase, cylinder, and head.

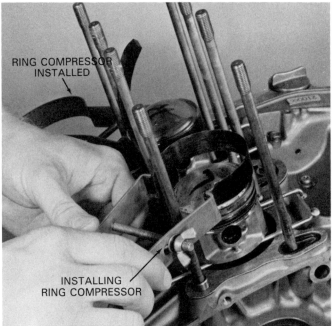

Fig. 16-75. Ring compressors reduce chance of ring breakage when cylinder is slid over pistons.

4. Use piston blocks, when possible, to hold the piston straight, Fig. 16-76.
5. Carefully install the cylinder. The cylinder must not be tilted or cocked when slid over the rings. Look at Fig. 16-77.

CAM TIMING

Cam timing determines valve movement in relation to piston movement. Cam timing is critical. Failure to properly set cam timing can cause the pistons to hit the valves. This can result in bent valves and damaged pistons. Timing (index) marks are provided on gears, sprockets, and crankshaft (alternator rotor or ignition advance unit). These marks must be used as specified by the service manual to time the camshafts

cylinder or case. See Fig. 16-73.
2. Properly position ring end gaps. This is shown in Fig. 16-74.
3. Use a ring compressor, Fig. 16-75.

Fig. 16-76. Piston blocks help keep pistons in position during cylinder installation.

Fig. 16-77. Be careful not to cock or tilt cylinder while slipping it over rings. Gently tap cylinder with heel of your hand or a plastic hammer to help move cylinder down. Remove ring compressors and piston blocks after rings are fitted into cylinder spigots. Then, slide cylinder all the way down until it touches base gasket.

with the crankshaft. Fig. 16-78 shows typical cam timing marks.

REASSEMBLY ADJUSTMENTS

Some normal tune-up adjustments are essential after engine reassembly. These include cam chain, valve clearance, and ignition timing adjustments. See Chapter 12, Tune-up and General Servicing, for these procedures.

FOUR-STROKE CYCLE ENGINE REASSEMBLY SUMMARY

The following list summarizes some of the most important aspects of four-stroke cycle engine

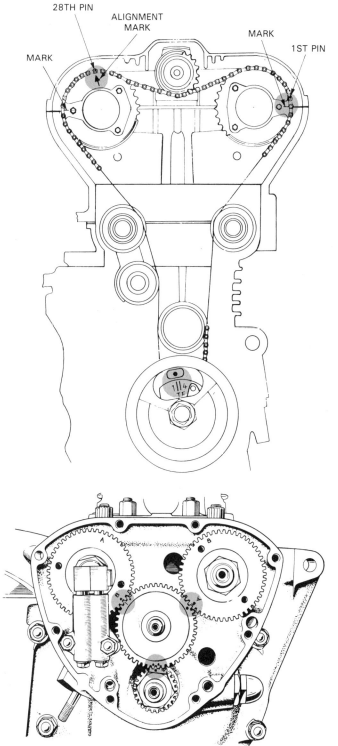

Fig. 16-78. Regardless of method for driving cams, index marks are given to simplify cam timing setting. With timing chains, marks must align with certain chain links. With timing gears, adjacent dots or lines must be lined up.
(Kawasaki Motors Corp., U.S.A.)
(Triumph Motorcycles [Meriden] Ltd.)

reassembly. Use your service manual for specific step-by-step instructions.

1. Lubricate all moving engine parts, Fig. 16-79.

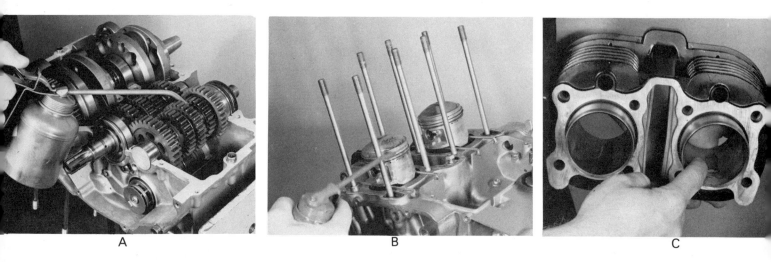

Fig. 16-79. Moving parts must be carefully lubricated before and during assembly. A—Lubricating gearbox components. B—Lubricating piston rings and piston. C—Lubricating cylinder.

2. Install new gaskets, seals, and O-rings.
3. Check crankshaft and gearbox shaft end play (where applicable).
4. Check for proper seal installation.
5. Make sure bearing locating half rings and dowel pins are installed properly.
6. Check that all crankcase dowel pins are installed.
7. Use new plain bearings.
8. Check that connecting rods have proper clearance (use Plastigage). Also check for proper rod, cap, and bearing shell direction. Torque connecting rod bolts.
9. Make sure all crankshaft bearings are installed properly (fully seated, proper direction, correct clearance).
10. Cam chain must be installed on crankshaft (OHC) correctly.
11. Make sure crankshaft assembly is installed properly. Use service manual directions.
12. Check for proper assembly of internal primary drive, Fig. 16-80.
13. Make sure gearbox assembly functions properly (See Gearbox Assembly Summary in Chapter 18).
14. Check installation of camshafts (push rod engine).
15. Use sealing compounds where needed.
16. Check for binding after each installation.
17. Carefully assemble crankcase halves.
18. Crankcase fasteners of different lengths must be in proper locations.
19. Use proper torque sequences and values. Refer to Fig. 16-81.
20. Make sure oil pump is in good condition and installed correctly, Fig. 16-82.
21. Check for proper clutch and external primary drive assembly. (See Clutch and Primary Drive Assembly Summary in Chapter 17.)
22. Check for proper piston ring installation. Be sure end gap was checked and adjusted.

Fig. 16-80. In this internal primary drive, crankshaft, primary chain, and jackshaft are installed together.

23. Inspect installation of cylinder base gasket, dowel pins, and O-rings.
24. Check for proper piston installation (piston direction, circlips).
25. Inspect piston ring end gap positioning on piston.
26. Check installation and condition of cam chain guides, Fig. 16-83.
27. Carefully install cylinder.
28. Check for proper installation of head gasket, dowel pins, and O-rings.
29. Install cylinder head using proper torque sequence and value.
30. Use proper installation techniques for valve train components.
31. Check timing of camshaft(s).

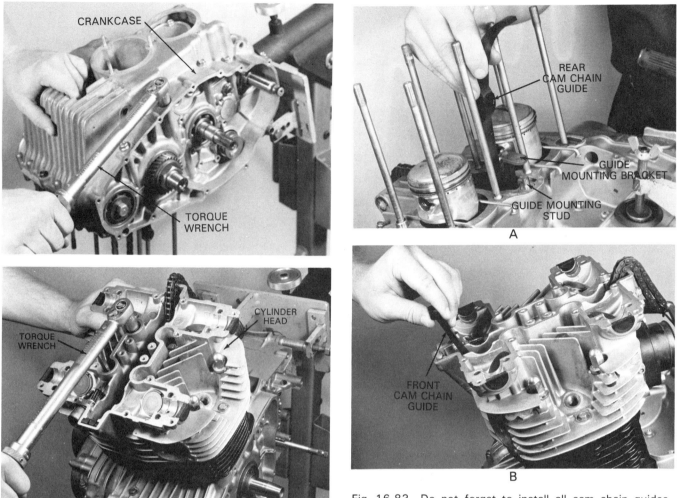

Fig. 16-81. Use a torque wrench and correct torque pattern to tighten crankcase bolts and head bolts.

Fig. 16-83. Do not forget to install all cam chain guides. A—In this engine, rear cam chain guide is installed into crankcase. B—Front guide is installed after cylinder and head are in place.

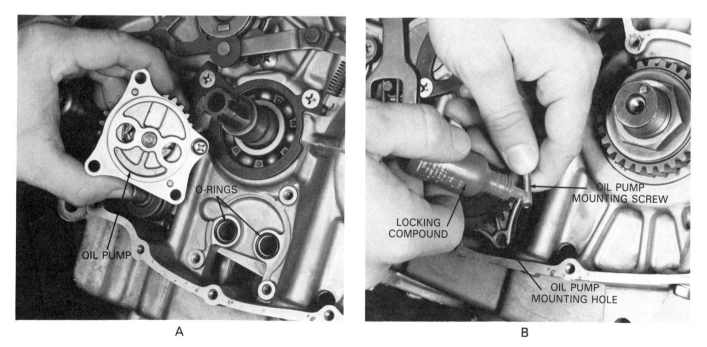

Fig. 16-82. A—Be sure to use new O-rings and gaskets when installing an oil pump. B—When service manual calls for it, use locking compound on oil pump mounting screws.

32. Double-check that alternator, electric starter, and ignition components are installed correctly.
33. Check for proper cam chain adjustment.
34. Valve clearance must be adjusted to specifications, Fig. 16-84.

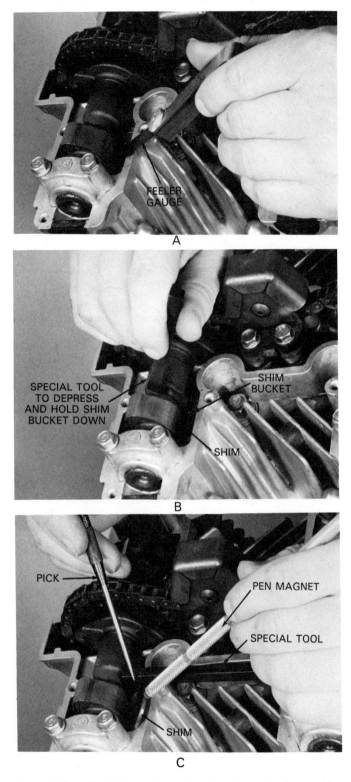

Fig. 16-84. A—Valve clearance adjustment is done after checking clearance with a feeler gauge. B—Special tool is used to hold shim bucket down so shim can be removed. C—Shim is being replaced with correct one using magnet.

35. Set static ignition timing, as in Fig. 16-85.
36. Make sure all engine covers (valve cover, primary case cover, etc.) are properly installed. Some covers may have to be left off until engine is installed.

ENGINE INSTALLATION

Although your service manual gives engine installation instructions, the following procedures are especially important:

1. Check for proper oil line connections (make sure lines are not crossed).
2. Clean and tighten electrical connections as needed.
3. Check that carburetor installation, initial adjustment, and fuel system hookups are correct.
4. The exhaust system at the cylinder head, crossover pipes, and mufflers should fit and seal properly.
5. Check for proper connection and adjustment of all control cables.
6. Check that drive chain is adjusted properly.
7. Check the connection and torque of shaft drive coupler.

INITIAL ENGINE RUNNING

Before starting the engine, you must make sure the lubrication system will function immediately. Initial lubrication is extremely important to prevent premature engine wear.

1. Fill the crankcase reservoir or oil tank with the proper grade and quantity of four-stroke cycle motor oil.
2. Prime the oil system (dry sump type) by filling the oil feed line and oil pump with motor oil. This is demonstrated in Fig. 16-86.
3. Lubricate valve springs and cam followers or rocker arms with oil.
4. Install an oil pressure gauge in the appropriate test port on the engine. See Fig. 16-87.

During initial engine operation, you should:

1. Check engine oil pressure.
2. Listen for unusual noises.
3. Look for oil and fuel leaks.
4. Check and adjust ignition timing (dynamic).
5. Check and adjust carburetor synchronization, pilot mixture, and idle speed.

WARNING! A freshly overhauled engine has very high internal resistance because of new parts rubbing against each other. As a result, the first time the engine is started, friction can cause the engine to heat up quickly. Be careful not to overheat and damage the engine while making initial adjustments. You may need to shut off the engine and allow it to cool down.

ENGINE BREAK-IN PROCEDURES

The break-in period of a four-stroke cycle engine is very critical to engine life and dependability. Since a

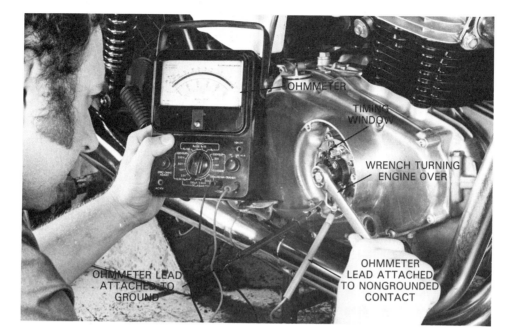

Fig. 16-85. To set static timing, hook one lead from ohmmeter, buzz box, or continuity tester to ground. Connect other lead to ungrounded contact. As engine is turned over with a wrench, infinite resistance, no buzzing, or lack of continuity will occur just as points open. Timing mark should be lined up just as points open.

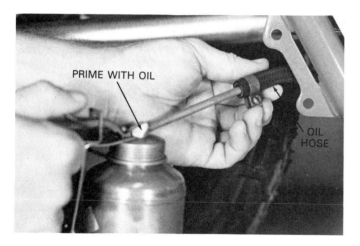

Fig. 16-86. Engines using a dry sump lubrication system should be primed. Fill oil feed line using oil squirt can.

four-stroke cycle engine has more moving parts which wear at a slower rate, the break-in period is longer than that of a two-stroke cycle engine. A typical break-in period is around 1,500 miles (2 413 km). Some engines may require more or less break-in time.

Important things to do during engine break-in are:
1. Do not accelerate abruptly.
2. Listen for abnormal engine noises.
3. Do not overheat, over-rev (race), or lug (operate at low rpm under load) the engine.
4. Do not cruise at a constant or high throttle setting.
5. Do not let the engine idle for long periods of time.
6. Monitor the oil level and add oil as necessary.

These recommendations help prevent overheating,

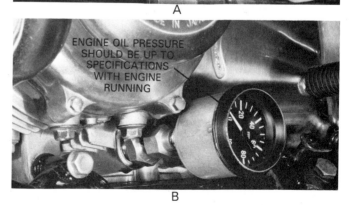

Fig. 16-87. Install an oil pressure gauge so that engine oil pressure can be checked when engine is first started. There is normally a threaded oil outlet near bottom of engine. A—Installing gauge. B—Ready to check initial engine oil pressure.

and inadequate lubrication which could ruin engine parts. Generally, keep the engine in midrange speeds and vary speeds occasionally.

POST-OVERHAUL CHECKUP

The break-in process is a controlled wearing in of engine parts. As parts wear from friction and gaskets settle from heating (expansion) and cooling (contraction) of the engine, clearances may change. The loosening or tightening of valve clearance is an example of this condition.

This initial seating in of parts will stabilize in two to five hundred miles (322 to 806 km) of riding. At this time, a post-overhaul checkup should be done.

Since the break-in process causes the oil to become contaminated with metallic particles (parts wearing in), always change the oil and filter after initial break-in.

The following list gives the specific adjustments and checks which should be made during post-overhaul checkup.

POST-OVERHAUL SUMMARY

1. Adjust valves.
2. Adjust cam chain.
3. Check cylinder compression.
4. Lubricate contact breaker cam.
5. Check and adjust contact breaker gap.
6. Check and adjust trigger clearance (electronic ignition).
7. Adjust carburetor pilot mixture (initial setting).
8. Check and adjust throttle free play.
9. Check and adjust throttle synchronization (cable operated systems).
10. Check spark plugs and set to proper gap.
11. Check and adjust ignition timing.
12. Adjust pilot mixture (engine running).
13. Synchronize carburetors (use vacuum gauges with engine running).
14. Change oil and filter.
15. Check and adjust primary drive chain (where applicable).
16. Check, lubricate, and adjust rear drive chain.
17. Lubricate and adjust clutch release and cable.
18. Road test.

KNOW THESE TERMS

Four-stroke cycle engine top end, Four-stroke cycle engine lower end, Camshaft base circle diameter, Cam lobe height, Shaft runout, Bearing inside diameter, Journal-to-bearing clearance, Cylinder head warpage, Worn valve guide, Valve margin, Valve face angle, Valve seat width, Valve seat contact position, Valve seat refacing, Valve spring installed height, Piston ring-to-groove clearance, Rod kit, Engine break-in.

REVIEW QUESTIONS—CHAPTER 16

1. Shim bucket _____ and bucket bore should be measured to determine bucket clearance.
2. What usually causes valve train noise?
3. What takes the place of a cam follower in some DOHC engines?
4. It is a good idea to replace the cam _____ during the overhaul of a high mileage engine.
5. Valve stem seals can usually be reused. True or False?
6. List the three major operations done during cylinder head reconditioning.
7. Most four-stroke cycle engine valves and seats use a _____ angle.
8. Valve spring installed height determines spring _____.
9. Progressively wound valve springs must be installed with the tight coils toward the _____ (upper, lower) spring collar.
10. What are three steps to remember when measuring four-stroke cycle cylinders?
11. If wrist pin clearance is too loose, but the wrist pin diameter is correct, the connecting rod must be _____ or _____.
12. Some four-stroke cycle crankshaft assemblies cannot be reconditioned. True or False?
13. Ball bearings must be checked for _____ play and _____ play.
14. Name the two oil pump checks completed during an overhaul.
15. Dry, seized, and burned engine components indicate a _____ system failure.
16. Engine balancers do NOT require any attention during overhaul. True or False?
17. What are the two methods of reconditioning for one-piece plain bearing type crankshafts?
18. Connecting rod big ends (two-piece types) should be measured for an _____ condition during an overhaul.
19. Give four adjustments which must be done during four-stroke cycle engine reassembly.
20. Failure to properly set cam (valve) timing usually results in:
    a. Connecting rod failure.
    b. Cracked cylinder head.
    c. Valve and piston damage.
    d. Excessive oil consumption.
21. List three important checks which must be done during initial engine start-up.
22. Define the term "break-in process."
23. Half rings and dowel pins are used to positively locate crankshaft and gearbox shaft bearings. True or False?
24. Improper use of sealing compounds during engine assembly can cause loss of oil pressure. True or False?
25. Two important aspects of torquing engine

fasteners are _____ and _____.

26. A ring expander must always be used to install piston rings. True or False?

27. An arrow stamped or cast into the piston crown indicates piston installation direction. This is important because:
    a. Offset wrist pins may be used.
    b. Valve pocket cutouts must match valves.
    c. Piston skirt length may be different from front to back.

d. Both a and b are correct.
e. All of the above are correct.

SUGGESTED ACTIVITIES

1. Complete a four-stroke cycle engine overhaul. Use a service manual and the information in this chapter.

2. Perform a post-overhaul checkup using a shop manual and the summary in this chapter.

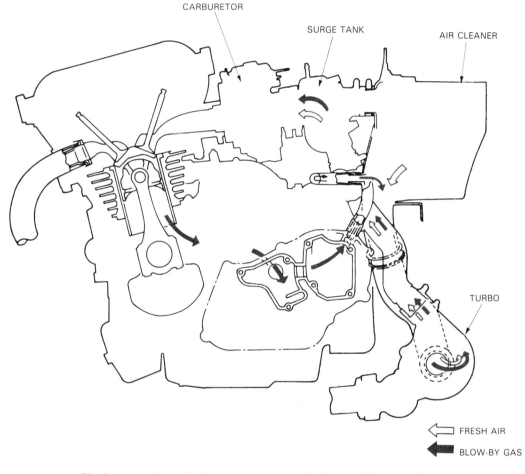

Air cleaner and ventilation system on a turbocharged, four-stroke cycle engine. Note flow of blow-by gases from crankcase into air cleaner. Toxic fumes are then burned in engine to prevent air pollution and sludging of engine. (Yamaha Motor Corp., U.S.A.)

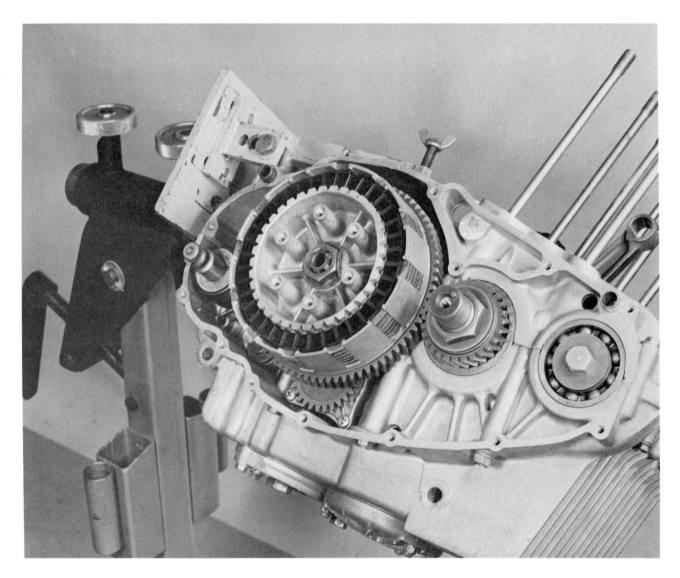

Clutch and primary drive overhaul is an important part of motorcycle mechanics. Study Chapter 17 carefully.

Chapter 17

CLUTCH AND PRIMARY DRIVE OVERHAUL

After studying this chapter, you will be able to:
- Correctly disassemble a clutch and primary drive.
- Properly inspect a clutch and primary drive for damage.
- Accurately measure clutch and primary drive part wear.
- Properly reassemble a motorcycle clutch and primary drive.
- Adjust a primary drive and clutch.

This chapter discusses the procedures for the proper inspection and overhaul of a motorcycle clutch and primary drive. Overhaul of the primary drive or clutch is necessary because of normal wear, improper adjustment, and physical damage to parts.

PRIMARY DRIVE SERVICE AND REPAIR

A PRIMARY DRIVE transfers all of the motorcycles engine power to the clutch and transmission. It must absorb tremendous shocks and changes in loading. With some designs, the chain or gears must be inspected periodically and even replaced after high mileage. Primary drive chains may also require periodic adjustment.

EXTERNAL CHAIN PRIMARY DRIVE SERVICE

An EXTERNAL CHAIN PRIMARY DRIVE operates off of one end of the engine crankshaft. Shown in Fig. 17-1, this type drive requires overhaul when the chain or sprocket teeth become worn or broken.

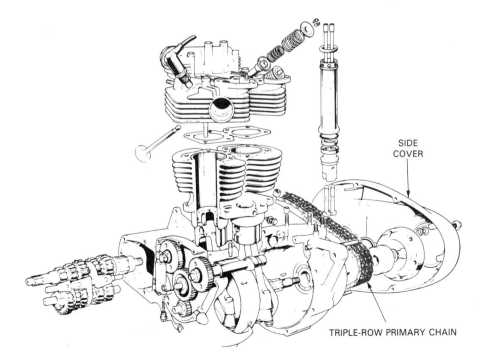

SIDE COVER

TRIPLE-ROW PRIMARY CHAIN

Fig. 17-1. External primary chain is used on this engine. Note how primary chain is mounted on one end of crankshaft. Chain can be replaced without major engine disassembly. (Triumph Motorcycles [Meriden] Ltd.)

Usually, a properly maintained primary chain drive assembly only requires chain replacement. The chain sprockets will normally be in satisfactory condition. Sprocket replacement may be needed when a badly worn or loose chain has been operated for a long period of time. A loose or worn chain will wear off and sharpen the teeth of the sprockets.

A loose primary drive chain is indicated when excessive noise (clatter or knocking) can be heard in the engine side cover. A clacking sound may be produced when changing from acceleration to deceleration or deceleration to acceleration. This will cause any slack or play in the chain to take up and slap loudly.

When there is no adjustment left on the chain tensioner, it normally indicates that the primary chain is worn out. A shop manual on the specific engine should be used to determine primary chain wear limits and procedures for repair.

INTERNAL CHAIN PRIMARY DRIVE SERVICE

Many recent motorcycle designs use an INTERNAL CHAIN PRIMARY DRIVE which locates the primary drive chain at the middle of the crankshaft. One is pictured in Fig. 17-2. Primary chain replacement for this design requires engine removal and disassembly.

The service life of an internal type drive chain is normally longer than that of the external chain primary drive. Replacement is usually not needed until the complete engine is ready for an overhaul.

EXTERNAL GEAR PRIMARY DRIVE SERVICE

The EXTERNAL GEAR PRIMARY DRIVE is a relatively trouble free system. When wear is suspected, inspection is an easy task. After removing the primary cover (clutch cover or engine side cover), check the primary drive gear TEETH for etching, chipping, breakage, and excessive backlash. Any of these problems will normally require primary gear replacement.

Primary drive gear backlash

Measurement of primary drive gear backlash (play between gears) identifies minor wear of the gear teeth. Fig. 17-3 illustrates the procedure for measuring primary gear backlash and wear. A service manual on the particular motorcycle will give specifications for primary drive gear backlash.

INTERNAL GEAR PRIMARY SERVICE

The INTERNAL GEAR PRIMARY DRIVE is housed within the engine crankcases. Engine disassembly is required for inspection and repair of this type of drive. As with the internal chain drive design, maintenance is normally not needed until a complete engine overhaul.

CLUTCH SERVICE AND REPAIR

A common cause of clutch wear and failure is improper clutch adjustment. When a clutch cable is too

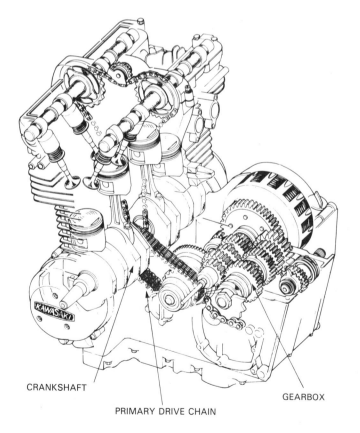

CRANKSHAFT
PRIMARY DRIVE CHAIN
GEARBOX

Fig. 17-2. This internal primary drive uses a hy-vo chain. It runs off of middle of crankshaft and is not serviced as easily as an external type primary chain.
(Kawasaki Motors Corp., U.S.A.)

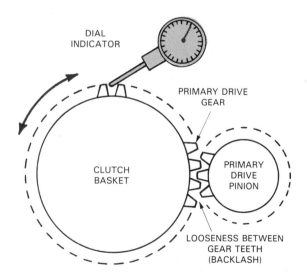

DIAL INDICATOR
PRIMARY DRIVE GEAR
CLUTCH BASKET
PRIMARY DRIVE PINION
LOOSENESS BETWEEN GEAR TEETH (BACKLASH)

Fig. 17-3. Wear and backlash in a gear type primary drive is measured with a dial indicator. Hold pinion gear steady while moving clutch gear back and forth. Indicator movement will show gear backlash. Excessive backlash would usually require gear replacement.

tight (no slack in release mechanism), partial release of the pressure plate can result. This can let the clutch discs slip and wear under heavy loads. A clutch cable release mechanism should always have some play to assure full pressure plate clamping action and disc lockup.

Accelerating a motorcycle from a dead stop, however, requires a certain amount of controlled clutch slippage. Depending upon the rider and the gearing of the motorcycle, some clutches may also be subjected to slipping during up and down shifting. Any slipping of the clutch wears the friction plates.

Another type of clutch wear is caused by rapid gearbox shifting, quick acceleration, engaging the clutch with the engine at high rpm, and abrupt changes in throttle opening. This type of abuse can cause severe loading and unloading of the clutch. As shown in Fig. 17-4, the following clutch components can wear and fail:
1. Clutch basket fingers.
2. Clutch cushion.
3. Drive plate tabs.
4. Clutch hub splines.
5. Driven plate tabs.
6. Clutch center bearing.
7. Clutch thrust washer.

Naturally, this type of abuse also causes unnecessary wear in the entire drive train (primary drive, gearbox, final drive).

CLUTCH BASKET AND BEARING WEAR

The clutch basket and bearing can wear in four places: basket fingers, basket cushion, basket center bearing, and center bearing thrust washer. These points should be closely inspected for excessive wear during clutch service, Fig. 17-4. If excessive wear is found at any of these inspection points, repair or replace the clutch parts as needed.

Clutch baskets which use a needle type center bearing have a very long service life and seldom fail. The clutch basket may also provide a mounting place for the primary kickstart gear. This gear should be inspected for wear and damage.

CLUTCH HUB WEAR

CLUTCH HUB WEAR is not very common, however, worn splines (internal and external) and worn keyways may be found occasionally. Keep this in mind when inspecting a clutch hub.

CLUTCH PLATE SERVICE

In many service manuals, the clutch plates are also referred to as friction and plain plates. The DRIVE PLATES (plates which engage with basket) are the friction plates. The DRIVEN PLATES (plates which engage with hub) are the plain plates.

Servicing friction plates

The clutch friction plates wear more than the plain plates. Inspection of the friction plates includes:
1. Checking for broken or damaged tabs.
2. Checking for a burned smell and glazing.
3. Measuring plate thickness.

Fig. 17-5, A, shows a worn clutch friction plate. PLATE THICKNESS must be measured and com-

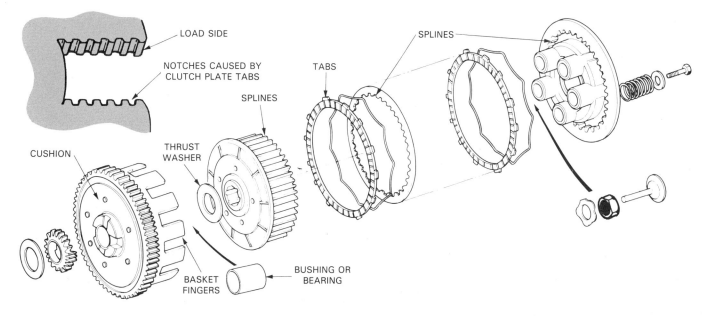

Fig. 17-4. These clutch parts in particular must be checked for wear. Common form of clutch basket wear is caused by drive plates. Tabs on plates wear notches in basket fingers. This can cause clutch drag, jerky engagement, and slipping. (Kawasaki Motors Corp., U.S.A.)

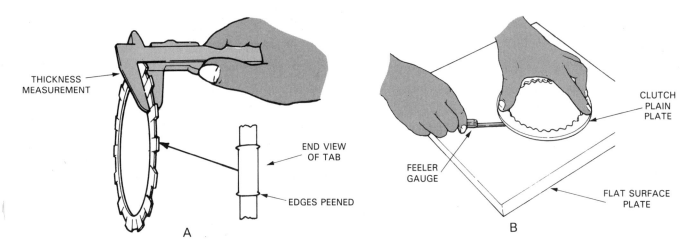

Fig. 17-5. A—Clutch friction plate thickness must be measured to check for wear. Also, if tabs on outside of friction plates are peened or damaged, plates must be replaced. B—Surface plate or sheet of plate glass and a feeler gauge are used to check clutch plain plates for warping. If specified gauge slides under plate, this indicates excessive plate warpage. (U.S. Suzuki Motor Corporation)

pared to specifications. If the discs are worn too thin, burned, or damaged, they must be replaced.

Servicing plain plates

Inspection of the plain plates, Fig. 17-5, B, includes:
1. Checking for broken or damaged teeth.
2. Checking for a burned or scored appearance.
3. Checking for warpage.

CLUTCH SPRINGS

CLUTCH SPRINGS acting against the clutch pressure plate provide the force needed to prevent clutch slippage. Four common causes of inadequate clutch spring pressure and CLUTCH SLIPPAGE are:
1. Defective (weak) clutch springs.
2. Worn clutch friction plates (reduces spring preload).
3. Improper clutch cable or release adjustment.
4. Improper clutch spring adjustment.

Clutch spring inspection

The condition of CLUTCH SPRINGS is determined by measuring spring free length, checking spring squareness, and testing spring pressure. Fig. 17-6 illustrates clutch spring inspection. By placing the spring on a flat surface and using a square, spring squareness and free height can be measured. Spring tension must be measured on a spring tester, discussed in Chapter 16. Compare your measurements to specifications to determine whether clutch spring replacement is needed.

CLUTCH TRUEING

Some clutch designs require trueing of the clutch pressure plate assembly. This is done by adjusting the

clutch springs to provide equal pressure and minimum pressure plate lateral runout (side wobble). Fig. 17-7 illustrates how each clutch fastener is tightened until equal clutch spring pressure and perfect clutch alignment is obtained.

Very few motorcycles still use an adjustable type clutch. In most cases, the clutch spring screws are tightened until they bottom. Uneven clutch spring pressure must be corrected by replacing all of the clutch springs as a set.

PRIMARY KICKSTART INSPECTION

A kickstart mechanism, that works through the clutch, is called a PRIMARY KICKSTART MECHANISM. When the clutch is disassembled, the primary kickstart is usually exposed. This permits easy inspection of primary kickstart gears, bearings, and ratchet. Kickstart mechanisms rarely cause problems. However, it is a good idea to visually inspect these components whenever possible.

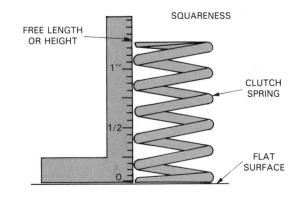

Fig. 17-6. With clutch spring on flat surface, square will show squareness and free height. If not within specifications, spring replacement is required.

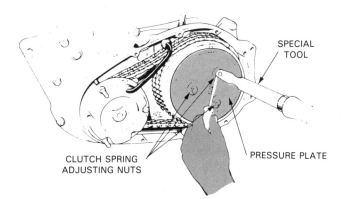

Fig. 17-7. Spring pressure is equal when pressure plate begins to lift at same time at each spring. Runout is checked by disengaging clutch and rotating pressure plate with kickstarter. (Triumph Motorcycles [Meriden] Ltd.)

PRIMARY DRIVE AND CLUTCH INSPECTION SUMMARY

During clutch and primary drive service, refer to your service manual for wear limits, specifications, and detailed procedures. The following summary provides a general outline for clutch and primary drive inspection during an overhaul.

CHAIN PRIMARY DRIVE

1. Check chain adjustment and amount of adjustment remaining.
2. Measure chain wear (stretch).
3. Inspect sprocket teeth condition.
4. Check chain tensioner for wear or damage.

GEAR PRIMARY DRIVE

1. Inspect gear teeth for etching, chipping, and wear.
2. Measure gear backlash.

CLUTCH BASKET

1. Check basket fingers for wear on edges.
2. Inspect the condition of clutch bearing surface.
3. Inspect kickstart gear for wear or damage.
4. Check shock absorber condition.

CLUTCH HUB

1. Inspect clutch hub driving splines.
2. Check for wear or damage of splines or keyway on ID (inside diameter) of clutch hub.

CLUTCH CENTER BEARING

1. Make sure clutch center bearing is not worn, scored, or discolored.
2. Check the thrust washer for grooving, wear, or other forms of damage.
3. Measure clutch basket-to-bearing clearance.

CLUTCH DRIVE PLATES (FRICTION)

1. Measure thickness of drive plates to determine wear.
2. Inspect condition of the tabs on the plates.
3. Inspect friction material on clutch plates.
4. Check for glazing or burning (burned smell) of friction plates.

CLUTCH DRIVEN PLATES (PLAIN)

1. Inspect the splines on the plates for wear or damage.
2. Check for burning or scoring of the plates.
3. Measure plain plate warpage.

CLUTCH SPRINGS

1. Measure free length of clutch springs.
2. Measure squareness of clutch springs.
3. Measure spring compressed tension or pressure.

PRIMARY KICKSTART

1. Check kickstart shaft for bent condition.
2. Inspect kickstart bushings for looseness or galling.
3. Check ratchet mechanism for damage and proper operation.
4. Inspect drive gear teeth for damage or wear.

PRIMARY DRIVE AND CLUTCH REASSEMBLY

Since there are so many variations in motorcycle clutches, the service manual must be followed for specific step-by-step disassembly and reassembly. The following list reviews some important aspects of clutch reassembly for most types of motorcycles.

1. Always use new seals and gaskets.
2. Use the proper special tools when needed.
3. Lubricate components as recommended with approved lubricant.
4. Install primary kickstart components before installing clutch basket, Fig. 17-8.
5. Properly preload and install kickstart spring.
6. Install snap ring correctly when used.
7. Install thrust washer and clutch hub bearing properly.
8. Correctly assemble lock washer concave side as shown in Fig. 17-9.
9. Torque drive gear or sprocket and clutch center nuts to specifications, Fig. 17-10. Then, bend lock tabs to keep nuts from loosening, Fig. 17-11.
10. Check the alignment of the gears or chain and sprockets.
11. Use the correct sequence and procedures for clutch pack assembly. Some clutch designs require timing (specific alignment) of the clutch plates. The thickness of some clutch plates may vary. Some clutches are assembled piece by piece. Other types require that the hub and plates are

Fig. 17-8. A—Since primary kickstart components are usually behind clutch basket, they must be installed first. B—Clutch basket can then be slid into place.

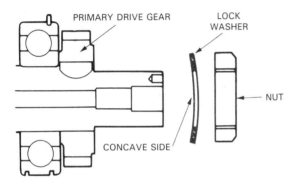

Fig. 17-9. When installing lock washer, concave side should face inward or away from nut.
(U.S. Suzuki Motor Corporation)

Fig. 17-11. Adjustable channel pliers make a neat, tight bend on lock tabs. Lock tab is splined to shaft. A properly installed and bent lock tab will prevent nut from loosening.

assembled before installation into the basket. Look at Fig. 17-12.

12. Install clutch push rod and other related parts correctly, Fig. 17-13.
13. Double-check that pressure plate-to-hub splines are properly indexed, Fig. 17-14.
14. Adjust (true) or tighten clutch spring bolts correctly, Fig. 17-15.
15. Adjust the primary chain correctly, Fig. 17-16.
16. Do not forget to install the outer kickstart thrust washer before installing the clutch cover.

This list is a guide to help you avoid some common mistakes when assembling a primary drive and clutch. The proper sequence of assembly for your clutch may be different from this summary. Always follow your service manual when in doubt.

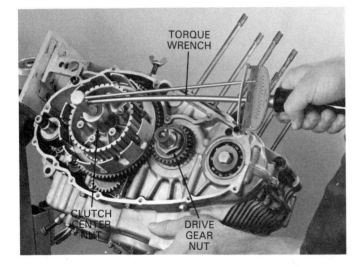

Fig. 17-10. Clutch center nut and drive gear nuts must be torqued to the recommended value.

KNOW THESE TERMS

Primary drive, External primary drive, Primary drive gear backlash, Internal primary drive, Friction plates, Plain plates, Clutch springs, Spring free

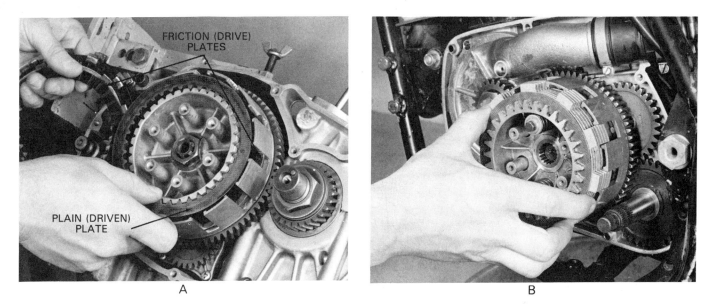

Fig. 17-12. Motorcycle clutch assembly procedures vary. A—This clutch must be assembled piece by piece. Clutch plates are installed before pressure plate. B—This clutch is installed as a single assembly.

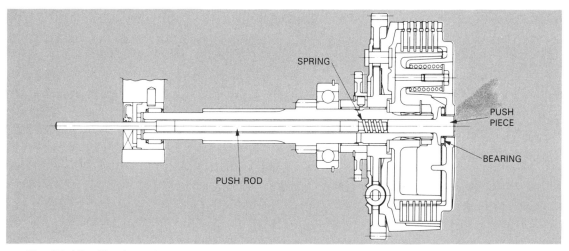

Fig. 17-13. Clutch push rod and related components must be installed in their proper positions. Note part locations in this clutch design. (U.S. Suzuki Motor Corporation)

length, Spring squareness, Spring pressure, Clutch trueing, Primary kickstart.

REVIEW QUESTIONS—CHAPTER 17

1. When all of the adjustment is used up on a primary drive chain tensioner, what does this indicate?
2. Measurement of backlash determines wear in gear type primary drives. True or False?
3. On internal gear or internal chain primary drives, the engine must be disassembled for inspection and repairs. True or False?
4. List four of the multi-plate clutch parts that will become worn as a result of harsh shifting, quick starts, and abrupt throttle changes.
5. Clutch drive plates engage with the clutch _____; the clutch driven plates engage with

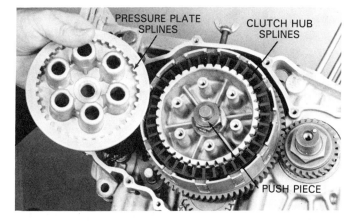

Fig. 17-14. Splines on pressure plate and clutch hub must be aligned (indexed) properly or clutch will not function. This clutch uses a push piece to disengage pressure plate. Push piece must be installed before pressure plate.

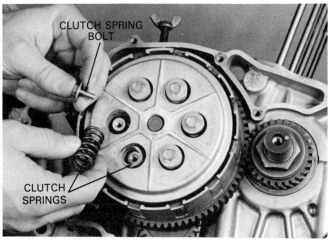

Fig. 17-15. After installing clutch pack and pressure plate, clutch springs are installed. Some springs must be carefully adjusted to true clutch. These clutch spring bolts are torqued to specifications.

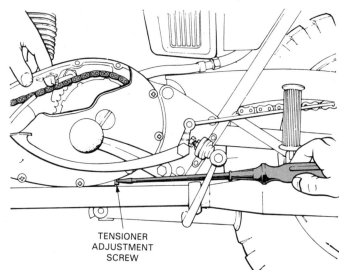

Fig. 17-16. Some primary chain drive systems provide easy access for checking and adjusting chain tension. Refer to your service manual for chain free play specifications. (Triumph Motorcycles [Meriden] Ltd.)

the clutch _____.

6. Which of the following is not a cause of inadequate clutch spring pressure.
   a. Missing push piece.
   b. Weak clutch springs.
   c. Worn friction plates.
   d. Improper clutch adjustments.
7. Inspection of plain clutch plates includes checking for broken tabs, burned surfaces, and warpage. True or False?
8. The condition of clutch springs is determined by:
   a. Measuring free length.
   b. Checking squareness.
   c. Measuring pressure.
   d. All of the above.
9. Write a brief definition of clutch trueing.
10. A primary kickstart mechanism does not work through the clutch. True or False?

SUGGESTED ACTIVITIES

1. Using the primary drive and clutch inspection summary in this chapter, perform all of the inspection procedures listed. Record your findings and make up a parts list to determine the cost of repairs.
2. Adjust a primary chain following service manual directions.

Chapter 18

GEARBOX OVERHAUL

After studying this chapter, you will be able to:
☐ List common motorcycle gearbox problems.
☐ Measure gearbox shaft end play.
☐ Check shift mechanism operation.
☐ Disassemble a gearbox.
☐ Inspect gearbox and kickstart components for wear or damage.
☐ Describe basic gearbox assembly methods.

This chapter describes the fundamental procedures for a gearbox overhaul. It starts out by covering typical gearbox problems. Then, the disassembly, inspection, and measurement of gearbox parts is explained. The chapter stresses the importance of proper organization and techniques when servicing a gearbox. The last section of the chapter summarizes the correct reassembly of typical motorcycle gearboxes. As a result, you should be prepared to use a service manual for an actual gearbox overhaul.

Note! A gearbox overhaul is frequently completed during a major engine overhaul. However, when a gearbox problem develops, the gearbox can usually be serviced without complete engine disassembly.

GEARBOX PROBLEMS

GEARBOX PROBLEMS usually produce obvious symptoms. Typical gearbox problems are:
1. Jumping out of gear (gearbox shifts into neutral).
2. Binding shift mechanism (difficult to shift gears).
3. Noisy operation (abnormal sounds in gearbox).
4. Gearbox locked up (gearbox shafts do not turn or shifter does not move).
5. Missing gear ratio (one speed or gear ratio does not operate).

Before disassembling a gearbox, you should check shaft end play, shift mechanism operation, and shift mechanism adjustment when possible. It may be possible to correct some gearbox problems without a complete teardown.

SHAFT END PLAY

On gearbox designs where shaft end play is adjustable and a specification is given, you should check shaft end play before disassembly. This saves time during reassembly in the event end play is incorrect. Fig. 18-1 shows how to measure gearbox shaft end play.

SHIFT MECHANISM OPERATION

Before tearing into the gearbox, it is also a good idea to check the operation of the shifting mechanism. Shift mechanism problems are quite common. Many gearboxes have been torn apart when the shift mechanism was the only problem.

When inspecting the shift mechanism, look for the following:
1. Freedom of movement.
2. Worn pivots in the shift arm, Fig. 18-2.
3. Worn pawls or damaged springs (ratchet type).
4. Proper adjustment of the shift stopper pin. Refer to Fig. 18-3.
5. Broken or damaged shift mechanism return spring.

Remember, when shifting the gearbox for a shift mechanism visual inspection, you must rotate the gearbox shafts.

GEARBOX DISASSEMBLY

Gearbox shaft assemblies are relatively simple. However, improper disassembly methods and poor organization can turn a gearbox overhaul into a "nightmare."

When disassembling a gearbox, it is important to check the position of shims, thrust washers, indexers, drain plugs, locating rings and pins. Also, check the location of circlips, shift forks, and gears. Note the direction of each gear on its shaft. Taking a little extra time during disassembly can save a considerable amount of time during reassembly.

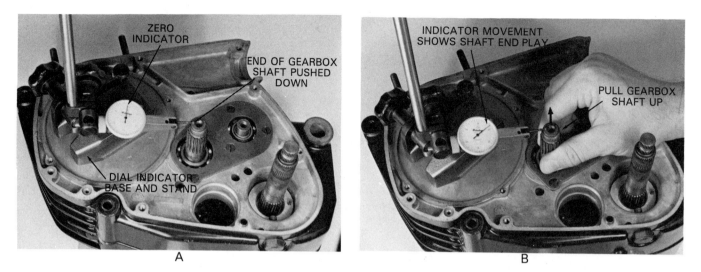

Fig. 18-1. A—Gearbox end play can be checked quickly and accurately with a dial indicator. A lever type indicator is shown here. Push shaft into case and zero dial indicator. B—Pull shaft up until it stops. Read dial indicator to obtain end play.

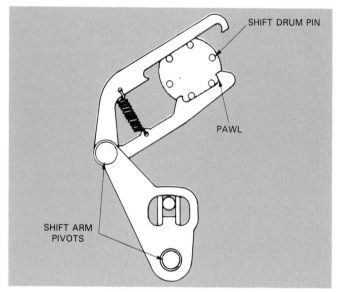

Fig. 18-2. Shift arm pivots must be checked for wear and looseness. Also, inspect pawls and shift drum pins for wear. (Kawasaki Motors Corp., U.S.A.)

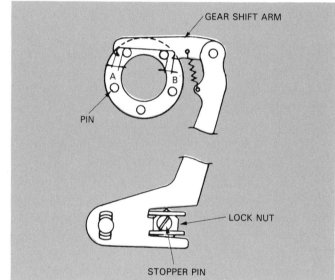

Fig. 18-3. In many designs, shift stopper pin is adjustable. Stopper pin must be adjusted so that distances A and B are equal. If stopper pin is not properly adjusted, shift drum will turn too far in one direction and not far enough in opposite direction. (Yamaha Motor Corporation, U.S.A.)

When removing the parts from a gearbox shaft, follow the specific directions in the service manual. Disassemble only one gearbox shaft assembly at a time. This will prevent you from mixing input shaft and output shaft parts. Fig. 18-4 illustrates the proper disassembly and organization of gearbox shaft components. Notice how all of the parts are arranged on the bench in an orderly manner.

Gearbox inspection

During and after gearbox disassembly, inspect the condition of each part closely. In particular, check for:

1. Etched gear teeth, Fig. 18-5.
2. Worn splines on shafts and gears.

3. Rounded engagement dogs and slots, Fig. 18-6.
4. Worn or scored bearing surfaces, Fig. 18-7.
5. Worn or scored shifting forks, Fig. 18-8.
6. Bent shifting forks.
7. Bent shifting fork shafts.
8. Worn shifting fork engagement pins, Fig. 18-9.
9. Free movement of shift fork on shift drum or shaft.
10. Free movement of shift drum or camplate.
11. Worn tracks on shift drum or camplate. Refer to Fig. 18-10.
12. Damaged or worn indexer.

Any of these components found to be defective must be replaced. Remember! If just one defective

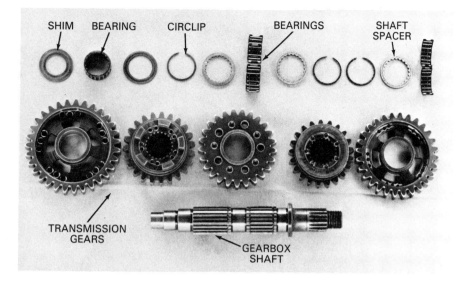

Fig. 18-4. Careful and organized disassembly of gearbox shaft components is necessary to prevent mixing and/or loss of parts.

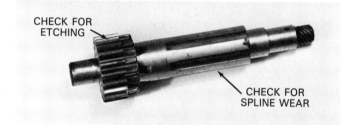

Fig. 18-5. Etching of gear teeth, if not caught during inspection, can eventually lead to broken gear teeth.

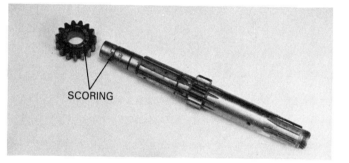

Fig. 18-7. Worn or scored bearing surfaces indicate lack of lubrication. Damaged parts must be replaced.

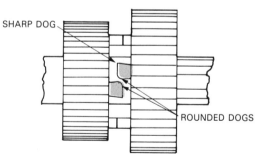

Fig. 18-6. Abuse and normal wear causes wear and rounding of gear engagement dogs. Load carrying side of dog becomes worn, while unloaded side remains sharp. Worn dogs can cause gearbox to jump out of gear.

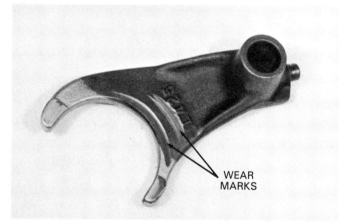

Fig. 18-8. Look for wear or score marks on sides of shift forks. Marks indicate that fork may be bent. Replacement of fork would be needed.

component is overlooked, the entire gearbox may have to be disassembled a second time.

GEARBOX MEASUREMENTS

There are three measurements that are very critical to the overhaul of a motorcycle gearbox. These measurements are:

1. Shaft runout (determines if shaft has been bent or damaged.).
2. Fork-to-groove clearance (detects wear between

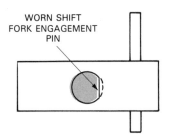

Fig. 18-9. Shift fork engagement pins can wear where they ride in shift drum or camplate tracks. This can cause poor transmission gear changes.

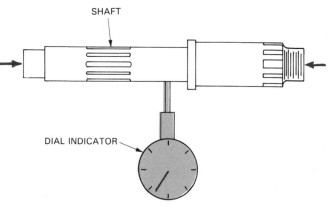

Fig. 18-11. Gearbox shaft is checked by mounting shaft in a trueing stand or on knife edge rollers. Then, a dial indicator is used to measure runout.

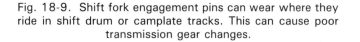
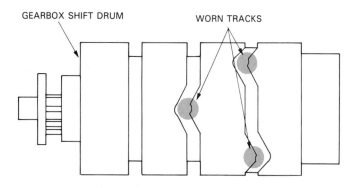

Fig. 18-10. Worn tracks on shift drums or camplates cause incomplete gear engagement, jumping out of gear, or rough shifting. Always check tracks closely.

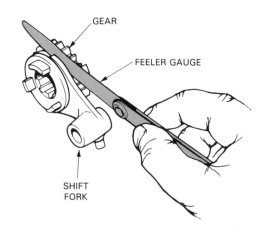

Fig. 18-12. Feeler gauge is used to check shift fork-to-groove clearance. If not within specs, part replacement is required.   (U.S. Suzuki Motor Corporation)

contact surfaces of fork and groove).
3. Gear backlash (checks clearance between gear teeth).

Figs. 18-11, 18-12, and 18-13 illustrate these gearbox measurements. Refer to the motorcycle's service manual for exact specifications (maximum runout values and clearances).

KICKSTART MECHANISM INSPECTION

Kickstart mechanisms are normally quite reliable. However, problems can develop after prolonged service. A few kickstart problems are ratchet wear, shaft wear, bearing wear in crankcase and cover, bent shafts, damaged splines, and broken or weakened springs. Check these parts closely during your inspection.

Due to the great variety of kickstart mechanisms, no single example is representative. Refer to the proper service manual for inspection and repair details.

GEARBOX REASSEMBLY AND SHIMMING

Some service manuals say, "Reassemble in the reverse order of disassembly." Although this is generally true, these are numerous checks that must be made during gearbox assembly.

Some gearboxes allow you to inspect gearbox operation after only partial assembly. Other gear-

Fig. 18-13. Dial indicator is used to check gear backlash (play between engaged gear teeth). One gear must be locked in place while other is moved back and forth. If backlash is greater than specifications, both gears must be replaced.

boxes, however, must be completely assembled before shifting through each gear. This is because motorcycle gearboxes are mounted and supported differently.

There are four basic variations in GEARBOX MOUNTING; they are:
1. The gearbox is supported by horizontally split crankcases, Fig. 18-14.
2. The gearbox is supported by vertically split crankcases, Fig. 18-15.
3. The gearbox and cover assembly are inserted into the crankcase cavity. This design is not very common.
4. A separate gearbox case is used (non-unit construction), Fig. 18-16.

Because of these variations, checking and adjusting shaft end play (shimming) is more difficult on some gearboxes than others.

Gearbox shimming procedures

GEARBOX SHIMMING and end play can be checked two ways: by external measurement (dial indicator) or by internal measurement (shaft and case measurement).

External end play measurement

Gearbox designs which allow EXTERNAL END PLAY MEASUREMENT should have been checked with a dial indicator during disassembly. This was described earlier.

Proper shimming and end play adjustment is accomplished by installing SHIMS (washer type spacers) which produce the proper clearance between

Fig. 18-15. Gearboxes mounted in vertically split crankcases usually cannot be shifted until cases are assembled.

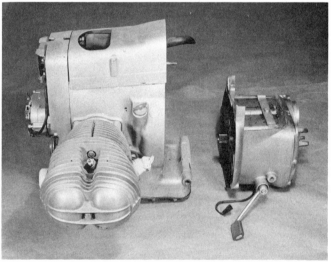

Fig. 18-16. Non-unit gearbox is a totally independent, self-housed assembly.

Fig. 18-14. Some gearboxes mounted in horizontally split crankcases can be shifted through gears before cases are assembled. This permits easy inspection of gearbox operation.

the gearbox gears and the engine case. Fig. 18-17 illustrates this procedure. A thicker shim would be needed to reduce gearbox end play. A thinner shim would increase end play.

Internal end play measurement

Gearboxes which require internal measurement for proper shimming are more difficult to check and adjust. Gearbox INTERNAL END PLAY MEASUREMENT usually involves:
1. Measurement of distance between bearing seats in the crankcase and/or cover. This procedure is illustrated in Fig. 18-18.
2. Measurement of the length of the assembled shafts

Fig. 18-17. Select shim thickness needed to achieve correct end play. Shimming procedure varies so be sure to check your service manual.

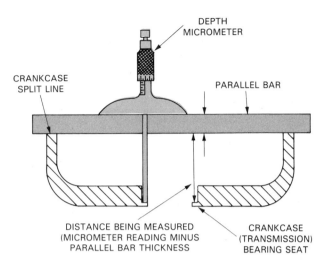

Fig. 18-18. A depth micrometer and parallel bar are used to measure distance between bearing seat and crankcase split line. Do this on each crankcase half. Depth of both crankcases would give internal width of case.

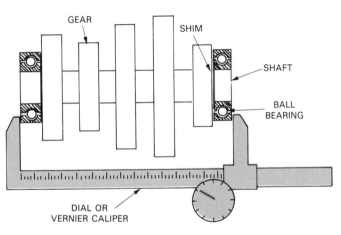

Fig. 18-19. Measure length of assembled gearbox shafts from bearing shoulder to bearing shoulder. This can be done with large dial or Vernier caliper.

(bearing shoulder to bearing shoulder), Fig. 18-19.
3. Measurement of the gasket thickness, if used.

END PLAY is determined by subtracting gearbox shaft length from crankcase width plus the gasket thickness. This calculation is detailed in the following discussion.

To find gearbox shaft end play: add left crankcase depth, right crankcase depth, and gasket thickness (if used); then subtract gearbox shaft width.

Example:
Left crankcase width   = 2.383 in.
Right crankcase width = 2.655 in.
Gasket thickness   = .012 in.
            Sum = 5.050 in.
Subtract transmission
  shaft width   5.045 in.
Shaft end play   = .005 in.

Add or subtract shim thickness to adjust shaft end play.

GEARBOX REASSEMBLY SUMMARY

Due to the variety of gearbox designs, a service manual should always be followed for specific step-by-step reassembly procedures. Use the following summary and your service manual to avoid making simple errors. Check for freedom of movement of all components throughout assembly of the gearbox.
1. Use new seals, gaskets, cotter pins, circlips, and lock tabs.
2. Lubricate all moving parts during assembly.
3. Use locking compound where recommended.

4. Check that shims, thrust washers, circlips, and gears are installed in proper order and direction, Fig. 18-20.
5. Make sure that bearing locating half-rings and dowel pins are installed properly, Fig. 18-21.
6. Double-check that bearings are properly seated on their shaft or in case.
7. Kickstart mechanism and return spring should be installed and checked for proper operation.
8. Shift forks must be installed and indexed correctly, Fig. 18-22.
9. Check that shafts are installed in the proper location, direction, and that forks are fully engaged.
10. Locators, indexers, and shift stopper mechanisms must be installed properly, Fig. 18-23.
11. Make sure shouldered bolts for indexers and stoppers are installed properly. Also, check that

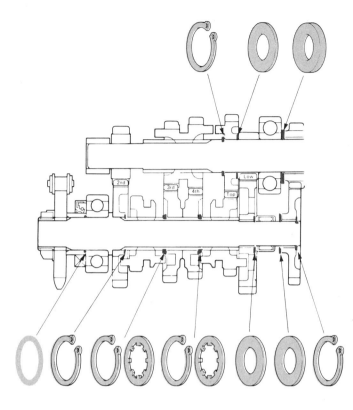

Fig. 18-20. As shown in this service manual illustration, make sure all circlips and washers are in their proper positions during assembly of gearbox shafts.
(U.S. Suzuki Motor Corporation)

screws of different lengths are in their proper holes, Fig. 18-24.

12. Check for proper timing and adjustment of the

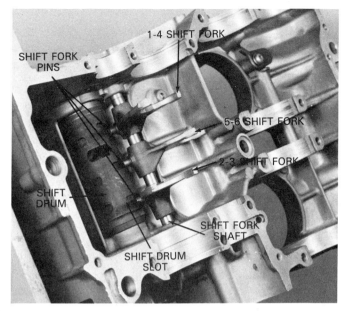

Fig. 18-22. Shift forks must be installed on shaft in proper sequence. Pins must be indexed into slots in shift drum.

shift mechanism, Fig. 18-25.

13. Double-check that the gearbox shifts through all gears properly.

14. Check freedom of movement after crankcase and/or cover fasteners are tightened. If binding is evident, investigate to determine the cause of the problem.

In most modern unit-construction engines, assembly of the gearbox also involves assembly of the engine lower end, clutch, and primary drive. Refer to

Fig. 18-21. Bearing dowel pins and half rings must be installed properly to accurately locate gearbox shafts.

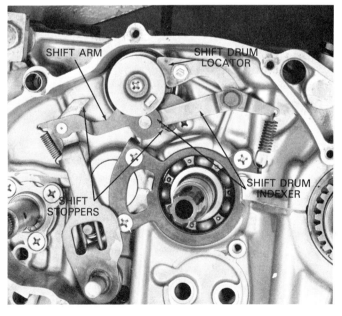

Fig. 18-23. All of these components must be installed correctly for proper gearbox shifting. Double-check everything during reassembly.

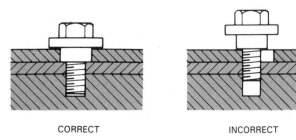

CORRECT   INCORRECT

Fig. 18-24. Shouldered bolts are commonly used as pivot points for shifting mechanism arms. Improper installation will prevent proper location and pivoting.
(U.S. Suzuki Motor Corporation)

the text's summaries for two-stroke, four-stroke, primary drive, and clutch reassembly as needed.

A correctly assembled gearbox will give smooth and dependable operation. Take your time and do it right the first time!

KNOW THESE TERMS

Gearbox overhaul, Shaft end play, Shift mechanism, Shaft runout, Fork groove clearance, Gear backlash, Dogs, Gearbox shimming, Gearbox external end play measurement, Gearbox internal end play measurement.

REVIEW QUESTIONS—CHAPTER 18

1. What are three of the most common gearbox problems?
2. Gearbox shaft _____ and shift mechanism operation should be checked before disassembling a gearbox.
3. It is not necessary to rotate the shafts when bench shifting a gearbox through all speeds. True or False?
4. List three checks you can make to prevent disorganization during gearbox disassembly.
5. Most gearbox checks (inspections) are done visually. True or False?
6. Name three general variations of gearbox mounting and supporting.
7. Write the formula for the internal measurement of gearbox shaft end play.
8. Which of the following is not a consideration

Fig. 18-25. Gear selector mechanism must be properly timed. Notice that ratchet gear teeth are centered on gear teeth of selector shaft shift arm.

during gearbox reassembly.
   a. Use a service manual.
   b. Lubricate parts.
   c. Replace all shims.
   d. Check for freedom of movement.
   e. Replace all seals and gaskets.
9. Define the term "gearbox shimming."
10. In most modern unit-construction engines, assembly of the gearbox also involves assembly of the engine top end. True or False?

SUGGESTED ACTIVITIES

1. Measure gearbox shaft end play. Compare your results to the specifications given in the service manual.
2. Check the operation of a shift mechanism. Use the list in this chapter as a guide.
3. Disassemble your gearbox shafts and perform all of the inspection checks listed in this chapter. Record your findings and make up a parts list.
4. Find examples of the different methods of gearbox mounting. Determine which method is most common.

Chapter 19

FRAME AND SUSPENSION SYSTEMS

After studying this chapter, you will be able to:
□ Describe the types of frames used on today's motorcycles.
□ Explain the action of front and rear suspension systems.
□ Change front fork oil.
□ Lubricate steering head bearings.
□ Describe the basic procedures for rebuilding a front fork assembly.
□ Explain rear swing arm and shock absorber construction.
□ Compare different types of suspension systems.
□ Inspect a frame and suspension system for signs of trouble.

It is very important for a motorcycle to handle properly over bumps, in turns, during acceleration, and when stopping. This is critical to both rider safety and comfort. The design of a frame and suspension system is a major factor controlling the handling characteristics of a motorcycle.

This chapter discusses frame and suspension designs and how they affect performance and dependability. The chapter also covers fundamental inspection, service, and repair procedures for frames and suspension systems.

FRAME TYPES

The FRAME is the "backbone" of the motorcycle. Virtually everything on the motorcycle is attached to the frame. A critical function of any frame is to provide a non-flexing mount for the engine, suspension, and wheels. Another primary job of the frame is to provide a rigid structure between the steering head (front wheel and fork assembly) and rear swing arm (rear wheel and suspension assembly). Cornering and acceleration tend to misalign these assemblies.

Motorcycles use three basic frame designs: cradle frame, backbone frame, and stamped frame.

Cradle frame

The CRADLE FRAME surrounds the engine, as shown in Fig. 19-1. This design derives its strength from the triangulation of support tubing. Almost anywhere you look on a cradle frame, triangles are formed at major stress areas. This principle is illustrated in Fig. 19-2.

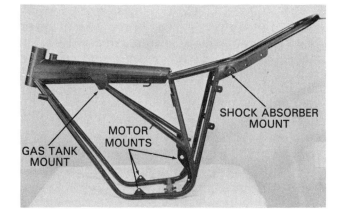

Fig. 19-1. Cradle frame uses tubing to surround engine and produce rigid mounting.

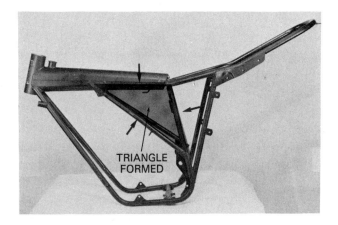

Fig. 19-2. Notice how triangles are formed at junction of most frame tubes. This makes cradle frame very rigid.

On large, high powered motorcycles, additional support may be provided by gussets, Fig. 19-3. A cradle frame is relatively lightweight and extremely strong.

Backbone frame

In the BACKBONE FRAME, the engine hangs from the top of the frame and acts as a structural member. This design requires the frame to be relatively heavy to provide adequate strength. Look at Fig. 19-4. Since the engine is NOT enclosed by lower frame tubes, engine service may be simplified with a backbone frame design.

Stamped frame

A STAMPED FRAME usually consists of two pieces of stamped sheet metal that are welded

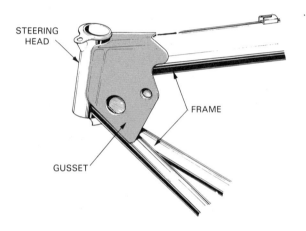

Fig. 19-3. Gussets reinforce area where steering head is welded to frame. (Triumph Motorcycles [Meriden] Ltd.)

Fig. 19-4. Backbone frame design. Engine hangs from backbone tube and acts as a rigid frame member.

together, Fig. 19-5. Frame strength in this design is achieved by the shape of the stamping. A stamped frame is the least expensive to produce and is normally used on inexpensive, small displacement motorcycles.

Motorcycle frame designs are constantly being updated. It is not uncommon to find frames which use combinations of these three designs. See Fig. 19-6.

FRONT SUSPENSION

The purpose of the SUSPENSION SYSTEM is to allow the wheels to follow an irregular road surface with a minimum amount of shock being transmitted into the frame. A few, old motorcycles used spring-loaded swing arms mounted on stationary tubes (Earls type front suspension). The arms would simply swing up and down to absorb bumps in the road surface. Today's motorcycles, however, use a telescoping fork type front suspension.

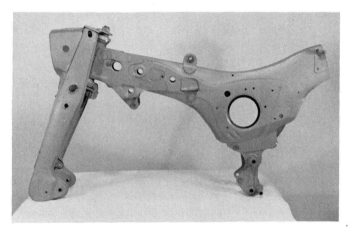

Fig. 19-5. Stamped sheet metal pieces are welded together to fabricate a stamped frame. Notice that this frame uses backbone design as well.

Telescoping fork

A TELESCOPING FORK assembly consists of two fork tubes, two triple clamps, a spindle (shaft mounted on lower triple clamp), and related fasteners. These parts are pictured in Fig. 19-7.

The FORK TUBES are shock absorbing devices that hold the front wheel in place. They are attached to the motorcycle by the triple clamps and spindle.

The TRIPLE CLAMPS secure the fork tubes to the frame and hold the tubes in alignment. The lower triple clamp is usually made as an integral part of the spindle.

The SPINDLE or steering stem on the lower triple clamp passes through the steering head (hole in the frame). This allows the fork to be turned to the right or left.

FORK SLIDERS (outer tubes) provide a mounting place for the front wheel axle. They slip over the

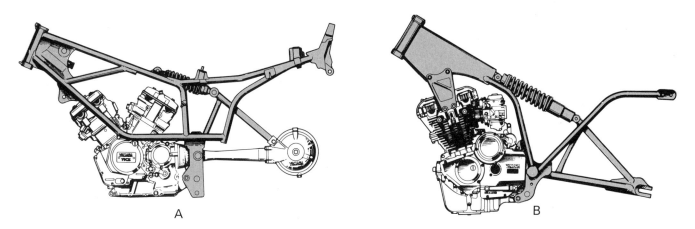

Fig. 19-6. Compare these frames to ones shown earlier. A—Frame for large displacement motorcycle with shaft drive. B—Modern backbone frame design with shock mounted in upper section of frame. (Yamaha Motor Corporation, U.S.A.)

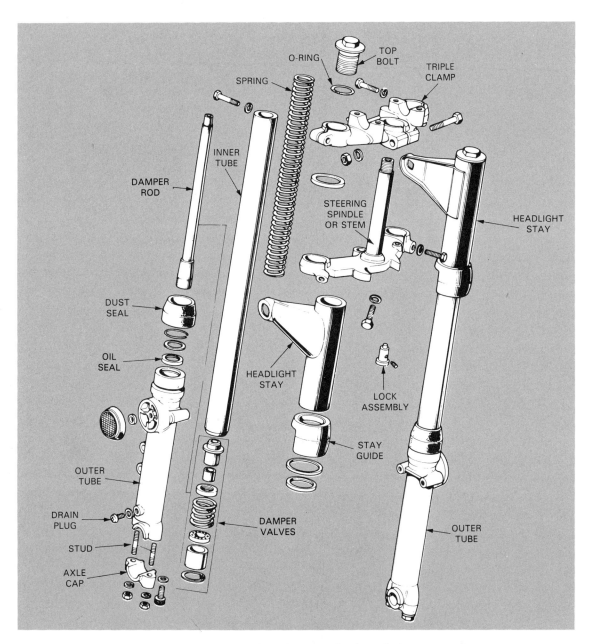

Fig. 19-7. This exploded view shows major front fork components.
(Kawasaki Motors Corp., U.S.A.)

bottom of the inner fork tubes, Fig. 19-8.

DAMPER RODS (cylinders) are attached to the sliders and project into the fork tubes. This is shown in Fig. 19-8. Damper rods serve two basic functions in most fork designs. They provide:

1. Compression damping (cushioning when forks are pushed inward).
2. Rebound damping (cushioning when forks extend).

Damper rods also prevent the sliders from falling off the fork tubes at full extension. Damper rods work in conjunction with fork oil and damper valves.

Coil springs are located inside the fork tubes and provide spring pressure to support the motorcycle, Fig. 19-9. To keep fork oil in and contaminants out, seals are located at the top of the fork sliders, as shown in Fig. 19-10.

While all telescopic forks work on the same principle, there are many design variations. For example, internal or external springs may be used. The axle may be mounted at the bottom of the slider or on the front side of the slider. Damping may be controlled by damper rods or orifices in the fork tubes. To provide adjustability of the suspension system, adjustable dampers and air assisted springing is also common.

Telescoping fork operation

Fork operation is usually described in two phases:
1. Compression stroke (inward or retracting movement of forks).
2. Rebound stroke (outward or extending fork movement).

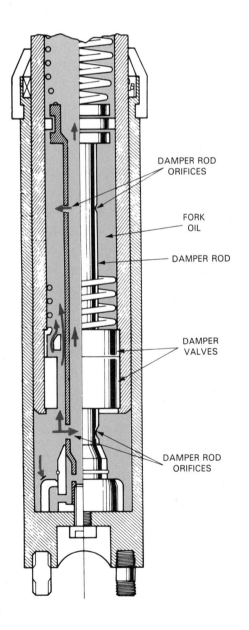
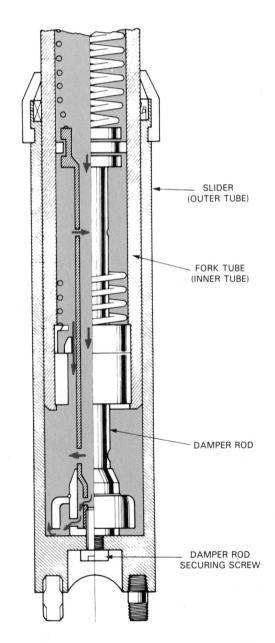

Fig. 19-8. Fork action is controlled by metering oil flow through damper valves and orifices in damper rod. Damper rod is attached to slider and protrudes into fork tubes. (Kawasaki Motors Corp., U.S.A.)

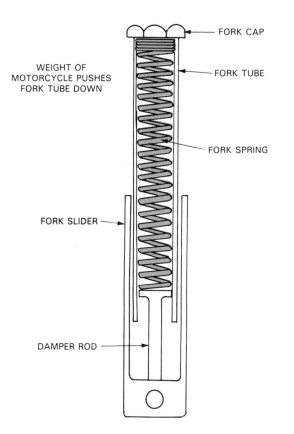

Fig. 19-9. A coil spring, which rests on damper rod, exerts pressure on fork cap to support motorcycle.

The FORK COMPRESSION STROKE is the movement of the fork tube into the fork slider, when striking a bump in the road. Oil trapped below the fork tube and check valve is forced to flow through the check valve and compression damping hole. Look at Fig. 19-11.

The amount of damping is determined by the size of the compression damping holes and the clearance between the check valve and check valve body. Generally, compression damping is relatively light since the fork spring provides most of the resistance to compression.

As the fork tube nears full compression, the fork tube collar blocks off the compression damping holes. This causes a partial HYDRAULIC LOCK which prevents mechanical bottoming (metal-to-metal contact) of the forks, Fig. 19-12.

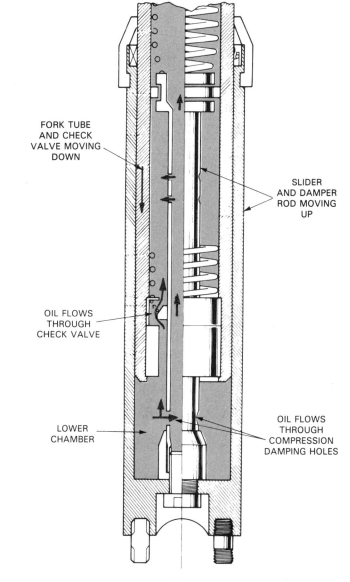

Fig. 19-10. A fork seal mounted at top of slider wipes fork tube, keeping oil in forks and preventing contaminants from entering fork.

Fig. 19-11. During fork compression, oil trapped in lower chamber flows through compression damping holes and damper rod check valve. (Kawasaki Motors Corp., U.S.A.)

During the FORK REBOUND STROKE, the fork spring causes the fork slider to extend. The spring pushes against the top of the damper rod. Oil above the damper rod piston flows freely through the damper rod into the bottom of the slider. See Fig. 19-13. Oil trapped between the damper rod piston and check valve is metered through the rebound damping holes before it can flow back into the slider. This restriction to oil flow provides the necessary rebound damping.

As the fork nears full rebound, the lower rebound damping hole is blocked off. This causes firmer damping. When the remaining damping hole is blocked off, a mild hydraulic lock is formed. A top-out spring provides the final cushioning of the rebound stroke. See Fig. 19-14.

There are many variations in fork design. The size and location of damper holes determines fork action. Suspension adjustment is accomplished by changing spring rates, oil viscosity, adjustable damping valves, or air pressure.

Anti-dive fork

Fig. 19-15 shows an anti-dive front fork design that uses brake fluid pressure to help prevent front end dive during braking. When the rider applies the brakes, the brake system master cylinder forces brake fluid into the inlet on the front fork. Pressure acts on a small plunger. The plunger slides in its cylinder and pushes on an oil flow control valve. The flow control valve then moves to restrict oil flow. This stiffens compression damping and reduces front end dive.

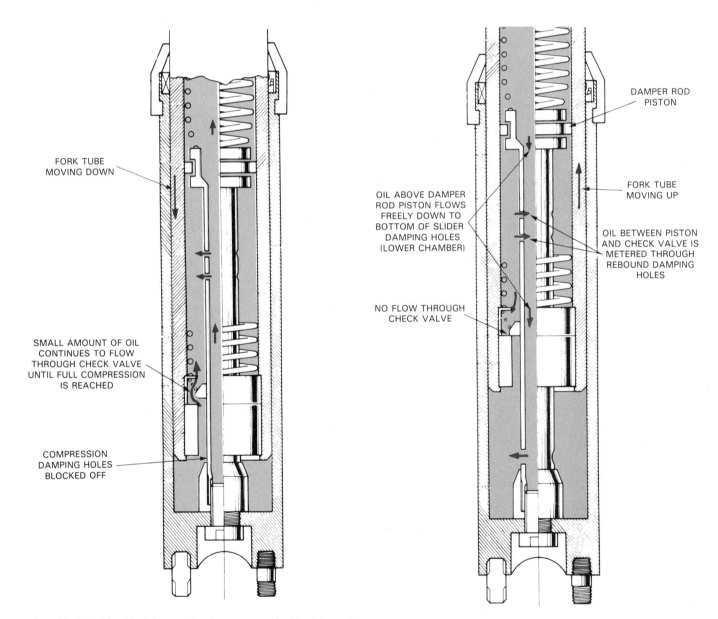

Fig. 19-12. Hard fork bottoming is prevented by blocking off compression damping holes just before full compression is reached. (Kawasaki Motors Corp., U.S.A.)

Fig. 19-13. Fork rebound damping is controlled by rebound damping holes. (Kawasaki Motors Corp., U.S.A.)

STEERING GEOMETRY

STEERING GEOMETRY refers to the position and angles formed by the various steering related components on a motorcycle. Factors which determine steering geometry are rake, trail, and offset.

Rake

RAKE is the angle of the forks from true vertical, Fig. 19-16. Rake angle may vary depending upon intended use of the motorcycle.

Generally, MORE RAKE (larger angle between fork centerline and vertical) results in slowed steering response and greater high speed stability. LESS RAKE (smaller angle between forks and vertical) quickens the steering, but increases the chance of high speed wobble.

Trail

TRAIL is the distance along the ground between a line down the centerline of the forks and a vertical line through the axle centerline. See Fig. 19-16. Trail gives the steering a self-centering effect.

As trail is increased, the self-centering effect improves stability. Rake and trail are interrelated. As rake is increased, trail also increases.

It is interesting to note that rake and trail change as the motorcycle is ridden. This is shown in Fig. 19-17. Today's off-road, long travel suspensions exhibit extreme rake and trail changes during the length of suspension movement.

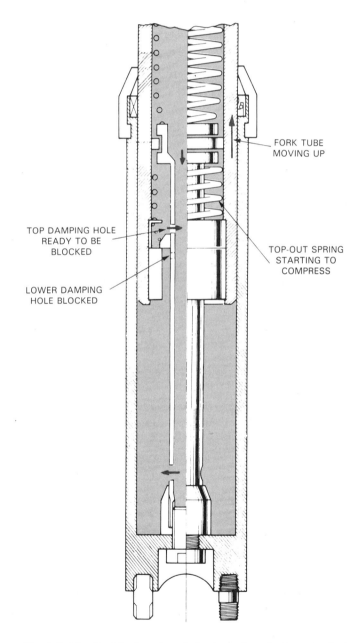

Fig. 19-14. Cushioning at end of rebound stroke is controlled by blocking off rebound damping holes and by use of a top-out spring. (Kawasaki Motors Corp., U.S.A.)

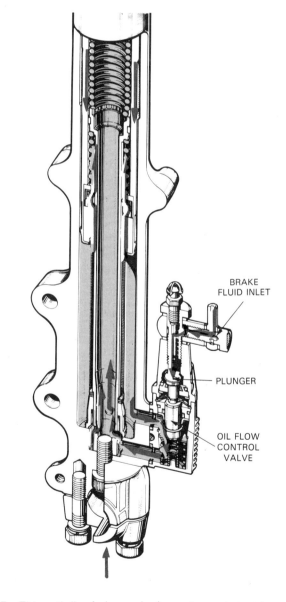

Fig. 19-15. This anti-dive fork uses brake system pressure to actuate flow control valve. Valve limits oil flow in fork during braking to help avoid nose dive. (U.S. Suzuki Motor Corporation)

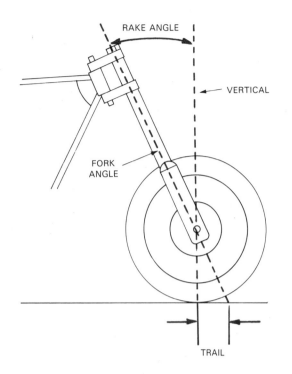

Fig. 19-16. Angle of fork tubes from vertical is called rake angle. Distance between fork angle and vertical line (through center of axle) is called trail.

Offset

OFFSET provides the proper steering arc. Offset may be achieved by either offsetting the fork tubes (triple clamps) or the axle, Fig. 19-18.

All these factors (rake, trail, offset) work together to give a certain steering feel and response. Other fac-

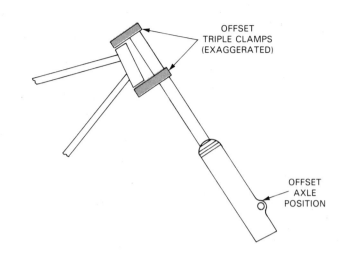

Fig. 19-18. Offset fork clamps or offset axles are used in conjunction with rake and trail to provide desired steering characteristics.

tors such as weight, center of gravity, and intended use determine the manufacturer's choice of steering geometry for a given motorcycle.

STEERING DAMPER

A STEERING DAMPER is a device which helps to eliminate unwanted steering oscillation (front wheel side movement). The two types of steering system dampers are:
1. Hydraulic (oil filled cylinder places drag on steering).
2. Friction (adjustable spring-loaded disc places drag on steering).

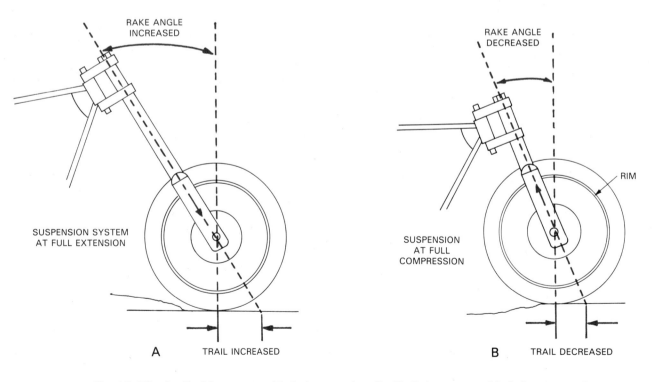

Fig. 19-17. A—Trail increases with fork extension. B—Trail decreases with fork compression.

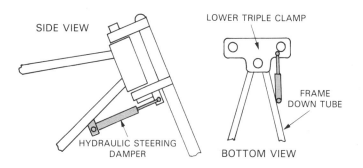

Fig. 19-19. Hydraulic steering damper attached between frame and lower triple clamp to help control steering oscillations.

A

Friction type steering dampers have been replaced by the more modern hydraulic type dampers. See Fig. 19-19. The cylinder usually connects between the frame and lower fork clamp.

SERVICING FRONT SUSPENSION COMPONENTS

Typical front suspension service consists of changing fork oil, lubricating and adjusting steering head bearings, and rebuilding the forks.

Changing fork oil

Fork oil must be changed because the oil can break down (change chemically). Also, the oil can become contaminated (filled with dirt, metal particles, and moisture).

The frequency of fork oil changing is determined by riding conditions and manufacturer recommendations. A motorcycle which is ridden in dirt, sand, rain, or mud requires more frequent fork oil changes than one which is not exposed to these elements. Even under the most ideal conditions, the fork oil should be changed at least ONCE A YEAR.

To change fork oil, pump out or drain the old oil, Fig. 19-20, A. Then, refill the fork with the proper weight and quantity of fresh oil, Fig. 19-20, B. Follow your service manual for specific instructions, specifications, and oil change intervals.

Lubrication and adjustment of steering head bearings

Lubrication of steering head bearings is not done as frequently as a fork oil change. However, adjustment of steering head bearings should be checked periodically. Two types of steering head bearings are used: ball bearings and tapered roller bearings.

BALL BEARINGS are the most common type of steering head bearings since they are inexpensive. TAPERED ROLLER BEARINGS have the advantage of extremely long service life and ease of assembly and disassembly.

REPACKING (lubrication) of steering head bearings requires disassembly of the triple clamps and

B

Fig. 19-20. A—To drain fork oil, remove drain screw and top nut. B—Use a graduated cylinder, baby bottle, or measuring cup to accurately measure fork oil. Do not forget to replace drain plugs before refilling forks. Refer to manual for proper weight and quantity of oil.

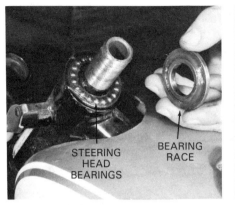 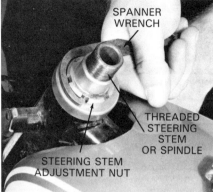

A—COMPLETE DISASSEMBLY OF TRIPLE CLAMPS IS NEEDED TO PROPERLY PACK STEERING HEAD BEARINGS WITH GREASE.

B—STEERING HEAD BEARING PRELOAD IS ADJUSTED BY TIGHTENING SLOTTED STEERING STEM NUT WHILE FOLLOWING MANUAL SPECIFIED PROCEDURES.

C—FINAL ADJUSTMENT OF STEERING HEAD BEARINGS IS DONE WITH FRONT SUSPENSION COMPLETELY ASSEMBLED. DOUBLE-CHECK STEERING ACTION AFTER ADJUSTMENT.

Fig. 19-21. Steering head bearing service.

spindle, Fig. 19-21. After cleaning and inspecting the bearings and races, repack them with a recommended type of grease.

STEERING HEAD BEARING PRELOAD adjustment is a simple task which does not require disassembly of the steering head. Fig. 19-21 shows how to change bearing preload. The adjustment must not be too tight or too loose. Improper steering head bearing adjustment would make the motorcycle dangerous to ride. Refer to your shop manual for specific instructions on disassembly, lubrication, reassembly, and adjustment of the steering head bearings.

Rebuilding forks

The most frequent cause of fork disassembly is leaking fork seals. Seal replacement only requires partial fork disassembly. However, if fork seals are leaking, other parts may be damaged. A complete fork rebuild is usually recommended during seal replacement. A fork rebuild involves complete fork disassembly and the inspection of all parts for wear, scratches, or other problems.

During a fork rebuild, follow the instructions in the service manual. It will describe important disassembly, inspection, and reassembly methods for the particular motorcycle.

When servicing a motorcycle fork, remember the following:
1. Check slider and fork tube bearing surfaces for wear.
2. Check all components for galling, nicks, straightness.
3. Replace all sealing rings and washers.
4. Replace all snap rings (circlips).
5. Use proper torque values on all fasteners.

CAUTION! Use extreme care when servicing front end components. Faulty service or repair methods can result in suspension failure, rider injury, and even death.

REAR SUSPENSION SYSTEMS

A typical motorcycle REAR SUSPENSION consists of a swing arm and one or two shock absorbers. See Fig. 19-22. One end of the swing arm pivots on the frame and the other end holds the axle and rear wheel.

A SINGLE SHOCK rear suspension, as implied, only uses one shock absorber mounted in front of the

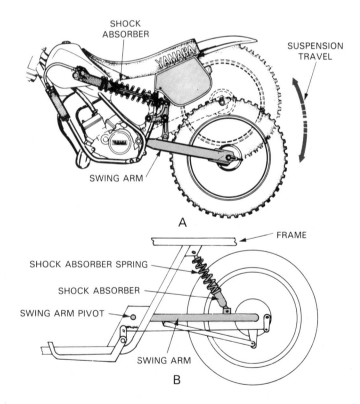

Fig. 19-22. Two basic rear suspension types. A—Single shock rear suspension uses one shock absorber between frame and swing arm. B—Dual-shock rear suspension places shocks on each side of motorcycle, between frame and swing arm. (Yamaha Motor Corporation, U.S.A.)

rear wheel. A DUAL-SHOCK rear suspension has a shock absorber on each side of the frame. With both types, the shock connects the swing arm and the frame to provide the necessary springing and damping action for the rear wheel.

SWING ARM

Many different types of swing arm designs are used. See Fig. 19-23. Swing arms may be made of steel or aluminum and may be either stamped or fabricated from tubing.

On shaft drive motorcycles, one leg of the swing arm houses the drive shaft, as shown in Fig. 19-24.

Swing arm mounting

The swing arm, Fig. 19-25, is attached to the frame with a swing arm pivot bolt or shaft. Bushings, needle

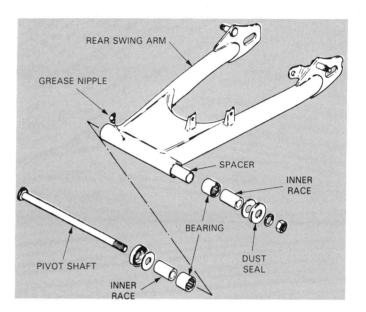

Fig. 19-25. This swing arm uses needle bearings for positive, accurate location and smooth operation of rear suspension. (U.S. Suzuki Motor Corporation)

Fig. 19-23. Notice rigid triangular shape of this single shock suspension. (Yamaha Motor Corporation, U.S.A.)

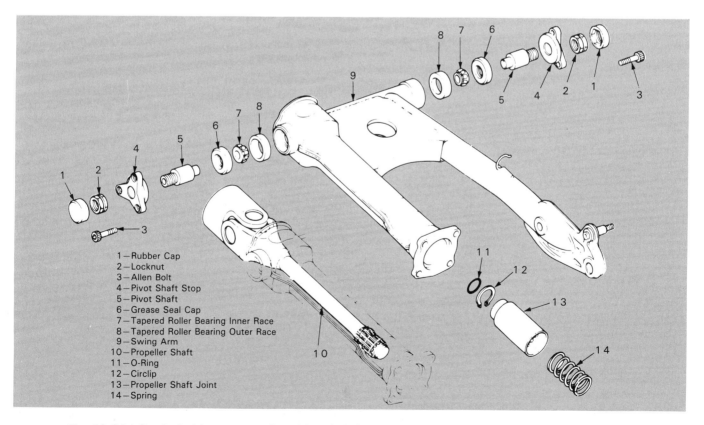

1—Rubber Cap
2—Locknut
3—Allen Bolt
4—Pivot Shaft Stop
5—Pivot Shaft
6—Grease Seal Cap
7—Tapered Roller Bearing Inner Race
8—Tapered Roller Bearing Outer Race
9—Swing Arm
10—Propeller Shaft
11—O-Ring
12—Circlip
13—Propeller Shaft Joint
14—Spring

Fig. 19-24. On shaft drive motorcycles, drive shaft (propeller shaft) passes through one leg of swing arm. Study parts of this assembly. (Kawasaki Motors Corp., U.S.A.)

bearings, or tapered roller bearings are used to provide smooth operation and accurate swing arm alignment. Some designs require periodic adjustment and lubrication. Refer to your shop manual for details.

SHOCK ABSORBERS

Shock absorbers work much like a front suspension telescopic fork. There are many different types of shock absorbers. Some have external damping adjustments. The most conventional type is the unpressurized, oil-damped shock, pictured in Fig. 19-26.

For severe applications (competition and off-road motorcycles), conventional shock absorbers can overheat and do not provide adequate damping. This is due in part to the small quantity of oil in the shock that provides damping. Large capacity, gas-oil shocks have been designed to meet this need, and are stan-

dard on most competition and off-road motorcycles. Look at Fig. 19-27.

Shock absorber springs

Shock absorber springs are mounted over the damper (shock) body. They are fastened to the shock absorber by collars or clips. This is pictured in Fig. 19-28. Three spring types are used:
1. One piece constant rate spring.
2. One piece dual rate or progressive spring.
3. Two piece dual rate springs.

Refer to Fig. 19-29. Additional springing may also be provided by internal pressure in GAS-CHARGED SHOCKS.

The lower spring platform on many shock absorbers also functions as a SPRING PRELOAD adjustor, Fig. 19-30. It can be adjusted to modify ride height.

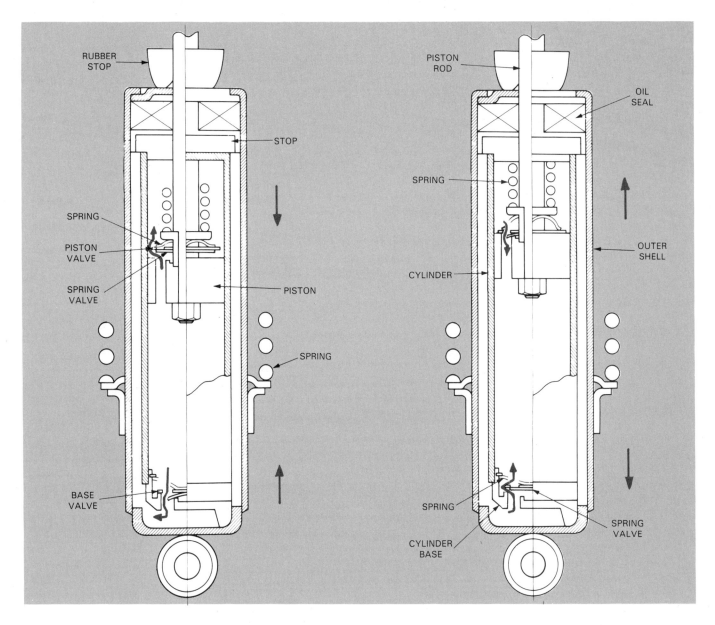

Fig. 19-26. A typical oil-damped rear shock absorber. (Kawasaki Motors Corp., U.S.A.)

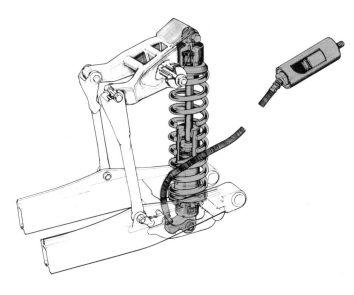

Fig. 19-27. This single shock rear suspension uses an adjustable rear shock system. Notice remote reservoir for additional oil capacity.   (U.S. Suzuki Motor Corporation)

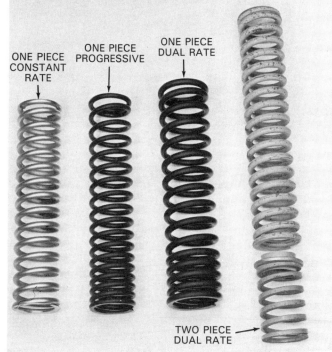

Fig. 19-29. Typical variations of rear suspension shock absorber springs. Coil design is used to help control suspension action.

Fig. 19-28. Spring collars or clips retain shock springs.

Shock absorber mounting

Shock absorbers are bolted to the frame and swing arm through rubber or steel bushings. Look at Fig. 19-31. The bushings allow the shock to swivel slightly on its mounting during suspension movement.

REAR SUSPENSION VARIATIONS

There are two basic rear suspension variations: conventional rear suspension and long travel rear suspension.

Conventional rear suspension

CONVENTIONAL REAR SUSPENSION systems usually mount the shocks vertically near the rear axle, as shown in Fig. 19-32. This design can provide low seat height and acceptable suspension travel for road bikes.

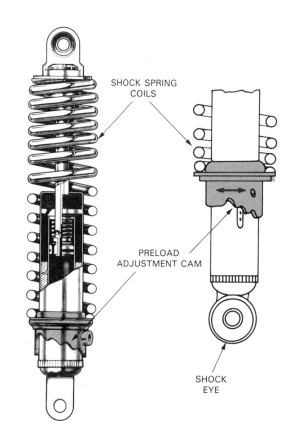

Fig. 19-30. More or less rear suspension spring preload is achieved by changing adjustment cam. Twisting preload cam changes compression of rear coil spring.
(U.S. Suzuki Motor Corporation)

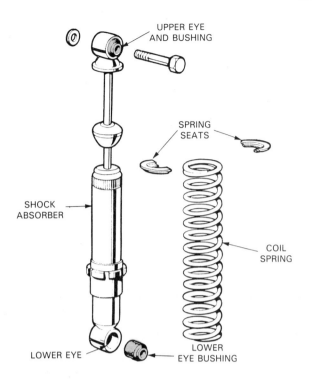

Fig. 19-31. Steel insert surrounded by a rubber bushing is used in shock eye. It provides a vibration resistant mounting for shock absorbers. (Triumph Motorcycles [Meriden] Ltd.)

Long travel rear suspension

LONG TRAVEL REAR SUSPENSION systems provide a softer suspension action over a longer distance of swing arm travel (suspension travel). This is ideal for competition and off-road motorcycles since it helps the wheel stay in contact with the ground.

There are three common long travel designs: laydown (cantilever), forward mount, and single shock absorber. They are pictured in Fig. 19-33. Each design has its advantages and disadvantages. Modern suspension design technology has made all three designs competitive and reliable.

Recently, single shock rear suspensions have become popular on road bikes as well as dirt bikes. This modern suspension design can provide "rising rate" operation. See Fig. 19-33, C.

FRAME AND SUSPENSION INSPECTION

You should inspect a motorcycle's frame and suspension system periodically. It is a good idea to check for any problems that could affect rider safety. Check in your service manual for routine inspection intervals. Generally, look for worn pivots, worn shock absorber bushings, loose fasteners, unlubricated grease fittings, suspension misalignment, and other similar types of problems.

NOTE! Frame and suspension system inspection is imperative when the motorcycle has handling problems or crash damage. You must locate and correct

every problem to assure that the motorcycle is safe to ride.

The following summary and your service manual will provide guidelines for a thorough frame and suspension inspection. Because there are so many designs, remember that the following summary is only a general guide. Items from Chapter 20, Wheels, Tires, and Brakes, appear in the summary because they can and will alter a motorcycle's handling characteristics.

FRONT SUSPENSION INSPECTION SUMMARY

1. Check steering head looseness and bearing condition.
2. Observe steering damper operation.
3. Check fork sliders or bushings for looseness.
4. Check wheel bearings for looseness.
5. Check trueness of wheels and tires.
6. Inspect tire for cuts, sidewall checking, and other damage.
7. Check spoke tension.
8. Measure tire pressure.
9. Check fork for loss of air pressure (air forks).
10. Check tightness of fasteners at fender brackets, brake plate brace, triple clamps, steering stem, steering damper, and axle.

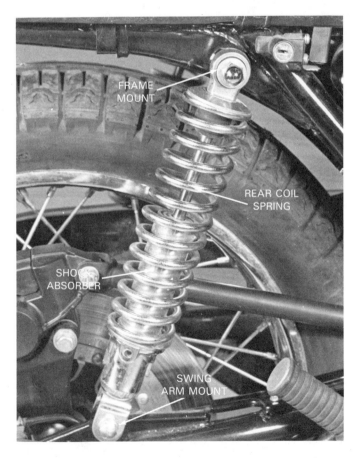

Fig. 19-32. Conventional or road bike rear suspension system mounts shock absorber close to rear axle.

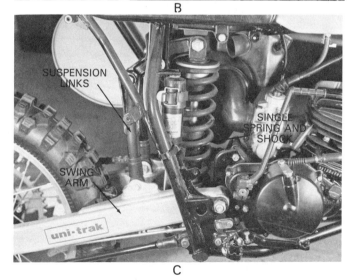

Fig. 19-33. Current long travel rear suspension types include: A—Laydown. B—Forward mount. C—This single shock rear suspension uses adjustable shock absorber, levers, and links to provide rising rate rear suspension.
(U.S. Suzuki Motor Corporation).

11. Check alignment of forks and steering head.
12. Measure fork tube height in triple clamps.
13. Check fork tube straightness.
14. Inspect fork seals for leakage.
15. Check condition of fork wipers or accordion boots.
16. Check fork tubes for scratches, nicks, dents.
17. Inspect steering neck, triple clamps, and front chassis for chipped paint, cracks, and straightness.
18. Change fork oil. If air suspension, release pressure before draining. Pressurize after filling. Refer to your manual.
19. Observe fork operation.
20. Check handle bar tightness and straightness.

MID-FRAME INSPECTION SUMMARY

1. Check mid-frame (center section of chassis) for chipped paint, corrosion, damage, and straightness.
2. Check the tightness of the fasteners on the engine mounts, side stand, center stand, brake pedal, and foot pegs.
3. Lubricate brake pedal, foot peg, center stand, and side stand pivots.

REAR SUSPENSION INSPECTION SUMMARY

1. Check swing arm looseness.
2. Inspect shock eye bushings for looseness.
3. Check wheel bearings and spokes for looseness.
4. Measure wheel and tire runout.
5. Check tire for cuts, checking, and other damage.
6. Measure tire air pressure.
7. Check swing arm straightness and alignment.
8. Grease swing arm.
9. Inspect shock absorbers for leakage (oil and air).
10. Check shock absorber rods for straightness.
11. Check shock absorber preload settings.
12. Observe shock absorber operation.
13. Check wheel and sprocket alignment.
14. Check tightness of fasteners at shock mounts, swing arm pivot, rear axle, brake plate brace, chain guard, passenger pegs, and fender brackets.
15. Inspect rear chassis, swing arm, and surrounding areas for chipped paint, corrosion, cracks, misalignment, and other signs of trouble.
16. If the motorcycle has a fairing, saddle bags, or a luggage rack, check for tightness, alignment, and cracked mounting brackets.

KNOW THESE TERMS

Cradle frame, Backbone frame, Stamped frame, Telescoping fork, Triple clamp, Spindle, Fork slider, Anti-dive fork, Steering geometry, Rake, Trail, Offset, Steering damper, Steering head bearing, Swing arm, Shock absorber, Long travel rear suspension.

REVIEW QUESTIONS — CHAPTER 19

1. Name three common frame types.
2. Triangulation and gussets add strength to frames. True or False?
3. List two functions of fork damper rods.
4. What are the two phases of fork operation?
5. Fork action is determined by the _____ and _____ of damper holes.
6. Rake angle is the same on all motorcycles. True or False?
7. The term "self-centering effect" is most closely related to:
   a. Rake.
   b. Offset.
   c. Trail.
   d. Camber.
8. A _____ _____ helps to eliminate unwanted steering oscillations.
9. The frequency of fork oil change requirements is determined by _____ _____ and manufacturer recommendations.
10. What advantage do steering head roller bearings have over ball bearings?
11. It is not necessary to replace sealing rings, washers, and O-rings during fork rebuilding. True or False?
12. A conventional shock absorber is unpressurized and _____ damped.
13. List the three types of shock springs.
14. When is frame and suspension inspection imperative?

SUGGESTED ACTIVITIES

1. Visit local motorcycle shops to find two examples of each of the three common frame types. Compare the frames, making note of:
   a. Triangulation.
   b. Gusseting.
   c. Diameter of frame tubes.
   d. Type and size of engine mounting brackets.
   e. Intended use of the motorcycle.
2. Complete the suspension inspection summary on an actual motorcycle.
3. From activity two, explain what should be done to improve the mechanical condition of the motorcycle.

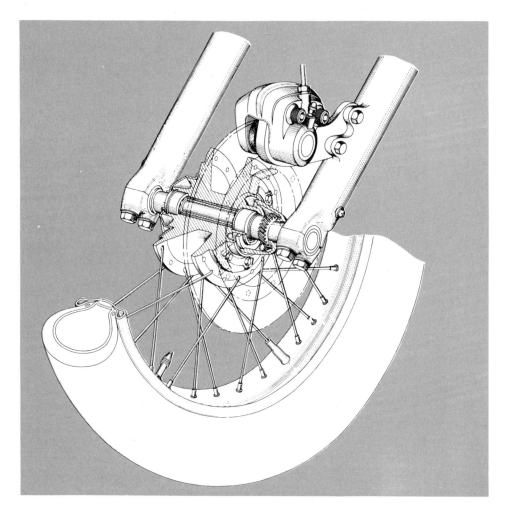

Can you identify the basic parts of this wheel assembly?   (Kawasaki Motor Corp., U.S.A.)

Chapter 20

WHEELS, TIRES, AND BRAKES

After studying this chapter, you will be able to:
□ Describe the types of wheels used on modern motorcycles.
□ Perform basic service and repair operations on motorcycle wheels.
□ Compare various tire designs.
□ Inspect, service, and repair tires.
□ Explain the operating principles of motorcycle brakes.
□ Inspect and repair a motorcycle brake system.
□ List safety rules for brake system service.

This chapter discusses the design and maintenance of motorcycle wheels, tires, and brakes. Improper maintenance and service of these components means the difference between a safe motorcycle and one which is a hazard to ride. Study this chapter carefully.

WHEELS

A motorcycle WHEEL rotates on an axle and supports the rubber tire. Three types of wheels are used on today's motorcycles: wire wheels, cast wheels, and stamped wheels.

WIRE WHEELS

A WIRE WHEEL consists of:
1. Hub (contains axle bearings and inner end of spokes).
2. Spokes and nipples (connects hub and rim).
3. Rim (supports tire).

Fig. 20-1 shows a typical wire wheel assembly. The hub is suspended from the spokes. The spokes are attached to the rim in a crisscross pattern. The spokes are secured to the rim by the spoke nipples.

The weight of the motorcycle is NOT supported by the lower spokes. The hub actually hangs from the top spokes, Fig. 20-2. As the wheel rotates, weight transfers from spoke to spoke.

With more spokes crossed in the lacing pattern, the wheel becomes stronger. This is because the load is

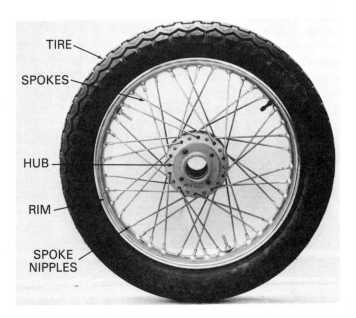

Fig. 20-1. Spoked wheel uses spokes and nipples to connect hub and rim.

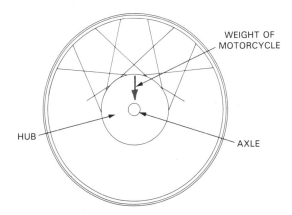

Fig. 20-2. Axle attaches wheel assembly to motorcycle. Hub, axle, and weight of motorcycle hang from upper spokes.

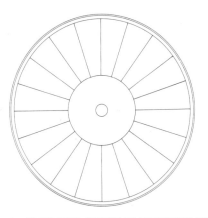

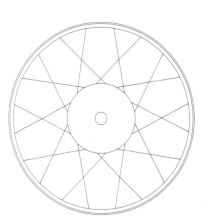

A—CROSS-ZERO PATTERN IS VERY WEAK AND SHOULD ONLY BE USED FOR SHOW. IT IS UNSAFE FOR STREET USE.

B—CROSS-TWO PATTERN IS COMMON, BUT PROVIDES MINIMAL SUPPORT.

C—CROSS-THREE PATTERN PROVIDES VERY GOOD SUPPORT FOR A STRONG WHEEL ASSEMBLY.

Fig. 20-3. Note different spoke patterns.

distributed over a wider area on the rim. Also, as the wheel rotates, each spoke is loaded and unloaded more gradually. Fig. 20-3 shows weak and strong spoke cross-patterns.

CAST WHEELS

A CAST WHEEL is manufactured by pouring molten metal (usually aluminum or magnesium alloy) into a mold. This makes the hub, spokes, and rim all one piece, Fig. 20-4. A cast wheel is a very strong and dependable type wheel.

STAMPED WHEELS

A STAMPED WHEEL consists of separate parts (hub, spokes, rim) fastened together. Unlike the cast wheel, the stamped wheel is either bolted or riveted together. It has the appearance of a cast wheel but is less expensive to manufacture. Refer to Fig. 20-4.

Hubs and bearings

In most wheel designs, ball bearings are located in the hub. An AXLE passes through the ball bearings and connects the wheel assembly to the rear swing arm or front fork legs. Fig. 20-5 shows a rear wheel hub. A spacer, installed between the ball bearings, allows the axle to be tightened without binding the bearing. See Fig. 20-6.

A HUB provides a mounting place for the brake drum or brake disc and sprocket (rear wheel). On some wheels, the rear hub also serves as a mounting place for the final drive shock absorber, Fig. 20-7. The hub must be strong enough to safely withstand braking, cornering, and driving loads.

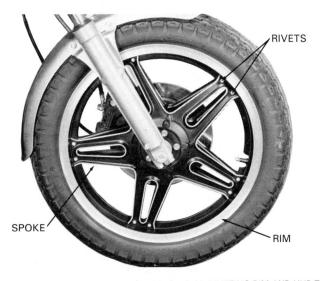

A—CAST WHEEL IS MADE BY POURING MOLTEN METAL INTO A MOLD. THIS PRODUCES A ONE PIECE WHEEL.

B—STAMPED WHEEL IS MADE BY BOLTING OR RIVETING RIM AND HUB TO STAMPED SPOKES.

Fig. 20-4. Compare similarities and differences between a cast wheel and a stamped wheel.

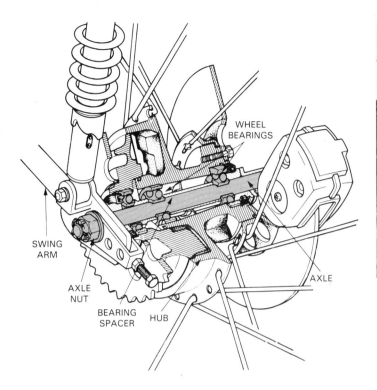

Fig. 20-5. Axle passes through swing arm and wheel bearings. When axle nut is tightened, axle and wheel are locked into position. (Kawasaki Motors Corp., U.S.A.)

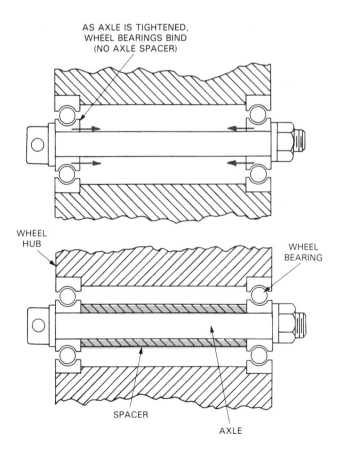

Fig. 20-6. A spacer is needed between bearings to prevent side loading of bearings when axle is tightened.

Fig. 20-7. This rear hub holds drive sprocket, final drive shock absorber and brake disc. Hub shock absorber reduces strain on parts during rapid clutch engagement or when tire becomes airborne under power.

WHEEL INSPECTION

Motorcycle wheels take a lot of abuse. Spokes may loosen or break. Rims may get dented. The wheel may develop runout. These problems can affect the handling and safety of the motorcycle.

To help prevent the possibility of failure, wheel inspection should be done on a regular basis. Typical wheel inspection requires that you:
1. Check wheel bearings for wear, Fig. 20-8.
2. Inspect wheel hub for cracks, Fig. 20-9.
3. Check for broken spokes, Fig. 20-10.
4. Check spoke tightness, Fig. 20-11.
5. Inspect rim for dents, Fig. 20-12.
6. Check spokes, rim, and hub on cast or stamped wheels for cracks, Fig. 20-13.
7. Measure rim runout, Fig. 20-14.

WHEEL SERVICING

Wheel servicing includes:
1. Repacking or replacing wheel bearings.
2. Tightening loose spokes.
3. Replacing broken spokes.
4. Replacing dented rim or damaged hub.
5. Lacing and trueing complete wheel assembly.

Repacking or replacing wheel bearings

Wheel bearings should be cleaned and repacked with grease at periodic intervals. Wheel bearing grease may become contaminated or break down from age or heat. Riding conditions determine how often wheel bearings must be cleaned and repacked. A dirt bike which is ridden in mud, water, or sand will need its wheel bearings serviced much more frequently than a road bike. Intervals listed in the owner's manual or service

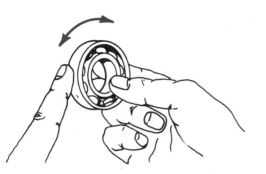

Fig. 20-8. Bearings must move freely and smoothly. Worn bearings have a gritty or catchy feel. (U.S. Suzuki Motor Corporation)

Fig. 20-11. Loose spokes can be detected by feel. Excessive flexing indicates looseness.

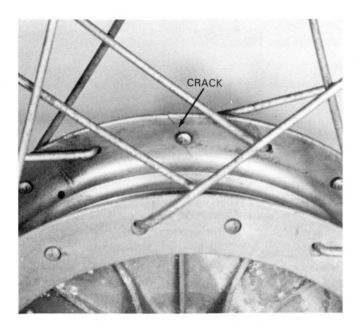

Fig. 20-9. Inspect both sides of hub flange for cracks. Replace hub if cracked.

Fig. 20-12. Most dents can be located visually. Small dents, however, may require you to spin wheel while watching rim.

Fig. 20-10. A broken spoke may be easily overlooked since only head of spoke may break off. Careful inspection is very important.

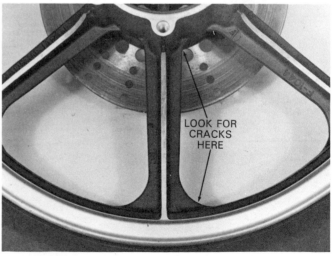

Fig. 20-13. Failure of an alloy wheel is rare but occurs occasionally. Thorough inspection is important.

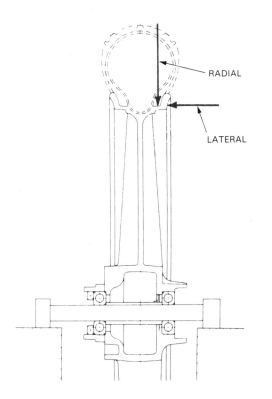

Fig. 20-14. Check areas shown using a stationary pointer or dial indicator while rotating wheel. Manual gives specs for wheel runout limits.   (Yamaha Motor Corporation, U.S.A.)

manual should be observed.

The method of bearing removal varies from wheel to wheel. Different methods are used for spacing, sealing, or securing the bearings into the hub. See Fig. 20-15. Once the bearings are removed, they should be cleaned in solvent and dried.

CAUTION! Do NOT use air pressure to spin bearings while drying. The bearings could fly apart with enough force to blind, break fingers, and even KILL.

Inspect bearings for pitting of the balls, rollers, and races. Check the bearing for smooth rotation and play. Roughness or catching indicates a problem, and the bearing should be replaced.

Once the bearings are cleaned and found to be reusable, or if new bearings are purchased, pack them with grease. A good grade of wheel bearing grease can be used. Fig. 20-16 shows how to properly pack a wheel bearing.

When reinstalling the bearings into the hub, make sure they are not cocked, and that they are seated completely. Also, do not forget the bearing spacers. Fig. 20-17 shows proper bearing installation.

Fig. 20-16. After placing a small quantity of wheel bearing grease in palm of one hand, rub into grease with outer bearing race. Continue doing this until grease is forced up through top of bearing.

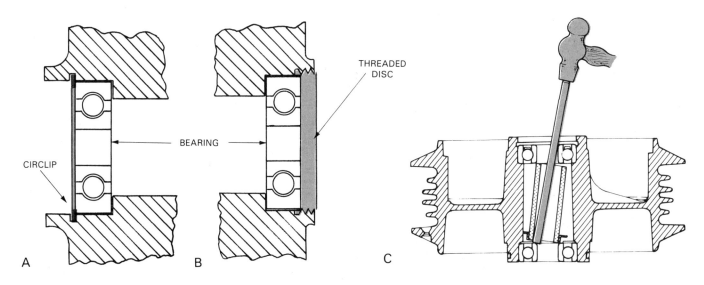

Fig. 20-15. A—Bearing is secured by a circlip. B—Threaded disc secures bearing. C—When removing wheel bearings, bearing spacer must be tilted to one side to gain access to inner bearing race. Using a drift and hammer, tap around inner race to remove bearings.   (Kawasaki Motors Corp., U.S.A.)

Fig. 20-17. When installing wheel bearings, use a bearing driver of slightly smaller diameter than outer bearing race. Remember to install bearing spacer.

A—FEEL SPOKES TO DETECT LOOSENESS. EXCESSIVE FLEXING INDICATES LOOSE SPOKES. TIGHTEN SPOKES UNTIL THEY FEEL EQUALLY STIFF.

B—SPOKE TONE, WHEN TAPPED WITH WRENCH OR SCREWDRIVER, INDICATES SPOKE TIGHTNESS. DULL TONE INDICATES LOOSE SPOKE. RING OR PANG INDICATES PROPERLY ADJUSTED SPOKE.

C—SPOKE TORQUE WRENCH IS AN ACCURATE WAY OF CHECKING FOR PROPER SPOKE TENSION. SOME SERVICE MANUALS GIVE SPOKE TORQUE SPECS.

Fig. 20-18. Note three common methods of adjusting spokes.

Tightening loose spokes

Because a wire wheel is continuously flexing, spokes have a tendency to loosen. LOOSE SPOKES, which have been neglected, can cause spoke, rim, and hub breakage. Spoke looseness should be detected during wheel inspection and should be corrected immediately.

There are three ways to check for loose spokes:
1. FEEL, Fig. 20-18, A. Grasp spokes above cross point and squeeze while feeling for tension. Excessive flexing indicates looseness.
2. SPOKE TONE, Fig. 20-18, B. Tap each spoke with a spoke wrench and listen for variation in tone emitted. Dull tone shows looseness.
3. SPOKE TORQUE WRENCH, Fig. 20-18, C. Check for unequal tension on spokes with spoke torque wrench or spoke wrench.

Spoke tightening should be done if only a small number of spokes are loose. If several spokes are loose, the wheel should be trued. For spoke tightening, let the air out of the tire.

CAUTION! If any spoke requires more than two turns when tightening, remove the tube so that threads protruding past the nipple can be ground off. If not ground off, the spoke could puncture inner tube. Refer to Fig. 20-19.

After tightening the spokes, the wheel should be checked for trueness (wobble). The service manual gives specifications for acceptable runout.

Replacing broken spokes

Broken spokes are usually caused by loose spokes. Loose spokes throw an excessive strain on surrounding spokes. Replacement of broken spokes usually requires:
1. Loosening of all the spokes.
2. Partial disassembly of wheel to gain access to the damaged spoke.
3. Trueing the wheel.

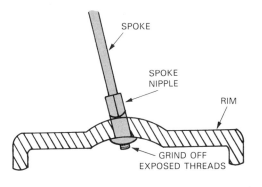

Fig. 20-19. If any spoke nipple requires more than two turns to achieve proper tension, there may be spoke threads protruding past end of nipple. These threads must be ground or filed off to prevent puncturing of inner tube.

Replacing dented rim

Replacement of a dented rim requires removal of ALL spoke nipples. Once the nipples are removed, the spokes can be pulled out of the rim. Before removing the rim, it is a good idea to tape or tie the spokes together where they cross. Look at Fig. 20-20. This keeps the spokes in proper position and makes reassembly much easier. Check the service manual to see if specific positioning of the rim is necessary. Rim replacement always requires wheel trueing.

LACING AND TRUEING WHEEL ASSEMBLY

WHEEL LACING is the building of a spoked wire wheel using a hub, spokes, and rim. Wheel lacing is necessary when:
1. A new wheel is built from scratch.
2. A hub is replaced (broken hub or worn out brake drum).

Fig. 20-20. Taping spokes at their crossing point before removal makes reassembly easier, since all spokes stay in position.

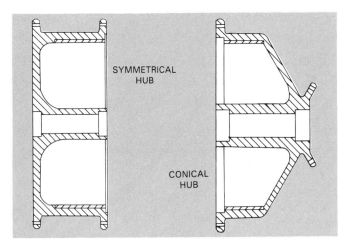

Fig. 20-21. Both sides of symmetrical hub are same diameter so spokes are all same length. One side of conical hub is smaller than other, so spokes on small side must be longer.

3. All spokes need replacement (spoke nipples seized).

There are numerous patterns and procedures for the start of a wheel lacing process. It is important to follow service manual instructions for the particular wheel being built. The two types of hubs are the symmetrical hub and conical hub. They are pictured in Fig. 20-21.

Before beginning to lace a wheel, you should always remember that there can be differences in individual spokes, spoke crossing patterns, and spoke angles. These factors affect how you lace the wheel.

The major DIFFERENCES IN SPOKES are length of the spoke, size of the spoke, angle and length of the spoke throat. Fig. 20-22 shows a few typical wheel

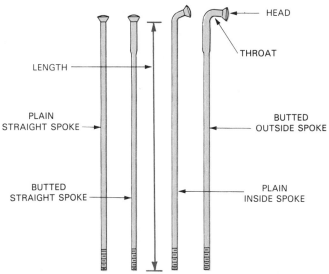

Fig. 20-22. Butted spokes are stronger than plain spokes at head and bend, where spokes usually break. Spoke length is measured from bend or base of head to threaded end. Overall length, spoke size or diameter, length, and angle of throat must be noted for proper wheel assembly.

spokes. The type of hub and the intended use of the motorcycle determines which type of spoke is used in the wheel.

The SPOKE CROSSING PATTERN refers to the number of other spokes a single spoke crosses on one side of the wheel. Common spoke crossing patterns are cross-two and cross-three. As more spokes are crossed, the wheel assembly will become stronger. For some extreme use applications, a cross-four pattern is custom laced to give added strength. Refer back to Fig. 20-3 as it shows spoke cross-patterns.

SPOKE ANGLE is the difference in width between the hub and rim spoke attachment points. Fig. 20-23 shows spoke angle and the difference between conical and symmetrical hubs. Because the angles differ from side to side on a conical hub, the holes in the rim must be at the proper angle. For this reason, a rim intended for a symmetrical hub cannot be properly laced to a conical hub and vice versa. A rim intended for a conical hub must be installed in the proper direction. If the rim is not marked as described in the service manual, it must be inspected to determine which side has the greatest spoke angle. This will normally be the brake side.

Wheel lacing procedure

A symmetrical wheel is one of the easiest wheels to lace. Fig. 20-24 shows the basic steps for proper lacing of this type wheel. First, select matching components and organize your spokes carefully. Insert inside spokes into hub. Screw nipples onto spokes and tighten nipples equally. Install outside spokes and screw on nipples. Snug nipples evenly. Then, tighten spokes to true wheel.

Wheel trueing

WHEEL TRUEING is the process of:
1. Adjusting rim offset.
2. Adjusting radial runout.
3. Adjusting lateral runout.
4. Maintaining proper runout adjustment during final tightening of spokes.
A wheel trueing stand and good quality spoke wrenches are required for accurate wheel trueing.

LATERAL RUNOUT indicates how parallel the rim is to the hub. Lateral runout causes side to side wobble.

RADIAL RUNOUT shows how concentric (round) the rim is with the hub. Radial runout causes up and down movement. Fig. 20-25 shows lateral and radial runout.

It is important to understand how lateral and radial runout are changed. Fig. 20-26 shows adjustment of lateral runout. Fig. 20-27 shows how radial runout is adjusted. When adjusting either lateral or radial runout, adjust the wheel area with the least runout.

It is best to make an initial adjustment of lateral

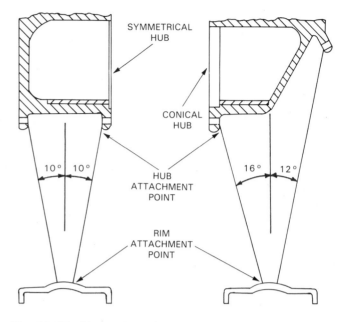

Fig. 20-23. Notice that spoke angle is same on each side of symmetrical hub, but is different on each side of conical hub.

runout first. This allows you to see how much radial runout is present. Next, make an initial adjustment of radial runout. At this point, all spokes should be snug. It may be necessary to alternately adjust lateral and radial runout.

Rim offset should now be checked, as in Fig. 20-28. The service manual usually gives rim offset specifications. RIM OFFSET is adjusted by loosening all the spokes on one side of the wheel and tightening all the spokes on the other side of the wheel. All spokes must be loosened or tightened the same amount to maintain minimum lateral and radial runout.

Important practices that make wheel trueing easier are:
1. Progressively tighten and loosen spoke nipples.
2. Keep all spokes at approximately the same tension (snug).
3. Lubricate spoke nipples and threads.
4. Do not try to change runout with only a few spokes.
5. Alternately check lateral and radial runout throughout trueing process.
6. Properly final tighten all spokes.

Final tightening of spokes

Proper final tightening of spokes should have minimal effect on runout. Use tape or crayon to divide the wheel into quarters (four sections), as illustrated in Fig. 20-29. Start by tightening quarter number one, then tighten number three, then number two, then number four. Make a final check of runout and offset. Also, check the spokes for the correct tightness. Use a spoke torque wrench or check them by tone.

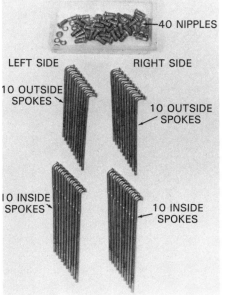

A—ORGANIZE ALL OF YOUR PARTS CAREFULLY.

B—INSTALL INSIDE SPOKES IN EACH SIDE OF HUB.

C—LAY RIM INTO POSITION AND START NIPPLES A FEW THREADS.

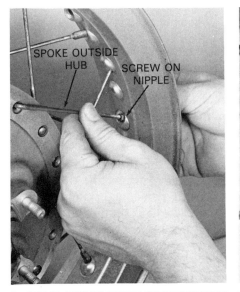

D—INSTALL OUTSIDE SPOKES. WORK YOUR WAY AROUND WHEEL, INSTALLING SPOKES ON ALTERNATE SIDES OF WHEEL.

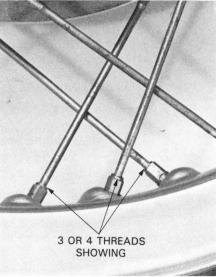

E—WITH ALL NIPPLES INSTALLED, EVENLY SNUG ALL NIPPLES WITH SPOKE WRENCH. TIGHTEN UNTIL THREE OR FOUR THREADS SHOW ABOVE EACH NIPPLE.

F—INSTALL WHEEL ASSEMBLY ON TRUEING STAND FOR FINAL TIGHTENING OF SPOKES AND TRUEING OF WHEEL.

Fig. 20-24. Study basic steps needed to lace a symmetrical wire wheel.

Maximum allowable runout will be listed in the service manual. It is best to get as close as possible to ZERO RUNOUT.

TIRES

Competent service methods and the correct choice of tire tread and size is essential to the safety of a motorcycle. This section of the chapter explains tire designs, sizes, markings, as well as maintenance and repair procedures. It will prepare you to use manufacturer recommendations when selecting and servicing motorcycle tires.

TIRE DESIGN

With the introduction of the "superbike," tire technology of the time became outdated. Recent years have seen staggering advances in tire design to accommodate today's motorcycles. Because some of these motorcycles are extremely powerful and heavy, better tires are needed to provide proper wear and handling characteristics. Some of the recent changes in tire design are:
1. New profiles (tire shapes).
2. Improved rubber compounds.
3. New tread designs.

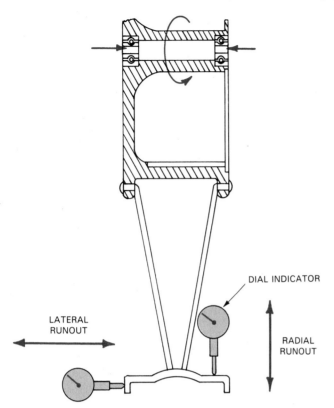

Fig. 20-25. Lateral runout is side to side movement or wobble of rim. Radial runout is up and down movement of rim. Note dial indicator positioning to measure each type of runout.

4. Introduction of tubeless tires.
5. Introduction of radial tires.
6. Sustained-speed tire rating.

There are basically three types of tires: road tires, dual-purpose tires, and off-road tires.

Fig. 20-30 shows an example of each type of tire. Because there are so many different designs available,

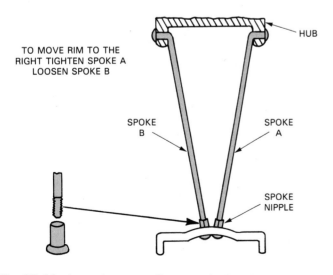

Fig. 20-26. Lateral runout adjustment is done by tightening or loosening spokes as shown.

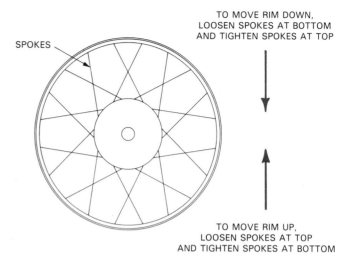

Fig. 20-27. Note basic method for radial runout adjustment.

it is advisable to follow manufacturer's suggestions regarding tire size and design.

TIRE SIZE

TIRE SIZE is determined by rim diameter and tire width at its widest point. Tire size markings are given on the tire sidewall. A typical tire size marking of 4.50H-17 means that the cross section (width) is 4.5 inches and is intended for a 17 inch rim.

Sustained speed tire markings

LETTERS appearing in the tire size markings indicate the sustained speed at which the tire is safe. For example, a tire with an "S" marking has been tested at a sustained speed of 112 mph (180 km/h) for six hours. The "H" rating indicates that the tire has been tested at a sustained speed of 130 mph (209 km/h) for six hours. A "V" rated tire has been tested at 150 mph (242 km/h) for six hours.

Maximum load rating and inflation pressure also appears on the sidewall. A tire balancing mark is provided and should be properly aligned. Refer to your service manual for details.

TIRE INSPECTION

For safety, tire condition should be checked occasionally. Visually inspect the tread and sidewall for cuts, aging cracks, and wear. Uneven tread wear can be caused by incorrect inflation pressure or an unbalanced tire. If a road hazard, such as a pothole, is struck it is very important to check the tire, rim, and spokes for possible damage.

TIRE SERVICE

Basically tire service includes changing a tire, repairing a flat tire, and balancing a tire and wheel assembly.

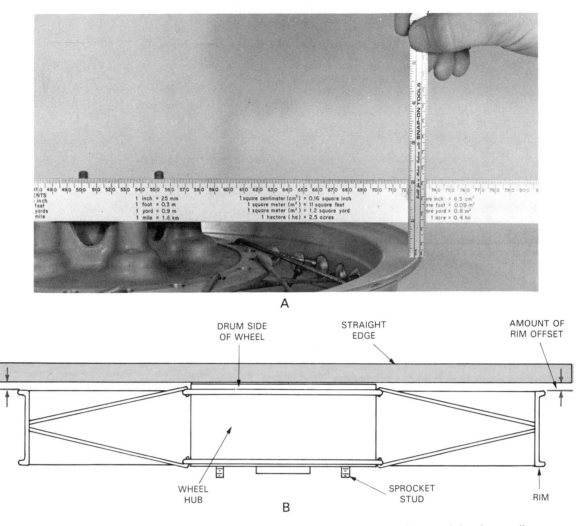

Fig. 20-28. Note procedures for adjusting rim offset. A—With disc brakes, place straightedge on disc mounting boss and measure to rim. B—With drum brakes, lay straightedge on drum edge and measure down to rim. Compare measurements with specifications. If specs are not given, rim must be centered.

Changing a tire

The basic steps for changing a tire are shown in Fig. 20-31. Refer to this illustration as each step is discussed.

To DEMOUNT A TIRE, unscrew and remove the valve core from the valve stem. This will deflate the

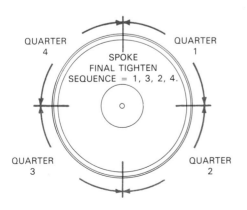

Fig. 20-29. Divide wheel into four sections to final tighten spokes. Tightening sequence is one, three, two, four. Tighten each spoke equally.

Fig. 20-30. Motorcycle tires vary in rubber compounds, profile, and tread pattern. A—High performance road tire suitable for "sport riding." B—Three universal designs are intended for use on road or in dirt. C—Trials universal design is also dual purpose but not as suitable for road use. D—Knobby design is strictly for off-road, dirt riding.

341

A—UNSCREW VALVE CORE AND STEM LOCKNUT.

B—FORCE TIRE OFF OUTER LIP OF RIM.

C—LUBRICATE TIRE BEAD TO AID REMOVAL.

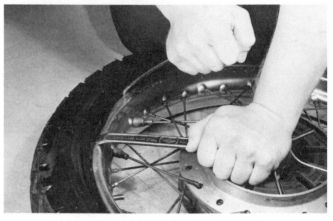

D—PRY BEAD OVER RIM WITH TIRE IRONS.

E—WORK WAY AROUND RIM WITH IRONS.

F—REMOVE TUBE AFTER FREEING ONE BEAD.

G—PRY OTHER BEAD OFF OF WHEEL.

H—CHECK UNDER STRIP FOR PROBLEMS.

Fig. 20-31. Study basic steps for removing a motorcycle tire from its wheel.

tire. Then, loosen the bead locks and remove the stem locknut.

Break the bead away from the rim. Stand on the tire or push the tire in with your hands. Lubricate the rim with rubber lubricant to aid removal and prevent tire damage.

Press one side of the tire into the drop center section of the wheel. This must be done for tire removal. Use a tire iron to pry the tire over the rim. Use two tire irons to pull the bead farther over the lip of the rim. Keep working the tire irons around the rim until the tire bead pops off the wheel.

With one bead removed, pull the tube out of the tire. Remove the other tire bead by prying with the irons. You may need to hit the tire with a rubber mallet to free it from the wheel.

After tire removal, pull the rubber rim strip off. Check under the strip for problems (rust, spokes protruding too far into wheel).

Tire installation is just as easy as removal. A tire changing machine makes tire changing easier and helps prevent damage to cast and stamped wheels.

Install a new inner tube when a new tire is installed or when the tube is punctured or has been previously patched.

To MOUNT A TIRE, follow the basic steps given in Fig. 20-32. Spray the tire bead with approved rubber lubricant. With the tire rotation arrow on the sidewall pointing in the right direction, force one bead over the rim. Pry with an iron. Keep the opposite bead held into the center of the wheel. Use two irons to work your way around the rim.

Carefully, fit the tube into the tire. Position the stem in the hole in the rim. Air up the tube to remove wrinkles which could damage the tube. Then, deflate the tube so that you can install the other bead.

Lubricate the other bead and work it over the rim with the tire irons.

CAUTION! Do NOT use screwdrivers to install a tire on a wheel. The sharp screwdrivers could damage the tube, possibly causing tube failure and rider injury.

A BEAD LOCK is a clamping device that pinches the tire beads against the rim. It prevents the tire from spinning on the wheel during periods of hard braking or rapid acceleration. Fig. 20-33 shows the

A—PUSH RIM INTO TIRE SO THAT ONE BEAD IS RESTING IN RIM STRIP AREA. PRY REMAINDER OF BEAD OVER RIM WITH TIRE IRON.

B—TUCK TUBE INTO TIRE. STICK STEM THROUGH HOLE IN RIM. SCREW LOCKNUT ONTO STEM ABOUT HALFWAY. AVOID KINKS IN TUBE.

C—PARTIALLY INFLATE TUBE TO REMOVE ANY WRINKLES OR FOLDS IN TUBE. THEN, DEFLATE TUBE BEFORE INSTALLING OTHER BEAD.

D—PRY OTHER BEAD OVER RIM WITHOUT PINCHING TUBE. INSTALL CORE. TIGHTEN STEM NUT AND INFLATE TIRE TO SPECS.

Fig. 20-32. Note basic procedures for installing a tire on a wheel.

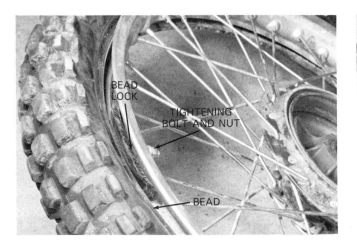

Fig. 20-33. A bead lock is used to prevent tire from slipping on rim. As bead lock is tightened, it pinches beads against rim.

Fig. 20-35. A tire pressure gauge is used to check air pressure in tires. This tire is inflated to 20 psi (138 kPa).

installation of a bead lock.

Before inflating the tire, double-check that the valve stem is straight. This is a common problem that can cause tube failure, Fig. 20-34. If the stem is cocked in the rim, remove one bead so that you can slide the tube around in the tire.

Inflate the tire and check that the tire beads are properly positioned on the rim. Use a pressure gauge to inflate the tire to exact specifications, Fig. 20-35.

Repairing a flat tire

It is not recommended to patch punctured or damaged inner tubes since it can cause an unsafe condition. This is especially true of road bike tires. Usually, a punctured tire can be repaired by installing a new tube. Be sure to remove the object that caused the puncture and thoroughly inspect the tire for sidewall damage, ply separation, or any condition that might make it unsafe.

Tubeless tires can sometimes be repaired with

special plug type patches. Follow the tire manufacturer's reommendations regarding repair of tubeless tires.

Balancing the tire and wheel assembly

Balance is changed whenever the tire is moved on the rim, or a new tire is installed. A bubble type balancing machine makes static (no movement) balancing a quick job. A bubble balancer suspends the wheel horizontally and uses a bubble to indicate the light side of the wheel. Lead weights are added until the bubble is centered, indicating the wheel is balanced, Fig. 20-36.

Fig. 20-34. A cocked valve stem can cause inner tube to rupture and leak where stem is bonded into tube. This produces a very dangerous situation.

Fig. 20-36. This type of balancing weight is slotted to slip over spoke and lock on spoke nipple.

BRAKES

Efficient operation of a brake system is of prime importance. To function safely, a brake system requires careful inspection and periodic maintenance. Important brake service considerations are:
1. Proper reassembly after wheel removal.
2. Maintaining proper brake adjustment.
3. Proper lubrication of mechanical components of the brake system.
4. Proper inspection to determine brake wear, and any need for brake service.

BRAKE OPERATION

A BRAKE is a device that changes kinetic energy (motion) into heat energy. Motorcycle braking is accomplished by the friction (resistance to movement) produced when BRAKE LINING (asbestos material) is forced against a rotating drum or disc. Friction between the linings and drum or disc stop wheel rotation, Fig. 20-37. Motorcycle brakes commonly use either hydraulic (fluid pressure) or mechanical (cable or linkage) mechanisms to apply the brakes.

Mechanical brakes

Shown in Fig. 20-38, a typical MECHANICAL BRAKE system consists of:
1. BRAKE LEVER (brake pedal).
2. BRAKE CABLE or rod (connects brake lever and cam arm).
3. STOPLIGHT SWITCH (operates brake light).
4. BRAKE CAM ARM (operates actuating cam).
5. BRAKE ACTUATING CAM (prys on and moves shoes toward drum).
6. BACKING PLATE (holds brake shoes and other parts).
7. BACKING PLATE TORQUE ARM (prevents rotation of backing plate).
8. DRUM (wheel hub friction surface attached to wheel).

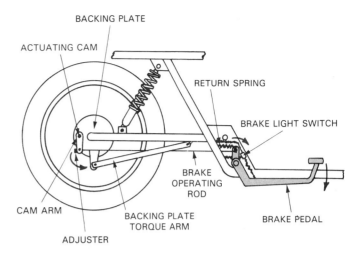

Fig. 20-38. Brake is applied by pressing down on brake pedal. This movement causes rotation of actuating cam which forces brake shoes into drum. Torque arm prevents backing plate from turning. Resulting friction slows down motorcycle.

9. SHOES (friction devices that fit into and rub on drum).
10. LININGS (asbestos friction material on shoes).
11. RETURN SPRINGS (hold shoes away from drum).

Movement of the brake lever or pedal, is transferred to the brake actuating cam by a cable or rod. Movement of the actuating cam forces the shoes into the drum, causing friction.

The stopping ability of the mechanical brake system is determined by:
1. The mechanical leverage of the system.
2. The surface area of the brake lining.
3. The composition of the brake lining.
4. The ability of the brake drum to dissipate heat.

A properly designed brake system will allow controllable lockup of the wheel.

HYDRAULIC BRAKES

In the hydraulic brake system, the lever or pedal as well as hydraulic fluid is used to achieve a mechanical advantage. The advantages of using hydraulic brakes are:
1. Equal pressure is provided in all directions within the system.
2. The system is self-adjusting.
3. It can produce very high pressure.
4. The system has low maintenance requirements.

A typical HYDRAULIC BRAKE system, Fig. 20-39, consists of:
1. BRAKE LEVER or PEDAL (pushes on master cylinder).
2. MASTER CYLINDER (produces pressure in brake system).
3. HYDRAULIC LINES (transfers hydraulic

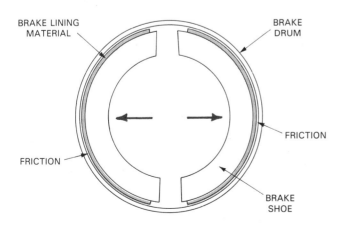

Fig. 20-37. Brake lining is forced outward against rotating drum. This causes friction and heat, which slows rotation of drum and wheel.

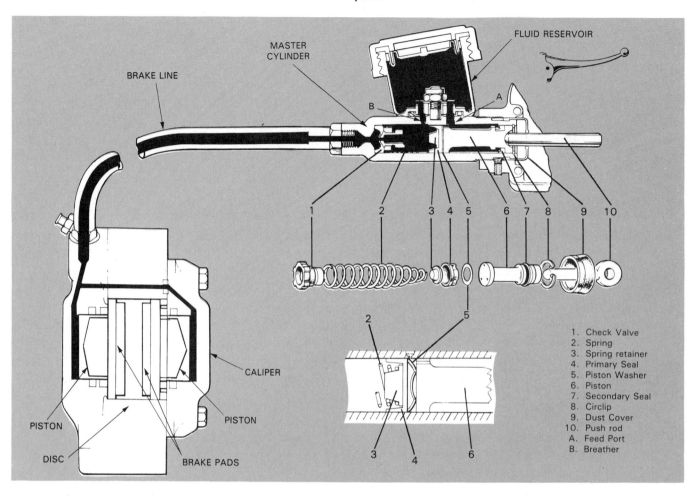

Fig. 20-39. When brake lever is pulled, it causes pushrod to move piston forward. Piston movement traps and pressurizes brake fluid in brake line and caliper. Line pressure causes caliper pistons to force brake pads against disc. (Triumph Motorcycles [Meriden] Ltd.)

pressure from master cylinder to wheel cylinder).
4. STOPLIGHT SWITCH (controls brake light).
5. CALIPER and WHEEL CYLINDER (clamp around disc).
6. DISC (attached to and stops wheel).

Movement of the brake lever or pedal causes the piston in the master cylinder to push fluid through the brake line. This fluid pressure is applied to the brake caliper piston, causing the brake pads to be squeezed against the disc. The clamping action causes friction, which slows the motorcycle.

Hydraulically operated drum brakes have been used on motorcycles but are no longer common. Hydraulic disc brakes are commonly used. The advantages of a hydraulic disc brake are: superior ability to dissipate heat, low maintenance requirements, and ease of maintenance.

HYDRAULIC THEORY

A hydraulic brake system is a closed system. When pressure is applied in a hydraulic system, it is transferred equally in all directions throughout the system.

A master cylinder, consisting of a piston, cylinder, and reservoir is used to apply pressure to the system. See Fig. 20-40. A piston and cylinder (caliper), mounted on the fork leg or swing arm, applies system pressure to the brake pads and disc.

Hydraulic brake systems are relatively simple if a few basic principles are understood:
1. Initial mechanical advantage is produced by the brake lever or pedal, Fig. 20-41. Pushing force going into the master cylinder is increased by the mechanical leverage of the lever arm.
2. Hydraulic fluid (brake fluid) in the system does NOT compress. This is important for proper operation.
3. Piston travel and pressure exerted is in direct proportion to piston sizes, Fig. 20-42.
4. Mechanical advantage is determined by comparing master cylinder and caliper piston sizes.
5. When pressure is released in the system, minimal clearance is maintained between the pad and disc.
6. Any air in the system will compress and drastically reduce braking effectiveness. The brake pedal or hand lever will feel spongy rather than solid.

Hydraulics, as applied to motorcycle brake

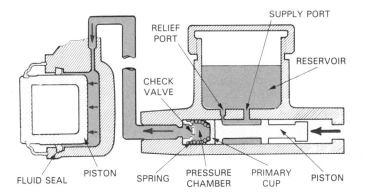

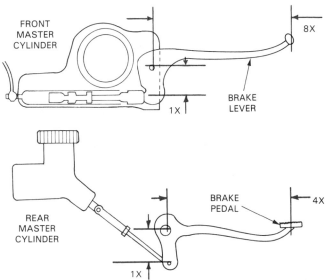

A—AS PISTON MOVES FORWARD IN MASTER CYLINDER, PRIMARY CUP PASSES SMALL RELIEF PORT. AS PRIMARY CUP CONTINUES FORWARD, PRESSURE IS BUILT UP IN SYSTEM. THIS PRESSURE IS EXERTED AGAINST CALIPER PISTON WHICH MOVES TOWARD DISC, PINCHING IT BETWEEN THE BRAKE PADS.

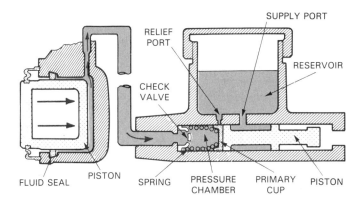

B—WHEN BRAKE PEDAL OR LEVER IS RELEASED, MASTER CYLINDER PISTON IS RAPIDLY RETURNED TO ITS REST POSITION BY SPRING. THIS ALLOWS PRESSURE TO DROP IN SYSTEM AS FLUID FLOWS THROUGH CHECK VALVE, RELIEF PORT, AND INTO RESERVOIR. CALIPER PISTON IS RETRACTED BY ITS SEAL.

Fig. 20-40. Study action of a basic master cylinder. (Kawasaki Motors Corp., U.S.A.)

Fig. 20-41. In a hydraulic brake system, initial mechanical advantage is provided by lever ratio of brake pedal or lever. With an 8:1 lever ratio, 1 lb. of pressure applied to brake lever results in 8 lbs. of pressure acting on master cylinder piston.

systems, provides mechanical advantage. A small cylinder and piston in the master cylinder operates a large piston and cylinder in the caliper. Piston movement in the master cylinder is greater than piston movement in the caliper. However, as shown in Fig. 20-43, clamping force (pressure) is much greater in the caliper.

BRAKE DESIGN

The two types of brake designs are the drum brake and disc brake. Both are used on today's motorcycles.

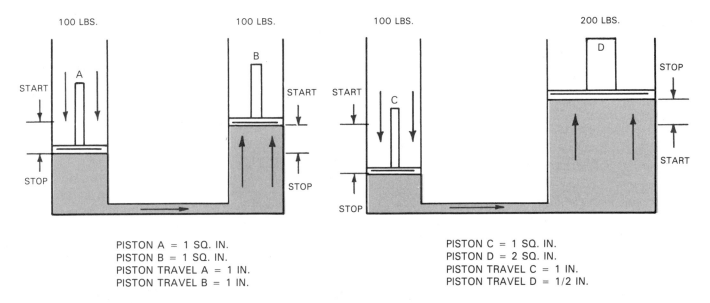

PISTON A = 1 SQ. IN.
PISTON B = 1 SQ. IN.
PISTON TRAVEL A = 1 IN.
PISTON TRAVEL B = 1 IN.

PISTON C = 1 SQ. IN.
PISTON D = 2 SQ. IN.
PISTON TRAVEL C = 1 IN.
PISTON TRAVEL D = 1/2 IN.

Fig. 20-42. Left. When hydraulic pistons A and B are same size, ratio is 1:1. Both pistons travel equal distance and exert equal pressure. Right. Piston D has twice the area of piston C. 100 lb. of pressure applied to piston C, results in 200 lb. of pressure at piston D. Also note difference in piston movements.

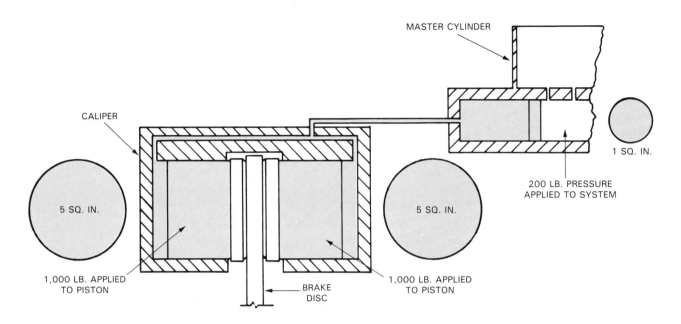

Fig. 20-43. When master cylinder piston has an area of one sq. in. and each caliper piston has an area of five sq. in., we have a ten to one ratio. Pressure of 200 lb. applied to system by master cylinder results in 1,000 lb. of pressure acting on each caliper piston. This gives 2,000 lb. of pressure applied to disc. Different hydraulic ratios are used depending on design and application.

Drum brakes

There are two basic drum brake designs: single-leading shoe and double-leading shoe.

Fig. 20-44 shows a simple SINGLE-LEADING SHOE type drum brake. As the actuating cam is rotated, it forces the shoes outward and into the brake drum. Notice that the shoes are supported by a pivot opposite the actuator cam.

A single-leading shoe brake has one shoe (leading shoe) being applied with wheel rotation, and the other shoe (trailing shoe) being applied against wheel rotation. See Fig. 20-45. As the leading shoe contacts the brake drum, it has a tendency to wedge itself against the drum. This wedging or self-actuating action causes the leading shoe to drag with more power than the trailing shoe.

If the drum was rotated in the opposite direction, the trailing shoe would then become the leading shoe. Single-leading shoe brakes are used on the front and rear of many dirt bikes, and also on the rear of a few road bikes.

A DOUBLE-LEADING SHOE brake uses an ac-

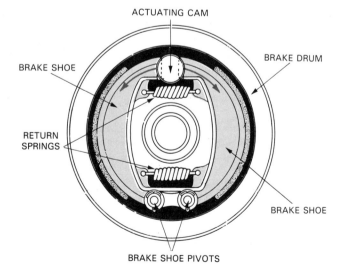

Fig. 20-44. Single-leading shoe brake uses one actuating cam to operate both brake shoes. (Kawasaki Motors Corp., U.S.A.)

Fig. 20-45. In single-leading shoe brake, notice that leading shoe rotates on its pivot in same direction as brake drum. Trailing shoe rotates in opposite direction. (Kawasaki Motors Corp., U.S.A.)

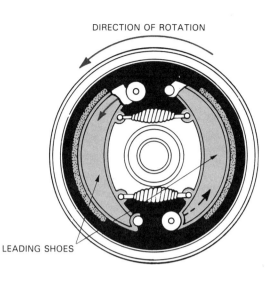

DIRECTION OF ROTATION

LEADING SHOES

Fig. 20-46. Double-leading shoe brake uses two actuating cams and two pivots. Both shoes rotate on their pivots in same direction as brake drum. (Kawasaki Motors Corp., U.S.A.)

tuating cam and pivot for each shoe, Fig. 20-46. Since each shoe can rotate into the drum as the brake is applied, both shoes are leading (self-actuating). This design provides greater braking force than the single-leading shoe design. A double-leading shoe brake is used on the front of some road and dirt bikes.

Disc brake

Disc brakes can be actuated hydraulically or mechanically. The hydraulic design is more common. However, mechanical calipers have been used. Hydraulic disc brakes use two types of calipers: single-piston floating caliper and double-piston caliper.

A SINGLE-PISTON FLOATING CALIPER has one moveable piston and pad and one stationary pad. This is shown in Fig. 20-47. As the brake is applied, force is applied to the piston. Piston movement causes the caliper to FLOAT (move on mount), pinching the disc between the pads, Fig. 20-48.

The advantage of this design is that it is inexpensive to produce. It also will compensate for slight disc runout (warpage) without severe vibration when braking.

A DOUBLE-PISTON CALIPER is rigidly mounted to the fork leg. Two moveable pistons and pads pinch the disc when the brake is applied, Fig. 20-49. Brake fluid is supplied to the caliper under pressure by a single line. A crossover passageway inside the caliper connects both halves of the caliper.

BRAKE INSPECTION, MAINTENANCE, AND REPAIR

Brake inspection should be done during routine maintenance or if a problem is suspected. A complete inspection of the drum brake system requires wheel

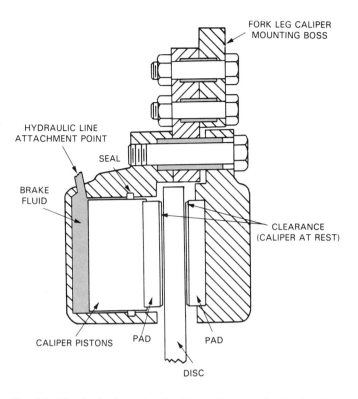

FORK LEG CALIPER MOUNTING BOSS

HYDRAULIC LINE ATTACHMENT POINT

SEAL

BRAKE FLUID

CLEARANCE (CALIPER AT REST)

CALIPER PISTONS   PAD   PAD

DISC

Fig. 20-47. A single-piston floating caliper applies hydraulic pressure to only one piston.

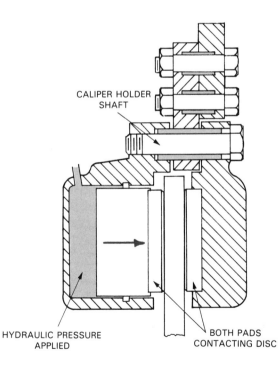

CALIPER HOLDER SHAFT

HYDRAULIC PRESSURE APPLIED

BOTH PADS CONTACTING DISC

Fig. 20-48. As hydraulic pressure is applied, piston moves pad toward disc. When it makes contact with disc, caliper body floats on caliper shaft. This brings caliper pad into contact with disc. As further pressure is applied, disc is pinched between both pads.

removal. A disc brake system can be checked without wheel removal.

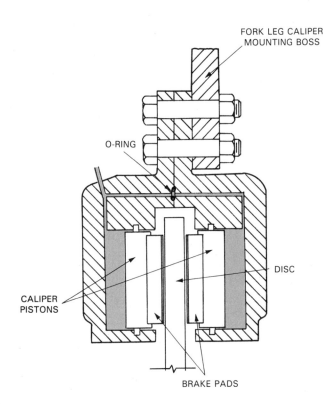

Fig. 20-49. Double-piston caliper is rigidly mounted to fork leg or swing arm. Hydraulic pressure is applied equally to pistons on each side of caliper.

NOTE! Any work done on a motorcycle brake system is a serious matter, a life or death matter. Brake repairs must be done carefully and accurately. The slightest mistake could cause an accident.

BRAKE INSPECTION involves checking for smooth operation and for worn or damaged parts. You must look for any problem that could make the system unsafe.

BRAKE MAINTENANCE is the routine adjustment and lubrication of the brake system. The service manual will give intervals for system maintenance.

BRAKE REPAIR is the replacement or repair of damaged or worn components discovered during brake inspection.

The three operations: inspection, maintenance, and repair, should be dealt with as one operation. It is imperative that the service manual be followed to insure accurate and safe brake service. Liability suits can result from inaccurate, unsafe brake system repairs. Also, pay special attention to vulnerable parts of the brake system if the motorcycle has crash damage.

DRUM BRAKE SERVICE SUMMARY

To help make sure that you do not forget any step during drum brake service and repair, use the following summary as a general guide.

1. Inspect the brake lever and brake pedal mechanism. Make sure they are in good

operating condition.
2. Check the brake cable and brake rod. Look for wear, damage, or improper adjustment.
3. Check the operation and adjustment of the brake light switches. Make sure the brake light functions.
4. Make sure the brake pedal and brake cable return springs are working.
5. Check the brake cam arm and backing plate torque arm.

NOTE! Wheel removal is required for the remaining operations.

6. Check backing plate for damage and wear.
7. Make sure the brake actuating cam is in good condition.
8. Inspect all grease seals for wear, damage, or leakage.
9. Check the wheel bearings. Make sure they are well lubricated and roll freely.
10. Inspect the brake drum. Look for wear, cracks, grooves, or other problems.
11. Check the brake shoe linings for wear. Also, check the linings for glazing (shiny, hardened condition due to overheating).
12. Inspect the brake shoe return springs. They should not be discolored from overheating and should be installed properly.

RULES FOR BRAKE REPAIRS

Listed are ten basic rules to follow when working on motorcycle brakes. They will help you complete a competent repair.

1. Do not inhale brake dust.
2. Use a service manual to compare measurements with specifications.
3. Components must be replaced if they do not meet specifications.
4. Use brake parts cleaner or alcohol to clean drum and shoes.
5. Do not get lubricants on brake lining or drum.
6. Refer to service manual for proper lubrication and reassembly procedures.
7. Always use new lock tabs and cotter pins.
8. Be sure cables are properly seated in sockets.
9. Adjust drive chain if rear wheel was removed.
10. Center the brake shoes by applying brakes before and while tightening axle.

RELINING DRUM BRAKES

RELINING DRUM BRAKES involves the replacement of the shoe lining material. All current designs use bonded lining (lining glued to brake shoe). Some earlier designs use rivets to attach the lining material to the brake shoe. When relining brakes which use bonded shoes, the complete shoe must be replaced.

CAUTION! Do not inhale brake dust. It contains ASBESTOS which is a CANCER causing substance.

To replace worn or defective shoes on drum brakes, follow the general steps listed below. Refer to a service manual for specific instructions.

1. Remove the wheel and completely disassemble the backing plate, Fig. 20-50.
2. Clean and inspect drum surface.

A—REMOVE WHEEL FROM MOTORCYCLE. THEN REMOVE BACKING PLATE.

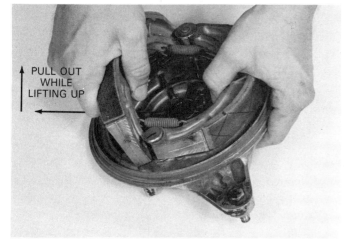

B—DISASSEMBLE BACKING PLATE. PULL OUT AND LIFT UP ON SHOES.

PULL OUT WHILE LIFTING UP

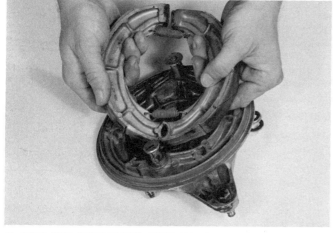

C—ONCE FREE FROM PIVOTS, SHOE AND SPRING ASSEMBLY CAN BE REMOVED AS A UNIT.

Fig. 20-50. Note basic steps for disassembly of drum brakes.

3. Measure drum inside diameter. Maximum serviceable diameter is usually found stamped inside the drum, or in the service manual. See Fig. 20-51.
4. Clean backing plate and actuating cam.
5. Put masking tape over the entire lining surface of the new brake shoes, Fig. 20-52. This reduces the chance of contaminating the linings with lubricants or brake fluid.
6. Lubricate actuating cam(s), Fig. 20-52. Make sure brake arm and cam are timed properly. Refer to your service manual.
7. Reassemble backing plate using new brake springs, Fig. 20-53.
8. Remove protective tape from linings.
9. Install wheel and brake assembly. Refer to your service manual.

HYDRAULIC BRAKE SYSTEM SUMMARY

The following summary provides general steps for inspecting, maintaining, and repairing a hydraulic

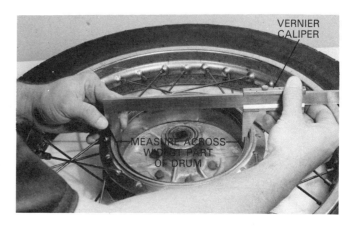

VERNIER CALIPER

MEASURE ACROSS WIDEST PART OF DRUM

Fig. 20-51. Use a Vernier or dial caliper to measure drum wear. Maximum allowable drum diameter is stamped inside drum. If diameter exceeds this specification, replace drum.

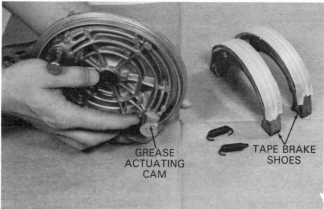

GREASE ACTUATING CAM

TAPE BRAKE SHOES

Fig. 20-52. Tape brake shoes to help prevent contaminating them during backing plate assembly. Lightly grease actuating cam with high temperature grease.

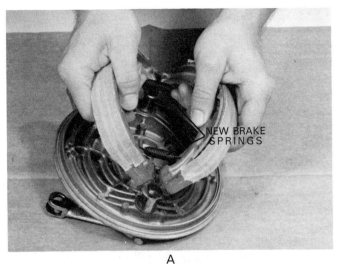

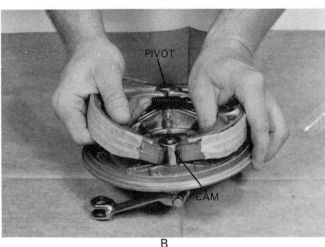

Fig. 20-53. Assemble backing plate using new brake springs. A—Begin by folding shoes into position over pivot and cam. B—Then push shoes flat against backing plate.

brake system. Use it and a service manual during actual service and repair operations.

BRAKE SYSTEM INSPECTION

1. Inspect the brake caliper mounting bracket.
2. Check the action of the brake pedal and lever.
3. Check the master cylinder linkage and fluid level.
4. Inspect the torque arm for signs of trouble.
5. Check the wheel bearings for looseness or roughness.
6. Inspect dust seals for deterioration or damage.
7. Observe the operation of the brake lights.
8. Check brake pad thickness. Many disc brake pads have wear indicators (tabs or groove) that allow inspection without disassembly.
9. Check the brake disc for wear, scoring, or cracks.

   If you find any problems during your inspection, correct them right away. Always remember that the brake system is critical to a safe motorcycle. It is up to you to keep the brake system in perfect operating condition.

IMPORTANT BRAKE SERVICE INFORMATION

1. Do NOT allow brake fluid to come into contact with painted surfaces. It acts like a powerful paint remover.
2. Use new DOT 3 or DOT 5 brake fluid. Refer to proper manual for details.
3. Do NOT allow grease or brake fluid to come into contact with the brake linings, disc, or drum.
4. Use service manual directions for carrying out all adjustments and repairs.

CHANGING BRAKE FLUID

Brake fluid should be changed every two years. This is necessary because brake fluid can become contaminated with moisture and other substances. The boiling point (temperature causes bubbles to form) of contaminated brake fluid is lower. Contaminated fluid can also corrode brake system parts.

Use the following procedures and Fig. 20-54 as a general guide for changing brake fluid:

1. Fit a piece of clear hose over the bleeder valve. Submerge the other end of the hose in a container of brake fluid, A.
2. Open the bleeder valve. Use a tubing wrench, B.
3. Pump the master cylinder until about 1/16 in. (1.6 mm) of fluid remains in the reservoir.
4. Use a clean shop rag or towel to soak up the remainder of the fluid in the reservoir. This will help to remove any dirt or other foreign matter from the bottom of the master cylinder, C.
5. Fill reservoir with new DOT 3 or DOT 5 brake fluid, D.
6. Repeat steps 3 and 5 until clear brake fluid comes out of bleeder valve.
7. Close bleeder valve and fill reservoir to proper level.
8. Check brake operation and bleed system if necessary.

BLEEDING HYDRAULIC BRAKES

BLEEDING HYDRAULIC BRAKES involves forcing any air bubbles out of the system. Air is compressible and will upset the operation of a hydraulic system. Air can enter a motorcycle brake system when a hydraulic component is removed for service. Air can also enter the system when the master cylinder runs dry or the system develops a leak.

Follow these basic procedures and Fig. 20-55 for bleeding a hydraulic brake system.

1. Fill reservoir to proper level.
2. Pump pressure into system using lever or pedal. Then, hold pressure on lever or pedal, A.
3. Open bleed valve, and watch air bubbles in clear tubing, B.
4. Close bleed valve, C.
5. Release lever or pedal.

A—CLEAR BLEEDING TUBE INSERTED INTO A CONTAINER OF BRAKE FLUID SIMPLIFIES BRAKE BLEEDING. BUBBLES ARE EASY TO SEE IN TUBE. AIR IS NOT EASILY PULLED BACK INTO SYSTEM AND THERE IS NO MESS TO CLEAN UP.

B—OPEN BLEEDER VALVE AND PUMP FLUID INTO BLEEDING CONTAINER. DO NOT PUMP FLUID RESERVOIR COMPLETELY DRY OR YOU WILL PUSH AIR INTO SYSTEM.

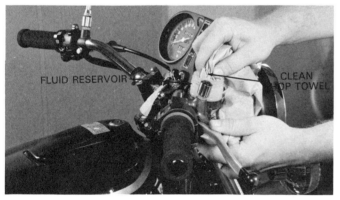

C—USE A CLEAN, LINT FREE SHOP TOWEL OR PAPER TOWEL TO CLEAN LAST OF FLUID AND SEDIMENT FROM FLUID RESERVOIR.

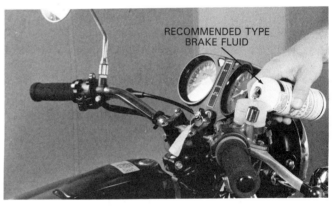

D—FILL RESERVOIR WITH PROPER FLUID. REFER TO MANUAL TO DETERMINE WHETHER DOT 3 OR DOT 5 FLUID SHOULD BE USED.

Fig. 20-54. Note general steps for changing fluid in a motorcycle brake system.

6. Bleed again as in steps 2 through 5 until there are no air bubbles visible when bleed valve is opened, D. Keep master cylinder full to prevent air from getting into the system.

MASTER CYLINDER AND CALIPER REBUILDING

Remember the following important information when rebuilding a master cylinder or caliper:
1. Always use new OEM (original equipment manufacturer) parts, if possible.
2. Use only alcohol or DOT 3 or DOT 5 brake fluid for cleaning parts which are exposed to brake fluid.
3. Discard all old brake fluid.
4. Use new DOT 3 or DOT 5 brake fluid for

assembly and servicing of the system.
5. Do NOT allow oil, grease, or brake fluid to come into contact with the brake disc or pads.
6. Refer to the service manual for exact specifications and procedures.
7. Always bleed the system after reassembly.

Master cylinder rebuilding procedures
1. Remove and disassemble master cylinder following manual instructions, Fig. 20-56.
2. Clean all parts thoroughly.
3. Check for blocked fluid passages.
4. Measure piston diameter, Fig. 20-57, A.
5. Measure bore diameter, Fig. 20-57, B.
6. Measure return spring free length, Fig. 20-57, C.

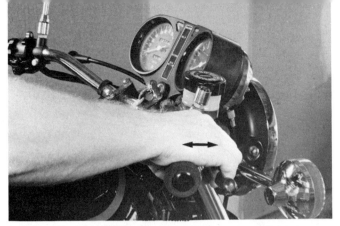

A—WITH STEADY STROKES OF LEVER OR PEDAL, PUMP PRESSURE INTO SYSTEM WITH MASTER CYLINDER.

B—MAINTAIN PRESSURE WITH LEVER OR PEDAL AND OPEN BLEEDER VALVE. NOTICE TINY AIR BUBBLES IN BLEEDING HOSE.

C—CLOSE BLEEDER VALVE BEFORE RELEASING LEVER OR PEDAL TO PREVENT AIR FROM BEING DRAWN BACK INTO SYSTEM.

D—CONTINUE BLEEDING UNTIL THERE ARE NO AIR BUBBLES IN BLEEDING TUBE.

Fig. 20-55. Study basic steps needed to bleed air out of hydraulic brake system.

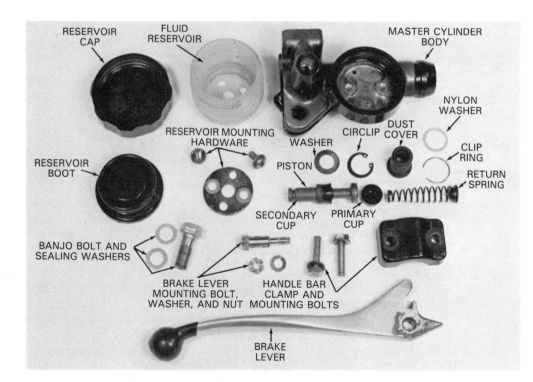

Fig. 20-56. Completely disassemble master cylinder before cleaning parts in brake fluid or alcohol.

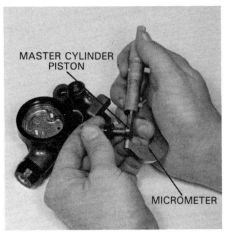
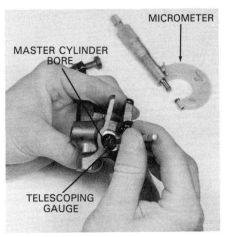
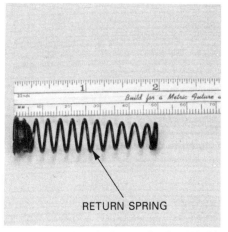

A—OUTSIDE MICROMETER IS USED TO MEASURE MASTER CYLINDER PISTON.

B—MASTER CYLINDER BORE DIAMETER IS MEASURED USING A TELESCOPING GAUGE AND OUTSIDE MICROMETER.

C—USE A MACHINIST'S RULE OR CALIPER TO CHECK RETURN SPRING FREE LENGTH.

Fig. 20-57. These three measurements are especially critical when rebuilding a master cylinder.

7. Inspect all parts for damage.
8. Replace all rubber parts, unless instructed not to by service manual.
9. Reassemble using new DOT 3 or DOT 5 brake fluid, Fig. 20-58.
10. Reinstall master cylinder.
11. Fill system with new DOT 3 or DOT 5 brake fluid.
12. Bleed brakes.

Caliper rebuilding procedures
1. Remove and disassemble caliper, Fig. 20-59.
2. Clean all parts except brake pads.
3. Inspect pads for wear, oil, grease, Fig. 20-60.
4. Measure caliper piston diameter, Fig. 20-61, A.
5. Measure caliper bore diameter, Fig. 20-61, B.
6. Inspect all parts for damage. Install new rubber parts.

7. Assemble using new DOT 3 or DOT 5 brake fluid, Fig. 20-62.
8. Install and torque caliper. Follow service manual instructions and torque specs, Fig. 20-63.
9. Connect hydraulic line, Fig. 20-63.
10. Fill system with new DOT 3 or DOT 5 fluid.
11. Bleed brakes.

KNOW THESE TERMS

Hub, Nipple, Cross-pattern, Cast wheel, Stamped wheel, Repacking bearings, Lacing, Trueing, Spoke Crossing pattern, Spoke angle, Lateral runout, Radial runout, Tire size, Bead lock, Bubble balancer, Mechanical brakes, Hydraulic brakes, Master Cylinder, Brake lining, Single-leading shoe, Double-leading shoe, Single-piston floating caliper, Double-piston caliper, Asbestos, Bleeding.

A—LUBRICATE ALL MOVING PARTS WITH CLEAN FLUID AND INSTALL RETURN SPRING.

B—SLIDE PISTON AND CUP ASSEMBLY IN MASTER CYLINDER BORE.

C—ASSEMBLE REMAINING PARTS, INCLUDING FLUID RESERVOIR.

Fig. 20-58. Use these fundamental steps and a service manual to properly reassemble master cylinder.

Fig. 20-59. To remove piston when disassembling a caliper, use compressed air to blow into brake line hole. Clean all parts in alcohol or new brake fluid.

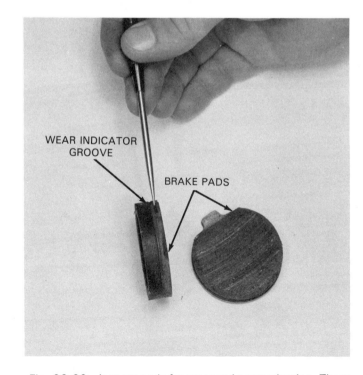

Fig. 20-60. Inspect pads for wear and contamination. These pads have groove type wear indicator. If worn to groove, pads are worn out.

REVIEW QUESTIONS—CHAPTER 20

1. The three types of wheels used on today's motorcycle are:
2. The weight of the motorcycle hangs from the top spokes of the wheels. True or False?
3. The spacer between the wheel bearings serves no other function than to direct grease to the bearings. True or False?
4. List four of the checks made during wheel inspection.
5. All wheel bearings are removed from the hub in the same manner. True or False?
6. What are the three ways to check for loose spokes?
7. It is usually necessary to completely disassemble a wheel to replace a few broken spokes. True or False?
8. After rim replacement, you must always _____ the wheel to prevent runout.
9. Define "Spoke cross pattern."
10. Conical and symmetrical hubs have the same spoke cross pattern and spoke angle. True or False?
11. A rim intended for a _____ type hub has a

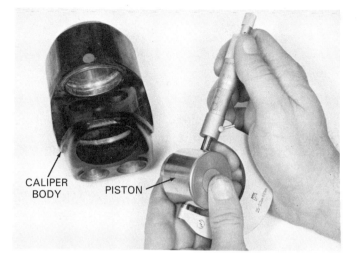

A—USE A MICROMETER TO MEASURE CALIPER PISTON DIAMETER.

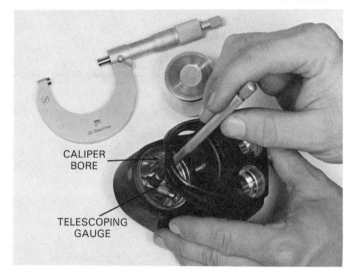

B—MEASURE CALIPER BORE DIAMETER USING A TELESCOPING GAUGE AND MICROMETER. ALSO, CHECK BORE FOR SCORING OR PITTING.

Fig. 20-61. Difference between piston diameter and caliper bore diameter determines piston clearance. If beyond specs, worn components must be replaced.

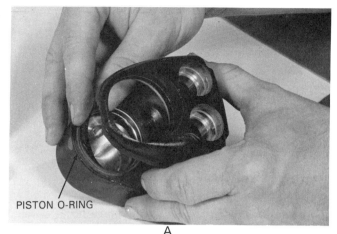

A

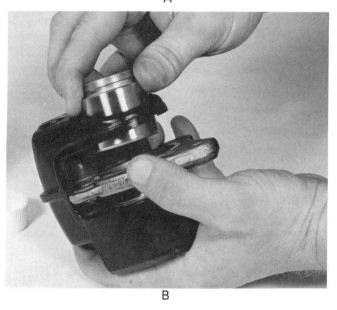

B

Fig. 20-62. When assembling a caliper, lubricate parts with new brake fluid. A—When installing piston O-ring, be sure it is not twisted. B—Install piston carefully.

left and right side and must be installed a certain way.

12. List four adjustments needed to true a wheel.
13. Name two factors that can cause uneven tire tread wear.
14. How do you tell the correct direction of tire rotation?
15. When should a new inner tube be installed?
16. A brake changes kinetic energy into _____ energy.
17. A _____ brake system uses rods, levers, and cams to apply the brakes. A confined fluid is not used.
18. A _____ brake system is self-adjusting and uses a confined fluid.
19. How many actuating cams does a double-leading shoe drum brake use?
20. Proper drum brake inspection requires wheel

Fig. 20-63. Install caliper and tighten bolts with a torque wrench. Then install brake line and bleed system.

removal. True or False?

21. Applying a drum type brake while tightening the axle nut actually helps to _____ the brake shoes.

22. Why is it necessary to change brake fluid every two years?

23. List three possible ways air can enter a hydraulic brake system.

24. To remove air from a brake system, you must _____ the system.

25. Which of the following is NOT done when bleeding brakes?
    a. Pump lever or pedal to build pressure.
    b. Open bypass valve.
    c. Fill master cylinder reservoir.
    d. Look for bubbles in hose.

SUGGESTED ACTIVITIES

1. Remove and install a tire.
2. Completely disassemble, lace, and true a wire wheel assembly, listing all problems.
3. Remove, clean, inspect, repack, and install a set of wheel bearings.
4. Change fluid and bleed a hydraulic brake system. Always refer to the proper service manual and note any safety instructions.

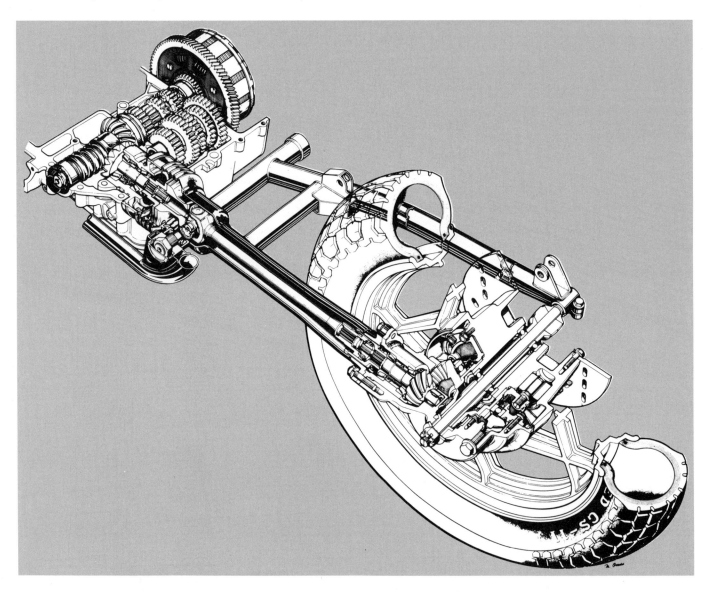

How many parts can you name and explain in this illustration?   (U.S. Suzuki Motor Corporation)

Chapter 21

FINAL DRIVE SYSTEMS

After studying this chapter, you will be able to:
- ☐ List the types of final drives used on today's motorcycles.
- ☐ Describe the operation and parts of chain, belt, and shaft type final drives.
- ☐ Summarize the procedures for inspecting, maintaining, and servicing final drive systems.

As you learned in Chapter 1, a final drive transfers power from the gearbox to the rear wheel. This chapter discusses, in more detail, how each type of final drive functions. The chapter also covers common adjustments, repairs, and maintenance operations performed on final drive systems.

FINAL DRIVE DESIGNS

There are three final drive designs: chain drive, belt drive, and shaft drive. It is important that you understand the similarities and differences of each design. This will help prepare you to work on any final drive system.

CHAIN DRIVE

The chain type final drive is simple, inexpensive, light weight, and easy to maintain. A typical chain drive is made up of a drive sprocket, drive chain, and driven sprocket. These parts are shown in Fig. 21-1.

Sprockets

The front sprocket (countershaft sprocket) and rear sprocket are made of sheet steel or aluminum. The countershaft sprocket drives the chain. The rear sprocket drives the wheel.

Roller chain

A ROLLER CHAIN is made up of pin links, roller links, and a master link.

A PIN LINK consists of two side plates with two steel pins riveted to the side plates, Fig. 21-2. The pin link connects the roller links.

A ROLLER LINK is made up of two side plates, two bushings pressed into the side plates, and two rollers surrounding the bushings, Fig. 21-3.

Fig. 21-1. With chain type final drive, small front sprocket drives roller chain. Chain drives large rear sprocket and wheel.

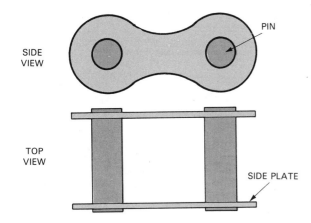

Fig. 21-2. A pin link consists of two side plates riveted to two pins.

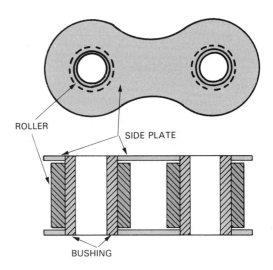

Fig. 21-3. A roller link is made up of two side plates pressed onto bushings. Rollers surround bushings.

A MASTER LINK is a pin link which has a removable side plate, Fig. 21-4. It allows the chain to be separated easily. For instance, the master link will allow chain removal without rear wheel removal.

Chain design variations

There are three basic variations in roller chain design. These include the O-ring chain, solid impregnated roller chain, and endless chain.

The O-RING CHAIN uses O-rings between the side plates of the pin and roller links. This seals in lubrication but keeps moisture and dirt out. Look at Fig. 21-5.

An impregnated SOLID ROLLER CHAIN uses a single nonrotating roller. This solid roller is filled with lubricant and takes the place of the bushing and roller.

An ENDLESS CHAIN is one which does NOT use a master link with a removable side plate. Instead, the master link is riveted in the same manner as all other pin links of the chain.

Note however, all three chain variations may be used in one chain.

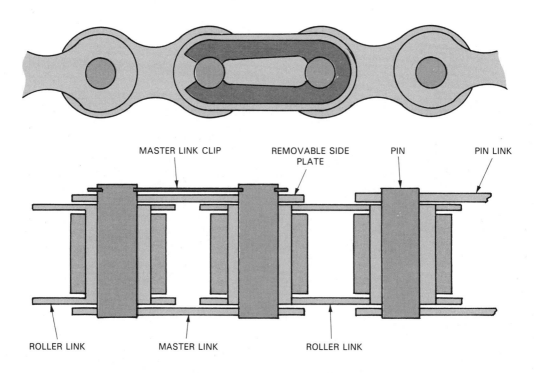

Fig. 21-4. A roller chain uses pin links to connect a number of roller links together. A master link is simply a pin link with a removable side plate. Side plate is held in place by a clip. This allows ends of chain to be connected and disconnected easily.

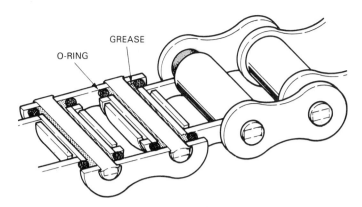

Fig. 21-5. O-ring chain requires minimal maintenance. O-rings between side plates seal lubrication in and contaminants out. Regular lubrication of rollers is required, however.
(U.S. Suzuki Motor Corporation)

Chain lubrication

Chain lubrication is necessary to prevent premature wear. A motorcycle drive chain is exposed to extreme loading, stress, and directional change. Proper lubrication is essential to prevent galling of

moving parts (rollers, pins, bushings, side plates, sprocket teeth). See Fig. 21-6.

BELT DRIVE

BELT DRIVE is similar in appearance to chain drive but uses a reinforced, toothed rubber belt and special sprockets. See Fig. 21-7.

A belt final drive system does not require as much maintenance as the chain drive system. Frequent adjustment is not needed and lubricant should NOT be used. A belt drive also is very quiet.

SHAFT DRIVE

A shaft drive is a fully sealed and internally lubricated final drive system which provides an alternative to chain drive. Shown in Fig. 21-8, a typical SHAFT DRIVE SYSTEM consists of:
1. A 90 deg. drive from the gearbox output shaft (only with transverse in-line engines).
2. Spline coupling (slip joint).
3. Universal joint (swivel joint).
4. Drive shaft (propeller shaft) and swing arm.

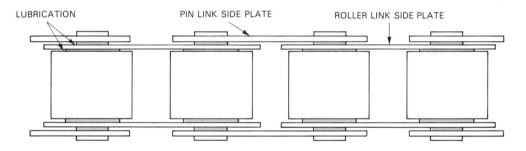

Fig. 21-6. Lubricant must be applied between side plates of pin links and roller links. Proper application allows lubricant to penetrate into space between pins and bushings, where it is needed most.

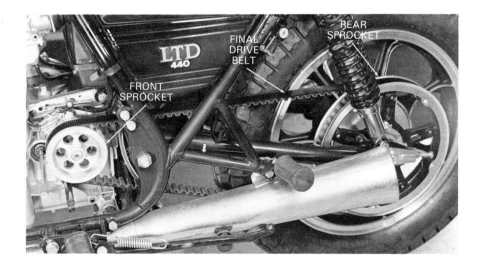

Fig. 21-7. Belt drive tension adjustment is done by moving rear axle. Set tension using service manual procedures.

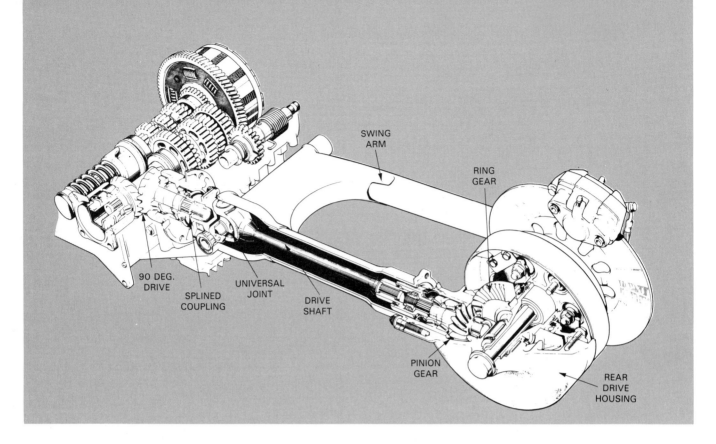

Fig. 21-8. Shaft drive uses setup similar to rear-wheel drive automobile. Study part names and locations. (U.S. Suzuki Motor Corporation)

5. Pinion gear (drive, spiral bevel gear).
6. Ring gear (driven, spiral bevel gear).
7. Rear drive housing (gear enclosure).

LUBRICATION for the shaft drive system is provided by gear lubricant (bath) in the rear housing and by grease in the sealed universal joint.

The advantages of a shaft drive system are:
1. Low maintenance requirements.
2. Self-contained lubrication.
3. Almost constant wheel base (distance between front and rear axles).
4. Quiet operation.
5. Long life.

FINAL DRIVE RATIO

OVERALL GEAR RATIO is the relationship of rear wheel speed to crankshaft speed. Discussed in Chapter 6, Primary Drive and Gearbox, there are three places for gear reduction: primary drive, gearbox, and final drive.

A chain type FINAL DRIVE RATIO refers to the number of teeth on the front sprocket versus the number of teeth on the rear sprocket. See Fig. 21-9. In a shaft drive system, this ratio refers to the number of teeth on the pinion gear versus the number of teeth on the ring gear, Fig. 21-10.

Changing final drive ratio

Chain drive ratio changes are accomplished by changing one or both sprockets. Shaft drive ratio

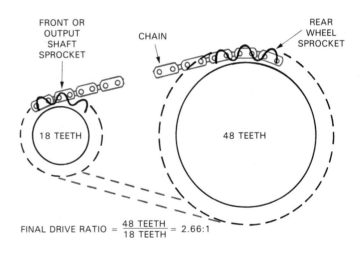

$$\text{FINAL DRIVE RATIO} = \frac{48 \text{ TEETH}}{18 \text{ TEETH}} = 2.66{:}1$$

Fig. 21-9. Final drive ratio is found by dividing number of teeth on rear sprocket by number of teeth on front sprocket.

changes require changing both the ring and pinion. It is costly and much more involved to change shaft drive ratio.

If a smaller front sprocket or larger rear sprocket is installed, this will generally increase acceleration but reduce top speed. A larger diameter front sprocket and smaller rear sprocket tends to reduce acceleration but increase top speed.

The same is true for shaft drive. A pinion gear with less teeth and ring gear with more teeth can improve acceleration but will reduce top speed as well as gas mileage. The opposite ratio change will have reverse

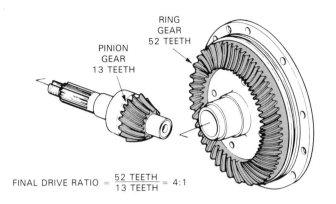

FINAL DRIVE RATIO = $\frac{52 \text{ TEETH}}{13 \text{ TEETH}}$ = 4:1

Fig. 21-10. Shaft drive final drive ratio is achieved by dividing number of teeth on ring gear (52) by number of teeth on pinion gear (13). In this example, final drive ratio is 4:1. (Kawasaki Motors Corp., U.S.A.)

effects on performance.

Normally, the stock ratio provides the best all-around performance. Manufacturers choose a final drive ratio which is suitable to the majority of riders. Final drive ratio may need to be changed when:
1. The motorcycle is used for competition purposes.
2. The motorcycle is heavily loaded (fairing, saddle bags, sidecar, touring equipment).
3. Better fuel economy is desired.
4. Higher top speed is desired.

CHAIN DRIVE INSPECTION, SERVICE, AND REPAIR

The chain drive system is an efficient and inexpensive means of transferring power from the gearbox to the rear wheel. However, the chain drive system generally requires more maintenance than a shaft drive system.

A chain drive system requires: lubrication, adjustment, alignment, and inspection for wear. Replacement of the chain and sprockets may also be needed from time to time.

CHAIN DRIVE LUBRICATION

A chain drive system may be lubricated two ways:
1. Automatic chain oiler (oil drips out of engine lubrication system onto chain).
2. Manual lubrication (rider must periodically apply oil to chain).
Chain lubrication intervals vary from motorcycle to motorcycle and with operating conditions. Frequent visual inspection is necessary to assure adequate lubrication. Never let a chain run dry or rapid wear will result.

CHAIN ADJUSTMENT AND ALIGNMENT

CHAIN ADJUSTMENT is the positioning of the rear wheel and sprocket to provide proper chain free

play (tension) and alignment. Look at Fig. 21-11. Chain adjustment is required because of chain and sprocket wear.

Chain tension and alignment can be adjusted by moving the rear wheel and axle or by moving the complete swing arm and wheel assembly. Movement of the rear wheel and axle is the most common method of altering chain adjustment. Moving the swing arm and wheel assembly for chain adjustment was used on some motorcycles. However, it is no longer common.

Most manufacturers provide INDEX MARKS on the chain adjusters and swing arm, as in Fig. 21-12. These marks assure proper sprocket, rear wheel, and chain alignment during chain free play adjustment.

To verify the accuracy of the chain adjusting index marks, measure from the center of the swing arm pivot to the center of the rear axle. This is illustrated in Fig. 21-13.

While adjusting chain free play, check for any tight spots caused by uneven chain or sprocket wear. Chain free play should be adjusted at the tightest spot. This prevents overtightening of the chain.

Some motorcycles require loosening and readjust-

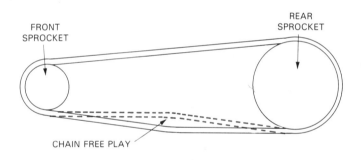

Fig. 21-11. Free play is measured in middle of bottom run of chain. Free play is distance chain moves from hanging slack until slight resistance is felt as chain is moved upward.

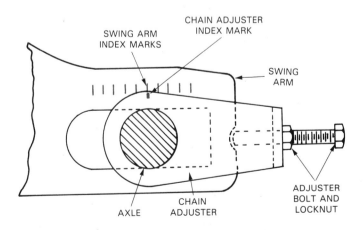

Fig. 21-12. Most chain adjusters have index marks which are used to accurately position rear axle for chain adjustment. Marks on each side should correspond. If not, rear wheel is misaligned.

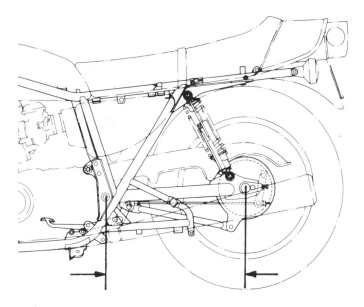

Fig. 21-13. Measure from center of swing arm pivot to center of rear axle on both sides of motorcycle. This verifies accuracy of swing arm chain adjuster index marks. (U.S. Suzuki Motor Corporation)

ment of the rear brake and brake light switch during chain adjustment. Follow the service manual for the motorcycle you are working on.

CAUTION! Use a new cotter pin in the axle nut following chain adjustment.

It is impossible to accurately adjust a chain which is not properly lubricated. A dry chain should be lubricated, and adjusted, and operated for a short time. Then, readjust the chain.

A dry, kinked, or rusted chain is usually unserviceable. It should be replaced.

CHAIN AND SPROCKET WEAR

Even with proper lubrication and adjustment, chains and sprockets will wear out. Wear of the pins and bushings account for what is commonly called CHAIN STRETCH (lengthening of chain). This is il-

lustrated in Fig. 21-14.

As the drive chain wears, the distance between its rollers increases. The worn chain will no longer mesh with the sprocket teeth properly. As a result, the stretched chain causes the sprocket teeth to wear very rapidly, as in Fig. 21-15.

An accurate method of checking chain wear requires measurement between a specified number of pins on the chain. See Fig. 21-16. A chain that is stretched 3 percent or more should be replaced.

If the sprockets are worn, always replace the chain and sprockets as a SET. This is important because worn sprockets will quickly wear out a new chain.

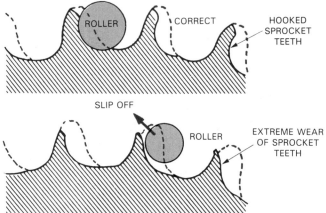
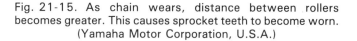

Fig. 21-15. As chain wears, distance between rollers becomes greater. This causes sprocket teeth to become worn. (Yamaha Motor Corporation, U.S.A.)

CHAIN AND SPROCKET REPLACEMENT

Depending upon which components need replacement and the type of chain being used (endless or conventional), several components may need to be removed. You may need to remove the swing arm, shock absorbers, chain guard, and other parts. Refer to your service manual for proper instructions.

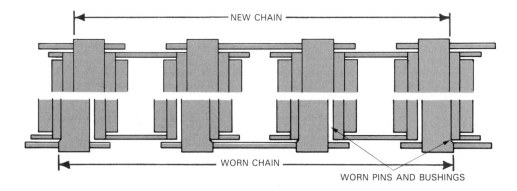

Fig. 21-14. Notice how much longer worn chain is than new chain. This is caused by wear on pins and bushings.

CHAIN SIZE	PITCH	NUMBER OF PINS TO MEASURE	NOMINAL INCHES-MILLIMETRES	SERVICE LIMIT INCHES-MILLIMETRES
35	3/8 × 3/16	21	7 1/2-191	7 11/16-196
420	1/2 × 1/4	21	10-254	10 5/16-261
428	1/2 × 5/16			
520	5/8 × 1/4	21	12 1/2-318	12 3/4-327
525	5/8 × 5/16			
530	5/8 × 3/8			
630	3/4 × 3/8	21	15-381	15 7/16-392

Fig. 21-16. After removing all slack from chain, measure distance between 21 pins. Use chart to determine chain condition. This is a 520 chain which measures 320 mm, so it is slightly worn. Do not forget to readjust chain after measuring wear.

SHAFT DRIVE INSPECTION, SERVICE, AND REPAIR

Shaft type final drive units are relatively trouble free. Some typical inspection and maintenance operations normally performed are:
1. Changing the lubricant in the rear housing, Fig. 21-17.
2. Inspection for oil leaks.
3. Inspection for universal joint looseness. This is pictured in Fig. 21-18.
4. Noise (clunking, whining) diagnosis.
5. Measurement of ring and pinion backlash. Refer to Fig. 21-19.

When repair of the rear drive unit is necessary, special tools may be needed and certain procedures must be followed.

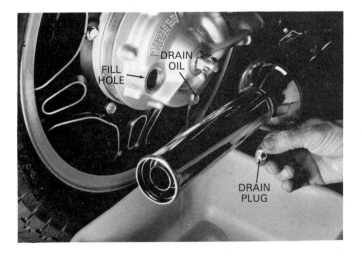

Fig. 21-17. Changing rear drive lubricant is a simple task. Use small lower hole for draining and larger upper hole for refilling.

Fig. 21-18. Universal joint looseness is easily determined by wiggling each joint section separately. In this illustration, motorcycle transmission has been removed.

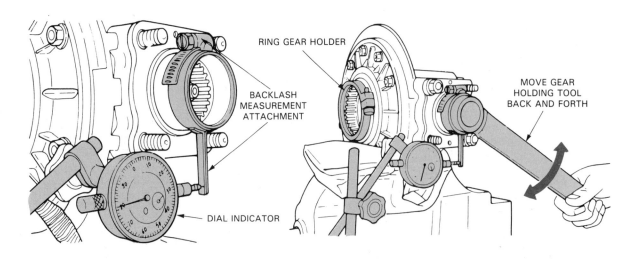

Fig. 21-19. Ring and pinion backlash is measured by holding ring gear and measuring pinion gear movement with a dial indicator. (Yamaha Motor Corp., U.S.A.)

SHAFT DRIVE DISASSEMBLY

Drain the oil and remove the rear wheel before attempting to remove the rear drive unit. Follow the service manual for proper disassembly steps and required special tools. Fig. 21-20 shows the breakdown of a typical rear drive unit.

REAR DRIVE UNIT INSPECTION

Clean all parts in solvent and inspect for damage.
1. Inspect the ring and pinion teeth for etching, chipping, and discoloration.
2. Inspect all ball and roller bearings for looseness, rough operation, and wear.
3. Inspect the condition of all oil seals and thrust washers.

REAR DRIVE UNIT ADJUSTMENTS

Whenever a rear drive unit is disassembled and especially when new parts have been installed (bearings, thrust washers, ring gear, pinion gear), it is essential to check and adjust ring and pinion backlash and tooth contact pattern.

Backlash adjustment

Fig. 21-21 shows how ring and pinion backlash is adjusted. Shims are used to move the ring gear into the pinion (reduce backlash) or away from the pinion (increase backlash).

Adjusting ring and pinion contact pattern

You must check ring and pinion tooth contact pattern to make sure the teeth of the ring and pinion mesh properly. To check contact pattern:
1. Make sure the ring and pinion are clean and free of oil and solvent.
2. Dab a small amount of machinist's dye or red lead and oil mixture on the teeth of the ring gear.

3. Install the ring gear and slowly rotate it. Keep the ring gear against its thrust washer.
4. Remove the ring gear and check the contact marks left by the pinion teeth.

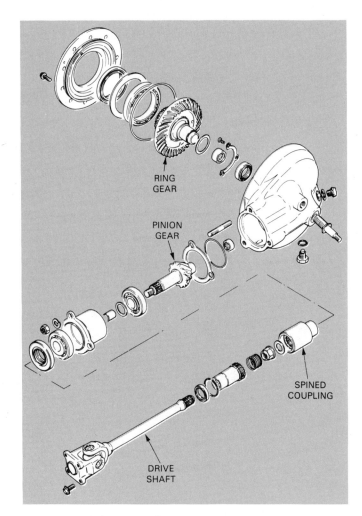

Fig. 21-20. Study this example of a rear drive unit. (U.S.Suzuki Motor Corporation)

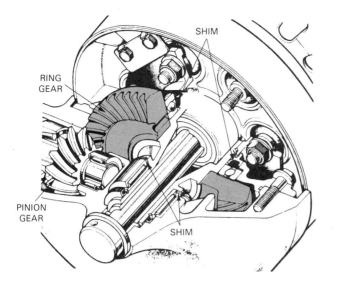

Fig. 21-21. Ring and pinion backlash is adjusted by shimming (moving) ring gear closer to or farther from pinion gear. (U.S. Suzuki Motor Corporation)

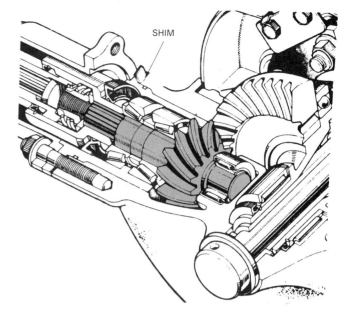

Fig. 21-23. Tooth contact pattern is altered by moving pinion gear closer to or farther from ring gear. Shim thickness change moves pinion gear and tooth contact pattern. (U.S. Suzuki Motor Corporation)

Fig. 21-22 shows typical contact patterns and the necessary adjustments for correction. Fig. 21-23 shows the shim that changes the tooth contact pattern.

Always recheck backlash after making any contact pattern adjustments. Accurate measurement and adjustment is needed for quiet and efficient ring and pinion operation.

KNOW THESE TERMS

Final drive, Roller chain, Master link, O-ring chain, Solid roller chain, Endless chain, Belt final drive, Shaft drive, Chain stretch, Final drive ratio, Ring gear, Pinion gear, Ring and pinion backlash, Ring and pinion tooth contact pattern.

REVIEW QUESTIONS—CHAPTER 21

1. What is the purpose of a master link?
2. List the three variations in chain design.
3. How is lubrication provided for a shaft drive system?
4. Three places for gear reduction are:
5. What components of a shaft drive system determine final drive ratio?

6. Motorcycle drive chains should not be lubricated until corrosion takes place. True or False?
7. What are two ways of changing drive chain tension?
8. Chain free play should be adjusted at the loosest spot. True or False?
9. What percentage of chain stretch is generally considered maximum?
10. It is always necessary to replace a chain and both sprockets as a set. True or False?
11. List three of the typical maintenance items performed on shaft drive systems.
12. What two gear adjustments must be checked during a shaft drive rebuild?

SUGGESTED ACTIVITIES

1. Verify chain adjuster index marks on a motorcycle.
2. Determine chain wear on a used final drive chain.
3. Check and adjust tooth contact pattern and backlash in a ring and pinion rear drive unit.
4. Remove and install a final drive chain using the master link.

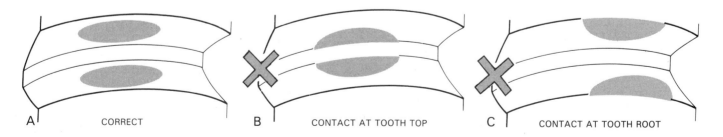

Fig. 21-22. A—Contact pattern is properly centered on face of gear. B and C—Shimming is required for proper contact. B—Pinion gear must be moved closer to ring gear. C—Pinion gear must be moved further from ring gear. (U.S. Suzuki Motor Corporation)

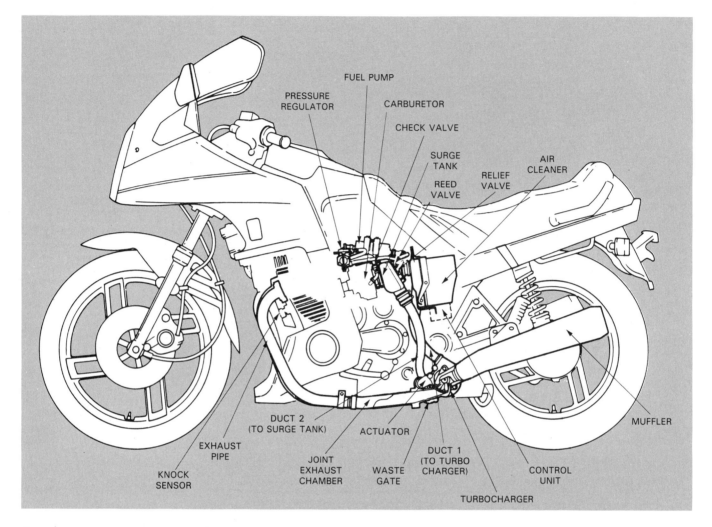

Note location of turbocharger and related components on this particular motorcycle.   (Yamaha Motor Corporation, U.S.A.)

Chapter 22

TURBOCHARGING AND EXHAUST SYSTEMS

After studying this chapter, you will be able to:

□ Explain the principles of supercharging and turbocharging.

□ List the basic parts of a typical turbocharger system.

□ Define the function of each turbocharging system component.

□ Summarize the advantages and disadvantages of turbocharging.

□ Describe the engine modifications needed with turbocharging.

□ Explain the design variations of different turbocharging systems.

□ Describe basic maintenance procedures performed on turbocharging systems.

Turbochargers have been associated with high performance for many years. Turbochargers have been used in a wide variety of applications, such as: aircraft, automobile, truck, and marine engines. In all of these applications, turbocharging provides increased air density in the engine's combustion chambers. This allows efficient burning of more fuel and results in higher horsepower output.

NORMAL ASPIRATION

Up to this point, all of the engines we have studied (two-stroke cycle, four-stroke cycle, carbureted and fuel injected) have been normally aspirated. An engine with NORMAL ASPIRATION uses atmospheric pressure and intake manifold vacuum to deliver the air-fuel mixture to the cylinders.

The most common method of improving engine power is by increasing engine displacement (size) or volumetric efficiency (breathing). These changes can be made in the factory design of the engine or by installing aftermarket modifications. In any case, there are limiting factors that determine the amount of usable horsepower available from a normally aspirated engine of a given displacement.

Any engine design has certain built-in compromises or trade-offs. For example, large displacement engines can provide high horsepower with good tractability, but they are usually bulkier and heavier than smaller displacement engines. Generally, larger engines also use more fuel than smaller engines.

SUPERCHARGING AND TURBOCHARGING

Another way of increasing engine power is by forcing more air-fuel mixture into the cylinders. This is done by using a COMPRESSOR (fan that increases air pressure). See Fig. 22-1. A compressor may be driven mechanically or by exhaust gases.

The term SUPERCHARGING refers to a mechanically driven compressor, Fig. 22-2. A cogged belt or a chain spins the compressor. The belt or chain is connected between the engine crankshaft and the com-

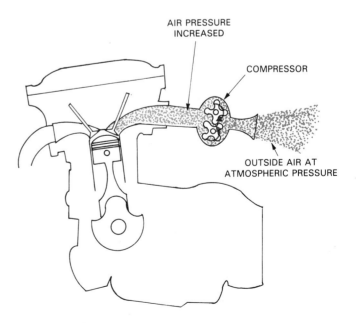

Fig. 22-1. Horsepower can be increased by using a compressor to force more air-fuel mixture into cylinders.

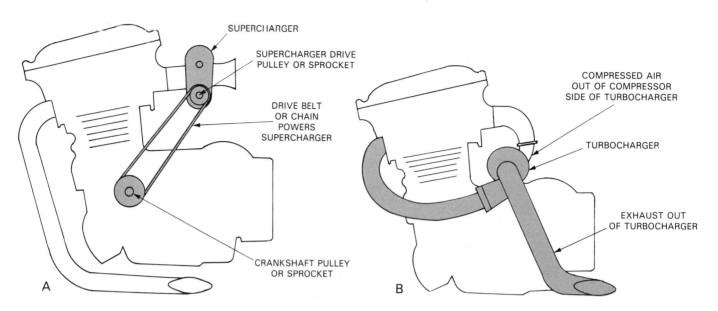

Fig. 22-2. Compressor can be driven either mechanically or by exhaust gases. A—Supercharger uses mechanical drive. B—Turbocharger uses exhaust gases to drive compressor.

pressor. When the engine is running, the compressor increases air pressure in the engine.

A TURBOCHARGER, often called turbo, is an exhaust driven compressor. Tubing carries engine exhaust gases to one end of the turbocharger. The gases blowing through the turbo are used to spin the compressor and form higher than normal air pressure in the engine. Look at Fig. 22-2.

Both superchargers and turbochargers increase power by pushing more air-fuel mixture into the cylinders than can be supplied by normal aspiration. In other words, "they force the engine to breathe better." This allows a smaller engine to produce the power of a larger engine.

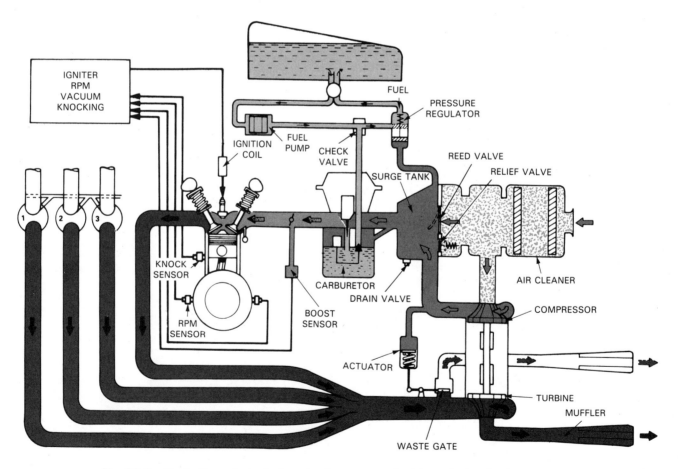

Fig. 22-3. Study flow of air, fuel, and exhaust gases in this typical turbocharger system. (Yamaha Motor Corporation, U.S.A.)

TURBOCHARGER OPERATION

A typical turbocharger system is shown in Fig. 22-3. This system can be broken down into the following parts:
1. Exhaust side.
2. Intake side.
3. Pressure control system.
4. Lubrication system.

Exhaust and intake sides

To explain turbocharger operation, it is easiest to first study the exhaust and intake sides of the system.

The EXHAUST SIDE of a turbocharger system uses exhaust gas energy to drive the intake side of the turbo. This is done by mounting a TURBINE WHEEL in the path of exiting engine exhaust gases, Fig. 22-4. The gases spin the turbine wheel. A shaft connects the turbine wheel to the compressor wheel in the intake tract. As a result, the compressor wheel spins with the turbine wheel.

The function of the COMPRESSOR WHEEL is to pressurize the intake tract. This is shown in Fig. 22-5. Pressure is built up in the intake tract as turbine and compressor wheel rpm increases.

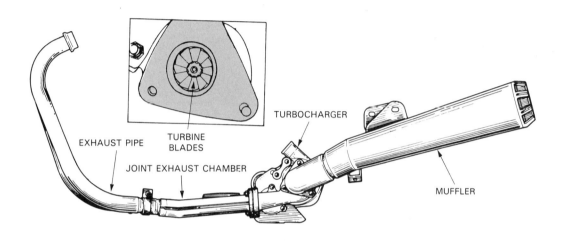

Fig. 22-4. Exiting exhaust gases spin turbine wheel. (Yamaha Motor Corporation, U.S.A.)

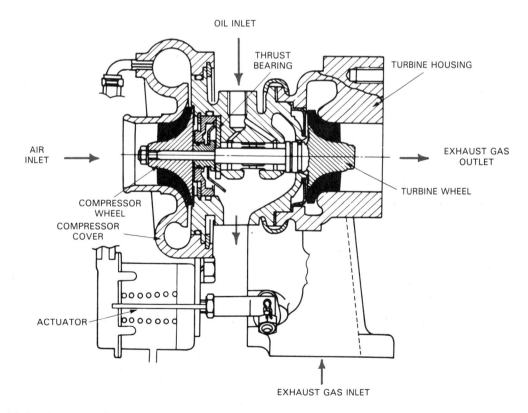

Fig. 22-5. Turbine wheel spins compressor wheel via a shaft. (Yamaha Motor Corporation, U.S.A.)

Exhaust gases from the turbine side are directed back to the normal exhaust system (muffler) after energy to drive the turbo has been extracted.

Filtered fresh air for the compressor side of the turbocharger is drawn in through the air cleaner (air box). Refer to Fig. 22-6. Fuel for mixing with the positive pressure (pressure above atmospheric pressure) intake air may be supplied by either carburetors or electronic fuel injection. This is discussed later in the chapter.

Pressure control system

In a well designed turbo system, the turbocharger is capable of making more BOOST (pressure) than the engine can use. A WASTE GATE is provided to prevent excessive boost pressure from damaging the engine. Fig. 22-7 illustrates waste gate operation.

The function of the waste gate is to bleed off excess exhaust gases when boost pressure reaches a specified limit. This reduces the amount of available energy to drive the turbine and limits boost.

Turbocharger lubrication

Due to the high rotational speeds of the turbine-compressor shaft and high temperatures present in the exhaust side, the turbocharger must be supplied with an adequate amount of clean, cool oil. Fig. 22-8 shows how oil circulates through a turbocharger.

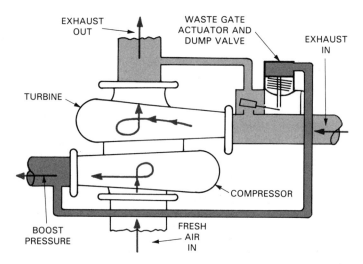

Fig. 22-7. A waste gate is like a pressure relief valve. When boost pressure reaches a preset level, waste gate opens, reducing amount of exhaust gas available to drive turbine wheel.

Turbochargers use floating type bearings. Oil is pressure fed to the turbo bearings by the engine lubrication system.

ADVANTAGES OF TURBOCHARGING

Both turbochargers and superchargers require energy for operation. Because a supercharger is mechanically driven by the engine, it absorbs horsepower and is in operation any time the engine is running.

A turbocharger uses exhaust gases to drive the compressor, and consequently, absorbs very little engine power. It also operates whenever the engine is running but affects performance only when the engine is under load, at relatively large throttle openings. This means that a turbocharged engine will operate very much like a normally aspirated engine at low engine speeds and under light load. Because the turbocharger is "freewheeling" when the engine is under light load, good fuel economy is also possible at cruising speeds.

DISADVANTAGES OF TURBOCHARGING

The transition to boost, as the throttle is opened rapidly, can cause a hesitation called TURBO LAG. Turbo lag has been greatly reduced with the recent development of turbocharger units that have been designed for specific motorcycle engines. Turbochargers used previously were designed for larger engines and adapted for use on motorcycles. These units generally suffer from severe turbo lag.

One of the major causes of turbo lag is the delay in time it takes for the exhaust gases to accelerate (rotate) the turbine as the throttle is opened. A lighter (smaller) turbine-compressor unit can accelerate more quickly, reducing turbo lag.

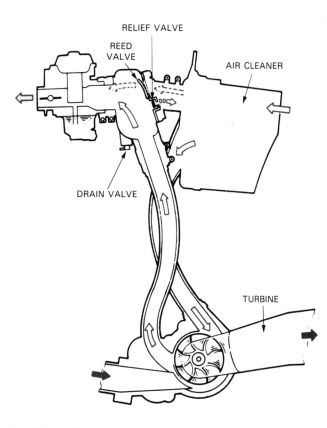

Fig. 22-6. Air passes through air cleaner to compressor and intake tract. (Yamaha Motor Corporation, U.S.A.)

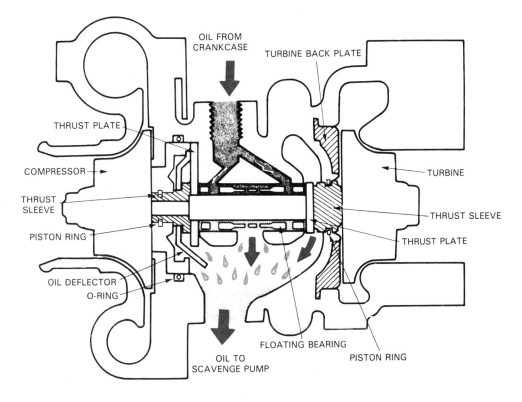

Fig. 22-8. Oil is pressure fed to turbo for lubrication and cooling of shaft.
(Yamaha Motor Corporation, U.S.A.)

TURBOCHARGED ENGINE DESIGN

Generally, a turbocharged engine makes more horsepower and heat than a normally aspirated engine of the same displacement. This is because the turbocharger forces more air-fuel mixture into the same space. Consequently, more heat and pressure is generated during combustion.

To maintain reliability, a turbocharged engine must be designed with extra stress and heat in mind. The following items must be given special consideration when designing a turbocharged engine:
1. Mechanical strength.
2. Turbocharger location and size.
3. Air-fuel delivery.
4. Control of detonation and engine heat.

MECHANICAL STRENGTH

Because of the extra horsepower and stress resulting from turbocharging, major engine and drive train components must be stronger. Typical components which may be designed differently are:
1. Crankshaft (stronger).
2. Connecting rods (stronger).
3. Connecting rod bearings and main bearings (larger, stronger).
4. Pistons and wrist pins (stronger, lower compression ratio).
5. Valves (better heat dissipation).
6. Clutch (stronger, more surface area).
7. Gearbox (stronger).
8. Final drive (stronger).

Whether a turbocharged engine is an all new design or a modification of an existing design, these factors are all considered in making the engine and drive train reliable.

TURBOCHARGER LOCATION AND SIZE

Ideally, the turbocharger should be mounted as close as possible to the exhaust valves to make the most efficient use of exhaust gas energy. However, there are no set rules which determine where the turbo unit must be located. Engine and frame configuration (available space) and fuel system design are the two major factors which determine torbocharger location. A look at the available turbocharged motorcycles demonstrates that different locations can work effectively.

Perhaps the most important factor in the selection of a turbocharger is the proper matching of turbo size to the engine. A properly matched turbo is one with the smallest, lightest turbine and compressor capable of providing the desired boost. Turbine size must be matched to the amount of available exhaust gas.

Since the inertia of the turbine-compressor must be overcome by exhaust pressure, a smaller unit is more responsive and is less likely to exhibit turbo lag.

FUEL SYSTEM

Like normally aspirated engines, turbocharged engines may use either carburetion or electronic fuel injection to supply the air-fuel mixture.

Carbureted fuel system

In designing a carbureted, turbocharged fuel system, it is possible to locate the turbocharger unit either before or after the carburetor. When the turbocharger is located after the carburetor, it is called a SUCK-THROUGH SYSTEM. When the turbocharger is located before the carburetor, it is called BLOW-THROUGH SYSTEM.

Suck-through turbocharging

The suck-through turbocharging system is common on after market turbocharger kits, because of its simplicity. However, a disadvantage of this system is that the turbocharger has a tendency to partially separate the air-fuel mixture into large droplets before it reaches the combustion chambers. This reduces low speed efficiency and tends to increase exhaust emissions (unburned hydrocarbons).

Blow-through turbocharging

The blow-through turbocharging system has been successfully used as original equipment. This system appears similar to a normally aspirated engine with the turbocharger installed before the carburetors. In this design, the turbocharger compresses only air. The carburetors must be modified to prevent boost pressure from forcing fuel from the float bowl back into the fuel tank. This is accomplished with the use of a fuel pump and pressure regulator, Fig. 22-9. They maintain a fuel pressure in the float bowl that is slightly above the pressure in the carburetor venturi. This pressure difference permits fuel to be metered into the venturi.

Electronic fuel injection

Because electronic fuel injection has the ability to precisely control the air-fuel mixture under varying conditions, it is an ideal fuel system for a turbocharged engine. The EFI system found on turbocharged engines is very similar to the type used on normally aspirated engines. It monitors the same type of information to determine how much fuel should be injected into the intake ports.

For a review of electronic fuel injection, refer to Chapter 9, Fuel Systems.

In addition to normal EFI monitoring devices, turbocharged engines may also have pressure sensors for altitude compensation, inlet air pressure, and turbo-boost pressure.

A typical, modern turbocharged electronic fuel injection system is illustrated in Fig. 22-10. Study all of the parts carefully.

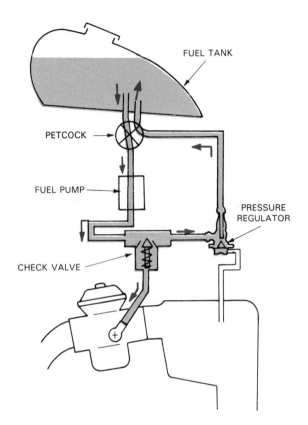

Fig. 22-9. In blow-through system, fuel pump and pressure regulator supplies fuel to float bowl at a higher pressure than boost pressure in venturi. This insures that fuel can flow through carburetor jets into venturi.
(Yamaha Motor Corporation, U.S.A.)

CONTROL OF DETONATION AND ENGINE HEAT

As you learned earlier, detonation and excessive heat can cause severe engine damage. Because of the extra air-fuel mixture packed into a turbocharged engine, pressures and temperatures in the combustion chamber are high enough that detonation is an ever present problem.

Detonation and engine heat are closely related. Detonation can be caused by excessive heat and extreme heat is produced by detonation.

Detonation control

Detonation is prevented by an electronic timing control unit. This unit adjusts ignition timing based on engine speed and boost pressure. As boost pressure increases, ignition timing is retarded to prevent detonation. However, with little or no boost, ignition timing will advance normally.

In addition, a knock sensor may also be used. A KNOCK SENSOR is a miniature crystal microphone mounted in the cylinder head to detect audible detonation. Signals from the knock sensor are sent to an electronic control box which retards ignition timing until the detonation ceases. The control box then begins to advance timing until detonation is detected

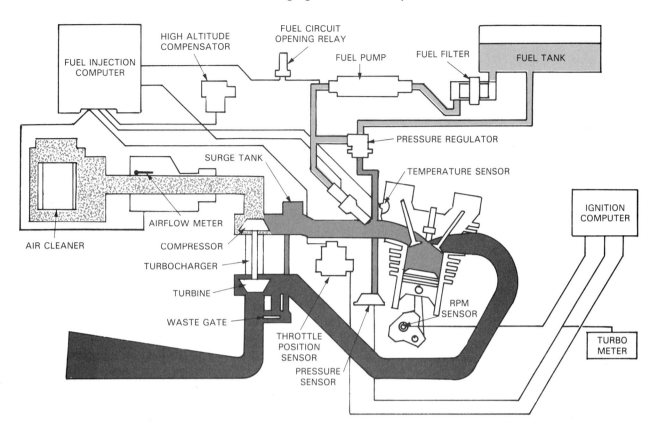

Fig. 22-10. Compare this EFI turbo system to blow-through system shown in Fig. 22-3. (Mark Wagner and Cycle Guide)

again. In this way, timing is constantly adjusted for maximum advance without detonation.

Engine heat

Due to the increased power available in a turbocharged engine, provisions must be made to keep engine temperatures down to an acceptable level. Just as changes are made to improve the mechanical strength of a turbocharged engine, similar changes must be made to control heat. Some of the changes which may be found are:
1. Lower compression ratio.
2. Oil spray to bottom of piston crowns.
3. Increased oil flow (increased oil pump speed or larger pump).
4. Addition of an oil cooler or larger oil cooler.
5. Increased oil reservoir capacity.
6. Oil passages near valve seats to help remove heat.
7. Increased cooling fin area (cylinder head, oil sump).
8. Cooling air ducts to direct airflow.
9. Increased water pump capacity (liquid cooling).

Some or all of these changes may be incorporated to insure adequate cooling of a turbocharged engine.

TURBOCHARGER MAINTENANCE

The turbocharger is not to be repaired in the field. If the turbo unit is damaged or does not operate properly, the entire unit must be replaced. Damage is usually caused by foreign material in the intake air or exhaust, or by a lubrication failure.

If severe engine damage has occurred (holed piston, broken valve), be sure to check the turbo unit for free operation and possible damage to the turbine blades. If there is any damage, the turbine unit must be replaced.

REMEMBER! The turbine and compressor wheels spin at up to 200,000 rpm. A tiny nick in a turbine or compressor blade could cause the turbo to explode.

The service manual outlines maintenance and safety checks for the turbocharger and waste gate, as well as routine inspection requirements.

Normally, a turbocharged engine requires no special maintenance or service. However, it is imperative to follow the manufacturer's recommendations for normal service items, such as oil and filter change intervals. Naturally, tune-up and periodic service items such as valve clearance adjustment, cam chain adjustment, and ignition timing adjustment are critical.

EXHAUST SYSTEMS

A motorcycle EXHAUST SYSTEM has three basic functions:
1. Route burned exhaust gases to rear of motorcycle.
2. Enhance power curve of engine.
3. Reduce engine exhaust noise.

Exhaust systems are normally made of steel,

covered with a layer of chrome plating or heat-resistant paint. A heat shield may be placed over the outer side of the exhaust system. The heat shield helps keep the rider from being burned on the hot pipe or muffler.

There are numerous exhaust system designs. Designs vary with the number of engine cylinders, engine type (two-stroke or four-stroke cycle), and application.

For example, a street bike normally has the exhaust system located close to the ground. This keeps exhaust heat away from the rider and helps lower the center of gravity. An off-road motorcycle, however, frequently has the exhaust system mounted higher on the side of the motorcycle. This provides more ground clearance for riding in rough terrain.

Four-stroke exhaust systems

As pictured in Fig. 22-11, the basic parts of a typical four-stroke exhaust system include:
1. HEAT DIFFUSER (finned flange to help dissipate heat and mount header pipe).
2. HEADER PIPE (exhaust pipe between engine and muffler).
3. MUFFLER (baffled container that reduces pressure pulsations and noise).
4. EXHAUST CLAMPS (devices for holding parts of exhaust system together).
5. EXHAUST GASKETS (heat resistant gaskets that prevent leakage between exhaust system connections.

After the power stroke, the engine blows extremely hot gases out the engine exhaust port. These gases enter the exhaust system header pipe. Some of the heat is dissipated into a diffuser to prevent overheating of the header pipe. The hot gases then flow through the pipe and into the muffler.

Since the engine is producing rapid pressure pulses during each exhaust stroke, the muffler contains baffles and inner chambers to dampen exhaust pressure pulses. See Fig. 22-12. The baffles and chambers are designed to quiet the exhaust with a minimum amount of backpressure.

Two-stroke exhaust systems

A two-stroke exhaust system can use many of the parts discussed for four-stroke engines. However, the internal design of the system is somewhat different.

An EXPANSION CHAMBER is used in a two-stroke exhaust system to help exhaust scavenging (removal of burned gases from engine cylinder), and to increase engine power. As shown in fig. 22-13, an expansion chamber consists of:
1. Header pipe.
2. Divergent cone.
3. Belly.
4. Convergent cone.
5. Stinger.

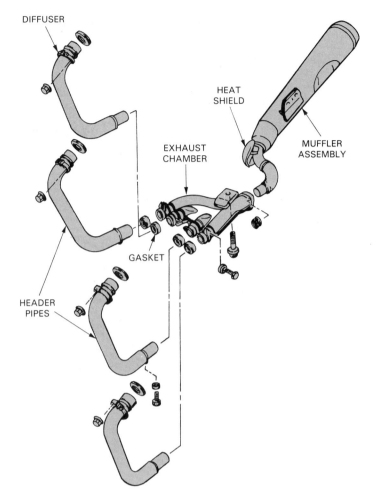

Fig. 22-11. Basic parts of exhaust system are diffuser, header pipe, clamps, gaskets, and muffler.

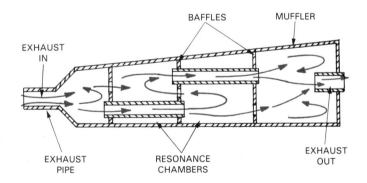

Fig. 22-12. Baffles form resonance chambers in muffler to eliminate pressure pulses and noise.

The length and angle of the cones determines the intensity and duration of the pressure waves in the expansion chamber. In two-stroke engines, a scavenging (positive pressure waves) effect is used to help pull burned gases out of the cylinder. Scavenging pulls fresh air-fuel mixture out of the engine and into the expansion chamber. An expansion chamber also produces reverse pressure waves that force the air-fuel

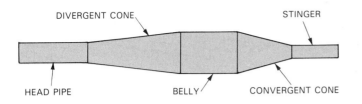

Fig. 22-13. Study basic parts of expansion chamber.

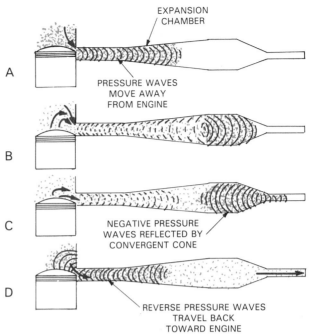

Fig. 22-14. Study basic action of expansion chamber. A—Exhaust positive pressure wave moves into expansion chamber. B—Vacuum pulls remaining exhaust out of engine cylinder. C—Negative wave is reflected from convergent cone back toward exhaust port as air-fuel mixture begins to flow into headpipe. D—Negative pressure waves force air-fuel mixture back into cylinder and exhaust gas is bled off through stinger.

mixture back into the cylinder, Fig. 22-14. A muffler is built into the stinger portion of all modern two-stroke cycle motorcycles.

KNOW THESE TERMS

Normal aspiration, Compressor, Supercharger, Turbocharger, Turbine, Compressor, Waste gate, Boost, Turbo lag, Suck-through turbo, Blow-through turbo, Knock sensor, Heat diffuser, Header pipe, Muffler, Expansion chamber.

REVIEW QUESTIONS—CHAPTER 22

1. The purpose of a turbocharger is to increase the density of the intake charge. True or False?
2. The _____ wheel is driven by the exhaust; the _____ wheel pressurizes the intake tract.
3. Name the two methods used for supplying air-fuel mixture to a turbocharged engine.
4. The waste gate is necessary to prevent excessive boost pressure. True or False?
5. Turbocharger lubrication is provided by an oil splash. True or False?
6. The delay in acceleration (rotation) of the turbocharger (turbine and compressor wheels) is sometimes called _____ _____.
7. List three engine components that must be designed stronger to withstand turbocharging.
8. A turbocharger spins whenever the engine is running, however, higher engine speeds and loads are necessary to pressurize the intake charge. True or False?
9. Define "blow-through" turbocharging.
10. List the two methods used to help control detonation.
11. List three typical changes in engine design for the purpose of controlling heat on a turbocharged engine.
12. Describe the inspection you would perform if a turbocharged engine sustained severe internal damage.
13. A typical turbo (turbine and compressor) may spin as fast as:
   a. 50,000 rpm.
   b. 200,000 rpm.
   c. 75,000 rpm.
   d. 25,000 rpm.
14. A well designed muffler produces minimum back pressure. True or False?
15. What is the purpose of an expansion chamber?

SUGGESTED ACTIVITIES

1. Compare turbine and compressor wheel size of several turbocharged motorcycle engines. Also, list the number of cylinders, displacement, compression ratio, maximum boost, and engine configuration. What conclusions can you draw?
2. Compare horsepower ratings of several turbocharged motorcycle engines to normally aspirated engines of the same displacement.
3. Compare differences in intake and exhaust system design of several turbocharged motorcycle engines (blow-through carburetion, fuel injection, turbo location).

Always observe all speed limits when riding. Top. Conventional instrument panel with cable driven tachometer and speedometer. Bottom. Modern electronic instrument cluster. Note digital readout speedometer and electronic movement tach.
(Yamaha Motor Corporation, U.S.A. and U.S. Suzuki Motor Corporation)

Chapter 23

LIABILITY

After studying this chapter, you will be able to:
☐ List possible component failures that can make a motorcycle unsafe.
☐ Explain the use of a release form.
☐ Describe how to inspect a motorcycle for safety related problems.
☐ Summarize the procedures needed to correct safety related problems.

This chapter will briefly explain some of the problems that could lead to rider injury and possible lawsuits. It also discusses how to avoid unsafe conditions through competent repair procedures, inspection techniques, release forms, and other shop practices.

The word LIABILITY means: "responsible under legal obligation." This implies that you are responsible for any work you perform on a motorcycle. The only way to satisfy this obligation is to always do quality, safety-oriented repair work. Safety-oriented repairs require you to use common sense and a conscientious work attitude.

UNSAFE CONDITIONS

A number of conditions can make a motorcycle unsafe:
1. Normal wear of components.
2. Improper service or repair procedures.
3. Aftermarket add-on accessories.

Normal wear of components

A good example of an unsafe condition caused by normal wear is a worn final drive chain. The chain can break, locking up the rear wheel. A serious accident could result.

It is up to the mechanic to find and correct normal wear problems that could cause injury to the rider.

Improper service or repair

An incorrectly routed throttle cable or a loose axle nut are examples of unsafe conditions that can be caused by improper service or repair operations. A mechanic could be liable for injuries caused by incorrect repairs of this nature. Always double-check your work.

Aftermarket add-on accessories

Aftermarket add-on accessories that can change aero-dynamic stability, cause overloading or change suspension geometry can upset normal handling and stability. This could make the motorcycle unsafe. Make sure any accessory is safe to use before installation.

Manufacturer recalls

All manufacturers make every effort to produce safe motorcycles of superior quality, and they have an excellent safety record.

A manufacturer recall occurs if a possible safety defect is discovered on a certain motorcycle model. Each customer and dealer is notified of the recall and what is needed to correct the situation.

Recalls are very rare and perhaps you will never deal with one. However, if you are working in a dealership and are involved in a recall campaign, make every effort to get the defective motorcycles into the shop for repairs as quickly as possible.

INSPECTING FOR UNSAFE CONDITIONS

Anytime work is done on a motorcycle, a quick safety check should be completed. A typical safety check involves inspection of the following:
1. Operation of the lights and horn.
2. Steering head condition and adjustment.
3. Condition of wheels and tires.
4. Tire pressure.
5. Chain condition and adjustment.
6. Tightness of the suspension components.
7. All fluid (oil, brake fluid, coolant) levels.
8. Condition of control cables.
9. Operation and condition of brakes.
10. Proper auto throttle return.
11. Tightness of important nuts and bolts.
Safety related inspection instructions are found

throughout most manufacturer's shop manuals and owner's manuals. The new mechanic should make a special effort to become familiar with these instructions before performing a motorcycle safety inspection.

CORRECTING UNSAFE CONDITIONS

When an unsafe condition is found, take immediate action to correct the problem. If the motorcycle is yours, fix it right away. If the motorcycle belongs to someone else, they must be notified. If the owner will not authorize the necessary repairs, make sure a proper release statement is filled out and signed by the owner.

Fig. 23-1 shows an example of a typical release statement. You would fill in the safety problem and have the customer sign the bottom. Motorcycle shops have work orders and prescribed plans for handling this situation. The customer's signature will help release the mechanic and shop from costly liability claims against the shop or mechanic.

PREVENTING LIABILITY PROBLEMS

A complete list of precautionary measures to prevent liability problems would be extremely lengthy. Below are a few thoughts that illustrate some of the precautions you should take.

1. In a motorcycle dealership, good communications between the sales and service departments can help in the selection of accessories. It is important that accessories are properly suited to the motorcycle, to the customer's riding style, and to the intended use of the motorcycle.
2. When replacing tires, do not make gross changes in tire profile or size and do not mix and match tires. On heavily loaded touring machines, make sure replacement tires have the proper ratings.
3. Do not patch inner tubes. Replace them! Also, do not attempt to straighten bent frames or suspension components.
4. Follow manufacturer's prescribed repair procedures. Do not take "shortcuts."
5. A neat, orderly work area, minimum interruptions while working, checklists, proper tool selection, and the desire to do things right will make it easy to complete a thorough repair job.
6. Remember! Common sense and a safety conscious attitude are mandatory in a motorcycle shop. You must "work at" being a responsible mechanic.

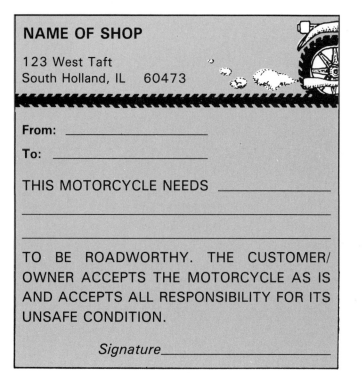

Fig. 23-1. This type form will help release mechanic and shop from possible lawsuits.

REVIEW QUESTIONS—CHAPTER 23

1. List four conditions that make a motorcycle unsafe.
2. Which of the following would NOT be an example of normal wear?
   a. Final drive chain stretch.
   b. No tread on tires.
   c. Cracked frame.
   d. Thin brake pads.
3. How can aftermarket add-on accessories alter the safety of a motorcycle?
4. If a possible safety defect is present on a certain model motorcycle, a _____ _____ will notify the customer or dealer of the problem and needed repair.
5. What is the function of a release form or statement?

SUGGESTED ACTIVITIES

1. Inspect several motorcycles for problems that could affect safety.
2. Obtain and read manufacturer recall notices. Note the types of problems and repairs.

Chapter 24

STORAGE

After studying this chapter, you will be able to:
□ Explain why a motorcycle should be properly prepared for storage.
□ List the basic procedures for storing a motorcycle.
□ Describe the fundamental procedures for returning a motorcycle to service after storage.

When a motorcycle is not going to be used for an extended period of time, it must be stored to prevent part damage. When a motorcycle sits for prolonged periods, condensation can cause rust and corrosion on numerous components. This is especially true in cold climates.

Improper preparation for storage can result in damage to the:
1. Lubrication system.
2. Fuel system.
3. Suspension system.
4. Ignition system.
5. Exterior appearance.

This chapter summarizes the most important preventive maintenance techniques for storing a motorcycle. It will help you keep your motorcycle in good condition, even after prolonged periods without use while in storage.

STORAGE PREPARATION PROCEDURES

The following list outlines the most important aspects for properly preparing a motorcycle for storage. Refer to the service manual and owner's manuals for more specific manufacturer's storage recommendations.
1. Degrease the motorcycle if necessary and thoroughly clean with soap and water. DUST and DIRT retain moisture which can accelerate rust and corrosion.
2. Apply a coat of wax to entire motorcycle (paint and chrome) to protect the finish. For extra protection, plated and aluminum surfaces may be coated with a light, petroleum based, protective spray.
3. Change all oil, including primary case, gearbox, and forks. Used oil contains contaminants that promote corrosion during storage.

   The engine should be at operating temperature before changing oil. After refilling with fresh oil, run the engine for a few minutes until oil has fully circulated.
4. If the bike is to be stored where the temperature will be BELOW FREEZING, remove the battery and store it in a warm place. Check battery every month or so and add distilled water to maintain level. If necessary, charge with a 1/2 to 1 amp charger to maintain a full charge.
5. If the temperature will NOT drop below freezing in your storage area, disconnect the battery terminals. It is best to store the battery in a warm place.
6. Wash any corrosion from battery, battery box, and terminals. Neutralize these parts with baking soda and water. Coat battery and cable terminals with petroleum jelly or white grease. If the battery box has been damaged by corrosion, it should be repainted after cleaning.
7. Drain fuel tank and carburetor float bowls, or completely fill tank and add the proper amount of gasoline stabilizer to prevent fuel deterioration (oxidation and gum formation) and condensation (water collection).
8. Squirt some #40 weight oil in the spark plug holes and turn the engine over a few times to coat the cylinders. Do this once a month to prevent the cylinders and rings from rusting.

   Be sure to remove the spark plugs before kicking the engine over. Oil does not compress. Serious damage to connecting rods and crankshaft may result if plugs are not removed. You may also install vapor plugs in spark plug holes to prevent moisture buildup or rusting of crank and cylinder.
9. Ignition points should be in the open position to prevent corrosion. A strip of paper may be placed between the contacts.

10. Clean and lubricate rear (final drive) chain.
11. Lubricate clutch, brake, and throttle cables.
12. Lubricate levers, brake pedal, and all grease fittings.
13. Inflate tires to the recommended air pressure.
14. Park the motorcycle on its center stand. If it does not have one, place it on blocks. The full weight of the motorcycle must NOT rest on the tires.
15. Cover the bike with a suitable dust cover. Avoid airtight covering material such as sheet plastic, since it can trap moisture and promote rust. If possible, check the bike every few weeks to make sure no rust is developing.

RETURNING THE BIKE TO SERVICE

After storage, a motorcycle should be serviced and closely inspected before being operated. You should perform the operations listed below.

1. If the bike has been stored with fuel tank empty, rinse with fresh fuel and clean the filter screen to remove any residue.
2. If the bike has been in storage several months and there has been considerable temperature fluctuation, change the oil, since there could be condensation in the oil.
3. Remove spark plugs or vapor plugs and kick the engine over vigorously several times to blow excess oil out of the cylinders.
4. Remove valve covers and squirt some oil on the valve stems, rocker arms, cam chain, and cam.
5. Check ignition timing, plug gap, valve clearance, and cam chain tension.
6. Check, adjust, and lubricate all cables and drive chains.

7. Check the operation of suspension components and electrical equipment.
8. Warm engine to operating temperature and adjust carbs.
9. Check all nuts and bolts to make sure they are tight.
10. Test ride slowly.

REVIEW QUESTIONS—CHAPTER 24

1. List five motorcycle areas that can be damaged by improper storage.
2. It is best to store a motorcycle with used oil and then change the oil in the spring after the first ride. True or False?
3. You should store a battery in a warm place. True or False?
4. What is added to gasoline to prevent deterioration and condensation?
5. Which of the following is NOT done when storing a motorcycle?
   a. Cover motorcycle.
   b. Squirt oil in spark plug holes.
   c. Tie suspension in compressed position.
   d. Inflate tires to specs.
6. Tune-up type adjustments may be necessary before removing a motorcycle from storage. True or False?

SUGGESTED ACTIVITIES

1. Using the information in your service manual and this chapter, prepare a motorcycle for storage.
2. Ready a motorcycle for use, after storage.
3. Make up a checklist for pre-storage and post-storage service.

Chapter 25

TROUBLESHOOTING

After studying this chapter, you will be able to:
☐ List the types of problems encountered when troubleshooting a motorcycle.
☐ Define the term "symptom."
☐ Use a systematic approach when troubleshooting.
☐ Discuss general techniques for troubleshooting the major systems of a motorcycle.

The purpose of this chapter is to explore the techniques used to troubleshoot motorcycle problems. The proper solution to a problem should not result from accidental hit and miss repairs. Logical step-by-step checks should be made until the problem is located.

Many shop manuals provide good troubleshooting charts that can and should be used as a guide. However, when tackling a troubleshooting problem, the competent mechanic must also rely on common sense, knowledge of motorcycle systems, and experience.

TROUBLESHOOTING, also called diagnosis, is the systematic and organized process of pinpointing the cause of a problem or failure. One of the things which makes troubleshooting a challenge is that you must be accurate in verifying the condition of a system and its components.

A good troubleshooter must be able to:
1. Make accurate tests and evaluations.
2. Digest and analyze test results.
3. Make the decision to continue testing, or to repair a discovered problem.

TYPES OF PROBLEMS

Troubleshooting problems fall into three categories:
1. Permanent failures.
2. Intermittent failures.
3. Failures caused by improper service.
The word SYMPTOM refers to the description of the problem. It is used in troubleshooting in much the same way as in the medical profession: "to describe an abnormal or out of the ordinary condition." One example, if a motorcycle does not accelerate well, the symptom is lack of power on acceleration.

Intermittent problems or symptoms are the hardest to diagnose because you must first duplicate the failure before beginning diagnosis. For example, the customer complains that the motorcycle runs for a while and then blows a fuse. If you cannot get it to blow a fuse, the problem may be hard to find. With an intermittent condition like this, it is more difficult to pinpoint the cause because everything may pass your tests.

HOW TO TROUBLESHOOT

To troubleshoot properly, you must first think about the problems. Ask yourself these kinds of questions:
1. What is the symptom (noise, performance problem, color of smoke)?
2. What system is involved (ignition, fuel, engine)?
3. Is there a possibility of more than one system being involved (starting, lighting, charging for example)?
4. Where is the most logical place to begin diagnosis?
Troubleshooting should begin with the easiest and most obvious checks. Progression to more difficult checks are done step-by-step.

One of the most common troubleshooting mistakes is to overlook the easiest or most obvious possible causes of a failure. More than one mechanic has serviced a carburetor when the actual problem was an empty fuel tank. When making these systematic checks, it is necessary to be 100 percent sure in verifying system or component condition.

IDENTIFYING THE SYSTEM

Some symptoms readily identify the system you must troubleshoot. For example, squealing brakes are obviously the result of some problem in the brake system. A discharged battery indicates a bad battery or weak charging system.

Other problems are more difficult to pinpoint. Poor engine performance may be caused by the fuel system, ignition system, or an engine problem. The troubleshooter must use available information to identify in which system the problem originates.

In an engine that accelerates poorly and overheats, a number of possibilities exist. A logical starting place is the ignition system (ignition timing). If the ignition timing is correct, it would be illogical to continue testing the ignition system before making some preliminary fuel system checks.

TROUBLESHOOTING CHARTS should be used to help you identify a logical starting point for a particular problem. The following text discussion suggests starting points for troubleshooting some common problem areas.

Charging system troubleshooting

The first thing to consider in troubleshooting a charging system is battery condition. The battery must be in good condition and fully charged before charging system components can be checked. This may require battery charging or battery replacement. Battery condition is very important since tests performed with a low or bad battery will be invalid.

Use a hydrometer, as in Fig. 25-1, to test the electrolyte. Charge the battery if necessary. Quite often, a suspected charging system problem is simply the result of a bad or discharged battery or corroded battery terminal connections. Visual inspection of wiring and connections is also important, and can be performed while the battery is charging.

Your service manual will provide testing procedures for the charging system and its individual components. These tests will require the use of a VOM (volt-ohm-milliammeter) to check continuity, voltages, and resistances of the system or its components. See Fig. 25-2. Read the manual carefully and perform all tests exactly as described.

Fuel system troubleshooting

Fuel system problems may cause an engine to run poorly or not at all. Your starting point will be determined by whether or not the engine runs. If the engine does not run due to a fuel system problem, you must check that there is fuel in the tank, that fuel is getting through the petcock and filters to the float bowl.

An engine that runs poorly in midrange, but runs fine below and above midrange, is obviously getting sufficient fuel to the carburetor. You must begin by checking components in the carburetor that affect midrange. Check parts for wear, maladjustment, and other problems.

Some useful tools for carburetor troubleshooting are shown in Figs. 25-3 through 25-6.

Ignition system troubleshooting

Like the fuel system, ignition system problems can cause the engine to run poorly or not at all. If poor performance is the problem, you should check the components which normally wear out or get out of adjustment (spark plugs, points, timing).

If a no start condition exists and the battery is fully charged, check for ignition spark and use a systematic approach to find the cause. If there is spark, try new

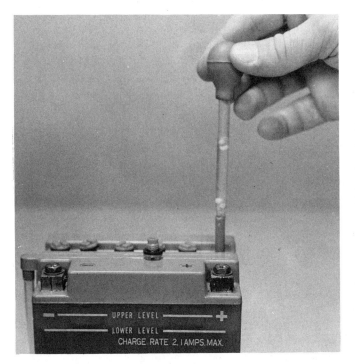

Fig. 25-1. A battery hydrometer is used to check electrolyte specific gravity.

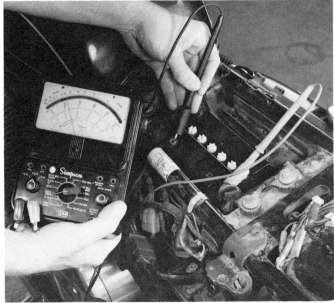

Fig. 25-2. In this illustration, a VOM or multimeter is being used to test charging system output voltage.

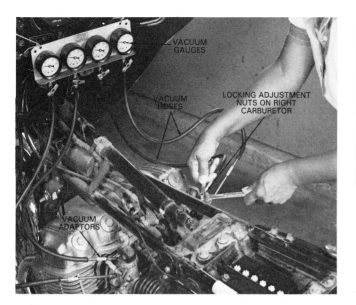

Fig. 25-3. Vacuum gauges are used for adjustment of carburetor throttle synchronization.

Fig. 25-4. Spark plug viewer (illuminated magnifier) is used to check carburetor jetting by inspecting spark plug color.

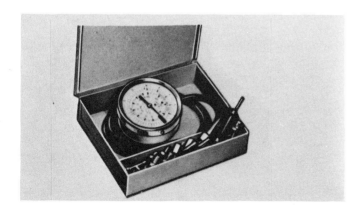

Fig. 25-5. A fuel pressure/vacuum gauge is useful for testing motorcycle fuel systems that have a fuel pump.

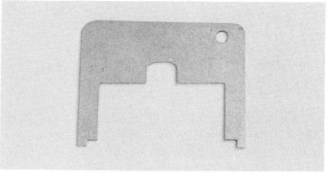

Fig. 25-6. A float level gauge helps to accurately adjust fuel level in carburetor bowl.

spark plugs and check engine compression before troubleshooting other components.

Some useful tools for ignition system troubleshooting are shown in Figs. 25-7 through 25-10.

Wheel and suspension troubleshooting

Symptoms resulting from wheel and suspension problems are classified as handling problems

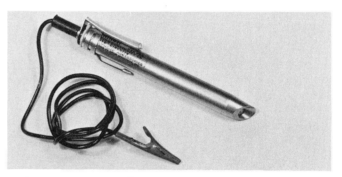

Fig. 25-7. Continuity light is handy for locating open circuits in ignition system wiring.

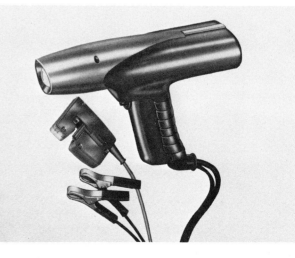

Fig. 25-8. Timing light is connected to battery and appropriate spark plug wire. It can then be pointed on timing marks to check ignition timing.

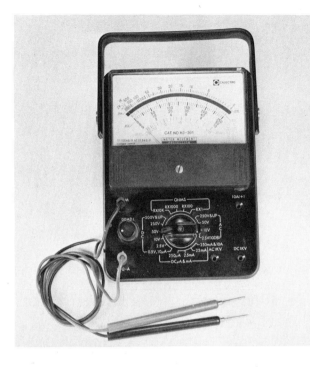

Fig. 25-9. VOM or multimeter will make accurate measurements of voltage, current, and resistance. If test value is not within specs, repairs are needed.

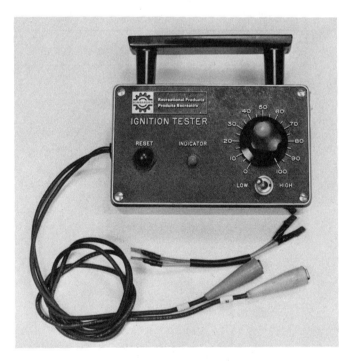

Fig. 25-10. Specialized electronic ignition tester is useful when diagnosing problems in modern ignition systems.

(wobbling, shimmy, vibrations). These problems can be caused by a number of conditions.

Whenever a handling problem is encountered, four easy checks which can be made are: steering head looseness, swing arm pivot looseness, wheel bearing looseness, and tire pressure. If these four quick checks do not reveal the problem, check:

1. Fork slider looseness and fork alignment.
2. Fork oil (proper type and quantity).
3. Rear shock condition.
4. Wheel runout.
5. Tire type and size, tire balance, and tire and wheel runout.
6. Wheel alignment.
7. Aftermarket components that might alter handling (forks, shocks, sissy bar, faring).

These components are critical to safety. When troubleshooting or working on wheels and suspension, carefully follow shop manual procedures and specifications.

Brake system troubleshooting

Brake system problems are usually related to normal wear and are generally easy to troubleshoot. Common brake system symptoms include spongy lever or pedal (hydraulic type system), fluid leakage (hydraulic type system), squeaking or squealing, and inadequate stopping power. The first things to check are fluid levels and wear indicators. Troubleshooting these problems is usually a simple matter of performing normal maintenance.

Follow your manual's instructions when doing any type of brake service to insure proper safety precautions.

Lighting system troubleshooting

Lighting system problems can be easy to troubleshoot (burned out bulb for example), moderately difficult (broken wire hidden in main harness), or very difficult (intermittent lighting failure—broken wire which opens and closes circuit).

Troubleshooting the lighting system requires the use of a multimeter or a test light and the wiring schematic. See Fig. 25-11. In order to troubleshoot a lighting system, you must check for voltage in the circuit, continuity of switches and wiring, and verify that a good ground exists.

The logical place to start troubleshooting is at the bulb, Fig. 25-12. If the bulb is good, check for power to the socket and proper grounding of the socket body. If everything tests good, make a visual check of the wiring, looking for any place where wires could get pinched or damaged. The remaining checks involve checking for power and continuity throughout the circuit. You may work from the bulb toward the battery or from the battery toward the bulb.

Before you start unplugging the wiring harness, make sure you understand the schematic and have decided the troubleshooting sequence you will follow.

Engine troubleshooting

Engine troubleshooting can generally be broken down into noise related or performance related problems.

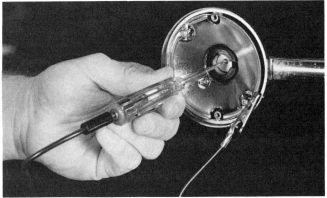

Fig. 25-12. A test light can be used to verify voltage at bulb socket.

Fig. 25-11. A multimeter or test light can be used to check for voltage at headlight plug connection.

Fig. 25-13. A stethoscope is helpful in determining origin of a particular engine noise. Noise will be loudest at its source.

Noise related problems are the result of wear, breakage, or need for adjustment. They should be localized if possible. Can you determine where the noise is coming from? A stethoscope may help, as shown in Fig. 25-13. Does the noise occur only when the engine is cold or hot? Does the noise occur only when the motorcycle is being ridden? You must use this type of information and common sense to determine where and how you will begin investigating the engine problem.

Performance related symptoms generally identify the problem area. For example, a four-stroke engine which performs poorly and has oily deposits in the exhaust pipes has an oil consumption problem. A gearbox that jumps out of gear has a gear selection adjustment problem or internal problem.

Any problem which might be cured by normal maintenance type adjustments (valve or cam chain adjustment, clutch adjustment, gear selector adjustment) should be done before major disassembly. Also, make use of engine test equipment such as compression gauge, oil pressure gauge, and crankcase leak tester. They will help identify problem areas. Checking engine oil for metallic particles and a burned smell can also be helpful. Refer to Figs. 25-14, 25-15, and 25-16.

If you determine that a teardown and overhaul is necessary, it should be done as outlined in the engine overhaul chapters of the service manual.

As you gain experience, you may have a tendency to second guess troubleshooting problems based on your experience. If you know the system well from previous repairs, this approach can be a time saver. However, if you guess wrong, a systematic approach

Fig. 25-14. A compression gauge is used to test engine top end condition.

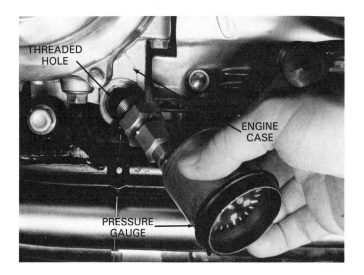

Fig. 25-15. An oil pressure gauge will help to determine condition of lubrication system.

must be utilized.

Troubleshooting should be broken down into six steps:

1. Collecting information pertinent to the problem (talk to customer and test ride if possible).
2. Symptom identification and system overlapping.
3. Systematic and accurate diagnosis.
4. Record keeping (know what you have done and what you plan to do).
5. Repairing the malfunction. (Perform only one repair at a time.)
6. Repair verification (test ride or tests).

HELPFUL INFORMATION

To make your troubleshooting job easier, it is important to gather as much information as possible.

Try to find out:

1. Service history of motorcycle.
2. When the problem first occurred.
3. If anyone else has tried to fix motorcycle. If so, what was done?
4. All the information possible about the symptoms of the problem.

THINKING OUT THE PROBLEM

Study and make use of all the information you have collected. If a motorcycle develops a problem while being ridden (no one has worked on it for quite some time), this indicates a normal type failure.

If a motorcycle has just been serviced and now it suddenly quits or performs poorly, this indicates improper service procedures. You, as the mechanic, must decide where to begin troubleshooting based on this type of information.

Your proficiency as a troubleshooter will increase with experience if you remember a few simple guidelines:

1. Think the problem through.
2. Do not overlook the obvious.
3. Do not assume there is only one problem.
4. Do not take shortcuts.

Troubleshooting problems can be tough for an inexperienced mechanic. You need not be apprehensive about troubleshooting if you have the right attitude. Follow the thought process we have described in this chapter, and use available information to your advantage. Figs. 25-17 and 25-18 are good examples of a "systematic approach."

Remember, the more troubleshooting you do, the more comfortable you will be about tackling

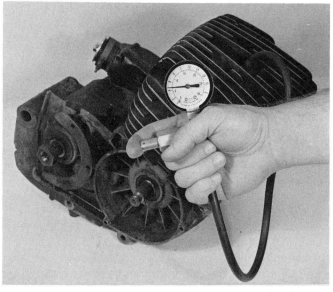

Fig. 25-16. A two-stroke cycle crankcase leak tester is used to test for engine air leaks.

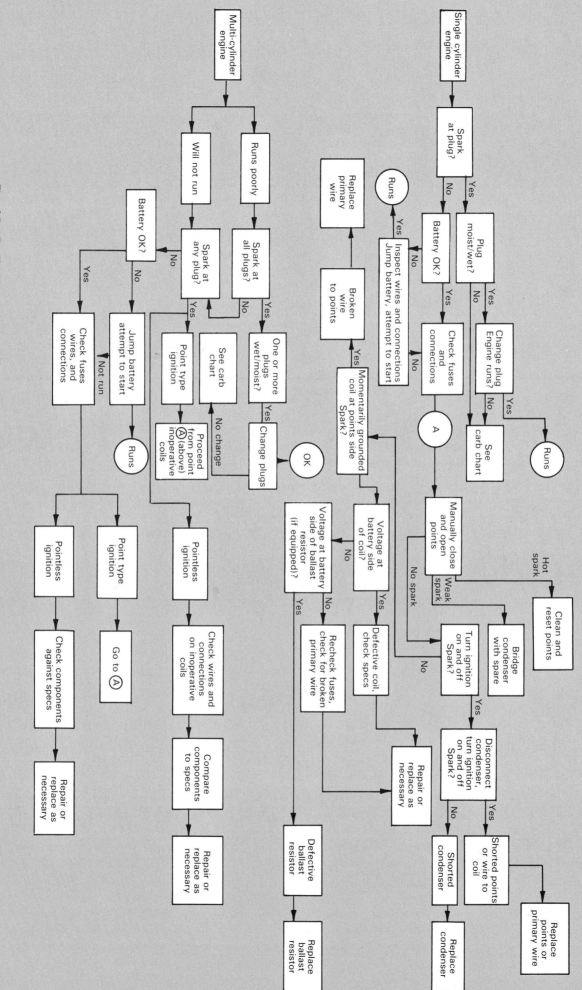

Fig. 25-17. Troubleshooting chart shows typical approach for finding a fault in an ignition system. (Cycle World)

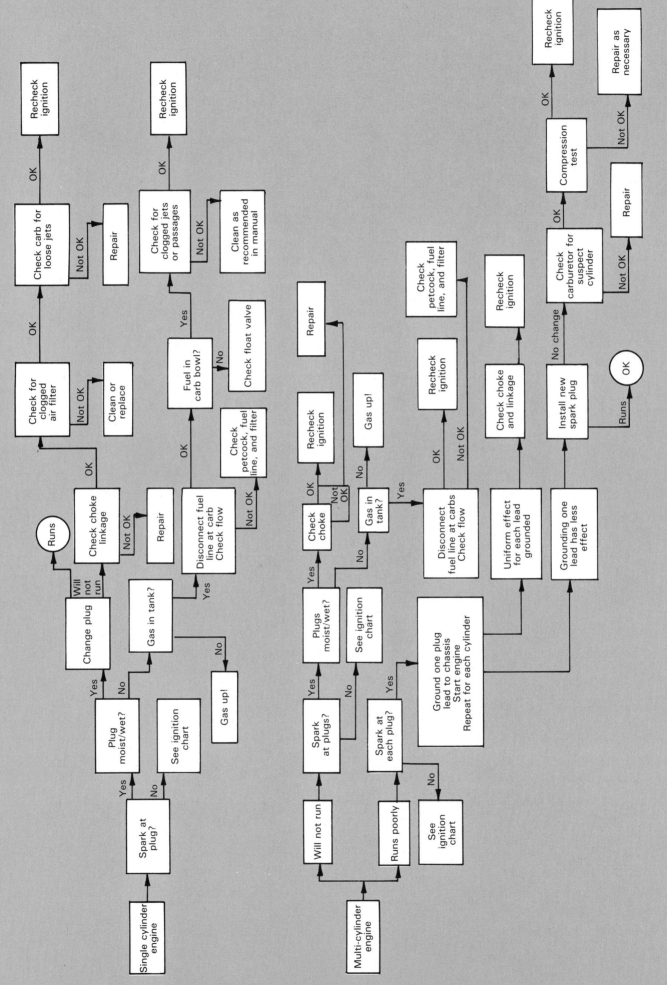

Fig. 25-18. This chart illustrates systematic approach for troubleshooting carburetors. (Cycle World)

troubleshooting problems. Developing confidence in your troubleshooting ability is a result of learning from experience. Finding the solution to a troubleshooting problem is very gratifying, and the more difficult the problem is, the better you feel when you solve it.

KNOW THESE TERMS

Troubleshooting, Intermittent failures, Symptom, Troubleshooting chart.

REVIEW QUESTIONS—CHAPTER 25

1. Define the word "symptom."
2. List the three types of troubleshooting problems (failures).
3. List four things you must think about when analyzing a troubleshooting problem.
4. A battery must be in good condition and fully charged before attempting to test the charging system. True or False?
5. List the four quick checks to be made when a handling problem is encountered.
6. When dealing with a brake system problem, you should first check _____ levels and wear _____.
7. What is the most difficult type of lighting system problem to solve?
8. An engine overheating problem can be caused by:
   a. Lubrication system.
   b. Ignition system.
   c. Fuel system.
   d. All of the above.
   e. None of the above.
9. When troubleshooting a lighting system problem, which of the following should be done first?
   a. Check that there is a good ground.
   b. Check for voltage in the circuit.
   c. Replace the bulbs.
   d. Clean all the harness connectors.
   e. Check continuity of switches and wiring.
10. A wiring _____ may be necessary for any electrical system troubleshooting.
11. What are two types of problems that commonly cause engine noise?
12. List the six steps involved in troubleshooting a problem.

SUGGESTED ACTIVITIES

1. Compile a notebook of troubleshooting procedures. Use information from various books, service manuals, and magazine articles.
2. Troubleshoot a motorcycle which has a problem or have a friend intentionally cause a problem (misadjust point, cross plug wires). Record each step of your troubleshooting procedure and continue until you have found the source of the problem.

METRIC TO AMERICAN CONVERSION TABLE

MULTIPLY	BY	TO OBTAIN
(LINEAR)		
Millimeters (mm)	.03937	Inches
Millimeters (mm)	.00328	Feet
Centimeters (cm)	.3937	Inches
Centimeters (cm)	.0328	Feet
(DISTANCE)		
Meters (m)	39.37	Inches
Meters (m)	3.28	Feet
Kilometers (km)	3281	Feet
Kilometers (km)	.6214	Miles
(AREA)		
Square Centimeters (cm²)	.155	Square Inches
Square Centimeters (cm²)	.001076	Square Feet
Square Meters (m²)	10.76	Square Feet
(VOLUME)		
Cubic Centimeters (cc) . .	.06102	Cubic Inches
Liters (1)	61.02	Cubic Inches
(LIQUID CAPACITY)		
Liters (1)	2.113	Pints
Liters (1)	1.057	Quarts
Liters (1)	.2642	Gallons
Cubic Centimeters (cc) .	.0338	Fluid Ounces
U.S. Gallons	1.2	Imperial gals.
Imperial gallons	4.537	Liters
Imperial gallons	277.274	cu. in.
(WEIGHT)		
Grams (gm)	.03527	Ounces
Kilograms (kg)	2.205	Pounds
(OTHER)		
Kilogram-Meters (kg-m) .	7.233	Foot-Pounds (Ft-Lbs.)
Kilometers/Liters (km/l) .	2.352	Miles/Gallon (mpg)
Metric Horsepower (ps)	1.014	Brake Horsepower (bhp)

AMERICAN TO METRIC CONVERSION TABLE

MULTIPLY	BY	TO OBTAIN
(LINEAR)		
Inches (in.)	25.4	Millimeters
Inches (in.)	2.54	Centimeters
Feet (ft.)	304.8	Millimeters
Feet (ft.)	30.48	Centimeters
(DISTANCE)		
Inches (in.)	.0254	Meters
Feet (ft)	.3048	Meters
Miles (mi.)	1.609	Kilometers
(AREA)		
Square Inches (in²)	6.452	Square Centimeters
Square Feet (sq. ft)	929	Square Centimeters
(VOLUME)		
Cubic Inches (cu. in.) . . .	16.39	Cubic Centimeters
Cubic Inches (cu. in.) . . .	.01639	Liters
(LIQUID CAPACITY)		
Pints (pt.)	.4732	Liters
Quarts (qt.)	.9463	Liters
Gallons (gal.)	3.785	Liters
Fluid Ounces (fl. oz.) . . .	29.58	Cubic Centimeters
U.S. Gallons	1.2	Imperial gals.
Imperial gallons	4.537	Liters
Imperial gallons	277.274	cu.in.
(WEIGHT)		
Ounces (oz.)	28.35	Grams
Pounds (lb.)	.4536	Kilograms
(OTHER)		
Foot-Pounds (Ft.-lbs.) . .	.1383 . .	Kilogram-Meters (kg-m)
Miles/Gallon (mpg)	.4252 . .	Kilometers/Liter (km/l)
Brake horsepower (bhp)	.9862 . .	Metric Horsepower (ps)

METRIC TAP DRILL CHART

	RECOMMENDED METRIC DRILL		CLOSEST RECOMMENDED INCH DRILL	
Metric Tap Size	Drill Size mm	Inch Equiv.	Drill Size	Inch Equiv.
M2 X 0.4	1.60	0.0630	#52	0.0635
M2.2 X 0.45	1.75	0.0689	—	—
M2.5 X 0.45	2.05	0.0807	#46	0.0810
M3 X 0.5	2.50	0.0984	#40	0.0980
M3.5 X 0.6	2.90	0.1142	#33	0.1130
M4 X 0.7	3.30	0.1299	#30	0.1285
M4.5 X 0.75	3.70	0.1457	#26	0.1470
M5 X 0.8	4.20	0.1654	#19	0.1660
M6 X 1	5.00	0.1968	#9	0.1960
M7 X 1	6.00	0.2362	15/64	0.2344
M8 X 1.25	6.70	0.2638	17/64	0.2656
M8 X 1	7.00	0.2756	J	0.2770
M10 X 1.5	8.50	0.3346	Q	0.3320
M10 X 1.25	8.70	0.3425	11/32	0.3438
M12 X 1.75	10.20	0.4016	Y	0.4040
M12 X 1.25	10.80	0.4252	27/64	0.4219
M14 X 2	12.00	0.4724	15/32	0.4688
M14 X 1.5	12.50	0.4921	—	—

Metric Tables

MILLIMETERS TO INCHES

mm.	Inches	mm.	Inches	mm.	Inches	mm.	Inches	mm.	Inches
.01	.00039	.41	,01614	.81	.03189	21	.82677	61	2.40157
.02	.00079	.42	.01654	.82	.03228	22	.86614	62	2.44094
.03	.00118	.43	.01693	.83	.03268	23	.90551	63	2.48031
.04	.00157	.44	.01732	.84	.03307	24	.94488	64	2.51968
.05	.00197	.45	.01772	.85	.03346	25	.98425	65	2.55905
.06	.00236	.46	.01811	.86	.03386	26	1.02362	66	2.59842
.07	.00276	.47	.01850	.87	.03425	27	1.06299	67	2.63779
.08	.00315	.48	.01890	.88	.03465	28	1.10236	68	2.67716
.09	.00354	.49	.01929	.89	.03504	29	1.14173	69	2.71653
.10	.00394	.50	.01969	.90	.03533	30	1.18110	70	2.75590
.11	.00433	.51	.02008	.91	.03583	31	1.22047	71	2.79527
.12	.00472	.52	.02047	.92	.03622	32	1.25984	72	2.83464
.13	.00512	.53	.02087	.93	.03661	33	1.29921	73	2.87401
.14	.00551	.54	.02126	.94	.03701	34	1.33858	74	2.91338
.15	.00591	.55	.02165	.95	.03740	35	1.37795	75	2.95275
.16	.00630	.56	.02205	.96	.03780	36	1.41732	76	2.99212
.17	.00669	.57	.02244	.97	.03819	37	1.45669	77	3.03149
.18	.00709	.58	.02283	.98	.03858	38	1.49606	78	3.07086
.19	.00748	.59	.02323	.99	.03898	39	1.53543	79	3.11023
.20	.00787	.60	.02362	1.00	.03937	40	1.57480	80	3.14960
.21	.00827	.61	.02402	1	.03937	41	1.61417	81	3.18897
.22	.00866	.62	.02441	2	.07874	42	1.65354	82	3.22834
.23	.00906	.63	.02480	3	.11811	43	1.69291	83	3.26771
.24	.00945	.64	.02520	4	.15748	44	1.73228	84	3.30708
.25	.00984	.65	.02559	5	.19685	45	1.77165	85	3.34645
.26	.01024	.66	.02598	6	.23622	46	1.81102	86	3.38582
.27	.01063	.67	.02638	7	.27559	47	1.85039	87	3.42519
.28	.01102	.68	.02677	8	.31496	48	1.88976	88	3.46456
.29	.01142	.69	.02717	9	.35433	49	1.92913	89	3.50393
.30	.01181	.70	.02756	10	.39370	50	1.96850	90	3.54330
.31	.01220	.71	.02795	11	.43307	51	2.00787	91	3.58267
.32	.01260	.72	.02835	12	.47244	52	2.04724	92	3.62204
.33	.01299	.73	.02874	13	.51181	53	2.08661	93	3.66141
.34	.01339	.74	.02913	14	.55118	54	2.12598	94	3.70078
.35	.01378	.75	.02953	15	.59055	55	2.16535	95	3.74015
.36	.01417	.76	.02992	16	.62992	56	2.20472	96	3.77952
.37	.01457	.77	.03032	17	.66929	57	2.24409	97	3.81889
.38	.01496	.78	.03071	18	.70866	58	2.28346	98	3.85826
.39	.01535	.79	.03110	19	.74803	59	2.32283	99	3.89763
.40	.01575	.80	.03150	20	.78740	60	2.36220	100	3.93700

ACKNOWLEDGMENTS

The authors wish to thank the individuals and organizations listed below for the valuable information, photographs and line drawings, facilities, and talents they so willingly provided.

Bombardier, Inc., Montreal, Quebec
Cycle, New York, NY
Cycle Craft, Woodstock, IL
Cycle Guide, Compton, CA
Cycle World, Newport Beach, CA
Cycle Werks, Barrington, IL
Elgin Community College, Elgin, IL
Fox Trail Motors, Algonquin, IL
Fox Valley Cycles, Aurora, IL
Fox Valley Yamaha, Elgin, IL
Harley Davidson Motor Co. Inc.,
    Milwaukee, WI
Kawasaki Motors Corp., U.S.A.,
    Santa Ana, CA
The L.S. Starrett Co., Athol, MA
Snap-On Tools, Kenosha, WI
Steier's Cycles Inc., Elgin, IL
Steven's Cycle, Aurora, IL
Tri City Suzuki, St. Charles, IL
Triumph Motorcycles (Meriden) Limited,
    Allesley, England
U.S. Suzuki Motor Corporation, Brea, CA
Waubonsee Community College,
    Sugar Grove, IL
Wildwood Suzuki, Elgin, IL
Yamaha Motor Corporation, U.S.A.,
    Cypress, CA

Betty Armstrong, Elgin, IL
Jim Carlson, Elgin, IL
Bob Conley, Aurora, IL
Lorna Cross, Albuquerque, NM
Ron Downen, Maple Park, IL
Denny Forni, Aurora, IL
Tom Foster, South Elgin, IL
Luke Gray, Streamwood, IL
Bonnie Guerra, Elgin, IL
Elmer Hansen, Elgin, IL
Chuck Horisberger, Elgin, IL
Larry Jones, South Elgin, IL
Bill Lilly, Algonquin, IL
Rick Lovens, Huntley, IL
Devin MacIntee, Mount Prospect, IL
Mike Markowitz, Algonquin, IL
Howard Marunde, Huntley, IL
Jim Moreland, St. Charles, IL
Bob Rewoldt, Carpentersville, IL
Ken Ronzheimer, Geneva, IL
Warner W. Riley, Skokie, IL
Craig Richie, Lake in the Hills, IL
Greg Smith, Elgin, IL
Albert Steier, Elgin, IL
Phyllis Taylor, Elgin, IL
Steve Ward, Gilberts, IL

DICTIONARY OF MOTORCYCLE TERMS

A

AC ARC WELDING: Welding method which uses alternating current to provide heat for melting and fusion of metal parts.

ACCELERATOR PUMP: A small pump that squirts fuel into throat of carburetor as throttle is opened.

ACCESSORY SYSTEM: Part of electrical system consisting of lights, horn, electric starter, turn signals, and warning systems.

ADDITIVES: Chemical compounds used to alter characteristics of lubricating oils and fuels.

AIR BOX: Plastic, fiberglass, or metal box mounted between carburetor and air filter. This box provides a volume of still, filtered air for induction into engine.

AIR COOLING: Use of fins to dissipate heat from part into air.

AIR FILTER: A device with paper, oiled foam, oiled gauze, or wire mesh to prevent entry of dirt or foreign particles into engine through air intake.

AIR-FUEL MIXTURE: Finely atomized mist of air and fuel necessary for combustion. This mixture consists of approximately 15 parts air to 1 part fuel (15:1) at cruising speeds.

AIR JET: A small jet in air passage of a carburetor. This jet meters amount of air fed to diffuser in an air bleed type carburetor.

ALTERNATING CURRENT (AC): Electrical current which constantly reverses direction and polarity.

ALTERNATOR: A crankshaft driven electrical generator that produces alternating current which must be rectified to DC current.

AMMETER: An instrument for measuring current flow in electrical circuits.

AMPERE (Amp): Electrical unit used to measure current flow.

ARC WELDING: A type of welding which uses an electric arc to produce necessary heat. Melting of base metal and welding rod join two parts.

ARMATURE: Portion of a DC generator housing generating coils.

ASBESTOS: Heat resistant material commonly used in brake and clutch linings. It is a known cancer causing substance if inhaled.

ATOMIZED: Tiny particles of fuel mixed with air, making a fine mist.

AUTOMATIC TRANSMISSION: A transmission not using a manually operated clutch.

B

BACKBONE FRAME: Frame which uses the engine as a structural member.

BACKLASH: The clearance between meshed teeth of two gears.

BALL BEARING: An anti-friction bearing consisting of inner and outer races separated by hardened steel balls.

BALL AND RAMP: A clutch release mechanism made of two stamped plates with three or four ramps. As one plate is rotated by clutch cable, balls climb ramps, forcing plates apart. This movement disengages clutch.

BATTERY AND COIL IGNITION SYSTEM: An ignition system with a battery as the source of primary ignition current.

BATTERY POWERED ELECTRICAL SYSTEM: An electrical system having a lead-acid battery as a source of power. The battery is recharged by a charging system using either a generator or alternator.

BATTERY SUPPORTED CDI: Capacitive discharge ignition system which uses a battery to supply primary ignition current.

BEARING: A part in which a journal, shaft, or pivot turns or moves.

BEARING PRELOAD: Amount of static pressure exerted on a bearing or a set of bearings. Preload is usually adjusted by a threaded collar or shims.

BEARING SPACER: A piece of tubing used between wheel bearing inner races to prevent unwanted bearing preload as the axle is tightened.

BENCH GRINDER: A power grinder with round abrasive stones mounted at either end of a special electric motor, for rough grinding of ferrous metals.

BLEEDER TYPE NEEDLE CIRCUIT: Air from carburetor air jet is mixed with fuel in body of needle jet making an air-fuel froth. This mixture is then metered into throat of carburetor by jet needle and needle jet.

BLOW-BY: Piston rings do not effectively seal combustion pressure, allowing hot gases to blow between rings and cylinder wall. This causes overheating of piston and poor performance.

BORING BAR: A machine tool used to accurately enlarge a cylinder bore.

BOTTOM DEAD CENTER (BDC): Lowest piston position in cylinder.

BRAKE ACTUATOR CAM: Small cam that pivots in brake backing plate and forces brake shoes into brake drum.

BRAKE CALIPER: Part of a disc brake which holds friction pads and encloses disc. As brake is applied, hydraulic fluid forces a piston in caliper toward disc, causing disc to be pinched between brake pads.

BRAKE DISC: A round, flat disc made of steel or cast iron. It is mounted on outside of wheel hub.

BRAKE DRUM: A circular ring of cast iron that is part of wheel hub. It provides a place for brake lining to be applied.

BRAKE LINE: Special hydraulic tubing made of steel, plastic, or reinforced rubber. Hydraulic brake lines must be capable of withstanding extreme pressure without deforming.

BRAKE LINING: A special high friction material made of asbestos and other materials bonded to brake shoes and brake pad plates. Brake lining produces friction and heat when it is forced against brake drum or disc.

BRAKE PAD: Small circular or square asbestos inserts in a wheel caliper. They produce friction and heat when forced against the disc.

BRAKE SHOE: A cast aluminum, half-circular shoe that holds a bonded brake lining material. When brake is applied, shoe forces lining into brake drum.

BRAKE WEAR INDICATOR: Index grooves, tabs, or reference lines to indicate amount of brake lining or pad wear.

BRAZING: Type of welding using a brass alloy filler rod.

BRIDGED PORTS: A vertical port division in a two-stroke cycle engine cylinder which allows use of a large port without danger of ring or piston catching.

BURR: A small, rotating cutter mounted in a rotary grinder and used for metal removal (rotary file). Also, sharp, rough area around a drilled hole.

BUTTERFLY CONTROLLED CARBURETOR: A carburetor using a flat plate between venturi and intake manifold to regulate airflow through carburetor.

BYPASS VALVE: Valve which allows fluid to flow around normal path of flow, used in oil filters.

C

CAM GROUND: Oval shape of a piston to control and compensate for expansion.

CAM LOBE: Protrusions on a camshaft that causes valve train parts to move as camshaft rotates.

CAM FOLLOWER: Component in valve train that rides on cam lobe.

CAM PLATE: Flat plate with slots that engage pins on shift forks. As plate is rotated, slots cause shift forks to move sliding gears or dogs, causing engagement and disengagement of gearbox ratios.

CAMSHAFT: Shaft with protruding eccentric lobes. As camshaft rotates, lobes cause reciprocating movement of other valve train parts.

CARBURETOR: Device that mixes and delivers proper amount of air and fuel to engine at a ratio of approximately 15 parts air to 1 part fuel.

CAST ALLOY WHEEL: A one piece wheel made of cast aluminum or magnesium alloy. This design is more rigid than wire spoked wheel.

CAST-IN SLEEVE: An aluminum cylinder block cast around an iron cylinder sleeve.

CAST IRON CYLINDER: A one piece cylinder assembly made of cast iron with a machined bore.

CAST PISTON: A piston made by pouring molten aluminum alloy into a mold of desired shape.

CAVITATION: Inadequate lubrication caused by air taking place of oil in pump.

CDI VOLTAGE AMPLIFIER: A device, used in a battery powered capacity discharge ignition system, that steps up battery voltage to provide high primary ignition voltage.

CENTER OF GRAVITY: Point at which any object is perfectly balanced.

CENTRIFUGAL CLUTCH: Clutch engaged by centrifugal force as engine speeds up.

CENTRIFUGAL OIL SLINGER: Cup shaped centrifugal oil filter mounted to end of crankshaft. As oil passes through slinger, centrifugal force removes impurities that are heavier than oil.

CHAIN DRIVE: Use of a chain and sprockets to connect gearbox output shaft to rear wheel.

CHAIN STRETCH: Wear of pins and bushings of a roller or hyvo chain, causing chain to lengthen.

CHAMFER: To bevel an edge of an object or to chamfer edges of port openings in a two-stroke cycle cylinder to prevent piston ring breakage.

CHECK VALVE: A spring-loaded ball or piston valve that allows flow only in one direction.

CHEMICAL REGULATOR: Voltage regulator with solid state electronic devices to regulate charging system output.

CIRCLIP: A circular clip or snap ring that fits into a groove, used to locate or retain a shaft or component.

CIRCUIT: An electrical path from a power source, through wire, to components, and back to source.

CLEARANCE: Amount of space between two adjacent parts.

CLOSE RATIO GEARBOX: A gearbox with gear ratios spaced close together.

CLUTCH: Device used to connect and disconnect engine power to gearbox input shaft.

CLUTCH BASKET: Part of clutch assembly containing drive plates. Primary drive gear engages teeth on outside of clutch basket.

CLUTCH HOLDER: Tool to secure clutch basket and clutch hub while loosening or tightening clutch securing nut or primary drive gear nut.

CLUTCH HUB: Part of clutch that engages with plain driven clutch plates. Clutch hub is mounted on gearbox input shaft.

CLUTCH PRESSURE PLATE: Part of a clutch assembly providing pressure against clutch disc or clutch plates.

CLUTCH RELEASE MECHANISM: Mechanism that moves clutch pressure plate away from clutch pack, allowing clutch to slip.

COATED BORE: Thin coating of chrome or iron applied to inside of cylinder by electroplating or wire explosion spray coating.

COIL BUILDUP: Buildup of a magnetic field while current is flowing through primary windings of coil.

COLD SOAK CLEANER: A strong cleaning solvent used to dissolve and remove varnish on carburetor parts.

COLOR CODE: Use of different base colors and colored tracers on insulation of electrical wire for purpose of identification.

COMBUSTION: Burning of air-fuel mixture in combustion chamber.

COMBUSTION CHAMBER: Area of cylinder head and cylinder above piston where combustion of air-fuel mixture takes place.

COMMON SUMP: Same oil is used to lubricate engine, gearbox, and primary drive.

COMPRESSION: Increased pressure caused as volume is reduced. Also, movement of suspension components against spring pressure caused by a force against wheel.

COMPRESSION GAUGE: Gauge which measures cranking pressure in combustion chamber.

COMPRESSION RINGS: Piston rings designed to seal pressure between piston and upper cylinder.

COMPRESSION STROKE: Movement of piston from BDC to TDC with valves closed, compressing air-fuel mixture for more violent combustion.

CONCENTRIC: When two or more circular parts have same centerline.

CONDENSER (Capacitor): Two metal sheets separated by an insulator used to store an electrical charge.

CONICAL HUB: A wheel hub (wire wheel) with spoke holes on brake side of wheel at a greater distance from center of hub than spoke holes on opposite side of hub.

CONNECTING ROD: A rod made of steel or aluminum, usually having an "I-beam" cross section. It connects piston to crankshaft.

CONNECTING ROD KIT: A parts kit consisting of connecting rod, crank pin, thrust washers, and roller bearing, used in reconditioning of assembled crankshafts.

CONNECTING ROD TIP: Amount of radial (side) play at top of connecting rod. Measurement of rod tip is one way of determining condition of rod big-end bearing.

CONTACT POINTS: Switching device used to start and stop flow of current.

CONTINUITY: A continuous path for current flow.

CONVENTIONAL REAR SUSPENSION: Suspension used on dual-purpose and road bikes which provides less than six in. (152 mm) of suspension travel.

COOLING FINS: Projections on cylinder heads cylinders and crankcases to increase surface area for more efficient heat dissipation into air.

COUNTERSHAFT SPROCKET: Output sprocket from gearbox. Mounted on output shaft in indirect drive gearbox and on high gear pinion in direct drive gearbox.

CRADLE FRAME: Frame built of tubing which supports and surrounds engine.

CRANKCASE: Castings that support and contain the crankshaft, primary drive, and gearbox.

CRANKCASE LEAK TEST: Pressure test done to a two-stroke cycle engine to determine if crankcase is properly sealed.

CRANKPIN: Pin or journal on which big-end of connecting rod rides.

CRANKSHAFT AXLES: Extensions at each end of crankshaft to provide a mounting place for main bearings, primary drive gear or sprocket, and alternator rotor or magneto flywheel.

CRANKSHAFT RECONDITIONING: Replacement of worn lower-end components in an assembled crankshaft. This involves pressing crankshaft apart, replacing crankpin, roller bearing, thrust washers, and connecting rod, pressing crankshaft back together and trueing it (assembled crankshaft).

CRANKSHAFT WHEEL: Portions of an assembled crankshaft that provide a mounting place for crankpin and crank axles.

CURRENT FLOW: Movement of electrons through a conductor.

CYCLE: A series of events which take place during a specific interval.

CYLINDER: A machined hole in cylinder block for piston, open at both ends.

CYLINDER BLOCK: Casting attached to crankcase which contains cylinder bore, cooling fins or water jacket, and provides a means of mounting cylinder head.

CYLINDER BORE: Diameter of cylinder opening.

CYLINDER BORING: Bore diameter machined (bored) to accept oversize piston. This renews a worn cylinder.

CYLINDER DEGLAZING: Use of a hone to slightly roughen walls of cylinder. It produces a crosshatch pattern which aids in seating of new rings.

CYLINDER HEAD: Casting that seals top of cylinder and provides a mounting place for spark plug. In four-stroke cycle engine, cylinder head also contains intake and exhaust ports. Both two and four-stroke cycle engines also have combustion chamber built into cylinder head.

CYLINDER HONING: Use of a parallel type cylinder hone to size a cylinder after boring. Proper cylinder honing provides proper texture and crosshatch.

CYLINDER LINER: Cast iron sleeve or tube pressed or cast into cylinder block to provide bore which piston moves in.

D

DAMPER: Device which uses oil metered through orifices to control abrupt suspension movement during extension and compression.

DAMPER ROD: Tube secured to bottom of each fork slider to hold slider onto fork leg. Damper rod controls movement of front suspension by metering hydraulic fluid through orifices in rod.

DECARBONIZE: To remove carbon buildup on piston, combustion chamber, and other parts.

DEPTH MICROMETER: A precision measuring tool used to take measurements of stepped surfaces.

DETERGENT OIL: An oil which keeps particles and contaminants in suspension and has ability to neutralize acids resulting from combustion process.

DETONATION: A condition where excessive temperature of air-fuel mixture in combustion chamber causes uncontrolled explosive burning. As detonated flame front collides with flame front initiated by spark plug, extreme pressure is often heard as "pinging" or "knocking." Detonation can be caused by incorrect ignition timing, lean air-fuel ratio, and improper fuel.

DIAGNOSIS: Process of determining cause of a failure.

DIAPHRAGM: A thin flexible disc of rubberized fabric which separates two cavities and uses vacuum or pressure for activation.

DIAL BORE GAUGE: A precision measuring tool which combines a telescoping gauge and dial indicator to give readings of inside diameter measurements.

DIAL CALIPER: A precision measuring tool used to determine inside, outside, or depth measurements. Measurements are displayed on a dial index.

DIAL INDICATOR: A precision measuring tool using a dial index to show linear movement of component being measured.

DIAPHRAGM SPRING: A slightly cone shaped metal disc which acts as a clutch pressure plate spring when flattened.

DIFFUSER: A projection in base of carburetor venturi and at top of needle jet that aids in fuel atomization.

DIODE: A solid state electronic device that permits current flow in only one direction.

DIRECT BEARING LUBRICATION: An oil injection system which feeds undiluted oil to two-stroke cycle engine main bearings and rod big-end bearing.

DIRECT CURRENT: A continuous flow of current in same direction.

DIRECT DRIVE GEARBOX: Power is transferred from clutch to input shaft (mainshaft), to layshaft, to high gear pinion, which has output sprocket mounted on it.

DISC BRAKE: A brake consisting of a flat circular disc attached to wheel. A hydraulic or mechanical caliper applies pressure to two brake pads to slow or stop disc rotation.

DOHC (Double overhead cam): Two camshafts located in cylinder head (one for intake, one for exhaust).

DOUBLE LEADING SHOE: A drum brake having two leading shoes and no trailing shoes. Each shoe has its own activating cam and pivot.

DOUBLE PISTON CALIPER: A hydraulic brake caliper with two pistons and provisions for applying hydraulic pressure equally to both pistons. The caliper body is fixed solidly.

DOUBLE-ROW CHAIN: A chain having two rows of rollers. Duplex (double-row) chains are used for primary drives.

DRIVE PLATE: A clutch plate which is indexed into clutch basket (outer hub) by tabs. Drive plate has friction material bonded to its surface. When clutch is engaged, drive plate transfers power to driven plate.

DRIVEN PLATE: A clutch plate which is indexed onto clutch inner hub by tabs or splines around its inside diameter. Driven plate is usually a plain plate (no friction material) and drives gearbox input shaft through clutch inner hub.

DRUM BRAKE: A brake consisting of two brake shoes mounted on a backing plate. One or two cams cause shoes to expand against inside of brake drum. Brake drum is part of hub or is bolted to hub.

DRY CLUTCH: A clutch assembly that does not run in an oil bath.

DRY SUMP: In this system, oil is gravity fed to supply side of oil pump from a remote oil tank. After oil has been pumped through four-stroke cycle engine, it is returned to oil tank by return side of oil pump.

DUAL-RATE CHARGING SYSTEM: A charging system that switches extra coils into charging system when lights are turned on.

DWELL: Length of time, in crankshaft degrees, that ignition contact points are closed.

DYKES PISTON RING: A piston ring with an L-shaped cross section designed to use combustion pressure to improve sealing.

DYNAMIC IGNITION TIMING: Use of a strobe light to check ignition timing with engine running.

E

ELECTRODE: Conductors at center and side of spark plug that provide an air gap for an electric arc to start combustion process in engine.

ELECTROLYTE: A solution of dilute sulfuric acid used to provide a chemical reaction in a lead-acid battery.

ELECTROMAGNET: A magnet which produces a magnetic field by passing electrical current through a coil of wire wrapped around a soft iron core.

ELECTROMAGNET ALTERNATOR: An alternator which uses electromagnets to produce a magnetic field.

ELECTROMOTIVE FORCE (EMF): Force that causes electricity to flow because of a difference in potential between two points.

ELECTRONIC IGNITION SYSTEM: An ignition system which uses a magnetic triggering device and solid state amplifier rather than conventional contact points.

ELEMENT FILTER: A disposable oil or air filter that uses gauze or paper as filtering material.

ELLIPTICAL PORT SHAPE: Rounded port shape designed to prevent ring catching in large ports of two-stroke cycle engine.

EMISSIONS: Byproducts of a running engine, including: exhaust pollutants, noise emissions.

ENDLESS CHAIN: A roller chain without a master link for connection of ends. All pin links are permanently riveted.

ENGINE: A machine that converts chemical energy into mechanical energy.

ENGLISH MEASUREMENT SYSTEM: A measurement using the foot (12 in.) as a standard.

ENRICHMENT CIRCUIT: A carburetor system with a plunger to open and close an air-fuel circuit which discharges a rich mixture into throat of carburetor for cold starting.

ERODED PISTON (Crown): A condition caused by detonation or preignition where temperatures are raised so high that part of piston crown is melted away.

EXHAUST PORT: An opening or passage which directs flow of exhaust gases out of engine. In a four-stroke cycle, it is located in the head. With a two-stroke cycle, it is in the cylinder.

EXHAUST (Port) TIMING: Amount of time two-stroke cycle exhaust port is open, expressed in crankshaft degrees or piston travel.

EXHAUST STROKE: With a four-stroke cycle engine, it is movement of piston from BDC to TDC with exhaust valve open, pushing burned gases out of cylinder.

EXTENSION: The return or stretching outward of suspension components (after compression) caused by spring pressure.

F

FASTENER: A device used to attach one part or assembly to another (nut and bolt, screw, rivet, etc.).

FEELER GAUGE: A measuring tool made of steel blades of precise thickness used for measuring distance between surfaces.

FIELD COIL: An electromagnet used in a DC generator or AC electromagnet alternator to produce a magnetic field.

FILLER ROD: A metal rod that is melted into welding puddle to provide necessary bead thickness.

FILM STRENGTH: Ability of an oil to keep moving parts from making contact with each other.

FINAL DRIVE: Chains and sprockets or shafts and gears used to connect the gearbox output shaft to rear wheel.

FLANGE MOUNT CARBURETOR: A carburetor mounted by a flange. The flange is bolted to a manifold on cylinder or cylinder head. An insulator block and gasket are used to seal and insulate carburetor.

FLYWHEEL: A weight attached to an engine crankshaft, providing crankshaft with added inertia. This helps to smooth out abrupt movement of crankshaft during power stroke, and helps keep crankshaft turning during non-power producing events.

FLYWHEEL MAGNETO IGNITION SYSTEM: An AC ignition system using a generating coil and either a magnetic trigger (CDI) or contact points as well as a flywheel to provide primary ignition current and triggering. An external ignition coil is used to provide secondary current.

FLYWHEEL MAGNETS: Magnets mounted on inside of flywheel in a flywheel magneto.

FLOAT ASSEMBLY: A carburetor device consisting of plastic or hollow brass floats attached to an arm. This assembly pivots on a pin and raises and lowers, opening and closing float needle to control fuel level in float bowl.

FLOAT LEVEL: Level of fuel maintained in carburetor float bowl. Controlled by float, float needle, and seat.

FLOAT NEEDLE AND SEAT: A carburetor valve, opened and closed by the float, that lets fuel into float bowl from fuel line.

FLUID PRESSURE GAUGE: Gauge for measuring fluid pressure in a system, such as oil pressure or fuel pressure.

FOAMING: Undesirable characteristic of oil being whipped into a froth (air and oil solution).

FOOT POUND: Amount of work required to lift one pound one foot, used to express torque.

FORGED PISTON: A piston made by hammering hot aluminum into a mold of desired shape.

FORK SLIDERS: Lower portion of fork which slides over fork leg.

FORK TUBES: Long sturdy tubes attached to triple clamps and fitted inside fork sliders.

FOUR-STROKE CYCLE: One cycle consisting of four distinct events, intake, compression, power, exhaust. One cycle requires two revolutions of crankshaft.

FRICTION: Resistance to movement between two

objects contacting each other, causes heat.

FRICTION PLATE: See drive plate.

FUEL FILTER: A small filter designed to remove dirt and water from fuel before it reaches carburetor or injection system. Filters may be made of metal or plastic screen, paper, or gauze. Filters may be located at fuel tank, in fuel line, or at carburetor.

FUEL LINE: A flexible fuel resistant hose that carries fuel from fuel petcock to carburetor.

FUEL PETCOCK: An ON-OFF valve located at bottom of fuel tank. It may provide for reserve fuel supply and may have a filter screen and sediment bowl. Fuel line to carburetor is attached to fuel petcock.

FUEL PUMP: A diaphragm or electric device that maintains proper fuel pressure to carburetor or injection system. A fuel pump must be used when fuel tank is located lower than carburetor and with all injection systems.

FUEL SYSTEM: System which stores, filters, and regulates flow of fuel to engine. It consists of fuel tank, fuel valve, fuel filters, fuel lines, air filter, carburetor, and carburetor mountings.

FUEL TANK: A reservoir used to store fuel for delivery to engine.

FULL-WAVE RECTIFIER: A rectifier that converts AC to DC by inverting negative portion of AC sine wave.

FUSE: A device used to protect electrical circuits from overloading. A link in fuse melts and opens circuit if current is above normal rating.

G

GAS CHARGED SHOCK ABSORBER: A shock absorber using a pressurized gas such as nitrogen to help prevent changes in damping as shock absorber heats up.

GEAR OIL PUMP: An oil pump with gear type teeth to move oil.

GEAR RATIO: Ratio of rotation of one rotating part compared to another rotating part.

GEARBOX (Transmission): A series of shafts and gears which varies ratio of engine to rear wheel speed. Motorcycle gearboxes use from two to seven speeds or ratios.

GEARBOX INDEXER: A plunger and spring or pivoted lever that indexes into dimples or slots in shift drum or cam plate. It provides positive positioning of shift drum or cam plate in each gear.

GENERATOR: A device which converts mechanical energy into electrical energy, producing direct current (DC).

GRADUATED CYLINDER: A container, calibrated in cubic centimetres or millilitres used for accurate measurement of fluids, such as fork oil and gearbox oil.

GUSSET: A reinforcing plate or boxed section used to prevent flexing of frame or swing arm.

H

HALF-WAVE RECTIFIER: A rectifier which blocks one-half of AC sine wave to convert AC into DC.

HEAT TRANSFER: Movement of heat from one area to another.

HELIARC WELDING: A type of electric arc welding which uses inert gas to shield area around arc.

HELICAL GEAR: A gear having teeth that are slightly angled. Helical gears (used for primary drives) are quiet in operation, but absorb a slight amount of power due to side thrust.

HEMISPHERICAL COMBUSTION CHAMBER: A combustion chamber shaped like a round dome, allowing use of large valves placed opposite each other in chamber.

HIGH GEAR PINION: Top gear on mainshaft in direct drive gearbox. All ratios drive through high gear pinion, which has output sprocket mounted to it.

HOLED PISTON: A condition caused by severe detonation or pre-ignition, where a hole is eaten or burned through crown of piston as a result of extreme heat and pressure.

HORSEPOWER: Amount of work required to lift 33,000 lbs. one ft. in one minute equals one h.p.

HYDRAULIC BRAKE: A brake system using hydraulic fluid, piston, and cylinders to provide extremely high pressure for brake application.

HYDRAULIC CLUTCH: A system which uses hydraulic pressure to disengage clutch.

HY-VO CHAIN: A very strong chain made up of toothed plates positioned side by side and held together by pins. Advantage of this type of chain is great strength and quiet operation.

I

IDLE MIXTURE: Air-fuel ratio with throttle twist grip closed. Idle mixture is controlled by pilot jet and pilot adjustment screw in carburetor or computer in electronic fuel injection system.

IGNITION COIL: A step-up transformer that uses induction to increase battery voltage to over 20,000 volts.

IGNITION GENERATING COIL: Coil in a flywheel magneto to provide primary ignition current.

IGNITION SYSTEM: Part of the electrical system responsible for providing a high voltage at proper time to ignite air-fuel mixture. Battery and coil, electronic, magneto, and CDI are the four systems commonly used.

IMPELLER: Finned wheel that produces pressure and flow when spun in enclosed housing of oil pump or water pump.

INDIRECT DRIVE GEARBOX: A gearbox where power is transferred from clutch to input shaft to output shaft. Output shaft has a sprocket mounted on one end.

INDUCTION: Production of current flow resulting from a magnetic field cutting through a conductor.

INERTIA: Tendency of a stationary object to resist movement or tendency of a moving object to continue moving in same direction.

INJECTION SYSTEM: An oil pump and oil lines that deliver oil to a two-stroke cycle engine as it is needed. Also, fuel system which meters gasoline into engine intake ports.

INLINE CYLINDERS: Cylinders positioned in a row or side by side.

INLINE FILTER: A small fuel or oil filter that replaces a section of line or hose.

INPUT SHAFT: Shaft of a gearbox which carries power into gearbox. Clutch assembly is mounted on gearbox input shaft.

INSIDE MICROMETER: A precision measurement tool used to take accurate measurements of inside surfaces.

INSULATOR BLOCK: A fiber or rubber block that insulates carburetor from engine heat, used with flange mounted carburetors.

INTAKE MANIFOLD: A sleeve or flange made of rubber or metal to attach carburetor to intake port.

INTAKE PORT: An opening or passage which directs flow of air-fuel mixture into engine. In a four-stroke cycle engine, intake port is located in cylinder head. In a two-stroke cycle engine, intake port is located in cylinder or crankcase.

INTAKE STROKE: In a four-stroke cycle engine, movement of piston from TDC to BDC with intake valve open, drawing air-fuel mixture into cylinder.

INTAKE TIMING: Amount of time two-stroke cycle engine intake port is open, expressed in crankshaft degrees or piston position.

INTERNAL COMBUSTION ENGINE: An engine that burns fuel inside rather than outside engine, as does a steam engine (external combustion engine).

J

JET: A carburetor component, usually made of brass, which meters flow of fuel to venturi. Fuel is metered by a small hole drilled through center of jet.

JUNCTION BLOCK: A device which transfers action of a single cable to two or more cables.

K

KENETIC ENERGY: Energy associated with motion. An internal combustion engine produces kenetic energy (crankshaft rotation).

KEY: Parallel-sided piece inserted into groove cut part way into each of two parts, which locates and prevents slippage between parts.

KEYSTONE PISTON RING: A piston ring with a tapered cross section designed to use combustion pressure to aid in sealing.

L

LATERAL RUNOUT: Side-to-side movement (wobble) of a wheel rim.

LATHE: A machine tool used to spin, cut, and shape a metal part with a movable cutting tool.

LAY SHAFT: Second shaft in a direct drive gearbox. It transfers power from input shaft to high gear pinion.

LEAN: An air-fuel ratio that contains extra air compared to fuel.

LEVER AND PIVOT: A clutch release mechanism in which a pivoted lever attached to clutch cable disengages clutch by pushing pressure plate away from clutch plates, allowing them to slip. Lever and pivot may act directly on pressure plate or through a push rod.

LIFTER: A hard surfaced short shaft with a radius or roller at one end that rides on cam lobe.

LIQUID COOLING: Use of liquid piped through water jackets, thermostat, and radiator to dissipate heat.

LONG TRAVEL REAR SUSPENSION: Suspension used on current competition dirt bikes to provide more than six inches of travel.

LOWER END: Portion of an engine from cylinder base downward including connecting rods.

LUBRICATING FILM: A thin coating of lubricant (oil) which prevents contact between moving parts.

LUBRICATION: Use of lubricants (oil, grease) to reduce friction.

M

MAGNETIC FIELD: Invisible lines of force surrounding a magnet or a conductor with current flowing through it.

MAGNETISM: An invisible force which attracts ferrous metals.

MAGNETO: See flywheel magneto.

MAGNETO SUPPORTED CDI: A capacitive discharge ignition using a generating coil in magneto to produce primary ignition current.

MAIN FUEL CIRCUIT: Carburetor circuit that controls air-fuel ratio from three-fourths to full throttle opening. Main jet meters fuel in this circuit.

MAIN JET: A carburetor fuel metering jet, usually mounted at base of carburetor body, to control air-fuel ratio from three-fourths to full throttle.

MANIFOLD INJECTION: Injector oil is pumped into the intake port of two-stroke cycle engine.

MASTER CYLINDER: Component in a brake system that produces hydraulic pressure for system.

MASTER LINK: A pin link which has one removable side plate located by a clip. This allows a convenient way of separating chain.

MATING PARTS: Two or more parts that contact each other during operation and set up wear patterns.

MECHANICAL BRAKE: A brake system which uses a mechanical advantage by way of levers and cables or rods to apply brakes. A brake system not using hydraulic fluids or hydraulics.

MECHANICAL CALIPER: A disc brake caliper actuated by a lever and cam rather than hydraulic fluid.

MECHANICAL VOLTAGE REGULATOR: A voltage regulator using an electromagnet to open or close contact points, varying output of a DC generator or electromagnet alternator.

METRIC SYSTEM: A measurement system which uses the meter (39.37 in.) as a standard.

MILD PORT TIMING: Two-stroke cycle engine ports open for a relatively short time, providing for a broad power band.

MOTORCYCLE: A two-wheeled vehicle powered by an internal combustion engine.

MULTI-GRADE OIL: An oil that flows like a thin oil when cold, but lubricates like a thicker oil when hot. For example, 10W40 at 0°F flows like a 10W oil; at 210°F, it flows like a 40W oil.

MULTI-PLATE CLUTCH: A clutch assembly using more than one driving plate and more than one driven plate.

MULTIPLE PORTS: Use of many small transfer ports rather than two large ports in two-stroke cycle cylinder. This can give improved scavenging.

N

NEEDLE BEARING: An anti-friction bearing utilizing hardened steel needle rollers between hardened races or parts.

NEEDLE CIRCUIT: Carburetor circuit that controls air-fuel ratio from one-fourth to three-fourths throttle opening. The jet needle and needle jet meter fuel flow in this circuit.

NEGATIVE: Terminal with an excess amount of electrons which flow toward positive terminal.

NEUTRAL INDICATOR SWITCH: A switch, usually mounted on end of shift drum, which completes circuit of neutral indicator light when gearbox is in neutral.

NON-PRIMARY KICKSTART: A kickstart system using gearbox input shaft and clutch hub to connect kickstart lever to crankshaft. For starting, gearbox must be in neutral and clutch engaged.

NON-UNIT CONSTRUCTION: Engine design with separate engine crankcase and gearbox case.

NYLON SCREW CLUTCH RELEASE: A clutch release mechanism which uses a coarse, square threaded nylon screw for clutch disengagement.

O

O-RING: A ring made of neoprene that is used to provide a positive seal. It usually fits into a groove slightly shallower than O-ring, and mated against a flat surface to provide a seal for oil, fuel, or air.

O-RING CHAIN: Roller chain which uses O-rings to permanently seal lubricant into area between pins and bushings.

OHM: Unit used to measure resistance in an electrical circuit or component.

OHMMETER: An instrument which measures resistance.

OIL BATH: Oil level is just high enough so it splashes around inside case or housing. Lubricates gearbox, primary drive, and ring and pinion.

OIL CONTROL RING: Piston ring designed to remove excess oil from cylinder wall, usually bottom ring.

OIL PUMP: A device which provides oil under pressure for engine lubrication.

OIL PUMP BLEEDING: Removal of air from supply line and pump in a two-stroke cycle oil injection system.

OIL SLINGER: A circular, lipped disc used in direct bearing oil injection to feed oil to rod big end.

OPPOSED CYLINDERS: Cylinders positioned opposite each other in same plane.

OUT-OF-ROUNDNESS: Cylinder wear caused by piston thrust. This results in wear to front and back of cylinder. Cylinder wears oval shaped rather than round.

OUTPUT SHAFT: Gearbox shaft that transmits power to final drive at a selected ratio.

OUTSIDE MICROMETER: A precision measuring tool for taking accurate measurements between outside surfaces.

OVERALL GEAR RATIO: Ratio of crankshaft revolutions to rear wheel revolutions.

OVERFLOW TUBE: A tube that is open at both ends and mounted in bottom of carburetor float bowl. If float sticks or float needle does not seat properly, excess fuel flows out overflow tube rather than into throat of carburetor.

OXIDIZED OIL: Oil that has been chemically combined with oxygen as a result of excessive heat, oil agitation, and exposure to combustion contaminants.

OXYACETYLENE WELDING: A type of welding (metal fusion) which burns a mixture of oxygen and acetylene to provide a high temperature flame.

P

PARALLEL CIRCUIT: A circuit where current is provided to each component independently (each component has own ground). The failure of one component does not affect rest of circuit.

PERMANENT MAGNET ALTERNATOR: An alternator using permanent magnets to produce a magnetic field for AC production.

PILOT AIR SCREW: A screw mounted on side of carburetor that allows fine adjustment of air-fuel ratio in pilot circuit of slide type carburetor.

PILOT CIRCUIT: A carburetor circuit that provides proper air-fuel ratio from approximately zero to one-eighth throttle opening. It basically consists of a pilot jet, pilot air screw or pilot fuel screw, and a pilot discharge port.

PILOT JET: Jet that meters fuel for pilot circuit.

PINION GEAR: A small gear that either drives or is driven by a larger gear.

PISTON (Brake system): A movable part of a master cylinder or wheel caliper. Master cylinder piston produces pressure and caliper piston applies that pressure to brake disc, slowing or stopping wheel.

PISTON (Engine): A cylindrical part, closed at one end, which moves up and down in cylinder. Open end is attached to connecting rod. Combustion pressure is exerted on closed end of piston, causing connecting rod to move and crankshaft to turn.

PISTON BLOCK: A slotted block used to support pistons for cylinder installation. Also may be used in conjunction with a piston pin to lock crankshaft.

PISTON CROWN: Top of piston, directly exposed to combustion pressure and heat.

PISTON PIN BOSS: A strengthened section of piston extending to inside of piston crown. It supports piston pin.

PISTON PIN HOLE: Machined hole through piston wall where piston pin and retaining circlips are mounted.

PISTON PORT: Two-stroke cycle piston skirt used to control intake port opening and closing.

PISTON RING END GAP: Distance between ends of a piston ring when installed in cylinder. This clearance is measured with a feeler gauge. Ring must be straight in cylinder as if installed on piston.

PISTON RING GROOVE: Grooves machined in piston to accept piston rings.

PISTON RINGS (Compression): A split cast iron band, sometimes chrome plated, designed to seal combustion pressure above piston.

PISTON RING (Oil control): A split cast iron or steel band, used to scrape excess oil from cylinder wall. Sometimes designed as a three-piece unit.

PISTON SEIZURE: Overheating of piston to point where it will no longer move freely in cylinder.

PISTON SKIRT: Part of piston below bottom ring and pin boss.

PLAIN BEARING: A split or circular type bearing in which a part slides, turns, or pivots.

PLAIN PLATE: See driven plate.

PLUNGER OIL PUMP: An oil pump that uses a piston or plunger and check valves to move oil.

POLARITY: Direction of current flow.

PORT WINDOW: Port opening in a two-stroke cycle engine cylinder wall.

POSITIVE: Electrical terminal having a deficiency of electrons and attracts electrons from negative terminal, causing current flow.

POSITIVE CARBURETOR LINKAGE: A carburetor linkage designed to positively open and close one or more carburetor throttles, actuated by one cable for opening and another cable for closing.

POWER: Ability to do work or rate of work being done.

POWER STROKE: In four-stroke cycle engine, movement of piston from TDC to BDC with intake and exhaust valves closed, after ignition and combustion of compressed air-fuel mixture.

POWER TRANSMISSION: A system of gears, chains, sprockets, and shafts that transfer power from crankshaft to rear wheel in varying ratios.

POWER TRANSMISSION SHOCK ABSORBER: A compensator cam, rubber pads, or springs in primary drive, gearbox, drive shaft, or rear wheel, provides means of cushioning loading of gearbox.

PREIGNITION: Premature ignition caused by "hot spots" in combustion chamber that ignite air-fuel mixture before spark plug "fires." This causes uncontrolled combustion and rapidly raises piston and cylinder head temperatures (similar to detonation).

PREMIX: Two-stroke cycle engine lubrication provided by oil mixed with fuel in fuel tank.

PRESSED-IN SLEEVE: Cast iron cylinder sleeve is interference fit into aluminum cylinder block.

PRIMARY CHAIN DRIVE: A primary drive design that uses a chain and sprockets to transfer engine power from crankshaft to clutch.

PRIMARY DRIVE: Use of chain, gear, or belt drive to connect crankshaft to clutch and gearbox input shaft.

PRIMARY IGNITION CIRCUIT: Section of ignition circuit including contact points, condenser, and primary windings of ignition coil, power supply (battery or ignition generating coil), kill switch, ignition switch, and related wiring.

PRIMARY KICKSTART: A kickstart system which connects kickstart lever to crankshaft through clutch basket. Gearbox can be in gear for starting if clutch is disengaged.

PRIMARY REDUCTION: A gear reduction usually about three to one, accomplished by primary drive.

PRIMARY TYPE NEEDLE CIRCUIT: Fuel metered by clearance between jet needle and needle jet is partially mixed with air from air jet and discharged into venturi of carburetor.

PRIMARY WINDING: Hundreds of turns of wire in an ignition coil to provide build up and collapse of a magnetic field, inducing voltage in secondary.

PROFILE: Contour or shape of camshaft lobe.

PUSH ROD: In four-stroke cycle engine, push rods provide means of transferring tappet movement to rocker arms, which open valves.

R

RACK AND PINION CLUTCH RELEASE: A clutch release mechanism using a pinion gear and a rack gear to disengage clutch.

RADIAL RUNOUT: Up and down movement of a rotating part (wheel rim, flywheel, etc.).

RADIATOR: A heat exchanger which reduces coolant temperature in a liquid cooling system.

RADICAL PORT TIMING: Ports open for a relatively long period of time.

REAR HOUSING: An aluminum case which provides a mounting place for shaft drive ring and pinion gears. This housing is sealed and carries oil which lubricates ring and pinion gears.

RECIPROCATING WEIGHT: Weight of any engine parts moving back and forth while engine is running: pistons, rings, piston pin and circlips, push rods, valves.

RECTIFIER: A device that converts AC (alternating current) to DC (direct current) for battery charging.

REED CAGE: An aluminum frame providing a mounting place for reed petals in two-stroke cycle engine.

REED PETALS: Movable part of reed valve assembly.

REED VALVE: A one-way valve placed in intake port of a two-stroke cycle engine. It prevents backward flow of crankcase air-fuel mixture.

REGULATOR: A device which controls alternator or generator charging current to battery.

RELIEF VALVE: A spring-loaded valve that regulates maximum pressure of enclosed system.

RESISTANCE: Characteristic of an electrical circuit to resist flow of current, measured in ohms.

RICH: An air-fuel ratio that contains extra fuel compared to air.

RIDGE: An unworn portion or ledge at top of cylinder formed above end of ring travel.

RIM OFFSET: Distance a wheel rim is set off-center (lateral) to a wheel hub. Rim offset is needed for drive sprocket clearance.

RIM STRIP: A rubber strip installed around center of a wire wheel rim to protect inner tube from being punctured by spokes.

RING AND PINION CONTACT PATTERN: Area of contact between teeth of ring gear and teeth of pinion gear. Checked with red lead.

RING GEAR: A large gear in shaft drive housing. It is driven by pinion gear.

RING LAND: Solid area of piston which supports rings, located between ring grooves.

ROCKER ARM: A pivoted arm that converts upward movement of push rod to downward movement of valve.

ROLLER BEARING: An antifriction bearing consisting of hardened steel inner and outer races, separated by hardened steel rollers.

ROLLER CHAIN: A chain made up of pins, side plates, bushings, and rollers. Roller links are connected by pin links to achieve desired length. Ends are usually connected by a pin link which has a removable side plate, called a master link.

ROTARY GRINDER: A high rpm hand held grinder using small grinding stones or burrs for metal removal in cramped or hard to get at areas.

ROTOR OIL PUMP: An oil pump which uses an inner and outer rotor to move oil.

ROTARY VALVE: A circular disc with a portion removed. It covers and uncovers intake port of two-stroke cycle engine. Disc is keyed to crankshaft.

RUNOUT: Out-of-round condition of a rotating part.

S

SCAVENGING: Inertia caused movement of gases through cylinder and exhaust system of a two-stroke cycle or four-stroke cycle engine.

SCHEMATIC: A diagram representing an electrical system.

SCRAPER RING: Dual-purpose piston ring which helps to seal combustion pressure as well as control oil.

SECONDARY IGNITION CIRCUIT: Part of ignition system consisting of secondary windings of ignition coil, spark plug wire, spark plug terminal, and spark plug.

SECONDARY WINDING: Thousands of turns of fine wire in an ignition coil. It uses induction to step up voltage as a magnetic field is rapidly collapsed in primary windings.

SEDIMENT BOWL: A cup located at bottom of fuel petcock, designed to prevent flow of dirt and water into fuel line.

SERIES CIRCUIT: A circuit in which current must follow a single path through each component in sequence before reaching ground. If one component fails, entire circuit is open.

SHAFT DRIVE: Use of a drive shaft, universal joints, and gears to connect gearbox output shaft to rear wheel.

SHIFT DRUM: A drum shaped gearbox component with slots around its outside diameter. It engages with shift mechanism and shift forks. As drum is rotated, drum slots cause shift forks to move sliding gears or dogs causing engagement and disengagement of various gearbox ratios.

SHIFTING FORK: A flat forked gearbox component which engages with a slot in a sliding gear or dog. Shifting forks slide back and forth on lateral shafts. Rotation of shift drum or cam plate causes shift fork to move its sliding gear or dog to engage with another gear, locking both gears to shaft.

SHIFT LINKAGE: Hinged lever or levers that transfer movement of shift lever to shift drum or cam plate.

SHIFT STOPPER: A fork or pin which limits movement of shift drum to prevent overshifting.

SHIM: A spacer used between two parts to achieve proper clearance.

SHIM BUCKET: A cylindrical shaped part in a DOHC (dual overhead camshaft) valve train. It is located between valve and camshaft and provides a receptacle for valve lash adjustment shims.

SHOCK ABSORBER: Rear suspension unit made up of a coil spring and a hydraulic damper. It prevents spring oscillations. Also, see power transmission shock absorber.

SIAMESED CRANKSHAFT: Crankshaft configuration where two rods are mounted on same crank pin (journal). One rod is forked, other rod is mounted on inside of fork.

SIDE-BY-SIDE CRANKSHAFT: Crankshaft configuration where connecting rods are mounted next to each other on same crankpin (journal).

SILENIUM RECTIFIER: A device which converts AC to DC through use of silenium plates.

SINE WAVE: A graphical representation of 360 degrees of rotation, representing change in direction of single-phase AC.

SINGLE-LEADING SHOE: A drum brake having two shoes; one is leading and one is trailing. Leading shoe tends to wedge itself into drum providing more braking action than trailing shoe.

SINGLE-PHASE AC: Alternating current which reverses direction of flow every 180 degrees.

SINGLE-PISTON CALIPER: A laterally floating disc brake caliper that uses one hydraulic piston to apply both brake pads. As pressure is applied to piston, it pushes one pad against disc. Other pad is solidly mounted on opposite side of caliper and makes contact with disc as caliper floats.

SINGLE-ROW CHAIN: A conventional roller chain with one row of rollers.

SLEEVE MOUNT CARBURETOR: A carburetor mounted on an aluminum manifold by a pinch bolt which clamps carburetor spigot over a plastic or fiber insulating sleeve.

SLIDE CONTROLLED CARBURETOR: A carburetor using a throttle slide (plunger) to regulate venturi restriction (throttle opening).

SLIDE CUTAWAY CIRCUIT: Carburetor circuit which controls air-fuel ratio from one-eighth to one-quarter throttle opening. Height of cutaway portion of slide controls how much air is mixed with fuel. Fuel is metered by pilot jet, needle jet, and jet needle.

SLIDING DOG: A gearbox component splined to its shaft and moved from side to side by a shifting fork. Dogs on each side engage with adjacent gears.

SLIDING GEAR (Dog gear): A gear splined to its shaft and moved side to side by a shifting fork. A sliding gear has dogs on its lateral face that engage with holes or dogs in adjacent gears.

SOHC (Single overhead cam): A single camshaft located in top of cylinder head.

SOLID ROLLER CHAIN: Roller chain using a one-piece roller and bushing assembly.

SPIGOT MOUNT CARBURETOR: A carburetor mounted by clamping spigot into a rubber sleeve manifold.

SPINDLE (Steering fork): A shaft which is secured to upper and lower triple clamps. It pivots on bearings mounted in steering head.

SPOKE CROSSING PATTERN: Number of spokes crossed on same side of hub by any one spoke.

SPOKED WHEEL: A wheel consisting of a rim, spokes, nipples, and hub. Spokes are laced between hub and rim and are attached to rim by nipples. Thirty-six or forty spokes are normally used.

SPOKE TORQUE WRENCH: A small torque wrench used to accurately adjust spoke tension.

SPRING PRELOAD: Static installed length of a spring subtracted from its free length. In suspension system, spring preload determines ride height of motorcycle.

SPRING TESTER: A device that measures spring pressure in relation to spring length.

SPROCKET: A circular plate with teeth machined around outside to engage links of a chain.

STAMPED FRAME: A frame stamped from pieces of sheet metal which are welded together to provide support for engine and suspension.

STAMPED WHEEL: A wheel assembly using stamped sheet metal spokes in place of small wire type spokes. A stamped wheel resembles a cast alloy wheel in appearance.

STANDOFF: Backward flow of air-fuel mixture in intake tract caused by radical port or cam timing.

STARTER SYSTEM: Carburetor system which provides a rich mixture for cold starting (tickler, choke, enrichment circuit). Also, electrical circuit for cranking engine, including: starter switch, relay, battery, and starting motor.

STATIC IGNITION TIMING: Use of a buzz box, test light, or ohmmeter to check ignition timing without running engine.

STEERING DAMPER: A device which uses friction or a hydraulic damper to reduce steering oscillation.

STEERING HEAD: Forward part of frame providing a mounting place for bearings which locate and support steering spindle and fork assembly.

STEERING OFFSET: Distance between steering axis and axis on which axle pivots. Steering offset is accomplished by offsetting axle or triple clamps.

STEERING RAKE: Angle of steering axis from vertical, given in degrees.

STEERING TRAIL: Distance along ground between lines drawn vertically through front axle and down center of fork tubes and sliders.

STRAIGHT-CUT GEAR DRIVE: A gear drive which uses gears having straight-cut teeth, used for one type of primary drive.

STRAIGHT-CUT OFFSET GEARS: A gear design using straight-cut gears installed side by side and one-half tooth out of phase. This gear design will eliminate noise caused by backlash common to conventional straight-cut gears.

STROKE: Movement of piston from TDC to BDC or from BDC to TDC.

SUMP: Lowest portion of crankcase, containing oil.

SURFACE PLATE: A block of granite ground and lapped to provide a very smooth, flat surface. It is used for checking straightness of cylinders, cylinder heads, crankcase joints.

SUSPENSION: Components which absorb road surface irregularities to smooth motorcycle ride. It is designed to permit controlled wheel movement over irregular surfaces. Basic parts include forks, swing arm, and shock absorbers.

SWING ARM: Main member of rear suspension that provides a mounting place for rear wheel and one end of shock absorbers.

SWING ARM PIVOT: Forward part of swing arm, where it is attached to frame and pivots on bushings or bearings.

SYMMETRICAL: Two sides or events being identical. For instance, two-stroke exhaust timing is symmetrical. Exhaust port opens and closes at same crankshaft position before and after TDC.

SYMMETRICAL HUB: A wheel hub (wire wheel) which has spoke holes on each side of hub at same distance from hub center.

SYNCHRONIZE: Adjustment of carburetor throttles on two or more carburetors so that all throttles are open same amount at any position of throttle twist grip.

T

TAPER: A smaller diameter at one end of part, for instance: tapered piston or tapered cylinder bore.

TELESCOPIC FORK: Front suspension unit made up of two fork tubes and two sliders that "telescope" up and down tubes against spring pressure.

TELESCOPING GAUGE: A "T" shaped instrument used to duplicate distance between inside parallel surfaces (cylinder bore for example).

THERMOSTAT: A temperature sensitive device used in a liquid cooling system to adjust flow of coolant as coolant temperature changes.

THREE-PHASE AC: Alternating current with a 120 degree phase difference. Three wires are needed to carry current.

THROTTLE CABLE: A cable consisting of an outer housing and an inner cable which connects carburetor to throttle twist grip.

THROTTLE STOP SCREW: An idle speed adjustment screw used in slide type carburetor. This screw contacts base of throttle slide. As screw is turned in, throttle slide is raised, increasing idle speed.

THROTTLE TWIST GRIP: A device mounted on end of handlebar which locates one end of outer throttle cable and pulls inner cable as twist grip is rotated.

THRUST WASHER: A washer used to bear side thrust loads or provide lateral location.

TICKLER SYSTEM: A spring-loaded plunger in carburetor that can be depressed to push float assembly down. This allows fuel to flow into float bowl, raising float level temporarily for cold starting.

TIRE PRESSURE GAUGE: A pressure gauge used to check tire air pressure.

TOP END: Part of an engine from cylinder base up, including pistons but not connecting rods.

TOP DEAD CENTER (TDC): Uppermost piston travel in cylinder.

TORQUE: A twisting force measured in foot-pounds or newton-metres.

TORQUE CONVERTER: A fluid turbine which takes place of clutch in primary drive. Oil is used to transmit power through torque converter depending upon engine rpm.

TORQUE PATTERN: A specific sequence of tightening fasteners to help prevent warping of components.

TORQUE WRENCH: A wrench calibrated to allow for accurate application of tightening force to fasteners.

TRANSFER PORT: Opening in cylinder wall of a two-stroke cycle engine which connects cylinder to crankcase.

TRANSFER (PORT) TIMING: Amount of time transfer port is open, expressed in crankshaft degrees or piston position.

TRANSMISSION: See gearbox.

TRIPLE CLAMPS: A pair of sturdy brackets that provide a mounting place for fork legs and steering spindle. Triple clamps attach forks to frame through spindle, steering head, and steering head bearings.

TRIPLE-ROW CHAIN: A chain having three rows of rollers. Triplex chains are used for primary drives.

TWO-STROKE CYCLE: A cycle of overlapping events (intake, transfer, compression, power, exhaust) which all occur during one revolution of crankshaft.

U

UNIT CONSTRUCTION: Engine design has one crankcase to house gearbox, clutch, primary drive, and engine.

UNIVERSAL JOINT: A flexible joint which allows changes in angle of drive shaft.

V

VACUUM: Pressure which is less than atmospheric pressure.

VACUUM CONTROLLED CARBURETOR: A carburetor using a butterfly to regulate airflow and a vacuum controlled piston to regulate venturi restriction.

VACUUM GAUGE: A gauge which measures pressures which are lower than 14.7 lb. per square inch (101 kPa) at sea level.

VACUUM PISTON: Throttle piston used in a vacuum operated CV carburetor. One type uses a diaphragm at top with a small diameter piston. Other type uses a large diameter piston in a vacuum cylinder.

VALVE: A device which controls flow by opening and closing. For instance, fuel valve controls flow of fuel from fuel tank to carburetor. Intake valve controls flow of air-fuel mixture into cylinder.

VALVE OVERLAP: Period of time when intake and exhaust valves in a four-stroke cycle engine are open at same time.

VALVE STEM: Portion of valve that slides in valve guide and provides a mounting place for valve spring upper collar and keepers.

VALVE TRAIN: All components which directly influence valve operation (cam, cam chain, cam followers, valves, valve springs, valve collars, and keepers in SOHC engine).

VARNISH: A buildup of oxidized oil or fuel.

VEE CYLINDERS: Cylinders positioned at angles to each other forming a "V."

VENT: A tube or drillway going from top of float chamber to atmosphere. This prevents buildup of pressure or vacuum in float chamber.

VENTURI: A restriction in a tube which causes an increase in air velocity, resulting in a decrease of pressure (increase in vacuum) at restriction.

VERNIER CALIPER: A precision measuring tool used to determine inside, outside, or depth measurements. A linear vernier scale is used.

VERTICAL MILL: A machine tool that removes metal with a rotating cutter mounted vertically.

VISCOSITY: An oil's willingness or resistance to flow (thickness or weight).

VOLTAGE: Force causing electron flow in conductor.

VOLTMETER: An instrument which measures electrical pressure (EMF, voltage) in electrical circuits.

W

WATT: Unit of measurement of electrical power (rate of doing work).

WEAR LIMITS: Minimum and maximum acceptable size of a component.

WELDING: Use of heat to fuse two pieces of metal together.

WET CLUTCH: A multi-plate clutch which runs in an oil bath (primary drive).

WET SUMP: Four-stroke cycle engine sump (crankcase) is oil reservoir.

WHEEL BEARING GREASE: A special, heavy duty, high temperature grease used to lubricate wheel bearings.

WIDE RATIO GEARBOX: A gearbox having wide ratio spacing between gears. A wide ratio gearbox is commonly used in enduro (off-road) and trials motorcycles.

WIRE GAUGE: A measuring tool made of precisely sized wire. It is for measuring distance between irregular surfaces (spark plug gap for example).

WIRE WHEEL: See spoked wheel.

Z

ZENER DIODE: A solid state device used to regulate voltage in motorcycle charging systems.

INDEX